Atlantic

TROPIC OF CANCER

BAHAMA IS.
(Los Cayos)

Watlings I.

Camaguey

B
A

Santiago

Tortuga
La Navidad

HISPANIOLA

San Juan
Virgin Is.

Anguilla
Saba
St. Martin
St. Eustatius
St. Christopher
Montserrat
Nevis
Guadeloupe
Marie Galante
Dominica

Barbuda
Antigua

PUERTO
RICO

Santo
Domingo

JAMAICA
Port Royal

A
N
T
I
L
L
E
S

LEEWARD IS.

i b b e a n   S e a

Martinique
Sta. Lucia
St. Vincent
Barbados

Grenada

Aruba
Curaçao
Buen Aire

WINDWARD IS.

Margarita I.
Gulf of Paria
Tobago
Trinidad

Rio Hacha

Coro
Pto. Cabello
La Guaira
Caracas
Cumaná

Santa Marta
Cartagena
Maracaibo

Porto Bello
Nombre de Dios

Gulf of
Darien

L.
Maracaibo

V E N E Z U E L A

ORO

Panama

Urabá
Darien

R.

G
U
I
A
N
A

R.

Orinoco

Cauca

Magdalena

Bogotá

CALUMET COLLEGE

WHITING, INDIANA

The Head of a Maize Goddess. (Courtesy of Clarence Kennedy, photographer, and the Peabody Museum)

A HISTORY *of* THE AMERICAS

From Discovery to Nationhood

by VERA BROWN HOLMES

PROFESSOR OF HISTORY
SMITH COLLEGE

THE RONALD PRESS COMPANY · NEW YORK

3

Library of Congress Catalog Card Number: 50-8490

To My Husband

JOHN HERBERT ARKWRIGHT HOLMES

WHOSE ENCOURAGEMENT AND GENEROUS COLLABORATION
HAVE MADE THIS BOOK AS MUCH HIS AS MINE

PREFACE

Colonial Americans north and south of the Rio Grande, despite their many differences and the paucity of communication in their age, were bound together in a common adventure. In a newly discovered hemisphere they were engaged in the experiment of applying the precepts and practices of western European civilization to the conditions of an Indian America. The various forms their efforts took—and how they fared—is the theme of this volume. The story begins with the Indian cultures of pre-Conquest days, extends through the colonial period when the two continents were organized in four empires—the Spanish, Portuguese, French, and British—and concludes, by the close of the first quarter of the nineteenth century, with the establishment of independence and the setting up of new governments.

This book is thus intended to give the reader a familiarity with the background and early history of the Western Hemisphere. A product of fifteen years spent in research and in teaching the history of the Americas, it is designed primarily for use in college courses in this field. It is hoped that it will also have correlative value in courses devoted to the United States, Canada, and Latin America, providing some of the larger perspectives within which these national histories have evolved. The volume, however, has not been written solely for the college student but is also meant for the general reader who desires an introduction to hemispheric problems. To this end an effort has been made to give continuity and interest to an account of the origins and early growth of the political and social foundations that underlie everyday life and international relationships in the Americas of the present time.

A work of such scope must necessarily rest on the specialized labors of numerous scholars and the resources of many groups and institutions. My gratitude for assistance reaches back through some years to certain scholarships—the Helene and Cecil Rubel Foundation Fellowship from Bryn Mawr College, a Grant-in-Aid from the Social Science Research Council, and a Fellowship from the John Simon Guggenheim Memorial Foundation—which helped to provide the opportunity for study in the archives of England, Spain, and Mexico of some of the imperial problems of the colonizing powers that are basic to such a work as this. Sabbatical leaves from Smith College have made possible additional travel in these lands and in South America.

I am under obligation for helpful criticism and fruitful suggestions to a number of colleagues at Smith College and friends elsewhere who have read the whole or single chapters of the manuscript. Here I would especially mention Professors Sidney R. Packard, Hans Kohn, Harold U. Faulkner, and Randolph Downs, now or formerly of the History Department of Smith College; Professor Jocelyn Gill read the entire manuscript with meticulous care; Dr. France V. Scholes of the University of New Mexico has read a large portion of the manuscript, especially the Latin American sections, and in many ways encouraged the completion of the book. Professors Howard Meyerhoff, Helen Stobbe, and Gladys Bryson have read chapters in their fields; Professors Laura Bornholdt and David Donald have contributed bibliographical suggestions; Professors Oliver Larkin, Marine Leland, and Helen Peirce have assisted with the illustrations. It was through the generous efforts of Mr. Victor Schroeter, Secretary of the Bolivarian Society of the United States, that the portrait of Simón Bolívar was secured. Others who have given valuable assistance are Professors Yvonne Imbault-Huart and Esther Sylvia and Miss Ruth Agnew. Professor Eleanor Duckett kindly read the proofs of a considerable portion of the book.

And to my husband, whose gift of lucid expression illumines many an otherwise dark passage, there should be particular recognition for the fortitude to assist throughout all phases of the preparation of this volume. For deficiencies that without doubt are still present I am of course wholly responsible.

To the museums, publishers, and individuals identified in the legends accompanying the illustrations I am under obligation for permission to reproduce their materials. I would especially recognize the kindness of Dr. Sigmund Samuel of Toronto for his permission to photograph several items in his valuable collection of Canadiana. To the officials and staffs of a number of organizations I am particularly indebted for favors and help that forwarded the preparation of this work. I would particularly mention the generous assistance received at the Royal Ontario Museum of Archaeology, Toronto; the Library of the University of King's College in Halifax, Nova Scotia; the Museo Nacional and the Museo de Historia of Mexico; the American Museum of Natural History; the Hispanic Society of America; the New York Public Library; the Library of Congress; and the Smith College Library. To these and all others who have been kind enough to help and encourage me, I should like to record my grateful appreciation.

Northampton, Massachusetts   VERA BROWN HOLMES
April 23, 1950

CONTENTS

PART III

Colonial Life and Culture

PART IV

Secession of America from the Old World

PART V

The Search for Satisfactory Forms of Government and Recognition

MAPS

ILLUSTRATIONS

A HISTORY OF
THE AMERICAS

INTRODUCTION: UNITY IN AMERICAN HISTORY

This volume attempts to present a comprehensive view of the historical development of the Western Hemisphere from its discovery to approximately 1830. We have long been accustomed to consider the history of Europe as something of wider and deeper significance than the mere summation of the national histories of its component units and have believed that a definite gain in perspective and proportion is secured from this approach. It would seem reasonable to expect that a similar treatment of the story of the American world should bring a comparable gain in illumination and comprehension. An effort has been made in this volume to give prominence to similarities, differences, and interrelationships between the major geographical and political divisions and to emphasize the rich opportunities for comparative studies afforded by the parallel development of New World communities and by the imperial attitudes and relationships of the founding states. There has been no conscious attempt to minimize the differences or magnify the likenesses in order to arrive at a more definite pattern, far less to propound any thesis of identity of contemporary experiences, outlook, or interests in any given period.

The general plan has been to treat the history of the Americas topically within an over-all chronological framework. Emphasis on comparative elements occurs not only in the individual chapters but in special résumés placed at the end of natural divisions of the material. In such a vast field it has seemed worth while, especially if the book is to be of use to college students for classroom purposes, to pause now and again to reconstruct a single major phase of the total picture, even though this inevitably requires a certain amount of repetition and involves hypotheses that still await detailed monographic studies for complete substantiation.

It is obvious that the Western Hemisphere has certain large elements of unity, both static and dynamic. There are the physical facts: that nature has joined the two American continents together, that they share the common and immensely important geographical factor of wide sea separation from the population centers of other land masses, and that they front on both the Atlantic and Pacific oceans in which they have like vital interests. They share also a prehistoric past in which their aboriginal populations were of one racial stock. Furthermore, within a period of a hundred and fifty years in the early modern age both American continents received their characteristic white populations from western Europe, from those nations whose homelands faced on the Atlantic, or had easy access to it, and whose cultures had developed under the influence of the Roman Empire. The whole New World was in consequence caught up in the political, economic, and religious currents of Renaissance Europe. It has been pointed out that the Spanish and Portuguese colonial movements came a century earlier and in spirit were closer to the age of the crusades than the French and English migrations, which were more intimately associated with the secular spirit of the seventeenth century.[1] But this difference, though immensely important, seems to be overshadowed by the dominant fact that all the American settlements represent the expansion of western European maritime powers whose overseas activities were marked by similar economic motives and by a colonial development in which the introduction of the Christian religion was a major feature. Had North America been colonized from China or Japan, and South America peopled from Europe or Africa, or the northern and southern continents populated in totally different ages, the unity of the Americas in historical experience would have been much less significant.

Since the age of discovery and settlement, the American peoples have by reason of their origins been part of an Atlantic world and have had their most important relations with Europe and Africa. Until near the end of the eighteenth century all sections were in a colonial relationship to Europe; then, within a space of fifty years, the French and the Thirteen English Colonies, followed by the Spanish and Portuguese holdings, were all severed from their mother countries by war or revolution, and started on their several ways. They either launched forth immediately as separate nations, or gradually, as in Canada, moved forward by a process of evolution towards political autonomy. Only in a few areas of the Caribbean and in the tropical Guianas on the coast of South America did the colonial political relationship persist into the nineteenth and twentieth centuries. Political rupture, however, did not altogether destroy many of the old ties, especially the cultural and commercial bonds; in some cases these were never broken, in others they were quickly re-established, though modified as new contacts were added to old associations. After a flurry of extreme nationalism which followed the achievement of independence and acted for a time as a disruptive or dispersive factor, two trends were to make themselves apparent: first, a tendency towards the reassertion of common cultural bonds, both in relations between former colony and parent state and among new states possessing a common cultural heritage; and second, a tendency for common interests to express

---

[1] *Cf.* S. A. Zavala, *New Viewpoints on the Spanish Colonization of America* (London: 1943), p. 3.

themselves in regional or inter-American conferences and in other quasi-constitutional forms.

During the colonial age and the early post-independence years, with which the present volume deals, the different sets of colonies were very generally marked by the survival of many elements emanating from their common European background. The strongest of these were feudalism and mercantilism. All except the English colonies suffered from the direct control of a paternalistic monarchy. Further, all except the English (and the transient Dutch and Swedes) derived their populations from states in which Roman Catholicism had succeeded in routing the forces of the Protestant Reformation. The colonial age in all the colonies saw the growth of American-born populations which drew from the New World environment a changed outlook as new needs, new ambitions, and different hopes replaced or were added to those of the Old World. As the colonial period wore on, the common practice of the home governments of restricting the highest positions in colonial administration, with their prestige and awards, almost entirely to members of the European ruling classes was everywhere increasingly resented and eventually was a large factor in bringing revolution. The various outbreaks not only aimed at shifting control to colonial hands but at making more extensive adjustments of old European institutions to American requirements and aspirations.

In this formative period two cultural Americas emerged, with the line of demarcation not at the Isthmus but approximately along the Rio Grande. South of that line all was Ibero-American except for some of the Guianas and the West Indian islands. North of it, beyond a hybrid border area, France and England for a hundred and fifty years waged a titanic struggle in which eventually France was defeated and forced to withdraw from continental North America as an imperial power, leaving the area predominantly Anglo-Saxon. After a few years the main body of her former colonists, those along the St. Lawrence, were combined with the dissatisfied and defeated English elements of the new United States to form in Canada a new colonial experiment under the aegis of Great Britain.

Neither north nor south of the Rio Grande could the Indian be ignored. Throughout the colonial period he constituted a persistent factor in influencing the white man's way of life and scheme of colonization. In the north, the pressure of his fierce resistance forced the whites, whether French *habitant,* pious Puritan, or pacifist Quaker, to consolidate their footholds in the coastal settlements, fortify and arm themselves, and build up communal strength before committing themselves to limitless expansion. The native was employed by both French and English for commercial ends in the gathering of furs and was also used as a military ally on either side, each bidding for his support and thus giving him for a time the strategic advantage of holding the balance of power. When France fell, the victim of her intrepid but unwise policy of overexpansion, the northern Indian's cause was lost. His retreat before the increasing strength of the Anglo-Saxon frontier farmer became inevitable, while the periodic warfare was to reduce his numbers to a fraction.

In contrast to the northern Indian's deteriorating position, that of the Indian south of the Rio Grande took on increasing significance. In part the difference was due to the vastly greater number of Indians encountered by the white men in the southern region, and in part to the greater proportion of Indians here who had acquired a degree of culture that made possible their incorporation into white man's society. Furthermore the Spanish and Portuguese temperaments showed little inclination to resist the court's policy of encouraging the intermingling of white and native blood with the deliberate intention of creating a colonial mestizo society.

The Negro's role in early America was of only less significance than that of the Indian. Distinctly an importation to bolster the white man's economy, he was the only major element to enter the population of the Americas involuntarily. Like the Indian, in those early days he played a larger role in Ibero-America than in Anglo-Saxon America, partly because of numbers and partly because in large areas, notably in Brazil and the Caribbean, his blood, like that of the American aborigines, entered the stream of the general population. In North America he was never incorporated socially and was not to win even partial political recognition until long after he had been a major, though innocent, cause of the worst civil war the American world was to know.

In the revolutionary era, sectional loyalties and regional unities, often resting on a basis of colonial administrative arrangements and boundaries, appeared throughout America as powerful factors in fostering national feeling and in producing the new nations. Spanish America broke up into entities that corresponded with the chief administrative units of the colonial system; independent Brazil held to the colonial unitary arrangement; the Thirteen English Colonies determined to preserve in peace a unity found necessary in war, and to remedy their demonstrated weakness of colonial times by combining in a single nation, while retaining in their federal system the state arrangements of the colonial age for purposes of local government. French colonial activities to a great extent determined the boundaries of Canada.

With independence won, all the American communities were stimulated to action by two major objectives. The first was the necessity to establish satisfactory and permanent forms of government within their several national boundaries. The former English colonies, the only ones to enjoy a representative form of government during their colonial experience, naturally succeeded first. Their principal problem was essentially the imperial difficulty of earlier times, that of reconciling effective authority in the central government with the preservation of local liberties. In what was to become Canada, the problem was how to devise a form of government that would be satisfying to the loyalist immigrants from the former Thirteen Colonies, long accustomed to representative government, and at the same time to provide adequate political direction and education for former French *habitants,* accustomed only to absolutist government and semifeudal organization. In Ibero-American lands the difficulties were both more numerous and more fundamental. Having no experience with any popular form of government, they felt the need to examine all types before making the fateful choice between a constitutional monarchy and a republic, between a unitary and a federal state, between a responsible and a nonresponsible executive. This difficult and momentous decision had to be made in the face of the fact that practically the whole electorate was illiterate and likely to remain so for a long time to come. Considering the complexity of the problem and the lack of political experience, it is not surprising that the search for constitutional stability was to extend for many members of the new American family of nations over more than a century.

A second matter of primary concern to the young American states was to secure from the rest of the world recognition of their independence, to compel respect for their new-found sovereignty, and to assure the appropriate rights of freedom on the seas and noninterference from abroad in their domestic affairs. The War of 1812 and the proclamation of the Monroe Doctrine, both emanating from the self-interest of the most firmly established of the American republics, were successful efforts to secure these ends, the benefits of which were ultimately to extend to the rest of the hemisphere—although without conscious intention on the part of the formulators. Curiously enough, these newly acquired benefits were to become effective mainly through the operation of British sea power.

There was, however, at the close of the revolutionary age, little conscious over-all American unity. While the newer American republics admired the eldest member of the family and paid her the compliment of imitation in many respects, there were few interests in common and fewer occasions for inter-American cooperation. The bases of unity, though fundamental, were as yet inchoate, unexpressed, and largely unrecognized. The American colonies had freed themselves from Europe but had not yet built a common house.

PART I

PRE-COLUMBIAN AMERICA

Chapter 1

THE AMERICAN SCENE

I. THE GENERAL PICTURE

It has been said that geography explains the history of the past and prophesies the story of the future. This seems pre-eminently true of the Americas. The dreams of ancient Greek geographers placed "the fortunate isles" in the West; and the New World, discovered for European man by Columbus at the close of the fifteenth century, seemed to a remarkable degree to fulfil this vision of an earthly paradise. Alone in the Western Hemisphere, reaching from the Arctic to the Antarctic region, situated between the two greatest seas of the world and generously provided with a varied soil and with rich agricultural and mineral resources, America was obviously destined for early political independence, commercial greatness, and that wealth in cultural life which variety in climate and contacts can alone insure. Its location on the Atlantic opposite Europe and Africa, with an eastern coast line adequately provided with rivers and harbors to serve the wealth and variety of the world's trade, gave promise of the continent's immediate and rapid development, while its Pacific shore line offered a wide base along the one other ocean that in time might rival the Atlantic in commercial and naval importance. Its position between these two seas and its great navigable rivers speeded the opening up of the whole continent, as the explorers of the several colonial powers frantically searched the eastern coast in a competitive race to find an interoceanic waterway leading to the fabled East, the original goal of the discoverers.

In the approaches to the continent, America was fortunate. Asia, the original source of her primitive population, is at only one point near her shores. By that far northern route came her first inhabitants, and the way was difficult enough to discourage the red man's entrance in such large numbers as might have offered a successful resistance to the imposition by the white man of his higher culture. On the other side of the continent the width of the Atlantic secured two advantages: a long-postponed discovery, and a body of settlers representing a highly developed modern culture and of an especially enterprising type. The delayed discovery gave time in America for the development of an Indian culture which was to provide individuality and variety in the history of the New World and gave time in the Old World for the harvesting of the early fruits of the Renaissance as Europe's first gift to America.

So far as records show, it was in the eleventh century that the Atlantic was first crossed. In its narrowest part, at the only place where landfalls are closely grouped, the first white men traveled towards America by the stepping stones of Norway, Iceland, Greenland, Newfoundland, and Cape Breton Island.[1] But this attempt by Europeans to lay claim to America proved abortive, partly because of the difficulties of the voyage and of maintaining communications with the home base, and partly because of the lack of immediately available plunder and attractive prospects at the points of landing. Permanent conquest awaited the passage of another five hundred years; it then came by a longer and more southern route, in the only other region where islands and land masses on either side of the Atlantic reach towards each other and encourage a crossing. The Canaries, the West Indies, Cape Verde Islands, and Brazil were the stepping stones for the later migration. With the eastern doorway open, sheer distance from Europe insured America a naturally selected population and a development of its own. None but the stout-hearted would voluntarily brave the discomforts and dangers of such a voyage when slow sailing ships were the only means of transport. Distance also led inevitably to a certain laxness of control by the motherlands and made possible the ultimate development of a spirit of independence.

The new continent was excitingly different from Europe in many ways. It was built on a far vaster scale. Proportions and atmosphere were entirely different, more like Asia and Africa in many respects than like Europe. Americans were to find that Nature herself forced a different approach to human problems and that the stern law of necessity demanded new solutions. Distance from all other lands and contact with two seas inevitably tended as time passed to give Americans not only an independent and detached but also an interested and enlightened outlook on world affairs and relationships.

In the course of three centuries of persevering exploration the white man discovered that his new American world comprised two triangular continents of nearly equal size, both broad in the north and tapering towards the south, and joined to one another by a long narrow mountainous isthmus that constitutes Central America. In the hollow thus formed lay the island-dotted twin seas of the Gulf of Mexico and the Caribbean. Each of the continents, he found, conformed in broad outline to other continental masses, possessing a structure characteristic of continents; each was mountain-bordered, fringed seaward by coastal plains

---

[1] See "The Voyages to Vineland" in *American Historical Documents*. Harvard Classics (New York: 1910), XLIII.

enclosing a center of plateaus and inland plains, and drained by great rivers which penetrate deep into the continental interior. In the mountain systems of both continents, the western cordillera, younger in the geological sense and therefore higher than the mountain ranges of the east, forms a practically continuous rocky backbone. Composed of folded and faulted structures, it is so wide for considerable stretches in both North and South America that the system falls into two distinct parallel ranges. The higher peaks and volcanic sections are found in South America, where the Andes constitute a greater barrier to east-west communication than does the western cordillera of North America. While not so wide as their northern counterpart, the Andes average six thousand feet higher, are steeper in approach, and possess far fewer useful passes—the lowest being three to six thousand feet higher than the passes in the North American system. The main range in South America was almost unconquerable for mechanical transportation until the day of the airplane.

One of the early discoveries was that South America is much nearer to Africa than North America is to Europe. To the geographers of that period there appeared to be a sort of curvature of the spinal column of the hemisphere, so pronounced as to place South America almost completely to the east of North America. This view of the geographical relationship of the northern and southern continents of the Americas was based on the belief that the western mountain ranges of the two continents constitute two lengths of the same system. Recent geological investigation has shown that this was a mistaken conception: that, as in the Old World, America in the tropical region possesses a transverse east-west mountain system, running practically at right angles to the north-south trend of the great cordilleras of the continents lying respectively to the north and south.[2] Actually, it is now known, the western cordillera of North America terminates in a belt of great volcanoes, many of which are still active, along the southern margin of the central plateau of Mexico, in a formation known as the Great Scarp of Oaxaca, about latitude 20° north.[3] Geologically speaking, this feature ends the continent of North America. Similarly, the Andes terminate their northern trend before reaching Central America, with one great spur bending eastward. The termini of these principal systems of the two continents are actually twelve hundred miles apart and between them stretches the Antillean mountain system with an east-west axis.

The portion of this Antillean range which lies in Central America— principally in southern Mexico, Guatemala, Honduras, and Nicaragua—

[2] *Cf.* C. Schuchert, *Historical Geology of Antillean-Caribbean Regions* (New York: 1935), pp. 9-11.

[3] O. G. Ricketson, Jr., "An Outline of Basic Physical Factors Affecting Middle America" in *The Maya and Their Neighbors* (New York: 1940), chap. ii.

consists of great folded and faulted rocks, the general east-west trend of which was long concealed by younger volcanic ridges and peaks arranged roughly in a north-south direction. Stretching from Colombia through southern Central America, these volcanic heights give the false impression of continuity. East of Central America, the Antillean mountain system finds a continuation in submarine ridges, some of which rise as the islands of the Greater Antilles. There are two main branches. One passes from Honduras and northern Nicaragua along a submerged plateau to Jamaica and from there continues into southern Hispaniola, the island first called by the Spaniards Española and today occupied by Haiti and the Dominican Republic. The other, somewhat farther north, extends from the ranges of Guatemala and British Honduras, through the Caymans and southeastern Cuba, and meets the more southern extension in the mountains of Hispaniola which rise to a height of nearly ten thousand feet. From this point the range continues as a single one through Puerto Rico and the Virgin Islands. From the eastern terminus of the Antillean system an arc of volcanic islands, known as the Lesser Antilles, or the Caribbees, runs in a southerly direction towards the northeastern corner of Venezuela, forming the eastern boundary of the Caribbean Sea. The southern frame of the Sea is formed by the coastal ranges along the northern margin of South America. These ranges, like the Antillean mountain system to the north, are predominantly east-west in their structural lines.

The whole region around the Caribbean Sea is rich in gulfs, bays, and harbors, and its soil is luxuriantly productive. In contrast to the mountainous shores that surround the Caribbean—"the American Mediterranean" as it has been called—are the extensive coastal plains which form the continental periphery of the neighboring Gulf of Mexico. The gulf itself, which covers 615,000 square miles, is characterized by a broad submarine shelf of shoal waters that, far out from the line of the present shore, suddenly gives way to ocean depths.

In this twin-sea area, during various periods in geologic times, the waters of the Atlantic and Pacific oceans mingled, finding their way by various channels through Middle America. Originally, it is thought, the Caribbean was a long, narrow mediterranean connecting the Atlantic and Pacific oceans, widely open at both ends, and completely separating the two continents of the Western Hemisphere.[4] Ultimately the land bridge at Panama was formed by mountain-making upheavals, and these in combination with volcanic action soon closed the other straits between the oceans. For instance there were: (1) the Balsas Portal in southern Mexico between the Great Scarp of Oaxaca and the Sierra Madre del Sur;

---

[4] Schuchert, *op. cit.*, p. 59.

(2) the Tehuantepec Portal north of Central America, reaching across the Isthmus of Tehuantepec; (3) the depression in southern Nicaragua, where Lake Nicaragua was once a gulf of the Pacific; and (4) the Atrato River route through northwestern Colombia. All these natural channels were eventually to attract the attention and invite the ingenuity of the modern engineer as possible canal routes.

In man's conquest of the continent it was to be of momentous significance that the eastern highlands of both North and South America are lower, more broken, and fringed with wider and more indented coastal plains than are the mountain systems on the western border. The Labrador hills, the Laurentian highlands, and the Appalachian chain in North America and the Guiana and Brazilian highlands of South America are all much older and considerably lower than either Rockies or Andes. Thus America lies more open to Europe than to Asia. The lower altitude of the eastern mountains and the occurrence of great waterways leading from the east into the interior invited the explorer, the trader, and eventually the settler from Europe into the very heart of the continent. The greatest of the breaks in the Atlantic mountain wall is that formed by the twin seas of the Caribbean and the Gulf of Mexico. It served to direct the first streams of colonial settlers by a water route to the plateaus of Central America and Mexico, across the continental divide at Panama to western South America, and, in North America, bypassing the Appalachian barrier, led to the Mississippi valley and, beyond that, to the very foothills of the western cordillera. A tropical climate and the formidable coastal rim of the east-west mountains of Venezuela and Colombia made the Caribbean Sea less important in the settlement of the northern portion of South America than the Mexican Gulf proved to be in the settlement of the southern section of North America.

Other breaks occurring at Hudson Bay, the Gulf of St. Lawrence, the Hudson River, and La Plata estuary also had a vital influence on the settlement of the New World. It is a remarkable fact that, of all the colonial peoples, the seafaring Englishman was the last to grasp the importance and take advantage of these strategic approaches. Only at the most northern gateway of Hudson Bay were the English the first and most forward of the nations to make use of this natural feature of the American world; elsewhere their settlements long clung to the coastal plain of North America, east of the Appalachian barrier, where they remained until the ejection of the French in the eighteenth century. The latter's more forward-looking dream of empire was based, from early exploration days, on control of the Gulf of St. Lawrence and the Mississippi valley. Had other factors been propitious this well-conceived plan would have confined the settlements of their English rivals to the narrow Atlantic seaboard and left open to French development the whole central portion of the continent.

Between the two mountain systems in both continents are wide rolling plains, intersected by rivers that behave in the two continents in a strikingly similar fashion. Those of greatest importance flow eastward and south-eastward. Streams of lesser consequence tend towards the north, while the westward-flowing rivers are shorter and more torrential in character. Each continent has two river systems of major consequence. The St. Lawrence and the Amazon run approximately parallel and flow towards the east. The Paraná and Paraguay rivers imitate the Mississippi and the Missouri by meeting each other halfway and then flowing southward to the ocean at right angles to the Amazon and the St. Lawrence respectively.

Certain geographical likenesses in the two American continents, however, have led to differences of life in large areas. From the fact that the broadest part of each continent is in its northern section comes the significant difference of dominant climatic conditions. The great bulk of North America lies in the temperate and arctic zones, with three fourths of its people living on plains of less than a thousand feet elevation. Most of South America, on the other hand, lies within the tropics. The southern continent, however, does not reap the full disadvantage of this location of its bulk because Nature has arranged that the highest altitudes should also occur in the tropical areas and thus provide living conditions so favorable that a large proportion of South Americans choose to live within the tropics.[5]

Both continents are richly stored with minerals and fuels providing in abundance both the precious metals so greatly coveted by the Europeans in the colonial age and the raw materials that were to furnish the basis of industrial life in the nineteenth and twentieth centuries. The distribution of these resources, however, especially of iron and fuels, was to differentiate the economic development of the two continents and of the various national groups. In the possession of iron and coal in close proximity to each other, a primary requirement for the production of steel, North America is infinitely more fortunate than South America. Whereas in the southern continent coal deposits are small, scattered, of medium quality, and far removed from iron resources, the North Atlantic basin on the American side is one of the richest coal and iron regions of the world, with these fundamental materials found close together and near cheap water transportation. The consequence has been that 7 per cent of the

---

[5] The temperature drops approximately three degrees for every thousand feet of elevation; the difference of one mile in elevation is equal to six to eight hundred miles of distance from the equator.

world's population living in this favored area today performs half of the industrial work of the world. On the other hand, although South America possesses in Brazil, Chile, and Venezuela the world's most abundant supplies of excellent iron ore, because it has less than 2 per cent of the coal reserves of the world the continent is compelled to export its metals and raw products for fabrication abroad. Lacking sufficient coal for a steel industry, it is unlikely that South America can ever duplicate the industrial development that has been the outstanding feature of the history of the United States in the last hundred years, unless man can find some way of converting iron ore without coke, that is, unless he can eliminate the blast furnace.[6] So far, efforts to make pig iron by the use of hydroelectric power have been uneconomic. It is to be noted, however, that for some of the less well-known ingredients needed to give certain desired qualities to steel, the world must turn to South America. Brazil, for instance, is one of the few manganese-producing countries of the world, and a minimum of fourteen pounds of manganese must go into the making of every ton of steel; Peru has almost a monopoly of the world's known supply of vanadium, another important alloy in steel production. While South America lacks coal, she has not been left without fuel, for, like North America, the southern continent is fortunate in possessing rich oil reserves. The petroleum fields of Venezuela and Colombia are among the greatest in the world. Ecuador, Peru, Bolivia, and Patagonia also contain oil resources, although the quantity present in these areas has not been fully ascertained.

In most of the other important minerals South America is well off; in fact, that continent is richer in minerals than is Africa. The copper deposits of Chile rank next to those of the Belgian Congo and northern Rhodesia in richness and importance; Peru also has a substantial supply of this metal. In tin, Bolivia is the world's second greatest producer; Colombia holds this same rank in the production of platinum. The only important deposits of natural nitrate lie in the Atacama Desert in northern Chile. From the huge deposits of bauxite in British and Dutch Guiana respectively, Great Britain and the United States derive their import requirements of aluminum. America's resources of lead and zinc, on the other hand, are found chiefly in the northern continent. To the American hemisphere as a whole nature has been abundantly generous in mineral resources, though these have not been so distributed as to insure an equal industrial development in each political unit. If in the future, however, international cooperation and enlightened exchange of complementary

---

[6] For a thoughtful study of the economic situation and possibilities see F. Tannenbaum, *Whither Latin America* (New York: 1934). The second World War, however, has served to spur the larger states of South America along the pathway towards industrialization and national self-sufficiency.

commodities can transcend national boundaries, the minerals, as well as the other natural resources, of the two Americas should prove fully adequate for the well-being of all the inhabitants of the Western Hemisphere.

Considered in respect to their physical outlines and the broadest of their geographical features, the two American continents show certain strong similarities. However, when details are considered, the differences are also outstanding; thus far, and in nearly every instance, they have been more favorable to man's rapid economic development in North America than in South America.

II. NORTH AMERICA

In North America the four great geographical divisions—high new mountains in the west, old low mountains in the east, the intervening plains between, and the coastal lowland rim around the whole—stand out more clearly than they do in South America, where the coastal plain for long distances narrows to the vanishing point. These physical features in the northern continent, where the grain runs definitely north and south, have little relation, of course, to the international boundaries marking off the United States from Canada on the north and from Mexico on the south by politically devised lines that run east and west.

In the west, North America, like the southern continent, is a complex of high mountains and plateaus, stretching from Alaska in the north through Canada and the United States to southern Mexico, and spreading from west to east in serried ranks from the coast to the interior plains. On the whole, the heights and passes are lower and the slopes gentler than in the taller Andean system, though there are a number of North American peaks towering above 14,000 feet. The tallest giants of the system are Mount McKinley in Alaska, 20,300 feet, and Mount Logan in the Yukon, 19,850 feet. The major difference in the two systems, however, is in width. The principal heights of the western cordillera of North America not only lie farther back from the coast than do the highest ranges of the Andes, but the whole mass is much broader, reaching a width of more than a thousand miles through much of the United States.

To the west of the Rockies, in Washington and Oregon, lie the Cascade Mountains, and in eastern California the Sierra Nevada ranges. The intermontane area between these two systems contains the Columbia Plateau of Washington and Oregon, the Colorado Plateau, and the Great Basin. Still farther to the west is the longer Coast Range. Between the latter and the line of the Cascades (called in Canada the British Columbia Coast Range) are a number of important depressions, notably the Inside Passage of British Columbia, the Puget Sound trough of Washington, the Wil-

1. REGIONAL NORTH AMERICA

lamette Valley of Oregon, and the Valley of California. In Canada the mountain system is more compressed and rugged, with the principal ranges reduced to two, the intervening valleys narrower, and the passes more difficult. Across the southern border, in Mexico, the cordillera appears in two widely separated ranges: one, the Sierra Madre Occidental, keeping parallel to the Pacific; and the other, the Sierra Madre Oriental, following the line of the Gulf of Mexico. Both are finally merged in the Great Scarp of Oaxaca marked by a line of active volcanoes. Between the two ranges of Sierra Madre lies the Mexican plateau which, beginning as a broken tableland near the Rio Grande, rises to an elevation of 7,500 feet in the vicinity of Mexico City. Loftiest among the spectacular volcanic heights in Mexico are Orizaba and Popocatepetl, both exceeding 17,000 feet. North of Mexico this high mountain area, like the desert regions of the continent, was to be late in development by the white man; finally, the lure of the precious metals brought exploitation and some settlement.

On the other side of the continent, corresponding in location to the Guiana and Brazilian highlands of South America and of much the same altitude, are the ancient highlands and mountains of the Laurentian Shield and the Appalachian chain. The Laurentian Shield, a wide plateau surrounding Hudson Bay, is geologically the oldest part of America. It takes the form of a U-shaped peneplain, nearly two million square miles in extent, of worn crystalline rocks averaging about a thousand feet in altitude.[7] Rising on either side of the waters of Hudson Bay, it reaches elevations of 6,000 feet or more in the Torngat Mountains close to the eastern coast, but on the west rolls away from the great bay in very moderate elevations. Its western edge is marked by a line of lakes stretching from the Arctic Ocean through the Coppermine Basin, Great Bear Lake, Great Slave Lake, Lake Athabaska, Lake Winnipeg, and Lake of the Woods to a point beyond Lake Superior in the United States. After embracing the iron region of Minnesota and the upper peninsula of Michigan, the southern line of the Great Shield extends through the southeastern part of Georgian Bay, loops southward to include the Adirondacks, then passes north of the St. Lawrence River to the vicinity of Quebec city, and thence moves eastward to include the Labrador peninsula. In the Ice Age this area was overlaid with a continental ice cap which as it spread out over the land scraped away the rich surface soil, carrying it southward and leaving the region for the most part a barren wilderness, full of swamps between the rivers and lakes and marked by rocky ribs showing through the thin soil. Most of its streams flow into Hudson Bay and are rich in potential water power. Some of its surface has sufficient depth of soil for tree growth,

---

[7] For a more detailed description of this area see C. L. White and E. J. Foscue, *Regional Geography of Anglo-America* (New York: 1943), pp. 487-516.

though generally not for agriculture. Well to the south of James Bay, however, there is an area known as the Clay Belt, the bed of an old glacial lake which is now believed to have agricultural possibilities for growing wheat. Although forbidding in appearance and as yet not completely explored, the Laurentian Shield has been found to possess considerable mineral resources. The exploitation of the narrow gold-bearing belts that, in bow-shaped formations, extend northwestward from western Quebec diagonally across Ontario into the Great Bear Lake country, has made Canada the third largest gold-producing nation of the world. Copper, iron, silver, platinum, asbestos, and the world's largest supply of nickel are other important minerals of this area. Apart from these mining resources, however, the Laurentian plateau has generally been regarded as Canada's heaviest handicap, a wedge-like barrier lying between the St. Lawrence lowlands and the interior plains, to a considerable extent uninhabitable and yet including more than half of the nation's land area.

The Appalachian highlands extend in three parallel bands southwestward from Newfoundland and the St. Lawrence to the states of Georgia and Alabama. Not so ancient as the Laurentian highlands, the Appalachians are irregular masses of heavily eroded, rounded, forested hills that seldom exceed six thousand feet in height. The most easterly band, starting in Newfoundland, runs through the Maritime Provinces of Canada and covers all New England, where the White, Green, and Berkshire Mountains are part of the system. As it passes southward through New York and northern Pennsylvania the range is little more than a series of rolling hills, but in southeastern Pennsylvania it picks up height and divides into the Piedmont and the forest-covered, massive, steep, irregular Blue Ridge Mountains. In the Piedmont section, as the plateau rises from the coastal plain, it is marked by a series of waterfalls and rapids at the zone of contact between the crystalline rocks of the plateau and the soft sediments of the coastal plain. This is the famous "Fall Line" of colonial times. On one side lies the Tidewater country and on the other the highly diversified Appalachian uplands. The Piedmont itself is a long belt of foothills extending from southeastern Pennsylvania to Alabama, one hundred miles wide in places—a land of varied soil, rich in water power. Towering behind the Piedmont are the high forms of the Blue Ridge Mountains. The second band, west of the most eastern section of the Appalachians, is a fertile region composed of great valleys and prominent ridges that extends southward from Lake Champlain and includes the Lehigh, Lebanon, Cumberland, Shenandoah, and eastern Tennessee valleys. Farther west is the third Appalachian band; it consists of the Allegheny plateau which stretches southward from the Mohawk Valley through the Catskill Mountains of New York, overlooks the Hudson River, and continues through

Pennsylvania, West Virginia, Kentucky, Tennessee, and on into central Alabama. At the eastern edge of this Allegheny plateau in northeastern Pennsylvania lie the finest anthracite coal deposits in the world. The development of these, and more especially of the vast fields of bituminous coal that extend completely under the western part of the plateau, has imposed a predominantly industrial economy upon this part of the country.

Between the Appalachian and Laurentian highlands of the east and the Rockies of the west, and reaching from the Gulf of Mexico to the Arctic, lie the interior plains of America, increasing in height towards the west. Particularly fortunate is that section which lies between the Ohio and Missouri rivers. Here in gently rolling country the fertile soil owes its richness to the great ice cap which brought along a wealth of surface soil from the Laurentian upland and, with the help of wind and rivers, spread it evenly over the area. Endowed also with a good climate, sufficient rainfall, fine water communications, and fuel close at hand, this plains area of the Middle West was to become one of the world's richest agricultural regions. It should be noted that north of the international border, except for a small extension in the southern peninsula of Ontario between lakes Huron and Erie, there is no corresponding rich "Middle West" in Canada. Its place is taken by the forbidding Laurentian Shield.

The western half of the American plains, rolling from South Dakota westward to the Rockies and stretching northward into the Canadian provinces of Manitoba, Saskatchewan, and Alberta, has a somewhat different character. The country is not so low, level, or fertile as farther east and is deficient in rainfall. The character of the country is more broken, with occasional heights rising to five thousand feet. Here and there lava-topped mesas, or volcanic ridges, are in evidence. Economically this section was to develop as a country of wheat and cattle farming. Southward from South Dakota and Wyoming to the Rio Grande lie the "high plains," the sheep- and cattle-grazing country of America.

In no feature of its topography does North America differ more significantly from South America than in its possession of an important Atlantic and Gulf coastal area plentifully supplied with excellent harbors. Providing a foothold and nursery for European colonization, this region offered, in its wealth and variety of resources and in its accessibility, substantial rewards to ingenious and persevering adventurers. The natural barriers of the Appalachian ranges, bordering the coastal plain to the west, gave a considerable measure of protection to the infant colonies from inland dangers and from a too early dispersal of strength in large-scale migrations or adventures into the interior.

The coastal area falls into a number of regions each having its own distinctive characteristics. That extending from Newfoundland through the Maritimes and New England has been called the "drowned North Atlantic coast." [8] It is a region of fine harbors and a narrow coastal plain flanked towards the interior by the heavily forested, often stony ridges and plateaus of the Appalachian uplands. A large part of the population, living nowhere more than thirty-five miles from the sea, early looked to the ocean for a livelihood and developed a great fishing industry based on the riches of the coastal and Grand Banks fisheries and on the skill of the inhabitants in building and sailing their famous schooners. Later, through exploitation of water power, available from the numerous streams plunging to the sea from the nearby highlands, the region was to develop as a great manufacturing and commercial section, with skilled mariners carrying the products of New England to all corners of the earth in their large and fast clipper ships. Such outlying areas as Cape Cod, Nantucket, Martha's Vineyard, and Long Island also belong geographically to the coastal plain area. South of New York the harbors continue fine. In early colonial times the most famous area in this region was the Tidewater country of Virginia, drained by its four major rivers, the Potomac, Rappahannock, York, and James. The soil is not as fertile as the best in the United States, as it is sandy, leaches readily, and is not well drained; but the early settlers found it possible to grow corn, tobacco, wheat, and garden vegetables in sufficient abundance for their sustenance and their limited export trade. The combination of advantages which the region offered, easy access to the sea and overseas markets, protection from the interior by the Piedmont, navigable rivers, and arable ground, was sufficient to make it the most attractive in colonial America.

From the Tidewater area, where it is approximately two hundred miles wide, the coastal plain continues along the South Atlantic border to include the peninsula of Florida and then, curling about the southern end of the Appalachians in Georgia and Alabama, becomes more important as it increases to a width of three hundred miles and extends along the Gulf of Mexico past the embayment of the Mississippi and on to the Rio Grande. The general features along the South Atlantic and the Gulf are very similar for long distances. Sandy outer barrier beaches are separated from the mainland by tidal lagoons or salt water marshes, with their rims frequently broken by tidal inlets or wide estuaries and submerged bays, such as Chesapeake Bay, Albemarle Sound, Galveston Bay, and Mobile Bay. The streams tend constantly to form deltas and need frequent dredging. Most of those on the east coast are interrupted by rapids as they drop from the Piedmont to the coastal plain. The region of the Carolinas is marked by numerous off-shore shoals lying between the coast line and the Gulf Stream. Florida represents a portion of the coastal platform that has been

[8] *Ibid.*, chap. iv.

warped upwards. The soil of the coastal area south of the Tidewater region is of great variety. In some places it is arranged in longitudinal belts lying parallel to the border of the plain, one strip being sandy, another of limestone, and a third of clay. Where the soil is sandy, farming is difficult; but in other places the rich alluvial soil, in combination with a warm climate, is ideal for the staple crop of cotton, as well as for the production of semitropical fruits.

III. SOUTH AMERICA

South America is a continent forty-five hundred miles long and three thousand miles across at its greatest width. It has a dramatic geographical framework and an exciting climate. In available natural gifts, however, it has been called the "Cinderella of the continents" because of its many extraordinarily unfavorable features as a habitation for man. Its widest part lies squarely across the equator, which makes it the most tropical of all the continents. At the same time, it is the most mountainous of the land masses. Its principal mountain system, made up of several ranges placed in echelon fashion, runs the entire length of the continent, with an average height of more than 10,000 feet, and reaches a width of approximately two hundred miles, except in the Bolivian area where it is four hundred miles across. Its numerous pinnacles, many of them volcanic, are among the highest of the globe. Volcanic activity is found principally in three zones: (1) southern Colombia and Ecuador; (2) southern Peru and along the border of Bolivia and Chile; (3) the southern part of middle Chile. Such giants as Chimborazo and Cotopaxi in Ecuador, El Misti overlooking Arequipa in Peru, Sorata and Illimani towering above La Paz in Bolivia, and, in western Argentina, Aconcagua (23,081 feet), the loftiest spot in the Western Hemisphere, all rise above nineteen thousand feet.

There are three main divisions of the Andes, southern, central, and northern. The southern Andes, extending southward from the Atacama region to the straits, are paralleled on the west by a coastal range; lying between the two is the fertile central valley of Chile, thirty to sixty miles wide, and in many ways reminiscent of the central valley of California. The coastal range gives to the shore line of southern Chile a greatly indented, fiord-like character similar to that of British Columbia and southern Alaska.

The central Andes, stretching from northwestern Argentina to southern Colombia, are wider, higher, and more complex. In the southern portion two main ranges enclose an elevated *altiplano* which has as one of its features Lake Titicaca (elevation, 12,507 feet above sea level), the highest fresh-water lake in the world. The northern Andes in Colombia are

2. Regional South America

more habitable than the southern sections. Here they lie in three major divisions. The western cordillera is separated from the Pacific by the Atrato River valley and a coastal range. The central cordillera is separated from the western by the Cauca River valley and from the eastern by the valley of the Magdalena River. Along the whole length of the Andean range, the eastern slopes towards the interior plains are very steep. As if it were not enough to have this mountain wall along the whole Pacific Coast, some spurs of the Andes, as they reach the northern end of the continent, sweep in a great curve to the eastward, helping to make the southern shore of the Caribbean a barrier to penetration of the continent almost as formidable as its west coast. The whole Andean system constitutes, indeed, the longest continuous mountain chain in the world, not only barring east-west communication between contrasted coasts that might otherwise be complementary, but effectively preventing north-south interchange as well. Most of the passes over the Andes are more than ten thousand feet above sea level—three to four thousand feet higher than those in comparable North American regions. Even today, after more than four hundred years of white settlement, only in two regions—through La Paz and Santiago—has the range been entirely crossed by transcontinental railways; though two shorter lines—the Central Railway of Peru and the Arica of Chile—overtop the western range and plans are in progress to connect the La Paz railhead with lines from Brazilian as well as Argentinian cities on the Atlantic. As yet, however, the oceans are still not only the chief means of approach to the continent from the outside world but the principal means, except for the airplane, of intercommunication.

The location of the Andes reduces the Pacific coastal plain to a very narrow strip, which averages only about forty miles in width and sometimes disappears altogether. The great height of the range, together with the influence of the Humboldt (or Peru) Current combine to make it largely a semiarid or totally desert region where agriculture is possible only in irrigated river valleys and in oases. The Atacama Desert of the central Andean area, stretching six hundred miles between Arica and Caldera, is one of the driest deserts of the world; it is utterly barren with little rain ever recorded. While nitrate wealth has made this bleak region of some service to modern man, its middle location between Chile, Peru, and Bolivia serves to perpetuate the isolation and the separation from each other of these western states. For the areas immediately north and south of the Atacama, which also receive very little rain, the western rivers provide the life blood, but as streams they are great disappointments, being for the most part unnavigable and more than half of them entirely seasonal.

Unlike the other continents, South America has not a single important river flowing westward. Nor is the Pacific coastal region adequately provided with good harbors. The Atacama Desert, with its steep coastal escarpment, has none; visiting ships have to ride at anchor some distance off the shore. With very few exceptions, this is typical of the entire coastline; trade is dependent either upon open roadsteads or harbors suitable only for small coastal craft. Progressing southward from Panama there is no port of significance until the good harbor of Guayaquil, Ecuador, is reached. Farther south the best ports are Callao, Peru; Mollendo, Peru; and Valparaiso, Chile, where man has increased anchorage protection from the sweep of the waves by constructing giant breakwaters.

Despite its many physical drawbacks, however, it was the semiarid region of the north and central Andes and the narrow valleys of the western rivers that sheltered and fostered the most advanced native cultures that South America produced. These locations offered many advantages. In the numerous protected valleys and the high plateau region about Lake Titicaca primitive man found a wonderful balance of the fundamentals needed for the development of a pastoral and agricultural society of a relatively advanced type. Here Nature offered an invigorating and varied climate; fertile soil suitable for intensive agriculture if irrigated; pasturage for his flocks; useful llamas, alpacas, vicuñas, guinea pigs, partridges, and other forms of animal life; raw material for pottery, basket-making, and textiles; stone for building; and, above all, protection from enemies, especially from the fierce, primitive tribes of the eastern lowlands.[9] These Andean cultures, on being brought under control by Spain, were not entirely wiped out but remained to play a significant role in colonial times. The Spaniards in settling Peru, like the Indians before them, used not only the mountain regions but also the Pacific coastal area. Depending as they did on control of the sea (such control being the first necessity in maintaining essential communication with the homeland), the Spaniards sought always to remain in contact with it, and their largest cities were located near the shore.

Exclusive of the Andean area, South America has a much greater proportion of her surface in highlands than has North America. The most striking of these are the old, worn-down mountains of the Guiana highlands north of the Amazon, and, south of that great stream, the Brazilian highlands. The Guiana highlands, covering a considerable area of southeastern Venezuela as well as of the Guianas, lie in the tropical region between the Orinoco and the Amazon rivers. They are steep, flat-topped mountains with narrow valleys and heavily forested, especially on their northern sides. Geologically they consist of a huge pedestal of crystalline rocks above which rise tablelands, increasing in height up to the 8,635-

---

[9] Cf. P. A. Means, *Ancient Civilizations of the Andes* (London: 1931), pp. 17-26.

foot eminence of Mount Roraima, and are located where the borders of
Venezuela, Brazil, and British Guiana meet. Though at present practically
inaccessible, wholly undeveloped, and unfortunately politically subdivided,
these mountains are a potentially habitable region of considerable possibilities. South of the Amazon, the Brazilian highlands cover a great area
including the richest and most beautiful sections of that country. Most
important of their assets are great natural fertility of soil, wide variety of
climate, numerous rivers and waterfalls, and immense and varied mineral
wealth. Increasing in height towards the southeast, these highlands reach
their greatest altitude in Pico de Bandeira northeast of Rio de Janeiro,
towering 9,462 feet. Along the seaboard the mountains so closely fringe
the ocean in the Great Escarpment as to leave, south of Salvador in Baía,
little or no coastal plain. Northward there is a gradual rise from the coast
towards the interior. Yet these eastern tropical and semitropical fertile
highlands and rolling plateaus of Guiana and Brazil, with their immense
forest and mineral riches, did not stimulate a high development of native
cultures comparable to those of the secluded, semiarid valleys and altiplanos
of the central and northern Andes of western South America.[10] Except
in terms of the human factor, this is hard to explain. In some way these
Brazilian and Guiana highlands failed to provide the balance of qualities
that the Indians needed for reaching maximum achievement. Perhaps
primitive man missed the greater protection from enemies that the higher
and more shut-in regions of the Andes offered. It is to be observed, however, that on the whole the natives in these eastern highland areas had
advanced in their culture somewhat beyond those on the nearby plains.

Distant and distinct in character from the true highland areas of the
northeast, and still more unfavorable to primitive man, is the high piedmont plain of Patagonia. This vast, dusty, wind-swept region of Argentina, analogous to the high plains of North America, reaches from the
Río Colorado on the north to the Strait of Magellan on the south. On the
west, Patagonia is separated from the Andes by a narrow belt of lowland;
on the east, it reaches the shores of the Atlantic. In general, the area is a
relatively level plateau rising towards the west, crossed from west to east
by a number of rivers—including the Colorado, Negro, Chubut, and Santa
Cruz—and cut by many deep canyons. As the desert cliffs of the plateau
touch the very water's edge of the Atlantic and extraordinarily high tidal
waves rush into the river mouths, the area has no good harbors. The river
valleys and canyon bottoms supply sufficient water to make possible only a

---

[10] There is an interesting discussion of the relation of primitive man to various South
American areas in C. F. Jones, "Geographical Background of the Colonial Period in South
America" in *Colonial Hispanic America*, edited by A. C. Wilgus (Washington: 1936),
chap. iii.

sparse population. Through the pre-Columbian period the inhabitants were mostly Indian nomads who made a precarious living by hunting with their stone slings, called *bolas,* the wild guanaco and rhea; later in the colonial age, Indians and mestizos of the region were given to supplementing their hunting operations by stealing cattle from white men in the border areas to the north and west.

Between the high young Andes of the west and the older highlands of the east, and between the coastal ranges of the north and the Guiana highlands, stretch the main lowlands of South America. On the whole they occupy a smaller part of South America than do the prairies in the northern continent. Moreover they do not include any considerable coastal plains, except at certain river mouths. But in the broad *savannas, llanos, campos, pampas,* and the Chaco, they include about one quarter of the continent. To the north of the Orinoco River, stretching towards the coastal mountains, lie the llanos of Venezuela: tropical, featureless, grass-covered plains, bisected by slow-moving, winding rivers, they are subject to alternate drought and inundation and are plagued with insect pests. Having few domestic animals, the Indians neglected these plains, but with the coming of the white man they became a great cattle-raising area. From colonial times herds of cattle, owned by absentee ranchers who for the most part made their homes in the more attractive central highland area, have been left to the care of nomadic half-breed llaneros who became typical of a distinctive way of Venezuelan life.

Farther south are the vast, tropical, forested plains of the Orinoco and the Amazon, the largest lowland area of South America, extending from the foot of the Andes, within three hundred miles of the Pacific, eastward across the continent. Contrary to the usual habit of river plains, these Amazon lowlands are much wider upstream than down, dwindling to a comparatively narrow floor plain in the lower reaches of the river. To the south, the plains of the Amazon join those of the Río de la Plata system in Mato Grosso. Between the Andean piedmont and the Paraná-Paraguay river system is an alluvial plain known as the Gran Chaco, composed of sediments brought down from the Andes. Though crossed by two considerable tributaries of the Paraguay, the Pilcomayo and the Bermejo, the Gran Chaco is an ill-drained, swampy, rather featureless area of open savannas, subject to annual floods and broken here and there by dense jungles in which grow the commercially valuable *quebracho* trees from which tannin is secured. It was in these hot, humid lowland jungles that the most primitive of the South American Indians dwelt.

On the eastward side of the Paraná-Paraguay system, towards the Río Uruguay, is a well-watered area, beautiful with spectacular waterfalls descending where highlands and plains meet. South of the Río de la Plata the great temperate Argentinian plains known as the pampas stretch away for fifteen hundred miles. The rainier and more fertile eastern area around Buenos Aires is known as the humid pampa, that farther to the west is called the dry pampa, or simply the pampa. In a temperate region of mild winters, and summers with sufficient rainfall, the pampa's great fertility is due to its deep alluvial soil, composed of hundreds of feet of loess—fine unconsolidated sediments borne thither on the winds from the drier regions to the west and south. Free of stones and covered with luscious grasses, it has become in modern times a paradise for the livestock industry, with an outlet to the world's markets through Buenos Aires. Its one disadvantage arises from deficient drainage; it is wholly flat, there are no good rivers, and hundreds of small ponds stand about. This region, like the other great lowland areas of South America, remained largely undeveloped until the close of the colonial period. The Indians had no use for open savannas; they possessed few domestic animals, and needed more adequate protection such as was provided by the tropical forest. The Spaniards, though they brought cattle, horses, and sheep, came primarily for quick wealth in the form of gold and silver and neglected the exploitation of the grasslands.

In her rivers, South America is less fortunate than North America. She has rivers more remarkable but not so useful. While possessing in the Amazon, Orinoco, and La Plata systems three of the most colossal stream arrangements in the world, with their headwaters so close together that they might easily be joined by canals, certain features have long restricted their usefulness as means of communication. That not one of the three led into lands rich in mineral wealth, the one product of vital interest to the Spaniards, greatly decreased their importance through colonial times. The usefulness of the Amazon, unequalled in the world for navigability (it extends from the Atlantic westward for twenty-three hundred miles) is much decreased by the fact that it flows through an equatorial jungle unsuitable for continuous white occupation. Moreover, while the main river itself is open, most of its great tributaries are interrupted near their junction with the Amazon by falls and rapids. The Orinoco also drains an extensive tropical region generally unsuitable to civilized man, though it has great importance as an entrance into the llanos and the Guiana highlands. The Plata system, in conjunction with the Paraguay and Paraná, forms a great waterway penetrating fifteen hundred miles through habitable country, but suffers from shifting channels and sand bars in the estuary.

In Brazil some of the largest rivers flow in the wrong direction to be of maximum utility. Rising in the southeastern highlands almost within sight of the Atlantic, a number of streams turn westward to find a way to the sea through the Río de la Plata system. Others like the São Francisco trace a northern course for many miles before finding a way through the mountain wall to the Atlantic. Because of resistance to erosion of the underlying volcanic structure, many eastern South American rivers are interrupted in their course by scenically magnificent but commercially obstructing waterfalls. The most famous are the Iguassú Falls on the borders of Brazil and Argentina, where the Rio Iguassú tumbles over the edges of the underlying diabase into the Paraná canyon, and the famous Guaíra Falls which occur on the Paraná River near the northeastern border of Paraguay. Of the northward-flowing rivers, the Magdalena River is the most important, providing a means of entrance into the highlands of central Colombia ever since the discovery of the continent. Navigation on its waters, however, has always been plagued by river shallows and numerous rapids.

Around all its coasts South America has poor harbor facilities. The deficiencies of the west coast have been mentioned. On the north coast the harbors have only limited protection. Even the east coast suffers serious disability. The harbor of Buenos Aires, the principal outlet for the produce of the Argentinian pampa, is kept open only by constant dredging. The magnificent Brazilian harbor of Rio de Janeiro has its usefulness as an outlet for interior produce greatly limited by the fact that immediately back of it are precipitous mountain slopes traversible only with great difficulty.

Chapter 2

INDIAN AMERICA

I. THE GENERAL PATTERN

The first known inhabitants of the Americas were northern Asiatics of a Mongoloid type, who arrived by way of Alaska in successive waves of immigration across Bering Strait some ten to twenty-five thousand years ago.[1] Striking evidence of at least this degree of antiquity for man in America came in 1926 with a purely chance discovery in an eroding arroyo near Folsom, New Mexico. Here were found a number of flint spear points and scrapers, obviously grooved and chipped by man, lying in close association with the huge bones of a type of bison known to have become extinct at least ten thousand years ago. The soil deposits in which these artifacts and animal bones occurred were of the same distant period. From a study of the region it was clear that man must have been in America early enough to find the now arid high plains still well watered and covered with lush grasses. Here was concrete evidence that the early Americans had known at first hand and hunted with the help of a spear, tipped with a flint point and probably flung with a spear-thrower, the straight-horned Taylor's bison that in great herds had found food and water in the area. Since those first finds, the pathway of the "Folsom hunters" has been traced back through dozens of camp sites across the United States and Canada to a starting point in Alaska.[2] Other archaeological discoveries at Sandía in New Mexico, in Cochise County, Arizona, and elsewhere have served to confirm the view that man had spread over a considerable part of North America at a period not far removed from the close of the last great glaciation. The earliest Americans may actually have seen the retreating continental glaciers! But nowhere have there been found any human remains of the Folsom man himself.

---

[1] For these figures, and the author's reasons for supporting them, see A. L. Kroeber, *Anthropology* (New York: rev. 1948), pp. 679-86; see also S. G. Morley, "Maya Civilization, —100% American," *Forum,* LXXXVIII (August, 1927), pp. 227-28. W. W. Howells in "The Origins of American Racial Types" (in *The Maya and Their Neighbors,* New York: 1940, pp. 3-4) states "Almost all authorities, in various fields, agree on a limit of ten or twelve thousand years (with conceivable maximum of twenty thousand) for the time since it began." A recent scholarly work by P. S. Martin, G. I. Quimby, and D. Collier, *Indians before Columbus* (Chicago: 1947, p. 15) places the beginning of immigration at some twenty thousand years ago.

[2] For a short, lively account of the Folsom finds see F. C. Hibben, *The Lost Americans* (New York: 1946).

Mastodon, Royal Bison, and Woolly Mammoth. Details of mural by Charles R. Knight, "Mastodon, Royal Bison, and Horse" in the American Museum of Natural History. (Courtesy of the American Museum of Natural History)

Model of an Old Empire Mayan temple at Tikal, Guatemala. (Courtesy of the
American Museum of Natural History)

New Empire architecture: in foreground, El Castillo; in background, the Temple of Warriors and the Court of a Thousand Columns, Chichén-Itzá, Yucatan.

Old Empire sculpture: stela from Copán, Honduras. (Courtesy of the American Museum of Natural History)

New Empire sculpture: columns in the Temple of the Warriors, Chichén-Itzá, Yucatan. (Courtesy of the American Museum of Natural History)

Whether a catastrophe in the old homeland or some fundamental change of circumstances, such as the pressure of overpopulation with diminishing food supply, drove these red men forth from northern Asia, we may never know. But we may be sure that they came and enough of them were able to maintain themselves to form the basis of a population for a hemisphere believed hitherto void of human inhabitants. Here probably were the real discoverers of America. It is not exactly known how these first Americans succeeded in crossing the fifty-six miles of ocean that separate America from Asia at the narrowest point. The feat, however, was not a difficult one. On fine days the American shore is clearly visible from the Asiatic coast. The beckoning headlands of Alaska may well have seemed to primitive man, once he had learned to make crude boats, no more unreachable than distant heights along his own shore. The centrally placed Diomede Islands would have helped as stepping stones, leaving the longest stretch of open water a mere twenty-five miles. The Eskimo of today in his primitive skin boat often makes the journey. However, an open-water crossing may not have been necessary. Some of the earliest Americans may have crossed on the drift ice that even today forms large fields north of the strait, and in the more severe winters of that age may have provided an ice bridge. Furthermore, it is possible that a land bridge, over which animals must have come to America in Pleistocene times, may have persisted long enough to permit early man to walk to America over land.

The origin of America's first inhabitants was thus Asiatic, and their advent came at a comparatively late date. Nowhere has there been discovered generally accepted evidence of a really primitive human type, nor are there any anthropoid apes. There have been found in America no human remains that scientists will agree correspond in age to the Heidelberg or Neanderthal man in Europe.

This indicates a unique prehistory for the continent and sets America definitely apart from the Old World where there are numerous traces of man and early simian types in Asia, Europe, and Africa of immense antiquity, in some cases hundreds of thousands of years in the past. The isolation of America and the remoteness of its avenues of approach from the original foci of population in the Old World offer at least a partial explanation why America alone among the continents remained uninhabited so long. Eventually, however, Asiatic man, probably in groups arriving hundreds of years apart and following in the footsteps of such Pleistocene mammals as the bison, the mammoth, the mastodon, the giant sloth, the great beaver, and the wild horse [3] and camel, reached the

[3] Like many of the other Pleistocene animals, the early American horse became extinct soon after man's arrival in America. A horse of different species was, of course, introduced thousands of years later by the Spaniards.

northwest corner of the American continent and opened the human chapter in the history of the Western Hemisphere.

These first American immigrants showed considerable diversity of physical form. While, like their descendants of today, they possessed in common yellow-brown to red-brown skins, high cheekbones, straight coarse black hair, scanty beards and dark eyes that appear oblique, in the more fundamental matters of stature and shape of head there was a good deal of variety. Some were longheads, some were roundheads; some were short in stature, and some were tall. Their culture does not appear to correspond exactly to any Old World classification, though it parallels the Upper Palaeolithic of Europe in time. They depended entirely for food and clothing on hunting the abundant and varied game they found on the continent, on fishing, and on the gathering of roots, seeds, nuts, and fruits. They had no knowledge of agriculture, weaving, pottery, or metals, though perhaps they had learned to make rude baskets and had domesticated the dog. Their principal weapons were the stone club, the spear with its skilfully chipped flint point, probably the spear-thrower, and the harpoon; the bow and arrow perhaps came later. Among their most useful implements were the flint knife, the scraper, the stone axe, and the fire drill. Their religion was probably a mixture of magic and animism. Social organization rested on a basis of blood, kinship, and contiguity, with communal and family responsibility well understood. An aggregation of family groups into a tribe led by a chief was an early gain, a step already taken by the more advanced of the migratory groups or taken soon after arrival in the New World. Of the stage reached in linguistic development among the aborigines, we know very little. If differentiation into a variety of tongues had not already proceeded apace at the time of crossing, divergence into numerous groups took place rapidly afterwards, largely because of the absence of the steadying influence of a written language and because of the ever-widening geographical barriers separating groups in the New World.

Once arrived in Alaska, and finding themselves unopposed by man or too formidable wild animals, the first immigrants soon moved southward either urged on from behind by new hordes or attracted from the bleakness of the first wilderness to the more moderate climate and the prospect of more abundant food ahead. It is of course impossible to follow with any exactness the ebb and flow of the tribes, or the routes pursued. The vanguard of the first immigrants may have reached the isthmus connecting the two American continents within a few hundred years. Here in the tropics the advance southward of the wanderers was slower as the geographical obstacles increased in difficulty, but by the close of two or three thousand years after the migration began, the wave of humanity had probably reached the southern tip of South America.

Through the following ten thousand years the red man lived in America unmolested and uninfluenced by Asia or Europe except by the arrival of new groups of his own people, and troubled only by internal dissension. Even this could hardly have been serious in view of the almost unlimited space available. Through those ages, as in all primitive society, the struggle upward was very slow. Except in certain favored areas, change took the form of variation and differentiation rather than progress. Differing environments played their part in causing physical variations in height and color, as well as in density of population, while geographical barriers and lack of communication produced an amazing number of languages.

The discovery of agriculture is now thought to have occurred independently in several areas in Middle and South America.[4] Inland valleys or plateaus of moderate altitude, in or near the tropics, and at some distance from the sea, appear to have provided originally the necessary favorable environment. Although in South America manioc and the white potato were under cultivation at an early date, by far the most important of the plants to be domesticated by the American Indian was maize, or Indian corn, which through adaptation long before the Christian era had become the staff of life in large areas of both North and South America.

For some reason at present not understood, the Western Hemisphere was much poorer in wild seed-grasses than the Old World, where, four or five thousand years before the Christian era, man possessed not only wheat, the basis of the dry-land civilizations of the Old World, and rice, the foundation of culture in wet lands, but also barley, oats, rye, and millet.[5] In America, the only known cereals that were indigenous were wild rice and teosinte, a native grass that grows on the Mexican plateau. The former the Indians never learned to cultivate though they used it in its wild state for food. But from teosinte, or some other pre-maize grass, they succeeded in developing the modern maize. Perhaps this first came about from an accidental spilling of seeds from a basket and their subsequent germination. However it happened, the results were

---

[4] For expressions of this view see *The Maya and Their Neighbors* (New York: 1940); R. Linton, "Crops, Soils and Culture in America," chap. iii, p. 34; A. V. Kidder, "Problems of the Highland Maya," chap. vii, p. 119; S. K. Lothrop, "South America as Seen from Middle America," chap. xxxi, p. 420. A recent discussion of the problem will be found in S. G. Morley, *The Ancient Maya* (New York: 1947), pp. 137-41. The author believes the weight of evidence to be in favor of the highlands of western Guatemala as the place of origin for domestication of maize.

[5] H. J. Spinden, "What is Civilization? Answer of Ancient America: Part I, Economic and Industrial" in *Forum*, LXXIV (August, 1925), pp. 162-71.

momentous. Not only did the new cereal prove to be one of the most adaptable and useful plants in the world, but its cultivation brought in its train a fundamental social change; for, once the idea was grasped that a steady supply of food could be secured from the systematic planting of seeds instead of its having to be sought in periodic migrations, the road of progress had opened for the Indian. Agriculture meant freedom from starvation, a permanent home, the growth of village communities, division of labor, and the possibilities of trade and commerce. These in their turn brought some degree of the leisure necessary for the development of art, education, and invention.

From the highlands of Mexico or Guatemala, where maize in North America was domesticated to dry-land conditions, it spread over the rest of Middle America, holding closely to the upland regions. Here it provided a basis for what is known as the Archaic culture in which primitive pottery and weaving, which now made their appearance in America for the first time, were accompanied by a rudimentary religion and simple art forms. All this was earlier than 1000 B.C.[6] The credit for the later adaptation of maize to humid tropical conditions should belong, it is thought, to Maya-speaking people who had been living a backward, nomadic, hunting and fishing life in the Petén Lake region of Guatemala, or possibly along the Gulf of Mexico south of the Pánuco River.[7] Learning of maize from their neighbors of the plateau, these primitive folk succeeded in adapting the new cereal to their own humid environment at least some six or seven centuries before the great period of Maya culture known as the "Old Empire." In the fertile soil of a region of heavy rainfall and continuous warm climate where minimum efforts brought maximum food results, the newly acquired staple became the basis of a highly developed culture. As food reserves accumulated, population increased and classes devoted to religion and aesthetic matters were able to arise. Pottery, weaving, and other arts in elaborate forms began to flourish. In the centuries after the advent of the Christian era, this Maya culture of Central America attained the highest level of achievement that pre-Columbian America was to know. It rested securely on the basis of successful agriculture, of which the production of corn was the principal element.

From Middle America[8] the cultivation of maize spread slowly northward as well as southward. It was very early associated with the domestication of squash. Beans, one of the two early protein plants of America,

[6] S. G. Morley places the first cultivation of maize "sometime during the third or second millennium before Christ." Morley, *The Ancient Maya,* p. 44.

[7] Final determination of the origin and trek of the Maya awaits further research. For a recent discussion of this subject see Morley, *The Ancient Maya,* pp. 39-45.

[8] Middle America includes Mexico, Central America, and the West Indies.

probably were a somewhat later development, but once their food value was understood they helped to free primitive American man from his dependence on hunting and on the gathering of wild nuts to balance his diet. Tobacco, probably used originally in its wild state, may also have been first cultivated in Middle America, although there are strong reasons to assign the plant a South American origin. In any case it was early known both north and south of the isthmus. In South America it took second place in popularity to the coca leaf which was chewed for its stimulating effects. In the dry-land areas these early staples were widely accompanied by tomatoes, chili peppers, and sunflowers, and in the wet-land areas were supplemented by manioc, sweet potatoes, cacao, and pineapples.

Agriculture among the Indians, however, even for those tribes that practised it most extensively, remained till the days of the Discovery in a primitive stage of development. Rotation of crops and fertilization of soil were little understood, and were practiced, if at all, only sporadically. Fallowing was the principal method the Indian knew for restoring used soil; this fact largely limited the size of settlements and forced frequent changes in the location of communities. Crude stone implements made impossible anything but elementary methods of cultivation. With only a flint axe and a stone-bladed knife at his disposal the Indian had to depend largely upon fire to clear his land. For the planting of seed he merely broke the surface with a sharp-pointed stick. Not until the Conquest was the plow or other implement for turning over the soil introduced into America. No practical application of the wheel assisted him in farming operations: he had no water wheel, windmill, potter's wheel, or spinning wheel, but relied on manpower and skill of hand alone. He ground his corn between two stones and twisted by hand the yarn he used. While a number of tribes made tools, utensils, and ornaments of native copper, as they did of silver and gold, they treated these metals for the most part as malleable stone and were far from a true metal age. Stone tools remained, till the time of the Discovery, the basis of the material culture of the vast majority of the Indian tribes. The amount of labor necessary restricted farming operations, determined the character of the red man's habitation, and severely limited his leisure.

This first American farmer also had few domestic animals. The early horse had become extinct soon after man crossed Bering Strait. Dogs and turkeys were eaten in a few localities, but even in these cases were luxuries. In South America the llama and related species were never milked and were considered so valuable as draft animals and for their wool that they were strictly protected and not killed for food except on great ceremonial occasions. But though severely handicapped in methods of husbandry, the Indian made a most notable contribution in the great number and variety of products of nutritional and medicinal value that he succeeded in developing from their wild state. To supplement the returns from his inadequate farm he turned to greater account than any other people of the world many wild plants, roots, fruits, berries, and nuts that the New World offered him. Quinine, coca, and other drugs, as well as cochineal, cacao, and various gums were all adapted to his use. Not all the tribes were equally proficient or well supplied, but in these matters most of them were far in advance of the Europeans. The Indian was also a good fisherman and supplemented his diet extensively with the teeming fish from the oceans, lakes, and rivers. On land the density of game was by no means the same in all regions, but fortunately was more abundant in those lands inhabited by the most backward groups. Even the least advanced were wise enough to be thrifty in the killing of game and carefully avoided practices that might lead to its extermination. Generally speaking, the Indians were fine naturalists, knowing well the life histories of the animals they hunted and recognizing them at every stage of development. The seasonal character of the wild food supply greatly affected daily life, particularly among the more primitive tribes. Frequent migrations meant temporary housing and poor living conditions; despite periodic moving, only a few groups could escape the stress of near starvation when game was scarce and weather conditions were unfavorable.

In social organization, the fundamental characteristic arrangement except in a few advanced areas (and even in these to some extent) was that of all primitive society, namely, the local group. This was a loose kinship band living in a small village under an elected or hereditary local leader, whose power, however, had distinct limitations. Some groups made a distinction between the permanent peace chief and the temporary war leader. For an enterprise requiring the services of a large group, such as a bison hunt or a raiding party, several villages would often join forces temporarily. Government for most of Indian America was not linked with the idea of boundaries, or country, or neighborhood, but lodged in the old, wise men of the community who administered customary law in which the individual counted for little and group welfare was the supreme consideration. Where the clan system was fully developed, it functioned for political as well as social and ceremonial purposes. Many of the most advanced tribes had matrilineal clan organization in which descent was reckoned in the female line, others followed a patrilineal pattern. In North America the highest form that political organization ever assumed was that of the loose confederation, such as the Spaniards found among the Aztecs of Mexico and the English and French met in the Iroquois of the Northeast Woodland. In South America, an absolutist, highly centralized state was discovered among the Incas of Peru. These examples, however, of the large, permanently organized political units were exceptions and not the rule. Real property was universally owned by the family group undivided. As land required co-operative effort to work and, as young and old were dependent on the able-bodied workers, this kind of communal ownership seemed to be the most natural arrangement. (For centuries after the Conquest, the Indian was to find it hard to comprehend what the white man meant by the buying and selling of land.) There was, however, some private property such as tools, clothes, and weapons. In the home, food and furnishings were owned or controlled by the women. Songs, magic spells, and dances might be owned by the individual—an interesting form of copyright. Slaves, too, might be privately owned. Marriage customs in general varied widely from the absence of any rite to strictly monogamous practice. Often priests, medicine men, chiefs, and other persons of distinction might have a plurality of wives where this was forbidden to lesser folk. Consanguineous alliances were strictly avoided by most groups. Chastity before marriage was not greatly insisted upon, but after marriage adultery was punished severely. Divorce, where it occurred, was mostly informal and accompanied by compensation.

Religion, chiefly in the form of a belief in the animation of nature, was closely entwined with every aspect of the life of the Indian community. Throughout America there was an unusual development of ritual and a fondness for symbolism and cult ceremonial. These, following the cycle of the seasons, were associated most frequently with maize, rain, fire, smoke, and sun. The four quarters of the world and the sacred number four were other common concepts ascribed mystic meaning. Underlying all this for the more enlightened was the idea of a Great Spirit; this was strongest on the plains. Everywhere the effort was made to learn by means of special revelation the divine will for the group, or the person, through lonely vigils or in public performances, in fasts, dances, and sacrifices. A rich mythology had as its most common feature the myth of the divine hero-civilizer or culture hero who, after dwelling for a time with men and establishing the existing order, takes his departure, promising to return. This story was but one of many widespread legends concerning imaginary beings, the most unique of which were the Thunderbird and the Plumed Serpent. The power of the medicine man, the shaman, associated with the faith in animism, differed from tribe to tribe. There were also religious prophets and other reformers. Burial customs varied from complete neglect and disposal of the corpse in the family rubbish heap to the careful construction of permanent stone tombs. Where cannibalism existed it was generally associated with religious ceremonial, but it is now thought not to have been as widespread as was once generally believed.

When Columbus arrived the American continents were inhabited from the Arctic to the Antarctic. Considering how much was virgin forest, the habitable areas were probably not too sparsely peopled, although there are few materials from which to arrive at any reliable estimate of numbers. Guesses run from eight and a half to fifty millions. A recent, careful statistical study places the probable number of natives in both North and South America at the time of the Conquest at 13,385,000 of which number 1,000,000 is assigned to the region north of Mexico, 4,500,000 to Mexico, 6,785,000 to South America. Such a low estimate is, however, disputed by many specialists whose figures for specific areas point to a much higher aggregate.[9] It is clear that the Indian population was by no means evenly distributed. Certain favorable regions, such as Mexico, Central America, Peru, Colombia, and the Mississippi area, were thickly settled. Others were very thinly peopled. In general the regions of greatest population were those of highest culture. North of Mexico there was great diversity of groups and modes of life, and among them all kinds of cultural cross-currents were discernible. This phenomenon can be accounted for by the fact that it sometimes occurred that two or more groups that had long lived together would separate, driven apart perhaps by food scarcity, and then would later come together again bringing with them the results of external contacts made in the interval of separation.

Students have attempted to classify the Indians in various ways, among others in language groups and cultural areas. On a linguistic basis the Indian peoples appear very diverse, especially in the northern continent. While the distinct speech families in the two Americas have been placed at eighty, the tendency now is to reduce this number as comparative linguistic studies reveal underlying unities.[10] North of Mexico some language families, like the Algonquian and Athapascan, occupied extensive areas. Each speech family was made up for the most part of tribes that had long lived near each other, but it also included groups that in the course of time had drifted apart or become characterized by different social customs.

In North America, the highly diversified Athapascans stretched generally through the far north, south of the Eskimo, but also included such distant relatives as the colorful Navaho and fierce Apache of the southwest. The Algonquins proper dwelt in the St. Lawrence valley, but related

[9] *Cf.* Angel Rosenblat, *La población indígena de América desde 1492 hasta la actualidad* (Buenos Aires: 1945). A critical review of this work appears in *Hispano American Historical Review* XXVI, 1946, pp. 353-56. For higher figures for special areas, see S. G. Morley in *The Ancient Maya* (New York: 1947), p. 316, who mentions 13,300,000 as a conceivable figure for the population of the Yucatan Peninsula at the height of Mayan development; also P. A. Means in *Ancient Civilizations of the Andes* (New York: 1942), p. 296, offers the figure 16,000,000 for the population of the Inca Empire.
[10] See Kroeber, *op. cit.*, p. 216.

groups extended along the Atlantic from Labrador as far south as Virginia
and the Carolinas and spread westward to include tribes of the Great
Lakes area, like the Illinois and Kickapoo, as well as Plains Indians like
the Blackfoot and Cheyenne, while others of this great family lived in far-
off California.[11] The famous Iroquois family included not only the "Five
Nations" of the Iroquois League living in western New York and Pennsylvania but also the Hurons of Ontario and the Tuscaroras and Cherokees
of the Carolinas. The Shoshonean group was one of great cultural contrasts not only comprising the Shoshones proper of the Rocky Mountains
and southern plateau area, but also the Comanches of the Plains, the Hopis
of the Pueblo region, the lowly Utes of California, and the highly cultured
Aztecs of Mexico. The Siouan family, whose original home was in southeastern United States but many of whose tribes came to live in the Plains
area, included such tribes as the Crow, Mandan, Omaha, Assiniboin, Win-
nebago, and Catawba.

In Middle America the more important of the larger linguistic groups
were the Nahuatlan, the Zapatecan, and the Mayan. In South America, in
the western cordillera and coastal regions, were the outstanding linguistic
families of the Chibchas of Colombia and western Ecuador, the Aymaras
and Quechuas of Peru and Bolivia, and the Araucanians of Chile. To the
east of the Andes, extending over the West Indies and Venezuela as well
as through the northern tropical forests of Brazil and the Guianas, were the
mild, agricultural Arawaks and the fiercer, more primitive Caribs. The
Tapuyan stock of Brazil were among the oldest people of the continent. To
the east and south were the Tupis, among whom the Guaranis of the
Paraguay River basin were the highest in culture. In the province of Jujuy
in the northern part of what is today the Argentine Republic there flourished the Calchaquí village culture reminiscent of the Pueblo culture of
southwestern North America. On the plains of Argentina were tribes
related in language to the Araucanians of Central Chile. In the far south
were the primitive Fuegians and "giant" Patagonians.

As many as twenty areas in pre-Columbian America have been recognized
as possessing distinctive cultural characteristics.[12] Among those lying north
of the Isthmus are the Eskimo, Northwest, California, Plateau, MacKen-
zie-Yukon, Plains, Northeast Woodland, Southeast Woodland, Southwest,
and Mexican. Those in South America include Chibchan, Andean, Pata-
gonian, the Tropical Forest, and Antillean. It is evident that geographical

---

[11] Some of the most colorful personalities of the colonial period were of Algonquian stock,
for example, Pocahontas, King Philip, Pontiac, and Tecumseh. Many Algonquian words have
passed into common American usage: moccasin, moose, caribou, raccoon, squaw, papoose,
tomahawk, toboggan, caucus, etc.

[12] For a recent classification see Kroeber, *op. cit.*, pp. 785-92; for a slightly different
grouping, cf. C. Wissler, *The American Indian* (New York: 3rd ed., 1938), chap. xiv.

environment had the primary influence in forming these cultural distinctions though similar physical conditions did not always produce the same culture among different racial groups. North of the Isthmus, the focal point of highest culture was in Middle America, and from there spread by diffusion in greater or less intensity to other areas. In South America the high point of culture was the Andean region, but its influence upon its neighbors is now believed to have been much more limited than that mediated by Mexico in the northern continent.

It is to be noted that it was in the areas where life was most primitive that hostility to the white man was longest continued and European settlement most delayed. Where the population was very largely nomadic, as in the Plains areas in both North and South America, assimilation was never to take place. The natives here were finally exterminated, scattered, or placed on reservations, and in consequence were to have little influence on subsequent culture. Spain, whose colonial empire was everywhere surrounded by a belt of nomadic life, made a long and sustained effort to bring this group under control through a system that combined the permanent mission and a line of military posts. She met with only partial and temporary success.

In the areas where some agriculture supplemented hunting and fishing and where the natives were higher in the cultural scale—as in most of the Brazilian area of South America, the coast of the Caribbean, the West Indian Islands, and eastern and southern United States—there was also a complete dispersal in the face of the white man's advance, either by flight, decimation by disease, or death in warfare. Depopulation after the Conquest was general and rapid. The Indians in these regions resisted forced labor in all its forms, and when caught in its toils proved unsatisfactory workmen. They were therefore, early in the colonial period, replaced by Negro slaves whose cultural mores were to make a far deeper mark on later American life. It was only in the regions of settled agricultural life and dense population that the American natives in any numbers survived the Conquest and, refusing to retreat before the European invasion, remained a lower and conquered class in colonial society, influenced by, and in turn influencing, the new masters. These areas lay entirely within the boundaries of the Spanish dominions.

II. MIDDLE AMERICA

The Mayas

The three main groups of Indians whose achievements in the pre-Columbian age are outstanding and whose influence on later development of American life possesses striking and permanent significance

were the Mayas of Central America, the Aztecs of Mexico, and the Incas
of Peru. It was not long after crossing the Atlantic that the Spaniards
moved into the areas of these most advanced American aboriginal cultures. Columbus on his fourth voyage cruised along the coast of Central
America; and his successors, soon after their occupation of the West
Indian islands, began the exploration of the Isthmus of Panama which
rapidly became a second focus of exploratory operations.

It was in 1517 that the first Mayan town in Yucatan was sighted, two
years later Cortés landed at Vera Cruz, and by 1527 Pizarro was on his
way to Peru. Though the Spaniards were amazed at the evidences of
high cultural achievements they encountered in these areas, cupidity,
religious zeal, and military necessity combined to effect at their hands
the speedy destruction of the native cultures. In later times, scholars have
been so impressed by the elaborate character of the social organization,
the art, architecture, and religion of these groups of Indians at the time
of the Conquest that some have gone so far as to speculate whether
this culture could really ever have been developed by the crude people
who came over Bering Sea. It has even been suggested that the attainments in this area stem from Egyptian culture that, passing through the
Near East, India, and the islands of the South Seas, reached Middle and
South America somehow across the Pacific. The majority of scholars,
however, basing their opinion partly on the study of the time element
involved, believe that the high Indian cultures really arose independently
in America and that the cultivation of maize provided the necessary
economic basis.[13]

Of the two major cultures of Middle America, the Maya and the
Aztec, the former is the older and more important. Indicative of the his-
toric and cultural place they occupy, the Mayas have been called the
Greeks of Indian America; the most exciting archaeological work proceeding in America is occupied with the records of their civilization.
From the study of such data, their cultural history has been divided into
two periods, the first being that of the "Old Empire" which, extending
over the fourth to the tenth centuries of the Christian era, reached its
height in the eighth. Specific dates for it have been suggested as 317-987
A.D., but antecedents stretch back to a much earlier time.[14] In this period
the Mayas thickly populated a territory covering most of modern Guatemala, contiguous western Honduras, British Honduras, and the eastern

---

[13] Morley, "Maya Civilization—100% American." *Forum*, LXXXVIII (August, 1927),
p. 235; also Spinden, *op. cit.*, p. 162. Also *cf.* Kroeber, *op. cit.*, p. 785.

[14] For Mayan chronology and its correlation with the Christian calendar, I have fol-
lowed the data as given in S. G. Morley, *The Ancient Maya* (based on the Goodman-
Thompson correlation). For a discussion of the factors involved, see the above work,
Appendix I, pp. 457-58, also pp. 51-54, 83-90.

half of the Mexican state of Chiapas, with the upper Yucatan Peninsula, a peripheral province lying to the north. Here in a highly favorable environment many city-states developed, each independent of the others though sharing in a common culture, and each probably ruled by a hereditary dynasty whose members exercised both ecclesiastical and civil authority. Below the ruling house there appear to have been four distinct classes in the community: nobles, priests, common people, and slaves.

3. Mayan, Mexican, and Pueblo Indian Areas

Probably the oldest and most important of the city-states of the Old Empire was Tikal in the northern Petén Lake area.[15] Others of comparable significance were Uaxactún, Copán, Quiriguá, Piedras Negras, Naranjo, and Palenque. Such a city-state had as its civic and ceremonial center a group of limestone or stucco temples and palaces built around open plazas on the top of great truncated pyramidal bases. In a wide area around each of these public centers there were a number of farms and villages where the common people lived in humble huts. For some reason

[15] For a description of Tikal see Morley, *The Ancient Maya*, pp. 320-23.

not yet understood, the Mayas, while at the height of their artistic achievement, abandoned this highly developed southern region and moved northward. Many possible causes for this dramatic migration have been suggested, including earthquakes, climatic changes, exhaustion of the soil, epidemic disease, war, and social upheaval, but no hypothesis seems wholly satisfactory, though failure of the agricultural system is perhaps the most likely. Whatever the reason, following in the wake of earlier Mayan settlers, they carried out a general northward trek into Yucatan and adjacent territories, and by the middle of the tenth century the Old Empire had been generally abandoned.

In the eleventh century, with northern Yucatan as the new center, Mayan culture underwent a renaissance and the history of the "New Empire" opened. This second period of Mayan history has been dated 987-1697 A.D.[16] Until recently the period of transition intervening between the Old and the New Empire has been obscure, but the tendency of recent scholarship is to shorten this interregnum and even to suggest that there was in Yucatan a culture contemporaneous with that of the Old Empire upon which the migrants built their New Empire.[17] Most of the city-states in this period centered about *cenotes,* or natural wells, on which the fertility of this region depended. Political life in the New Empire through the first two hundred years, approximately the eleventh and twelfth centuries A.D., appears to have come increasingly under Mexican influence. New leaders, at least some of whom are representatives of Toltec culture [18] then flourishing in central Mexico, brought about a league or confederacy of the three city-states of Chichén-Itzá, Mayapán, and Uxmal which came to dominate the whole land though it continued to be Mayan in speech. This union succeeded in keeping order among the numerous settlements and in maintaining a high level of economic prosperity, as is shown in the magnificent new architectural and other artistic and intellectual achievements that flourished, especially in the three dominant cities. One of the

---

[16] Morley, *The Ancient Maya,* p. 83.

[17] J. E. S. Thompson, "Archaeological Problems of the Lowland Maya," in *The Maya and Their Neighbors,* chap. viii, pp. 131-32.

[18] The Toltecs (preceding the Aztecs) have been thought to be the earliest of the recorded Nahuatl-speaking peoples to rise to fame on the Mexican plateau. Much obscurity still surrounds their history. Their name means "master builders" and they appear to have developed an advanced culture after the middle of the eighth century, which lasted till the twelfth century. During this time they extended their power well beyond the plateau. The vast ruins of great dignity at San Juan Teotihuacán, some miles from Mexico City, have been associated with their name. Their great culture hero-god, credited as the bringer of civilization and the author of advanced ideas in astronomy and mathematics, was Quetzalcoatl whose symbol, the feathered serpent, was the dominant artistic motif in their buildings. The Toltecs are supposed to have been the Mexicans who were so influential in Yucatan, helping to establish the worship of Kukulcan at Chichén-Itzá and assisting Mayapán in its rise to dominance among the Mayan cities. For a recent treatment of the Toltec problem see Kroeber, *op. cit.,* pp. 801-03.

leaders responsible for the new era is believed to have been a former Toltec ruler whose Mexican name, borne in honor of the feathered serpent deity, was Quetzalcoatl. The Mayas, however, called him Kukulcan, the Mayan term for bird-serpent. Although this notable person apparently reached Yucatan as a prisoner of war destined for sacrifice, he presently appears— having somehow escaped his grim fate [19]—as the powerful and enlightened ruler of Chichén-Itzá. Under his dominance, this city became the center of the worship of the god whose name the ruler bore and in whose worship the two beings became thoroughly confused. The feathered serpent motif was spread broadcast over the handsome new temples and palaces of the reigning city.

After the breakup of the league of the three cities in 1194—brought about by the jealousy of Mayapán for Chichén-Itzá—the hegemony passed to Mayapán. For the next two and a half centuries, from the beginning of the thirteenth to the middle of the fifteenth century under the misrule of the dominant dynasty of Mayapán which maintained its oppressive rule by the use of Mexican garrisons, Toltecan political and cultural ideas continued to rule the land while bitter civil war raged much of the time among the rival cities. The destruction of Mayapán in 1441 put an end to centralized government in Yucatan and brought political disintegration to the country in general. The wars, aided by hurricanes, pestilence, and famine, caused the abandonment of the larger cities, exhausted the people, and devastated the land. When the Spaniards first sighted Yucatan in 1517, the Mayan remnants were still occupying the territories of modern Yucatan, Tabasco, Chiapas, Quintana Roo, and the Lake Petén region, but their glory had departed. Politically the erstwhile great confederacy had declined into a number of petty provinces which the Spaniards were soon to find no great difficulty in conquering. Mérida was founded as the Spanish capital in Yucatan in 1542.

Mayan culture in both the Old and New Empires was an agricultural civilization based on the cultivation of maize. Farming methods were elementary in the extreme. Lands were cleared of forest and underbrush by girdling the trees with deep cuts through the bark. Then, leaving the trees to die, the Mayan farmer tore out the roots of smaller brush by hand, and when all was dry, burnt over the whole field. Kernels of corn, beans, and squash seeds were then dropped into holes made in the ground by a sharp stick and the earth was scraped back with the planter's bare foot. In the same field crops were frequently mixed. When the soil became exhausted

---

[19] It has been suggested that possibly Kukulcan had been actually hurled into the Sacred Well at Chichén-Itzá in the fashion Mayan ritual prescribed, and managed to survive the experience, a fact which the Maya accepted as evidence of his divine mission to be their ruler. cf. Gann and Thompson, *History of the Maya* (New York: 1937), pp. 82-83.

the fields were allowed to return to woodland for five or ten years before being burnt over again. Besides the basic maize, squash, and beans, other crops that became common included sweet potatoes, tomatoes, chili peppers, and cacao. Tobacco was used largely for incense in the temples. The cultivation of cotton made possible an advanced textile art. A large cooperative element seems to have marked Mayan farming life. At planting and harvest time, cooperative bands of workers passed from farm to farm. Hunting operations were also frequently on a communal basis.

While the great mass of the people were farmers, there is some evidence of a fairly extensive commerce which was carried on in large canoes equipped with oars and sails. Cacao beans, shells, and quetzal feathers were used as currency. As was true of other American Indians, the Mayas had failed to domesticate animals to practical use or to develop a knowledge of the principle of the wheel. They were, however, good engineers and through their difficult country constructed, perhaps primarily for ceremonial purposes, stone-surfaced roads that were well drained, as well as bridges, retaining walls, and fortifications.

The most striking achievements of the Mayas, however, were in the realm of art and the intellectual sciences. In art they excelled in both architecture and sculpture. In both the Old and the New Empires they built great stone or stucco-covered buildings for ceremonial religious purposes, to house their priest-kings, or for other public use. The high pyramidal bases for these buildings were constructed of rubble and faced with dressed stones; they rose in several terraces which were often decorated with friezes showing sculptured animals or geometric designs. A great stairway led up one or more sides of the pyramid to the platform which might hold one or several buildings, or might form the base for lesser truncated pyramids which in their turn carried a number of structures as well as open plazas for ceremonial uses. Columns, colonnades, and fine stairways were effectively used for decorative purposes. Stelae, many rising nine or twelve feet above ground, were erected to mark regular intervals of time. These were carved on one or more sides with figures in elaborate ceremonial attire and were inscribed with hieroglyphics. A feature of the plazas, especially in the period of the Old Empire, they serve today as our most useful guide in the dating of events of Mayan history.

The buildings, though usually only one story in height, were obviously designed to be seen from a distance and were constructed with an eye to external magnificence. Many of them, especially those erected during the New Empire, were highly ornate, their exterior walls elaborately carved, or embellished with elaborate designs molded in lime stucco. As the principle of the keystone arch was not understood, the doorways were narrower at the top than at the bottom, and were made of overlapping courses that finally terminated in a single stone. Many of the buildings had corbeled stone roof vaulting. The long, narrow rooms within were often barbarously gorgeous with bright colors—especially red, blue, and green. The building material most generally used was hard limestone, which the Mayan builders embedded in mortar. The accuracy of adjustments was remarkable considering the absence of precision tools.

The sculptural work on the buildings and monuments of the Old Empire, though in smaller amount than in the later structures, is especially notable for fineness of workmanship. Beautifully sculptured altars and figures in the round, as well as the intricate designs in bold relief on façades and stelae, show a high degree of artistic skill and a remarkable acquaintance with the principles of foreshortening and composition. A striking feature is the frequent use of the diagonal or slanting line. During the New Empire, sculpture as an independent art tended to decline and become a mere handmaiden of architecture devoted to façade decoration. The later designs are chiefly geometric in pattern, though human, serpent, bird, and animal forms are also frequent. The highly conventionalized subject matter of much Mayan art, featuring beast gods with human attributes, masked figures, jaguars, and feathered serpents, tends to make it seem bizarre and unpleasant to many modern eyes, despite the technical excellence and generally magnificent effect.

The religion of the Mayas, with which art as well as all other phases of public and private life was intimately associated, centered about a pantheon of gods in which Itzamna, the lord of the heavens, the god of light and learning, appears to have held a place corresponding somewhat to that of Zeus among the Greek gods. Chac, the benevolent rain god, was given a prominent place by this agricultural people. He had a fourfold character as the deity of the cardinal points of the compass, each of which was assigned its own special color. The protruding snout of the rain god is a frequent device in many temples. The young corn god, who often wore an ear of corn as his headdress, was also a friendly deity. Kukulcan—The Feathered Serpent—whose image was much in evidence on the temples and statues when the Spaniards arrived, was closely associated with the yearly calendar, was revered as a builder of cities, and honored as a great teacher of law and order. Numerous temples and buildings at Chichén-Itzá took their decorative motifs from his wavy, scaly body. His head, with its plume of feathers and open mouth, often holding a human skull, frequently formed the ends of balustrades whose rails were his elongated body.

The most feared among the gods of evil was the death god, Ah Puch, always depicted as a skeleton with a rattle about his throat. He was the chief of the forces of darkness opposed to those of light and fertility. His com-

New Empire architecture: Palace of the Governor, Uxmal, Yucatan. From Desire Charnay, *Cités et Ruines Américaines.*

(*Left*) Xochipilli, god of flowers. (*Right*) Quetzalcoatl. (Courtesy of the Instituto Nacional de Antropología e Historia, Museo Nacional, Mexico)

The Plaza, Mexico City, in pre-Columbian times. From a copy of a drawing. (Courtesy of the American Museum of Natural History)

Panoramic view of summit remains, Monte Albán, southern Mexico. A. Main southern terrace with pyramids. B. Great Plaza. C. Central group of pyramids. D. Eastern range of pyramids. E. Western range of pyramids. F. Great northern group of pyramids. G. Spur with ruins. H. The lesser Albán. I. City of Oaxaca. J. Hills crowned with ruins. (Courtesy of the American Museum of Natural History)

Ruins at Mitla, southern Mexico. Inner Chamber of Palace II. (Courtesy of the Instituto Nacional de Antropología e Historia, Museo Nacional, Mexico)

 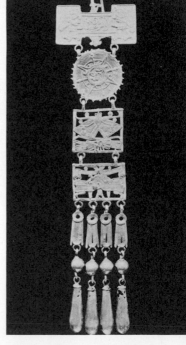

(*Left*) Gold pectoral of the Jaguar Knight (representative of the god of death) from Tomb VII, Monte Albán. (*Right*) Gold pendant made of seven symbolic elements. (Courtesy of the Instituto Nacional de Antropología e Historia, Museo Nacional, Mexico)

Oldest house at Massett, Queen Charlotte Islands, British Columbia. An example of Haida carving. (Courtesy of the American Museum of Natural History)

Pueblo of Taos, New Mexico. (Courtesy of the American Museum of Natural History)

Cliff-dweller remains, Mesa Verde, Colorado. (Courtesy of the American Museum of Natural History)

Cliff-dweller remains, Canyon de Chelly, Arizona. (Courtesy of the American Museum of Natural History)

panions were the dog, the owl, and the moan bird,[20] all omens of evil. A close associate was the god of war and human sacrifice. While human sacrifice went to no such lengths among the Mayas as among the Aztecs, purification by blood sacrifice held a prominent place in Mayan religious ceremonial. The killing of animals and birds on the altar was always a feature of the worship, and in the later years, when the religion had grown more cruel under Mexican influence, the sacrifice of human beings became a common practice and took a form very similar to that in use in Mexico; especially were notable prisoners of war likely to be offered to the gods. On certain great religious occasions high-born maidens, decorated with flowers and jewels, were thrown into a sacred well as living sacrifices, to become brides of the rain god. Male victims might also at times of national crisis be cast into the well of sacrifice and along with them various articles of value as gifts from the attending pilgrims. Persons dying in sacrifice were held to be sure of immortality. Others promised heaven were warriors who died in battle and persons who committed suicide.

A near handmaiden to art and religion was learning in all its forms, especially the highly intellectual sciences of astronomy and mathematics. Naturally the chief duty of the numerous priests who served the Mayan pantheon was to discover the will of the gods for the people of earth and guide the latter into acceptable ways of propitiating the divine beings, or turning aside their anger. In their efforts to find out the mind of the gods the priests were early led to the study of the heavenly bodies; this they found required mathematics and a system of writing for the keeping of records. Their achievements in this field resulted in their possessing, at the time of the Conquest, a calendar more accurate than the one the Spaniards were using. Their observations of sun, moon, and stars were accurate enough to enable them to adjust their calendar to an accuracy of 11/100 of a day in 206 years.[21] Their numerical system, devised several centuries before Christ, was based on a unit of 20 instead of 10 as in our system, enabling their priest-astronomers to deal more readily with the large numbers called for by astronomical observations. They had also early reached an understanding, for the first time in history, of the place value of numbers, involving the concept of zero.

For their religious needs and the calendar the Mayas had developed a graphic system of writing which, though devised later in time, represents an earlier stage of development in the history of writing than do Egyptian hieroglyphics. The Mayan glyphs were not merely pictures of the idea to

---

[20] Moan bird, a member of the falcon family.
[21] H. J. Spinden, "What Is Civilization? Answer of Ancient America: Part II, Artistic and Scientific," in *Forum*, LXXIV (September, 1925), pp. 371-79. This article draws an interesting comparison between the contribution to civilization of Indian America and that of Greek culture.

be conveyed but more or less conventionalized symbols representing abstract ideas, in other words true ideographs representing a stage in development midway between pictorial and true phonetic writing in which the characters denote sounds only. Finding it impossible to learn this written language but convinced that the hieroglyphic manuscripts, painted in colors on paper made from wood fibers and coated with a wash of fine white lime, probably bore on pagan religious matters, the Spanish missionaries in an excess of zeal burned in the public square as many of them as they could collect. Only three are known to have survived. These are known as the *Codex Dresdensis,* the *Codex Tro-Cortesianus,* and the *Codex Peresianus,* now in the Dresden, Madrid, and Paris museums. The contents appear to be devoted almost entirely to the calendar as it relates to the Mayan pantheon religious functions. There is a pictorial representation of gods and animal figures of mythological significance. At present the codices are only about 50 per cent readable, as unfortunately there is no "Rosetta stone." By far the greatest amount of extant Mayan writing, however, is not in "books" at all, but in the form of inscriptions carved on stone monuments. Even these, if they could be wholly deciphered, would apparently enlighten us very little concerning either Mayan history or its great figures, as they also deal principally with arithmetical and calendrical data.[22] The Spanish missionaries gradually learned the spoken language of the Mayas and set about recording it phonetically in Spanish characters. The natives adopted this form of their written language, and there is now a considerable amount of literature, dating from the Conquest, in the Mayan language written in European symbols, much of it relating to native customs, myths, rituals, and other cultural matters. As a group, the native manuscripts in European characters have been called the *Books of Chilam Balaam.* Some are undoubtedly literal translations of the now lost native chronicles originally written in hieroglyphics.

The Aztecs

North of the Mayas, beyond the Isthmus of Tehuantepec, were the Aztecs, a group of Nahuatl-speaking people and the last Indian group on the Mexican plateau to develop a characteristic culture. On the foundation of earlier Archaic-Middle and Toltec cultures, and greatly influenced by Mayan inventions, the Aztecs in the fifteenth century rose to a commanding position in the central valley of Mexico. Following obscure beginnings in the north, they reached Mexico in the twelfth century and by 1325 had established themselves on the western shore of Lake Tezcoco with their head-

---

[22] S. G. Morley, "Maya Epigraphy," in *The Maya and Their Neighbors,* chap. ix, pp. 139-49.

quarters on a nearby strategic island which they called Tenochtitlán, now Mexico City. Here, in the course of the next hundred years, they became a relatively strong power and early in the fifteenth century (1437 A.D.) strengthened their position by making an alliance for mutual defense and military advantage with two other lake cities, Tezcoco and Tlacopan. Under the leadership of Montezuma I (1440-1469) the allies entered upon a career of conquest and, in a series of wars, brought much of the country east, west, and south of the central valley—from the Atlantic to the Pacific —under their sway. To the north and northwest their efforts were less successful.

The territory which this Aztec confederacy controlled when the Spaniards arrived in the early sixteenth century was not an empire as it is sometimes called, but rather it was ruled by a dominating partnership for military and tributary purposes. Beyond the territories of the three chief members of the confederacy were a large number of tribal groups in various stages of vassalage. Some of these paid tribute regularly to officials of the confederacy, others paid only occasionally and were in a perpetual state of revolt, and still others, like the Tlaxcalans of Pueblo, whom the Spaniards were to find so useful, had never been subdued. All the groups were practically independent in local affairs, as they were only visited by tax agents of the confederacy and were free from the control of permanent garrisons. At times, however, an Aztec governor would be imposed on a recalcitrant tribal group. Unsubdued tribes were frequently raided and numbers of both sexes were carried off to be placed in slavery or sacrificed on the altars of the voracious Aztec gods. In all joint military operations— and the confederacy was aggressively militaristic—the ruler of the Aztecs of Tenochtitlán was war chieftain though spoils of victory were supposed to be divided in the proportion of two fifths to the Aztecs, two fifths to the Tezcocans, and one fifth to the Tlacopans.

In local Aztec affairs the "Chief of Men" was far from wielding unlimited authority. Although chosen from a single powerful family or lineage and often closely related in blood to his predecessor, he was minutely advised by a tribal council made up of important officials, priests, and representatives of the twenty Aztec clans. His power was greatest in military and extra-tribal affairs, but even in these matters it varied a good deal according to the personality of the ruler and the composition of the tribal council. Highly venerated and surrounded with a complicated court and religious etiquette that prescribed his every movement, he was decidedly not an absolute ruler. Highest authority in internal affairs was vested in an individual who, regardless of sex, was officially known as the "Snake Woman" and who was largely independent of the "Chief of Men."

The rank and file of the nation was organized into twenty clans, membership in which was originally based on blood. The principal function of the clan officials was the allotment of land to heads of families; for land belonged in theory to the community and not to the individual. A certain proportion of the land, worked cooperatively or by hired or slave labor, was set aside for the support of government officials and for the upkeep of religion. The clans, which were the basic units, were in turn grouped for certain military and religious functions into larger organizations called phratries. There was also an elaborate system of law courts which administered a severe legal code in which the death penalty was very common and extraordinarily cruel. The expenses of government were provided for principally from taxes and tribute, paid in kind into the public treasury, and supplemented by the income from state lands.

In the Aztec economy, though the cultivation of corn was the basis of life, trade and commerce enjoyed a higher prestige than is usually found among a primitive people. The Aztecs linked trading operations closely with conquest and empire building, and provided the swarms of travelling salesmen (who overran much of present-day Mexico) not only with protection but with an ominous military threat to insure the success of their commercial ventures. Woe betide the town or tribe that refused a welcome to an Aztec trading caravan bearing agricultural products, cotton textiles, pottery, jewelry, cochineal dye, drugs, implements, and other handicrafts and also, of course, Aztec ideas and standards. Barter was the principal form of exchange, with cacao beans customarily used as a currency to adjust small inequalities and quills filled with grains of gold to take care of large amounts. Prices were generally determined by rarity and desirability. Gold and silver were not as highly prized as the scarcer turquoise and jade. Other precious stones widely sought for use in an elaborate jewelry craft were emeralds, opals, and moonstones. Copper, too, bore the value of a scarce article. Rare feathers were eagerly sought for the popular feather mosaics for which the Aztec artists were famous.

Religion was an integral part of every phase of Aztec life. There was a multitude of gods, some of them old tribal Aztec deities, and others taken over from the conquered peoples. Huitzilopochtli (Hummingbird-Wizard), the terrible god of war, and Tezcatlipoca, the sky god, were examples of the former, while Tlaloc the rain god and Quetzalcoatl, the god of civilization and the renewal of life, were apparently legacies from the Toltecs. Many other deities were associated with agricultural life. The numerous religious festivals connected with the huge pantheon were often celebrated by human sacrifices on a scale to be found nowhere else in America. After the immolation and offering of the still-beating hearts of the victims, who usually were prisoners secured in wars fought primarily for their capture, the bodies were thrown down from the *teocalli,* dismembered, and eaten by men and animals. The Spaniards were horrified at the religious practices in Mexico—the most frightful in their experience. Not all the Mexican deities, however, demanded lives of human beings in return for the gifts of rain and life. Many might be propitiated with gifts of incense, flowers, and fruits. Associated with religion was a widespread belief in signs and portents and in the use of magic, as well as a firm faith in life after death. Despite his warlike propensities, the ferocious character of his religion, and the widespread presence of slavery, the ordinary Aztec of the sixteenth century seems to have possessed many attractive qualities: he was artistic in temperament, loved birds and flowers, was fond of poetry and music, delighted in the dance and the drama, and excelled at games.

Some of the thousands of priests employed in the Mexican temples were especially engaged in educational work, and many were occupied with the study of astronomy, primarily for the calculation of dates for religious festivals. Astronomical science in Mexico, however, never attained the accuracy that it achieved in the lands of the Maya.[23] The priests also prepared the manuscripts in which calendrical records, tribute lists, and other similar memoranda were kept. Their method of writing was cruder than that of the Maya, closer to the pictograph than to the hieroglyphic form. In Aztec art forms there appears to have been comparatively little originality; the best elements came from Mayan sources. Architecture also was quite similar to that of the southern neighbor, though sculpture did not play so great a part as in the Mayan area.

The special function of the Aztec contribution to American development was not so much the creation of a distinctive and original culture as the accumulating of the gifts of other groups, the incorporation of these into the texture of their own tribal life, and the imposition of the resulting civilization on a wide population in the greater part of the Mexican territory.

III. NORTH AMERICA

Pueblos, Iroquois, and Others

In North America, north of Mexico, the picture in pre-Columbian times is one of many tribes in various stages of development. Only a representative few can be briefly surveyed here.

---

[23] The famous Aztec calendar stone was made in 1479 when Aztec art was in its flower. It was designed as a religious object and originally set up before the Temple of the Sun in Mexico City. Its carved circular face, twelve feet across, bears, in addition to the central sun image, the divisions of the calendar and a representation of Aztec cosmology.

In the southwest, the sedentary Pueblo Indians are associated in their history with parts of present-day New Mexico, Arizona, Colorado, Utah, and adjoining Mexican regions. Coming originally from several distinct linguistic stocks, they early adopted a common way of life and attained a high degree of culture, though not one on a level with the most advanced forms in Mexico and Central America. This achievement was the greater because it was accomplished despite the discouragements of a semidesert environment and harassing raids from Navahos, Apaches, and other enemies of lower culture. To this well-integrated culture has been recently given the name "Anasazi."[24] The history of its development is of considerable interest.

Early in the Christian era the ancestors of the Pueblo people, whom the archaeologists now conveniently identify as "Basket-makers" from their skill in weaving of fibres, cultivated maize, squash, and pumpkins and supplemented these foods by gathering wild seeds, nuts, and fruits. They appear to have lived at this time mostly in shallow caves—though some were in the open. Slowly they rose through various stages, learning in the course of time to cultivate beans, to domesticate the turkey, to grow and weave cotton, and to manufacture first simple, and later decorated, pottery. The development of their dwelling places seems to reflect a close association between the habitations of the cliff dwellers and the great apartment-like community houses so familiar to present-day visitors to Indian pueblos. Somehow the descendants of the Basket-makers acquired the skill to construct in stone or adobe these great, fortress-like blocks of buildings, consisting of large numbers of adjoining rooms, sometimes four to six stories in height, with each level terraced back from the one below and with all doors and windows opening on a central court. Kivas, or circular council chambers used for religious ceremonial purposes, were originally built underground within the community house itself, but later were likely to be placed separately in the plaza. Some of these community houses were built within caves high in the canyon walls, others under the shelter of overhanging ledges, but mostly they were constructed in the open, sometimes on the top of broad mesas, sometimes in fertile valleys.

Each pueblo was a politically self-contained communal state, democratically governed by its own elected officials and council, and never allied, except temporarily, with other pueblos. There is no trace of a common ruler of the pueblo territory. Socially, each pueblo was inhabited by a number of related clans. Clan descent was reckoned from mother to daughter, the sons marrying out of the clan, sons-in-law being acquired from neighbor-

---

[24] The student is referred for greater detail to Martin, Quimby, and Collier, *Indians Before Columbus* (Chicago: 1947), chap. xii, "The Anasazi Culture."

ing clans.[25] Religious and political duties were the special functions of the men. Boastful individualism in any form was heavily frowned upon. Exaltation of the clan or the tribe was the paramount consideration. The community, not the individual, was the unit. In the economic sphere, each pueblo assumed ownership both of the ground on which it was established and of the surrounding farming lands, which were periodically distributed among the cultivators. The sites of some of the larger towns covered as much as ten or twelve acres, but many were much smaller.

The pueblo people were a conservative, peaceful folk in whose religious faith and practice the conceptions of God and nature were essentially blended. The characteristic religious ceremonies centered about the changing seasons of the year and were marked by elaborate ceremonial and rich symbolism. Ritualistic dances, designed to invoke the supernatural powers that could cause their crops to grow, were a manifestation of their religious life. Their decorative arts provided a medium and expression to the same end.

In its great period (c. 1050-1300 A.D.) Pueblo culture extended over a much larger territory than it occupies today. At that time three principal cultures stood out as marking a high tide of achievement: along the San Juan River basin; at Mesa Verde in southwestern Colorado; and in the Chaco Canyon in northwestern New Mexico.[26] But at the end of this period some disaster or other unknown factor caused a great exodus southward. The more northern sites, including Mesa Verde and the Chaco Canyon, were abandoned and a general decline in population set in. This recession in the fortunes of the Pueblo people cannot be blamed in the first instance on the white man, for it occurred two hundred years before he appeared on the scene. Pressure of nomadic enemies, epidemic disease, severe drought threatening starvation, or internal dissension could be surmised, but there is nothing certain. When Coronado and his Spaniards arrived in 1540 they found eighty inhabited towns where there had formerly been hundreds.[27] Spanish activities hastened the process of destruction. In the next century the Pueblo revolt of 1680 brought further decimation.

Today there remain only seventeen villages along the Rio Grande in New Mexico, together with the Zuñi (Coronado's "Seven Cities of Cíbola") in the western part of the state, and eight Hopi towns in Arizona. Among them, four different languages are spoken. The best known of the surviving pueblos are Taos, Isleta, Cochiti, Santo Domingo, Santa Clara,

---

[25] On community organization, see E. L. Hewett, *Ancient Life in the American Southwest* (New York: 1943), pp. 69-73.

[26] Hewett, *op. cit.,* chap. iii, treats the history of these three sections.

[27] *Ibid.,* p. 67.

Jémez, and Acoma. The last named is an outstanding example of a pueblo perched on the top of a high mesa and probably represents a city of refuge for the fugitives from Mesa Verde.

Turning now further east in North America: Along the lower Mississippi and its tributaries the Spanish were astounded to come upon a large number of great artificial earthworks. Some were long earthen walls enclosing circles or squares, others were mounds in various shapes, some truncated pyramids, others conical, some terraced. When examined, most of these were found to be burial mounds in which the dead had been laid with greater care than has been discovered elsewhere in North America, with the bodies surrounded with an abundance of weapons, tools, and ornaments. Other mounds were apparently used as the bases for temples. The wall enclosures, at times hundreds of feet in length, were at first thought to be fortifications, but may have had a religious ceremonial use. These terraces and mounds and their contents gave abundant evidence that their builders had possessed a knowledge of the use of copper, great skill in the working of silver and gold, fine pottery techniques, and a social organization capable of cooperative effort on a large scale. There had also obviously flourished an elaborate religious cult. Everything pointed to a culture far in advance of the capacities of the simple tribes then dwelling in the area. Here was evidence of a sedentary agricultural civilization furnished with a great body of artisans skilled in many types of artistic work and supported by a trade that brought in materials from far and near.

Later discoveries have revealed similar mound monuments scattered thickly over a wide territory of North America, stretching from the Atlantic to beyond the Mississippi and from the Gulf of Mexico to central Wisconsin. It is now thought that this culture, at its height in a period estimated to have been from the tenth to the fourteenth century, had its principal location in southern Ohio in a phase of development called by archaeologists the "Hopewell culture." [28] There were subsidiary centers in Pennsylvania, New York, Tennessee, Indiana, Illinois, Iowa, Wisconsin, Michigan, and Kansas.

The large Hopewell villages, each with its odd enclosures and great mounds, while able to furnish well-made utilitarian tools, utensils, and weapons, could also produce fine pottery in many styles—some decorated with finely stamped bird designs—as well as excellent wood carving and metal work superior to any other found in North America. From copper, meteoric iron, silver, occasionally gold, mica, shell, and animal teeth were made elaborate head ornaments and breast plates, ear spools, and necklaces,

---

[28] For a more detailed treatment of this culture see Martin, Quimby, and Collier, op. cit., pp. 267-78.

with the jewelry at times decorated with pearls. Stone tobacco pipes made in effigies of men, birds, and animals were also products of this culture.

The discovery of this mound-building culture immediately stimulated much fantastic speculation concerning its origin. The suggestion was made that the mound builders may have been a pre-Indian race that had vanished before any known Indian tribe had come upon the scene. But students of this barbaric culture now are convinced that it represented the work of some branch of the general Indian population of America, though its relationship to other phases of Indian culture—particularly that of the Mayas—is still a matter of contentious debate.

The inland Plains area lying between the Mississippi and the Rocky Mountains is another region showing a highly specialized culture. The first inhabitants were Folsom hunters. Later groups coming from the east along the river valleys brought a knowledge of simple agriculture and pottery and equipped the hunter with the bow and arrow. Many of these early Plains folk lived in semisedentary communities of earth-covered lodges, located on ridges along the rivers.

The great cultural change in the Plains came with the arrival of the European horse. Originating, of course, with the Spaniards of Mexico the horse began to appear on the southwestern Plains as early as 1540. Eagerly adopted by the Plains Indians and traded or stolen from tribe to tribe, it spread rapidly over the whole area and revolutionized the life and culture of the region. More than a hundred years were to pass, after the horse became common, before the white man himself came in any numbers to this inland area. Meanwhile there developed a new mode of life that centered around the pursuit of the bison from horseback.

This possession gave man a new mastery over a wider environment. Mounted on swift horses and armed with the quick-firing bow and arrow, the Indian could follow the bison herds, covering great distances and traveling wherever necessary in search of water and vegetation. At first it was the sedentary farmers already in the Plains area who took up this nomadic life, abandoning their fixed lodges for movable tepees for at least part of the year. But presently other Indians, hitherto dwelling on the fringes of the plains to the north, south, east, and west, were attracted to the area to share in the excitement and expanded life horsemanship made possible.

The population of the Plains soon became a conglomerate one, made up of Indians from many widely differing linguistic stocks and widely separated cultural backgrounds; thirty-one tribal groups have been counted.[29]

---

[29] See C. Wissler, *The American Indian* (New York: 3rd ed., 1938), p. 218.

But whatever their past, the newcomers, whether Blackfoot, Crow, Dakota, Pawnee, Cheyenne, Comanche, Assiniboin, Arapaho, Mandan, or another, all came to share certain common traits that marked them as Plainsmen and members of a Plains culture.

The outstanding feature of this culture was dependence on the buffalo, whose meat, hide, sinews, and bones provided nearly everything needed in

Redrawn from a map prepared by Clark Wissler
4. INDIAN CULTURE AREAS OF NORTH AMERICA

daily life. Adjusting to the new economy, the Plains Indians adopted a different mode of living and with it developed products and skills that became characteristic of the area as a whole. Typically they lived in movable tepees, dried their meat on high frames, did notable work in skins and beads, developed a sign language, practiced sweat-house observances, and were famous for certain ceremonial dances, especially the Sun Dance. There were variations here and there; tribes such as the Mandan combined two types of life, carrying on fairly extensive agriculture, basketry, and pottery-making along with bison hunting, while others were content with little more than hunting.

Across the western cordillera in the North Pacific area in what is today northern Washington and British Columbia, far removed from Central America and its influence, there developed among the Northwest Coast Indians [30] a peculiar culture. On the one hand it was nonagricultural and nonpottery-making, on the other it was marked by a highly developed social organization in which class distinctions, slave-holding practices, and an emphasis on material wealth were strong. The potlatch ceremony flourished among them with its curious mixture of acquisitiveness and boastfulness in which a man, having accumulated considerable wealth, might divest himself of it in a single gesture, distributing most of what he possessed to his friends and neighbors.[31] For food these people depended largely on fish and game, cooked with hot stones in boxes and baskets. Their houses were large rectangular buildings of wooden posts and planks, some, in the north, with gabled roofs and others, in the south, with sloping shed roofs, each capable of holding many families. These people excelled in basketry and tattooing, and preferred bone, horn, and shell rather than stone for implements. Their most notable artistic gift was their skill in woodcarving which early appeared in huge grave figures, adorned their dwellings, utensils, helmets, facial masks, and smaller objects and, in later times, found remarkable scope in the construction of totem poles, depicting a mythical line of animal ancestry.

Southward on the Pacific coast and in the Great Basin were more primitive tribes, eking out an existence on acorns, berries, wild seeds, roots, insects, small game, and fish. Among these were the so-called "Digger" Indians of California whose shelters were primitive brush lean-tos. Though living on the coast, they had no canoes but used rafts. While they were good basketmakers they did only poor work in wood, skins, bone, and stone and knew nothing of metal work, pottery, or weaving.

On the other side of the continent in the Northeastern Woodland area the dominant tribes were the Iroquois and many Algonquian groups. They are of special interest because of their association in colonial times with the efforts of the French and English to build rival empires in these regions. Of the two, the Iroquois had the more distinctive culture and

---

[30] Tlingit and Haida were prominent members of the northern group and the Coast Salish and Nootka in the south.

[31] For a description of Potlatch, and also cannibalistic practices among these Indians, see: Wissler, *op. cit.,* chap. xiv, "The Capitalists of the North."

waged the fiercest and most intelligent struggle to preserve their independence. The center of their power in early historical times lay east of the Great Lakes in the central valleys of what is now New York state. Culturally, however, they seem to have come within the radius of the influence of the Hopewell culture and to have had southern rather than northern roots.[32]

Iroquois economy combined intensive agriculture, pottery-making, and superior bone work with hunting and fishing. Their settlements, enclosed in palisades, consisted of a number of rectangular, bark-covered "Long Houses," one hundred or more feet in length and fourteen to twenty-four feet wide, designed for sixteen to twenty-four families apiece. Each was equipped with four to six centrally placed stone fire hearths and had bunks and shelves along the walls. Casks and pits held their food supplies.

Clan development among the Iroquois was strong, with descent reckoned in the female line and exogamous marriage insisted upon. Woman had a uniquely strong position in tribal life, having a large share in the appointment of officials and the ownership of property, as well as a decisive role in determining the fate of prisoners. Elaborate song rituals, long mourning rites, and masked societies had developed to a marked extent among them. The trumpet-shaped pottery tobacco pipe of distinctive design was a prized possession. They were skilful canoemen and used the birchbark canoe extensively to navigate the many lakes and rivers of their territory.

But the most remarkable achievement of the Iroquois was in the realm of politics. They were undoubtedly the most politically minded of the tribes of North America. They early adopted a policy of aggressive expansion and made this effective, not only by the zest with which they fought, but also through the organization, about 1570, of the famous Iroquois League of the Five (later Six) Nations. Not all the Iroquois-speaking peoples were included. Those within the League were the Mohawk, Oneida, Onondaga, Cayuga, and Seneca, and, with lesser rights at a later date, the Tuscarora.[33] Under the direction of a council of fifty sachems, the League embarked on an imperialistic career and at one time controlled a military empire of remarkable extent and great strategic dominance.

Thus in North America beyond Mexico there was a wide range of cultural expression from that of the simple Californians to the achievements of the able Iroquois and the advanced cultures of the Hopewell and Pueblo peoples. The variety of skills among them, both in degree and

---

[32] Martin, Quimby, and Collier, op. cit., p. 258. The culture is named "Hopewell" after the owner of a site in Ohio.

[33] Some of the best-known Iroquois-speaking groups not in the League were the Huron, Neutrals, Erie, and Cherokee.

kind, point to a high level of adaptability to environment, while many similarities and common traits so noticeable in their religious outlook, social organization, and political structure suggest a family likeness.

IV. SOUTH AMERICA

Chibchas, Amazonians, and Incas

South of the Isthmus of Panama the cultural picture in the centuries preceding Columbus is a distinctive one, though recent archaeological studies emphasize the considerable interchange of cultural elements that took place both by land and sea between the two continents. In continuation of the great development in the highlands of Middle America, the center of the greatest achievement in the southern continent was in the Andean area extending from Colombia southward to Chile, flowering especially in the mountains and the coastal areas of Peru. Here, as in Middle America, on the basis of a settled agricultural life, the native Indians were able to advance to complex cultures marked by extensive political and economic organizations and high intellectual and artistic achievement.

The most northerly people in this area were the Chibchas of Colombia and northern Ecuador. They were divided into many small communities ruled by autocratic, hereditary *caciques* whose mutual jealousies kept their people politically feeble. Their economic life, however, was rich and varied. While their chief occupation was agriculture, they were also skilled metallurgists, doing fine work in gold and silver, using alloys, and carrying on an extensive trade in emeralds and copper in which their land abounded. Both their language and metallurgy were carried northward into the Isthmus as far as Honduras. The most famous myth of South America, that of El Dorado or the Gilded Man, has been found to be based on an ancient practice of the Chibchas. In the course of religious ceremonies that marked his coronation a young chief was customarily taken to the shores of Lake Guatabita where he was coated with gold dust by the priests and placed in a boat laden with gold and emeralds which he offered to the gods as a sacrifice for the welfare of his people and the prosperity of his reign. Other religious practices of the Chibchas, who were nature worshippers and practiced human sacrifice, were less attractive.

South of the Chibchas, stretching away to Chile, lay the lands, peoples, and cultures that were eventually brought into the empire of the Incas. The equatorial plateau that formed the northern portion of this state had once been the land of the Quitus and continued to be called the Kingdom of Quito. South of the Inca empire, beyond the Maule River in Chile, were the sturdy Araucanians who, in their fierce love of freedom, their cruelty, their drunkenness, and their mixed hunting and farming economy, have often been likened to the Iroquois of North America.

At its center, the level of ultimate achievement in this highest cultural area of South America was comparable, if not superior, to the standard reached by the Mayas and Aztecs of Middle America. Its emphases, however, were different from those north of the Isthmus. If the Middle American peoples excelled in architecture and sculpture, in mathematics and

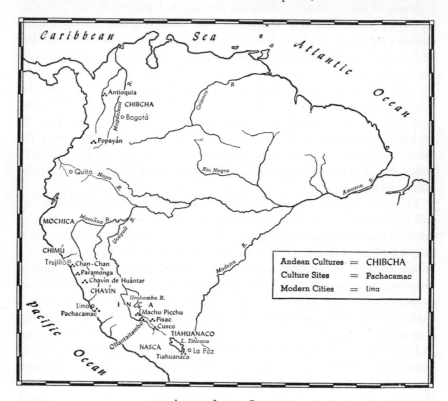

5. ANDEAN INDIAN CULTURES

astronomy, and in the production of a written language, the Peruvians were superior in the engineering arts of roadmaking, terracing, and the building of bridges, aqueducts, and fortifications, as well as in the handicrafts of textiles and ceramics. Furthermore, no other American Indian group achieved such an elaborate and efficient social, economic, and political organization as that through which the Inca ruled his vast empire. On the other hand, formidable mountain and jungle barriers confined this area of high culture to the Pacific slopes of the Andes, so that in South America there was nothing comparable to the wide-spreading influence of the Maya-Aztec culture of Middle America among the peoples of the rest of the continent.

Of the Indian tribes in the tropics, east of the Andes, the most important were the Arawaks, the Caribs, and the Tupi-Guarani. Among these, the Arawaks were the most widely extended and the most advanced culturally. They were probably of Amazonian origin.[34] In Columbus' time they occupied many of the larger islands of the Caribbean, as well as the Bahamas, where he first encountered them. On the South American mainland they lived along the numerous water courses of Venezuela and the Guianas, and inhabited the basins of the Orinoco, the Amazon, and the Río Negro as far westward as the borders of Peru. Other scattered Arawak groups reached southward as far as the Gran Chaco in Argentina. Primarily an agricultural people, they possessed maize, manioc, potatoes, beans, and peppers. Equipped for travel with the dugout canoe and the balsa raft and armed with the javelin, the spear-thrower, the bow and arrow, the blowgun, and the war club, and organized in a close-knit social group, the Arawaks were able to penetrate and become dominant in many areas of tropical South America, though in their island homes in the Caribbean they suffered severely from the raids of the fierce and more primitive Caribs.

The Caribs (whose Spanish-given name was to cling permanently to the great sea that has been called the "American Mediterranean") were very different from the relatively gentle and more highly cultured Arawaks. Though rather similar in their material possessions the social patterns, religious concepts, and fierce war practices of the Caribs marked them as definitely more primitive. In the sixteenth century they were found principally south of the Amazon, between the rivers Xingú and Tapajoz, though earlier they had been north of the great river and spread through the Guianas. Bold and expert in the management of boats, some of which had three sails of cotton or palm leaf and carried as many as fifty persons, they frequently raided the Caribbean Islands. Here, especially in the Leeward and Windward Islands, some settled down and were later encountered by the Spaniards, who were horrified at their practice of eating male prisoners and at their habit of deliberately using terror as a method of warfare. Their culture was essentially South American in origin, and to them that continent is said to owe the useful inventions of the large dugout canoe and the hammock. Though they understood the preparation of manioc and learned from the Arawaks how to cultivate maize, they were primarily

---

[34] See *Handbook of South American Indians,* ed. J. H. Steward (Washington: 1948), Vol. IV, p. 507. But *cf.* P. Radin, *Indians of South America* (New York: 1942), 45-46. Here it is suggested that the Arawaks shared many cultural traits with the people of southeastern United States and may have been purveyors to the Amazonian world of cultural elements originating in far-off Mexico.

hunters and fishers. They were eventually to find it impossible to come to terms with European civilization, meeting its advance merely by a further withdrawal into the wilderness.

The Tupi-Guarani were a more southern group than either the Arawaks, who on the whole were centered north of the Amazon, or the Caribs, who lived on both sides of the great river but in a fairly restricted area. An early home of the Tupi may have been in the area between the Tapajoz and Xingú and the northern tributaries of the Paraguay River, from whence some of them found their way to the delta of the Paraná. The Tupi were also in great strength through eastern coastal Brazil, dominating the shoreline from the mouth of the Amazon southward as far as Rio Grande do Sul and appearing in groups as far as Río de la Plata. They also penetrated far up the Amazon.[35] They were great wanderers and their culture showed elements from many sources. From the Arawaks they learned the cultivation of maize, though they got their living chiefly from hunting and fishing. They were famous for their bravery and gave themselves the name of "Guarani," which means warrior. Like the Caribs they were cannibals.

Besides these three principal groups, there was a great diversity of small primitive tribes in the Amazonian area, each intent primarily on the problem of survival. While they understood the preparation of manioc they were ignorant of maize and were for the most part hunters and fishers. They possessed no clan organization. Among them fighting was practically perpetual and trade nonexistent. The blowgun and the signal drum were old possessions. Most of them lived in large, thatched community houses holding as many as sixty individuals. These dwellings could be approached only by circuitous paths in the jungle and for greater security were moved every two or three years.

In the northern part of the great temperate plains area which stretched south of the tropical forest—in the Gran Chaco and among the Ge-speaking peoples of Brazil—cultural traits were varied. The basic occupation was agriculture, but mixed with hunting. There was some pottery and weaving. Like the Plains Indians of North America these groups readily adapted themselves to an equestrian life once they acquired horses from the Spaniards. Among them were the Tapuyas, a northern group bordering on the Tupi, whom the Portuguese called *Botocudos,* or "peg-lips" from their warriors' custom of ornamenting their lower lips with a peg for each

---

[35] On the Tupi see: *Handbook of South American Indians,* IV, pp. 69-72, 95-97, 883-86; also *cf* D. G. Brinton, *The American Race* (Philadelphia: 1901), pp. 229-31 and P. Radin, *op. cit.,* pp. 78-79.

Monolithic gateway, Tiahuanaco, Bolivia. A splendidly executed frieze in bas-relief. The central figure probably represents the creator god, Viracocha, on each side of whom are shown twenty-four attendants.

Ruins at Machu Picchu, Peru.

Mochica water jugs, or stirrup-mouth jars. These well illustrate the extraordinary realism of Mochica ceramics.

Chimu vessel with storytelling decoration. Another type of stirrup-mouth jar.

Chimu gold earplug.

Ancient arpa, or harp. This Inca musical instrument is still played by the Peruvian Indians.

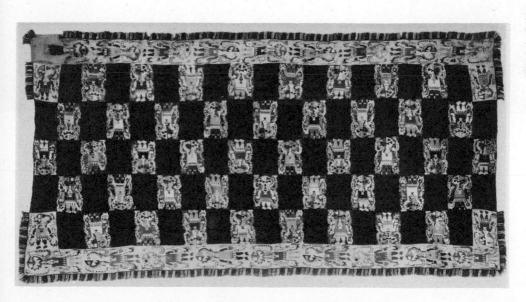

An Inca tapestry poncho in the Museo Nacional at Lima.

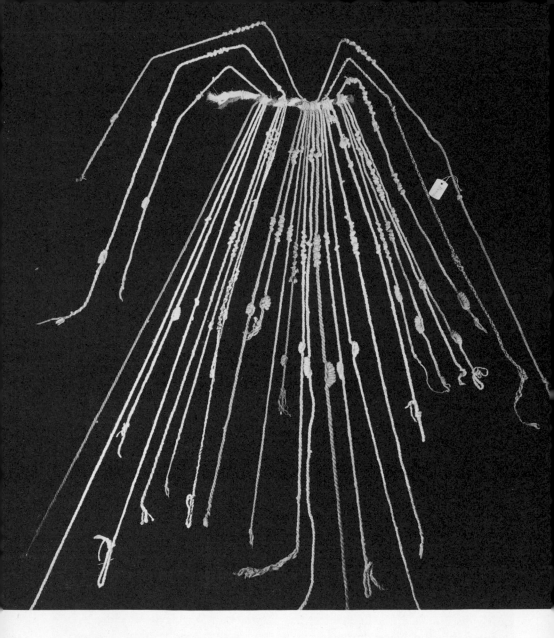

A quipu, a device for computing and recording. The smaller cords are of various colors, each having a specific meaning, as gold, corn, soldiers, etc. Knots in the smaller cords represent definite numbers. Used in Peru from the period immediately preceding the rise of the Incas. (Courtesy of the American Museum of Natural History)

enemy killed in battle. South of the Tapuyas were the Charruas who dwelt along the banks of the Uruguay River and were noted bola throwers and chicha drinkers. Farther south were the more nomadic tribes and the primitive Patagonians and Fuegians.

The area of South America occupied by the tribes of low cultural attainment was by far the greater part of the continent and included many of the regions today considered most desirable, but in the colonial age, and in the general cultural history of America, the truly significant area was the Andean region—the home of the Inca culture. We now turn for a more detailed consideration of the history and achievements of that area.

The Incas

In the Andean region the Spaniards encountered the largest and most firmly organized of the native states in America, the Inca Empire. By the sixteenth century it had been a unified and conquering state for four hundred years and then extended from Quito, in present Ecuador, southward fifteen hundred miles along the mountain and coastal plains of the Pacific to the River Maule in Chile. Notable for their political and military genius, the Incas had subjugated and incorporated within their domain a number of peoples whose culture had reached remarkable heights at an earlier period.

At sometime in the last millennium B.C. a knowledge of agriculture had reached this region, either invented by the South American natives themselves or adopted through cultural contacts with Central America along paths which we today cannot completely retrace. A rich variety of food sources, including manioc, maize, and potatoes, along with such plants as cotton, tobacco, and coca, were domesticated, making possible a settled life in which pottery, textiles, and the building arts made their appearance and were developed to a state of high perfection. Within the area that eventually fell under the Inca sway, two centers of earlier wide-spreading highland cultures were notable, each associated with specific coastal developments. The earlier centered at Chavín de Huántar with its influence clearly discernible in the localized cultures of the coastal valleys—Mochica in the north and Nasca farther south.[36] The second was based at Tiahuanaco, south of Lake Titicaca within the border of modern Bolivia. This may have been the capital of a pre-Inca empire but at least was the center of a great religious cult. Of the contemporary coastal cultures one was the Empire of Chimú, a descendant of Mochica culture. Its capital was Chan

---

[36] See Kroeber, *op. cit.*, pp. 827-31. For a comparative table of Central American and Andean cultural history, see P. A. Means, *Ancient Civilization of the Andes* (New York: 1937), p. 47.

Chan, located not far from modern Trujillo. Its ruined site today, covering eleven acres, is marked by burial mounds of rubble and clay built in the form of pyramids, and picturesque ruins of miles of adobe walls, many with arabesque designs. After 1200 A.D. this highland-based culture fell before the advance of another sierra people, the Incas, who from their stronghold at Cusco, in a fertile mountain valley two hundred miles north of Lake Titicaca, began to build their empire. For a time the coastal cities were free and enjoyed a brief renaissance and then they also became subject to the Incas.

The archaeological remains of these earlier cultures give evidence that, in the centuries when the Mayan culture was flourishing in Central America, Peru was likewise showing a great development of the arts. In these large, well-organized states under the semitheocratic rule of priest-kings, the arts of pottery and weaving were carried to great perfection. In beautifully modeled and colored pottery forms, often cast in the shape of animals or portrait heads of human beings and decorated with realistic scenes from daily life, the early Mochica and Nasca Indians left a record of their skill and a picture of their times that go far to compensate for the absence of written accounts. From the fleece of the domesticated alpaca and llama and of the wild vicuña, fine textiles were woven in intricate and beautiful patterns. Lace-making, embroidering, knitting, and crocheting were also carried to great proficiency. At Tiahuanaco, highland culture expressed itself in an advanced building art. Temples, palaces, and fortresses constructed from huge blocks of stone, accurately cut, fitted, and locked into place without the use of mortar, bear testimony to a numerous, well-organized, and disciplined population.

In the twelfth century the Incas, a warlike, highland people, who some centuries earlier had come to the headwaters of the Ucayali River from farther east, began to build their empire on the ruins of earlier states. Their own traditions declared them to be "children of the sun," led to their new home by a ruler named Manco Capac whose golden divining rod, sinking into the earth, had indicated the location of their capital city of Cusco. Tradition also said that twelve successors had followed Manco Capac before the coming of the Spaniards. Sober history indicates that from Cusco the Incas extended their territories, first to the Lake Titicaca area, and then through the highland regions to the north, west, and south, reaching in the early fifteenth century present-day Ecuador, Chile, and northwestern Argentina. The Peruvian coastal states were among the last to be added. A systematic program of deportation, assimilation, and indoctrination aimed at integrating as rapidly as possible the new conquests with the older portions of the empire, and in large measure succeeded. For the incorporation of conquered peoples, the Incas resorted to transfer of population, particularly of agricultural colonies. Care was taken to settle the alien folk in fertile but hitherto uninhabited valleys where conditions were not too dissimilar to those with which they had been familiar. Through the time of adjustment, encouragement was provided by special concessions. Far from their former ruler and kinsfolk, carefully supervised, and not permitted to move, the new colonists had hardly a chance at successful rebellion and seldom attempted it.

The ruler of this state, the Sapa Inca, was a supreme, hereditary monarch who wielded despotic authority as befitted a descendant of the sun god, which he was believed to be. Both a ruler and a god, the head of the priesthood as well as of the state, and the source of all law, he was regarded with the utmost awe and reverence. Even the highest nobles entered his presence in a stooping position and bearing a burden. Ideally, at least, his wife should be his own sister, as only the eldest son of such a marriage was considered qualified to inherit his absolute power.[37] His court was held in great magnificence at Cusco, and when he traveled to visit the provinces he was borne in a richly adorned litter on the shoulders of the greatest lords of the realm; at all times he was surrounded by great pomp and show of power.

The empire that he ruled—as large as modern France and Spain combined—held a population that has been variously estimated at from four to sixteen millions.[38] For administrative purposes, it was divided into four provinces over each of which was placed a governor or viceroy who was usually a kinsman of the Inca. The provinces were in their turn divided and subdivided on a decimal basis until the fundamental administrative unit or *chunca* of ten families had been reached. Socially, the old *ayllu* or tribe was the fundamental unit throughout all Andean society. The Incas had originally been merely one of the highland ayllus. Under their domination the whole Peruvian social order became organized in a caste system in which there were four principal classes. The first comprised the high nobility, made up of the descendants of the original Incas, who filled all the highest civil and religious posts in the land. They lived luxuriously, dressed in fine woven mantles, wore caps that indicated their rank, and ornamented themselves with elaborate jewelry, especially bracelets, chains, and huge earrings of gold and precious stones. It was from this latter peculiarity that they earned the nickname from the Spaniards of "Big

[37] A recent monograph points out that there is considerable evidence that this dynastic qualification had not always been strictly adhered to; that, in fact, the rule only reached its final form late in Inca history, and that there always existed the possibility of its being set aside for the older Indian tradition—originally shared by the Inca tribe—of a nonhereditary or, at most, a semihereditary principle of succession asserting itself. See C. Gibson, *The Inca Concept of Sovereignty and the Spanish Administration in Peru* (Austin, Texas: 1948), chap. ii.

[38] For the larger figure and the reason on which the author bases it, consult Means, *op. cit.*, p. 296.

Ears." A second class consisted of a lesser nobility which included in its ranks the deposed heads of the conquered peoples. From this group the host of lesser officials was drawn. The third class consisted of the great mass of the craftsmen and farmers, classified according to their occupation. A fourth group was made up of hereditary servitors called the *Yana-conas.*[39]

Economically the empire was managed as a single unit and worked co-operatively. Private ownership of land was not permitted. Land tenure was conceived of as falling into three categories: (1) that belonging to the Inca, (2) that belonging to the priests for the service of religion, and (3) that belonging to the tribes. Of the latter, each family was allotted a portion considered sufficient for its needs, and this must be cultivated under the supervision of state officials. Different classes of land were worked in regular succession. First came those sections belonging to religion; next, the fields of women, children, the aged, and the sick who were not able to work for themselves; third, the lands of the workmen themselves; finally, the lands of the state. Careful attention was given to the storing of surplus food in state storehouses against the time of famine. Each member of society had his place and his assigned task; each was provided by the state with the food and the materials that he needed for his work. No one might change his occupation, move from his locality, or marry, without special permission. Absolute obedience and submission were required. Agricultural and pastoral pursuits absorbed the energies of the great majority of the people. The advanced techniques used in terracing, irrigation, and fertilization amazed even the Spaniards who in these matters had been the pupils of the Arabs, respected in the Old World as expert gardeners. As an inheritance from older times, the Incas, like the peoples of Middle America, raised a wide range of grains and vegetables, including maize, manioc, the white potato, squash, beans, tomatoes, and peppers.

To an extent greater than elsewhere in America, the Incas had the help of domesticated animals, using the llama, their one beast of burden, the alpaca, and the guinea pig. These were, however, strictly under state control, and fresh meat was a rare item in the diet of the ordinary man. From the wool of the alpacas, vicuña, guanacos, and llamas, as well as from cotton cultivated in the valleys of the coast, the Incas wove textiles that exceeded in beauty even the finest achievements of the Mayas.

But all the people were not farmers or shepherds. The land was rich in metals. Gold, silver, copper, tin, platinum, and lead were mined, or taken from the beds of rivers, and the native craftsmen showed great skill in working these metals into useful and beautiful utensils, implements,

---

[39] For greater detail on this interesting group, consult Means, *op. cit.,* pp. 296-97.

images, and ornaments. The processes of casting, soldering, welding, and hammering were understood. Bronze, an alloy of copper and tin, was common. There were also jewelers skilled in cutting and polishing precious stones. As potters, Incan craftsmen were efficient and tasteful workmen, though their designs were simpler than those of their predecessors on the coast. Images of gold and silver and models of plants and flowers were frequently and expertly made.

As builders the Incas used both stone and adobe. Their skill in stone-cutting and in fitting without mortar was greater than that of any other of the American builders. Every stone—and some weighed several tons—in their earlier fortifications, walls, and palaces, was specially shaped to fit its own particular niche. Their structures have withstood centuries of earthquakes. The architectural forms were simpler, more solid, and less decorative than those of earlier cultures. Richness in appearance was achieved by the lavish use of gold and silver. The most famous building was the Temple of the Sun at Cusco, some of the walls of which were said to be plated with gold. Gorgeous mural decorations in feathered mosaics and intricate tapestries were also used to add color to the walls of palaces and temples.

Towns and provinces were linked together by a great system of roads, without which the empire could hardly have functioned. Like Roman roads, the Inca highways ran as straight as possible. As they were intended only for foot passengers they were narrow. Long stretches were paved, graded by steps, walled, here and there planted with shade trees, and marked at regular intervals by post houses, storage bins, and inns. They were intended to serve primarily for the use of the Sapa Inca on his progresses, the army in service, and the liveried runners who, with regularity and rapidity, bore the orders of the ruler from end to end of the long narrow state. Some of the bridges over the great gorges and swift rivers of this mountainous land were made of stone and wood, but many more were simply swinging ropes of osiers or fibre. The ingenuity of their construction was a marvel to the Spaniards who were themselves no mean engineers. There were two principal highways: one extended along the highlands of the great sierra from Quito by way of Cusco to Chile; another ran through the level country between the mountains and the sea. It is said that a message could reach Cusco from Quito, a distance of twelve hundred miles, by relay runners in eight days. These runners at times carried fresh fish and game for the ruler's table. Use was also made of signal fires. Besides the network of roads and constant visitations by high officials, the bond of a common language held all Inca land together. The Quechua dialect was declared the official language which all must learn, and in it there developed an unwritten literature of poems and stories.

An elaborate ritualism marked the worship of the sun, moon, Venus, and other heavenly bodies represented in the pantheon of the official Inca religion. The incarnation on earth of the sun god was the Inca ruler. Images of the local gods of conquered peoples were always brought to the Temple of the Sun in Cusco and were given a minor though honored position and incorporated in the pantheon of the state religion. The high priest was a near relative of the Inca. Every town had its temple with attendant priests, divines, and virgins. The usual offerings were flowers, fruits, precious metals, and garments which were burnt upon the altar. At times llamas were offered, and on occasions of great importance even human beings, often children, were sacrificed; but human sacrifice never was carried to such lengths as among the Mayas and Aztecs. Beyond this pantheon that satisfied the majority, there seems to have existed for the intellectual few the higher and nobler conception of a more spiritual creator-god, who was worshipped under the name of Pachacamac, or Viracocha, of whom the sun itself was conceived to be a visible symbol. The moon, as the sister-spouse of the sun, was also greatly revered. Probably to the masses neither Viracocha nor the official religion meant very much, except at great feasts and on splendid ceremonial occasions. Even in these the people had little part; their faith and fears centered in numerous *huacas* or sacred objects of nature or ancestor worship, such as rocks, lakes, stones, stars, animals, and mummies. Every locality and every family had its special huacas. Mummification of the dead and homage to ancestors were widespread customs. The body at burial was placed in a sitting position and, in the case of important individuals, was surrounded with utensils, implements, arms, and clothing that might be needed in the world after death.

In no other aspect of the cultures of North and South America are there greater differences than in the field of religion. In the north there is nothing to parallel the cult of the divine origin of the Sapa Inca; nor in the south is there any approach to the bloodthirsty ceremonial of the Mexican war gods. It is interesting to note, however, that it was in the northern lands of the more barbarous religious practices that scholarship made the greater progress. While as "children of the sun" the Peruvian priests were naturally much interested in the movements of the heavenly bodies and had made considerable progress in the study of mathematics and astronomy, even devising a fairly accurate calendar, their achievements cannot be compared to those of the Mayas and Aztecs. Neither did they ever succeed in inventing a system of writing. In the Inca civilization, great as it was in many respects, there is nothing comparable to the hieroglyphic codices that marked Maya and Aztec cultures. The greatest achievement of the Peruvians in the field of record-keeping was the invention of the *quipu,* a fringe of colored and knotted strings, used to help in the keeping of accounts, census figures, and other facts connected with statistical matters. This system, however, required considerable oral information to make it intelligible.

In another branch of science—medicine and surgery—a good deal of progress was made. In stimulants and narcotics the Inca possessed the coca leaf (containing cocaine), which they chewed; tobacco, which they used as a kind of snuff; and a potent variety of beer called chicha, which they made from maize. From the bark of the cinchona, which they cultivated extensively, they secured the all-important quinine. In surgery their most astonishing feat was the difficult operation of trepanning for the relief of pain resulting from depressed fractures. To judge from the appearance of skeletal forms it was evidently performed frequently and with success. Instruments used were made of bronze and obsidian. The patient was soothed with coca leaves. In addition to their possessing this ancient form of anesthetic, the number of cures would indicate that the native doctors had some means of preventing infection.

A complete regulation of life in the interests of a sort of aristocratic state socialism, presided over by an absolute ruler, remains the outstanding impression left by a study of the Inca system. For the individual it had certain undoubted advantages which go far to account for his submission to it over a prolonged period. Its greatest blessing was the considerable degree of economic, social, political, and military security which it provided. It also involved for the common man a welcome lack of responsibility, while at the same time the high degree of governmental efficiency, which made crime rare and graft unknown, seemed to indicate that all was well. The political wisdom that left undisturbed many local customs and lightened the year's drudgery by many colorful feasts and festivals helped also to make the system acceptable.[40]

The mortal weaknesses, however, of the basic principles on which the whole fabric rested, namely the removal of individual responsibility and the subjection of the individual to the supposed welfare of the state, made themselves at once apparent when a greedy conqueror made his appearance on the shores of Peru. The long absence of individual freedom not only meant the utter collapse of the state when the recognized leader had

---

[40] The reader should realize that the traditional conception that the Inca state functioned as an extremely successful form of state socialism under a benevolent autocrat rests largely on the authority of one famous book, *Commentarios Reales que Tratan del Origen de los Yncas* (Lisbon: 1608 or 1609), written by Garcilaso de la Vega. A half-breed descendant of a Spanish conquistador and an Inca "princess," Garcilaso, after a youth spent in Cusco, went to Spain where he wrote his interesting book, partly as a justification for the culture of his mother's people and partly as a consolation for himself. Modern research in contemporary writings and evidence as turned up by archaeology have been casting doubts on the accuracy of the picture.

been captured or killed by the enemy, but also involved the gradual elimination over a period of centuries of sufficient incentive and initiative in the character of the people to organize a resurgence of national life at a time of crisis. The first stirrings of the Indian people in the post-conquest period occurred, not in those regions where pre-Columbian government was most efficient, but in the areas where the looser confederation was the prevailing form and where man was not so closely harnessed to the chariot wheels of the state.

In fairness to the remarkable political system that the Incas devised, it has to be remembered that the white man arrived in the midst of perhaps the most serious crisis that ever shook the Inca throne. It was almost as if "the stars in their courses" fought against the red man. When Pizarro and his adventurers landed, a civil war was in progress. The cause of this struggle, according to the traditional story, involved the very vitals of the theory on which the fabric of the Inca state rested, namely the godhead of the Sapa Inca himself. The last Inca, Huayna Capac, according to one version, had been unable to resist the temptation of leaving a part of his great inheritance to a favorite but illegitimate son, thus defying the dynastic tradition—reputedly of divine origin—that the realm must pass entire to the legitimate eldest son of the official sister-wife. To Atahualpa, the son of the Inca and a princess of Quito, a secondary wife, was left the northern part of the kingdom centering at Quito, while Huáscar, the legitimate son, was ordered to be satisfied with the southern part of the kingdom with its capital at Cusco. The break with tradition was made the more serious when, in the civil war that naturally followed, it was Atahualpa who succeeded in re-establishing the unity of the state by conquering the southern half, making prisoner the true Inca, and setting up his only half-divine self as successor to Huayna Capac on the Inca throne. Recent studies have raised a number of questions concerning this traditional story: (1) whether the outbreak of civil war between Huáscar and Atahualpa was as unique an event as the official Inca chroniclers make out; (2) whether there had been for any length of time an inviolable rule that the *borla,* or royal headdress, must pass to the eldest son of the principal wife; and (3) whether Huáscar was in fact the eldest legitimate son of Huayna Capac.[41] But whatever the view taken of these matters, the fact remains that the Inca territories were staggering under the impact of a civil war over a disputed succession when the Spaniards arrived to make full and unscrupulous use of the opportunities before them. Still more fundamental in the disaster that overtook the Inca people was the reaction of the individual subject and his helplessness in the face of this crisis.

[41] *Cf.* C. Gibson, *op. cit.*

PART II

DISCOVERY AND ORGANIZATION BY THE WHITE MAN

Chapter 3

THE SPIRIT OF DISCOVERY

A new epoch in the history of the Americas began with the close of the fifteenth century when the existence of this hemisphere first dawned upon the mind of a Europe recently reawakened by the impact of the Renaissance and tingling with the spirit of adventure. The discovery of America in 1492 was the climax of a great Age of Discovery that had been in progress since the thirteenth century. During these three hundred years Europe had been passing through a period of transition from the medieval towards the modern world in which a number of new political, social, and intellectual forces had been gaining momentum and direction.

Politically the outstanding feature of this time of revival was the rise of the national states and the weakening of the concept, inherited from Rome, of a universal empire. All semblance of the ideological unity that had held together the whole of western Christendom in the Middle Ages as one religious and political society gradually dissolved and the modern nations of France, England, Portugal, and Spain became fully self-conscious national entities, each possessed of clearly defined geographical boundaries. These states bordering on the Atlantic had never territorially been parts of the Holy Roman Empire of which Germany and Italy were the principal components. They now emerged from even the shadow of the imperial nexus under the stress of great military events of the fourteenth and fifteenth centuries, which brought to them all a great access of national pride and a strong sense of self-sufficiency. In England and France the Hundred Years' War, and in Spain and Portugal the final expulsion of the Moors from the Iberian Peninsula, endowed these countries with strong confidence in their respective national destinies.

This spirit flowered in an outburst of energy and accomplishment. In England, patriotic exultation in the stirring victories of Crécy, Poitiers, and Agincourt finally welded Normans and Anglo-Saxons into one nation. By the middle of the fourteenth century, English as the national tongue had come into use in the law courts and Parliament, as well as in the development of a vernacular literature under the inspiration of Chaucer and Langland. The House of Commons found the courage in the first century of its existence to depose two unsatisfactory kings. In the same century Wycliffe's independent thought foreshadowed the day when a religious reform movement would succeed in establishing the independence of the national church from continental ties. Meanwhile, in France, the failures and successes of the Hundred Years' War brought a closer union between king and people and prepared the way for a Jeanne d'Arc who, in the darkest hour of the war, inspired a national movement which snatched victory from defeat and carried the king to a throne more national in character than it had ever been. The close of the Hundred Years' War in the middle of the fifteenth century was followed in both countries by civil wars that undermined the power of the feudal barons and established strong monarchial governments which, though highly centralized and despotic in many ways, derived their real power, both national and international, from the support of the trading classes. The Wars of the Roses in England closed with Henry VII, the first of the strong Tudors, on the throne; and in France, the Burgundian wars established Charles VII as the national monarch.[1]

In Spain, also, civil war brought national unity and a stronger monarchy.[2] A long period of internal anarchy was brought to an end by the marriage on October 19, 1469, of Ferdinand of Aragon and Isabella of Castile, a marriage which united the two largest and strongest states among the five independent political units in the Iberian Peninsula. Two of the three remaining states were added to the Spanish crown during the reign of the joint Catholic sovereigns. Of these, Granada fell by conquest in 1492, closing a long crusading struggle of nearly eight hundred years against the Moors for possession of the national soil and bringing the land under the exclusive dominance of the Cross. Navarre was won in 1512, partly by conquest and partly through dynastic claims, and became a part of the Aragonese inheritance. For the incorporation of the fifth state, Portugal, Ferdinand and Isabella laid many schemes, mostly matrimonial, which in time were to be temporarily successful, but for the moment Portugal escaped the net and the Iberian Peninsula entered the sixteenth century under the divided control of Spain and Portugal.

Internally, both Castile and Aragon were in chaos when Ferdinand and Isabella took up their tasks in 1469. Heedless of what it might cost in the loss of hard-won representative institutions and local liberties, the common people, especially in Castile, in desperation were ready to fling themselves into the arms of any ruler, whatever his political principles, who would deliver them from the turbulence and tyranny of the nobles and bring order out of anarchy. Ferdinand and Isabella, both able and

---

[1] The student is referred to the classic essay on "Nationality" in A. F. Pollard's *Factors in Modern History* (various editions), chap. ii.

[2] Cf. R. B. Merriman's *The Rise of the Spanish Empire in the Old World and the New* (New York: 1918-34), Vol. II, chap. xiv, pp. 78-79.

personally ambitious, took full advantage of the situation to establish their own absolute and centralized power. While they conciliated popular favor by a restoration of order and the securing of life and property through reforms in army, police, and the courts, they quietly allowed representative institutions to fall into disuse. They introduced royal agents into traditionally self-governing towns, converted popular and aristocratic institutions into royal ones, reduced the nobles in power and prestige through a scrutiny of their land titles, and, by substituting lawyers in new offices with

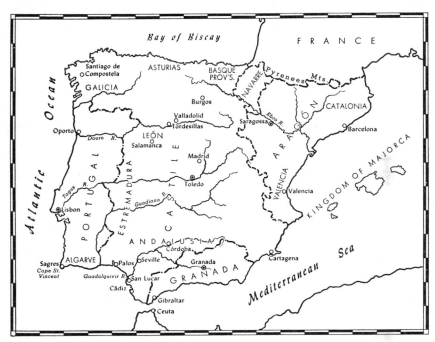

6. The Iberian Peninsula at the Accession of Ferdinand and Isabella

effective powers in place of hereditary nobles in the great offices of state, encouraged the aristocracy to become a mere courtier class. The Inquisition was introduced not primarily as a religious weapon but as a politically unifying instrument to help the crown deal with alien elements in the middle class, the Jews and the Moors. These two groups, having been forced into a nominal Christianity, nevertheless were believed to retain secretly their old religious habits. The avowed ideal of the sovereigns was political unity based on religious uniformity. Although more scrupulously thorough and more completely ambitious to achieve absolutism, their methods differed little from those employed by contemporary rulers of other national states.

As a result of their work, Spain at the beginning of the sixteenth century stood well abreast of the other rising nations. She opened the first century of modern times with the process of regional and political unification well on the road to completion, despite having to overcome greater geographical, racial, and historical obstacles than were faced by either France or England. In the development of the *cortes* she had behind her a long and honorable tradition of popular participation in the government; she possessed able rulers on her throne and a succession of eligible heirs in view. Her population was vigorous, varied in blood, richly endowed along many lines, and had shown itself possessed of sufficient persistence and unity of national purpose to carry through the *reconquista*. Her soldiers were known as the best in Europe; the country was filled with bold, adventurous characters keen to undertake any new enterprise; the glory of the recent conquest of Granada was fresh upon her. She was apparently ready for a truly great future.

That this glory was to be short-lived and her pre-eminence was to last for not more than a single century was not apparent to contemporaries, though actually Spain carried within her organism the seeds of an early decline. The repression of all free thought by the Holy Office of the Inquisition, the determination of the rulers to use all the resources of faith and order in the church to enhance their own prestige and power, the stifling of the voice of true representative government by ingenious curbs upon the cortes, the depriving of the nation of the natural leadership of its upper classes in the interests of absolutism, the bleeding of the nation's economic vitality by the expulsion of the industrious and resourceful Jews and Moors, and the discouragement of commercial initiative by heavy taxation and a system of rigid state direction and control, all these factors in their cumulative weight were to prove too great for her own reserves of strength and the resources of the vast empire she was about to acquire.

The unification and centralization of authority, achieved by strong national rulers in all the maritime states of western Europe at the close of the fifteenth century, provided a conscious foundation of strength and an indispensable backdrop for the display of Renaissance genius in many directions. Another dominant note of the age was a revival of interest in classical learning which carried with it a freer, more naturalistic attitude towards the search for truth in many fields of thought and action. Supernaturalism and the spirit of subordination to accepted authority, so prevalent in the Middle Ages, began to decline and be replaced by a greater interest in direct observation and investigation of natural phenomena at first hand. Medieval myths and legends began to lose their hold as reports of discoveries and the results of scientific experimentation and observation poured in. As early as the thirteenth century Roger Bacon

(1214-1292), obtaining many of his ideas from Greek, Hebrew, and Arabic sources, had been a herald of the new age of experimentation.

In the center of this development during its flowering in the sixteenth and seventeenth centuries (1543-1687), was the work of the astronomers. The epoch-making study by Copernicus, *De Revolutionibus Orbium Coelestium,* was published in 1543. Its principal contribution was the revival of the heliocentric hypothesis which places the sun at the center of the planetary system. This thesis had been set forth centuries earlier by the great Greek teacher Aristarchus of Samos (310-250 B.C.), but afterwards lost sight of. The work of Copernicus stimulated the thought and experiments of scientists for the next hundred years and brought in its train a procession of revolutionary achievements. The observations of heavenly bodies made by Tycho Brahe (1546-1601) and Galileo (1564-1642) proved that all the planets, including the earth, moved around the sun. After incredible labor on Tycho Brahe's observations, Kepler (1571-1630) arrived at the elliptical form of the planetary orbits and established his famous laws of planetary motion. The climax came at the end of the seventeenth century with the publication of Sir Isaac Newton's *Principia* (1687), which presented the motions of the planets simply as manifestations of his universal law of gravitation. An immediate and practical outcome of the new science in the sixteenth century was a keen interest in the invention and perfection of scientific instruments, both for the pursuit of pure astronomy and as aids to practical navigation. The earlier invention of the printing press (1455) made possible a wide dissemination and popularization of the new learning. That so many factors—an awakened spirit of scientific investigation, a keenness for adventure, a new exuberance in the enjoyment of literary and artistic forms—were practically contemporary with the discovery of America, ought surely to have started the New World off with a rich endowment of Old World culture. How faithful to their opportunity the bearers to America of Renaissance gifts proved to be is another story.

It is to be noted that while the centrifugal forces of emergent nationalism were among the factors leading to the discovery of the New World, the loss of religious unity more directly affected the form its settlement should take. While the Reformation movement was not in full swing until settlement in America was well under way, signs and portents were plentiful well in advance. One of the most notable of these was the Conciliar Movement, an expression of the rising political and constitutional temper of the fourteenth century. It demanded that the Pope should recognize the authority of representative general councils as supreme in interpreting the voice of the whole church. The failure of this movement led inevitably to the revolt of northern Europe under Luther, Zwingli,

Calvin, and other Protestant leaders of the sixteenth century and eventually sent thousands of dissatisfied folk flocking to America. Meanwhile, the Papacy was caught up in the dazzle of the Renaissance movement in its artistic and literary aspects and awakened to the need of a counterreformation too late to save the religious unity of Europe.

Along with fundamental political and religious changes that marked the Age of Discovery came sweeping economic and social readjustments. Western society in the Middle Ages had been organized in a feudal structure with its attendant manorial system. This was a complex form of organization in which economic and social life, as well as political relationships, was based on the tenure of land which in ultimate theory belonged to the king. Feudalism had come into existence to meet the exigencies of a time when the central government had been too weak to deal successfully with both turbulent internal conditions and the threat of foreign invasions. It had offered a practical remedy, involving grants of land to local strong men who in return had the responsibility of raising military levies in any emergency to serve as units in an easily assembled army. Under this system of lords, vassals, and serfs, each unit of society was a group of men attached to a hereditary superior in a pyramidal structure that found its apex in the royal power. Each man owed military service to his immediate superior from whom he claimed protection and from whom he held his land. The system involved summary methods of government and a perpetual struggle for existence between the various groups. The lower stratum of society, constituting the majority of the population, consisted of serfs bound to the soil, only partly free and only remotely connected with the central government. The basis of wealth was agriculture, organized in large estates, with the goal of each unit economic self-sufficiency. Industry and commerce were localized as far as possible. Towns and businessmen fitted awkwardly into the framework, as the goal was production for sustenance rather than for profit. Barter methods and fixed prices made the merchant unpopular and his way difficult.

This feudal order of society prevailed generally in all western Europe from the tenth to at least the beginning of the thirteenth century. The principal problem after the eleventh century, when foreign danger was no longer acute, was how to make innocuous the power of the feudal lord who had degenerated from being the savior of society to its worst enemy. The Crusades of the twelfth and thirteenth centuries helped greatly to reduce the power of this class by drawing off to the East many of the most obstreperous spirits and by financially ruining many of the great houses of Europe. Cities and towns in increasing numbers found it possible to struggle free from the burden of aristocratic control and to create a trade that made them wealthy enough to defy their feudal suzerains, or to buy charters of liberty. The kings, jealous of the overweening power of the great landowners, for the most part sided with the cities and revoked many of the powers and privileges that earlier had devolved upon their vassals. After the thirteenth century, feudalism was definitely on the decline, though ideas emanating from it were not to die out for centuries. Some of these conceptions, though surprisingly few, were transported to the New World.

One of the most crippling features of feudalism had been the submergence of the individual within the group, which alone had importance as a unit in medieval society. With the crumbling of feudalism, this limitation was lifted and "man won back his ancient right to count as an individual." The emancipation of the spirit that followed the throwing off of feudal fetters of convention and custom, the illumination of mind that came with the revival of learning, and the new opportunities offered to his imagination and energy in the wider field of the national state and in the opening of world trade and adventure gave individual man a new stature and dignity. He acquired new skills, invented new devices, found courage to face new dangers, lifted his eyes to new horizons, and found an ability to adapt himself to new conditions. Among the many fruits of the Renaissance, these qualities were essential for the discovery and the successful colonization of the New World. The explorers and colonists of America were the logical inheritors of the new spirit of courage and individual initiative, as well as trustees of the social, cultural, and political forms being evolved in the fourteenth and fifteenth centuries in Europe.

Exploration to a great extent was the work of the middle class that arose out of the changing complex of the declining medieval system.[3] Indeed, it has been pointed out that the most extraordinary thing that the middle class did in rising to strength was to discover the hitherto unknown lands beyond the European world—to strike out for America, Africa, and Asia—and to establish relationship with people of the yellow, black, and red races. For three centuries a flow of middle-class adventurers, who were both romantic and practical in temperament, was constantly issuing from European ports in search of places with such thrilling names as Bokhara, Khiva, Karakoram, Pekin, Ormuz, the Gold Coast, the Cape of Good Hope, Mexico, and Peru. They were looking for regions promising high adventure, pushing on in search of such goals as the Island of the Seven Cities, the Kingdom of Prester John, the Fountain of Youth, El Dorado, and the Seven Cities of Cíbola; they were in search of lands where there was plenty of gold, silver, and gems, and where, returning travellers reported, instead of the dull diet of Europe it was possible to have turkey

---

[3] Pollard, *op cit.,* chap. ii, "The Advent of the Middle Class."

for dinner, along with sweet potatoes and red tomatoes, pineapple or straw-berries for dessert, and coffee with a pipe of tobacco afterwards. Those affected with the wanderlust were for the most part people of the new towns—of all elements in the population the freest from feudal obligations. The country dwellers, mostly still enmeshed in feudal service, did not at first take much part in the overseas movement.

The noble houses, great and small, whose fortunes and doings had played such a large part in the history of Europe since the decline of Rome, were but sparsely represented in the voyages of discovery. When, however, the principal business in the new lands took the form of adminis-tration and systematic exploration rather than discovery, the ranks of the nobility were drawn upon to serve as governors and viceroys, charged with the responsibility for law and order and to act as custodians of the interests of the crown. Their conservatism and lack of fluid capital prevented their playing in the new age the conspicuous role they had filled in the old. Inheriting a traditional scorn for trade, their wealth was mostly frozen in landed property. It was therefore largely the middle class that provided both the personnel and the necessary resources for the new adventures. It was soon found, however, that no single individual from any class could finance successful colonization. For the first two colonial enterprises—those of Spain and Portugal—the kings largely underwrote the bills, mak-ing, however, careful provision for reimbursement from the hoped-for treasures of the new lands. The French, English, and Dutch, who were denied this help, ran into immense difficulties and could not successfully get under way until, at the beginning of the seventeenth century, the device of the joint-stock company took practical form. Under this scheme a number of individuals could pool their resources and assume limited responsibilities for losses and yet have a chance for a handsome profit by buying shares of stock in an "adventuring" company. Eventually all colo-nial nations employed the joint-stock company device.[4] The most famous of these companies were the various East and West India companies and the Hudson's Bay Company. Thus colonization on its business side was an expression of the new Europe for which town and city life provided the needed impetus.

The one traditional institution which retained its vitality and func-tioned continuously as a principal factor in colonial enterprise for three hundred years was the monarchy. Kings and queens not only provided financial resources for the early voyages of discovery, but gave the sanction

---

[4] A short, clear account of the development from the regulated company to the joint-stock company and the relation of the latter to the chartering by governments of commercial undertakings will be found in L. B. Packard's *The Commercial Revolution, 1400-1776* (New York: 1927), chap. i, pp. 15-19.

of sovereignty to the national settlements. Discoveries were made in the name of the king, the royal flag was planted, and title to the new territory was claimed for the crown. The greatest care was always taken to safeguard royal rights. The discoverer might explore, but the king was determined to hold the title and intended to rule.

The motives that inspired the members of all these classes, from king to common sailor, were of course as varied as the individuals themselves. One motive affecting all was curiosity, aroused by stories of the rich and fabled Orient; cupidity followed on the heels of curiosity, stimulating the trading instincts of the new middle class; opportunity for daring and romantic deeds appealed to the young and adventurous; religious feeling moved many who felt the call to win souls for the Church.

The lands that were eventually opened up in the great Age of Discovery—whether in Asia, along the coast of Africa, or in the American hemisphere—were all more or less incidental to the ultimate purpose: reaching the golden East. To whatever point of the compass the traveler directed his way—whether east or south or north or even west—he was always seeking an unrestricted passage by which the Atlantic nations of Western Europe might come into direct contact with China, India, and the Spice Islands of the Pacific. This dream had especially haunted and tantalized European man since the mid-seventh century when the great wave of Arab conquests, following the rise of Mohammedanism, had flowed over the shores of Africa and the Near East and created a formidable Moslem barrier between Europe and farther Asia. The stiffening of this barrier by the conquests of the Mohammedan Seljuk Turks in the twelfth century had helped to produce the Crusades. Although these heroic enterprises failed to make an appreciable dent in the barrier, they succeeded in stimulating the European appetite for the luxuries of the East. In the following centuries Italian merchants grew rich on the profits of an increased trade in oriental goods—spices, silks, and gems—secured from Moslem middlemen at the western termini of the southern oriental trade routes, the ports along the Levantine coast of the Mediterranean. But this devious and costly interchange (from which only the Italians profited) was far from satisfying to the western and northern nations.[5]

A new effort to open a direct and independent route to the Orient came in the thirteenth century in the wake of a wave of Tartar conquest.

---

[5] For the continued prosperity of the Levant trade until well into the sixteenth century, and an emphasis on the view that the Mediterranean conquests of the Ottoman Turks came too late and from other considerations cannot be held responsible for the economic urgency behind the search for direct sea passages to the Far East—and the discovery of America, consult A. H. Lybyer's article "The Influence of the Rise of the Ottoman Turks upon the Routes of Oriental Trade," *Annual Report* of the American Historical Association, 1914, Vol. I, pp. 127-33.

Sweeping westward from centers in eastern Siberia and China, these barbarians succeeded in breaking through the northern portion of the Mohammedan barrier, overflowing the plains of southern Russia, and engulfing the Black Sea coast. Although Europeans were at first terrified by the appearance in eastern Europe of the brutal Asiatic horsemen of Genghiz Khan, presently bolder spirits believed they saw a possibility of converting these Mongols to Christianity, making allies of them against the Mohammedan Turks, and perhaps through them opening the coveted Far Eastern trade. For a time these dreamers were encouraged by the tolerant attitude of the Tartar Grand Khan who sought to have the merits of all religious creeds explained to him.

With this encouragement, a period of land travel into Asia opened which lasted for approximately one hundred and twenty years. From 1245 to 1368 missionary friars, emissaries of the Pope, ambassadors from European courts, and finally private traders from Italy, France, Spain, Holland, and Germany made great overland journeys into the Orient. They not only succeeded in spreading over the East a thin network of Christian missions but brought back the first reliable record of what the East was really like. Missionaries and traders alike were keen observers. Pian de Carpini in Mongolia, William of Rubruck in Central Asia, Friar Oderic in China, Jordanus in India, and Marco Polo in Turkestan, Mongolia, Cathay, India, and the Indian archipelago, were immensely interested in everything to be seen and brought back eyewitness accounts and stimulating observations.[6] Of these chronicles, the *Book of the Ser Marco Polo* was the foremost record of overland exploration and the best geographical survey that the thirteenth century bequeathed to later times. Its author, Marco Polo, was the son of a Venetian jewel merchant who became a highly trusted emissary of the Grand Khan. While the narrative is marked here and there by exaggeration, hasty generalization, and a childlike credulity in accepting reports of the marvelous, it nevertheless shows the writer to have been not only a careful observer and a wonderful raconteur of curious customs, but a man endowed with the spirit of the new age. Belonging to the world of business, alive to the value of money, and genuinely interested in trade routes and other commercial matters, Marco Polo took special note of such novelties as coal, oil, and asbestos.

Marco Polo's *Book*,[7] available in many manuscript copies in the fourteenth and fifteenth centuries before the days of printing, was studied with

---

[6] On the Tartars and their relations to Asiatic exploration, *cf.* E. Power, "The Opening of the Land Routes to Cathay," in *Travel and Travellers of the Middle Ages*, edited by A. P. Newton (London: 1926), chap. vii, pp. 126-37.

[7] The standard English edition is that in the Hakluyt Society Publications, *The Book of the Ser Marco Polo, the Venetian, Concerning the Kingdoms and Marvels of the East*, edited by Sir Henry Yule.

the greatest care by the geographers and explorers of those centuries. When Prince Henry the Navigator, the Portuguese founder of scientific exploration, visited Marco Polo's city of Venice in 1428 he was presented by the Seignory with a handsome edition of Marco's *Book*, together with a map illustrating the route that the famous Venetian had followed. Many of Prince Henry's captains were familiar with the work. We know also that Columbus studied the *Book* with the greatest care and that it became the chief source of his geographical views. His copy of it, preserved in the Columbian library in Seville, is filled with marginal notes in the Admiral's own handwriting, especially those portions referring to Cipangu— the rich island of Japan—placed by Marco Polo fifteen hundred miles off Quinsay, capital of the easternmost province of China.

In the end, the overland movement towards the Orient proved to be merely "a splendid failure." Not only did the Mohammedans eventually triumph in the religious issue and the Khan and his Mongol subjects embrace Islam, reversing their attitude towards the Christian missionaries and traders, but the Mongol empire itself soon fell to pieces. But, while not successful, this frontal overland attack on the East in the thirteenth and fourteenth centuries laid a foundation of essential information for ultimate success by the round-about maritime route. Because of this knowledge, the seamen of the fifteenth century in striving for a seaway to India could move forward with the certainty that the golden prize which they were seeking really existed.

Already in the thirteenth and fourteenth centuries the earliest steps in maritime exploration had been taken by the Genoese and Catalans, who were apparently the first to adventure southward along the west coast of Africa. They were soon joined by the French and the Portuguese. Exactly what their achievements were, it is difficult to determine. The Canary Islands we know were discovered, and other island groups may have been visited. By the close of the fourteenth century the seamen had equipped themselves with serviceable maritime instruments and maps. They had a practical compass, maritime quadrant, astrolabe, and more or less accurate coastal charts. They also possessed gunpowder which had been introduced from the East in the late thirteenth century.

The golden age of maritime discovery was the fifteenth century. Portugal, occupying most of the Atlantic coast line of the Iberian Peninsula, was the center of the most exciting activity of this age. About 1420 began the systematically planned oceanic exploration under the direction and financial assistance of Prince Henry the Navigator (1394-1460), who set up his nautical headquarters at Sagres, near Cape St. Vincent. This famous prince was the third son of João I of Portugal and his English queen, Philippa of Lancaster, the daughter of John of Gaunt. The conquest of

Ceuta—a knightly task entrusted to Prince Henry, it is said, by his English mother on her deathbed—stimulated his interest in Africa and started his dreaming of the possibility of reaching the East by turning the flank of the Moslems in Africa.[8] He knew of the legend that somewhere along the coast of West Africa was to be found the mouth of a "western Nile," a river that was thought to run from east to west across Africa. Along its banks, it was believed, lay the realms of the Christian king, Prester John, who could be relied upon to welcome and give aid to his coreligionists (a legend probably based upon rumors of Abyssinia).[9]

Progress southward began along the African coast in 1420 with the rediscovery of the Madeira Islands. In 1434 Cape Bogador was passed, a feat considered in that time equal to one of the labors of Hercules.[10] Seven years later the first slaves and the first samples of gold dust and ivory were brought back and swung popular interest to the support of the new venture. Henceforth Prince Henry was no longer accused of being a mad dreamer. By the time of his death in 1460, the Cape Verde Islands had been discovered and shortly afterwards the Grain, Ivory, and Gold Coasts were explored and the great bend of Africa was turned. Step by step, the line was pushed to the south. The equator was crossed in 1472, the mouth of the Congo reached in 1484, and finally, in 1488, Bartholomeu Dias rounded the Cape of Good Hope and sailed to the northeast of it for two hundred miles. At this point his sailors, fearing that they might never be able to get back, refused to go farther and forced his return home. At the reception that welcomed him in Lisbon, Christopher Columbus was probably present. The death of King João II in 1495 caused so long a delay in renewed efforts that six years before the Portuguese reached India, as they did under Vasco da Gama in 1498, Christopher Columbus, sailing under Spanish colors, reached what he called "the Indies" by a rival route.

The excitement created by these Portuguese voyages down the African coast (obviously intended to discover a southern route to the East) helped to revive an alternative idea, conceived originally by the Greeks eighteen hundred years earlier, of the feasibility of reaching the Orient by a westward journey. Ptolemy's *Geography,* recently recovered and greatly venerated by all scholars, not only emphasized this potentiality of the earth's sphericity, but calculated the distance between western Europe and the eastern shore of Asia. Other old accounts, theories, maps, and legends

---

[8] *Cf.* S. de Madariaga, *Christopher Columbus* (New York: 1940), pp. 71-76.

[9] On the African projects and activities of Prince Henry, see E. J. Payne, "The Age of Discovery," in *The Cambridge Modern History* (Cambridge: 1902), Vol. I, pp. 10-16. But cf. E. Prestage, "The Search for the Sea Route to India," in *Travel and Travellers of the Middle Ages,* pp. 203, 214-16. See also H. V. Livermore, *A History of Portugal* (Cambridge: 1947), p. 187.

[10] Prestage, *op. cit.,* 205.

were resurrected and studied. By the time of the Navigator's death in 1460, these researches had crystallized in a general belief that somewhere in the western ocean between Europe and Asia there existed a large island which would form a halfway station and whose discovery was a necessary first step in the achievement of the westward passage. The Portuguese, whose ships year after year plied the seas to the west of the Azores looking for such an island, spoke of the object of their search as Antillia or as St. Brendan's Isle; English seamen out of Bristol, searching for a similar island, spoke more frequently of "Brasil." The Italian scientist, Toscanelli, assumed the fact of the existence of such an island and, in 1474, indicated on a chart for Portuguese seamen a large island in the midst of the Atlantic.[11]

The early British and Portuguese voyages to the west came to nothing largely because, after sailing some distance westward, one explorer after another became firmly convinced that he had somehow missed his objective and would turn about in a vain search for it. Columbus, too, hoped to find one or more islands on his way to Cipango; however, he seems not to have made this a *sine qua non,* but instead fixed his mind on the ultimate goal which he conceived as attainable only by a direct westward passage steadily persisted in.[12]

The traditional story of Columbus' efforts in one European court after another, to secure the three ships, provisioned with food for twelve months and well stocked with trading goods that he reckoned necessary for his enterprise, is a classical example of courage and persistence eventually rewarded. He made his first formal application for aid to the King of Portugal, probably in 1484. From his youth he and his brother, Bartholomew, who were Genoese by birth, had been in the maritime service of Portugal. For some time they were engaged in the chart-making business in Lisbon, where Christopher married a Portuguese. In early life he had sailed repeatedly on voyages of exploration to the West African coast, and is said to have made journeys to England, Ireland, and Iceland. His experience, acquired mostly under the Portuguese flag, covered, he claimed— he was not a modest man—"all that to our day is navigated" from the Arctic to the equator.[13] The reigning sovereign, King João II, a highly respected authority himself in navigation matters, turned Columbus' proposition over to his marine advisory committee. This body was not favorably impressed. The explorer's plan was simply that of sailing directly westward until he reached "Cipango" (Japan) and the eastern shore of Asia in the

---

[11] For mythical Atlantic islands see S. E. Morison, *Portuguese Voyages to America in the Fifteenth Century* (Cambridge: 1940), pp. 15-29.

[12] E. J. Payne, *op. cit.,* pp. 20-21.

[13] Columbus' Letter to the King and Queen of Spain, March 23, 1502.

province of "Quinsay," fifteen hundred miles beyond the rich outlying island. His estimate of distance seemed—as it was—preposterously small, the details of the scheme vague and imaginary, and Columbus' pretensions and demands exorbitant.[14] Furthermore it was exceedingly questionable, the committee probably felt, whether from the royal point of view the success of such a journey was desirable. The circumnavigation of Africa was well within sight and such a route to the East would be practically a Portuguese monopoly which would be definitely jeopardized by the opening of a western route. Columbus' scheme was therefore discouraged.

If, as has been suggested, Columbus sought help about this same time from Genoa and Venice and was turned down, it is easy to understand his rejection, as these Italian trading states had their eyes on the Mediterranean and were still prospering from their Levant commerce. Columbus realized that he must fix his hope on one or other of the western powers whose maritime fortunes were still in the future and obviously in the Atlantic. In 1485 he dispatched his brother Bartholomew to France to endeavor to secure the needed support, failing which he was to make an appeal to the English king. In the meantime Columbus himself left for Spain to approach the Spanish sovereigns.

Leaving his young son Diego at the monastery of La Rábida near the port of Palos, Columbus passed on to Seville and applied for assistance to a number of wealthy Spanish grandees. One of these, the Count of Medina Celi, the owner of a merchant fleet, thought seriously of supplying the needed resources but decided that the proposed undertaking ought to receive the royal approval and so referred Columbus directly to the Spanish sovereigns. The time, however, was unpropitious. Ferdinand and Isabella were completely absorbed in the last phases of the conquest of Granada and had small time to spare for the consideration of fanciful overseas projects. They, however, listened graciously and turned the project over to an advisory commission where it remained shelved for four years. They were, however, sufficiently interested to give Columbus a retaining fee to hold him in Spain.

Through these hard waiting years Columbus probably lived in Córdoba, perhaps earned a little money making maps, and filled in his time studying geographical works, especially Marco Polo's *Book*, Pierre d' Ailly's *Imago Mundo* (a world geography written about 1410), and a volume by Aeneas Sylvius entitled *Historia Rerum Ubique Gestarum* (1477). In 1488 his hopes were raised by a letter from King João II summoning him to Portugal and offering a reconsideration of his proposition. However, it all came to nothing. He had barely arrived when Bartholo-

---

[14] Morison discusses these Portuguese negotiations in his *Admiral of the Ocean Sea,* 2 Vols. (Boston: 1942), Vol. I, pp. 93-96.

meu Dias returned with the news of his successful venture round the Cape of Good Hope into the Indian Ocean.[15] Columbus' project was summarily and permanently dropped at the Lisbon court. Portugal now had one passage to the Indies and that was enough. Columbus returned to Spain.

Here he found the sovereigns in a more favorable frame of mind, but the Moorish war was still on and, in 1490, a further setback came in an adverse report from the special committee investigating his proposed enterprise. It declared the whole proposition "vain and worthy of rejection." This decision had turned on the question of the width of the Atlantic Ocean which the scientists knew Columbus was underestimating. The gracious and intelligent queen, however, gave him permission to reopen the project when the war was over. Completely discouraged, Columbus set out for France.

On the advice, however, of Fray Juan Pérez of the Monastery of La Rábida, where Columbus stopped to pick up his son, he was induced to wait in Spain and try again. A letter from the monk to the queen brought a royal summons to Columbus to return again to the court. He arrived just in time to take part in the jubilant procession into the fallen last stronghold of the Moors in Spain. Again a commission met to reconsider the vexed question of the proposed expedition. Again it was turned down, this time on the ground of the explorer's exorbitant demands. Once again he departed completely discouraged. But ten miles from the city he was overtaken by a messenger with an urgent summons to return. The queen had been persuaded by her chancellor, Luis de Santangel, not to refuse so little risk for so vast a gain. The chancellor offered to put up the money himself. The queen was willing, she said, to pledge her crown jewels. Finally the 2,000,000 *maravedis* ($14,000) came partly from the royal treasury, partly from Santangel, and partly from Columbus' own friends.[16]

The contract was signed on April 17, 1492. Its terms secured to Columbus, in addition to the usual rewards of maritime enterprise—one tenth of the gold and silver and other merchandise that might be discovered or produced—certain advantages of a personal and political kind that Columbus insisted upon. These included the hereditary dignity of Admiral of the Ocean Sea and, also to be hereditary, the authority in the new lands that should be discovered of Viceroy and Governor, with the hereditary title of Don.

Palos, a small port town, was ordered by the sovereigns to provide Columbus with the necessary vessels. Eventually three adequate vessels were secured. The town provided two caravels—the *Niña* and the *Pinta* —and Columbus himself chartered the largest—the *Santa María*—of 100

---

[15] Morison, *op. cit.,* Vol. I, p. 99.
[16] For these negotiations in Spain see Morison, *op. cit.,* Vol. I, pp. 131-38.

tons or less.[17] Most of the 90 men and boys comprising the crews were from the seafaring families of Palos and its vicinity. No men-at-arms, gentlemen-adventurers, or priests were carried on this voyage. It was to be purely a voyage of discovery. For such a purpose it was well organized and thoroughly equipped. The little fleet set sail from Palos on August 3, 1492. Just twenty-four hours earlier a mournful fleet had left Cádiz bearing into exile in North Africa and the Levant a great body of unfortunate Jews, whose expulsion from the land where they had made their home for centuries had been ordered in a royal decree of March 30, 1492, issued as a thank-offering for the fall of Granada.[18] The two fleets were symbolic of the Spanish life of the day: on the one side, courage, persistence, individual initiative, and imagination; on the other, religious fanaticism, intolerance, cruelty, and lack of economic sense. Together the two were prophetic of what was in store for that unknown hemisphere across the Atlantic for which Christopher Columbus was setting out.

The momentous journey westward could hardly have been more fortunate. After a stop in the Canary Islands for water, wood, and fresh provisions, Columbus set his course directly westward. This meant that he had the advantage of the northeast trade winds whereas a journey due west from Spain would have encountered the westerly gales of the North Atlantic. The more southern route also had the advantage that the Canaries lay, according to the best globes, in the same latitude as the hoped-for goal of Cipango and could therefore be reached, no matter how distant it proved to be, if a due westerly course were pursued. Fair winds held throughout the voyage and, though the leagues were more numerous than his calculations had led him to suppose and his sailors became increasingly nervous lest they should never see home again, Columbus was filled with a wonderful confidence, springing from an inward assurance that he was the appointed of the Lord to find the new way to the Indies.

Two days before sighting land disaffection almost caused outright mutiny, but Columbus persuaded his men to continue three days more and, thirty-three days after leaving the Canaries, land was sighted, a reasonably fast passage for the ships of that day. On October 12, 1492, a date of fateful significance in the world's history, Columbus and his captains "with the royal standard displayed" landed on an island, knelt in thanksgiving and, while friendly natives looked on in wonder, took possession of it in the name of their Catholic Majesties, calling it San Salvador. It has been identified as Watlings Island, one of the Bahamas, a low, sandy, coral island thirteen miles by six. The natives called it Guanahani.

---

[17] On the probable size of the Santa María and later models and pictures, see Morison, *op. cit.,* Vol. I, pp. 155-60.

[18] For a description of this other sailing, see Morison, *op. cit.,* Vol. I, p. 194.

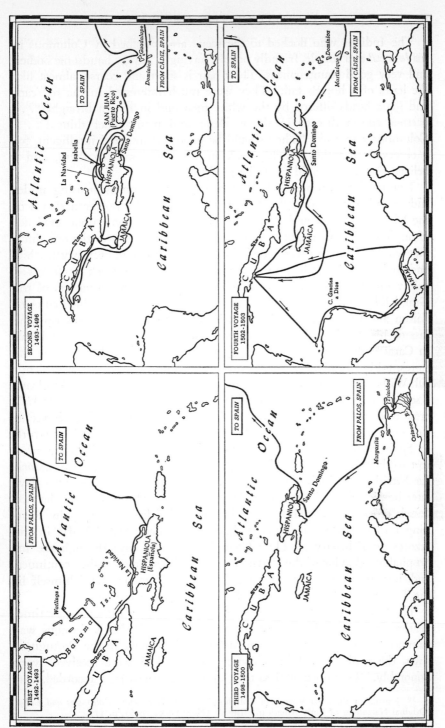

7. The Four Voyages of Columbus

The Indians who flocked to the scene are described by Columbus in his *Journal* as a simple, friendly people, having ". . . very handsome bodies, and very good countenances. Their hair is short and coarse, almost like the hairs of a horse's tail." They were much interested in the red caps and glass beads offered by the white men and in return brought ". . . parrots, cotton threads in skeins, darts, and many other things; . . ." Columbus remarked, "They should be good servants and intelligent, for I observed that they quickly took in what was said to them, and I believe that they would easily be made Christians. . . ." [19]

Not until Columbus had spent nearly three months cruising under Indian guidance among the Bahamas and along the northern shores of the Islands of Cuba and Española (Haiti), did he come upon evidence of any considerable quantity of the gold that he knew was the one thing that would make his sovereigns feel that the journey had been worth-while and their confidence in him well placed. Week after week he followed vainly one lead after another in his search for the headquarters of the Grand Khan or any evidence of the neighborhood of the fabled cities of Zaitun and Quinsay. It was on Christmas Day, 1492, after suffering the loss of his flagship, the *Santa María,* which ran ashore on a coral reef in Caracol Bay, that a native chief, whose people helped to salvage the stores, told Columbus of a valley in interior Haiti where gold was plentiful. With evidence in hand that this was true, Columbus decided to leave a settlement on the shore of the island. The members of the *Santa María's* crew were induced to remain behind by the prospect of a first chance at this golden treasure. Meanwhile, he and the others prepared to return to Spain with the wonderful news. After ordering the building of a fort to defend this first settlement in the New World, which he named La Navidad, Columbus weighed anchor on January 4, 1493. Two days later he picked up the *Pinta* on the long homeward journey and the two vessels crossed the Atlantic, intending to make directly for Spain. Running into a storm, the *Niña* with difficulty made Santa María in the Azores on February 18. Here Columbus lost ten days through the inhospitable behavior of the Portuguese authorities. Bad weather continued and, instead of reaching the Spanish coast, Columbus found himself in the Tagus estuary, in the power of the Portuguese sovereign.

The Portuguese king and queen were absent from Lisbon at the time, visiting at monasteries some thirty miles distant. Hither Columbus was summoned. In spite of what was definitely bad news to the Portuguese ruler, the explorer and his accompanying Indians were received "very honorably." Though doubtless true, as an eyewitness later recorded, that

---

[19] "Journal of the First Voyage of Columbus" in *The Northmen: Columbus and Cabot* (Original Narratives of Early American History) (New York: 1906), p. 111.

the king was "irritated and inwardly enraged" at "the tale of gold, silver and riches," which Columbus "made seem much greater than it was," he preserved an outward civility. He expressed, however, his belief that the discoveries would prove to be within his own domain of Guinea as guaranteed by papal bulls and recognized under treaty with Spain.[20]

The famous letter to Ferdinand and Isabella in which Columbus announced the success of his journey and gave a brief description of his voyage had already, with some astuteness, been despatched before the interview with the Portuguese king. When free to sail from the Tagus, Columbus went to Palos where he arrived on March 15, 1493, after an absence of seven months and twelve days. The same tide brought in the long-lost *Pinta,* whose crew were much surprised to find the *Niña* safely berthed. Great was the rejoicing in this home port. With little delay Columbus set out with his ten Indian captives for Seville, then *en fête* for Holy Week, to await orders from the royal court sojourning at Barcelona.

The royal summons addressed to "Our Admiral of the Ocean Sea, Viceroy and Governor of the Islands that he hath discovered in the Indies" arrived on Easter Day. It conveyed their Majesties' ". . . much pleasure in learning whereof you write, and that God gave so good a result to your labors, and well guided you in what you commenced, whereof He will be well served and we also, and our realms receive so much advantage." [21] He was bidden to make haste to Barcelona but commanded first to set in train preparations for a speedy return to the Indies.

Acclaimed all along his route across the peninsula by excited and admiring throngs, Columbus reached Barcelona between April 15 and 20, 1493, where he was received with extraordinary honors by Ferdinand and Isabella, who rose from their thrones and bade the kneeling Admiral rise and sit beside them on the royal dais. They plied him with questions, viewed with intense interest his Indian captives with their ornaments and trappings, the parrots and other curiosities, and examined with enthusiasm the specimens of fine gold that he had brought from the Indies. Then the whole assembly—the sovereigns, the nobles, and court officials —accompanied Columbus to the royal chapel where a solemn Te Deum was sung.

Already, before the explorer's arrival at Barcelona, negotiations had been opened by Ferdinand and Isabella at the papal court for a confirmation to them of the lands which Columbus had discovered. It had long been an accepted principle in western Europe that the Pope might determine the sovereignty of any lands that had not hitherto been in possession of any Christian prince. On the basis of a series of papal bulls, modified by

20 Morison, *op. cit.,* Vol. I, p. 439.
21 Quoted in Morison, *op. cit.,* Vol. II, pp. 7-8.

a subsequent compromise with Portugal recognizing that country's claims, the Treaty of Tordesillas of June 7, 1494, laid down an agreed line of demarcation running from the north to the south pole, 370 leagues west of the Cape Verde Islands, as the boundary between their spheres of colonial enterprise. Lands to the west of this line, by whomsoever discovered, were to belong to Spain, and those to the east to Portugal. It was on this treaty, supported by the papal bulls, that Spain based her claims to all America, except Brazil, which was later seen to fall to the east of the Tordesillas line and thus to accrue to Portugal.

After the determination of the demarcation line, a furious race ensued between Spain and Portugal to reach the real Indies, with each nation following its own particular route. The Portuguese achieved the goal first when Vasco da Gama, in 1498, rounded the Cape of Good Hope and crossed the Indian Ocean to the harbor of Calicut on the west coast of India. This momentous journey marked the beginning of a Portuguese commercial empire in the East which in time came to embrace trading stations on the coast of India, the Malay Peninsula, and the Spice Islands of the South Pacific. Meanwhile, the Spaniards for some years continued to believe that they had reached an outer fringe of islands guarding Japan and China and certain unknown parts of the Asiatic continent, and were constantly searching for evidences of the civilization and wealth of the Grand Khan.

Columbus made three additional voyages of exploration to the western world. The second, in 1493, was a magnificent expedition, made with seventeen ships and fifteen hundred men, which gave him a more extended knowledge of the West Indian Islands. Deliberately following a more southerly route than that of his first voyage, he came upon, and named, Guadalupe, Dominica, and other islands in the Leeward and Virgin groups, and coasted along the southern shore of Puerto Rico before revisiting Española. Here he was appalled to discover that every member of the Santa María's crew left at La Navidad had perished at the hands of the Indians—a fate brought on by their own rapacity and cruelty. Choosing a location somewhat further to the east, he established a second colony at Isabella and then, leaving his brother Diego in charge, he set out westward for further exploration.

During the next five months Columbus coasted slowly along the southern shore of Cuba, sailed nearly all the way round Jamaica and, on the way back, inspected the southern shore of Española. He was specially charmed by the beauty of southern Cuba and felt sure that he had reached a peninsula of the mainland of China—Marco Polo's "Mangi." The west end of Cuba he never rounded and so remained in ignorance of the fact that it was an island. This western region he took to be "the Golden Chersonese" as Marco Polo named the Malay Peninsula.

On his return to Isabella he was greeted by his brother Bartholomew, recently arrived from Spain, whom Christopher had not seen for five or six years. In the months that followed, he and his brothers, under fear of royal displeasure if gold were not forthcoming in quantity, embarked on a policy of systematic reduction and exploitation of the natives of Española —the most sinister phase of the explorer's career. Using dogs to hunt them down, and at times employing torture, he compelled the Indians to pay regular tribute in gold. But in spite of all the pressure that he could exert, the amount of precious metal dwindled progressively as native hoards became exhausted and no new resources could be found. The only gold that the island possessed came from stream washing, with nuggets here and there. To make good the financial expectations Columbus turned to slavery, sending home at every opportunity hundreds of Indians to be sold in the slave market. This procedure was directly contrary to the Queen's expressed wishes and did the explorer's standing with her no good. In Española this slave raiding, combined with other forms of cruelty, had a most disastrous effect on the native population, which by 1496 had been reduced to two thirds of its original three hundred thousand.

Indication that the crown realized that all was not well in the infant colony came in October, 1495, with the arrival of a royal commissioner to investigate complaints against the Viceroy's administration. Eventually Columbus himself was charged with the conveyance of the sealed report when he sailed for Spain in the spring of 1496. Despite his fears and the critical attitude of many, the king and queen received him graciously, appeared satisfied with his explanations, confirmed his rights and privileges, and agreed to equip another voyage.

The primary purpose of this third voyage was to test the theory of the King of Portugal that a great continent lay to the westward in the South Atlantic, for, if true, it was highly important to discover whether all or any portion of it lay within the Spanish sphere.[22] Sailing from Spain with six ships, three of which went directly to Española, Columbus himself sailed westward from the Cape Verde Islands with the other three ships and came upon the Island of Trinidad and the northeastern shore of South America. After exploring the Gulf of Paria, north of the Orinoco River, he made his way through the dangerous passage—the *Boca del Drago*—and surveyed the northern shore of Venezuela as far as the Island of Margarita before turning away northward for Española. As he pondered these experiences he became convinced that he had found

---

[22] Morison, *Portuguese Voyages to America*, pp. 131-32.

"a very great continent" which "until today has been unknown." [23] He concluded, however, that this new continent was somehow related to southeastern Asia, for his mind was wholly preoccupied with the lore from Marco Polo's *Book* and he was still hoping to find the Grand Khan. Unfortunately for his reputation, his haste to return to Española prevented him from exploring the vicinity of Margarita and he missed finding the rich pearl fisheries behind that island—a piece of bad luck which told heavily against him when used in accusations by his enemies as evidence of selfish concealment of riches.

Arriving at the end of August, 1498, at Santo Domingo, whither the Spanish settlement had now been moved, he found sedition rife among the colonists and his brother Bartholomew, whom he had left in charge, unable to cope with the situation. The next two years were filled with administrative difficulties of all kinds. From an early regime of too great leniency when he should have been firm, he veered to one of extreme severity when it was too late. After two years of disastrous oscillation a second royal commissioner, Francisco de Bobadilla, arrived at a bad moment. As he sailed into the harbor he was confronted by the sight of the bodies of seven rebels hanging on gibbets and learned that five more were awaiting a similar fate the next day. Moreover the governor was temporarily absent. Bobadilla felt that drastic action was called for, and Columbus and his two brothers were arrested and sent to Spain in chains.

Six weeks elapsed after the ship reached Cádiz before the king and queen, who were at the moment deeply immersed in Italian diplomacy and plans for a number of royal marriages, ordered the chains removed and the three Columbus brothers to appear at the royal court then sitting in the Alhambra at Granada. On the day of the royal audience Ferdinand and Isabella were as usual gracious in their bearing and ordered that the explorer's titles and property should be at once restored to him, but concerning his reinstatement as viceroy and governor of the Indies they would make no promises. As the months went by Columbus came to realize that his viceregal functions had been suspended. Not only were licenses being granted (without reference to him) for other adventurers to go exploring, but in September (1501) came the shock of the news that Nicolás de Ovando had been appointed the new royal governor and chief justice of the islands and mainland of the Indies. Five months later the new ruler set sail with a magnificent fleet of thirty ships and thirty-five hundred marines and colonists.

It was probably with a desire to soften this blow, as well as to rid themselves of the constant importunity of the man to whom they owed

---

[23] "Narrative of the Third Voyage of Columbus as Contained in Las Casas's History," in *The Northmen: Columbus and Cabot*, pp. 358-59.

so much, that the sovereigns acquiesced in Columbus' request and in the month after Ovando's departure authorized his fourth voyage. The expedition, four caravels and 135 men, sailed from Seville on April 3, 1502.

The special objective of Columbus on this voyage was to sail to the far western end of the Caribbean and there search for a strait which he felt must exist somewhere west or southwest of Cuba and which he expected to be a western passageway to India, possibly enabling him to return to Spain by circumnavigating the globe. A second objective was to discover a land richer in gold than Española had proved to be. On his way westward he was refused permission by Ovando to land at Santo Domingo though a terrific storm was brewing, but managed to survive the experience. He arrived in August, 1502, on the Central American coast in the region of the Bay Islands off the coast of Honduras, and in the months that followed coasted southward along the shores of present-day Honduras, Nicaragua, Costa Rica, and Panama. He found the Indians more advanced, more eager for barter than in the islands, and better supplied with gold ornaments. He gathered from them that he was on the eastern coast of an isthmus between two oceans and that on the other side was what he took to be Marco Polo's "Cochin China," but that across the isthmus there was no waterway. He therefore abandoned the idea of finding a strait and concentrated on gathering gold. After spending some time near the present entrance to the Panama Canal, he paused at the later famous colonial harbor of Porto Bello and then set out for home, satisfied that, though he had found no strait, at least he could report to his sovereigns the discovery of a land possessed of a goodly amount of gold.

The homeward journey was difficult and disastrous. The two remaining vessels became unseaworthy in June, 1503, and had to be beached on the northern coast of Jamaica. There Columbus and his crew put in a miserable year waiting for help from Santo Domingo. When finally he arrived in Spain on November 7, 1504, it was to be greeted with the news that his protectress and best friend, Queen Isabella, was dying. With her passing, on November 26, went Columbus' last hope for the lifting of the ban on the exercise of his viceregal rights. Little further notice was taken of him for the next two years. He died at Valladolid on May 20, 1506, leaving considerable wealth to his descendants and claims upon the crown, which were ultimately partially recognized in his son's lifetime, for the transmission of his hereditary titles and privileges.

It is unfortunate for the reputation of the Great Discoverer that from the outset of his American career he was saddled—at his own demand—with the burden of administration. Had the energy and time which he exhausted in carrying out these duties, for which he had no real gift, been devoted to exploration, Columbus might have revealed much of the American coastline. Even so, despite administrative shortcomings that sullied the laurels won as a discoverer, Columbus set the stage for a series of magnificent achievements.

Within thirty years of his death, the general shape and relative position of the two American continents had been revealed. In 1513 Vasco Nuñez de Balboa sighted the Pacific from a height in Darién. In the same year Ponce de León discovered Florida which became a point of departure for the exploration of the northern shore of the Gulf of Mexico and for expeditions northward along the Atlantic coast of North America. In 1519 Magellan started on his voyage round the southern tip of South America for the first circumnavigation of the globe. In the same year Cortés embarked for the conquest of Mexico and the eventual exploration of northern Central America and the Gulf of California. Five years later, in 1524, Pizarro set out from Panama on a series of expeditions which, within a dozen years, placed him in Cusco, master of Peru. Within the same decades Portugal took possession of Brazil, and Jacques Cartier, crossing by the route of John Cabot, explored the St. Lawrence in the name of France. Representatives of all the colonizing European powers were engaged in the widespread activities that were to lead to the establishment of rival empires throughout the length and breadth of the New World upon which Columbus had focused the first gleam of light.

Chapter 4

DISCOVERERS AND EXPLORERS OF THE SIXTEENTH CENTURY: HISPANIC AMERICA

I. THE SPANISH CONQUISTADORES

The Islands, Isthmus, and Northern South America

The first interest of the Spaniards in the West Indies was to lay hands on the last ounce of gold to be found in the island of Española.[1] With the exhaustion of this limited supply, they began a series of voyages of exploration to other islands and to the mainland surrounding the Caribbean, while still making the port of Santo Domingo in Española their headquarters. Even when, somewhat later, Cuba became the base for major exploratory operations, Santo Domingo continued for over forty years to be the administrative capital of the New World and the principal port for ships traveling to and from the Old World. Although many early explorations were unsuccessful, the hope of gold, the profits to be found in opening new slave districts, and the love of adventure led the explorers on and on until the northern and eastern coasts of South America, the Isthmus of Panama, Mexico, and the southern shores of North America had all known the visits of Spaniards, and the geographical outlines of the whole Caribbean had become familiar to western Europe.

Long before the neighboring island of Cuba (a portion of whose shore Columbus had visited on his first voyage) or its sister islands of Jamaica and Puerto Rico were regularly colonized, several attempts were made to open up the northern part of South America and the Isthmus of Panama. Columbus had made the first discovery of the mainland of South America when he landed at Paria, somewhat to the north of the mouth of the Orinoco River, in the course of his third voyage in the year 1498. In the next few years various contemporaries of Columbus explored the greater part of the northern and eastern coasts of the southern continent. Southward in 1499 went Vicente Yáñez Pinzón of a famous family of Palos; while he commanded the *Niña* on Columbus' first journey, a brother, Martín, had been in charge of the *Pinta*. Landing on the most easterly projection of the Brazilian coast (February 7, 1500), Pinzón continued south

---

[1] The Spanish name for the island later called Hispaniola, on which today are located the Dominican Republic and the Republic of Haiti.

99

for a short distance before turning north. During this latter part of his voyage he discovered the mouth of the Amazon River and then sailed on as far as Central America. In the same year, the jovial boisterous fighter Alonso de Ojeda, with the two famous geographers in his company—Juan de la Cosa and Amerigo Vespucci—landed on the coast of Surinam, two hundred leagues southeast of the Orinoco estuary, and from thence followed the shore, which he named Venezuela, northward and westward beyond the Gulf of Maracaibo to Cape de la Vela. Two letters written in Europe by Amerigo Vespucci in 1503 and 1504 describing the New World resulted in his name being bestowed upon the whole western hemisphere.[2] With the discovery of pearls, said to be as "plentiful as chaff," the Venezuelan coast became known as the Pearl Coast, and from it not only pearls, but gold, logwood, and other prized articles were long obtained. Farther to the west, Bastidas explored the region of the Gulf of Darien.

Among the earliest efforts at permanent settlement on the shoreline were the twin expeditions of Nicuesa and Ojeda in 1508-1509. Diego de Nicuesa was a man of good birth, gallant bearing, and some scholarly and artistic attainments, who had come to Española with Ovando, its second governor, and grown rich there. While on an embassy from the colony to Spain, Nicuesa was granted the governorship of the province of Veragua, extending from the Isthmus of Panama to Cape Gracias a Dios, a territory which had been discovered by Columbus on his fourth voyage. Nicuesa returned to the New World prepared to stake his whole fortune to found a colony in this region which he called "Castilla de Oro." At this same time the uncouth but daring and well-connected Ojeda, in reward for past exploring feats, was appointed governor of the province of Urabá (in modern Colombia), adjacent to and very like the swampy, mosquito-haunted, tropical territory granted to Nicuesa. Agreeing on the river Darién (now the Atrato) as the boundary line between their territories, both explorers set sail from Santo Domingo in 1509, Ojeda with three hundred men and twelve horses and Nicuesa with seven hundred men and six horses. From the flattering account of its wealth given by Columbus, Ojeda's province had acquired the name of Nueva Andalucía. Its first Spanish governor, attempting to land near modern Cartagena, was received

<hr>

[2] The Florentine Amerigo Vespucci is the most controversial figure in the history of American discovery. The number, dates, and itineraries of his voyages, the date of one of his important letters, his claims to fame, and his character are all in dispute. He claimed to have made four journeys to America; (1) 1497, (2) 1499-1500, (3) 1501-1502, (4) 1503-1504. It is now thought that he probably made only two, of which the one under Ojeda was the first. The two letters, written to the Florentine ruler Lorenzo di Medici and to an old friend Piero Soderini, described the new lands he had visited. The second of these letters was published at St. Dié in Lorraine in April, 1507, by Martin Waldseemüller in a book entitled *Cosmographiae Introductio* in which the geographer makes the suggestion that the new world should be called America "because Americus discovered it." In this way the western hemisphere got its name of America.

by the natives with showers of poisoned arrows and pursued with such determined attacks that all save two of the landing party of seventy, including Juan de la Cosa, were wounded, killed outright, or died, swollen and raving from the effects of the poison. Ojeda himself escaped, though his shield had twenty-three arrow marks on it. The arrival of Nicuesa's fleet on its way to Veragua enabled Ojeda to inflict merciless punishment on his unsubmissive Indian subjects and establish a settlement farther west on the Gulf of Urabá. Here the improvident Spaniards were soon in a famishing condition and their commander was forced to undertake a terrible journey back to Española for supplies. Shipwrecked on his way and penniless when he arrived, Ojeda was unable to secure the help and re-enforcements needed and a few years later died in poverty and neglect at Santo Domingo.

Ojeda's men, left behind on the shores of Urabá, had among them Francisco Pizarro, the future conqueror of Peru, at this time as yet undistinguished. They were making preparations to leave this inhospitable land when their plans were changed by the arrival of a relief expedition under Ojeda's partner, a lawyer named Enciso. But presently the loss of a provision ship in a storm placed the group, now greatly enlarged, again in a hazardous position. From this, Vasco Núñez de Balboa, an adventurer originally from Badajoz who had shipped with Enciso at Santo Domingo as a stowaway, hiding himself in a barrel to escape creditors in Española, rescued the party, by suggesting that they sail to Darién, a place which he remembered having passed while on an earlier journey and where the Indians did not use poisoned arrows.

Few expeditions have had such a gathering of famous men as the one which Balboa now led in safety to Darién. The new leader, in addition to possessing useful knowledge of the locality, was a genius in handling men, and an adventurer of a much higher type than most of the men of the time. After a successful skirmish with the Indians, he was able to secure provisions in abundance in the new locality. Presently he seized the authority from Enciso and with general consent became *alcalde* of a newly founded city which he called Santa María la Antigua del Darién. The ousted Enciso retaliated by sending a messenger to Nicuesa, in whose territory the party now was, to urge him to come and take command. Nicuesa and his party of settlers, after leaving Cartagena, had suffered shipwreck, hunger, and sickness. Within a few short months his brilliant expedition had been reduced from seven hundred to forty wretched, starving men gathered for fear of the Indians at Nombre de Dios. When Nicuesa arrived at Darién in response to Enciso's invitation, he was prevented from landing by a body of men under Balboa; in the end, he was placed in a wretchedly provisioned brigantine and set adrift, and was never heard of again.

After Nicuesa's expulsion, Balboa got rid of Enciso by forcing him to undertake a visit to Spain to tell his story at the royal court and was then left to do as he pleased on the Isthmus. The absence of any spectacular success had dampened enthusiasm in Santo Domingo for further exploration; for four years Balboa's colony remained practically unnoticed, visited only at rare intervals by a relief ship. During these years Balboa ranged up and down the coast in his brigantine and made long excursions inland. He held the factiousness of the Spaniards in check by a combination of astuteness and fairness, and, avoiding the worst ruthlessness of other Spaniards in his treatment of the natives—though at times he used torture to discover the whereabouts of local hoards of gold and provisions—he succeeded in keeping his colony alive and finally winning a great reward. The story is told [3] that the son of a chief, while watching Spaniards weigh out gold, struck the scales from their hands, pointed to the south and exclaimed that in that direction lay a land where gold was plentiful but to find it they must cross the mountains until they came to another sea.

At first incredulous, Balboa decided to put the story to the test; with 190 Spaniards and a number of savage dogs he forced a trail through the tropical jungle until, from a ridge which he climbed alone and with the Atlantic at his back, he looked out upon another open sea. Falling upon his knees, he raised his hands in thankfulness for being permitted to discover the "Sea of the South" before summoning his companions—among them Francisco Pizarro—to share his great discovery. The day was September 25, 1513, twenty-one years after the discovery of the first land in America. Balboa was not the first European to gaze at the Pacific Ocean—Marco Polo had seen it—but Balboa was the first to see it from American shores. Some days later the expedition reached the shore of the Gulf of San Miguel and, wading breast deep into the waves and holding aloft the banner of Castile, Balboa took possession for Spain of the Pacific Ocean and adjacent lands. Not long afterwards he found the valuable pearl fisheries of the Bay of Panama.

Sending word to the king of all his wonderful discoveries and accompanying his message with rich gifts, Balboa then set to work to gather materials on the west coast of Panama for some brigantines with which to carry out further explorations of the Pacific shores and investigate the rumors of a land of gold to the south. While he was so engaged in June, 1514, news reached him that a new governor, Pedrarias Dávila (Pedro Arias de Ávila) had arrived with twelve or fifteen ships on the Atlantic

---

[3] F. A. Kirkpatrick, *The Spanish Conquistadores* (London: 1934), p. 53.

seaboard with a company of fifteen hundred persons—one of the most splendid expeditions so far sent to the Indies. Among those with him in an official capacity, Balboa heard, was his enemy Enciso. It became clear that King Ferdinand had listened to Enciso and appointed an elderly man of high rank as governor, though Balboa had been given the title of *Adelantado* of the South Sea and allowed the governorship of two Pacific provinces. Balboa accepted with loyalty this decision giving him a secondary position, welcomed Pedrarias with respect and at first worked in harmony with him, even becoming engaged to his daughter. In 1517, however, an untrue report that Balboa was intending to slip away and make discoveries on his own account reached the ears of the jealous and avaricious governor, and, on a trumped-up charge of treason, the discoverer of the Pacific was imprisoned, condemned to death, and beheaded with four of his friends. Just four years had passed since he had first beheld the western ocean and four vessels stood all but ready to carry him to the south to find the rich lands of which the Indians had told him. His death at the age of forty-two was one of the disasters of early American history. Had he, and not the ignorant and coarse Pizarro, led the Spaniards south, the history of the Peruvian region might have been very different.

Under Pedrarias, who thus inauspiciously began his career in Central America and who remained as governor for sixteen terrible years, Panama City was founded in 1519. From it as a base, the work of discovery—accompanied by frightful atrocities against the Indians—went steadily forward until all Darién, Costa Rica, and Nicaragua had been explored. A man who deserves to be honorably remembered for his work in the exploration of Central America from Panama was Gil González de Ávila. Pushing along the western shore, he explored from the Gulf of San Miguel beyond the great gulfs of Dulce and Nicoya and well into Nicaragua. Here he is said to have landed and proceeded to the margin of the great Lake Nicaragua, into whose waters he rode his horse and, sword in hand, took possession in the name of the King of Spain. The Indians of this area were not unfriendly and Gil González claimed to have made Christians of 32,264 of them.[4] Farther on, other natives were not so complacent and González was forced to retreat. He took back with him to Panama, however, 146 pounds' worth of pearls and some gold.[5]

Pedrarias then sent Hernández Gonzalo de Córdoba, a very different person from Gil González, to carry forward the work of exploration. He divided the Indians "like flocks of sheep" amongst the Spaniards, and it was said that under him "there was no outrage of which the natives

---

[4] R. C. Murphy, "The Earliest Spanish Advances Southward from Panama along the West Coast of South America," in *Hispanic American Historical Review*, XXI, 1921, p. 20.

[5] *Ibid.*

were not victims." Pedrarias eventually got himself appointed Governor of Nicaragua. When he died in 1530, the historian Oviedo y Valdés, who had accompanied him to Panama and knew him well, declared that he was responsible for the death or enslavement of two million Indians. The cruelties of the Nicaraguan conquest were among the worst in America.

In Veragua along the eastern Caribbean shore of Central America, ill luck dogged all efforts at settlement. The conquest of Costa Rica, especially, was a prolonged and terrible business. The struggle was one with the unhealthy climate of the coast, with the forests and mountains, as well as with the bold and irreconcilable Indians who would neither work for the conquerors nor, if they could help it, submit to becoming the basis for a half-caste race. Not until 1563 did the final conqueror of Costa Rica appear. This was Juan Vásquez de Coronado whose famous brother had headed an expedition from Mexico in search of the Seven Cities of Cíbola. He carried through a series of carefully organized expeditions and finally succeeded in establishing Spanish authority on the central plains. Today, Costa Rica is the one white country of Central America boasting that the settled areas of the upland villages have a population of predominantly white stock. The final conquest of the land was only won by torrents of blood.

While these events which center around the names of Ojeda, Nicuesa, Enciso, Balboa, Pedrarias, and their successors in Central America were in progress, expeditions led by Spaniards of lesser fame were opening up the great islands of the West Indies.

Jamaica, discovered in 1494, was colonized in 1509 by Juan de Esquivel of Seville, who was sent from Española by Diego Columbus. Two years later, in 1511, the same governor dispatched Diego Velásquez, a reputable man of wealth and one of the companions of Columbus, to undertake the subjugation of Cuba, of which little was known except that it was an island, although nearly twenty years had passed since Columbus had first sighted it. Landing on the southeastern shore, Velásquez and his lieutenant, Pánfilo de Narváez, gradually worked their way westward, driving before them the miserable natives whose primitive weapons made resistance useless and flight their only recourse. Step by step the island of Cuba, seven hundred miles long, became what the Spaniards called "pacified" under the pressure of characteristic methods of subjugation. Several small towns were founded here and there along its coasts—Trinidad, Santiago, Habana, San Salvador. Mines were opened and lands and Indians were granted in *repartimiento* and *encomienda*. Two early famous Cuban *encomenderos* were the priest Bartolomé de Las Casas, afterwards "Protector" of the Indians, and Hernando Cortés, future conqueror of Mexico.

Puerto Rico was colonized in 1508 by Ponce de León and later became the site of several towns founded by Governor Ovando. But none of the early settlements on the Greater Antilles flourished. Gold was the one commodity that the Spaniards coveted and it could be found in the islands only in the smallest quantities. There were some attempts at sugar raising, but this required too close application and permanent settlement to find favor with the *conquistadores*. It was finally discovered that the most satisfactory investment was to take horned cattle to the island, turn them loose, and then after a period of years hunt the savage herds for their hides and tallow to be shipped for sale in Europe. Although the early settlements in these naturally fertile islands were poor and unprosperous, they served for many years as convenient starting points for exploring expeditions to the surrounding continental areas.

For the primitive natives of these islands, who were living on the Archaic level of culture, the coming of the white man, whom they pathetically mistook for visitants from a heavenly world, proved an unmitigated tragedy and brought almost complete extermination. Their simple tribal organization and their primitive weapons drew only scorn, while their possession of a small amount of gold served to whet the appetites of the voracious newcomers. Of the two Indian races inhabiting the islands, some of the tougher Caribs survived, fighting off the would-be enslaver or escaping by flight to the safety of northern South America whence they had come. The meeker, less robust Arawaks died like flies under the unaccustomed toil, lack of freedom, and terrible cruelties. Española, the first of the islands to be settled, had a population of at least 100,000—perhaps three times that number—when first discovered; by 1514 it could boast of not more than 30,000 persons.[6]

Mexico

The Spaniards had been roving and fighting in the Caribbean area for a full quarter of a century before the first rumor of the existence of Mexico reached them. It was brought to Habana in 1517 by a group of adventurers of whom Bernal Díaz del Castillo, the future historian of the conquest of Mexico, later claimed to be one.[7] These men after a wretched experience in Darién under Pedrarias had recently secured three ships and a license from Governor Velásquez of Cuba for an expedition of discovery

[6] P. A. Means, *The Spanish Main* (New York: 1935), pp. 14-15.

[7] Bernal Díaz del Castillo not only claimed to have been a member of Córdoba's party but also one of the later expedition under Grijalva. There are, however, reasons to doubt his acquaintance with Mexico earlier than his participation in Cortés' enterprise in which he served as a common soldier in Alvarado's company. See article by H. R. Wagner, "Bernal Díaz del Castillo." Three studies on the same subject, *Hispanic American Historical Review*, XXV, 1945, pp. 155-211.

and slave raiding. Sailing westward from Cuba under the energetic leadership of one Francisco Fernández de Córdoba they had come upon the coast of Yucatan at a point somewhat farther north than Columbus, Nicuesa, or other adventurers. Here they saw from the sea an Indian town larger and more impressive than anything yet found in America. As they coasted along beyond Campeche as far as Champotón they stared in amazement at lofty stone temples and other elaborately carved buildings, inhabitants clothed in colored costumes, and on all sides cultivated maize fields and other evidences of a culture far in advance of the naked Indians and poor villages of the islands and shores they had hitherto visited. Well might they marvel! They had chanced upon an area of Maya culture, the most highly developed and artistic then existing in America. When they attempted to land on the excuse of carrying on barter or securing fresh water, they found the Indians, who apparently had heard of the Spaniards, far from friendly; they were finally driven off with the loss of half their men by showers of stones and arrows, though not before they had secured some specimens of gold. With these and their exciting news, they hastened back to Cuba.

Governor Velásquez was sufficiently interested to fit out a larger fleet and dispatch it in April of the following year under the command of his cousin, Juan de Grijalva, a former companion of Columbus and a man of prudence and dependability, with instructions to carry out a more thorough investigation. In a coasting voyage that finally carried him from Cape Catoche to the Pánuco River, the explorer first visited the island of Cozumel and then sailed along the coast, where at Campeche and Champotón there was again serious fighting. At Tabasco, he learned that farther to the west there was a country called "Mejico," where gold was to be had in abundance, and where a great emperor called Montezuma held sway. Continuing north along the Caribbean shore of present-day Mexico, they encountered more friendly natives and landing parties obtained, for the merest trifles, a quantity of gold and hundreds of axeheads of a metal that later proved to be copper. At Vera Cruz they were entertained at a feast and, being fed on "the fowls of the country," were probably the first Europeans to taste turkey. They carried back to Cuba a report of having seen a rich country, thickly populated and throbbing with activity, of having caught glimpses of many large pueblos, and of having beheld pagan temples with ghastly rites of human sacrifice. Their enthusiasm left no doubt that in Mexico there was wealth beyond the wildest dreams. All Cuba was immediately filled with a fever of excitement.

Velásquez already had preparations in hand for an expedition to take possession of the rich mainland which were now rushed to completion. Disgusted with Grijalva for having carried out his cautious instructions so conscientiously, the governor appointed a bolder spirit to be captain-general of the new expedition. The new leader, Hernando Cortés, was a typical Spanish cavalier, thirty-four years of age. The son of an infantry officer and a native of Medellín in Estremadura in Spain, he had come to the Indies in 1504 to seek his fortune, after a commonplace career at the University of Salamanca. In Española, however, he had taken an effective part in the pacification of the island, was given a repartimiento and had become a planter. Finding settled life monotonous, he accompanied Velásquez to Cuba in 1511. His audacity in love affairs and a capacity for getting into mischief caused Velásquez considerable exasperation, but his military ability, independence of spirit, and sociable ways won for him the governor's liking and favor, securing for him grants of land and an appointment as alcalde of Santiago. By 1519 he had collected a considerable fortune.

Before the fleet of eleven ships had set sail from Cuba on the Mexican venture, Velásquez had begun to fear that he had not chosen his leader wisely, that Cortés would prove too independent and would fail in loyalty to him. He twice sent messages to revoke the appointment, but Cortés disregarded these and sailed in February, 1519. His entire force consisted of 508 soldiers, 109 seamen, and 16 horses. Officers and men were devoted to him: "We would have died for our leader, Cortés," declares Bernal Díaz,[8] who was a foot soldier.

Among his captains, the most outstanding was Pedro de Alvarado, the future conqueror of Guatemala, who had been with Grijalva and now had four brothers with him. Other leaders later to win fame were young Gonzalo de Sandoval and Cristóbal de Olid, who in later years was beheaded on Cortés' order for rebellion while engaged in the conquest of Honduras.

But these events were hidden in the mists of the future as Cortés, preparing to follow in the route of Grijalva, made his first stop at the island of Cozumel. Here he marveled at the stone temples, seen by him for the first time, and here he rescued a Spanish castaway named Aguilar, who had lived for eight years among the Mayan Indians and so proved immensely valuable to Cortés as an interpreter. Doubling Cape Catoche and keeping close to the shore, Cortés next came to Tabasco where he fought and won

---

[8] Bernal Díaz' *Historia Verdadera de la Conquista de la Nueva España* is a lively biographical account of his own adventures in which he mixes extravagant praise of Cortés with bitter criticism of his leader, especially of his failure to give due credit to the soldiers who helped him conquer Mexico. Recent studies have thrown doubt on the long-accepted view that the whole book was written, largely from memory, by Díaz in his old age when living in Guatemala, for the express purpose of combating errors in a work by López de Gomara entitled *Conquista de Mexico* published in 1552. The composition, it is now thought, covered a longer period and had simpler aims. Díaz' narrative ends in 1568. The book however remained long in manuscript, not being published till 1632. For a discussion of this work in its historical setting, see Wagner, *op. cit.*

a battle with the Indians, who, Díaz says, numbered twelve thousand, but whose native javelins, slings, arrows, and lances were no match for the steel swords, muskets, and cannon of the Spaniards. At Tabasco, Cortés insisted upon the native caciques swearing fealty to King Charles and promising that they and their people would become Christians. Included in a propitiatory gift of twenty slaves offered by the Indians was a native Mexican girl named Marina who had been sold in childhood as a slave to the Mayas by an Aztec mother. An intelligent woman, Marina naturally felt no loyalty to either Aztecs or Mayas and yet spoke both languages. She was of invaluable service to Cortés as interpreter and later, becoming his mistress, served him with the utmost loyalty and devotion. With Aguilar and Marina both in his company as he left Tabasco, Cortés had the means of communicating with both Mayas and Aztecs.

Arriving in the vicinity of Vera Cruz, in the territory under Aztec domination, Cortés dispatched to the ruler, Montezuma, messages and gifts that purported to come from the Spanish king. As a matter of fact, this Aztec monarch had been kept informed (by picture records painted on sisal cloth by skilled scribes) of every movement that the white men had made on Mexican soil since Grijalva's arrival. He had long been pondering with his councilors the best method of dealing with the fair-skinned visitors who might possibly be the returning gods prophesied in an old native legend. His final decision was to send representatives with welcoming words and rich gifts of fine cotton cloth, gorgeous feather work, incense, beautifully wrought ornaments, and a golden disc "as large as a cartwheel" representing the sun, and a smaller one of silver representing the moon, in the hope that the visitors would be satisfied with these presents and go away. Unfortunately for the Aztecs, such evidences of wealth had exactly the opposite effect on the Spaniards.

Cortés and his men, who had landed on Mexican soil on Good Friday, 1519, spent four months near the coast. During this time, in line with Spain's methods of conquest since medieval times, Cortés and his men founded a city as a permanent base of operations; he then opened negotiations with subjugated, non-Aztec tribes of the vicinity for an alliance. If they could detach outlying provinces and persuade some of the Indians to fight with them as allies, the Spaniards might not be so hopelessly outnumbered. Not all the followers of Cortés approved of this course which obviously implied an attempt at conquest of the whole country with the small forces then in hand. Some adherents of Velásquez thought that the captain-general was exceeding his authority, while others felt that the odds were too great and favored returning forthwith to Cuba. Cortés took swift action. He imprisoned the dissenters, resigned his original commission from Velásquez to the council of the new municipality, and induced it to elect him captain-general. He then dispatched a ship to Spain with devoted friends on board to explain his action to the king. Finally, to bind all his followers irrevocably to his enterprise—the conquest of all Mexico—on which he was determined, Cortés scuttled or burned his remaining ships. With the loss of their only means of returning to Cuba, there was nothing left but to undertake the march to Montezuma's capital. They must succeed or perish in the attempt.

Leaving behind at Vera Cruz only a small garrison, Cortés, in the middle of August, with a small army of four hundred men, six cannon, and fifteen horses, began his famous march inland to Tenochtitlán, lying two hundred miles away beyond a mountain barrier on a plateau 7,500 feet above sea level. The journey took three months.

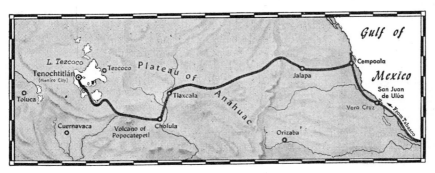

8. March of Cortés to Mexico City

John Fiske has said that the very stars in their courses seem to have fought for Cortés. The most marvelous good fortune attended his small band from the moment of his departure from the coast. Perhaps the greatest assistance came from the existence of the prophetic legend previously mentioned. This centered about the beneficent culture god, Quetzalcoatl, reverenced by all Nahua peoples, who after having taught their ancestors the arts of a higher culture, departed with a few youthful followers to the east, promising to return some day. A cycle of Mexican stories concerning this tall, fair-bearded god was told to every Nahua child. When Spanish ships came from the east bearing fair-skinned, bearded men who assumed a haughty demeanor, wielded thunder and lightning, and dared to ride the swift-hoofed animals that accompanied them, the question rose in every Indian mind whether this was the return of their long-expected Quetzalcoatl whom it would be sacrilege to resist.

A more favorable situation could not have been imagined, and Cortés had the boldness and political acumen to make the most of this and other fortunate opportunities. His lordly attitude towards the altars of the pagan gods, and the crusading ardor that he displayed for a new and apparently gentler religion, fell into line with what the Indians might have expected from the true Quetzalcoatl. Moreover, Cortés displayed to the Indians an uncanny knowledge of their customs and their present grievances under their Aztec rulers. In the latter respect, Cortés' native acuteness and Marina's knowledge aided the leader, while his experience in Cuba had taught him that if the native chiefs were captured and held as prisoners, Indian resistance became practically paralyzed, partly through lack of individual initiative and partly because native custom forbade the election of a new chief during the lifetime of the old. For this reason, Cortés was careful to secure alive the chiefs along his line of march and to see to it that no ill befell them; in addition, he encouraged revolt in those subject pueblos that had no greater desire than to overthrow the hated Aztec domination.

The two principal towns through which he had to pass before reaching Aztec territory at Cholula were Cempoala and Tlaxcala. At the first he persuaded a very "fat cacique" [9] of the Totonac tribe to revolt against Montezuma and to provide him with four hundred Indians, porters, and other assistance. When he came to Tlaxcala, he found a fierce and warlike tribe with whom he had to fight two sanguinary battles before they would acknowledge his leadership. The Aztecs claimed that they had permitted the Tlaxcalans to remain free in order to have near at hand a strong enemy whose hostility would keep their own warriors in fighting trim and meanwhile provide them with prisoners of war for their incessant human sacrifices. Once Cortés won the respect of the Tlaxcalans by his skill and courage they became his allies against their old enemies and remained faithful both in prosperity and adversity. Even when the Spaniards later were temporarily defeated, the Tlaxcalans did not desert them. Henceforth the small band of white men was supported by an Indian army that, even before Cortés' coming, had proved to be almost a match for the Aztecs.

While still at Tlaxcala, an invitation to Mexico City arrived from Montezuma. A warning from their allies that this meant treachery was verified at Cholula, where only Marina's keenness and loyalty enabled the Spaniards to turn a massacre planned by the Cholulans under Montezuma's inspiration into one of Cholulans by the Spaniards. From Cholula, Cortés led his men, now re-enforced by a formidable body of Indian allies, towards the city of Tenochtitlán, built on an island in the midst of a lake and connected with the mainland only by causeways. This was the famous capital of the Aztecs who dominated the confederacy that held much of

---

[9] Bernal Díaz tells this story.

central Mexico under tribute. Montezuma's mounting anxiety at the approach of the white men who had detached his coastal tributaries and made allies of his bitterest enemies may be imagined. Deciding to welcome them in their ostensible character as emissaries of another great emperor, he received them in a ceremony of barbaric splendor, assigning them and their allies quarters in what had been a great tribal council house. Bernal Díaz can hardly find words to express the wonder and amazement of the Europeans at the splendor and strength of the city: "We were astonished and kept saying it was like the enchanted things which they tell of in the book of Amadis." [10] But as Cortés regarded the causeways that could be so easily blocked, cutting off his only retreat, and realized that familiarity might well breed contempt for the number and character of his forces, he formed, after a week of anxious thought, an audacious plan for gaining possession of Montezuma, as he had of other chieftains on previous occasions.

Pretending that Montezuma had been implicated in a recent murder by an Aztec officer of some Spaniards on the coast and also had been involved in the trouble at Cholula, Cortés succeeded in forcing Montezuma to take up his residence in the white man's building, where he was practically a hostage for the good behavior of his people. Henceforth, though he was treated with every respect, he had to rule his kingdom under Cortés' eye, and was accompanied everywhere by Spaniards armed to the teeth. Furthermore, he was forced to go through a ceremony in which he declared himself to be a vassal of the Spanish king, and to send orders throughout his kingdom that tribute should be gathered for transmission to Spain. His subjects were at first stunned and allowed months to go by in sullen silence without taking action, but Cortés realized that they would not long delay the election of a new ruler to lead them against the intruders.

The situation became seriously complicated when, in the spring of 1520, the news came that eighteen ships, carrying eight hundred infantry and eighty horsemen, had arrived at Vera Cruz under the command of Pánfilo de Narváez, who bore an order from Velásquez to supersede Cortés and return him to Cuba in irons for insubordination. On arrival in Mexico, as Cortés found out, Narváez had opened negotiations with the Aztecs, promising release of their ruler if the Indians would rise against Cortés. In this crisis Cortés as usual kept his own counsel while he planned swift and decisive action. Pretending to be pleased and writing friendly letters to Narváez, he put Alvarado in charge in Mexico City, leaving him a small force, while he himself led the remainder—some seventy men—back to the

---

[10] Díaz' colorful, detailed account of the capture of Tenochtitlán is the most satisfactory part of his interesting book.

coast. Arriving at Vera Cruz he attacked the new expedition by surprise, succeeded in capturing Narváez, and persuaded the latter's followers to change sides and share with him the plunder of Mexico.

Meanwhile news came that a revolt had broken out in Mexico City, precipitated by a stupidly brutal act by Alvarado. This report caused Cortés to hurry back to the rescue of the endangered Spaniards. With an army gathered en route, he forced his way after severe fighting into the beleaguered Spanish quarters where, in an attempt to quell the storm, he induced Montezuma to appear on the walls arrayed in his imperial robes, with pacifying words to the besiegers. The Aztec chief, however, was stoned by his own subjects, and so seriously injured that he died a few days later. A kinsman, Cuitlahuac, who had directed the attack on the Spaniards, was saluted as his successor, and the situation for the Spaniards became so hazardous that it soon became clear to Cortés that, if they were to survive at all, they must force their way out of the city. The night of June 30 (1520) was fixed upon for the attempt and has ever since been called *la noche triste*. Though eventually the Spaniards succeeded in fighting through the streets and across the causeway to the mainland, their losses were tremendous. Many trying to escape were drowned in the lake; others, cut off as they retreated, were carried back to the city for sacrifice. Not until they reached the land of their allies, the Tlaxcalans, did the Spaniards find respite and opportunity to reform their company and devise new plans. Bernal Díaz says that nine hundred men were lost in the retreat.

A year later, in May, 1521, Cortés attacked Tenochtitlán by water from a base at Tezcoco on the east side of the lake. From here he launched a number of brigantines which he and his allies had built to convey his men to the inland city. For three long months the grim struggle went on. When at last it was over in August, 1521, most of the people lay dead and the great buildings which the Spaniards had so greatly admired were in ruins.

A new Spanish city was still building when, in October, 1522, Cortés received his commission from Charles V as Governor and Captain-General of Mexico. He went steadily forward with plans of expansion that eventually enabled him to boast with a good deal of justice that he had given to the Spanish king "more provinces than he had possessed cities before."

After the fall of the capital, the rest of the Aztec dominions, extending from the Mexican Gulf to the Pacific, fell section by section to the arms of Cortés' group of able conquistadores as they spread out in separate armies over all the country. Rumors of gold, or sheer curiosity, led the Spaniards ever onward to new regions, while the growing reports of the invincibility of Spanish arms, supported by their redoubtable Indian allies, led to the paralysis of native defensive efforts. Even beyond the boundaries of Aztec domination these famous captains of Cortés and their successors pushed huge salients into the great unknown, bequeathing to the next generation extensive areas that remained permanently conquered and that only needed the missionaries, soldiers, miners, and farmers to occupy and hold.

The advance southward into Central America was especially rapid, partly because of the rumor that in this region there might be found a strait that would lead through the obstructing land mass toward the long-sought Spice Islands of the East, and partly because it was known that exploration was being pushed northward from Panama, which, it was feared, might anticipate efforts from Mexico. Alvarado followed this will-o'-the-wisp to Tehuantepec and then on to Guatemala, where he conquered the highland Mayas and founded Guatemala City. Olid went by sea to Honduras, and in 1525 was followed by a land expedition captained by Cortés himself. Francisco Montejo and his son spent years in Yucatan trying in a series of terrific campaigns to subdue the fiercely independent and cultured Mayas, whose conquest had not been even approximately accomplished. Mérida was finally founded as the new capital in 1542.

Failing to find the long-sought strait in the south, Cortés turned his attention to the west coast, planning to extend exploration by water northward along the Pacific Ocean. An expedition dispatched by him in 1533 discovered Lower California, which for a time was thought to be an island. The early discovery of rich pearl fisheries in the Gulf led to great interest in the western region. Before the close of the first half of the sixteenth century, the whole west coast as far north as Oregon had been explored through the efforts of Ulloa, Cabrillo, and Ferrelo. These voyages led to expeditions being sent farther out into the Pacific, one of which in 1564 took the Spaniards to the Philippines. The conquest of these islands, which now became a dependency of New Spain, brought in its train a rich trade by means of the "Manila galleon" which henceforth for two hundred and fifty years traveled once a twelvemonth between the Mexican Pacific port of Acapulco and Manila.

Meanwhile by land into the northwest from Mexico City went Núñez de Guzmán, who in the years 1529-1531 conquered by fire and sword the territory as far north as Culiacán in Sinaloa. This general region was organized in 1550 as the *audiencia* district of New Galicia with a center first at Compostela and later (1560) at Guadalajara.[11] Within twenty-five years this region had fifteen hundred Spaniards living in some thirty-two settlements and mining camps. Another great expedition into the northwest was that of Francisco Vásquez de Coronado who, stimulated by Indian tales of seven rich cities in a northern region called Cíbola, in 1540-1542 led a large expedition to investigate the reports. Financed by the crown it-

[11] See Chapter 6, pp. 171 and 174.

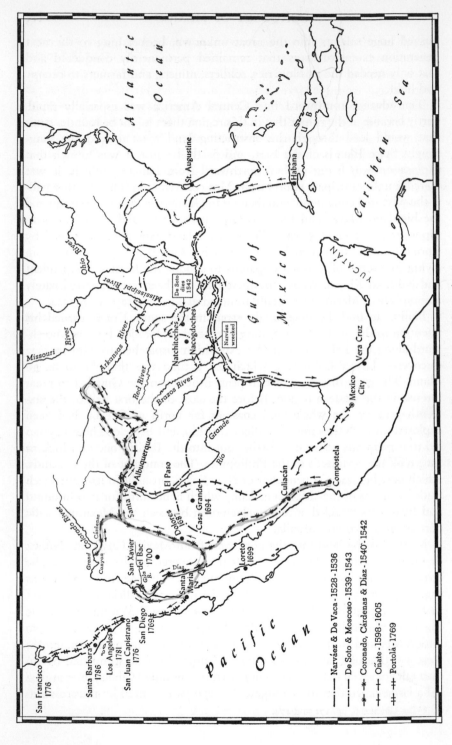

9. Early Spanish Explorations in North America

self, his entourage, consisting of some three hundred Spaniards and eight hundred Indians, was supported by a great pack train and aided by two vessels operating in the Gulf of California. In 1540 both land and water forces set out from Culiacán. The sea force under Hernando de Alarcón sailed to the head of the Gulf and explored the Colorado River for some two hundred and fifty miles; the land force under Coronado, passing through Sonora and Arizona, wended its way into New Mexico, Texas and Kansas. Though Coronado found that Cíbola was nothing but a group of humble Indian pueblos and his second objective, Quivira, was little better, his explorations made known a large part of what is now north-western Mexico and southwestern United States. In this same geographical area the expedition of Juan de Oñate, setting out from Mexico City, conquered New Mexico in 1598, visited Kansas and reached the Colorado River in 1604.

Meanwhile, during these years of stirring events in Mexico, there set out from Cuba a number of expeditions into what is now the southeastern part of the United States, all of which, though dogged with ill luck, eventually opened this region to later settlement. In 1513 a patent had been given to Ponce de León under which, while searching for the Fountain of Youth, that explorer had discovered Florida. After his death at the hands of the Indians in 1521 while he was attempting to colonize the west coast of the peninsula, his patent was transferred to Pánfilo de Narváez of Mexican fame. This conquistador in 1528 set out for Florida with an expedition of five ships and some four hundred and fifty men, and landed at Tampa Bay. Later, sending his fleet along the coast, he led a party inland to search for certain prosperous cities which the Indians had described to him in glowing terms, but on the return journey he lost contact with his fleet. His men were soon in so desperate a plight that they constructed five small boats, hoping to be able to follow the coast along to Mexico. They probably passed the mouth of the Mississippi, but only one of the five boats was ever heard of again. Of the score of men in it, only four, headed by Cabeza de Vaca, after an incredible journey on foot across the whole continent to California, lived to reach Mexico City five years later and tell one of the most remarkable stories that the sixteenth century affords.

Another famous adventurer asked to be appointed to the place left vacant by León and Narváez, and to be allowed to explore in the Florida area. This was the wealthy Hernando de Soto, who had made a name for himself in Central America and Peru, and who now turned his attention to southeastern North America in the years when Coronado was roaming the southwestern section. With a fleet of seven ships and six hundred men, de Soto landed at Tampa Bay in May, 1539. Searching for the same will-o'-

the-wisp by which the natives had lured Narváez to his death, de Soto wandered for two years through what are now the states of Georgia, North and South Carolina, Alabama, and probably Tennessee, eventually reaching the Mississippi near Memphis in November, 1541. Crossing the river, he explored Arkansas and Oklahoma and was at one time near Coronado's party. He followed the Arkansas River to its mouth in the Mississippi and was about to descend it to the Gulf when he succumbed to fever and discouragement, and, after appointing a successor, Luis de Moscoso de Alvarado died in May, 1542, and was buried in the Mississippi River. Eventually the survivors, numbering about half the original band, managed to build boats and float down the Mississippi to the sea and follow the coast to Mexico which they reached in September, 1543. Other early efforts at colonizing Florida were failures. Two decades later, however, the Spanish crown, driven by the fear of foreign settlement, bestowed a patent with wide powers on the noted admiral, Pedro Menéndez de Avilés, and he, in September, 1565, with a great following of twenty-six hundred persons, founded the city of St. Augustine, the first permanent Spanish settlement within the boundaries of the present United States.

But before the full harvest of Cortés' conquest of Mexico could be reaped, the career of this most famous of the conquistadores of the New World came to an end. As early as 1528 his powers as governor were turned over by the king to an audiencia, though Cortés himself in the same year was received with the greatest honor at the Spanish court and given the title of Marquis del Valle de Oaxaca with a princely estate consisting of a repartimiento that included the city of Oaxaca and twenty-eight dependent villages. Returning to Mexico as captain-general, Cortés a few years later was much mortified to find, when the first viceroy assumed his office in 1535, that among that official's powers was the right to suspend Cortés as captain-general at any time the royal representative judged fit. Humiliated by all the contentions over his claims and privileges, and discouraged over the failure of an attempt to colonize Lower California, Cortés in 1539 sailed for Spain and never again returned to Mexico. In the homeland he found himself coldly received at court, and died in Seville in 1547 at the age of sixty-three, feeling almost as neglected and unhappy as had Columbus forty years earlier.

The Conquest of Peru

The discovery of Peru was closely associated with the work of colonizing the Isthmus of Panama and the plans that eventually led to it first took shape in the lively imagination of Darién's first governor, Vasco Núñez de Balboa. His execution in 1517 at the hands of the jealous second governor, Pedrarias, resulted in a delay of seven years before the first exploring

expedition set out for the land of the Incas. In this interval two of the
world's most famous events were in progress contemporaneously: the
conquest of Mexico and the first voyage around the world. Cortés was
leaving Vera Cruz in August, 1519, for his amazing march to Mexico City,
just as the experienced Portuguese explorer, Ferdinand Magellan, sailed
from Seville under Spanish colors with a commission from the Emperor
Charles V to find a western sea route to the Spice Islands. Three years
later, the one surviving vessel of the expedition—the *Vittoria*—after passing

10. PIZARRO'S EXPEDITION TO PERU

through the strait since called by the name of its discoverer, crossed the
Pacific, visited the Philippines—where Magellan was killed—surveyed the
Spice Islands, and completed the first voyage around the world by the Cape
of Good Hope. The famous vessel limped into its home port on the Guadalquivir in September, 1522, with thirty-one exhausted survivors of the original 270. By this time in Mexico Montezuma was dead, his capital was in
process of being rebuilt as a Spanish city, and Cortés was on the point of
receiving his coveted commission as governor and captain-general of New
Spain.

It was two years after these events that an old comrade of Balboa,
Francisco Pizarro, who had been with him on the Ojeda expedition, took

up the task of exploring the "South Sea." During the intervening years more evidence had accumulated supporting the truth of the rumors that far to the south lay lands of marvelous wealth and, in 1524, Pizarro was one of a group of three to receive an appointment from Pedrarias to follow up these leads.

Pizarro was a very different man from the gently bred and fairly well-educated Balboa, though both were natives of Estremadura—that extraordinary province of Spain that produced so many of the conquistadores. Francisco Pizarro was an illegitimate son of a Spanish officer. His mother, a woman of poor and humble birth, brought him up in the meanest of circumstances. It seems to be true that he was for a time a swineherd and certainly he was without formal education, never learning even to write his name. Though somewhat coarse-fibered, he was a man of great determination, extraordinary courage, and endowed with robust health. In America he is first heard of as a member of Ojeda's expedition in 1509. Later he took service under Balboa and was with him when the Pacific was sighted. Serving under Pedrarias he engaged in a number of exploring expeditions about the Gulf of Miguel, and it was he whom the jealous governor employed to arrest his old chief, Balboa, and lead him to trial and execution.

In Panama, where he was an encomendero, Pizarro became friendly with Diego de Almagro, whose background of peasant upbringing and lack of education was not unlike his own, though Almagro's genial, sociable ways made him more generally liked. The two friends became associated with a more highly placed and better-educated man, Hernando de Luque, who was a well-to-do priest and a friend of Governor Pedrarias. All three became intensely interested in the work of southern exploration and especially in the rumors of a rich *Birú,* and finally drew up articles of partnership for its discovery. Their plans provided that Luque should remain in Panama, act as business agent, and provide the funds, while Pizarro and Almagro, though both were over fifty, were to go south. Almagro's special duty was to maintain connections with the base at Panama while Pizarro was to give his first attention to the advance. The partners procured the governor's sanction for their enterprise by promising him a substantial share of all treasures that might be found. The cost of the expedition was estimated at 20,000 pesos de oro.[12]

It was in November, 1524, that Pizarro finally set out southward with two vessels and a canoe, carrying in all one hundred twelve Spaniards, of whom eighty were soldiers; and there were also seventy Indians and Negroes and four horses. Almagro followed in a second vessel four months

---

[12] Murphy, *op. cit.,* p. 20.

later. Both expeditions were forced to turn back to their base. This was but the first of a number of disappointments. During the next three years no less than three fresh starts had to be made, both Almagro and Pizarro returning several times to Panama for re-enforcements and supplies as the difficulties increased with the lengthening distance.[13] Funds and official sanction naturally became increasingly hard to obtain, especially after Pedrarias was superseded as governor by Pedro de los Ríos in July, 1527. Only the most indomitable perseverance carried the Peruvian project forward. Again and again the enterprise was at a standstill with the survivors half naked, starving, and despairing. On one famous occasion Governor de los Ríos, determining to put an end to an enterprise so costly in men and money, sent a ship to the island of Gallo where Pizarro and his men were stranded in a state of starvation and semimutiny, with definite orders for all to return to Panama. Pizarro, still determined to go on, drew a line in the sand with his sword and stepping across invited those who still preferred to follow him to further adventure, hardship, and glory to cross the line. An immortal thirteen white men and one mulatto did so.[14]

After seven more wretched months of torrential rain, mosquitoes, lack of food, and hardships of every description,[15] Almagro arrived late in 1527 with a relief ship and the little company embarked southward on a further reconnoitering expedition under the guidance of the loyal pilot, Bartolomé Ruiz de Estrade, who months earlier on a scouting expedition had crossed the equator and encountered signs of an advanced civilization. On this occasion the Spaniards put into the Gulf of Guayaquil and anchored off the town of Tumbes on the southern shore. Later, clad in armor and bearing a cross, the visitors went ashore and were hospitably received by the amazed inhabitants. Visiting several other places and realizing that he was but on the outskirts of a great empire, whose capital was far inland, Pizarro was careful to make no armed demonstration but decided to return once more to Panama and from there, if necessary, make his way to Spain to enlist the support of the crown.

In Spain where he supported his magnificent story by displaying some llamas, textiles of vicuña wool, and vessels of gold and silver (and no doubt was helped by recent Mexican discoveries), Pizarro met with no great difficulty in securing royal countenance for an attempted conquest of Peru. The agreement was signed on July 26, 1529. By it Pizarro was made governor and captain-general, adelantado and *aguacil mayor,* for life, with a

---

[13] For sequence and dates of events from the preparations of the three partners for the enterprise to the death of Atahualpa (May 17, 1524-November 16, 1532), see Murphy, *op. cit.,* pp. 20-28.

[14] *Ibid.,* p. 25.

[15] These months were spent on the Island of Gorgona, some seventy miles northeast of the Island of Gallo—smaller but more easily defended.

handsome salary and generous administrative powers in a Peruvian dominion yet to be won. The two absent partners came off less well. Almagro
was appointed Governor of Tumbes with a salary half as great as that of
Pizarro; Luque was to be Bishop of Tumbes and Protector of Peruvian
Indians. The loyal pilot, Ruiz, was made Grand Pilot of the Southern Seas,
while the thirteen faithful companions of Pizarro were made *hidalgos*. On
leaving Spain for America, Pizarro took with him his four brothers [16]
and a cousin.

When this conquistador arrived in Panama troubles began again. His
partners, especially Almagro, were bitter at the outcome of the Spanish
visit and the suffering of earlier trips made it difficult to secure men for the
new undertaking. Eventually, however, late in December, 1530, or early
in January, 1531, Pizarro's final southern expedition was ready. It consisted
of two vessels and several dugouts and included 150 Spanish soldiers in
a total complement of two hundred thirty souls and twenty-seven to forty
horses. On this voyage there were a number of ecclesiastics, the most conspicuous of whom was the Dominican friar, Vicente de Valverde. Shortly
after arriving on the Peruvian coast this force was strengthened by one
hundred men and fifty horses coming from Nicaragua and Guatemala
under the leadership of Hernando de Soto. With the combined force,
Pizarro captured Tumbes in January, 1532, and began the consolidation
of a foothold in northern Peru.

The empire that the Spanish conquistadores had now invaded was a
very different organization from the tribal confederacy of the Aztecs with
which Cortés had been faced. The Inca from his capital in mountain-girt
Cusco aimed not only at extorting tribute from conquered peoples but
also at maintaining a military despotism. His well-knit, centralized empire
stretched from Quito in what is now Ecuador on the north to the River
Maule in Chile, and from the Pacific to the high Andes east of Lake Titicaca—a long, narrow land, twenty-seven hundred miles in length by three
hundred to three hundred fifty miles in width. The social system of this
empire, like the political, was in advance of that of the Aztecs. It was a
type of paternal autocracy, under which the submissive Indians were accustomed to direction and stern discipline; they were well fed and cared for,
but were left little individual initiative.

The Spaniards were fortunate in the time of their arrival. When
Pizarro had been on the Peruvian coast in 1525 the Inca, Huayna Capac,
could have led a united people against any threat of foreign danger, but
in 1532 this ruler was dead and the state was still staggering from the
effects of a civil war for possession of the crown waged between his two

---

[16] Hernando, Juan, Gonzalo, and a half brother Francisco Martín de Alcántara.

sons, Huáscar, the legitimate heir, and Atahualpa, the son of a favorite concubine, between whom the king in his will had divided the inheritance. When Pizarro arrived in Tumbes in 1532 Atahualpa had just won a crushing victory, captured Huáscar and taken the capital of Cusco, and was consolidating his conquests.

After securing Tumbes Pizarro's next step was to march twenty-five leagues south to San Miguel on the Piura River where he established a more convenient base for further operations. Here he took the characteristically Spanish measure of laying out a town, with a central plaza surrounded by a number of public buildings with streets radiating from the center. He also provided from among his Spanish followers a city government of magistrates and councilors, and assigned the Indians in encomienda to householders or *vecinos*. From this base he was determined to visit Atahualpa who was stationed near Cajamarca on the central plateau, as yet undecided whether the white visitors were men or gods. On the perilous march through narrow defiles and up the freezing Andean heights, Pizarro had with him sixty-two horsemen, one hundred and six infantry, and a few small cannon. Along the way the Spaniards were met by a succession of messengers bearing gifts from the Inca ruler.

At Cajamarca one of the most dramatic events of history took place. Here on November 15, 1532, the Spaniards were received with great dignity by Atahualpa who entered the principal square of the city, accompanied by five thousand followers from an army of thirty thousand Indian warriors near the city. The Inca, clad in gorgeous raiment adorned with enormous emeralds [17] and wearing the imperial fillet,[18] was seated in a golden litter under a canopy of brilliant feathers. The Spaniards through Vicente de Valverde, the Spanish chaplain, who held a crucifix aloft, made the perfectly incomprehensible demand that Atahualpa should acknowledge papal supremacy and give allegiance to Charles V. When a Bible was handed to him the Inca in ignorance or in regal indifference let it fall to the ground, whereupon the Spaniards who had been concealed in the surrounding houses, professing horror at the sacrilege, raised the battle cry of "Santiago," and with their cannon and horses killed or wounded thousands of the Inca's followers and made Atahualpa himself prisoner. One of those present later reported, "As the Indians were unarmed they were defeated without danger to any Christian."

In captivity, Atahualpa was treated with a measure of dignity and respect, and is said to have learned to play chess and to converse with his captors. To prevent the assumption of the throne by his recently conquered brother, the royal prisoner managed to convey an order for Huáscar's

---

[17] Emeralds were the insignia of Quito.
[18] The "borla" as Child of the Sun.

assassination. However, he realized that this was not enough to meet the emergency; with his dazed and docile people leaderless everything depended upon his own release. Having observed that the Spaniards would do anything for gold, he decided to make a great bid for his freedom; making a mark upon the wall of the room in which he was confined as high as he could reach with his hand, he offered as his ransom sufficient gold and silver to fill the room up to that height. Pizarro professed himself ready to accept the offer, and the task of collecting the metal was begun. Day by day the pile rose as Atahualpa's subjects brought in on their backs vessels of gold and silver; sheets of gold from the Golden Temple at Cusco, objects of art, and every kind of article made of the precious metals. When the gold was weighed it totaled 13,265 pounds and the silver amounted to 26,000 pounds. To the horror of the artistically minded Indians, Pizarro had all this treasure, except that intended for the Spanish king, melted down to bars of gold and silver of equal weight which he then apportioned to his followers. Pizarro's own share represented an enormous fortune. Every cavalryman received nearly ninety pounds of gold and one hundred eighty of silver; the infantrymen, less; but to every Spaniard was given an amount which, if it had been thriftily used, would have made him wealthy for life. Almagro's men arriving late were given less and felt themselves cheated. After the apportionment Hernando Pizarro, the only one of the Pizarro brothers who was a man of education with manners fit for a court, was dispatched to Spain to carry the king's share to Charles V. The bearer, upon arrival at the court, was awarded the Cross of Santiago and dispatched back to Peru with titles, honors, and commissions for all the leaders.

With the ransom in hand and the Inca entitled to his release, the great problem before the Spaniards was what was to be done with him. It was obviously inexpedient to set him free, so it was finally decided to accuse him of treason and conspiracy against the white man and of other crimes. De Soto and Hernando Pizarro, who were opposed to extreme measures, were sent to investigate the rumor of gathering Inca forces and returned to report that there was not an armed Indian to be found in the land. But they were too late. At a mock trial on August 29, 1533, Atahualpa was condemned to be burnt at the stake. On his consenting to be baptized, the sentence was commuted to the milder one of strangling, and he was permitted Christian burial. After commending his children to the care of Pizarro he met his fate with Indian stoicism. The crowds of natives who looked on "lay upon the ground like drunken men." Some of the women hanged themselves.[19]

---

[19] Kirkpatrick, *op. cit.*, pp. 157-66 gives an eloquent description of Atahualpa's tragedy.

After Atahualpa's death, the Spaniards hastened on to Cusco, easily overcoming the weak resistance to their advance offered by the remnants of the dead Inca's army. Pizarro entered the capital of the empire at the head of an army of 480 Spaniards on November 15, 1533, just one year after his entry into Cajamarca. The Spaniards gave themselves over to a great sack of the city, stripping palaces, temples, and sepulchers of their treasures of gold and silver and other objects of value. To give a constitutional aspect to their conquest, Pizarro organized Cusco as a Spanish municipality, providing it with a town council, eight councilors and two alcaldes. On the council sat two brothers of the governor, Juan and Gonzalo Pizarro. Every Spaniard settling in the city was provided with a house within the town, a strip of agricultural land outside, and an encomienda of Indians as a labor force. To meet the problem of Indian government, Pizarro proclaimed that Huáscar, now dead by order of Atahualpa, had been the legitimate heir, and set up his brother, Manco Capac, as puppet ruler. Manco Capac's quiet behavior gave no indication of future trouble, the Indians gave him their loyalty, and the Spaniards were for a time well satisfied with their settlement of the Indian problem. It appeared that the despotic form of Inca government and the communal system of property holding had so reduced private initiative that to conquer the country it had only been necessary to capture the Inca and take possesssion of the capital, the two centers of administrative and military authority.

In 1535 the Spaniards felt their position so secure that they set up a new center of Spanish power on the coast as being more convenient than Cusco for administrative and trading purposes. The result was the founding by Francisco Pizarro in January, 1535, of *Ciudad de los Reyes,* now Lima, two leagues from the harbor of Callao at the mouth of the Rimac River. The conquest of Peru now seemed over except for the work of consolidation, but in reality a chapter of violence and disaster lay ahead. There were too many ambitious and cruel conquistadores in Peru for peace, either among themselves or with the natives. Among the contending elements Pizarro was unable to wield the same undisputed authority that Cortés had exercised in Mexico.

While Pizarro was engaged in laying out the streets of Lima, putting up houses and building a palace for himself, his elder brother Hernando arrived from Spain bearing with him a royal patent creating Francisco a marquis and describing the territory subject to him as extending southward for 270 leagues from the river Santiago lying a little north of the equator. Almagro was given the title of adelantado and appointed governor of the country to the south of Pizarro's, covering much of what is now Chile. Feeling himself to have been pushed out of his rightful share of the rich Peruvian discoveries, Almagro very sulkily betook himself with

570 Spaniards, some Negroes, and several thousand Indians, along with a large number of horses and a flock of llamas, to his new dominions. Though an able leader, his experience for the next two years was bitter. Many of his followers died from the hardships of the southward journey which, in the depth of winter, lay over a long mountain road skirting the western shore of Lake Titicaca, traversing the bleak Bolivian plateau and thence over the cordillera to the coastal plain of Chile at Copiapó. On his arrival in Chile he was greatly disappointed to find that the portion of the New World allotted to him had no rich cities, was barren and cold, devoid of rich metals, and filled with a vigorous, fighting native population. He decided to return to Peru and enforce his claims in that country. He found affairs in Peru in great turmoil.

Almost immediately upon Almagro's departure the most serious rebellion which the Incas ever attempted broke over the heads of the Pizarros. With astonishing suddenness the natives in central Peru, led by Manco Capac who escaped from Cusco in 1536, rose against the white man, cut communications between Cusco and Lima, and closely besieged Cusco where there was a small band of Spaniards that included three Pizarro brothers. Juan Pizarro was killed in a sortie, but the other two, Hernando and Gonzalo, with a few companions contrived to maintain themselves against immense odds for six months when the approach of winter and news of Spanish re-enforcements induced the Indians to retire. Meanwhile, from Lima, Francisco Pizarro sent for aid to Panama, Mexico, and Guatemala.

When the rebellion had proceeded thus far, Almagro suddenly returned from Chile in April, 1537, and, hearing of the situation in Cusco, marched thither. Chancing upon the main Inca army as it retired from the siege of Cusco, he attacked it and inflicted a severe defeat. By this victory he assisted greatly in suppressing the native revolt, though its embers continued to glow for another two decades. Not until 1559 did Manco's son, apparently recognizing that the struggle against superior weapons was hopeless, make peace with the Spaniards and abdicate in favor of Philip II of Spain. His two brothers, however, continued to claim the royal authority and to hold on in the remote mountain fastness of Vilcabamba in the Andes with a remnant of their people. The survivor of these, Tupac Amaru, fell into the hands of the Spanish viceroy, Francisco de Toledo, in 1571 and was put to death.

Almagro's presence in Peru brought on a civil conflict among the Spanish conquerors almost as tragic as that befalling the unhappy Indians. Before his departure for Chile he had claimed that the city of Cusco properly fell within the limits of his territory, and he now determined to enforce this claim. Attacking the city, he took it by surprise and imprisoned the two Pizarro brothers. This act by Almagro opened a period of eleven years of civil war in the course of which all the principal actors were swept from the stage. Almagro himself was finally defeated in the battle of Las Salinas, brought before a court for sedition, sentenced to death by Hernando Pizarro and strangled in a prison in Cusco in July, 1538.

In the following year, Hernando Pizarro was sent by Francisco to Spain with an enormous quantity of gold for the king. His story, however, was only half believed, for friends of Almagro had preceded him. Before long he was seized and imprisoned for twenty-two years in the castle of La Mota at Medina del Campo for his share in causing the native uprising and Almagro's death. Eventually released, he lived to a great age—one hundred, it is said. He was the only Pizarro brother who did not meet a violent end. The Marquis Francisco Pizarro was murdered in Lima in an assault by several of the men of Chile on June 26, 1541. His rival's son, called Almagro the Lad, was proclaimed governor of Peru in his stead, but on arrival of the king's commissioner, Cristóbal Vaca de Castro, was defeated in battle, tried for treason, and executed. The last of the Pizarro brothers, Gonzalo, who as governor of Quito won fame as an explorer during Francisco's lifetime, later became conspicuous by placing himself at the head of the fierce opposition aroused in Peru by the publication of the "New Laws." For two years he was master of Peru, but was then defeated (1548) in battle and beheaded, along with eight or nine other leaders of rebellion by order of the governor; with him ended the sway of the Pizarros over the land of the Incas. Disorders continued for some years after Gonzalo's death, but with decreasing violence. With the appointment in 1551 of the experienced Antonio de Mendoza, who had earlier served fifteen years as viceroy of Mexico, an era of peace and order opened for Peru, and the period of the Conquest was over.

Exploration based upon Peru for a time had to take a secondary place because of the heavy fighting, though even in the midst of civil war an astonishing amount was accomplished in opening up new territory. As lieutenant and deputy-governor for Francisco Pizarro, Sebastián de Benalcázar—the son of a peasant of Estremadura who had run away from home and joined Pedrarias' expedition—subdued and occupied Quito in 1534 while his chief was occupied with Atahualpa and the capture of Cusco. From Quito, Benalcázar pushed north into southern Colombia, explored the Cauca valley, and founded Cali and Popayán, of which latter place, where he found much gold, he eventually became governor. From there in 1538 he set out eastward in search of a rich Indian kingdom of which he had heard and arrived at Santa Fé de Bogotá in the land of the Chibcha Indians in 1539, only to find that he had been anticipated by two other explorers who had come from the Caribbean shore. One of these, Gonzalo Jiménez de Quesada, had come up the Magdalena River from Santa Marta; the other, Nikolaus Federmann, had arrived over the mountains from Venezuela. As months of negotiations failed to settle their contentions all three men returned to Europe and laid their respective claims before the emperor. Only one of the rivals won a prize—Benalcázar was confirmed as governor of Popayán. Though Bogotá was the grave of many fond hopes the discovery of this plateau land of the Chibchas proved to be the beginning of a century's treasure-hunting in all directions and led to exploration of great areas in northwest South America.

One of the explorers in this region was Gonzalo Pizarro who, in his early Peruvian days, along with his brother Hernando, had made a considerable reputation for himself as explorer and conqueror in present-day Bolivia, then called Las Charcas. In 1539 he was appointed governor of Quito and in 1541-1542 set out to carry through extensive explorations eastward from Ecuador in a search for new wealth. He was looking, he said, for the "province of Cinnamon and the Lake of the Gilded King." His own achievements on the eastern slopes of the Andes were not great, but one of his officers, Francisco de Orellana, in charge of a foraging expedition on the Napo River, achieved a great victory. Carried onward by the force of the current and the unwillingness of his followers to attempt a return journey to the parent expedition, Orellana, in the course of nine months, sailed all the way down the Napo River to its junction with the Amazon, and then onward down this great river to its mouth, from where he made his way to Spain. Attempting to return under a royal commission to establish a colony he was killed at the mouth of the Amazon.[20]

The subjugation of Chile was closely linked to that of Peru. On the whole it was a land of great disappointment to the Spaniards. Almagro in 1536-1537 had stayed long enough to discover that it was an agricultural country apparently lacking in the great mineral wealth that made Peru so attractive. The work that he abandoned in disgust was taken up by Pedro de Valdivia, who had fought among Almagro's enemies at the battle of Las Salinas and whose prowess on that occasion commended him to Francisco Pizarro; Pizarro gave him a commission in 1539 to consolidate Spanish dominion in Chile and to speed its colonization.

An Estremaduran, generous and good-humored, Valdivia was a leader much beloved by his men. Persistent and determined, he left no one in doubt that he meant to finish his task. He spent arduous years in the Chilean undertaking, founding the cities of Valparaíso, Santiago, and Concepción. After a "starving time" and the discovery of some gold

[20] For a well-written, more detailed account of this famous expedition, see Kirkpatrick, pp. 229-42.

mines near Concepción, the colony was eventually established. The final subjugation, however, of the Araucanian Indians in southern Chile was a different matter. In fighting off a revolt of these determined natives Valdivia was captured and tortured to death, January, 1554. Valdivia's successors to the end of the century found how difficult was the task the founder had set for himself and learned how stubbornly brave an American native group could be. It has been estimated that eventually Spain spent more blood and treasure in reducing the Araucanian Indians than in all the rest of America. Some of their virile blood flows in the veins of many Chileans today.

Already in Valdivia's time, explorations and colonizing expeditions were pushing eastward from Chile across the Andean barrier and into what is today Argentina. The Tucumán region of the northwest was colonized from Peru; the city of Tucumán was founded in 1565. From Chile settlers spread eastward into the province of Cuyo (across the Andes from Santiago); Mendoza and San Juan were founded in the 1560s. This colonizing of Argentina from the west, in a kind of long-range continuation of the enterprises of Pizarro and Almagro, was carried on by small groups of frontiersmen who planned to live permanently in the land. It was more closely related in character to the genuine colonizing activities that had marked the advance into Chile than to the greed for gold that furnished the original impulse in Peru. As was to be true for all Argentina, there was no supply of semicivilized agricultural Indians to form a servile labor population. The colonists for the most part became stock farmers, and the few Indians of the territory went the way of the red men in North America—to extermination or reservations.

Meanwhile the continent was being opened from the east. In 1515 the famous explorer, Juan Díaz de Solís, looking for a strait to the east, discovered the estuary of La Plata and proceeded some distance up the river, where he was killed by the Indians. A survivor from this expedition, a Portuguese by the name of Alejo Garcia, with three or four other men, found their way sometime between 1520 and 1526 into Bolivia, but were massacred on the return journey.

Solís' work on the Plata was continued by Sebastian Cabot who, in 1527, secured a commission from the Spanish king to go to the Far East. Along the way he was to determine the line of demarcation in South America and then, before following Magellan's route, explore the west coast of South America. Arriving on the coast, Cabot abandoned these plans. He may have decided that the difficulties were overwhelming, or heard diverting rumors that tempted him to seek his fortune, or possibly have followed secret instructions; in any case, he pushed up the Plata River. After exploring the Paraná for hundreds of miles, he ascended the Paraguay as far as its junction with the Pilcomayo, and sent home tall stories about the silver in the area, built up on the basis of some silver articles secured from the river Indians. It was he who bestowed the name Río de la Plata, "River of Silver," on the estuary that Solís had discovered. A small party of Cabot's men, sent out under Captain Francisco César in 1528 or 1529, appears to have succeeded in crossing the Andes and reaching the Atacama region of the Inca empire where they were kindly received and presented with gifts and guides and returned safely.

Arriving at the royal court with this news Sebastian's emissaries found that they had been anticipated by Francisco Pizarro who had won the king's support for a conquest of Peru based upon Panama. Consequently, little attention was paid to Cabot's report and the explorer was left to get home as best he could. However, during the next few years many followed in Cabot's footsteps, hoping to find a really practical water or land route from the east coast through which to tap the gold and silver treasures of Peru. With this end in view, in 1536 a large Spanish expedition under Pedro de Mendoza, a gentleman of the royal household, attempted to found a colony at Buenos Aires, but sickness and Indian raids caused its abandonment. One year later, however, a member of his expedition succeeded in establishing the first permanent colony in the region when he founded Asunción at the junction of the Paraguay and Pilcomayo rivers, almost a thousand miles from the sea. For a long time this was the only settlement in the Plata basin.

Contact was not made between the eastern and western enterprises until the late forties when the king's commissioner, Vaca de Castro of Peru, gave a concession to a party of Peruvian adventurers to go into the province of Tucumán. One of these "men of the *entrada*," Francisco de Mendoza, on reaching La Plata River in 1546, came upon the ruins of a Spanish fort and found some Indians speaking Spanish. The two streams of Spanish exploration, one from the Atlantic and one from the Pacific, had met. For a time they threatened to clash, but eventually the river region was assigned to the men of Paraguay, while the inland was left to the men of Peru and Chile.

After several failures to colonize the banks of the estuary of La Plata, an expedition from Asunción in 1580 succeeded in refounding, this time permanently, the city of Buenos Aires. By the beginning of the seventeenth century, it had a population of 3,000, and was on the way to the pre-eminent position in this part of the world which it was to maintain continuously thereafter.

The permanent founding of Buenos Aires in 1580 is noteworthy as marking the completion in rough outline of the work of Columbus and the sixteenth century conquistadores. By this date these energetic path-

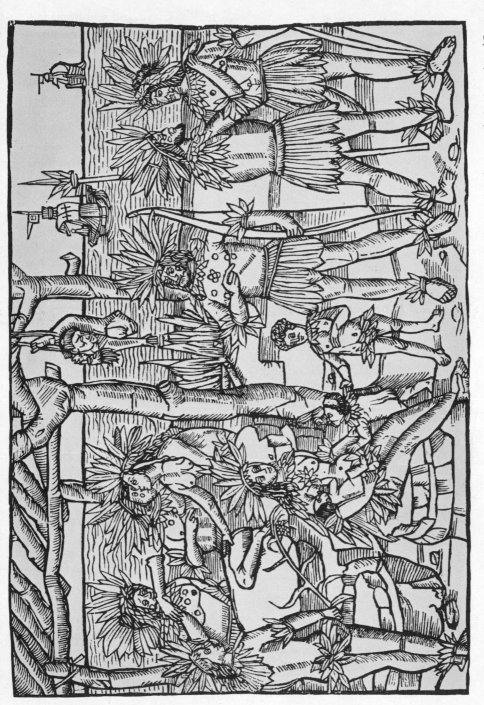

Wood engraving of South American Indians, 1505. Earliest known pictorial representation of Indians made in America. (Courtesy of the New York Public Library)

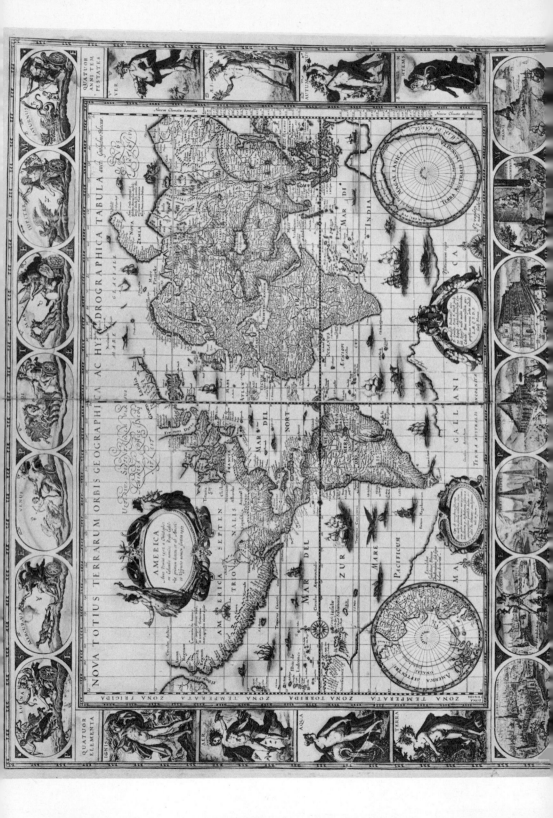

Incas bringing in Atahualpa's ransom. From DeBrye. (Courtesy of the New York Public Library)

(*Opposite*) The World about 1600. Border pictures illustrate the Four Elements, the Seven Principal Heavenly Bodies, the Four Seasons, the Seven Wonders of the World. A contemporary map by J. A. Vanden Ende, published by Guilelmo Blaeuw, Amsterdam. (Courtesy of the Royal Ontario Museum of Archaeology)

Hernando Cortés. Engraved by W. Holl. From a picture in the Florence Gallery. (Courtesy of the New York Public Library)

finders had completed two great semicircles of exploration and conquest
that met in the West Indies. The more northern crescent curved about the
Gulf of Mexico. Starting in Española it stretched through the islands of
the Greater Antilles, took in the lands of Central America north of Panama, included Mexico and the discoveries northward to the Seven Cities
of Cíbola, and wandered thinly along the northern shore of the Mexican
Gulf to Florida, where the founding of St. Augustine in 1565 permanently
anchored the Spanish flag in a location suitable for the protection of the
vital Bahama straits. The southern crescent curved about the Portuguese
possession of Brazil. It began at the Gulf of Paria, somewhat to the north
of the Orinoco (discovered by Columbus in 1498), followed along the
northern coast of South America, passed through the Isthmus of Panama
and then bent southward to include the Pacific shores of Colombia, Ecuador, Peru, and Chile before crossing the Andes and the pampas to anchor
at Asunción and Buenos Aires on the Paraná.

The record was an extraordinary one, not only in the amazing extent of
territory traversed with incredible rapidity, but in the methodical effectiveness with which the first discoveries were followed up and Spanish control
was extended inward to a considerable depth. The Spanish explorers by no
means remained satisfied with a fringe of coastal settlements or the establishment of shore trading posts, but from the beginning pushed inland in
a series of spectacular marches aimed at overthrowing the various centers
of native power, all located far from the coast. Leaning on their old
Roman training, re-enforced by centuries of struggles against the Moors
for the reconquest of Spain, they pursued the invariable policy of establishing municipal foundations as bases from which to carry on the work
of military conquest. By the close of the sixteenth century Spanish America was thickly dotted with *municipia,* each with its surrounding territory
constituting a kind of city-state, that provided a local focus of strength
for the work of exploration and conquest. Thus from the very beginning
Spanish colonial life was organized to center in cities. Beyond their
borders, *haciendas* (estates of vast extent), worked by gangs of semien-
slaved Indians, early took shape. The conquistadores organized as they
moved and forced the large native population of agricultural Indians into
conformity with their colonial pattern.

An outstanding feature of the conquest was the notably close combination of effective royal direction with a maximum amount of individual
initiative. Columbus did not dream of setting his sail westward until he
had a signed and sealed contract promising royal backing. In a very real
sense the Spanish expeditions that opened up America were royal undertakings. Not only were they made originally at the crown's expense, but
those taking part in them continued always to look to the crown as the

source of their authority and the fountain of office, honor, justice, and reward. Individual initiative and ambition, however, felt in no sense cramped. Spanish conquistadores of the sixteenth century seemed to have no difficulty in linking their personal hopes with loyalty to a distant king. On his part, the king showed himself always ready to receive them in audience, listen to their stories, read their dispatches, judge between them, and provide as intelligent and detailed direction from home as he could devise. To this overseas supervision, Spaniards on the whole obediently bowed; however fiercely the conquistadores might quarrel in America, they rarely disputed the royal decision.

From another aspect, the conquest was a religious crusade, an eager venture of faith, as well as a military undertaking. Being Spanish it was reasonable that this should be so. Those who took part in it had been drilled through centuries of conflict with the unbeliever to associate the sword and cross, to combine adventure, greed, and the clash of arms with crusading and religious ardor, and they naturally experienced no difficulty in transferring this combination to the New World.

The conquest was also essentially an undertaking by the Spanish common man. Most of the conquistadores were definitely from the middle class, though there was a sprinkling of wealthy men and some from the lowest class. It was in no sense an effort to relieve overcrowded jails at home; on the contrary the absence of condemned criminals in any large numbers and of such unpopular elements in Spanish society as heretics and Jews was notable. To all who came, America provided excitement and adventure. To some of the conquistadores she gave great riches, though few lived long to enjoy them. Most of America's conquerors died violent deaths, usually at an early age, in the land they came to conquer; of the few who finally returned home, many died in poverty and neglect.

II. THE DISCOVERY OF BRAZIL

Portugal's claim to a place in the colonial sun was recognized by Spain in the Treaty of Tordesillas in 1494. Primarily, the little Iberian nation owed this chance to build the second colonial empire in America to her unparalleled reputation as a pioneer in oceanic exploration. The immediate stream of events leading to the famous treaty started on March 4, 1493, when Columbus was forced to seek shelter from a storm in the harbor of Lisbon on his homeward journey from his first transatlantic voyage. At this time King João II [21] learned from the explorer that he was about to report to the Spanish court the discovery of new lands which he called

---

[21] King João II ruled Portugal, 1481-1495, carrying on the exploration policies of Prince Henry the Navigator.

"the Indies," filled with inhabitants—some of whom he had brought with him—whom he referred to as "Indians." The king naturally concluded that this man had been visiting lands that belonged to the Portuguese crown. They must surely, he thought, be part of those "Indies" which had been so persistently sought by Portuguese explorers since the early years of the fifteenth century.[22] Five years previously, in 1488, these efforts had culminated in Bartholomeu Dias' magnificent achievement of rounding the Cape of Good Hope. Although India itself had not yet been reached by a Portuguese ship, all the world knew that it was practically in sight and surely would be attained by the next properly equipped expedition. Morally, if on no other ground, the indignant João II felt that the Indies already belonged to Portugal. Furthermore, by international documentation Portugal held titles to the Indies. A papal bull of 1456 had conferred on Portugal all territory lying south of capes Bogador and Nam "through Guinea," not already held by any Christian prince, and also all lands lying beyond the southern coast of Africa "as far as the Indians." [23] All this the Spanish crown had recognized in a treaty of 1479. Portuguese claims had been further strengthened by the bull *Aeterni Regis* of 1481, which, in Portuguese understanding, conferred upon it everything south of a horizontal line running east and west through the Canaries. King João therefore felt himself justly incensed and entitled to protest.

He was especially aroused to vigorous action when he presently learned that Pope Alexander VI, a Spaniard by birth and under great obligation to King Ferdinand, had, in his role as the recognized international authority of the day, so far acquiesced in an application from Ferdinand and Isabella for a grant to the Spanish crown of lands visited by Columbus as to proclaim in a series of bulls dated in May, 1493, an official perpendicular line of demarcation. This was described as drawn from the north to the south pole and lying 100 leagues to the west of the Azores and Cape Verde Islands; to the west of this demarcation all new lands were to be acknowledged as Spanish.[24] This line, it is now clear, had been suggested by Columbus who thought it represented the middle of the Atlantic.[25] Although the form of this action gave evidence that the Pope recognized that in the complicated situation there ought, in all fairness, to be some division of the rewards of exploration, King João was far from satisfied

---

[22] See Chapter 3, pp. 92-93.

[23] M. W. Williams, "The Treaty of Tordesillas and the Argentine-Brazilian Boundary Settlement," in *Hispanic American Historical Review*, Vol. V, 1922, p. 3.

[24] This was the third of the papal bulls issued and was the second *Inter caetera*. The first of the two *Inter caetera*, and *Eximiae devotionis*, had merely confirmed to the Spanish crown the sovereignty of the newly found lands. If the hundred-league line had been retained it would practically have shut Portugal out of America. It was, however, never acted on, and was withdrawn within a year.

[25] S. E. Morison, *Admiral of the Ocean Sea*, Vol. II, pp. 24-25.

and became seriously alarmed when, in September, 1493, under further pressure from Spain, the Pope issued another bull, *Dudum siquidem,* which revised and amplified the earlier bulls in favor of Spain, actually bringing into question Portuguese claims on their old routes to the south and east.[26] It declared open to both nations the whole field of maritime exploration with the provision that Spain should approach from the west and Portugal from the east. Despairing of Rome, the king opened direct negotiations with the Spanish court and suggested a conference.

The outcome was the Treaty of Tordesillas, June 7, 1494, which made no mention of papal bulls but was more favorable to Portuguese claims. Its terms provided that a line 370 leagues to the west of the Cape Verde Islands should be regarded as the boundary line between the colonial claims of the two crowns, Spain taking the lands to the west and Portugal those to the east. It was further agreed that a joint expedition should sail west a stipulated distance and where the line cut the land set up markers. A supplementary pact in the following year agreed that this surveying expedition should be postponed. Actually it never sailed and the ambiguities and vague expressions of the treaty were to prove sufficiently indefinite to keep the exact landfall of the famous line in dispute, in its entirety for 250 years, and in certain of its details till the end of the nineteenth century.[27] The advantages from the uncertainty were to accrue to Portugal. Though early in the sixteenth century Spain gave evidence that she considered as belonging to her all territory west of a meridian passing slightly to the east of the right mouth of the Amazon,[28] the Portuguese paid no heed and pressed on westward. In the eighteenth century, in the treaties of Exchange (1750) and of San Ildefonso (1777) Portugal was finally able to secure from the Spanish court treaty recognition of territory several times as extensive as that to which she had been originally entitled, even under her own early interpretation of the Treaty of Tordesillas.[29]

This smaller Iberian nation, whose splendid record of systematic exploration in Africa had thus won her an opportunity in America, was a people closely akin in race, language, and historical experience to the Spaniards from whom they had separated politically in the twelfth century. Events, however, were to prove that they differed sufficiently to enable them to produce, with the help of environmental differences, a distinctive colonial society in South America that was by no means a mere

---

[26] The bulls and the negotiations associated with them are discussed in detail in H. Vander Linden's article "Alexander VI and the Bulls of Demarcation," in *American Historical Review*, XXII, 1916, pp. 1-20.

[27] Williams, *op. cit.*, p. 22.

[28] *Ibid.*, p. 8.

[29] *Ibid.*, p. 10. See also V. L. Brown, *Studies in the History of Spain in the Second Half of the 18th Century*, pp. 89-92, Smith College Studies in History, XV, October, 1929-January, 1930.

duplicate of the neighboring Spanish colonies. By the close of the fifteenth century the Portuguese were a sturdy, alert nation of about 1,120,000 [30] people enjoying a European reputation as pioneers of oceanic exploration and maritime enterprise—outlets for energy that had been naturally suggested and favored by their geographical location. Prince Henry the Navigator's center for naval scientists and seamen at Sagres, with its emphasis on the study of applied astronomy and cartography, had achieved wonders in laying the technical foundations for the later voyages.[31] By the close of the fifteenth century, Portuguese ships had long excelled all others in the skilful use of the compass, the astrolabe, the quadrant, ocean maps, and other nautical aids which made possible deep-sea navigation on a hitherto undreamed-of scale.

To a greater degree than any other nation of the age, the Portuguese also possessed historical traditions and experience likely to be useful in the government of an overseas empire. Seven hundred years of fighting side by side with the Spaniards to expel the Moors from the Iberian Peninsula had provided valuable lessons in continuous fighting and in frontier settlement and organization. The emergence during this time of a monarchy powerful enough to triumph over baronial anarchy at home gave a sense of strength and national unity. The work of the fifteenth century, in establishing stations along the west African coast and in the task of rediscovering, conquering, and administering the Azores, Madeira, and Cape Verde Islands, had provided intimate knowledge of the needs of a colonial empire. Their record as traders in the Mediterranean markets and in West Africa had made them familiar with trading companies, commercial monopolies, and the exploitation of trade opportunities in a wide field.

In temperament, also, the Portuguese had many qualities that fitted them for success in colonial competition against the larger maritime powers of western Europe. Combining the crusading spirit, with its love of military adventure and religious fervor, with a truly modern keenness for commercial advantage, the Portuguese were more adaptable, easy-going, and tolerant than the more orthodox and military-minded Spaniards. Nearer than the contemporary Englishman to the Mediterranean crossroads of the Renaissance world, they were endowed with a wider outlook and yet were possessed of fully as much commercial initiative and

---

[30] This figure is one of the lower estimates of the population. G. Barros suggests three million. For a discussion of this subject see Fidelino de Figueredo, "The Geographical Discoveries and Conquests of the Portuguese," in *Hispanic American Historical Review*, Vol. VI, 1926, pp. 48-49.

[31] Figueredo discusses the achievements in some detail in the article cited, pp. 50-60; but for a different point of view, one emphasizing the medieval character of Prince Henry's plans and outlooks and protesting against Sagres being regarded as a school of scientific seamanship, cf. E. J. Payne, "The Age of Discovery," *Cambridge Modern History*, I.

business acumen, and were much more imbued with missionary zeal. Compared with the French colonial builders of their age, the Portuguese shared the same background of frugality and hard work; emotionally, however, they were not so tied to the homeland nor were they so dependent on state supervision in their enterprises. In willingness to intermarry with darker races and settle down as permanent citizens of new lands, the Portuguese probably surpassed all other western Europeans. Their most serious handicap as colonizers was a small, rather poverty-stricken home base and a consequent lack of numbers and resources.

The effective discovery of Brazil was made by Pedro Álvares Cabral who sighted its coast near Port Seguro in Baía on April 22, 1500. The traditional story is that on the advice of Vasco da Gama Cabral sailed on his way to India far to the westward to escape the calms of the Gulf of Guinea and by chance thus came upon the Brazilian shore. He landed on what he assumed to be an island, remained for eight days trafficking with the natives, and then on May first sailed again for India. Before sailing he took formal possession of the country for Portugal, naming it "Ilha de Vera Cruz," and despatched a vessel home loaded with brazilwood, monkeys, and parrots to inform King Manoel [32] of his discovery. Brazil in this account appears to have been a kind of by-product of Portugal's interest in the African route to India. Some modern scholars, especially of Portuguese and Brazilian origin, have thrown doubt on both the chance element in Cabral's journey and its primacy in the record of Portuguese voyages to Brazil. They stress the fact that the later Portuguese rulers of the House of Aviz,[33] following a rule imposed by Prince Henry, were notorious for pursuing a policy of absolute secrecy in their maritime operations, forbidding their subjects and others who served them to publish any accounts, maps, charts, or other data of their exploring activities. In their version, Cabral's visit to Brazil appears to have been merely one of a number of Portuguese voyages which were despatched deliberately, though secretly, across the Atlantic by the Portuguese kings who wished to be better informed concerning the lands falling to them under the Treaty of Tordesillas.[34]

Whatever the reality of the vague early Portuguese journeys may have been, Cabral was long given the credit for being the first of his countrymen to touch Brazil. It was, however, well known to his contemporaries

[32] Manoel I, succeeding João II, reigned from 1495 to 1521.

[33] This dynasty ruled in Portugal, 1385 to 1580.

[34] According to this version a certain Duarte Pacheco Pereira was probably on the Brazilian coast with a Portuguese fleet in 1498. The Cortereals' expedition to Newfoundland is considered to be another journey in the same series. Cf. F. de Figueredo, op. cit., pp. 60-62; also C. E. Nowell, "The Discovery of Brazil, Accidental or Intentional?" in Hispanic American Historical Review, XVI, 1936, pp. 311-38; and J. P. Calogeras, A History of Brazil, translated by P. A. Martin (Chapel Hill, N. C.: 1939), pp. 3-4.

that he had not been the first European there but had been preceded by two months by a Spaniard, Vicente Yáñez Pinzón, sailing under orders from Ferdinand and Isabella. Driven by a violent storm Pinzón, on February 7, 1500, had landed on the easternmost coast of Brazil near Pernambuco, some hundreds of miles north of the point later reached by Cabral. He had then turned northward and traced the Brazilian coastline for two thousand miles, discovering on his way the mouth of the Amazon River. Although Portuguese claims to Brazil rested legally on the terms of the Treaty of Tordesillas, and not on mere discovery, King Manoel realized the advantage of having juridical claims supported by exploring operations, and shortly after receiving Cabral's messenger dispatched in May, 1501, three vessels to the Brazilian coast to make further explorations and to skirt the coast far enough southward to be sure that the demarcation line had been passed. Amerigo Vespucci, who claimed to have accompanied this expedition, described it in two famous letters which circulated widely in manuscript; one of them finally resulted in his name becoming attached to the whole New World. Vespucci also claimed that he went along on a later expedition to the Brazilian coast, leaving Lisbon on May 10, 1503, and returning a year later. Great uncertainty, however, surrounds all Vespucci's American voyages.[35]

Through the first three decades of her history, Brazil gave no evidence of the remarkable development that was subsequently to be hers. Portugal in these years was giving her full attention to the golden East. Her sailors visited, as the first Europeans to come by sea, the coasts of China and Japan and explored the Islands of southeastern Asia. Eventually they brought into being a maritime empire of trading posts, and opened an enormously profitable direct trade in spices and pepper between the Orient and Lisbon.

In the midst of the excitement over the East, there was no enthusiasm to spare for the American possession which was later to be the principal bulwark of her overseas empire, and she almost totally neglected it. In the first thirty years of its history Brazil was apparently regarded as both unprofitable and inglorious. Compared with the rich and desirable Spanish holdings, or with Portugal's own eastern empire, Brazil in these days appeared poor and full of fierce, cannibalistic Indians among whom were interspersed a few unfortunate individuals, the majority of them unwanted in Europe. These consisted mostly of shipwrecked mariners, adventurers, criminals, and Jews, many of whom had been sent over to America to relieve the overcrowded jails or followed in the wake of the 1496 expulsion of Jews from Portugal. A certain number of private trading expeditions

---

[35] See Footnote 2.

were made, and a small amount of desultory trading in tropical products went on, especially in brazilwood, but this was accorded no state aid or protection and suffered heavy losses from the depredations of French privateers operating off the coast. But though unprofitable, Brazil was useful in these years as a refreshment point on the ocean route to India as well as as being a foothold in America of possible future value.

In 1530 a new page was turned. The East by this time was beginning to lose a little of its early glitter as it was found that "every grain of pepper exacted a drop of blood" and it became doubtful if Portugal could succeed in permanently holding her Asiatic empire against the increasing numbers and strength of the aggressive Dutch and English competitors now appearing on the Indian and Malayan coasts and among the Spice Islands. Not only had the flood of gold and silver of recently discovered Mexico and Peru given an enhanced value to all American holdings, but there had recently been rumors of the discovery of silver in the Plata area. Meanwhile increasing French depredations threatened Portugal's foothold in the western hemisphere. King João III [36] determined to undertake seriously the colonization of Brazil and explore its resources. His first step was to despatch in 1530 a fleet of five ships under the capable admiral, Martim Affonso de Souza, with the threefold commission of waging an exterminating war against the French corsairs, verifying the report of silver in La Plata, and putting into operation along the Brazilian coast a plan of colonial settlement that had been found successful in the Azores.

After studying the contours of the land, Souza divided the Brazilian coast, between São Vicente on the south and the mouth of the Amazon on the north, into fifteen sections, forming from them some twelve or thirteen captaincies which the king granted to a corresponding number of favored subjects as *donatarios,* or hereditary landlords, who should undertake to settle and defend their new acquisitions at their own expense.[37] Theoretically the sections were of the same size, measuring fifty Portuguese leagues [38] along the coast and running inland to the demarcation line. In practice, however, there were great discrepancies and the captaincies varied considerably in size, shape, and potentialities.

In his work as a colonizer and organizer, Souza received most valuable assistance from two white patriarchs, castaways surviving from the earlier period. Diogo Alvares, of uncertain social origin, known to the Indians as Caramurú, had been shipwrecked probably as early as 1510; João Ra-

---

[36] João III reigned 1521-1557.

[37] See accompanying map for names and locations of the captaincies. For the names of the original grantees see H. G. James, *Brazil after a Century of Independence* (New York: 1925), pp. 64-67; *cf* also C. E. Chapman, *Colonial Hispanic America* (New York: 1933), p. 74, on the uncertainty of the numbers of the captaincies.

[38] Approximately 150 miles.

malho, Portuguese sailor, had suffered a similar fate some two years later. Succeeding in making friends with the Indians and marrying daughters of Indian chiefs, both men had become fathers of amazingly large families and persons of great influence in the native community. Souza found Ramalho established near his own captaincy of São Vicente. Diogo Alvares

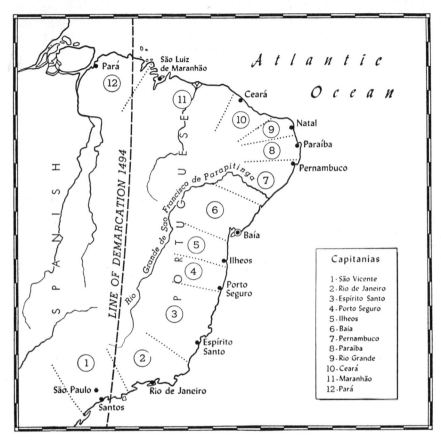

Capitanias
1 - São Vicente
2 - Rio de Janeiro
3 - Espírito Santo
4 - Porto Seguro
5 - Ilheos
6 - Baía
7 - Pernambuco
8 - Paraíba
9 - Rio Grande
10 - Ceará
11 - Maranhão
12 - Pará

11. Capitanias of Brazil in the Sixteenth Century

was the first white settler in beautiful Baía de Todos os Santos. While both were friendly and extremely useful to the later white comers, they used their influence to curb the excesses of their countrymen towards the Indians.

In this scheme of captaincies, the principal idea of the king was to provide for the organization, settlement, and development of the colony in its early expensive years with a minimum outlay from the crown. To induce wealthy and vigorous individuals to shoulder the burden, the donatarios were endowed with political, military, and economic powers that were hereditary in character and almost sovereign in extent. The new rulers might wage wars against the natives or enslave them, found towns, distribute lands, carry on trade, appoint officials, establish courts, levy taxes and tithes, impose banishment, and, in some places, even inflict the death penalty. They owed a certain proportion of the taxes and revenues to the crown and were prohibited from coining money but otherwise the king imposed a minimum of restraint.

A number of the donatarios arrived in Brazil in 1534 and 1535, and for the next fifteen years the plan of the captaincies was tried out. The greater number of donatarios were men drawn from the lesser nobility or from the middle class. Some had been in government or military posts in the East where they had made fortunes; others were wealthy landowners from Portugal; all were intent on investment in Brazil.

These Brazilian captaincies showed an interesting combination of feudal and early capitalistic elements. While feudal in that they provided for the grant of land and political power on a hereditary basis in return for services partly military in character, they also partook of the new capitalistic spirit of the age in their emphasis on trade and profits. Within the captaincies, the social and economic relationships were not feudal. Not only was labor provided by slaves—not serfs as in the medieval pattern— but the relation of the white settlers to the donatarios did not carry traditional feudal obligations, nor was land held on feudal tenure. Both the donatarios and the white settlers, in a modern capitalistic manner, were primarily interested in making their fortunes from the growing of sugar. This plant had been introduced from Sicily into the Madeira Islands where the Portuguese had become familiar with it. They soon discovered that the cane flourished wonderfully in Brazilian soil and climate. Soon after landing and running up a few temporary houses and some form of fortification, it was usual for both the donatarios and other white settlers to turn their attention wholly to laying out sugar plantations in the neighborhood of the new town, and presently to furnishing these with *engenhos,* or mills, for the grinding of the sugar. Military duties concerned with keeping the surrounding Indians in check were usually delegated to mercenary soldiers. By 1545 the donatario of São Vicente,[39] the first captaincy to be established, possessed six mills and 6,000 slaves. Besides São Vicente, only one other captaincy stood out as really prosperous. This was Pernambuco with its capital at Olinda, lying on the bulge of

---

[39] In the south near the present port of Santos, Martim Affonso founded, in 1531, a settlement which he called São Vicente. Farther inland he established another colony which became São Paulo.

Brazil to the north of the São Francisco River. Like São Vicente, Pernambuco was predominantly a sugar colony.

While the Portuguese experiment of colonizing Brazil under donatarios was under way, Spanish explorers, half by chance and half by intention, anticipated Portuguese action and succeeded in tracing the course of Brazil's greatest river, the Amazon, from one of its western tributaries to its mouth on the Atlantic. In 1539 a Spanish exploratory expedition of 300 men and thousands of Indians under the leadership of Gonzalo Pizarro set out from Quito to find a fabled "land of cinnamon" across the eastern cordillera of the Andes. When starvation overtook the expedition on the Napo River, one of Gonzalo's men, Francisco de Orellana, was sent ahead with a party of fifty men to investigate reports of the neighborhood of a larger river on whose banks there was said to be food. Finding the great river and being carried swiftly eastward on its current, and being moved also by a hope of personal advantage, Orellana decided not to return and report to his chief as he was obligated to do. Gonzalo was thus left to struggle back as best he might to his starting point, while Orellana and his followers continued down the full length of the mighty stream—which they named the "river of the Amazons," from the fighting native women along its banks—and finally reached the ocean in August, 1541. When this deserter finally presented himself to the Spanish court he was commissioned by the Emperor Charles V to conquer and govern the region which he had found. On the return journey Orellana died, and the great Amazon basin was left for incorporation into Portuguese holdings.

By 1549 the Portuguese crown had reached the conclusion that, from the national point of view, the captaincies had been a failure. There were obviously many weaknesses. One of the greatest was the artificiality and unreasonableness of the boundaries of the grants. Based on meridians and parallels, the sections lacked economic unity and natural cohesiveness. Settlers, instead of being concentrated at a few points on the coast within reach of help from each other and from the motherland in case of need, had been encouraged to scatter over a wide area. They appeared as small islands of settlement severally attached to the motherland by a precarious and tenuous thread of communication. Furthermore, as a class the donatarios had clearly been granted too much power; from the first they had behaved practically as independent rulers and carried on almost perpetual war with one another, showing little sense of national mission or obligation. Economically, also, the plan left much to be desired; while a few of the donatarios had grown rich from trade in sugar, brazilwood, and other tropical goods, others had been ruined. On the whole, it was clear that private resources were inadequate to carry out the expensive tasks involved in clearing the jungles, settling white colonists on the land, carrying on perpetual war against the natives, and keeping the trade routes clear of European rivals. If Brazil was to flourish even as a flanking base for India, the crown must play a stronger hand.

In all these circumstances, it was decided to put into operation a compromise plan: to leave the donatarios their lands, but to revoke by royal decree their political powers and centralize the administration in the hands of a royally appointed governor general, whose seat should be at Baía (or São Salvador) in the beautiful Baía de Todos os Santos [40] and whose principal responsibility should be the strengthening of the royal interests and the unification of the scattered settlements. The choice for the first Governor-General of the new viceroyalty was Thomé de Souza. With his arrival at Baía, the history of Brazil as a royal colony really began. Eventually all the original captaincies reverted to the crown, either by confiscation, abandonment, or purchase. Three had already become royal property by the close of the sixteenth century and the last fell to the king in the eighteenth century. Throughout its history, however, Brazil was to bear the marks of the period of the captaincies. Not only did their boundaries remain substantially unchanged as provincial frontiers, but their separatist spirit lived on to diversify Brazilian life and perpetuate a strong sentiment of decentralization and local autonomy.

---

[40] This territory was bought back by the crown from heirs of the first donatario who had been devoured by his irate Indian subjects. Baía remained the capital till the eighteenth century.

Chapter 5

DISCOVERERS AND EXPLORERS OF THE SIXTEENTH CENTURY: NORTH AMERICA

I. FRENCH ENTERPRISE

During the sixteenth century, while Spain was systematically discovering, conquering, and organizing her great empire in the New World, French colonial efforts in America were spasmodic. Like her neighbors, Spain and Portugal, France had attained national unification and a strong centralized monarchy by the close of the fifteenth century and was equipped to embark on new adventures, predatory and otherwise. Through the first century of modern times, however, these activities were centered in Europe and not in America. The primary goals were the realization of old French claims in Flanders, Navarre, and along the eastern frontier, and the fulfilment of new dreams in Italy. Everywhere French ambitions were thwarted by the Spanish-Hapsburg alliance. Francis I, on coming into possession of the French crown in 1515, found his lands practically hemmed in by those of Charles V, on whose head by 1519 rested the crowns of Spain, Burgundy, Austria, and the Holy Roman Empire. It was therefore but natural that Franco-Spanish hostility should be the dominating thread weaving in and out of European politics for the next half century. While this bitter struggle lasted, the French kings had little thought to spare for adventuring in the New World. When, in the second half of the century, the Spanish menace lessened with the death of Charles V and the separation of the Spanish and Hapsburg inheritances, France fell almost immediately into civil and religious warfare at home which absorbed most of her national energies for another fifty years.

Despite her foreign and domestic distractions, however, France did not allow the whole first century after the discovery of the New World to go by without making some effort to stake out future American claims. When the report of the Spanish and Portuguese arrangements for the division of the unknown world reached Paris, Francis I (1515-1547) is said to have flown into a high rage, declaring that he "would like to be shown the will of our Father Adam, bestowing the world on these two neighbors." When the news of Magellan's momentous journey was followed quickly by the discovery of Mexico by Cortés, Francis decided that it was time for him to join in the game of the search for the northwest passage, and dispatched an able Italian seaman in his employ, Giovanni da Verrazano, to scour the coast north of the Spanish holdings for such an opening. In 1524 Verrazano reached America in the latitude of North Carolina and, sailing northward, explored the east coast of the present United States, examining, among other indentations, the mouth of the Hudson River.[1] Rumors of this prospective journey led Charles V to hurry to America a Portuguese sailor, Gómez, who actually preceded Verrazano and sailed along the entire coast from Cape Breton to Cuba.[2] Nothing came of either voyage except that rival French and Spanish claims were established to the lands which had been skirted.

Ten years later Francis took advantage of the recent acquisition of Brittany by the French crown to commission a Breton sailor of St. Malo, Jacques Cartier, to explore North America again in behalf of French interests. Sailing on April 20, 1534, with two ships and sixty men, Cartier arrived three weeks later off the east coast of Newfoundland. After refreshing his company, he passed through the Strait of Belle Isle, examined the southern coast of Laborador for a short distance, and then went southward along the west coast of Newfoundland, proving it to be an island. Buffeted by strong winds, he turned westward and came upon Prince Edward Island and the coast of New Brunswick. Bay Chaleur was especially a disappointment as its fresh water made it evident that it would never lead to China. In the Bay of Gaspé, before a concourse of Indians, Cartier planted a large wooden cross at the entrance to the harbor and at the center of it hung a shield with three fleurs-de-lis, above which was carved the legend "Vive le Roy de France." [3] At Gaspé, Cartier carried on some trade with the Indians, two of whom he persuaded to return with him to France. As autumn was approaching with its dangerous storms, Cartier, after rounding the eastern end of the island of Anticosti, decided to return to France and report to the court. His claim of sovereignty for France had been preceded in the same general region by that of Cabot for England by thirty-seven years.

The following summer (1535), Cartier was back in the Gulf of St. Lawrence with three vessels and a company of one hundred and twelve persons, plus two Indian guides who could now speak French. This time he made his way up the St. Lawrence River. Sailing past Murray Bay and the Île d' Orléans, he arrived on September 7, 1535, at the Indian settlement of Stadacona, near present-day Quebec, where the Indians were

---

[1] G. M. Wrong's *Rise and Fall of New France,* 2 vols. (New York: 1928), I, pp. 47-48. H. P. Biggar in *The Precursors of Jacques Cartier, 1497-1534* (Ottawa: 1911), Introduction, p. xxv, indicates that Verazzano explored the coast from Florida northward to Cape Breton.
[2] Wrong, *op. cit.,* I, chap. iv, p. 46. Biggar, *op. cit.,* Introduction, pp. xxvi-xxix, discusses this journey in some detail.
[3] Wrong, *op. cit.,* I, chap. iv, pp. 53-54.

friendly. Leaving here the bulk of his party in a new fort, the French leader with fifty men pushed further up the river. At Hochelaga—the modern Montreal—he was given a riotous welcome by a thousand savages who danced and shouted and showered his boats with bread and fish and later showed him Mount Royal with its magnificent outlook and told him of the Ottawa River and the Lachine Rapids. After an expedition lasting twenty-two days he returned to Quebec where he and his men spent the winter in a fort at the junction of the Lairet and the St. Charles, suffering much from cold and scurvy and fear of possible treachery from the Indians. On May 3, 1536, Cartier claimed the country for his sovereign by erecting on the bank of the St. Charles a cross thirty-five feet high with the inscription "Franciscus Primus Dei gratia Francorum Rex regnat." Three days later he sailed for France carrying with him a dozen Indians and vague rumors of a land of Saguenay "where is infinite gold, rubies, and other riches." [4]

Five years elapsed before Cartier was able to return to Canada. This third and longer expedition of 1541 had as its primary purpose the establishment of a permanent French colony on the St. Lawrence and the possible conquest of the "kingdom of Saguenay." With Cartier, now titled "Captain General and Master Pilot," was associated Jean François de La Roque, Sieur de Roberval, an aggressive, determined noble of New Rochelle, who was named "Viceroy and Lieutenant-General of Canada, Newfoundland, and Labrador." The two leaders, bound together in the same enterprise by the king, were far from seeing eye to eye on the plans and objects of their voyage, and their strained relations are indicative of the rivalry and diverse interests of the explorer and the businessman so closely associated in the French undertaking.

Misfortunes beset the expedition from the outset. The group of colonists included many condemned criminals and the expedition was short on munitions of war. Preparations in France miscarried and were unduly prolonged. Cartier finally sailed in May, 1541, with five ships, but Roberval, who was to have followed as soon as possible, delayed until 1542. The two leaders merely encountered each other in Newfoundland where Cartier, after a terrible winter spent at Cap Rouge near Stadacona, stopped for refreshment on his way home with the survivors of the colonists who had accompanied him. He had visited Lachine Rapids, but otherwise had added little to his earlier knowledge.[5] After a repetition in the following winter of the same frightful experiences that Cartier had suffered in the

---

[4] *Ibid.*, pp. 64-65.
[5] For further details concerning the Cartier voyages see H. P. Biggar, *A Collection of Documents Relating to Jacques Cartier and the Sieur de Roberval* (Ottawa: 1930), Introduction, pp. xvii-xxxvii.

previous year, Roberval too returned to France, leaving Canada to the Indians and Newfoundland to fur traders and fishermen for another sixty years.

Cartier, the discoverer of the St. Lawrence, is the most attractive of the explorers France sent to America in the sixteenth century. At the time of his visits to Canada he was an energetic man in the prime of life, an able navigator, religious, humane, thoroughly intelligent, sensible, and yet a dreamer and an adventurer. In his work in Canada Cartier pursued a policy toward the Indians that the best of his countrymen followed, showing none of the arrogance and cruelty that marred the efforts of many contemporary Spaniards. Persistently in his dealings with the red men he strove to avoid all show of hostility, to trade with them, and through friendly relations to secure needed information and supplies. He reported to the king that he found the Indians everywhere glad to exchange their furs for knives, iron tools, combs, red hats, beads of glass, and other trifles of small value. "They gave us whatsoever they had, not keeping anything, so that they were constrained to go back again naked." Although keenly disappointed at not finding the pathway to the east for which he was searching, Canada's first explorer was filled with enthusiasm over the natural beauty of the land. Despite many hardships, Cartier went home with an abiding affection for the St. Lawrence countryside.

In the second half of the sixteenth century, when France was torn by religious strife between Protestants and Catholics, the most notable of the French overseas adventuring activities were two efforts made by the Huguenots to found colonies in America where they might pursue their religious faith in peace. Both of these were founded far south of the St. Lawrence where the first colonial project had failed. One was located in a region to which Portugal considered that she held title, and the other in land claimed by Spain. France, however, had never admitted the claims of the Iberian powers to possession of the whole of America.

In 1555 Nicolas Durand de Villegagnon, Vice Admiral of Brittany and Knight of Malta, led a colonizing expedition of some six hundred persons to the harbor of Rio de Janeiro in Brazil where, on an island in the bay, he established a fort and colony which he called "Fort Coligny and Antarctic France." He knew that Portugal claimed exclusive sovereignty there, but he hoped to be strong enough to defy her. A soldier of fortune with extremely tolerant religious views, Villegagnon wished to found in this far-off, fertile region a colony where a new community might prosper and where God could be worshiped without persecution. Coligny and Calvin encouraged the project under the impression that the leader was a Protestant, while Henry II gave him money and two vessels with no

Queen Elizabeth. Engraved by Isaac Olivier. No date. (Courtesy of the New York Public Library)

Sir Walter Ralegh. Engraved
in 1821 by J. Fitler, A.R.A.
From an original picture in the
collection of Her Grace the
Duchess of Dorset. (Courtesy
of the New York Public Library)

Sir Francis Drake. Engraved by S. Freeman.
No date. (Courtesy of the New York Public
Library)

Queen Elizabeth knighting Drake on the deck of the Golden Hind at Deptford,
April 4, 1581. From a drawing by Sir John Gilbert, R.A.

Typical ships of the discovery era. (*Left*) facsimile of an armed British ship such as was used by Sir Walter Ralegh and others. From a treatise on "Nauigation, late collected out of the best Modern writers thereof, by Mr. Blundiuile," published in 1595. (*Right*) Henry Hudson's ship shown below the Palisades of the Hudson River. Drawn by L. Simond and engraved by A. B. Durand. (Both courtesy of the New York Public Library)

The burning of San José de Oruna, Spanish capital of Trinidad, by Sir Walter Ralegh in 1595. (Courtesy of the New York Public Library)

Henry Hudson by Paul Van Somer. (Courtesy of the New York City Art Commission)

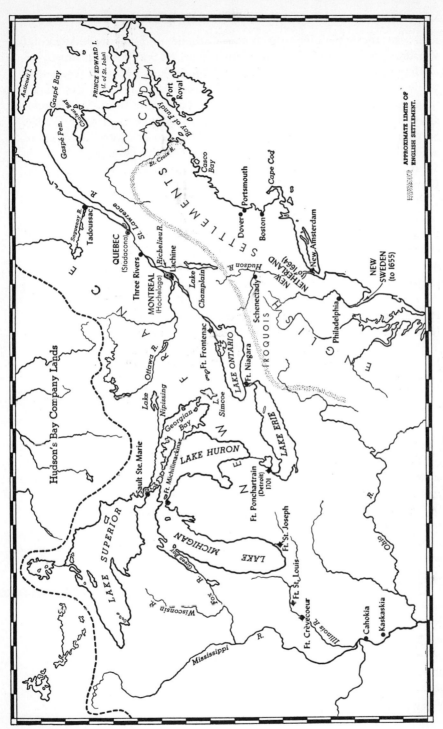

12. Lands of Early French Exploration and Settlement

idea that the expedition was not a Catholic undertaking.[6] A second squadron in 1557 brought to Rio three hundred additional colonists, including some Protestants from Geneva. Famine, however, soon threatened, while religious dissension between the Roman Catholics and the Protestants early broke the colonies into two contending factions. Villegagnon sided with the Catholics and finally in 1559 set out in disgust for France. Some of the colonists followed him home, while others, after a successful attack by a large Portuguese expedition under the Governor, Mem de Sá, in March, 1560, scattered to live among the natives. Thus the second French colonial experiment failed.

Five years later France made a third effort, this time in Florida, to which the court now laid claim on the basis of Verrazano's discoveries. Previous to 1561 the Spaniards, as the French well knew, had carried on active colonization in this region, reputedly rich in gold and silver, but had become discouraged and abandoned their efforts. They continued however to claim sovereignty over this section of the coast on the basis of the work of Ponce de León, De Soto, and others. The new French venture was planned by François de Coligny who, in 1562, sent Jean Ribaut, a capable, debonair leader and strong Protestant, with a little company of settlers, most of them Huguenots, to the Florida coast. In designing this venture the Admiral was not only planning a haven of refuge for his persecuted coreligionists, but acting in the larger interests of France; he realized the strategic importance of such a colony located within easy striking distance of the Florida channel through which the Spanish silver fleets passed on their way home. In other words, the planting of the colony was a move in the long and bitter drama of Franco-Spanish rivalry. On arrival at the mouth of St. Johns River Ribaut reared a stone column bearing the arms of the King of France, but settled his colony farther north on the coast of what is today South Carolina near the site of the abandoned Spanish settlement of Santa Elena. After building a fort called Charlesfort to protect this new settlement, which he named Port Royal, Ribaut returned to France for more settlers. The colonists whom he left behind barely managed to survive a winter of starvation and in the spring built a ship and sailed for home.

Despite this inauspicious beginning, Coligny persevered and in 1564 sent a larger group to the same general location under the leadership of René de Laudonnière, a Protestant noble of fine character. Laudonnière established his colony on the Florida coast where Ribaut had erected the column at the mouth of St. Johns River, and built a fort called Fort Caroline. Famine, disease, and discontent followed; eighty of the men mutinied,

---

[6] Wrong, *op. cit.*, p. 79.

put Laudonnière in chains, and went off on a piratical expedition to Española and Jamaica where most of them were caught by the Spaniards. Those left at Fort Caroline tried in vain to secure food from the natives and were making ready to depart for France in a ship secured from a chance visit by the English John Hawkins when, on August 28, 1565, Ribaut arrived with seven ships and a reinforcement of three hundred men. This new group had had barely a week to establish itself when a Spanish fleet under Pedro Menéndez de Avilés arrived off the French settlement with a commission from Philip II to extirpate the French heretics and hold Florida for Spain. A bitter fight of many incidents ensued, in the course of which Menéndez's men massacred most of the men, women, and children at Fort Caroline and treacherously put to the knife an armed force under Ribaut that, sailing to attack St. Augustine, had been driven by storm and starvation into the hands of the Spaniards. Able Jean Ribaut who "could do more in one year than another in ten" was stabbed to death. When the struggle was over a thousand Frenchmen had perished; the Spaniards were firmly established at St. Augustine, and the French had lost all hold on Florida.

This was no chance exploit on the part of the Spaniards. Although a merciless religious bigot, Menéndez must be credited with competence and statesmanship of a high order. He was probably one of the ablest naval strategists that Spain ever possessed. He fully grasped the transcendent importance to the continuance of Spanish power in the Caribbean of putting an end to French intrusion in Florida. Captain-General in charge of the Indies trade, he had devoted himself for years to perfecting the convoy system and had long been urging upon the court the construction of a Spanish fortress on the Florida coast for the defense of the vital Bahama Channel. His plans for such a rampart of empire were already far advanced when the French appeared. The Coligny project threatened his whole scheme of defense for the trade of the Indies and he felt that a bitter and ruthless lesson was necessary.

Thus within twenty-five years in the middle of the sixteenth century (1541-1565), France had failed in three attempts to establish a permanent colony on the mainland. The object of the first, on the St. Lawrence, was the creation of a center for the fur trade and a base for further exploration, especially in the hope of the discovery of a northwest passage. There were no active rival European claims in this Canadian region, but cold and fear of the Indians broke up the settlement. The second attempt was made in Brazil at the expense of the Portuguese, whose claims were known, and followed a half century of contraband trading activities along the South American coast. The aim here was a double one: on the part of the king to plant a colonial establishment in America, on the part of the Huguenot settlers to found a colony where they could worship as they pleased. Religious dissensions ruined the settlement. The third attempt, made on the Florida coast in lands claimed by Spain, was a private venture supported by Coligny and, like the Brazilian undertaking, had a double purpose. It aimed at founding a settlement where freedom of religion might exist, and at the same time proposed to establish a useful overseas base against the colonial possessions of the Hapsburg rival. It failed because of vigilant Spanish hostility. All three attempts were made in different localities; all were at least double efforts at settlement and had more than one purpose; all involved a large measure of private enterprise, and in every case the leaders were intelligent and high-minded men who were both able and persistent. In the last two attempts the heretical element was large. Invariably it proved hard to find French colonists, and many men of all the expeditions were sweepings from the French jails.

The explanation seems to be that in this century the European commitments of France were too great to permit success in establishing any well-founded, permanent colonial settlements. European wars drained away any surplus in the population and absorbed the energies and resources of the government. Such overseas undertakings as there were in the sixteenth century reflected in many respects the European issues of the age. In his struggle with Spain the French king was glad of an opportunity to dispute his rival's colonial claims; meanwhile, the religious conflicts in Europe were responsible for the Huguenot element in the colonial ventures, as well as the rivalries of Protestants and Catholics within the colonies and the bitter attacks of Spanish Catholics on French Protestants.

The most persistent French challenge to Spanish and Portuguese monopolistic claims came from the pirates, contrabandists, and privateers who swarmed about the coast of both American continents, insistently contesting throughout the sixteenth century the claims of the Iberians to exclusive rights in the waters off their shores and resisting especially the effort of Spain to make the Caribbean a *mare clausum*. In the first half of this sixteenth century the French far outnumbered all other contenders for the freedom of the seas. The Brazilian coast, long lightly held by Portugal, was early the scene of contraband activities. From 1504 onward, bold individual French traders were constantly reported to Lisbon as trading along that coast. So serious had the menace become by 1530 that the Portuguese king complained to the French court that the corsairs in a single year had captured three hundred of his ships and caused him a loss of half a million *cruzadas*.[7] It was his fear as to where these French

---

[7] H. I. Priestley, *France Overseas through the Old Regime* (New York: 1939), p. 39, note.

activities might lead that decided him to tighten Portuguese control of Brazil by the establishment of the captaincies.

The challenge to Spanish dominion began as early as Columbus' second journey, on the return from which the explorer found a fleet of French privateers waiting for him between the Azores and the Spanish coast. This area for a time became the principal scene of piratical operations. Here in 1523 units of the fleet of twenty or thirty armed vessels, directed and partly owned by the notorious Jean Ango of Dieppe, succeeded in cutting off two of the richest of the galleons bringing the treasures from the conquest of Mexico despatched by Cortés to the emperor. Years later, in 1537, the same fleet intercepted nine of the vessels bringing home the booty from the conquest of Peru.[8]

In time the corsairs moved westward across the Atlantic and made the Caribbean, with its ample hiding possibilities, their principal headquarters. Here they preyed upon coastal shipping and dreamed of, and at times succeeded in, cutting off strays from the silver fleet. In the decade of the 1540's there were at least eight major corsair attacks on Spanish shipping.[9] The same period also saw a number of damaging raids on Spanish-American harbors: Santa Marta was sacked in 1542 by eight hundred French pirates, and Cartagena in the following year suffered a like fate at the hands of three hundred French and English corsairs who carried off thirty-five thousand gold pesos. In the next decade the piratical attacks eased somewhat, though in 1555 Habana was mercilessly sacked for eighteen days and then burned by French Huguenot pirates who claimed to be friends of Admiral Coligny.

In their efforts to force the freedom of the seas, the freebooters paid little attention to official declarations of war and peace, though the depredations were usually stepped up in time of war. By 1559, when the Treaty of Cateau-Cambrésis was signed, bringing to a close a period of sixty years of Valois-Hapsburg warfare, the pirates had compelled the tacit recognition by the maritime powers of the principle of "no peace beyond the line." This meant that in the area lying west and south of the right angle formed by the meridian passing through the Island of Ferro in the Azores and the Tropic of Cancer as it cuts across that meridian eastward, no breach of the peace was to be held as affecting international relations in Europe. As hostility between the French and Spanish crown lessened after the treaty of 1559, and with the beginning of the reign of Queen Elizabeth and her tacit (and sometimes avowed) encouragement of English buccaneering at the Catholic King's expense, the relative numbers of

[8] A. P. Newton, *The European Nations in the West Indies, 1493-1688* (London: 1933), chap. iv, pp. 48 and 52.
[9] Priestley, *op. cit.*, p. 39.

French and English corsairs in the Caribbean came to be reversed, though France could still send 260 vessels from a single port on predatory trans-Atlantic voyages in the period 1571 to 1588.[10]

By the second half of the sixteenth century, Spanish methods for protecting her silver fleets, and to a lesser extent Caribbean coastal cities and trade, had reached a creditable standard of efficiency, considering the immensity of the task. By 1556 the fleet system had been fully organized and ordinances governing it had been elaborated. The *flota* and galleons, each separately organized, traveled under the escort of units from the *armada de la carrera*.[11] While straying vessels were sometimes caught by pirates, it was eighty years before a whole fleet was captured, although hundreds of pirates were every year scheming to bring off such an exploit. The shore defenses were more vulnerable to attack, though the strategically more important harbors associated with the transatlantic trade were given a measure of protective attention. Between 1560 and 1566 Habana, the assembly port for the silver fleet, was heavily fortified, and in the same decade St. Augustine was strengthened with a view to guarding the dangerously exposed Bahama Channel.

Provision for the purely local policing of Caribbean waters fell far short of being adequate. Now and again units from the armada de la carrera would be temporarily detached to chase away the pirates, but as soon as the warships had resumed their primary escort duty the "black brethren" would always return and roam the Caribbean at will, pouncing on any coastal settlement or vessel engaged in coastwise trade which they thought would repay plundering. The organization in 1582 of two light police flotillas, known as the *armadas de barlovento* or Windward squadrons, for a time greatly improved the security of the Caribbean shores, but they were not consistently maintained in strength. In her efforts to make the Caribbean a closed sea and prevent access to all American lands, whether occupied or not, Spain was attempting the impossible; however, the complete break-through by her rivals did not come until the sixteenth century had closed.

II. THE FIRST ENGLISHMEN IN AMERICA

England entered late into the race for colonial possessions, and it was not until the seventeenth century that her first permanent colony was planted on the American continent. There were many reasons for the delay. Unlike Spain, Portugal, and France, England was geographically far

---

[10] *Ibid.*, p. 77.
[11] For the work of Menéndez de Avilés in this connection see P. A. Means, *The Spanish Main* (New York: 1935), pp. 81-82 and also Newton, *op. cit.*, pp. 82-84.

away from the crossroads of world trade which until late in the sixteenth century continued to be the Mediterranean area. England was even practically excluded from the nearer Baltic, as this trading area in the sixteenth century was monopolized by the Hanseatic League. As for the Atlantic, Spain under the "Catholic Kings" was mistress of the sea, and continued so until the defeat of the Spanish Armada at the close of the century. English sailors possessed little technical seamanship or the knowledge of charts and instruments that was to distinguish them later. Italians, because of their centuries of experience in the Mediterranean, were the first seamen of Europe, though Spanish and Portuguese sailors were now threatening to surpass them. The English Royal Navy, as the sixteenth century opened, was small and of little account. It was not until well into Henry VIII's reign that the fleet was transferred from its medieval base on the south coast to a headquarters in the Thames and was given the support of docks and arsenals constructed for its use. English ships were few and English sailors scarce.

Economically England was still a small nation of six million people and was only just beginning to struggle out of the agricultural swaddling clothes of the Middle Ages. English cities were small and English merchants comparatively few in number and not yet of the moneyed class. Wealth was still largely invested in land, and liquid capital for overseas or other adventures was consequently almost totally lacking. Spain, Portugal, and France had all struggled out of the turmoil of the fifteenth century earlier than England and secured the national unification needed to provide a conscious background of strength at home so necessary before overseas adventures could be successfully embarked upon. Even when, with the succession of Henry VII, England had finally secured a strong royal house and able rulers, the lack of a wholly clear hereditary title to the crown made it advisable for the early Tudors to use extreme caution before embarking on high adventures. Furthermore, the first Tudor, Henry VII, was a frugal man and not naturally inclined to adventures of doubtful profit. His son, Henry VIII, became immersed in controversies growing out of his marital difficulties with the Church, Parliament, and foreign powers. Edward VI and Mary were both greatly absorbed in the issues of the Protestant Revolt. In the light of these circumstances it is not strange that in the first half of the sixteenth century there was relatively little English activity overseas. The country possessed neither the capital, sea power, nor freedom from distraction at home needed for such undertakings.

The first English voyages to America, however, came in this period, and though they were not followed up at the time and were long considered of little consequence, they later acquired importance as the basis on which England founded her claims to North America. The first

English discovery in America came through her connection with the spice trade and was part of the excitement that followed the news of Columbus' first voyage. Its leader, John Cabot, was a member of that Italian nation which supplied all the Atlantic nations with their ablest and most imaginative navigators. When this naturalized Venetian citizen—he was born in Genoa—settled as a merchant in England (c. 1484) and became interested in trading ventures out of London and Bristol, he continued to keep in touch with Mediterranean commerce in which he had earlier been actively engaged. Having visited Mecca, the great emporium for the exchange of eastern and western goods, he fully realized the wealth to be had from the eastern trade in spices, silks, perfumes, and gems. With the support of Henry VII, English merchants had recently forced their way into a share of the commerce and carrying trade between England and the Mediterranean. But this was a comparatively small matter. If only there were some way of tapping the rich treasure house of the East directly across the Atlantic, and one in which England could share! Cabot was a student of maps and globes and grasped the significance of the progress of Portuguese voyages along the west coast of Africa, culminating in Bartholomeu Dias's feat of 1488. In the early 1490's, however, that nation had not yet proved its point by reaching India and opening for itself a superior route to the East, though the achievement could hardly be far off. Over that trade route when opened, however, Portugal would exercise a complete monopoly. A way to the East by a western route was what was needed.

Under John Cabot's encouragement and perhaps personal direction, ships from Bristol were searching the seas west of Ireland for unknown islands in 1491 and 1492. Columbus's voyage seems to have excited him greatly. Like every other intelligent person in Europe, he was familiar with the idea that the world was round and he appears to have believed that Columbus had reached the true East. Somehow in the sympathetic atmosphere of the time he managed to interest a group of Bristol merchants and with their backing secured in 1496 a royal patent entitling him "to saile to all parts, countreys, and seas of the East, of the West, and of the North, under our banners and ensignes . . . to seeke out, discover, and finde whatsoever isles, countreys, regions or provinces of the heathen and infidels . . . which before this time have bene unknowen to all Christians . . ." [12] The crown would be entitled to one fifth of the returns, although it contributed nothing but the charter. This first English overseas venture, like so many later ones, was financed by private money.

---

[12] Hakluyt's *Principal Navigations, Voyages and Discoveries of the English Nation* (Everyman edition), V, p. 83. "Letters patents of King Henry the 7 . . . granted unto John Cabot and his 3 sonnes. . . ."

Setting out on May 2, 1497, and crossing the stormy North Atlantic in the *Matthew* of eighty tons with a crew of eighty men, John Cabot reached land in the general region of Newfoundland, southern Labrador, and Nova Scotia, possibly, there is reason to think, on a western extremity of Cape Breton.[13] He seems optimistically to have believed, though he saw no inhabitants, that he had arrived on the coast of the realms of the Grand Khan, but north of where he wished to be. Near his landfall he erected a cross and planted the royal standard of England, alongside which he hoisted the banner of Venice to indicate his own leadership of the expedition.[14] Within three months he was back in England, where he was received with enthusiasm and was feasted at court. The king was so pleased with his report that he rewarded some of the English sailors, ordered Cabot to be paid £10 and granted him a pension of £20 a year.[15] On the basis of this first success, Cabot secured in the following year a second patent and more backing and was able to set out on the second voyage in May, 1498, with two ships and 300 men. This time the king advanced considerable sums towards the expenses. It was hoped that he would return with his ships laden with eastern silks, spices, and gems.

It is now thought that on this second journey Cabot first steered far to the north, along the Greenland coast and then, when stopped by icebergs, turned southward and skirted the North American mainland, passing along the shores of Labrador, Newfoundland, Nova Scotia, New England, and proceeded possibly as far south as Chesapeake Bay.[16] From this point, we know little about Cabot. On his return to England he could only have made the disappointing report that he had not found the East but new, cold, bleak, mostly uninhabited lands from which there could be no hope of gold or profitable oriental trade. He was probably considered a failure and dropped into obscurity. The results of Cabot's work, however, were extensive and important. The individual to profit most from his enterprises was his son, Sebastian Cabot, whose facile pen enabled him in later years, after he had won a glamorous reputation in the service of Spain, to magnify the part he claimed to have taken in the first of the northern voyages and thereby gain greatly enhanced prestige.[17] After his death, John Cabot's adopted country, England, used the two early Cabot voyages as the basis for her claims to all North America.[18]

---

[13] Biggar, *The Precursors,* Introduction, p. x.

[14] Wrong, *op. cit.,* I, p. 41.

[15] *Ibid.;* also, Biggar, *op. cit.,* Introduction, p. xi.

[16] Biggar, *op. cit.,* Introduction, pp. xii-xiv.

[17] An unflattering account of the much disputed Sebastian Cabot is given in Henry Harrisse's *John Cabot and His Son Sebastian* (London: 1895).

[18] The Portuguese attempted to find a northwest passage to the Indies in the vicinity of Cabot's activities. Between 1500 and 1503 they dispatched three expeditions to the region under one or other of the two Corte Real brothers, both of whom met death in the enterprise.

For a time after John Cabot's death, interest in American exploration temporarily waned in England, though a trickle of concern in western voyaging persisted in maritime circles. In 1527, John Rut, a master mariner in the navy, traced the whole Atlantic coast from Newfoundland to the Caribbean, but his work attracted little attention. It was clear to most Englishmen of that day that the new lands opposite their island possessed no treasures that could be immediately turned into cash and made to pay for further adventures. And so for some years more North America was left to the fishermen who, from Cabot's time onward, frequented the Newfoundland banks in increasing numbers but were interested in nothing more romantic than the lowly cod.[19]

By the middle of the century, the situation had somewhat changed and vigorous interest in exploration revived in England. This came about in part from an economic depression caused by the progress of the English enclosure movement. Landowners, whose estates had become infertile through constant use without rotation of crops and who found sheep raising more profitable with the expansion of the wool trade, began to enclose their fields and turn them over to pasturage. As this movement gathered strength it came to assume the proportions of an economic revolution. The common lands tended to vanish behind fences and great numbers of agricultural workers found themselves without employment. Only an increased foreign trade seemed likely to meet the situation. Interest in overseas adventure therefore revived, this time with an economic drive behind it. If only some way could be found to share in the rich spice trade, prosperity might return. Magellan's success in finding a route around South America to the spice islands inspired suggestions that there might be similar routes via the northwest and the northeast.

The arrival in England at this time of Sebastian Cabot stimulated speculation on the possibility of reaching India via a northeastern sea route. Eventually the navigator, now famous, secured a royal license for such a venture and organized a company which finally took the name of the Muscovy Company.[20] The new corporation was erected on the basis of a novel financial device, its capital of £6,000 being raised by the sale of shares each costing £25. This meant that men of very moderate wealth could participate in overseas ventures and that large-scale enterprises might be undertaken that would have been impossible if dependent upon the investment of a single individual or of a partnership. The expedition sailed in May, 1553, under the command of Sir Hugh Willoughby with Richard

---

[19] Some detail on the Newfoundland fisheries in the early sixteenth century will be found in my article: V. L. Brown, "Spanish Claims to a Share in the Newfoundland Fisheries," in *Canadian Historical Association Annual Report*, 1925.

[20] For the Charter of the Marchants of Russia granted by King Philipe and Queen Marie see Hakluyt, *op. cit.*, I, p. 318.

Chancellor as pilot-general.[21] Although this venture failed in its original objective—discovering a northeastern passage—and half of its members perished, it brought a number of important results in its train. Not only did it open a new northern sea route to Russia and set a pattern in financial organization for the future exactly fitted to English circumstances, but it also revived interest in the other northerly passage to Cathay, that by the northwest.

One of the most influential Englishmen to become interested in the northwest passage was a gallant young army officer, Sir Humphrey Gilbert, an elder half-brother of Sir Walter Ralegh, and a man of family, wealth, and learning. In a widely read pamphlet entitled "A discourse written by Sir Humphrey Gilbert Knight, to prove a passage by the Northwest to Cathaia, and the East Indies," [22] he identified America with the legendary island of Atlantis and concluded that there must be a strait to the north as well as the southern one which Magellan had found. Over this northwestern route, Gilbert pointed out, England could exercise a monopoly. With encouragement from Queen Elizabeth, through the next half century expedition after expedition left England determined to pass the obstructing mass of North America, reach the golden East, and open a direct spice trade to England. It was in the course of these voyages that the bays, straits, and headlands of the bleak areas north of Newfoundland acquired their English names years before the more hospitable lands of the now heavily populated regions of the temperate zone received theirs.

One of the first to put Gilbert's theories to the test was Martin Frobisher, a sea captain of good birth and reputation, whom a group of London merchants placed in charge of an expedition of two small undecked ships, carrying thirty-four men in their crews with instructions to look for the northwest passage. Sailing from the Thames in 1576 with Queen Elizabeth's "good liking of our doings," Frobisher passed south of Greenland in waters so rough that at times his men had to be lashed to the mast to prevent them from being swept overboard. He came at last to a bay on the Labrador coast to which he gave his name, hopefully mistaking it for the northwest passage. At this point he was induced to turn back to England by the discovery, on a headland which he called Meta Incognita, of ore containing some shining metal which he believed to be gold. When the royal assayers declared Frobisher's ore to be rich in true gold, the stock of the Company of Cathay boomed and there was no difficulty in fitting out two large expeditions. These sailed in 1577 and 1578 for Meta Incognita and there loaded with 200 tons of shining stones and made plans for a

---

[21] For the orders and instructions of Sebastian Cabot to Sir Hugh Willoughby and his fleet, see Hakluyt, *op. cit.*, I, p. 232.

[22] Hakluyt, *op. cit.*, V, p. 92.

permanent settlement.[23] What was the disgust and disappointment when the assayers reversed their first opinion and declared the ore to be worthless pyrites, or "fool's gold." [24] The bubble burst and popular interest in the northwest passage dropped to the vanishing point.

Some navigators, however, continued to follow the old will o' the wisp. John Davis in 1585-1587 led three expeditions into the region between Greenland and North America in search of a northwest passage and succeeded in discovering Davis Strait and Cumberland Sound and tracing the line of the Laborador coast, where he is said to have played football with the natives. On returning home, he drew attention to the seal and other fisheries of this region.[25] This report, however, aroused little popular interest.

The most notable of the seventeenth century navigators to sail into icy northern waters in search of the fabled strait was Henry Hudson. In 1610 he visited Frobisher's Strait, Davis' "Land of Desolation," and finally entered Hudson Bay. Here, after a winter of intense suffering, he and his son were set adrift in a small boat by his mutinous crew and were never heard of again. In the belief that Hudson had been successful, Thomas Button, in 1612, was despatched by Prince Henry of England into Hudson Bay to search its western shore for a break. In 1615 and 1616 Robert Bylot and William Baffin also explored Hudson Strait and Cumberland Sound and returned home with the words, "Doubtless there is a Passage." But no passage around the north was to be found until the nineteenth century, and then it was to prove impracticable for trading purposes.

The new direction of adventure after Davis' time came in the train of a changing foreign policy. As the years of Elizabeth's reign drew on, it became clear that the old friendship with Spain was vanishing. For years it suited the Queen's policy to spar with Philip, but deep world currents had carried the interests of the two nations far apart. England had become the chief Protestant power while Spain used the resources of the Indies to bolster her position as the leader of the Catholic forces of Europe. Elizabeth, in preparation for inevitable war, was ready to encourage unofficial attacks upon Spain by individuals. As this situation unfolded itself in the 1560's and 1570's it was seen to offer golden opportunities for profitable overseas adventures and trade in regions hitherto regarded as a Spanish preserve, and the search for the northwest passage was cast wholly into the background. Why worry about such cold, bleak regions with sunny

[23] *Ibid.*, V, pp. 131-65.

[24] For further detail on the life of this very able seaman and naval hero see R. Collinson, ed., *The Three Voyages of Frobisher* in Hakluyt Society Publications, XXXV (London: 1867) and also J. Corbett, *Drake and the Tudor Navy*, I, *passim*.

[25] For accounts of Davis's journeys see Hakluyt, *op. cit.*, V, pp. 281-336.

Spanish America open? Why not seize a part of Spanish wealth in undeclared warfare?

The first phase came in the form of slave trading that violated the rights
and codes of both the Portuguese and the Spaniards. A certain John
Hawkins of Plymouth, whose father had long made his living by raiding
the Portuguese West African coast settlements for gold and ivory, turned
to slave trading on a large scale. In all, the son made three famous voyages
to America. On the first in 1562-1563, with a small English fleet, Hawkins
succeeded in capturing six Portuguese slave vessels and carrying them
still loaded to the great market for slaves, the Spanish settlements of the
Caribbean. Here he knew black labor was greatly needed for the sugar
plantations and the mines, but the slaves were not supposed to be purchased except from Portuguese merchants who held a contract from the
Spanish government. Disregarding all such regulations, Hawkins sailed
into a number of harbors on the northern shore of Española, not troubling
to conceal the number and size of his guns and ostentatiously offered to
pay all royal dues and behave as a friendly trader. He should not be mistaken, he declared, for one of the outrageous French corsairs whose conduct he loudly denounced. The Spanish officials decided that it would be
only prudent to do business with him, and he was allowed to dispose most
profitably of both his slaves and a general cargo of European manufactures.
On a subsequent voyage (1564), which like the first brought rich rewards,
the officials were even more friendly and Hawkins apparently imagined
that it would be possible for English traders to win from Spain by peace-
able means a recognized status in the Caribbean trade. However the
second voyage produced such strong diplomatic protests from Spain that
Queen Elizabeth forbade a third. But Hawkins was not deterred and this
time (1567) met disaster. His fleet of four vessels and two armed convoying ships was attacked on its homeward journey while it lay at anchor in
the Mexican port of San Juan de Ulúa and in the ensuing bitter fight four
of his six vessels were destroyed.[26] Henceforth, unofficial warfare raged
unceasingly between the two nations until it merged into open hostilities.
With Hawkins at the time of his disaster was Francis Drake, another
English "sea dog" of Plymouth.[27] The avowed intention of Francis Drake
and his kind, for which they enjoyed the support at home of the war party
in the government, was no longer to carry on peaceful trade but openly
to attack Spain, capture Spanish ships, and raid Spanish American coastal
towns, while at the same time continuing contraband trade in Negroes and
manufactured goods. Drake was a violent Protestant and combined in an

---

26 For Hawkins's career *cf.* J. Corbett, *op. cit.,* I, chaps. ii-iii and Newton, *op. cit.,* chap. v.
27 On Drake's exploits see J. Corbett's *Sir Francis Drake* (London, 1911) or relevant
chapters in the same author's *Drake and the Tudor Navy,* 2 vols. (London, 1912).

odd blend religious bigotry with patriotism and greed. The first of his openly piratical voyages (1572-1573), was confined to the Caribbean. In its course, he carried out an audacious raid on Nombre de Dios on the Isthmus of Panama where he and a handful of men with him caught a glimpse in the cellar of the governor's house of an immense store of silver treasure awaiting shipment to Spain. In another attack there fell into his hands three mule trains of treasure so rich that all in the raiding party were made wealthy for life. Finally, in February, 1573, some natives from the neighboring Spanish settlements led him to a notched tree on the ridge of the isthmus from where he could see both the Atlantic and Pacific Oceans.

Drake's second great voyage, on which he embarked in 1577 with five ships and one hundred and fifty men, carried him through the Strait of Magellan and into the Pacific. South of the Strait he discovered the islands about Cape Horn, and then, proceeding up the west coast, mercilessly raided the undefended Spanish American harbor towns as far north as Panama, sweeping in great booty which included a number of Spanish treasure ships. Not wishing to pass through the Strait of Magellan a second time and holding Frobisher's belief in the existence of a northwest passage, or "Strait of Anian," Drake sailed northward looking for a passage which might lead him back to the Atlantic. Finally somewhere between 43 and 48 degrees north latitude he became discouraged by the cold and fog and turned southward again. In a bleak harbor on the north Pacific coast he proclaimed Queen Elizabeth the ruler of New Albion[28] and then, on July 2, set out westward directly across the Pacific. After visiting the Carolines, the Philippines, the Moluccas, and Java, he sailed around the Cape of Good Hope and, with his ships laden with wine, gold, and gems, triumphantly re-entered Plymouth harbor in September, 1580. Queen Elizabeth, to mark her lack of displeasure at this unlawful adventure, knighted her audacious subject on the deck of the *Golden Hind,* and henceforth wore one of Drake's jewels in her crown.

In 1585, Drake again sailed for the West Indies on a bold raiding expedition. This time he had with him a fleet of twenty-eight privateers and two ships of the royal navy with a complement of twenty-three hundred men. The city of Santo Domingo was attacked and plundered of twenty-five thousand ducats, suffering a blow from which it never recovered. Cartagena, despite the strength of its natural defenses, was also taken, completely devastated, and forced to disgorge one hundred and twelve thousand ducats as ransom, and the new St. Augustine was also ravaged and its defensive works were destroyed. When Drake returned to England

---

[28] For a discussion of this incident, see H. R. Wagner's *Sir Francis Drake's Voyage Around the World* (Glendale, Calif.: 1926), chap. vii.

he bore a booty worth more than three hundred thousand pounds, and had done immense damage to Spanish prestige. The arrival of the Spanish Armada in the English Channel was now made certain. When it appeared in 1588, the English "sea dogs" trained in such exploits as those of Hawkins and Drake played major roles in its defeat, thus giving the *coup de grâce* to Spanish sea power.

Meanwhile there had arisen in England the determination to establish a permanent plantation in America. It would provide, it was thought, an American starting point for further search for the northwest passage. It might conceivably serve as a local base of operations from which Spanish possessions could more easily be attacked and Spanish expansion and Catholic propaganda more effectively counteracted, as well as provide an overseas home for the new poor of England. With both these ends in view, the first charter "for the inhabiting and planting of our people in America" was granted by Queen Elizabeth to Sir Humphrey Gilbert in 1578.[29] It permitted him to take possession of lands not actually in the possession of any Christian power. After one preliminary disaster, Gilbert sailed in 1583 for Newfoundland. There in a formal, dignified ceremony at St. Johns, before his own company and other men from some thirty-six fishing vessels in the harbor, he annexed that island as a "territorrie appertaining to the Queene of England."[30]

On the homeward journey, when near the Azores, his tiny vessel of ten tons was lost with all on board.[31] His patent went to his half-brother, Sir Walter Ralegh, who made two costly attempts to carry out the project of planting a permanent, self-sustaining English colony in the New World,[32] this time in closer proximity to the Spanish settlements. The first attempt was made in 1584 when Ralegh dispatched an expedition to explore the Atlantic coast of Virginia and the Carolinas, and Roanoke Island was decided upon as a site. In the following year several shiploads of colonists were dispatched thither, but when Francis Drake shortly afterwards stopped by chance at the island, the homesick colonists thankfully seized this first opportunity to return to England. Undiscouraged, Ralegh in 1587 sent another group under John White to Roanoke. This settlement became the "lost colony of Roanoke." A supply expedition in 1591 could find no trace of the settlers save the word "Croatoan" carved on a tree trunk.[33] It was generally believed in England that the Spaniards

---

[29] Hakluyt, *op. cit.*, V, p. 349. For biographical details see W. G. Gosling's *The Life of Sir Humphrey Gilbert* (London, 1911).

[30] Gosling, *op. cit.*, pp. 238-40.

[31] For Edward Haies's account of this famous voyage see Hakluyt, *op. cit.*, VI, pp. 1-38.

[32] For the letters patent to Sir Walter Ralegh see Hakluyt, *op. cit.*, VI, p. 115.

[33] For an account of this voyage see Hakluyt, *op. cit.*, VI, pp. 211-27.

had destroyed them. This disaster put an end to English colony planting in the sixteenth century.

Thus when the Elizabethan age closed England possessed no permanent colony on the mainland in America; the Iberians alone had a solid footing there. English seamen of the sixteenth century, however, had sailed to the remotest regions and carried the name of England around the globe. The records of their amazing adventures and achievements were gathered by Richard Hakluyt, greatest of Elizabethan editors, in his *Principal Navigations, Voyages, Traffiques and Discoveries of the English Nation*—a work undertaken ". . . to commend our nation for their high courage and singular activitie in the Search and Discoverie of the most unknowen quarters of the world." [34]

---

[34] Hakluyt's Epistle Dedicatorie in the first volume of the second edition (1598) of his *Principal Navigations*.

Chapter 6

THE SPANISH COLONIAL SYSTEM

I. THE POLITICAL STRUCTURE

It was during the first two decades after the Discovery, while the seat of government for all the Indies was still at Santo Domingo on the southern shore of Española—the West Indian island on which the first white settlement was made—that Spanish colonial administration took shape and the relationship of the new discoveries to the motherland was evolved. Here under the first four American governors—Christopher Columbus (1492-1500), Francisco de Bobadilla (1500-1502), Nicolás de Ovando (1502-1509) and Diego Columbus (1509-1523)—Spanish rule developed the principal features that were to distinguish it through the next three centuries. Rapidity of expansion from a local base was from the beginning the general procedure and, within a quarter of a century, resulted in bringing under the Spanish flag the other West Indian islands, the northern shore of South America, and the southern half of Central America. The immediate reduction of the semicivilized Indians to a servile state and the extermination or reduction to slavery of those who would not submit provided a rough and ready solution of the native problem. The introduction of a colonial government combining detailed direction from special councils resident in Spain with local administration in America in the hands of royally appointed single officials and collegiate bodies set the political pattern. The assumption by the crown of responsibility for the conversion of the natives as well as for the spiritual welfare of the colonists made it clear that the close association of Church and State, which had been such a prominent feature of medieval Spain, was to be continued in America. The earliest island settlements also showed the same striking combination of a genuine crusading ardor for the salvation of the souls of the Indians with a ruthless cruelty in their economic exploitation that was to mark the whole Spanish colonial record. Finally, the subordination in this early colony of all other considerations to the securing of the precious metals in the greatest possible quantities was prophetic of the years to come. In other words, in Española the first quarter century of Spanish rule in America foreshadowed in microcosm much of the later history of Spanish America.

In relation to the homeland, Spanish America was regarded from the outset not as a national colony, but as a separate royal domain which in time came to comprise a group of mutually independent units directly under the crown, associated with Spain and with each other only through a common allegiance to the king. Both Queen Isabella's financial backing of Columbus' venture and the Pope's action in conferring on Ferdinand and Isabella by papal bull the title to the new-discovered lands were conducive to this view. The subsequent administrative arrangements were all made on the assumption that the American lands were not colonies of the Spanish people after the pattern of later colonial empires, to be administered by national officials, but were royal holdings to be provided for independently.

In line with this view there was gradually built up by royal fiat a separate organization consisting of a number of new councils, institutions, and officials specifically charged with American affairs. Some of these bodies and officials resided in Spain, some in the Indies. Generally speaking, they followed the pattern of characteristic Spanish institutions and offices, modified to meet the new conditions.

First in rank was the *Consejo de las Indias,* or the Royal and Supreme Council of the Indies, which by 1524 had taken definite shape. Its membership usually comprised a president, a grand chancellor, two secretaries, a *fiscal* or crown prosecutor, and a varying number of councilors—five to ten or more—besides a number of minor officials. Required to reside at court, it was frequently presided over by the king in person. In order that this important body might possess firsthand information of the matters with which it had to deal, it became the king's policy to appoint some of its members from persons who had had experience in royal service in America.

To the Council of the Indies was committed supreme jurisdiction in the affairs of the American colonies in all branches of government—legislative, judicial, and executive. By it the laws for the colonies were prepared for the king's signature. These, in 1680, were codified in the famous *Recopilación de Leyes de los Reinos de las Indias* which for their time displayed a breadth of vision and a concern for colonial welfare that is not to be found in any other empire code. In its judicial capacity, the council customarily acted as a court of final appeal in civil cases from the highest tribunals of the colonies, and exercised primary jurisdiction in suits involving encomiendas, as well as in all cases arising in Spain that concerned the Indies.[1] As an executive body, it advised the king on all points of importance in connection with the administration of the Indies,

---

[1] C. H. Haring, *The Spanish Empire in America* (New York: 1947), p. 107.

assisted in all appointments and, through a correspondence with officials all over the Indies, supervised the whole colonial structure. Its greatest weaknesses were long deliberation and procrastination. This supreme central body continued to function for more than three centuries, though after 1714, when the first Bourbon king of Spain appointed a minister of the Indies, the council's functions were much reduced in importance. It continued in existence, however, till 1834.

Another important administrative body, also located in Spain, was the *Casa de Contratación,* or House of Trade. Though eventually subordinate to the Council of the Indies, it was the older institution, having been founded in 1503. To it was assigned the immediate superintendency of all commercial and economic matters relating to the Indies. Though the fundamental policies and laws in this field, as in all others, were determined by the crown in consultation with the Council of the Indies, their execution and the drawing up of regulations concerning their enforcement rested in the hands of the *Casa.* Its center was in Seville in the *Casa de las Indias,* especially erected for its accommodation near the shipyards. The civil authorities of Seville were specifically forbidden to interfere with the Casa's affairs which, from the first, increased rapidly in volume and prestige.

As its functions included the control of everything that concerned the economic or commercial affairs of the Indies, or had to do with the king's revenue from America, the House of Trade in many respects entered more immediately into the practical day-to-day life and administration of the Indies than did the Council of the Indies. No ship might sail without its license; no goods might be exported to or imported from the colonies without having been registered by its officials. It not only had the power to equip and provision ships and to issue instructions for loading and sailing, but it possessed the right to exercise civil and criminal jurisdiction in all cases involving owners of vessels, sailors, and factors, or other persons violating its regulations, or in cases of crime committed on the voyage to and from the Indies. Appeal from its sentences lay only to the Council of the Indies. An important aspect of the work of the Casa was the supervision of emigration to the colonies. Its special concern, however, was to restrict the trade with America to a rigid monopoly, and this task it performed with a thoroughness unapproached by any other colonial power.

The first step in carrying out this restrictive commercial policy was to limit the commerce with America to a single Spanish port. Seville was the privileged port for about two hundred years. Mariners complained bitterly that this port, twenty leagues up the winding Guadalquivir River, interrupted by a dangerous sandbar at Sanlúcar, was a poor location for the Casa and put a great burden on trade, pointing out that Cádiz, with its commodious harbor on the sea, would be infinitely more convenient. The influence of the powerful merchants of Seville, organized in a *Consulado,* or consulate, however, was sufficient to override all opposition; for long years the most the rival interests could obtain was the location at Cádiz of a deputy of the Casa with strictly limited powers. Only in 1717 was the Casa itself finally established at Cádiz, and not until the close of the eighteenth century were other Spanish ports open to American commerce.

The Consejo de las Indias and the Casa de Contratación were the two institutions created by the king to assist him from Spain in the government of the Indies, but the direct management of colonial affairs was vested in officials and councils located in America. The most important of the officials were the viceroys, captains-general, governors, presidents, *oficiales reales* and the alcaldes of the municipalities. Among the collegiate bodies, the audiencia and the cabildo were the most prominent. All these were subordinate to the king and the Council of the Indies. The functions of all were designed to serve the two great ends of Spanish colonial policy: the establishment of royal absolutism in the political sphere and, in the world of industry and trade, the imposition of a strict system of monopoly in the interests of Spain and the royal revenues.

The establishment of the audiencia marked the determination of the crown to recover some of the authority which, in the first flush of enthusiasm following upon the Conquest, it had too generously dispersed into the hands of adelantados and other private individuals, as well as to provide a check on the decisions and actions of powerful governors and other high officials. Staffed almost entirely from *peninsulares,* the audiencia to the close of colonial times was to remain the important resident agency of royal control in America. It bore a name which in Spain signified the supreme judicial tribunal. In America, the term was applied not only to the highest judicial court, but to the district over which it held jurisdiction. In time every portion of Spain's colonial empire fell within some audiencia district.

Actually, the authority and functions of the court as a colonial body were much extended to include not only judicial duties of the highest order but wide authority in many other fields of government as well. Its legislative functions were of least importance. Laws for the Indies were decrees of the king, forwarded to the proper audiencia for implementation; consequently, enactments of the audiencia were usually only regulations for the execution and administration of the royal decrees and therefore were of comparatively minor importance. The executive functions of the audiencia, on the other hand, were both extensive and important. In this branch of government the audiencia acted as an advisory council to the viceroy or governor of the district who was under obligation to consult it on certain matters. In this capacity it usually sat with him and the officiales reales three times a week in a *consulta* at which royal instructions were read, measures adopted for putting them into effect, and general matters of policy and administration determined. In its primary function as a judicial body, the audiencia was the highest court in America, regularly hearing cases in appeal from all lower courts in its district—even from decisions by the viceroy in certain fields—and trying certain types of cases in first instance, especially those in which the crown had a large stake. In criminal cases there was ordinarily no appeal from a sentence of the audiencia; in civil suits—after 1542—only cases involving more than 10,000 pesos de oro could be carried from the appropriate audiencia in America for review by the Council of the Indies. The viceroys had the usual right of royal reprieve and pardon, but very rarely exercised it.

The first royal audiencia in America was established in Santo Domingo in 1511 while Diego Columbus was governor. Composed of a president, who was usually the governor, and three (later four) royally appointed *oidores,* or judges, it was for a number of years the chief governmental agency in the Indies. Its jurisdiction not only extended over all the West Indian islands, but also over the mainland as it was opened up. After the establishment of the second audiencia in Mexico City in 1527, the new court took charge of the areas near its seat; with the creation of additional audiencias, that of Santo Domingo gradually declined in importance, although until the eighteenth century the Venezuelan coast, as well as the islands, remained under its jurisdiction.

As Spanish dominion spread and the districts under the charge of the later audiencias increased in size, the composition of the courts tended to become more elaborate. Especially was this true of the courts designated as *audiencias-pretoriales* established in the two viceregal capitals of Mexico City and Lima that had the important function of advising the viceroy and other exceptional duties. In these cities the audiencias, following the precedent of the *chancellería* of the homeland, developed two *salas* or chambers, one with a bench of eight to ten oidores to deal with civil cases, and the other staffed with four to five *alcaldes del crimen* to exercise criminal jurisdiction. Two *fiscales,* or crown attorneys, one for each *sala,* were attached to these two audiencias. The president in each case was the viceroy. In the less important provincial capitals, the audiencia's duties were chiefly judicial; these had presidents of their own and consisted of but one sala, usually with four oidores who exercised both criminal and civil jurisdiction. Territories controlled by an audiencia whose president was neither a viceroy nor captain-general were known as *presidencias.*[2]

---

[2] On territorial organization and the historical development of the various colonies, consult Haring, *op. cit.,* chaps. iv and v.

It was during the first fifty years after the Conquest that the audiencias exercised greatest power. Later they tended to dwindle in influence before the rising importance of such royal representatives as viceroys and captains-general who had easier access to the ear of the king. It remained true, however, that if these royal officials exceeded their authority it was the audiencia that had the duty of calling them to account, and in case of the absence or death of the viceroy, it was the senior oidor of the court in the viceregal capital who exercised viceregal functions in the interim. The court's continuity of function gave it an advantage over those officials who came and went. As time wore on, aspirations towards regional autonomy, sometimes approaching an incipient nationalism, tended to find expression within the audiencia districts. It is significant that the identity of the national states of the post-independence age followed closely the boundaries of the colonial audiencia districts, as they in turn had borne an approximate relationship to earlier native groupings.

Another body of continuing significance was the cabildo. Because it was customary from the very first for the conquistadores to mark their conquests by founding cities, municipal organization early became, as in Spain, of fundamental importance. The Spanish colonial cities often included extensive territories, at times being practically coterminous with the provinces in which they lay. Their vaguely defined boundaries made an overlapping of jurisdiction inevitable and were often the cause of bitter disputes. On the other hand, municipalities were the centers of such culture and enlightenment as colonial times enjoyed, and were among the most valuable contributions that Spain made to the New World. The tradition of municipal consciousness and civic pride that today marks Spanish America clearly stems from early colonial times.

Town government centered in the cabildo, or town corporation, which represented in America the fine tradition of the Spanish *ayuntamiento* and was the only institution in the Spanish colonies in which there was any form of representative government. While at first the members of the cabildo were often appointed either by the adelantado or by the individual founder, they were later generally elected annually by the retiring cabildo from among the more substantial inhabitants of the settlement. The right of election was granted by Charles V in 1523 and, to some extent at least, was preserved throughout the sixteenth century, though the Crown took various measures to keep a tight rein over the concession and tended to narrow its popular character.

A cabildo was usually composed of one or two *alcaldes ordinarios* (magistrates) and a council of *regidores* (councilors) varying in number from four to twelve according to the size of the town, and had attached to it a number of administrative officials, such as a constable, a procurator,

a notary, and others. At times, a particular cabildo would have its independence limited by the addition of a number of royally appointed members to sit with the elected ones. In some cases, oficiales reales also had
the privilege of ex-officio membership, as also did the provincial governor.
In many instances the governor might preside at meetings of the council,
and in such cases it was necessary that he approve its decisions. The normal
functions of a cabildo generally included the appointment of lesser magistrates; the organization of the local police force; the inspection of jails,
hospitals, and orphan asylums; the care of roads and public works; the
granting of building and other licenses; and the issuance of local regulations concerning trade, public health, and social welfare. Above all, the
cabildo jealously guarded the right of protest and petition against the pretensions of the royal officials. The alcaldes had duties not unlike those of
English justices of the peace, acting as judges in first instance in both civil
and criminal cases of minor importance.

The most serious handicap under which the cabildo labored was that,
unlike the English municipal corporation, its members had very little
control over financial matters. The revenues of the cities, as of all other
parts of the provinces, early came under the charge of the oficiales reales,
or "royal officials"; these functionaries were members of a special treasury
department of government, or royal exchequer, known as the real hacienda,
whose special duty it was to collect, supervise, and expend the crown's
revenue from all sources. In the capital of every province there was a treasurer and a comptroller and sometimes also a factor, or business manager,
and a *veedor,* or overseer of mining revenues.[3] In the principal port cities
deputies of these officials carried out similar functions. The oficiales reales
often lived in a special building called the *casa real* where the strong box
(*caja real*) was kept; each official possessed a key to this box but it could
be opened only in the presence of all. The cabildos might recommend the
expenditure of certain sums, but the oficiales reales, who were responsible
to the casa de contratación, held final decisions entirely in their hands.
The separation of the department of finance, in which the treasury and
customs house were combined, from all other branches of the administration, was from the first one of the cardinal principles of Spanish policy,
and in the field of municipal administration contributed to the growing
weakness and deficiencies of the cabildos.

By the beginning of the seventeenth century the elective character of the
cabildo had largely disappeared, either through royal measures taken to
raise revenue by the sale of cabildo offices, or because of a local decision to
make the offices hereditary, or by the assumption on the part of the retiring

---

[3] See C. H. Haring's article, "The Genesis of Royal Government in the Spanish Indies," in
Hispanic American Historical Review, Vol. VII, 1927, p. 152.

members of the cabildo of the right to sell their seats to the highest bidder. In some of the most important cities the council became practically moribund,[4] the feeble tool of a small hereditary clique whose members possessed no real power but enjoyed a certain social prestige from their connection with it. Nevertheless, though it preserved more shadow than substance in this age of growing centralization of authority, the continuance in existence of the cabildo provided a nucleus around which new forces and rising aspirations might find embodiment should opportunity present itself. One feature which was to bear important fruit in the period of the struggle for independence originated early and persisted throughout the colonial period. This was the occasional summoning by the cabildo of important townspeople to an open town meeting, or *cabildo abierto,* for the purpose of hearing a special announcement, discussing some important matter of general interest, or determining popular action in a crisis. Though the decision taken on these occasions was not held to be binding on the regular cabildo, such meetings provided practice and precedent of democratic action.

Early in the sixteenth century some interesting attempts were made by a number of municipalities to combine for cooperative action on a wider scale. Several towns took the step of appointing delegates to meet with others for the discussion of common problems and joint action—a procedure that might easily, if encouraged, have led to the creation of a colonial cortes. Disapproval came promptly from Spain, Charles V in 1530 despatching the specific order: "Without our command it is not our intention or will that the cities or the towns of the Indies meet in convocation." [5] Though their constitutional wings were thus early clipped by royal fiat, the cabildos continued to provide practically the only training schools in which the creoles, or American-born Spaniards, had any opportunity to acquire political experience. Even though this was confined to the affairs of a single municipality and developed but a limited outlook, it proved immensely valuable when the cabildos became the nuclei of revolutionary activity and subsequent reorganization. Thus while Santo Domingo still carried the principal responsibility for the government of the colonies, the four major collegiate bodies of Spanish Colonial administration, namely, the Council of the Indies, the *Casa de Contratación,* the *audiencia,* and the *cabildo* were all instituted and their fields of work determined.

Of those officials residing in America, the most important was the viceroy. He was the personal representative of the king and ordinarily had the titles and duties of viceroy, governor, captain-general, superintendent of

---

[4] C. H. Haring, *op. cit.,* p. 176.
[5] *Recopilación de Leyes de los reynos de las Indias* (Madrid: 1681), 4 vols., lib. iv, tit. 8, ley 2.

real hacienda and president of the royal audiencia in one or other of the major divisions. Sent to America to preside over the colonial government, the viceroy was usually chosen from the ranks of the higher nobility and was a person of prestige, proved loyalty, and known executive ability. Given a handsome salary[6] with a palace in the viceregal capital, and entitled to the royal salute, he was expected to maintain an almost royal entourage and conduct his court and public appearances with great pomp and dignity. He was also instructed to hold himself socially aloof from his subjects in the viceroyalty; he and his children were not allowed to marry in America during his term of office; he was forbidden to engage in any business enterprise, to acquire landed property, or to pay private social visits. As the monarch's personal representative in a kingdom far removed from any hope of prompt advice from Spain, his discretionary authority had to be very wide. He headed the armed forces that protected the viceroyalty; advised the king on appointments, both temporal and ecclesiastical; had in his charge the special duty of protecting and Christianizing the Indians; functioned as president of the audiencia that met in his capital city and supervised other audiencias of his jurisdiction; exercised the pardoning power; initiated public works; pushed forward exploration on the frontiers; and, in short, directed every branch of the administration of his viceroyalty. In times of danger he was expected to cooperate with the heads of other viceroyalties and captaincies-general for the protection of all Spanish America from the foreigner.

The most effective checks on the arbitrary power of the viceroy were those exercised by the appropriate audiencia, by the occasional appointment of a *visitador général* (inspector-general), and by the fact that at the expiration of his term of office the viceroy, like all other administrative officials, had to undergo a *residencia,* or judicial review, of his conduct while in office.[7] Before commissioners especially appointed for the purpose, all persons with grievances or complaints had the privilege of bringing their charges against a retiring official during a period of six months. The report from the commissioners, or judges of residencia, was sent to the Council of the Indies which made the final decision. Though the procedure was often a farce, a favorable report was a strong argument for continued royal favor and so was greatly coveted. Such checks on official conduct, while ineffective in many individual instances, when combined with the charac-

---

[6] The first viceroy of Mexico, Antonio de Mendoza, was paid a salary of 6,000 ducats and given an addition of 2,000 ducats for his bodyguard. By the middle of the seventeenth century, salaries had reached 20,000 ducats for the viceroy of Mexico and 30,000 for the viceroy of Peru. In the middle of the eighteenth century, the Mexican viceroys were raised to 40,000 and one received as high as 80,000, the equivalent of $160,000 to $200,000. *Cf.* C. H. Haring, *Hispanic American Historical Review*, II, 173-87.

[7] For details on the residencia and visita consult Haring, *Spanish Empire,* pp. 148-57.

teristic Spanish reverence for the sovereign and the great monetary rewards of office in salary and opportunity for graft, were sufficient to hold these powerful and distant officials loyal to the king. In the long history of Spanish America, during which sixty-two viceroys ruled in New Spain and forty-one in Peru, there is no instance of an attempt on the part of a viceroy to lead a rebellion against the crown. On the other hand, few of these officials left a record of distinction. The majority were both mediocre and venal and helped build a tradition in Spanish America of corruption in office that has had unfortunate repercussions and widespread imitation to our day.

The first viceroy was Antonio de Mendoza, a Castilian nobleman appointed in 1529 to head the newly organized viceroyalty of New Spain which included all Spanish territory in the New World and had its capital in Mexico City. Taking charge in 1535, Mendoza in fifteen years of office set a fine precedent in efficiency, moderation, and loyalty. He was of the careful, hard-working, and not brilliant type of man approved by the Hapsburg rulers. Professor Merriman has said that Mendoza "showed his Spanish training and traditions when he told his successor that the secret of good ruling was to do little, and to do that slowly, since most matters lend themselves to that kind of treatment. . . ." [8] Following his term in Mexico, Mendoza was transferred to Peru where he died in office. In 1629 the viceregal term was limited to three years, though in practice it could be extended or shortened at the pleasure of the king. The second viceroyalty, with its capital at Lima, Peru, was created in 1544, after the completion of Pizarro's conquest of the empire of the Incas. Of immense size at first and the source of great mineral wealth, the viceroyalty of Peru came to be regarded as the greater of the two major colonial honors within the gift of the king, a view supported by the larger salary attached to the Peruvian post. Frequently a successful viceroy of New Spain was promoted to the viceroyalty of Peru. Of the forty-one viceroys of Peru nine had previously held similar office in Mexico. [9]

From the middle of the sixteenth to the close of the seventeenth century Spanish America continued to consist of these two viceroyalties. That of New Spain comprised Mexico, Central America, and all the mainland north of the Isthmus of Panama, together with the West Indies and that part of North America which is now Venezuela. The viceroyalty of Peru, established in 1544, included the Isthmus from Panama southward and comprised all the territory of South America from the border of New Spain to the Strait of Magellan, except Venezuela, and of course Brazil. Eventually, after varying periods of evolution, both of these viceroyalties

---

[8] R. B. Merriman, *Rise of the Spanish Empire in the Old World and in the New*, Vol. III, pp. 650-51.

[9] Haring, *op. cit.*, p. 128.

were subdivided for administrative purposes into a number of subordinate provinces, often referred to in official papers as "kingdoms," each of which was ruled by a governor and possessed its own audiencia. The viceroy's relations to these different units might vary considerably, and also change from time to time. Over the kingdom in which he had his viceregal seat, he ruled directly as governor and acted as president of the audiencia. Over the provinces (or kingdoms) that had the standing of presidencias, where the provincial audiencia had a presiding officer of its own who in the seventeenth century usually also bore the title of governor, the viceroy exercised considerable authority in matters of major policy. In other kingdoms, called "captaincies-general," the local governor, though theoretically under the supervision of the viceroy, was practically independent and presided ex officio over the audiencia in his own capital—was in fact a "little viceroy." Thus the underlying conception for the viceroyalties of Spanish America was the same as that in Hapsburg Spain itself: namely, that the crown, or the viceroyalty, comprehended within its sovereignty a group of kingdoms, not all necessarily having the same status but each capable of having its own special relationship to the common monarch.

The two viceroyalties by 1700—at the close of the Hapsburg age—were subdivided into ten audiencia districts, or kingdoms, of which, in America, three were captaincies-general and the rest presidencies. Thus the viceroyalty of New Spain comprised: (1) the huge audiencia district of Mexico; (2) the captaincy-general of Santo Domingo, which included the West Indies and the Venezuelan coast; (3) the captaincy-general of Central America centering in Guatemala City; (4) the presidency of New Galicia, a frontier area in northwestern Mexico with its capital, after 1560, at Guadalajara. Outside America, but officially attached to the Viceroyalty of New Spain, lay the captaincy-general (after 1583) of the Philippines, centering at Manila. The viceroyalty of Peru in 1700 contained: (1) the audiencia district of Lima; (2) the captaincy-general (since 1563) of New Granada with its capital at Santa Fé de Bogotá; and the presidencies of (3) Quito in Ecuador, including a much larger territory than the present republic, (4) Charcas in Bolivia, (5) Panama (since 1568), and (6) Santiago in Chile.

In the eighteenth century under the Bourbon regime, the growing complexity of colonial administration and the danger of foreign aggression forced a number of major changes, among them the creation of two new viceroyalties, both erected in large part from the huge territories originally included in the viceroyalty of Peru. The viceroyalty of New Granada was definitely established in 1739 [10] with a capital at Bogotá and included in

---

[10] A short-lived experiment of a separate viceroy for New Granada had been made in 1717.

Map labels:

Atlantic

Ocean

D. GOLD

Mississippi R.

VICEROYALTY

Guadalajara

MEXICO CITY

Acapulco   Vera Cruz

OF

NEW SPAIN

TO THE
PHILIPPINE IS.

•Guatemala

Habana   Puerto Príncipe

CUBA   HAITI
(French)

SANTO
DOMINGO

TO SPAIN

FROM SPAIN

PUERTO
RICO

FROM SPAIN

Porto
Bello

Cartagena

Santo Domingo

Caracas

Panamá

VICEROYALTY OF
NEW GRANADA

BOGOTÁ

Guiana

Quito

BRAZIL

VICEROYALTY OF PERU

LIMA

Callao   Cusco

Chuquisaca

VICE-

ROYALTY

OF

LA PLATA

Asunción

BANDA ORIENTAL

Montevideo

Santiago

BUENOS AIRES

Pacific

Ocean

13. SPANISH AMERICAN VICEROYALTIES AT THE CLOSE OF THE EIGHTEENTH CENTURY, AND
SPANISH COLONIAL TRADE ROUTES

its jurisdiction the northern section of South America—the territories now included in the republics of Colombia, Panama, Ecuador, and Venezuela, the last named being permanently detached from the viceroyalty of New Spain. In 1776 the viceroyalty of La Plata was established with a capital at Buenos Aires. This potentially rich area had hitherto been severely restricted in its development because of the fears of the Spanish merchants that trade through its favorably located port could not be sufficiently controlled. Its affairs, except for one decade in the seventeenth century (1661-1671) when it was a presidency, had been administered under the audiencia of Charcas. The new viceroyalty was given control of the administrative districts of Buenos Aires, Paraguay, Tucumán, Charcas (detached from Peru), and Cuyo (detached from Chile); in other words it covered the area included today in the states of Argentina, Paraguay, Uruguay, and Bolivia.

Another important administrative change of the eighteenth century occurred in North America. In the viceroyalty of New Spain in 1776, the same year in which the new viceregal administration was set up in Buenos Aires, the northern regions of Mexico, together with present-day California, New Mexico, and Texas, were combined in a new administrative division called the Commandancy-General of the Internal Provinces and placed under the authority of a commandant-general. This official established his capital at Chihuahua and exercised nearly the same degree of autonomy as a captain-general, though he possessed not quite the same level of prestige nor had he the support of an audiencia of his own.[11] Apparently the change took this peculiar form chiefly for economic reasons, because of the poverty and undeveloped state of the region. As an experiment it was not wholly a success and underwent many changes in a few years.

Thus by the close of the eighteenth century, on the eve of the wars of independence, Spanish America consisted of: the four viceroyalties of New Spain (1535), Peru (1544), New Granada (1739), La Plata (1776); four captaincies-general of Guatemala (1560), Cuba (1764), Venezuela (1777), Chile (1778) and the Commandancy-General of the Internal Provinces (1776). These major divisions embraced twelve audiencias: Mexico City (1528), Lima (1544), New Galicia (1548), Guatemala (1549), Bogotá (1549), Charcas (1559), Quito (1563), Santiago in Chile (1609), Buenos Aires (1783), Caracas (1786), Cusco (1787), Cuba (1797).[12] Two of the earliest audiencias had by this time disappeared: Panama (1538) had been incorporated into the audiencia district of Bogotá in 1751 and the oldest of all—Santo Domingo (1511)—had vanished from the system when Spain ceded the eastern part of the island of Española to France in 1795.

---

[11] Haring, *op. cit.,* p. 87.
[12] Dates represent the date of original establishment.

In the organization and administration of local government, the territorial units smaller than provinces or kingdoms differed greatly in size and importance. They were presided over by various grades of local officials who were usually chosen from the creole class and were very numerous and wretchedly paid. Divisions of importance, especially in South America, were the *corregimiento* under the *corregidor* and the *alcaldia mayor* under the *alcalde mayor*.[13] There was, however, no uniform pattern in terminology, functions, or relationship among the various local authorities.[14] In the older areas the organization was more complete and consistent than in the frontier regions. Among the busiest of the local functionaries was the corregidor who had a great variety of special duties, some of which were of an economic character, such as the general encouragement of agriculture and the supervision of weights and measures; but primarily he served as a kind of Indian agent for the collection of tribute and for the promotion and regulation of trade between Spaniards and the natives, with the special charge of protecting the Indians from unjust treatment by the white man. In this latter capacity the corregidor was far from being a success. The Indians often found him their most oppressive enemy, having his attention solely fixed on retiring from his corregimiento a wealthy man. It was the unbearable cruelties of a local corregidor that in 1780 caused a bloody uprising of the Indians, led by Tupac-Amaru, a descendant of the royal Incas who then was acting as a petty Spanish official.

This revolt hastened a general investigation into the system of local government and brought the introduction of fundamental reforms. The principal change came in the suppression of the corregidores and the introduction of a system of intendants. The four viceroyalties were now subdivided into intendancies over each of which was placed an intendant. Each intendancy was again subdivided into districts over which a subdelegate was placed. The viceroyalty of Peru, for example, was divided into eight intendancies and fifty-seven districts and Mexico was given twelve intendancies. Often the former corregidores and *gobernadores* became subdelegates. In the capital city of each viceroyalty was an intendant-general to whom all the intendants reported.

The chief purpose of the new system was to relieve the overworked viceroys by providing them with assistants who would exercise a more effective check on the minor officials and the municipalities. Primarily, the intendants were financial agents in charge of all revenue and commerce, including that of the Indians. In all matters touching the treasury they were

---

[13] The functions of the corregidor and the alcalde mayor were often much alike, the official in different regions being known under one or other of the titles.

[14] Haring, *op. cit.*, p. 139.

practically independent of the viceroys, but in other fields—and their functions touched the administration on many sides—they were subordinate to the viceroys. The system was complete by 1790. In spirit it was in line with the whole program of administrative reform carried out in Spain and Spanish America by the Bourbon kings of the eighteenth century—reforms aiming at the introduction of French ideas of centralization and efficiency into the slacker Spanish system.

Instituted late in the colonial period, the Spanish American intendancies did not have a long history; it is therefore not easy to assess the value of the changes that they represented. The viceroys, feeling their own power and prestige lowered by the presence of the new officials, resented them. While it appears that only men of mediocre caliber were attracted by the new office, there is some evidence that this institution did inject new vigor into local government and gave the Spanish colonial regime an extension of usefulness.[15]

A weakness in colonial administration that the intendancies did not succeed in curing was the general corruptness and mediocrity of its personnel. The crown was constantly trying various devices to insure honest government; it insisted on detailed instructions to all officials, elaborate oaths of office, and itemized reports. It maintained a system of checks and balances in official relations which, however, did little but foster an active espionage. Furthermore, systematic review of official actions of all royal appointees was provided by the system of residencia and spasmodic inspections of visitadores-générales. In spite of these precautions, corruption continued to pervade the whole colonial structure from the highest to the lowest officeholder. It has even been suggested that at times the Spanish government itself actually connived at the widespread system of graft as a means of keeping the officials satisfied and saving itself the expense of high salaries. Spain, of course, had no monopoly on venality in colonial administration; her colonial rivals were only slightly better. In passing judgment, slowness of communication and the other immense difficulties of colonial administration at the time must be borne in mind, as well as the fact that Spain had a task incomparably greater in magnitude and complexity than that of any rival.

By the close of the eighteenth century the shape of Spain's policy in the American colonial field was clearly delineated. Following deeply seated national traditions, the Spanish sovereigns had created in the several viceroyalties and captaincies-general (each containing one or more audiencias) a number of distinct political societies that were practically separate state

---

15 Cf. L. Fisher, "The Intendant System in America," in *Hispanic American Historical Review*, Vol. VIII, 1928, p. 13.

systems, were attached severally to the Spanish crown, and had very little intercourse with each other. This separation was partly due to geographical barriers and physical difficulties of communication, but it was also the outgrowth of deliberate royal policy. Under the Hapsburgs this formation of a number of political entities seemed a natural development, but in the eighteenth century the Bourbon sovereigns, under the influence of French imperial ideas, modified the system. They inaugurated a number of reforms intended not only to improve colonial administration but to break down the isolation of the colonies from each other, to strengthen the ties with the motherland, and to unify the empire in the interests of a common defence against the foreign aggressor. But the creation of new viceroyalties at Bogotá and Buenos Aires, the formation of captaincies-general in Venezuela, Chile, and Cuba, the institution of the system of intendancies, and the substitution of "free trade" [16] in place of the old fleet system seemed only to accelerate colonial tendencies towards a local nationalistic self-consciousness that had long been latent in the audiencias.

In the holocaust of the independence struggle, the framework of the larger units of the viceroyalties and the captaincies-general disappeared. But the imprint of the pattern, first laid down by the Hapsburgs, of large-scale territorial sovereignties lingered on and through the next 150 years continued to tantalize some of the best minds among the Spanish-American leaders, evoking repeated aspirations and efforts to recreate territorial unions along the broader lines of the old empire. These larger units of viceroyalties and captaincies-general had never had the tough cohesion and practical utility of the "kingdoms" and consequently, under pressure of a great crisis, dissolved into their smaller component parts. But the memory of the old system continued to retain sufficient vitality to keep the hope alive that, if given enough stimulus and the right occasion, the dream might some day come true. Meanwhile, at the end of the colonial age, the audiencia districts proved to be the more naturally cohesive units of nationhood and are still represented by the present system of Spanish-American republics.

The Spanish colonists had become habituated politically to a hierarchical system that found its apex in a highly honored king who was regarded as an almost quasi-divine source of authority, justice, and honor. This absolute sovereign made his paternalistic will effective through a vast correspondence and by royal decrees that were the Laws of the Indies—through various grades of royal officials and appointed councils, located some in the New World and some in the Old. The confusion and overlapping of the powers exercised by these agents acted as a rough-and-ready system of

---

[16] Not international free trade, but trade free to all Spaniards.

checks and balances. In practice the system tended to favor the individual official at the expense of his group of advisers. It provided no room whatever for anything like a democratically representative assembly. This is not surprising since the national cortes of Spain itself, despite a proud history, was at the time of the discovery of America fast dying out under the determined absolutism of Ferdinand and Isabella. It would have been strange if the Catholic kings had permitted anything of the kind to show itself in their new overseas dominions. The only place in Spanish colonial life where the elective principle was permitted to operate, even for a short time, was in the smallest of the political units, the local cabildo, and this was eventually to prove an effective instrument for overthrowing the royal power.

But, while the Spanish colonists had thus been trained to accept a despotism, they had also been trained to expect a benevolent despotism. From the beginning the Spanish crown had been confessedly actuated by high religious and ethical motives and a strong sense of responsibility for the welfare of its subjects. While many ideals failed of consistent execution, they were constantly reiterated in royal instructions and measures of reform and set a standard of political thinking for the future.

II. THE SPANISH COMMERCIAL AND ECONOMIC SYSTEM

Fleets and Fairs

At this time when the spirit behind organized life in Spain was one of increasing acceptance of the strengthening of royal absolutism, the Spanish colonies were drawn into the economic system of Spain quite as completely as into the framework of her political institutions. Spanish economic technique was not particularly original. In so far as it was not opportunistic, it rested on the generally accepted concepts of the mercantilism of the age. This system set for itself, as an over-all goal, the strengthening of the national state in competition with other states, and regarded the use or sacrifice of the individual for this end as natural and proper.[17] In general, the immediate economic aims were the maintaining of a favorable balance of trade, the barring as far as possible of the foreigner from participation, the gathering in and hoarding at home of as much gold and silver as possible, the monopolizing of colonial trade in the interests of the homeland, the prohibiting or limiting of colonial industries that might compete with those of the metropolis, and the general acceptance of the view that colonies existed for the benefit of the motherland. In the colonial sphere these same ideas were later to be practised by the French, English, and

---

[17] E. F. Heckscher's *Mercantilism*, 2 Vols. (translated by M. Shapiro) (London: 1935), Vol. II, chap. i.

Dutch as well as the Spaniards; where the Spanish system was to differ from the others was in the much higher degree in which the king personally and directly entered into business dealings in the colonies, in the thoroughness and persistence with which royal authority was asserted over every detail of economic activity, and, finally, in the elaborate mechanism for the enforcement of its numerous regulations. Behind the measures taken by the "Catholic Kings" for the exploitation of the wealth of the new discoveries and in enforcing their royal rights was doubtless the view that the crown had contributed the major part of the expense of the original venture and consequently should reap the major part of the benefits accruing from it.

The first intention of Ferdinand and Isabella seems to have been to impose a complete royal monopoly on all trade to and from the new lands, modified only by the share promised to the discoverer. They soon found, however, that they would need the assistance and support of the private initiative and capital clamorously offered by their Castilian subjects and, by 1495, the Indies were opened to the latter on certain conditions. Slowly these terms were defined, with royal rights jealously guarded at every step by the imposition of definite percentages reserved for the crown on all colonial gains, whether arising from trade, confiscations, or discoveries of treasure.[18] But within a decade of Columbus's first voyage it was found advisable to establish a definite organization on a permanent basis to be especially charged with the financial and economic administration of the expanding Indies.

The first important step in this direction was taken in 1503 with the creation of the Casa de Contratación, or House of Trade, as a central agency of superintendence resident in Spain. Located in Seville, the richest port city of Castile, the Casa was composed at first of three royally appointed commissioners who acted respectively as comptroller, treasurer, and factor, each with his own staff of lower officials.[19] As explained earlier, the new organization wielded authority in all fields of government—legislative, judicial, and executive—the Spanish administrative practice of the time knowing little of the separation of the functions of government. In legislative and judicial matters the Casa was subject to the veto of the Council of the Indies, but in executive matters it had a fairly free hand. In pursuit of its primary business of enforcing a strict monopoly over all commerce and travel between Spain and the colonies, the Casa maintained a rigid system of registration of every person and article passing to and from the Indies. Thus immigration into the colonies was regulated; the

---

[18] C. H. Haring, *Trade and Navigation between Spain and the Indies in the Time of the Hapsburgs* (Cambridge: 1918), pp. 4-5.
[19] *Ibid.*, p. 7.

flow, both in kind and amount, of exports and imports was controlled; customs duties were collected; the special convoy tax was imposed and royalties from American mining operations were secured; in general, the Casa acted as a clearing house for all business transactions touching the economic and financial life of the Indies.

Second only in importance to establishing the Casa with its elaborate regulations as a means of carrying into practice the economic and financial policies of the crown, was the gradual evolution of the fleet system.[20] Its purpose was to provide transport across the Atlantic for the valuable American gold and silver shipments, to confine the trade—and so safeguard the monopoly—to one Spanish port in the homeland and to three designated colonial harbors with their attendant fairs. By restricting the merchant vessels and their warship convoys to a definite sea lane, it was hoped to secure maximum protection against roving pirates and the hijacking of jealous traders of other nations.

The fleet system was not fully developed until 1564. In the early sixteenth century, when gold and silver consignments from America were not as heavy as they later became, any ship might sail from Spain when ready, from any one of a number of ports. In 1543, however, a rule was laid down for the periodic sailing of ships in convoys of at least ten vessels, to be protected by men of war, and in the next two decades—partly because of a great increase in piracy—the system of fleets was further elaborated, made obligatory, and the fleets were given their respective organizations, duties, and goals. Henceforth until 1748, two fleets were supposed to go annually to America to carry the whole of the trade between the Spanish colonies and the mother-land. One of these fleets, known as the flota, was bound for Vera Cruz to serve the needs of the Greater Antilles, northern Central America, and all Mexico; the other, called the "galleons," was routed for Cartagena and a port on the Isthmus—in the early days Nombre de Dios, but later Porto Bello—where the trade of all South America and southern Central America was concentrated. Through the greater part of the colonial period there were no other official ports of entry on either the Atlantic or Pacific shores of Spanish America.

In the heyday of the silver fleets, the southern convoy—the "galleons"— usually sailed from Seville in the late part of the summer, though it was found impossible to adhere strictly to a regular timetable. Towards the end of the sixteenth century, this fleet consisted of thirty to ninety merchantmen, escorted by five to eight warships, and was accompanied by a number

---

[20] The outstanding authority on the fleet system is C. H. Haring. He has treated this subject in detail in *Trade and Navigation between Spain and the Indies in the Time of the Hapsburgs,* especially chaps. ix, xi, and xii; and more briefly in the Introduction to *The Buccaneers in the West Indies in the XVII Century,* pp. 13-23, and *The Spanish Empire in America* (New York: 1947), chap. xvi, "The Spanish Commercial System."

of despatch boats. A frequent procedure was for the galleons to go first to the Canaries and then sail directly west to the South American coast, passing between Tobago and Trinidad in a strait known as "Galleons' Passage." It then proceeded along the northern coast of South America until its first port of call, Cartagena, was reached. In the Caribbean, despatch boats were dropped off to carry the news of the fleet's arrival to Margarita, Cumaná, and Caracas and to collect revenues from these localities. Often individual merchantmen slipped off surreptitiously by night on private ventures to La Guaira, Santa Marta, or other trading centers and later rejoined the convoy. Reaching Cartagena, usually some two months after having left Seville, the ships were supposed to remain a week in port but often stayed much longer as there was a rich cargo of indigo, tobacco, cacao, leather, cochineal, emeralds, and pearls to be collected and loaded in exchange for the manufactured goods of Europe. Meanwhile, couriers to Porto Bello, Panama, Lima, and Santa Fé spread the news throughout Central and South America of the annual fleet's arrival.

From Cartagena the fleet moved on to Porto Bello on the Isthmus, for a more protracted stay during which a great fair was held, at which an enormous business [21] was done with profits ranging as high as 500 per cent. When the fair was over the fleet returned to Cartagena for ten or twelve days, and then proceeded through the Yucatan Channel to Habana, where it might spend the winter. Here it would probably be joined by the flota and the two together sail for home in the middle of March via the Bahama Channel and the Azores, having taken eight or nine months in all for its journey.

The northern fleet or flota was smaller than that of the galleons, consisting usually of fifteen or twenty merchantmen guarded by two warships. It either left Spain in April and returned in September or left in June or July, wintered in America, and returned with the galleons the following spring. From the Canaries it entered the Caribbean near Guadeloupe, then proceeded northwestward along the southern coasts of Puerto Rico, Española, and Cuba, and passed finally through the Yucatan Channel to Vera Cruz.

At times the two fleets sailed westward together as far as Guadeloupe before separating for their different destinations. In some years, because of war or for other reasons, there was no fleet; for example, in the last twenty years of the sixteenth century, only eleven fleets reached Vera Cruz, while in the seventeenth century there were only sixty-six in all. By the second half of the seventeenth century the whole system was in decline, fleets

---

[21] It has been estimated that at the beginning of the eighteenth century transactions at the Porto Bello fair amounted to 35 to 40 million pounds sterling. See Haring, *Buccaneers in the West Indies in the XVII Century* (New York: 1910), p. 19.

were smaller and sailed less frequently, and those to Vera Cruz were larger than those to the Isthmus. In the fleetless years, despatch boats known as *avisos,* or small armed vessels called *azogues* loaded with quicksilver for the mines, would be allowed to convoy six or seven merchant vessels. Also, there were occasionally special single ships called *registros,* which served such neglected ports as Caracas and Buenos Aires. After 1749, when the fleet system was practically abandoned, the single-register ships became more frequent. In the eighteenth century, the experiment was tried of giving a monopoly of trade in certain restricted areas to commercial companies. Two of the most famous of these were the Honduras Company, founded in 1714, serving Central America, and the Guipúzcoa (or Caracas) Company which operated, for some years after its establishment in 1728, in the Venezuelan area.[22] Monopolistic trading companies, however, never played as great a part in Spanish colonial commerce as they did among the Dutch, English, and French.

Most interesting of the voyages, other than those of the annual fleets, was that of the Manila Galleon. The annual sailing of this ship was inaugurated at the instance of the monopolists of Seville to prevent the unrestricted filtering of Chinese goods into the colonies through the Philippine Islands, a permanent Spanish settlement after 1565. This arrangement restricted trade between the Philippines and Spanish America to one annual vessel of 500 tons, sailing from Manila to Acapulco on the Pacific coast of Mexico. The value of the cargo was supposed to be limited to 500,000 pesos at Acapulco, but often reached many times that amount. The west-bound cargo of the Manila galleon was light, consisting mostly of silver and other American luxuries, but the east-bound cargoes were remarkable for their bulk and value. The ship was then piled to the rails with Chinese goods, chiefly silks, cottons, and porcelains. The westward journey to the Philippines, taking some two or three months, was relatively easy, but the return voyage was long and hazardous, as it necessitated a long run to the northeast to take advantage of the Japan current before the vessel turned south to follow the California coast to Acapulco. Long before reaching her harbor, the heavily loaded and crowded ship carried a miserable complement of sick and dying. The potential profits from such a journey, however, were fabulous, and there were always persons willing to take the risk for such high stakes. An investment of 10,000 pesos could be counted on to bring a profit of at least 100,000 to 200,000 pesos. This trade filled Mexico with Chinese merchandise. Some found its way out by Jalapa to Spain, some eventually reached Peru by way of two vessels which

[22] R. D. Hussey's *The Caracas Company, 1728-1784* (Cambridge: 1934) throws light on many aspects of the economic life in the last of the colonial centuries.

for a time were allowed to come to Acapulco to carry a limited amount of the Chinese goods to South America—one of the few instances of a permitted interprovincial trade.

The fairs at Porto Bello [23] on the Isthmus and at Jalapa near Vera Cruz in Mexico deserve special mention. These became great distributing centers, made necessary by the fleet system. The fair at Porto Bello, on the Atlantic side of the Isthmus, was one of the great markets of its kind in the world. European commodities destined for such distant parts as Potosí in Upper Peru (Bolivia), Chile, Tucumán, and Buenos Aires as well as Central America were all brought to this fair. Here they were purchased by agents of South and Central American merchants and transported across the Isthmus by mules, Indian porters, and river boats to Panama, whence they were distributed to their ultimate destinations. The cargoes for Spain travelled the same long and difficult road in the other direction. When news reached the viceroy at Lima that the galleons had arrived at the Isthmus, it was his duty to order "the Armada of the South Sea" to prepare, meanwhile sending word by runners to Upper Peru, Chile, and other places within his jurisdiction, to forward the royal revenues to be sent to Spain. In its northward journey the Armada of the South Sea touched at Paita, where it was joined by the "Navio del Oro" carrying the contribution of precious metals from Quito; then the two ships proceeded to Panama where their rich cargoes were unloaded and transported by mules and Indians across the Isthmus to Porto Bello, either by the trail through the jungle—dignified by the name of *el camino real*—or by a route that utilized the Chagres River. Other items besides gold, silver, pearls, and precious stones included in this colonial trade for Europe were cochineal, indigo, vanilla, cacao, quinine, tobacco, hides, cotton, wool, copal, gum, coffee, and many other American commodities.

The actual fair lasted from two weeks to forty days, or as long as the unhealthful nature of the place permitted. The sanitary conditions were past belief, the heat was terrific, rain poured in torrents, and disease of every variety flourished unchecked. In addition to the throng of merchants, commercial agents, and Indian porters collected with their paraphernalia from all over the vast region served by the fair, sometimes as many as five thousand soldiers and sailors arrived with the galleons. The resulting strain on accommodations and the soaring rents may be imagined. In the crowded streets and squares, among the bundles of merchandise, chests of gold, and heaps of silver wedges, gamblers and thieves plied their trade, sailors ran candy booths, and professional players provided entertain-

[23] Earlier at Nombre de Dios.

ment.[24] Commodities from Spain included such finished goods as fine textiles, shoes, hardware, furniture, rope, paper, glassware, clocks, spices, and tiles. Business was on a cash basis and prices were very high. Double the price of the article in Spain was the minimum; 300 per cent profit was quite common, and still higher prices often prevailed. In Peru 500 or 600 per cent advance on the original cost was usual.

The Jalapa and Cartagena fairs, serving smaller areas, were not so important as that held at Porto Bello. Of the European goods sold at these fairs, Spain provided a progressively smaller amount as the industrial situation at home declined; finally 95 per cent was English, French, or Dutch in origin. The fact that these goods were subject to duty in Spain before being shipped added to their high cost in America.

It was the principal weakness of the fleet system and the commercial policy of which it was a part that the Spanish possessions, throughout the colonial age, were kept chronically understocked in essential European commodities, with prevailing prices always maintained at exorbitant levels. At the same time, the almost total prohibition of intercolonial trade stifled any spontaneous growth of an indigenous American prosperity on anything larger than a local scale. In fact, the effect of the fleet system was the perpetual exploitation of the colonial public in the interests of a comparatively small number of large Spanish commercial houses that enjoyed the patronage of the crown and the favor of the Casa. Organized in the *gremios,* or guilds, of Madrid and in the *consulados,*[25] or consulates, of Seville and Cádiz and parallel institutions in Mexico and Lima, these large interests easily pushed aside both the small Spanish merchant and the small colonial tradesman; neither of these had any real opportunity for a fair share in the profits of the trade carried on between the colonies and the motherland.

To such lengths was the exclusive port system carried that huge fertile regions, like present-day Argentina, were deliberately left unpeopled and undeveloped. Seeing no way to exercise an effective control and fearing the possibility of a leakage of unregistered Peruvian treasure, as well as the possibility of the development of contraband if Argentinian ports were opened, the monopolists refused to allow the establishment of a direct trade between the Plata area and Spain. For more than two hundred years, this policy forced trade between this rich pampa region and Spain to

---

[24] A contemporary seventeenth century account of the fair at Porto Bello by the English Dominican friar, Thomas Gage, who came out to Mexico and Central America in 1625, is *A New Survey of the West Indies.* (Recent edition, New York: 1928). For a modern account of the Fair see the article by A. C. Loosely, "The Puerto Bello Fairs" in the *Hispanic American Historical Review,* XIII, 314-335.

[25] For a special study of the *consulado,* see R. S. Smith, *The Spanish Guild Merchant. A History of the Consulado, 1250-1700* (Durham, N. C.: 1940).

follow the unnatural route over the Andes, up the Pacific coast, and across the Isthmus to the fair at Porto Bello. The inevitable results were a powerful stimulus to smuggling and the abandonment of Argentina to living standards of the most primitive kind. In general, throughout the colonial period the Spanish restrictive trade policy resulted in shortages of goods, exorbitant prices, depressed living standards, universal smuggling, and wholesale bribery from one end of Spanish America to the other.

Spanish Colonies in Their Economic Aspects

Economic life within the colonies was based on mining, grazing, and agriculture. These were the occupations that were the chief concern of the Spaniards and were of primary importance in their own country. With few exceptions, there was comparatively little manufacturing anywhere in Spanish America, partly because of the inherited Spanish disdain for industry which had long been associated with the despised Jews and Moors, and partly because of discouraging, though intermittent, interference from home. The acquisition of precious metals was from the first the primary concern of the Spaniards in the New World. The conquistadores in the early days secured the gold and silver by robbing Indian temples and graves and by forcing donations from native hoards. As these sources of supply became exhausted there occurred in the 1520's and 1530's the conquests of Mexico and Peru with their war spoils of immense confiscated wealth. Then in the 1540's and 1550's came the discovery of the great mines of Mexico and Peru; henceforth mining furnished the bulk of the coveted treasure.

There are no reliable figures for the output of the Spanish American mines, but it is certain that the flood of gold and silver that reached Spain from America, and through Spain Europe, in the colonial age was prodigious and one of the greatest additions of precious metals ever made to the world's store. It provided, just when needed most, the exchange medium required by the expanding commercial activities of western civilization, and this despite the fact that the mineral resources of the Spanish American areas had been barely tapped.

The earliest gold discoveries occurred in river washings in the island of Española, but the richest deposits of silver were uncovered in the middle of the sixteenth century in Mexico, in New Granada, and Upper Peru. The important mine of Espíritu Santo, near Compostela, was opened in 1543; the fabulously wealthy Zacatecas deposits, first worked in 1548, were among the earliest of the great Mexican silver areas to become the object of a mad mining rush with all its lawless accompaniments. Other Mexican mining areas with extremely wealthy diggings were Guanajuato, Taxco, and Michoacán. The 1540's also saw the opening of the richest of all the silver mines, Potosí (1545) in Upper Peru. Two years later the royal city of Potosí was founded and soon became the most famous of the mining capitals of the New World. By 1650 it had a population of 160,000, making it the largest city in America.[26] An idea of its wealth may be gathered from the fact that in 1556, within a decade of its founding, the city spent eight million pesos in celebrating the accession of Philip II.[27] The mines of Potosí rapidly became the greatest source of silver in the world and ran the silver output of the Indies far ahead of the gold, though the latter remained considerable.

A new method of extracting gold and silver from ore by the use of mercury was discovered in 1557, considerably increasing the yield of the mines of the New World. The needed quicksilver was at first supplied from the Almadén mines in Spain, but later in the sixteenth century rich deposits were discovered near Huancavelica in Peru and importations from Europe were no longer necessary for South America, though shipments continued to New Spain.[28] Gold and silver were only the richest of many minerals found in the Spanish Indies. Copper, lead and, later on, tin were secured in quantity; pearls, emeralds, and other precious and semiprecious stones were also extracted.

Under an old Spanish law, ownership of the surface land did not carry with it proprietary rights to the subsoil, so that in theory all mineral wealth belonged to the crown; a few mines were, in fact, worked directly for the king. To induce his subjects to find and work the mineral treasure became one of the primary objects of royal colonial policy. The mining class, though it included many undesirable persons, was favored above all other colonists for many years. The usual crown fee required was a fifth of the output; this became famous as the "royal fifth," or the *quinto real*. This amount, even if paid in full (as it seldom was), allowed a most generous reward to mineowners.

Among the most prized favors enjoyed by the mineowners was the *mita*, a kind of *corvée* or forced labor system, under which from 1549 on a large part of the supply of Indian labor for the mines was secured.

In the exploitation of America, next in interest to mining were the pastoral industries, which were also of traditional importance in the Spanish homeland. This industry had to be built from the ground up as there were no domestic animals native to America except the llama; but with vast tracts of land and limitless feed available and, in many sections of the colonies, a temperate climate, the fundamental conditions for a successful pastoral industry were present. In the small vessels of that age only a few

[26] C. E. Chapman, *Colonial Hispanic America* (New York: 1933), p. 149.
[27] *Ibid.*
[28] See A. P. Whitaker's *The Huancavelica Mercury Mine* (Cambridge: 1941).

animals could be brought from Spain at a time, but every ship carried some—cattle, horses, swine, or sheep—and the rate of natural increase in America was soon found to be tremendous. By the seventeenth century there were many owners of forty thousand head of cattle.[29] On some of the West Indian Islands, for example on Española, a few animals were turned loose and left to multiply and then in later years hunted for their hides. The Plata region of open pampas with a temperate climate and no mining activity to distract attention became famous for its cattle-raising industry. Great wild herds were soon roaming the pampas. Only skins and tongues were taken, the carcasses being left for dogs and vultures. The Spanish government strongly favored this industry and encouraged the export of hides and raw wool.

Agriculture was another industry favored by the crown, though generally hated by the colonists who preferred quicker ways to wealth. However, much was achieved in this field. The government sent seeds and plants on practically every ship and, as far as possible, these were suited to every variety of climate. Through its efforts, sugar cane, coffee, rice, lemons, and oranges were introduced into the tropical and subtropical areas, and to the highland regions were despatched cereals, fruits, vegetables, flax, and hemp from the plateau areas at home. The government also encouraged the development on a larger scale of such native crops as maize, cotton, sarsaparilla, vanilla, and cacao. On the other hand, agricultural industries so definitely competing with those at home as the vine, silk, and olive culture were at times vigorously discouraged, though the restrictions were not consistently enforced and many vineyards and olive and mulberry plantations flourished.

Further to help the Spanish farmer in America, the crown constantly offered special inducements to farm laborers from Spain and the Canaries to migrate to the colonies. These men, however, were prone to desert and leave the work to be done by Indians, Negroes, and half-breeds while they sought less laborious and more lucrative and exciting occupations. Partly because of this individual dislike of farming, and partly because of the effect of a system of inheritance by primogeniture which kept large holdings intact, vast plantations became a characteristic feature of Spanish America. Both the favored Church and the heavily rewarded conquistadores soon built up huge landed estates which they worked with servile labor and with primitive methods of agriculture, actually cultivating only a small portion. This wasteful form of farming prevailed throughout the colonial age and its effects continued to mark Spanish American life into modern times.

---

[29] Chapman, *op. cit.*, p. 153.

The immense timber wealth of America remained relatively unex-ploited, although some finer woods, such as mahogany and rosewood, were shipped to Europe in moderate quantities. Dye-producing trees of the tropical areas in Central America and Mexico were, however, eagerly sought. Especially popular were logwood—from which black dye was se-cured—and fustia wood used in making a yellow dye. Another source of dye, widely cultivated in Mexico, Central America, New Granada, and Peru, were the cochineal insects that flourished on the cactus plant and yielded fast scarlet and orange dyes.

On the whole, manufacturing was distinctly limited. Certain missions, towns, and areas developed characteristic industries, such as the casting of cannon and church bells and the making of carriages, furniture, and silver articles, and everywhere such small trades persisted as those of the shoe-maker, harness maker, weaver, tanner, smith, and miller. A considerable textile industry flourished, not only in the coarser blankets and woolen and cotton cloths for universal use, but also, in certain areas of Mexico and Peru, in fine silks, velvets, and linens. Leather goods and pottery also were widely developed.[30] Towards these industrial activities which undoubtedly cut down imports from Spain, the crown in the sixteenth and seventeenth centuries developed a paternalistic attitude: not entirely prohibiting but frequently issuing minute regulations and imposing restrictions. The latter, however, were not enforced consistently nor do they seem to have been imposed with mercantilist theories in view. There were two schools of thought in Spain as to the desirability of manufactures in the colonies. One group wished to prohibit stringently all colonial manufactures that would compete with those of the motherland; a more liberal group inclined to the view that the prosperity of the colonies in the long run would redound to the benefit of Spain. The crown oscillated between the two.

In the king's revenue from America, the quinto or "the royal fifth" usually imposed on precious metals represented the largest item. Thus of the total receipts in the viceroyalty of New Spain in the decade 1550-1560, amounting to 4,867,000 pesos, the quinto accounted for 2,131,000, and in approximately the same period in Peru, of a total revenue of 6,752,000 pesos the quinto amounted to over 5,225,000.[31] This famous tax by no means represented all the revenue drawn from gold and silver. It has been calculated that a variety of other duties collected at various stages came to fully 11 per cent.

The second largest source of income was Indian tribute. This was a

---

[30] For industrial development in the colonies see L. E. Fisher, *Viceregal Administration in the Spanish American Colonies* (Berkeley: 1926), pp. 111-19.

[31] C. H. Haring, "Ledgers of the Royal Treasurers in Spanish America in the XVI Century," in *Hispanic American Historical Review*, Vol. II, pp. 178-80.

royal capitation tax on all male Indians between the ages of eighteen and fifty. In New Spain in the decade quoted above, it amounted to 1,381,000 pesos and in Peru to 445,500 pesos, each Indian paying approximately one to three pesos.[32] This tax, usually collected in kind, varied in different areas. After 1574 it was made applicable to Negroes and freedmen as well as to the Indians. In the frontier areas, little of this tax could be collected.

Items of lesser importance in the large and complicated list of revenue receipts came from (1) judicial fines and confiscations; (2) customs duties, roughly 7½ per cent ad valorem on goods imported from Europe; (3) the *alcabala* or sales tax—a legal essential of every sale and the most hated of all imposts, first introduced into America in 1574 and thereafter varying from 2 to 4 per cent ad valorem; (4) the *avería,* a special tax levied on imports and exports to meet the expense for the protection of the fleet to and from America; (5) the tithe, granted by Alexander VI in 1501 to Ferdinand and Isabella, collected from whites and natives alike on the gross production of the grains, vegetables, fruits, flocks, hides, silk, cheese, and other articles and used to provide for ecclesiastical livings, the building of churches, and charitable institutions; (6) the *cruzada,* another ecclesiastical tax of the nature of an indulgence or dispensation, extended to America in 1578; (7) income from royal monopolies such as those on mercury, playing cards, pepper, salt, and tobacco; (8) proceeds from the sale of public offices; and (9) items from "benevolences" or forced gifts to the king. As the economic situation of Spain deteriorated after 1600, these last two items became of increasing importance. All in all, Spanish taxation in America was not light.

This does not mean that the king received in Europe the total royal American income. He was fortunate if he eventually secured one half. Before being shipped from the New World all expenses of the American government were deducted. These included the civil list, the cost of ecclesiastical establishments, military expenses, subsidies for such areas not self-supporting as Florida, Cuba, the Philippines, and Puerto Rico, and the very considerable cost of transportation and protection of the remainder while on its way to Spain. As colonial administrative machinery became more elaborate, the expenses of colonial government mounted. Haring has calculated that in the sixteenth century—after the creation of the viceroyalties—expenses probably consumed 50 per cent of the revenues, whereas by the end of the seventeenth century administrative expenses were taking 80 per cent or more.[33] The balance, representing the bulk of

[32] *Ibid.* Also Fisher, *op. cit.,* 320.

[33] *Ibid.,* p. 178. Of the total Mexican revenue of 4,867,000 pesos in the decade 1550-1560 there were sent to Spain 1,769,500 pesos. At the close of the seventeenth century the amount transferred across the Atlantic was only 926,000 pesos out of a total revenue of 14,750,000.

the king's profits from the colonies, was weighed, stamped, and boxed and then shipped to Europe in the form of metal bars. Its care from the mines to the royal treasury was the duty of the hacienda real. The amount that eventually arrived in Spain, however, was sufficient to provide the life blood that nourished the grandiose program of foreign policy of the Hapsburg monarchs in their ambitious attempt to play the role of champion of Roman Catholicism in Europe.

Whether in the final balance sheet Spain profited from her vast efforts in America is debatable. During the first half of the sixteenth century Spain held the premier position among the powers of Europe with a home population virile, adventurous, imaginative, and persevering; she was mistress of the seas and had secured almost exclusive access to the greater part of the American hemisphere which contained mineral resources in unimagined quantities, was endowed with inexhaustible timber wealth, stored with hundreds of varieties of fruits, vegetables, and medicinal plants, and possessed an abundance of the finest agricultural and pasture land of the globe. From this American treasure house a stream of wealth poured into Spanish coffers in the form of bullion, precious stones, and vast sums in tribute, taxation, and excise such as no other nation ever enjoyed.[34] Yet despite these unparalleled riches, during the remainder of the colonial period the homeland grew steadily weaker in population and wealth, while the promising colonies early reached relative stagnation. In other words, neither Spain nor Spanish America grew truly wealthy in the colonial age.

The explanation appears to lie partly in economics and partly in foreign policy. The Spanish home population was relatively small—about seven million in 1500—and could badly spare the drain of the bolder and more ingenious elements needed for successful colonization, and the prosecution at the same time of great foreign wars. Moreover, the Spaniards were not a manufacturing people, while most of the colonists were occupied in mining, agriculture, or sheep raising. After the fanatical expulsion from Spain of the Moors and Jews with their genius for trade and industry, the nation was apparently incapable of developing the industrial life needed to supply the requirements of a growing colonial empire and to absorb and convert into true wealth the raw materials that the American colonies were able to export. As a result, an increasing quantity of American treasure poured into the hands of enterprising foreigners in payment for the needed manufactured goods to be sent to the colonies, while a comparatively idle Spanish population at home was called upon to pay the higher prices which the

---

[34] For some years after 1550 the annual average income from the Indies was one million ducats, increasing in the reign of Philip II to two to three million. See Haring, "The Early Spanish Colonial Exchequer," in *American Historical Review*, Vol. XXIII, 1918, p. 780.

mere influx of the gold and silver from America sent soaring. The monopolistic trade carried on with such regulations principally benefited only the
small group of favored merchants in Seville, Cádiz, and Madrid. The immense treasure flowing into the Spanish ports had the further evil effects
of giving a false sense of wealth, and of providing the sinews of war for
an insanely ambitious foreign policy directed against the rising Protestant
powers of Europe. In America, oppressive regulations faced the colonists
with the three alternatives of accepting an undersupply of manufactured
goods at exorbitant prices, utter stagnation, or the demoralizing resort to
smuggling with its attendant bribery of officials and the consequent rid-
dling of the whole colonial administration with corruption.

III. SPANISH NATIVE POLICY

From the beginning, the attitude of the Spaniards towards the native
population of America was essentially different from that of the later English, French, and Dutch colonists. Unlike these latter groups, it seems not
to have occurred to the Spaniards to deal with the Indians as with independent tribes, to be made military and commercial allies if they should
prove friendly or to be exterminated if they were hostile.[35] The Spanish
national temperament, domineering and strongly marked by proselyting
zeal, together with the natural climatic conditions of the regions in which
they first found themselves, combined to set a different and distinctive
pattern for Spanish native policy.

Moreover, it was early evident that the natives of the new lands were
too numerous to be exterminated or confined to reservations. Exact figures
are unobtainable but it seems probable that, in those parts of the Western
Hemisphere destined to become Spanish, there was living at the close of
the fifteenth century a population of twelve to thirteen millions, of which
four and a half were in Mexico and three millions in Peru.[36] The early
discoveries and settlements were made in the most heavily populated areas,
where the numerous inhabitants obviously could not be easily "liquidated,"
even if the Spaniards had had any desire for an empty, though rich, empire.
Such, however, was far from their thoughts. The great majority had come
to the New World as adventurers and seekers after quick wealth; they
were not true colonists in the sense of their being immigrants fleeing an
overcrowded homeland or oppressive political conditions in Europe to
seek new permanent homes in America. All had inherited a disdain for

---

[35] *Cf.* E. G. Bourne, *Spain in America*, 1450-1580 (New York: 1904), p. 253.

[36] See the chronological table in A. Rosenblat, *La Poblacion indigena de América desde
1492 hasta la Actualidad*, (Buenos Aires, 1945), p. 109. See also a critical review of this
study by J. H. Stewart in the *Hispanic American Historical Review*, XXVI, p. 354.

manual labor which, in any case, was practically out of the question for white men in the tropical and subtropical Caribbean regions where the first settlements were made. What was needed most was a servile native population capable of being put to work in the mines and on the plantations in the interest of the newcomers. The availability of millions of docile Indians inevitably determined the trend towards exploitation and the eventual establishment of a system of practical serfdom.

The earliest royal instructions, however, directed that the inhabitants of the new lands were to be Christianized, civilized, and absorbed into the economic and social fabric of the new colonial society. A great body of paternalistic legislation, dating from the earliest days of the Conquest and unequalled in the record of any other colonial people, was slowly hammered out, which, though often evaded, in practice eventually gave to the Indians the protected status of wardship. Though legally minors all their lives, they came to enjoy the special care of the crown and were the particular charges of the king's personal representatives in the colonial organization. And though they occupied a humble position in society, the crown insisted that they should be recognized as fellow subjects of the conquistadores and "free persons" possessing legal rights, not merely as chattels of the white colonists. The intermingling of races was actively encouraged and very soon a large mestizo class, half white and half Indian, had made its appearance and showed evidence of becoming an increasingly important element in the population.

In this process of incorporation into a civilization technically far in advance of their own, the Indians paid a heavy price. In numbers they were reduced by more than a third, falling from a possible twelve and a half millions at the Conquest to some seven and a half millions by the close of the colonial period.[37] Many perished in the actual Conquest, and many more died from exhaustion and the cruelties they suffered in the mines and on the plantations. Worry, unhappiness, and white man's diseases accounted for many more thousands annually.

It was not, however, only in numbers that the Indians suffered; they suffered also, and more disastrously, in morale. In courage, hopefulness, and initiative the Conquest took a fateful psychological toll. This was partly due to the circumstances of the Conquest, as well as to its completeness. Its rapidity and unexpectedness were of themselves overwhelming. The newcomers arrived from the sea in ships of unheard-of size, were accompanied by terrifying animals, and were armed with devastating weapons—muskets, cannon, and gunpowder. These strange white men—in glittering armor and at first reputed to be immortal—struck sharp and

---

[37] Humboldt's well-known figure for 1823 was 7,530,000. For his table showing the relative position of the different groups in the population, see Chapman, *op. cit.,* p. 189.

paralyzing blows. Advancing swiftly in strategically brilliant thrusts to the great centers of native military and political strength—though these were placed far inland from the coast—the newcomers overwhelmed or forestalled successful resistance. Furthermore, with fiendish ingenuity or good fortune, the strangers seemed able to make the very legends, prophecies, and customs of their victims work to their own advantage and contribute to native confusion and ultimate collapse. For example, the beloved Aztec legend, prophesying the return some day from the East of the fair culture-hero who would lead his people to a golden age became a veritable agency of death for the Mexicans, while the widespread native custom, by which a new chief was not appointed in the lifetime of the old, was made use of as a paralyzing military device by the Spanish practice of imprisoning the chief. The natives were further dismayed by the desecration of the temples of their gods and the general discredit thrown on their religion. Early bereft of the direction of their political, religious, and military leaders—the first to be seized—and meeting consistent and humiliating defeat at the hands of the relatively small Spanish forces, the great mass of Indians became demoralized and seemed unable to improvise either new organizations or effective methods of defense. In the long run, this loss by the natives of confidence in themselves was probably the most devastating and permanent aspect of the Conquest. It left them in a state of mind to permit, in the age that followed, their own natural cultural trends to be smothered by the superimposed techniques of their conquerors, and made possible the almost complete diversion of their labor and efforts from their own interests and concerns. The Spanish American culture of the future was impoverished by the very completeness of the Conquest.

For the Indians who survived the invasion, the greatest danger to be feared was outright slavery. From this fate they were saved by the humanitarian impulses of the crown, supported by the more or less consistent protests of the Church, whose representatives were early on the scene in considerable force. Christopher Columbus, from the first, apparently took for granted the enslavement of the American natives, following the practice already in operation in the Spanish and Portuguese possessions in Africa with which he was familiar, but he met with stiff opposition from the crown. To its enduring credit, the Spanish monarchy set its face from the beginning against the evils of slavery for the red men. Apart from very limited exceptions—and those only for a short time—the Spanish sovereigns in a long and honorable struggle compelled their subjects, even the first excited conquistadores, to be satisfied with something less than slavery.

The key institution which determined the Indians' status in colonial society more vitally than any other was the semifeudal encomienda,[38] the practical effect of which was to make the Indian little better off than the medieval serf. In origin the encomienda (literally recommendation) was an apportionment of Indians—often, in the first instance, made temporarily by a conquistador to certain of his followers as part of their reward for successful conquest and remuneration for their out-of-pocket expenses. In theory it was a grant from the crown permitting certain "well-deserving persons" to collect for their own benefit the royal tribute due from a specified group of Indians. It was first established, at least in germ, during the governorship of Christopher Columbus who authorized the acceptance of labor in lieu of the money tribute which, it was laid down, all the Indians owed to the crown in token of vassalage. In a relatively short time the whole island of Española came to be divided into repartimientos (allotments), each usually comprising one or two native villages of tribute-owing inhabitants. The same conquistador might hold a repartimiento or other grant of land as well as an encomienda of Indians, but the two were not necessarily associated; the encomienda did not of itself carry a title to land. Neither were any judicial or other jurisdictional rights conveyed to the encomendero. Although normally granted for the lifetime of two generations and often permitted to continue longer, the encomienda in its strict sense was not hereditary, nor had the encomendero the right to transfer his privileges to another individual. These fundamental features sharply distinguished the encomienda from the medieval European feudal fief.[39]

Having experienced in Spain the disadvantages to the crown that resulted from excessive powers in the hands of ambitious feudal lords, the Spanish kings of the sixteenth century were careful not to allow the creation of such conditions in the New World. The crown hoped, however, to garner some of the advantages associated with the feudal tie. Thus, in return for the privilege of collecting and using the Indian tribute, the encomenderos were expected to reside in the district in which the Indians

---

[38] Most recent scholarship on the encomienda is represented by S. A. Zavala, *New Viewpoints on the Spanish Colonization of America* (Philadelphia, 1943), chap. vii, "The Encomienda as a Political Institution"; viii, "The Encomienda as an Economic Institution"; ix, "The Evolution of the Labor System"; and C. H. Haring, *The Spanish Empire in America* (New York: 1947), chap. iii, "Race and Environment: El Pueblo Indigena." For a somewhat older detailed study of the encomienda see L. B. Simpson, *The Encomienda in New Spain: Forced Native Labor in the Spanish Colonies, 1492-1550* in University of California Publications in History (Berkeley: 1929) Vol. XIX. His general conclusion is, on the whole, favorable to the Spanish crown's course of action, maintaining that in the light of contemporary conditions the encomienda was a "logical and wholly justifiable organization of society in the Spanish colonies." *Cf.*, however, an older work, *The Spanish Conquest in America* (London: 1855-1861), 4 Vols., by Sir Arthur Helps who is bitterly critical of the encomienda system.

[39] For a further elaboration of the relationship of the encomienda to feudal conceptions see Zavala, *op. cit.*, pp. 72-79, 80-83.

lived, protect it, and provide for the conversion and nurture in the Christian faith of its inhabitants and, in a general way, assume responsibility to the crown for the welfare of their charges.

But the system was open to terrible abuses. Although the king might think of the encomienda as vassalage in terms of tribute, the Spanish conquerors regarded it as primarily valuable as a fruitful source of labor. For the Indians, it carried in practice the possibility of a double burden of excessive oppression in tribute and labor. The crown was early (1503) induced to assent to the general principle that the Indians might be compelled to work for the encomenderos. For any labor, however, over and above the amount required to pay the tribute, the encomenderos were expected to pay wages. The Indians, the crown insisted, were to be considered free men, entitled to a return for their work. In almost universal practice, however, the Indians thus placed in encomienda were regarded by their encomenderos, whose greatest need was labor, as their own to do with as they saw fit. They were compelled to render services far beyond the tribute due and were deprived, except for mere nominal sums, of the wages that should have been paid, according to royal instructions, for the extra labor. In short, the simple-minded Indians, with no knowledge of money value or wage contracts, fell easy victims to outrageous exploitation.

The system spread with extraordinary rapidity, each new area being engulfed as the Conquest spread. Not only individuals but corporations and ecclesiastical establishments hastened to share in the profits of the system. The royal officials, the municipalities, the Church and the monasteries were soon vieing with the conquistadores for the best and largest encomiendas and it was a poor individual Spaniard who did not hold at least a few Indians in encomienda and feel himself entitled to their free services.

For the crown, the encomienda represented an attempt to reconcile what it felt to be the economic needs of the time with idealistic principles bearing on the fundamental human rights of the Indians. Labor for the mines and plantations must come from somewhere and the Indian population was the natural source. The inherent indolence of the red men could not, the sovereigns felt, be allowed to prevent the economic development of the colonies and interfere with the flow of the much-needed American revenues. On the other hand, they sincerely deplored the abuses to which the Indians were subjected and the resulting decimation of the population. They persistently applied considerable pressure in the form of restrictive legislation to ameliorate the Indians' lot. As early as 1512 a code known as the "Laws of Burgos" defined the rights of the Indians and placed limitations on the exactions that might be made. As specific dangers presented themselves, further paternalistic regulations followed in rapid succession: the Indians might not, even with their own consent, be used in certain dangerous and heavy industries, such as the pearl fisheries, the grinding of sugar, and the preparation of indigo; burdens must not exceed a certain weight, nor the march exceed a certain distance; neither must the Indian be transferred to regions of a radically different climate or too far from home; they must not be employed as household servants and must be allowed time to work on their own farms; they must not be whipped or maltreated, and so on.[40] Viceroys, governors, judges of audiencia, and visitadores generales were all given strict instructions to see that these regulations were enforced. But opposing the well-intentioned and enlightened royal decrees were the inertia and evasion of the self-interested Spanish colonials, from the highest officials through all ranks down to the smallest encomendero, and even in many cases to the appointed protectors of the natives—the Indian village *cura* and the corregidor.

The most famous opponent of the encomienda system was Bartolomé de Las Casas [41] whose forty years of devoted and single-minded labor prepared the ground for the abolition of the most pernicious aspects of the system and earned him the title of the "Apostle of the Indies." Las Casas reached America at the age of twenty-eight, just a decade after its discovery, arriving in Española in the retinue of Governor Ovando. His father had been with Columbus on his second voyage and aroused his son's active interest in the New World by presenting him with a young Indian lad whom he had carried back with him to Spain and who henceforth became Las Casas' close companion. A man of some private fortune, Las Casas was not long in acquiring encomiendas in both Española and Cuba, just then being opened up. For some time, as he tells us himself, he lived thoughtlessly on the labor of his Indian serfs, enjoying the exciting life of the two Spanish islands whose populations were largely picturesque adventurers and where every day brought news of thrilling new discoveries. A strong movement, however, under the courageous leadership of Dominican friars, was in progress against the oppression of the encomenderos. Their practical enslavement of the natives, under the guise of encomienda rights, presently touched the heart and conscience of Las Casas. Gradually he became obsessed with the conviction that it was his mission to try to lighten the miseries under which the Indians were suffering. Relinquishing his own encomiendas and becoming a priest in 1510—the first to be ordained

---

[40] *Cf.* Bernard Moses' *The Spanish Dependencies in South America* (London, 1914), 2 Vols. Vol. I, pp. 206-7.   Also Fisher, *op. cit.,* pp. 320-21.

[41] Two very readable though uncritical accounts of Las Casas are: F. A. MacNutt, *Bartholomew de Las Casas* (New York: 1909), and John Fiske, *Discovery of America,* 2 Vols. (Boston: 1892).   Vol. II, pp. 427-82.

in the New World—he bent his versatile abilities as a preacher, diplomat, and writer to remedying the evils around him.

In the long crusade on which he now embarked, Las Casas placed his chief reliance for effective assistance on the crown, which he believed properly bore the same relation to the Indians as to the Spaniards and, as "the fount of justice," should be equally concerned for their prosperity and happiness. In 1515 he made the first of fourteen long journeys across the Atlantic to denounce in person before the Spanish court, with all the vehemence that was in him, the terrible exploitation and cruelties practised by the encomenderos. Though his visit fell in the interval between the death of King Ferdinand and the assumption of power by King Charles, he made a strong impression and was fortunate enough to secure the sympathy and support of the Regent, Archbishop Cisneros. His denunciations were bitter, circumstantial, and devastating, even raising the question whether the Spaniards were fit to be in America at all. In any case, he maintained, the encomienda system, which the crown had hoped would be a means for the moral and religious improvement of the Indian, was proving itself the exact opposite. It was rapidly bringing about, he asserted, not only the destruction of the Indian population but the demoralization of the whites. He recommended that the whole institution should be abolished, or at least strictly limited by drastic laws. In the end, Archbishop Cisneros gave the earnest, eloquent priest the official position of "Protector of the Indians" and sent him back to America, along with other missionaries, to try to effect at least some of the reforms he advocated.

There followed many years of earnest, crusading work, punctuated by other visits to the Spanish court for supporting legislation. Las Casas' fertile brain and untiring energy in this period devised, encouraged, or carried into practice a number of experiments involving profound social changes that are of great interest. As an expedient to meet the labor shortage, he urged as a substitute for forced work from the Indians an increased importation into America of African slaves, some of whom had been in use there already before his arrival. He came later bitterly to regret his support of this compromise when he observed the wretchedness of the enslaved Negroes; but he had thought of the black men as "natural slaves" and physically better able to stand the rigors of bondage than the Indians. He could not, however, reproach himself with having inaugurated Negro slavery in America, as it had preceded his advocacy of it by some years.

With an ideal picture of peaceful Spanish colonization before his eyes, and in the hope of encouraging settlements of a kind radically different from those being made by the warlike conquistadores, Las Casas, with the approval of the crown, on two occasions stumped the whole Spanish peninsula and succeeded in inducing a number of genuine peasants to migrate to America. His idea was that they should live on terms of equality with the Indians, intermarry with them and till the soil. But these enterprises failed. This was partly because the several sites chosen for the utopias were on the Venezuelan coast where they fell heir to the odium created by Spanish slave-raiding in the neighborhood, and partly because the Spanish peasants immediately fell into the practice of forcing the Indians to do their work for them.

A later experiment, with a stronger missionary flavor, was carried out in Central America where Las Casas became Bishop of Chiapas, at that time a province of Guatemala. This undertaking was designed to prove to the crown that, if missionary enterprises were left to the religious and given a pacific character, and if secular influences were excluded, the American natives could be won over both to the Christian faith and to loyalty to the king. It would be accomplished, Las Casas thought, much more effectively than by the current practice of first establishing dominion by force and subsequently entrusting the propagation of the faith to the lay hands of self-seeking encomenderos. Las Casas' experiment, carried out amid originally hostile Indians at Vera Paz in the heart of Guatemala, was an outstanding success and had a marked effect on later Spanish policy.

Subject to frightful abuses as were the Indians in the encomienda, there were other American natives, as Las Casas knew only too well, who were even worse off. These were the outright Indian slaves who did not enjoy even the questionable "protection" of the encomenderos and were definitely excluded from the paternalistic legislation of the crown. Many of the earlier of these Indian slaves were inhabitants, such as the Caribs, of the smaller and more remote West Indian islands, who had been captured in the frequent raids by the Spaniards from Española or Cuba to replenish their diminishing labor supply. Later Cortés and other conquerors on the mainland made slaves of many war captives. Under Spanish law, for almost fifty years after the Conquest, these unfortunates might legally be enslaved under the pretext that they were perpetual rebels, or prisoners taken in a "just war." [42] Another fruitful source of Indian slaves was the process of *rescate,* which was a system of barter or purchase from slave-holding Indian chiefs; under certain conditions the courts of law might condemn criminals to the penalty of slavery; and at times slaves were accepted from the Indians as tribute. [43]

The crowning achievement of the "Apostle of the Indies" came in 1542

---

[42] On the concept of "just war," Zavala has a most illuminating chapter; *op. cit.,* chap. iv, "The Doctrine of Just War."

[43] Zavala, *op. cit.,* chaps. vi and vii, discusses the system of *rescate* and other aspects of Indian slavery.

with the enactment of the "New Laws of the Indies." This famous code of colonial laws, of which twenty-three of the fifty-four articles concerned the Indians, definitely outlawed the practice of their enslavement. It did not, however, completely abolish the system of encomienda, though it forbade the granting of any new encomienda and provided that the existing ones should revert to the crown on the death of the present holders—thus forecasting the eventual extinction of this form of personal service. In the meanwhile, all officials, priests, and religious institutions were ordered to give up their encomiendas forthwith, as were those encomenderos who had been guilty of abusing their privileges. Unfortunately the time was not yet ripe for these drastic changes and the "New Laws" proved an empty triumph for Las Casas. So great was the opposition in a number of places among the colonists, notably in Peru where an armed revolt occurred, that it was found impossible to carry out the reforms. Some of the most vital sections of the new code had actually to be repealed, while others suffered modification. The encomienda system, however, had received a definite check.

In 1547, depressed and practically forced out of the colonies by his enemies, Las Casas returned to Spain for the last time. He spent the remaining nineteen years of his life in the Dominican college of San Gregorio in Valladolid, writing voluminously in support of the cause to which he had given his life. In 1552, he published a series of tracts, the subject of all contained in the title of the first: "A Very Brief Relation of the Destruction of the Indies." *La Brevissima Relación* was probably the most widely read account of the Indies in the sixteenth century. In it Las Casas gave the court and all Spain an annotated indictment of the evils suffered by the American natives in the Spanish conquest of the New World, in which, according to him, fifteen millions of Indians had perished. A jealous and competitive world was also here presented with the basis of "the black legend" of "Spanish cruelty" that, translated into many languages, was a potent propaganda weapon to be used against Spanish interests throughout the colonial age. A more extensive and scholarly work, one less marked by overemphasis, exaggeration, and special pleading, was Las Casas' more detailed work, *História Général de las Indias.*

In the meanwhile, as the result of legislation in the 1540's, the lot of the Indians had been immensely improved. Not only had the essential steps been taken in the New Laws to free them from slavery, but after a law of February 22, 1549, the substitution of personal service to the encomendero in lieu of tribute became unlawful. This marked the legal end of the encomienda as a labor system.[44] Henceforth, while the encomienda

---

[44] *Ibid.*, p. 85.

lingered on, it was primarily a system of tribute which had to be paid in money or kind.[45]

Beginning with the second half of the sixteenth century, therefore, the encomenderos were faced with the necessity of devising other plans for securing the labor needed in their mines and on their plantations. For a time a system of free contract or voluntary wage work was tried. It failed to produce the needed quota of labor and in consequence the state felt itself driven, in the public interest, to countenancing a plan of enforced labor for wages. In this system the state itself, through government officials, acted for a time as an intermediary between the natives and their white employers, summoning and assigning the Indians to their work.

This forced labor, or *corvée,* was called the *cuatequil* in Mexico, the *mita* in Peru. It was in addition to the tribute requirement. Under this system the Indian communities were divided into mitas, or shifts, with a fixed proportion of the male population subject to be drawn upon in turn for the needed work—in Mexico 4 per cent, in Peru 7 per cent being always thus occupied at any one time. Under the system the Indians were obliged to work in the mines at a legally stipulated wage and for a strictly enforced period of service. In Peru, especially, this often involved transportation to a considerable distance for months at a time. The sanitary conditions in the mines were unspeakably bad, incidence of occupational disease was terrific, the treatment of the natives cruel and abusive, and the wage a mere pittance. The mita, or cuatequil, was the most dreaded aspect of the labor system, and in some districts summons to it was regarded by the natives as equivalent to a sentence to death.[46]

In the seventeenth century, the harsh conditions of mita and cuatequil were considerably lightened. Mitigating legislation permitted the natives, though still forced to work, to choose among the jobs offered instead of being summarily assigned. As the century wore on, the shift system tended to disintegrate as large plantation owners—in desperate need of labor—induced many Indians, by offering to pay their tribute, to leave their native communities and settle on the plantations. Here these agrarian Indians speedily fell into debt to the *hacendados* (landowners) and were started on their way to the evils of debt peonage in which they were still

---

[45] Of the tribute collected, which varied in amount at different times and in different localities from four reales to two or three pesos annually from each adult male Indian, about three quarters went to the encomendero, or to the crown, and the remaining fourth was expended on local administration and the Church. In the middle of the sixteenth century it has been estimated that a fairly prosperous Indian town would pay the encomendero 2,000 pesos a year, more or less, while a poor community would turn in not more than 200 pesos annually. See Zavala, *op. cit.,* p. 89.

[46] See A. P. Whitaker, *The Huancavelica Mercury Mine* (Cambridge, 1941), and L. E. Fisher, *Viceregal Administration in the Spanish-American Colonies* in University of California Publications in History (Berkeley, 1926), Vol. XV, p. 117.

to be found in the nineteenth century. In certain other fields of labor, notably in the mines and sugar mills, the trend was away from the use of compulsory labor, on which severe restrictions were placed by law, towards the progressively greater use of free contract labor.[47]

Taken as a whole, the colonial age showed definite stages of improvement in labor conditions—though the evils died hard and were by no means extinct—at the coming of independence.

---

[47] For greater detail on the progressive changes in the labor system in New Spain, consult Zavala, *op. cit.,* chap. iv, "Evolution of the Labor System."

Chapter 7

BRAZIL AND THE PORTUGUESE COLONIAL SYSTEM

I. POLITICAL ORGANIZATION

With the abolition of the political power of the donatarios in 1549 and the appointment of the able Thomé de Souza as the first governor general of Brazil, Portugal abandoned the idea of the maintenance of several equal administrative centers for her American holdings and adopted the principle of a single, highly centralized government. Unlike Spanish America, where there came to be four viceroys and four captains-general, all Portuguese America from 1549 to 1808, except for two short periods, was ruled by one supreme governor general whose seat was at Baía until 1763, when Rio de Janeiro became the capital. To him the governors of the several provinces, or captaincies, and all other royal officials were in theory strictly responsible. Near him, to assist in the work of the central administration, were an *ouvidor-geral,* or chief justice, a commissioner-general of finances, and a captain-major of defense, to each of whom provincial representatives in their respective departments were subordinate.

But despite this centralized framework and the exertions of a number of able governors-general, regionalism flourished sturdily in Brazil throughout the colonial period. It found political expression partly in the independent spirit of the provincial governors and partly through the provincial town councils. The tradition of local one-man government coming down from the days of the donatarios, combined with the difficulties of effective control from a distant capital and the paucity of communications over enormous distances, often rendered it comparatively easy for many of the provincial governors either to overlook their official superior in Baía and deal directly with Lisbon, or to act in their provinces as well-nigh autonomous rulers. Any slackness in Baía usually accrued not so much to the immediate benefit of the town councils as to that of the provincial governors.

Less openly challenging to central authority, but frequently very effective in that direction, were the pretensions and practices of the provincial towns. As in Portugal, the larger Brazilian communities were generally in possession of town charters, the provisions of which secured to them the right to elect their own magistrates and municipal councils or *camaras.* The procedure was fairly simple. The *homens bons,* or "good men" of the town—comprising a list of persons of "uncontaminated blood" [1] whose names alone were on the voting list—chose electors who in turn named the members of the camara—usually one judge and two *vereadores*. The functions of this body embraced the whole field of local government and at times, despite royal orders to the contrary, strayed well beyond these limits. Performing such services as appointing city officials, imposing local taxes,

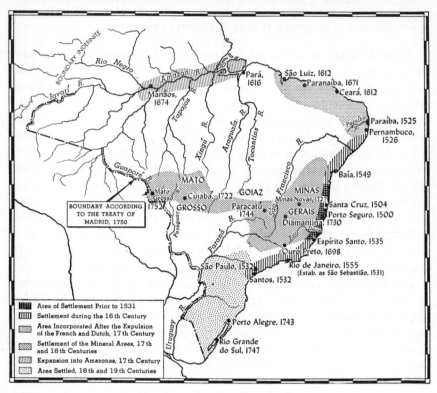

14. THE SETTLEMENT OF COLONIAL BRAZIL

fixing prices, wages, and tribute for their areas, supervising the police, constructing streets, overseeing the water supply, and at times planning the despatch of *bandeiras* and missions involving matters of war and peace, the camaras regarded themselves as the defenders and caretakers of regional interests.

Although membership in these bodies soon came to be designated largely by royal officials who presided at the elections, once in office their

---

[1] The possession of Jewish or Negro blood, the practice of any mechanical trade, or the direct selling of merchandise was held to constitute such a bar. *Cf.* A. Manchester, "The Rise of the Brazilian Aristocracy," in *Hispanic American Historical Review*, Vol. XI, 1931, p. 161.

powers, granted or assumed, though not intentionally undermining to centralized authority, were significant factors in the continuance of the spirit of localism which represented the first stage on the road towards ultimate independence for the whole colony. Moreover, like the Spanish cabildos, the Brazilian camaras provided the only experience in political practice open to large numbers of American-born Brazilians in colonial times. Unlike the English colonies, there was in Brazil no representative government on a provincial or national scale. Nevertheless, the administration of the local camara, restricted in membership and limited in functions to a narrow field as it was, pointed the way towards a future development of democratic institutions.

To strengthen the central authority and to offset the dangers of regionalism from an imperial point of view, the experiment was tried on two occasions, each for a period of five years (1572-1577 and 1608-1613), of dividing the huge colony into two captaincies-general—one in the north with Baía as its capital, and the other in the south based on Rio de Janeiro. Each time, however, the division was found to create more evils than it cured and the administration was again unified. To enhance the prestige of the king's representative, the title of viceroy was bestowed in 1640 upon the governor-general, though the colony itself was not designated a viceroyalty for another century.

A major administrative feature of Brazilian government in the early colonial period is the fact that the Portuguese crown, unlike the Spanish, did not immediately create in the homeland special governing bodies for colonial holdings, but ruled the American territories through the existing political machinery in Portugal. The colony of Brazil appeared, therefore, not as a separate realm of the crown, as was the case with New Spain, but more in the nature of a dependency of greater Portugal.

In 1580, following the death of Henry, the cardinal-king, and the lack of a direct heir in the House of Aviz, Philip II of Spain, as grandson of Manoel, inherited the Portuguese crown. During the ensuing sixty years of Spanish control, Portuguese political machinery was brought into closer likeness to the Spanish system, and a special administrative body for the colonies was established in Lisbon, paralleling in many of its functions those performed for Spanish holdings by the Council of the Indies. After 1640, the Portuguese Council of the Indies (renamed the Transmarine Council), like many other administrative arrangements, was retained by the House of Braganza and continued to function as the supreme colonial authority in civil, military, and religious matters. It remained deficient, however, both in financial control and in power of appointment to the highest offices, limitations which prevented it from achieving the same prestige that surrounded its Spanish counterpart. These limitations, it is to be noted, were consistent with the different conceptions of the relationship between crown and colonies that characterized Spanish and Portuguese political theory. In the more casual and less carefully planned Portuguese colonial system the king was less hampered by powerful collegiate bodies, both in the homeland and in the colonies, and played a more personal role in the routine management of colonial affairs than did the sovereign in the more elaborate Spanish organization. The royal representatives in Brazil also enjoyed, in relation to the colonial collegiate bodies, a greater degree of real power than was the case in the Spanish colonies.

The Portuguese king was particularly fortunate in his choice of early governors-general. With the arrival in Brazil in 1549 of the capable Thomé de Souza, a Portuguese noble who had already had a notable career in Africa and India, the new royal administration got off to a good start. Though de Souza's immediate successor was not particularly brilliant, his short occupancy was followed by the long term of distinguished service of Mem de Sá who remained in America for eighteen years and proved one of the ablest executives Portugal ever sent to Brazil. Through the efforts of these and other early governors the warring donatarios were gradually brought under a measure of control, the neglected financial interests of the crown were cared for, the Indians were pacified or driven back, immigration on a large scale was encouraged, sugar, tobacco, and cotton plantations were laid out, cattle and other domestic animals and a great variety of plants were introduced, and serious attention was given to the pressing economic and social problems that beset the new colony.

Little was done, however, to correct the notoriously corrupt and inefficient administration of justice in the courts, which was one of the weakest features of the Portuguese colonial system. This inadequacy was in part due to the small delegation of authority from Portugal. Only comparatively minor cases could be tried in the Brazilian courts even by the ouvidor-geral himself. All suits involving severe penalties or sums of more than $300, and in any case those touching persons of high rank, had to go for final decision to Lisbon.

II. PLANTATION SYSTEM

In the century and a half from Thomé de Souza's arrival in 1549 till the close of the seventeenth century, Brazil remained primarily an agricultural colony with its principal development occurring in the sugar states along the eastern and northeastern coasts of the "bulge." The royal captaincy of Baía, or São Salvador, with its splendid harbor of Todos os Santos and its broad fertile plains, became the center of this development.

It had been purchased by the crown from the son of the first donatario, whose cruelty and incompetence had brought devastating Indian attacks on his unfortunate captaincy and accomplished his own destruction at the hands of his outraged savage subjects, who finally literally devoured him. Under the new regime, Baía in 1549 was designated as the seat of the general government and took on a new lease on life. It occupied a strategic position. Immediately to the north was the rich captaincy of Pernambuco, with its two rival but prosperous settlements of Olinda and Recife. Still farther north were the regions of Paraíba, Rio Grande do Norte, and Ceará which were pacified in the last two decades of the sixteenth century and developed as rich sugar colonies. Through the seventeenth century, tobacco and cotton, both indigenous plants in Brazil before the white man's arrival, became lucrative export crops. Cacao, too, was cultivated, after its introduction in 1665, but never became economically important in the colonial age. Southward from Baía in Espírito Santo and in the more temperate regions about Rio de Janeiro, and in the southern captaincy of São Vicente with its more important inland colony of São Paulo—economic life, though still to some extent based on sugar, tobacco and cotton, tended to be more varied. Here cattle raising and the growing of cereals and fruits diversified the agricultural scene. To the west, along both banks of the São Francisco River, and in the backlands of Baía, Pernambuco, and Paraíba, an enormous cattle industry developed supplying *zarque* or "jerked beef" as a basic article of food for all Brazil, as well as providing the leather for which colonial life found numerous uses in the manufacture of furniture, implements, garments, and shoes.

Until the close of the seventeenth century, however, "sugar was king" and the land on which it could be grown the most sought-after possession. A writer of 1711,[2] who was severely punished and his work confiscated by a secretive Portuguese government for giving away to outsiders so much valuable information, described Baía as possessing at that date 146 sugar mills that annually produced a surplus for export of 14,500 cases of sugar, each weighing 35 *arrobas*.[3] Pernambuco, he said, sent abroad from its 246 mills 10,300 cases, while Rio with 136 mills exported 10,220 cases. The world, however, stood in no need of these figures to be made aware that Brazil was supplying most of the sugar consumed by Europe. In return she received through Lisbon such manufactured goods as the colonists required.

Within Brazil itself, plantation life was the characteristic feature of the period and found its center in the "casa grande," the residence of the plantation owner. This served at once as a social center, office, fortress,

---

[2] André João Antonil, a Jesuit priest. See Manchester, *op. cit.*, footnote 2, p. 152.
[3] An old Portuguese weight used in Brazil. It was equal to 32.38 pounds avoir.

school, hospital, bank, and guest house for an integrated community that was to a high degree self-contained, self-sufficient, isolated from its neighbors, and patriarchal in character.[4] Each individual unit was large, not only because the original government grants had been lavish but also because the plantation from the beginning showed a constant propensity to grow at the expense of the small independent farmers. Many of the latter, giving up the unequal struggle, came eventually to work for the large proprietors in return for shelter, clothing, and food, becoming practically a peon class. Others more fortunate rented land from the plantation owner and were under contract to send their sugar to the *senhor's* mill. In some fashion the great majority of the rural population, especially in the north, came to be attached to the life of the plantation. Virtually a petty kingdom ruled over by the senhor, the plantation offered a variety of occupations that provided recognition for varying class and professional distinctions. From the priest who acted as chaplain through the overseers, carpenters, millers, cobblers, blacksmiths, carters, cattlemen, house servants, workers in the mills, and field slaves—of which a large plantation might have a hundred and fifty to two hundred—all looked to the senhor as master. The symbol of the latter's wealth and position was the sugar mill—the *engenho*—which, it has been pointed out,[5] conferred on the owner much the same kind of prestige in sixteenth and seventeenth century Brazil as did a castle in medieval Europe.

Life in the casa grande was as luxurious as the owner could make it, reflecting the extravagant and ostentatious standards of the age. Contemporary writers describe with relish the velvets, damasks, and silks worn by the women and children of the casa grande, the blooded horses that every senhor prided himself on possessing, and the lavish hospitality that he delighted to dispense.[6]

This powerful landed aristocracy, living on isolated plantations with their fortunes identified with the economic life of the colony, was a characteristic Brazilian development and tended to give a distinctive flavor to Portuguese America. These senhors, unlike the wealthy Spanish colonists, showed no tendency whatever to congregate in towns. Though they were careful to retain the legal right to vote in the elections of the nearest town, and so in a measure to control local politics, they definitely preferred to live on their *latifundia*. The towns and the commercial occupations within them were left to Portuguese middle-class immigrants, the majority of whom clung to the hope of making a quick fortune and returning home to

---

[4] J. A. Martin, "Portugal in Brazil," in *Hispanic American Historical Review*, Vol. XVII, 1937, p. 195.

[5] *Ibid.*, p. 189.

[6] *Ibid.*, pp. 195-96; also *cf.* Manchester, *op. cit.*, pp. 153-55.

Europe. They were despised by the Brazilian aristocracy, both for their interest in trade and their nostalgia.

III. NATIVE POLICY

The greatest problem of the plantation period in Brazil, as it was also of the later mining age, was the deficiency of manpower. The efforts of the Portuguese to solve this difficulty produced the most complex set of social problems with which any colonial society in America had to deal. Although most of the Portuguese, like the later immigrants into the Thirteen Colonies, were true colonists in that they were willing to sell all that they had in the homeland, transport their families across the Atlantic, and throw in their fortunes completely with the New World, they faced in Brazil a task which was notoriously the most difficult in colonial enterprise;[7] they had to establish in a tropical land a successful plantation colony on the economic basis of a staple money crop. Obviously the first requirement was a sedentary native population, one that was accustomed to persistent labor in a tropical climate and from which could be drawn unlimited slave labor. At first the Portuguese believed that the Brazilian Indians could be made to serve this purpose. Only by painful degrees did they learn that these natives were not a type suitable to their purpose and need.

In no circumstances could Portugal itself conceivably furnish the required labor supply. From its population of little more than a million it was with difficulty that a small cross section could be spared to serve as a nucleus of the new society. The white group dispatched from Portugal to colonize Brazil was exceedingly mixed. At the top were the donatarios and the planters—the *fidalgões*—some of whom had indeed come from the finest of the old landowning families of Portugal, but included among them were also many adventurers of middle-class origin. As a social group they constituted a landowning, hard-fighting, able, ruling class that heartily despised manual labor and based its great creation—the sugar-tobacco-cotton kingdom of the sixteenth and seventeenth centuries—firmly on slave labor.

Accompanying the wealthy fidalgo element were a considerable number of poverty-stricken but sturdy peasants and artisans, who were lured to the New World by the prospect of owning land and slaves and generally improving their fortunes. Eventually many from this class came to serve the planters as overseers and soldiers. Many Jews were early on the scene. Some were of Spanish origin, having fled into Portugal after

---

[7] Manchester points out that the subjugation of Portugal by Philip II caused many Portuguese families of the best type to flock to Brazil and that in their wake so many voluntary settlers of all classes followed that the total population was raised from 57,000 in 1584 to 150,000, possibly even 200,000, in 1640. *Op. cit.*, pp. 147-48.

the great expulsion of 1492, and were now fleeing again before the establishment of the Inquisition in 1536 in Portugal. In Brazil they tended to constitute a wealthy, intelligent, capitalistic element in the middle class of shopkeepers, businessmen, and moneylenders of the towns. On the whole they were an exceedingly useful group, helping to finance the erection of sugar mills and the large-scale marketing of plantation crops.

Among the less respectable and fortunate elements of the Portuguese society who came along with their betters were a considerable number of convicts; many, however, had been guilty of nothing more serious than one or another of the two hundred minor offenses that in the sixteenth century were punishable by banishment.[8] Even heretics were admitted into tolerant Brazil in the pre-Spanish period. Every ship from Europe in the early years of the colony carried a cargo of socially diverse human beings for incorporation into the Brazilian melting pot. Thomé de Souza, for example, was accompanied by four hundred convicts and six hundred soldiers besides officials and half a dozen Jesuit fathers. Shortly thereafter, as in French Canada, cargoes of female orphans were imported to become wives of some of the many white men who had originally come alone.

On the whole, the majority of early white immigrants into Brazil were representative of the rougher and more energetic elements of a Portuguese society, that had in its background a long acquaintance with the cruelty, bloodshed, pillage, and religious persecution characteristic of the southern European world of the sixteenth century.

These white elements on entering Brazil learned by degrees that the new country they had come to was inhabited, though somewhat sparsely, by a native population largely of seminomadic, warlike, cannibalistic Indians living under tribal chieftains. Unlike the majority of the American natives early encountered by the Spaniards, the Indians of Brazil were in a relatively low stage of cultural development. Some were completely nonagricultural, others almost wholly so. In large areas what crop raising was undertaken at all was performed by the women, all but a few were ignorant of metals, their industries were in a primitive stage. Great numbers were constantly on the move in search of new areas of natural foods or on the warpath against their enemies. Primitive, superstitious, and revengeful, they were an aboriginal group with which it was exceedingly difficult to deal.[9]

Racial crossings began at once, and the theft of native women by the Portuguese was a major irritant in the bloody quarrels between the white

---

[8] Martin, *op. cit.*, pp. 189-90.

[9] *The Tropical Forest Tribes*, Vol. IV of the *Handbook of South American Indians*, edited by G. H. Steward (Washington: 1948), deals in great detail with the Arawaks, Caribs, and Tupi-Guarani of the Brazilian area.

and the red men that soon were raging on every side. Another cause of enmity was the determination of the Portuguese to reduce the natives to slavery. Associated from their earliest days as a nation with slave-holding Arabs and Moors, and accustomed through close contacts with Africa to the idea of slavery as a right justly pertaining to conquest and superior force, the Portuguese were further stimulated in their impulse to enslave the Brazilian natives by their desperate need of labor for their plantations. At first they confined outright slavery, at least theoretically, to cannibals or to prisoners taken in "just wars," but in practice they soon abandoned all pretense of legality and seized Indians wherever they could. As in their possessions in Africa, the Portuguese were soon organizing slave raids, or *razzias,* into the far interior, passing well to the west of the Tordesillas' line of demarcation. The natives naturally struck back at the whites with as much force and cunning as they could command, repeatedly, in the early years, wiping out white settlements and forcing the Portuguese to maintain expensive fortifications and militia for protection.

But the razzias expanded, both in size and daring, and became a regular feature of the Brazilian frontier. Lured by the hope of fabulous profits, the spice of adventure, and the possibility of discovering mineral treasure, a band of one hundred to two hundred or more men, called a *bandeira* or entrada, would elect a natural leader and set off for the interior, staying away sometimes for several years. Frequently accompanied by women, and always taking along sufficient horses, cattle, and swine for immediate needs, these bands moved by stages, living off the land and raising brief crops as they went. Their range through the pathless wilderness was almost incredible, reaching at times from Pernambuco or São Paulo to the foothills of the Andes. The free and easy life of the *bandeirantes,* as the members of these expeditions were called, was punctuated by recurrent attacks on Indian settlements whose inhabitants they enslaved. Eventually they returned to the coast, sometimes with several hundred, often several thousand, captives. These cruel and bloody expeditions, organized on a large scale and backed by public approval, though deplorable from a humane standpoint, were the greatest factor in the exploration of the vast interior of the country, serving to push back the Indians and open up the interior to settlement. The bandeiras constitute the Brazilian counterpart of the westward movement in the Thirteen Colonies and Canada.

The region about São Paulo soon became the organizing center for these raiding activities. The very geography of this region, with its rivers draining from the eastern coastal range towards the Paraná River, seemed designed by nature to invite and assist an ever-continuing penetration westward. No single crop in this Paulista area provided the rich returns that sugar did in the north, partly because of the more temperate climate and partly because the mountains in this area rise directly from the sea and leave no coastal plain. From earliest times many of the inhabitants were *mamelucos,* or Indian-white half-breeds, intensely proud of their paternal ancestry and keen to prove the dominance of the white element in their blood by the harshness of their behavior towards their mothers' people. Drawing from their Indian ancestry great powers of physical endurance as well as a considerable knowledge of woodcraft, and from their fathers' people ambition, acquisitiveness, and a spirit of adventure, the mamelucos or Paulistas, as they became known, made very effective frontiersmen and soldiers and the pure-blooded Indians' most determined foes.

The enslaving of the Indians, however, did not really solve the labor problem, partly because the Brazilian native when captured proved a very inferior type of slave. Though physically strong, he was unaccustomed to persistent labor and confinement and, when forced to submit to life on the plantations, in most cases either ran away, committed suicide, or died at his work. Many also perished from white men's diseases. In southern Brazil, Indian slavery was destined to persist a long time, but in the north it was soon evident that another source of supply must be found.[10] In their predicament, the northern plantation owners naturally turned in thought to the Portuguese African possessions and the inexhaustible supply of Negro slaves that was available there; and by the middle of the sixteenth century African blacks were arriving in the slave ships to the number of many thousands annually.

The arrival of the African Negro brought to Brazil the third basic racial element that was to enter the blood stream of the population. Henceforth the three strands of Portuguese, Indian, and Negro were to be crossed in every imaginable combination and in the course of time were to be woven into the population pattern of Brazilian life. Of these three, the black man henceforth provided most of the labor. Culturally, he was on a higher level than the Indian of this area. He was a natural agriculturist, a skilled worker in metals, understood pastoral pursuits, and showed himself capable of being taught the skilled use of the white man's tools. He was also more immune to the white man's physical maladies. Even in the most unpropitious conditions of slavery in a tropical land he prospered and increased in numbers, the Negro birthrate being the highest of the three Brazilian strains. He became an indispensable element in the sixteenth and seventeenth centuries in the patriarchal unit that was the plantation, and in the eighteenth century a valued worker in the mines. He was

---

[10] Martin points out that the only occupations the Brazilian natives ever excelled in were those already familiar to them before the conquest, such as paddling canoes and fighting. *Op. cit.,* p. 192.

probably not usually ill-treated. His very economic value protected him, and a long series of royal decrees furnished some safeguard of his most elementary rights. The easy-going temperament of the average white Brazilian did not lend itself naturally to unrelenting cruelty, and even provided some check on the animosity of the Negro's worst enemy, the mulatto overseer. But his own happy, child-like disposition was the Negro's greatest asset, enabling him to survive and even wring some happiness from conditions that overwhelmed the stolid and unadaptable Indian.

The fact, however, must not be obscured that a terrible price in human suffering was paid for the prosperity that the Negro's coming brought to Brazil and for his own incorporation into Brazilian society. First came the unspeakable cruelty of the voyage from Africa to the American shores in the "floating coffins" that were the slave ships, which regularly showed a mortality of 30 to 40 per cent. Packed like sardines into the holds of the small and slow-sailing slave ships, and denied air, space to move, decent food, and adequate water, only the hardiest could survive. Once in Brazil, the Negro had to face the same horrible conditions that marked slavery elsewhere. The slave market, the whipping post, the iron collar, and the slave prison were all parts of the system; while any slackness in labor or the failure to meet the demands of the overseer brought the lash. There seems no doubt that conditions grew worse with the discovery of precious metals at the close of the seventeenth century. Not only was the black man then transferred from the coastal plantations to the mines of the interior, where he was deprived of many of the amenities of a patriarchal society that had hitherto made his life tolerable, but also working and living conditions were much more harsh and degrading. The numbers brought in at this time added immensely to the sum total of human misery. There are no reliable statistics, but it has been estimated that possibly the annual importations of the eighteenth century touched 55,000 per annum.[11]

Despite their large numbers, the Brazilian slaves seldom attempted serious revolt, though on some plantations and in some cities, among them Baía, they outnumbered the white man twenty to one. A mitigating feature of Brazilian slavery and one that in part accounts for the absence of rebellion was the fact that many slaves had the hope of eventually achieving freedom. From the earliest days, the manumission of faithful slaves was a favorite Brazilian form of celebrating festive occasions; also, certain classes of slaves were allowed time in which they might work for them-

---

[11] J. P. Calogeras, *A History of Brazil,* translated by Percy A. Martin (Chapel Hill: 1939), p. 28. *Cf.,* Martin, *op. cit.,* p. 198, who gives the lower figure of 30,000 to 40,000 per annum as the average through long periods of the colonial age. He remarks that it is estimated that in the period 1530 to 1850 three to six millions of slaves were imported.

selves and so accumulate funds with which to purchase their own freedom; but the greatest hope for most lay in successful flight. The goal of such fugitives was usually one of the *quilombos,* or colonies, entirely populated and defended by runaway slaves. By the close of the colonial period there were literally hundreds of these, spreading from the very outskirts of towns such as Baía, Recife, and São Paulo, to the far interior of such western areas as are now the states of Mato Grosso and Amazonas. The most notorious of these fugitive colonies was the quilombo of Palmares in the interior of the present state of Alagoas. This settlement at one time had a population of twenty thousand and survived nearly fifty years until overwhelmed in 1696 by a white army of seven thousand men. The colonists seem generally to have acquiesced in the existence of these places of refuge as a normal phenomenon of colonial life, recognizing possibly that they provided a necessary safety valve, and even winked at a certain amount of trade between them and the legitimate settlements.

The Negroes constituted the lowest social stratum in Brazil. Above them came the Indians and above the pure colored groups came the rapidly growing class of half-castes, within whose ranks were innumerable gradations of color and social consequence. Highest were the mestizos, the cross between whites and Indians. Known locally as mamelucos, or *cabocles,* they were usually children of a white father and an Indian mother. It was from this class that the razzias were largely recruited. Intrepid soldiers and skilled woodsmen, these mamelucos were a major factor in opening up the interior, penetrating in their forays as far as the Andes. In the west they were the frontiersmen; in the east they provided the backbone to the resistance of foreign encroachment. All in all, the mamelucos played an enormously effective role throughout the colonial period. The mulatto, on the other hand, did not come into his own in the colonial period; in fact, it was not until the later years of the nineteenth century that he had found his way into nearly every walk of life. Below these two groups were the various mulatto-Indian and Indian-Negro combinations.

In this highly stratified colonial life the moral problems were serious and complex. Indeed, all sense of moral values and spiritual discipline threatened for a time to vanish. The donatarios had concerned themselves very little with religion and the number of secular priests to settle in the captaincies was totally inadequate, even if the priests had possessed the capacity to make any impression on the behavior of the whites. The majority of the clergy, however, exposed to this environment, tended to become degenerate and corrupt, mere hangers-on of the planter group.

With the establishment of direct royal government, the crown determined to take the religious situation more firmly in hand. Like the

Spanish monarch, the Portuguese king possessed direct responsibility for the state of the faith in his overseas possessions. A papal bull of 1551 made this charge more precise by bestowing on João III and his successors, in their character as Grand Masters of the Order of Christ, complete control over the Church in the colonies. This gave the king the right to make the higher ecclesiastical appointments, collect tithes, and hear cases in appeal from the ecclesiastical courts. An early step in fulfilment of his religious obligations was the dispatch by the king, in 1552, of the first bishop of Brazil. This dignitary for the next century had the whole colony for his diocese. Another early royal decision in relation to the Church, and one made on petition of the clergy themselves, was the abolition of the system of tithes as a basis for the Church's support and the substitution of fixed salaries from the state. This measure had the effect of binding Church and State more closely together, but also carried with it certain disadvantages. The consequent subservience of the Church to the State, combined with the gradual lowering of the real value of a fixed salary, tended in time to have the effect of drawing to the clerical profession a class of men of less eminent spiritual and intellectual powers. The lack of independence in both policy and resources, and the restrictions placed by the crown on the disciplinary powers of the clergy, confined the Brazilian Church to a sphere of secondary importance compared with that of the powerful and wealthy Church in the neighboring Spanish Indies. The Inquisition also played a very different role in Brazil from that exercised in the Spanish dominions. Although subject to the Portuguese Inquisition, whose agents were at times active in the colony, no separate tribunal of the Holy Office was ever set up in Portuguese America. Indeed, in general, far less emphasis was given to orthodoxy in Brazil than was the practice under the less tolerant Spanish crown.

The greatest name in the religious history of Brazil in the colonial period was that of Father Manoel de Nobrega who, as the leader of a group of six missionaries, accompanied Thomé de Souza to Baía in 1549. He and his fellow-workers belonged to the newly organized Society of Jesus which, on a rising tide of enthusiasm, determined to sweep into the Church as many souls in the New World as had been lost to Protestantism in the Old. Working in northern Brazil, with Baía as headquarters, the Jesuits succeeded in making a deep and lasting impression on Brazilian colonial society.

Nobrega himself played a role in Brazilian history comparable to that of Las Casas in the Spanish Caribbean and Central American possessions. Fearlessly and tirelessly, he denounced to the whites their special sins of concubinage, cupidity, and cruelty to the natives, not less than the more general evils of violence, gambling, and drunkenness, threatening with exclusion from the sacraments those who failed to heed his words. He had, however, less success among the hardened colonists than among the Indians. Among the latter his goals were nothing less than their conversion to Christianity, the stamping out of polygamy and cannibalism, and the protection of the red men from enslavement and exploitation by the whites. In the mission field he encouraged his fellow workers to use every device of drama and music that ingenuity could suggest in order to make the Christian story appealing to the native mind and to induce the Indian to accept baptism and the obligations of Christian discipline and worship. To lead them to adopt civilized ways, as well as to protect them from their enemies the bandeirantes, Nobrega and his Jesuits developed a system of gathering their charges into permanent mission-villages, or *aldeas,* where they tried to teach the rudiments of Christianity, the standards of civilized living, the production of marketable goods, and elementary measures of self-defense. The aldea has been described as a "combination of an Indian agency, an ordinary mission, and a thriving plantation." The system served at once as a school of religion, an interesting experiment in social welfare, and a means of protection for the Indians. It may also have proved a safeguard for the Portuguese that prevented possibly disastrous outbreaks of native violence and despair hurled against the encroaching foreigner.

In carrying on his activities Nobrega, like Las Casas, again and again appealed to the king for royal decrees in behalf of his Indian charges, using his powerful Jesuit group in Brazil to see that these ordinances did not remain a dead letter. Inevitably the difference in outlook, and particularly the success of his campaign against the exploitation of the Indians as a source of slave labor, aroused the bitter enmity of the planters and their agents, the mamelucos. War became the normal state of affairs between the two sets of interests, and eventually even the missions themselves were openly and repeatedly attacked by the slave-raiding *Paulistas* under the excuse that they were competing economic enterprises. Nobrega died in 1572, two years after his greatest triumph, the securing of the royal decree of 1570 which definitely prohibited Indian slavery in Baía—a prohibition which his enemies feared, justly as events proved, might be extended to the whole of Brazil.[12]

A contemporary of Nobrega who carried on work of parallel importance in southern Brazil from São Paulo as a center was José de Anchieta who arrived in the colony at the head of a second company of Jesuits in 1553. A learned and versatile man, at once priest, physician, artificer, and an accomplished linguist who became skilled in Indian tongues, Anchieta was the first of his order in Brazil to give timely attention to the establishment of schools. In this field he set a pattern that, faithfully followed

---

[12] A royal decree of 1640 extended that of 1570 to include all of Brazil.

by his successors, eventually placed education in the colony largely in Jesuit hands. A monument to his interest in education remained to later times in the college of São Paulo, founded originally as a school for Indians.

A worthy successor to these pioneer missionaries of the sixteenth century was Antonio Vieira, whose activities in the seventeenth century were associated with the far north. His notable reports on the cruelties suffered by the natives on the tobacco plantations of the lower Amazon resulted in the creation in Lisbon of a council of missions entrusted with the special task of caring for the welfare of the natives in this region.

The Jesuits reached the peak of their power in Brazil in the seventeenth century after the restoration of the Braganza dynasty, an event which their order had helped instigate. But despite its power, twice in this century opposing interests were sufficiently strong to secure the temporary expulsion of the order from Brazil. Given royal support, however, the Jesuits managed each time to return and carried on their labors until the middle of the eighteenth century when the powerful José Carvalho, Marquis of Pombal, became the dominant figure at the Portuguese court. A central plank in his political platform was the merciless pursuit and final suppression of the Jesuits. In 1757 a royal decree peremptorily ordered the Jesuits to turn over the control of their Indian charges to the civil authorities. The Indians were declared free before the law, and the missions were transformed into villages with directors replacing the missionaries. Two years later an order was issued for the total suppression of the order throughout Brazil and the expulsion of the fathers from the country— a measure which was carried out with great gusto and cruelty by their long-standing enemies.

In any estimate of Jesuit contribution to Brazilian history, many factors enter. The labors of the fathers in protecting Indian freedom were only partially successful, even in the sixteenth and seventeenth centuries. Much of their mission work failed, as many of the Indians eventually relapsed into savagery. Furthermore, offsetting even the moderate gains they made in the Indian field was their attitude towards the institution of Negro slavery, which they did little to hinder, if they did not actually encourage it, in the hope that thereby the Indians might be spared. The Jesuits can be credited, however, with checking the process of native extermination sufficiently long to ensure to the Indians a permanent place in the racial amalgam that today makes up the Brazilian population. From another point of view, it may also be said that the Portuguese settlers probably owed to the Jesuits the immunity they long enjoyed from disastrous Indian uprisings. The colony was also certainly indebted to Jesuit influence among the natives for the success of Portuguese efforts in resisting the encroachments of the French and Dutch heretics.

IV. STRUGGLE AGAINST FOREIGN ENCROACHMENTS

The force that did more than anything else to weld the diverse elements of colonial Brazil into a nation was the never-ending struggle against envious European rivals. All the maritime powers of western Europe—the French, English, and Dutch—coveted Brazilian riches and were determined that Portugal should not be allowed to possess and monopolize them. This struggle had a number of distinct phases.

In the sixteenth century the most serious challenge came from the French who from the earliest days had appeared constantly about the coast on piratical expeditions. In the middle of the century, the challenge became direct in the form of two serious attempts to establish a permanent colony in the Bay of Rio de Janeiro. The first of these was an effort in 1555, under the leadership of Nicolas Durand de Villegagnon, a friend of John Calvin, to set up an "Antarctic France" where religious tolerance might flourish. His enterprise had the approval and support of France's great Admiral Coligny, who was anxious to find a colonial refuge for his persecuted fellow Protestants. An island commanding the narrow entrance to the world's most beautiful harbor was seized, fortified, and named Fort Coligny, and a settlement established on the mainland. As in Canada, the invading French in Brazil were soon on friendly terms with the neighboring Indians, with whom they carried on a brisk trade, exchanging small European gadgets for brazilwood. The colonists, however, were a mixed Protestant-Catholic group and religious dissension soon broke out. Villegagnon himself gave up in despair in 1557 and returned to France. The settlement he left behind was obviously so weak that in 1560 the Portuguese governor, Mem de Sá, though he had but a small force at his disposal, dared to attack it. Somewhat to his surprise he succeeded in capturing and destroying Fort Coligny and in driving the French from Rio. They did not, however, go far, merely taking refuge in the interior with their Indian friends. Here they were soon able to organize a general rising against the Portuguese, in the course of which they were able to reoccupy Rio. A decimating war raged for three years, and for a time it seemed likely that this native support might prove decisive in making the French settlement in Brazil permanent. But eventually the efforts of the Jesuit missionaries, especially Nobrega and Anchieta, both interested in excluding heretics from Brazil, were successful in persuading most of the Indians to make peace and to leave the contest at Rio to be fought out between the two groups of whites. In 1565 the Portuguese, under cover of a considerable fleet, founded a Portuguese settlement in another part of the bay, and two years later, after a lackadaisical siege, succeeded in forcing the French to sail away.

An early Brazilian sugar mill. From a lithograph in *Voyage pittoresque dans le Brésil* by J. M. Rugendas, Paris, 1835, Vol. IV. (Courtesy of the Library of Congress, Prints and Photographs Division)

The planter's family. From a lithograph in *Voyage pittoresque dans le Brésil* by J. M. Rugendas, Paris, 1835, Vol. III. (Courtesy of the Library of Congress, Prints and Photographs Division)

Rue Droite in Rio de Janeiro. From a lithograph in *Voyage pittoresque dans le Brésil* by J. M. Rugendas, Paris, 1835, Vol. III. (Courtesy of the Library of Congress, Prints and Photographs Division)

The Church of Nossa Senhora de Pilar Salvador in Baía. Erected in the late eighteenth century. (Courtesy of the Library of Congress, Archive of Hispanic Culture)

While the double failure at Rio put an end to the most serious French attempts to colonize Brazil, it was not until well into the seventeenth century, when French colonizing activities were definitely centered in the St. Lawrence valley in North America, that the contest between France and Portugal along the Brazilian coast reached a final conclusion. Until then French trading posts, which quickly became centers of native revolt, were persistently appearing here and there along the Brazilian littoral and having to be reduced. One of these was founded in 1594 by the notorious corsair, Jacques Riffault, who landed in Maranhão and established with the Indians of this area a lucrative trade which, with the support of the French crown, a few years later developed into a new French colony and fort called St. Louis, now São Luiz on the island of Maranhão. The latter colony was intended to serve as a center for an "equatorial France" which, it was hoped, would in time extend its control over the mouths of the Amazon and well up the reaches of that great river. But lack of consistent support from home and the appearance on the scene of a considerable Portuguese expedition under the mameluco leader, Jeronymo de Albuquerque, compelled the surrender in November, 1615, of the French garrison and put an end to the dream of a French empire in Brazil.

The English, like the French, were a scourge to colonial Brazil, especially in the sixteenth century when the sacking and burning of coastal towns by English pirates was a recurrent experience. This menace was particularly grave in the decade following the defeat of the Spanish Armada, when a comparatively easy way of "singeing his Catholic majesty's beard" was to attack his newly acquired Portuguese holdings in America. Pernambuco was set upon by Drake, Cavendish, and Lancaster in 1595, and its two principal settlements of Olinda and Recife were sacked. In the second half of the seventeenth century the English menace passed away as the English acquired from the restored Portuguese monarchy such commercial privileges as made piratical and contraband activities on the Brazilian coast not worth while.

The most serious foreign threat to Portuguese exclusive dominion in Brazil, however, came from the Dutch. When Portugal fell under the Spanish crown in 1580, all the Portuguese colonial possessions became fair game to the Dutch, who were at the time at war with Spain in a long-drawn-out struggle for independence. In the East Indies they succeeded in taking over most of the Portuguese Spice Islands and continental naval and trading posts. In the American area their efforts to occupy Brazil, either in whole or in part, eventually failed, but not without a prolonged struggle. Their first serious effort to establish a permanent settlement on the Brazilian coast followed the creation in 1621 of the Dutch West India Company. The charter of this new venture bestowed wide territories, then belonging to the Portuguese and Spaniards, along the South American and South African coasts, together with a twenty-four-year monopoly of trade therein. Three years later a Dutch fleet of twenty-six ships and some thirty-five hundred men under Admiral Heyn captured and sacked Baía. Though retaken two years later by a Spanish fleet, the Dutch returned to Holland enriched with the immense booty they had acquired, leaving a ruined city for the Portuguese to reoccupy. In 1630 a larger Dutch expedition of 38 ships and seven thousand men succeeded not only in capturing and plundering both Olinda and Recife but in bringing the whole Bay of Pernambuco under Dutch domination. From here they expanded north and south and, in spite of considerable guerrilla resistance, managed to gain control of the whole northeastern coast from Maranhão to Sergipe. Spain was too deeply involved in the Thirty Years' War in Europe to be able to render effective help. Brazilian settlers, slaves, and the natives of the region found themselves obliged to surrender to the Dutch and accept what terms of submission they could obtain.

In 1637 Count Maurice of Nassau, a Prince of the House of Orange, was sent out as governor of the new Dutch conquests, which included the territory in the present states of Maranhão, Piauí, Ceará, Rio Grande do Norte, Paraíba, Pernambuco, Alagoas, and Sergipe—in all a region larger than that of the Thirteen Colonies.[13] A far-seeing statesman and wise administrator, Count Maurice did his best to persuade the Dutch West India Company to consolidate its already huge holdings before adding new ones. But his views were overridden. The Company was intent on organized trade—legal or illegal—carried on from shore installations, rather than on building a genuine colonial empire, and ordered an attack on Baía. When this failed, Maurice settled down to suppressing lawlessness in the territory already acquired and putting into effect his own enlightened views on colonial administration: instituting religious tolerance, freedom of commerce, state-aided agriculture, and even setting up a colonial representative legislative body. The Brazilian planters were induced to return to their old *fazendas,* and were encouraged by large importations of Negroes from the Gold Coast. Olinda and Recife were rebuilt and, to mark the intended permanence of the Dutch regime, a sumptuous palace in a tropical style of architecture was built for the government near Recife. The West India Company, however, showed itself unappreciative and so parsimonious that the governor's plans were largely frustrated; the army went unpaid; traders were interfered with; and his own administrative duties made more difficult. Problems became so overwhelming that Mau-

---

[13] C. E. Chapman, *Colonial Hispanic America: A History* (New York: 1933), p. 87. See footnote.

rice resigned in 1644 and returned to Europe, bringing to a close the only hopeful phase of the Dutch occupation.

In 1640, while Maurice was still governor of the Dutch colonies in Brazil, the Portuguese in Europe began their war of independence against Spain to secure the restoration of their own national monarchy. This struggle was to last the greater part of three decades, 1640 to 1668. In furtherance of this object, the national government in Lisbon signed with the Dutch an alliance against Spain which practically legitimized continued Dutch appropriations in Brazil. The native Brazilians were not long in making clear that they held different views. In 1643 they staged an uprising against the Dutch in Pernambuco, which gradually expanded into a general war of thirteen years' duration (1641-1654) aimed at the total expulsion of the Dutch from Brazil. Although, after the expiration in 1651 of the alliance with the Dutch, the Lisbon government gave some assistance to the Brazilians, the success of the conflict was primarily a colonial triumph, the result of an extraordinary wave of patriotism which swept all classes.

The moving spirit and principal patriot leader was João Fernandes Vieira, who had originally come to Brazil from Madeira. During the early years of the Dutch invasion he had fought bravely against the intruders and then, perusaded that further resistance was hopeless, had yielded and settled down as a planter under their regime. While he enjoyed many favors under the new rulers, and had come to be implicitly trusted by them, he never forgave them for their persecution of his coreligionists, and laid careful plans for a revolt which, once started, spread like wildfire. Heated by the fires of racial, religious, and national hatred, the war was waged with great ferocity and cruelty on both sides. The Dutch eventually made peace. By a treaty of 1661 they finally agreed, for a consideration of four million cruzados ($400,000), to relinquish their Brazilian holdings and withdraw from the land. Their decision to evacuate was in part due to their becoming embroiled in hostilities with the English. Their departure from northern Brazil predated their withdrawal from New Netherlands on the Hudson by three years. The conflict left behind distinct beginnings of a Brazilian nationalism. This was composed partly of pride in local achievement and partly of a feeling of resentment against a mother country that had shown herself ready to sacrifice the interests of her colony to further her European interests.

V. DISCOVERY OF GOLD

The most significant development in the colony in the seventeenth century was the growth of a distinctly Brazilian self-consciousness, the emergence of which was both provoked by and developed during the struggle against the Dutch. As the century closed this spirit found new sources of power and self-confidence in the discovery of immense mineral wealth. The new riches came as one of the results of the activities of the bandeirantes, who in their exploring and slave-raiding expeditions always had an eye open for the possible discovery of gold, silver, and precious stones.

In 1673 one of the most spectacular and experienced of the bandeirantes, a rich, iron-fisted Paulista named Fernando Dios Paes Leme, with a commission "to seek out and discover emerald mines," led a great entrada into the mountainous area around the headwaters of the Rio São Francisco and the Rio Doce in the western part of what is today the state of Minas Gerais. After four years of incredible hardship, he made the first rich strike, finding on the shores of a lake precious stones that he took to be the long sought emeralds. Though the "emeralds" turned out to be tourmalines, they were prophetic of great riches to follow.[14] In 1680 gold was found in the same region of Minas Gerais, and the discovery of diamonds occurred about the same time.

By 1700, Brazil was in the grip of one of the wildest series of gold and diamond rushes in the world's history. A kind of delirium passed over the land. Men, women, and children from every walk of life, both slave and free, threw down their accustomed tools and abandoned their usual occupations to take part in a mad rush westward to the new gold and diamond districts of the highlands of central Minas Gerais and eastern Goiaz. Plantations were abandoned, factories were left idle, and ships in the harbor were deserted, while thousands swarmed into the mushroom mining camps and boom towns that sprang up over night. Sugar was no longer sole king; his troubles, in fact, were just beginning. In the second half of the century the Brazilian planter not only had to face the competition of the mining industry in the labor market, but also—in the markets of the world—he had to meet the competition of the British, French, and Dutch West Indian growers, then in their heyday, all this while suffering a drastic fall in sugar prices.

The gold period, like so many economic phases of Brazilian history, was transitory, lasting not quite a century. Through the first half of that period the output of the gold mines was great, though the methods of extraction were crude in the extreme. Eighty thousand persons were said to be engaged in mining in 1750, but shortly thereafter a rapid decline in output set in, and by 1800 the gold-bearing gravels and stream beds had become exhausted. Interest in the diamond industry also had declined as the price of the stones dropped in the European market. However, many effects of

---

[14] Martin, *op. cit.,* p. 203.

the gold and diamond age were permanent. The most outstanding was the expansion of the country's area. As a result of eighteenth century development, Brazil became practically double the size originally envisaged. Hitherto penetrations west of the demarcation line had been only sporadic raiding and exploring expeditions, but now numerous permanent settlements were established and revision of the international line became imperative. In the treaties of 1750 and 1777, Spain bowed to the inescapable logic of the situation, and agreed to relinquish her rights under the Treaty of Tordesillas and recognize a new boundary line based on the doctrine of *uti possidetis.*

An immediate result in Brazil itself of this discovery of the new mining wealth was the emergence of a striking dualism in the economic and social life of the country. The north, with its capital at Baía, remained a region of great plantations in possession of a slave-holding aristocracy; while the southern region, centering at São Paulo and Rio de Janeiro, became a mining and pastoral area, inhabited by a more polyglot and democratic society. In this southern area, the great migration of all classes into the interior in search of the precious metals had been a great democratizing and unifying factor, breaking down social barriers and producing sharp economic changes.

Portentous of future developments was the fact that the bandeira movement that had led to the mineral discoveries had been almost wholly a Brazilian phenomenon and owed little to the mother country, though the crown, through its assertion of rights to the "royal fifth," profited enormously. By the close of the eighteenth century Brazil, with such an imposing series of assets as her plantations, mines, cattle, and timber, already surpassed the mother country in resources, wealth, and population. Brazil, though still a colony, had obviously come of age, and notions of nationhood and independence had been born.

Chapter 8

THE ESTABLISHMENT OF FRENCH COLONIES

I. THE FOUNDING OF NEW FRANCE: THE AGE OF CHAMPLAIN

Champlain and the First Half of the Seventeenth Century

In the early seventeenth century the St. Lawrence River and its Gulf, which had been the scene of Cartier's activities seventy-five years earlier, again became a center of intense colonial enterprise by France. Only in this region had sixteenth-century French efforts borne any fruit and laid a basis for future development. Annually since Cartier's time, scores of Breton and Norman fishing vessels from St. Malo, Dieppe, and Honfleur had continued to find their way to the Newfoundland Banks and the St. Lawrence to fish for cod and to barter with the Indians for furs. These traders did not venture beyond Tadoussac at the mouth of the Saguenay River, or attempt any permanent settlement, but by the opening of the seventeenth century they had built up a profitable business.

By this time, too, the European situation had become more favorable for French colonial expansion. France was now the first military power in Europe and the Spanish danger had subsided. Following the success of the Dutch revolt and the defeat of the Spanish Armada at the hands of the English in 1588—and the consequent loss of control of the seas—Spanish fortunes had begun to decline and were to sink lower as time went on. Germany, separated from Spain since Charles V's time, was on the eve of the Thirty Years' War over the Protestant-Catholic question and was no longer a menace to France. The English, in dispute with their Stuart kings over constitutional and religious issues, also seemed to be effectively shackled. Furthermore, the domestic situation in France had again reached equilibrium and prosperity. Henry of Navarre was king and had settled the religious problem by a formal profession of Catholicism to please the majority of the nation and by the issuance of the tolerant Edict of Nantes in behalf of his former coreligionists. Though it was to be a mere matter of time till, with the disappearance of the personal influence of the king and his friendliness towards them, the Huguenots would be shut out of colonial enterprise, at the moment France had in this Protestant group a vigorous colonizing element whose interest in overseas land and trade was shared by a growing middle class.

In the colonial movements of the seventeenth century that were to challenge Spain and Portugal, the influence of the middle class was at first predominant and the commercial motive frankly uppermost. Only later, and then spasmodically, was this feature modified by glamorous dreams of empire and an occasional revival of romantic interest in the old search for the northwest passage. As the century opened there was a general theory abroad that colonies should be self-supporting. For France, this meant that colonizing activity must be harnessed to the fur trade, which in turn implied a northern empire and a policy of conciliation towards the Indians who provided the furs. Enthusiasm for the enterprise came at first almost entirely from individual merchants and explorers. Neither the king nor his chief minister, the Duc de Sully,[1] was much interested. Henry IV had his mind on the reorganization of France after a half century of civil conflict. Sully considered northern colonies a mistake, especially so since they could only be financed through monopolies, of which he thoroughly disapproved. It was therefore evident that a French colonial empire, if it was to be constructed, must start without that warm support from the crown which had been the mainstay of Spanish and Portuguese colonial efforts, though jealousy of glory and profits flowing to rival monarchs could be counted on to provide a certain stimulus to royal interest.

The merchant capitalists of France, however, were convinced that a colony would provide a practical base of operations for a monopoly of the fur trade and, in return for a charter, were willing to promise to carry out to the New World, for a greater or shorter length of time, a specified number of colonists per annum and to fulfil other conditions. Many companies were organized. Till 1627, the dominant influence in the various partnerships and companies was Huguenot, though some groups were of mixed Catholic and Protestant membership. But the story was always the same. After securing its monopoly the company would be confronted with religious dissension, the violent jealousy of excluded traders, a lack of willing colonists, and the consequent necessity of taking overseas a large percentage of beggars and criminals who were unthrifty and made the worst possible use of their opportunities. In consequence the company would fall into the practice of taking out to New France each year fewer and fewer immigrants and of spending less and less on fortifications and other colonial needs, until finally a wrathful government would cancel the charter before the date of its expiration. Many of the leaders of these enter-

[1] Maximilien de Bethune, Duc de Sully, a Protestant, became Henry IV's sole Superintendent of Finance in 1598 and remained in this post until a few months after the king's assassination in 1610. An able man of business, Sully held many offices. He opposed Henry's colonial policy partly because he held that overseas colonization was not in keeping with the French character.

prises were capable and inspiring men and some of the companies built up flourishing businesses. Their failure as colony builders was due partly to the poor quality of the rank and file of Frenchmen who were available as colonists, partly to the lack of support from the crown, and partly to jealousy of the merchants in the home markets. For all these reasons New France, by 1627, had fewer than one hundred inhabitants. Meanwhile English Virginia, planted only one year earlier than Quebec, had a population of over four thousand and had built up a flourishing trade in tobacco with the mother country.

Through the first thirty-five years of the seventeenth century, the outstanding figure in French Canada was that of Champlain, a man of the middle class, born about 1570 at Brouage, near La Rochelle. Though a sincere Catholic himself, he was a follower of Henry of Navarre, having been with him in the war against Spain, and thus had long been accustomed to cooperation with Huguenots. He had spent two years in the West Indies, Mexico, and Panama studying the Spanish colonial system. His primary interest in Canada from the beginning was in exploration, not in fur trading, though he realized that this latter element alone provided the necessary economic basis for a colony in the north. He made his first trip to North America in 1603 as Geographer Royal in an expedition financed by a group in which Ayman de Chaste, Governor of Dieppe and a friend of the king, was most prominent, and Pontgravé, a trader of St. Malo, was commander. Although the two vessels were gone from France only five months in all, they traveled up the St. Lawrence as far as Lachine Rapids and Champlain was able to make brief side trips up the Saguenay and Richelieu rivers.

After a shift in the organization at home, by which Pierre du Guast, Sieur de Monts, another Protestant follower of the king, was given a monopoly of the fur trade of the St. Lawrence and Acadia and made lieutenant-governor of Acadia, Champlain in 1604 made a second voyage that took him to Acadia and kept him in the New World through three winters. One winter season was spent on an island at the mouth of the St. Croix River and two across the Bay of Fundy at Port Royal in Annapolis Basin, a location which Champlain himself discovered and recommended as a base.

The principal object during these years was to carry on explorations and to discover if possible a more southern center of operations than the St. Lawrence with its bitter climate and ice-locked channel. Seeking this goal, Champlain made three long journeys from Acadia along the Atlantic coast as far south as Nantucket Island, exploring Mount Desert, the Penobscot River, and Cape Cod. He was the first to chart in any detail the Atlantic seaboard from Cape Breton to Cape Cod and, considering his instruments, he did it with amazing accuracy. No doubt in the winter evenings of 1605-1607 at Port Royal he spent long, absorbed hours on his great map of the Atlantic coast. In these years, neither the Dutch nor the English had established a foothold on these shores and the French might have established a future New York or a Boston, but Champlain thought the Indians of the region a "poor thieving lot" and seems not to have considered seriously any scheme of permanent settlement. Probably he realized that for an empire resting on furs the base must be well to the north; in any event, he did not pursue farther his southward explorations.

After a brief visit to France in 1607, Champlain returned for the third time to Canada, and on this occasion went up the St. Lawrence, resolved to establish a colony. On July 2, 1608, on the site of the old Stadacona, he founded Quebec as a foothold for France in the New World. This settlement encountered great hardships but managed to endure. As there were still a few Frenchmen at Port Royal in Acadia, and the de Monts Company was determined to maintain it, France had now two colonies far separated from each other in North America.

In Quebec as in Acadia, Champlain was happiest when he could slip away accompanied by an Indian guide and explore unknown rivers and lakes. In 1609 he accompanied a band of Indians up the Richelieu River, which he named for the chief minister of France, and discovered Lake Champlain. Here on this inland lake, as the ally of the Algonquian Indians whom he accompanied, he had his first brush with the Iroquois—an unfortunate encounter which bore bitter fruit through half a century after his death.[2]

Led on by a vision of the acquisition of vast new territories for France, the hope of finding the magical route to Cathay, and sheer love of exploration, Champlain devoted the years 1613-1616 largely to discovery. In 1613, led on by a romancing young Frenchman [3] who claimed to have been at Hudson Bay, he partially explored the Ottawa River in search of a passageway to this great northern sea from which he hoped to find the northwest passage to China. Though disappointed of his immediate objective, his interest in the river two years later brought a great reward. Following the Ottawa to the mouth of the Mattawan and from there going by way of Lake Nipissing and French River, he came to Georgian Bay in Lake Huron, thus discovering for France an inland waterway to the upper Great Lakes comparatively free from the depredations of the fierce Iroquois who were a constant peril along the more southern Lake Ontario route

---

[2] G. M. Wrong, *The Rise and Fall of New France* (New York: 1928), 2 vols. Vol. I, pp. 176-80, gives the details of this encounter.

[3] Nicolas Vignau. For the full story see Wrong, *op. cit.*, Vol. I, pp. 190-95.

to the west.[4] Turning southeast from Georgian Bay, Champlain pursued his way by Lake Simcoe and the River Trent until he came to Lake Ontario. Continuing south of it, he penetrated the Iroquois country—this time as the ally of the Huron Indians. After a winter spent with the Hurons (1615-1616), Champlain returned to Quebec where his career as an active explorer really came to an end, though he continued to live, except for one prolonged absence in France, as the honored Lieutenant-General of New France in the city he had founded, held in greatest respect and esteem until his death in 1635.

Thus Champlain, who was always in search of a passage to China, was a leading figure in pioneering work in Acadia, the earliest chartmaker of the Atlantic coast, the founder of Quebec, the discoverer of Lake Champlain and explorer of the Ottawa-Nipissing canoe route to Lake Huron. Widely esteemed as a man of breadth of view, courage, and fervent religious piety, he gave an air of distinction to the French colonial venture in Canada. "Half monk and half crusader," he looked for neither comfort nor personal gain and succeeded through a long life in holding the respect of both savage and civilized man.

Two other great explorers of the age, younger than Champlain, were Etienne Brûlé and Jean Nicolet. Brûlé, a retainer and close companion of Champlain for some years, was probably the first Frenchman to visit both Lakes Ontario and Huron and to shoot the Lachine Rapids. As an explorer, fur trader, and interpreter, he led a life of great adventure, early becoming familiar with much of the modern province of Ontario, with Georgian Bay, and Lakes Huron, Ontario, and Superior and, to the south, exploring northern New York and Pennsylvania. In the latter region he traveled down the Susquehanna River to Chesapeake Bay. In 1632 he met the fate of many less well-known pioneers, being clubbed to death and eaten by the Hurons. Nicolet, a man of great dignity and high character, arrived in New France in 1618 just after Champlain had retired from active exploration. After learning the Algonquian language while in the Ottawa River area, he went westward and was evidently the first European to enter Lake Michigan (1634), visiting Sault Ste. Marie and entering Green Bay on the northwestern side of the lake. Here he became acquainted with the Sioux, Assiniboine, and Illinois Indians and learned something of the Great Plains. Under commission from Champlain to find a passage to the South Sea, Nicolet followed the Fox River as far as the portage to the Wisconsin and, hearing from the Indians of the "Great Water" (the Mississippi), concluded that he was not far from the mysterious "South Sea" or "Sea of the West"; his report strengthened the view held in

---

[4] Wrong, op. cit., Vol. I, pp. 201-2.

Quebec that the Pacific Ocean and the St. Lawrence were not far apart and that a little more effort would open the way to China and Japan.[5]

In Champlain's lifetime, therefore, exploration centered around the St. Lawrence River and the Great Lakes. All the lakes were discovered before his death, but no one went beyond Lake Superior or into the country west of Lake Michigan. There was, however, considerable southward exploration, despite the presence of the Iroquois in western New York and Pennsylvania. North of Lakes Ontario and Erie, much of the modern province of Ontario was traversed. The best fur hunting grounds were found to be north and west of the Great Lakes, and for the pelts of this region there developed a great rivalry between the French of the Great Lakes and the Dutch who were continuously active along the Hudson after 1614. Until the middle of the century, these hunting regions were ranged over by the Algonquins, Hurons, and Neutrals. The Algonquins and Hurons sold only to the French, the Neutrals to both the French and the Iroquois. The route in most frequent use by the French was Champlain's Ottawa-Nipissing route, as the St. Lawrence-Lake Ontario route was terrorized by the Iroquois.

Nearly a decade before Champlain's death in 1635 a fundamental change took place in the organization of the French colony. This came in the wake of the rise to power of the great French organizing genius, Cardinal Richelieu, who after 1624 became possessed of such authority as no French minister of the crown ever had wielded before. Jealous of the incomparably better showing as colony planters of the Portuguese, Spaniards, English, and Dutch, convinced that the Hapsburgs must be fought in America from whence they drew their wealth, as well as in Europe, and urged on by the Jesuits for religious reasons, Richelieu determined to launch France on a logical and forceful colonial program which should be more in keeping with the pre-eminent position he designed for his country in Europe. He fully realized that the English had been in Virginia less than twenty years and already had a flourishing agricultural colony of four thousand persons carrying on a profitable tobacco trade with England, whereas the French, who had known of the St. Lawrence and its resources for nearly 100 years and had been settled in Quebec since 1608, had succeeded in planting only seventy-five colonists in Quebec and less than one hundred in all New France—and these were living in misery, "exchanging yearly the hunger of winter for the starvation of spring."

Convinced that the policy of strong trading companies such as the English and Dutch were using was the only practical method of colony

---

[5] For the work of both Brûlé and Nicolet see *Canada and Its Provinces*, edited by Shortt and Doughty (Toronto: 1913), Vol. I, "The Pathfinders of the Great Lakes," by J. H. Coyne, pp. 56-61.

founding, Richelieu decided that the French should follow suit; at the same time, he resolved to eliminate religious diversity as the most fertile source of dissension. In 1627, therefore, he took decisive steps to deprive the comparatively small Huguenot company, headed by William and Emery de Caens, Rouen merchants, of the charter that had been granted in 1619, on the ground that, like preceding companies, this one had not lived up to the terms of its contract. To replace it, the minister founded the "Company of the One Hundred Associates," or "The Company of New France," made up of a group of wealthy nobles and traders who were each to subscribe 3,000 livres and were all to be Catholics. To this new company was given the whole of New France in full property with a per-petual monopoly of the fur trade and exclusive rights to all other trade, except the cod and whale fisheries, for fifteen years. Richelieu himself was president of the company and head of a board of twelve directors. In return for such concessions the company undertook to settle two hundred or three hundred Roman Catholic settlers in New France each year and to assist them in getting a start by supplying necessities for three years. It further promised to fortify and protect the country, to provide each settlement with three priests, and to make an effort to effect the conversion of the Indians.[6]

The results were disappointing. There was no great difference in the essential character of the new company from that of its predecessors, except that the new project had stronger court support and patronage and that all elements were of the dominant Catholic faith. These elements Richelieu had hoped would secure greater vigor in the true work of colonization and eliminate religious dissensions. But the primary weakness remained as it had always been, lack of willing colonists. France with a rich soil and a population of eighteen millions had no surplus population: all French-men could live, if meagerly, in France, and all preferred to do so except the Huguenots who, by the terms of the charter, were now forbidden to emigrate to New France. Richelieu, too, lacked the gifts that might have aroused popular enthusiasm for the new undertaking. Soon new domestic and European complications added to the already considerable number of the enemies of New France and brought disaster and destruction. In 1628 a Huguenot revolt, which had English backing, brought about the loss of a great fleet of twenty vessels filled with colonists and supplies which the new company sent to New France. David Kirke, an English adventurer who had been brought up in France, in command of a small fleet of Eng-lish privateers operating near Tadoussac, captured nineteen of the twenty

---

[6] Wrong, *op. cit.*, Vol. I, p. 254, points out that the total capital, 300,000 *livres*, of the new company, was only equal to £ 12,000 or £ 13,000 and was not one fifteenth as much as the English spent on establishing Virginia, and later Massachusetts.

French ships. In the following year a similar fleet under two of Kirke's brothers attacked Quebec and forced its surrender. Champlain and his half-starved garrison were given passage to France, and Quebec remained in English occupation for three years. It was then, along with Acadia which also had been captured, returned to the French by Charles I under the terms of the Treaty of St. Germain en Laye (1632).[7] By this time the Company of New France had lost much of its original enthusiasm and the home government was so immersed in European affairs that there was little time, money, or interest to expend on colonial matters.

From 1632 until 1663—while Richelieu, and later Mazarin, directed French policy in Europe, guiding French fortunes through the Thirty Years' War, the continuation of the War with Spain, and the treaties of Westphalia and the Pyrenees—the home government gave little attention to its American colonies. In 1645 the Company of New France handed over to the settlers, organized as a corporation of leading merchants called the *Compagnie des Habitants,* its trading and governing monopoly in return for 1,000 pounds of beaver skins a year, the assumption of its debts, and provision for paying the salaries of the government officials and the priests. Its rights as landowner and its privilege of naming the governor it retained, keeping, said its critics, its most valuable privileges and getting rid of its obligations at a high price. The operations of the new company soon brought agitation for the establishment of a council to assist the governor in the administration of the colony; this activity was successful in 1647, when the king ordered that there should henceforth be a council composed of the governor, the superior of the Jesuits (until there should be a bishop) and the commandant of troops in Montreal. A year later the council was expanded to include two leading citizens to be selected by the rest of the council. Syndics, or representatives, elected annually by the towns-people of Quebec, Three Rivers, and Montreal, might appear before the council and represent the views of the people, though they could have no vote in the decisions taken. Thus an originally autocratic system of government was succeeded by one in which the colonists had some influence, though by no means did they have representative government.

Little general progress, however, was made by New France in these years, largely because there was a renewal of Indian warfare that ruined the fur trade, obstructed exploration, and made normal life impossible. The decades of the thirties and forties were hideous with Indian strife. Wishing to be sole middlemen in the fur trade of the northern and western tribes with the Europeans, among whom they favored the Dutch and the

---

[7] Population of Quebec at this time was less than one hundred persons. *Cf.* H. I. Priestley, *France Overseas through the Old Regime* (New York: 1939), p. 72. For greater detail, see Wrong, *op. cit.,* Vol. I, pp. 257-63.

English, the Iroquois were determined to destroy the Hurons, a distant branch of their own race, and to subjugate as far as possible the other southern tribes. Again and again they fell on the settlements of the Hurons, burned the huts, slaughtered many of the inhabitants, and carried as many as possible off for torture. They constantly plundered the furs being carried to the French settlements and seized possession of the axes, knives, blankets, kettles, and other stores that were kept at the French missions and trading posts among the northern tribes.

In the course of the years 1649 and 1650 the best beaver grounds of Ontario were seized by the Iroquois. The territory between the lakes became depopulated as the remnants of the Hurons, Neutrals, Algonquins, and other Ontario Indians moved west to the Lake Michigan and Lake Superior regions. The triumphant Iroquois sold furs to the Dutch and English, and French trade slumped badly. Lake Ontario and Lake Erie became practically closed waterways because of the Iroquois settlements along their northern as well as their southern shores. Even in the French settlements of Montreal, Three Rivers, and Quebec, the inhabitants went in terror of their lives and hardly dared to pass beyond the stockades.

In these circumstances there was only one direction in which any energy could be displayed in the following decades, and that was the mission field. The first Canadian missionaries were the Récollet friars, a branch of the Franciscans. Invited to the New World by Champlain, they arrived in 1615 and for ten years struggled with the gigantic task of converting a sea of Algonquins and Hurons to Christianity. They met with scant support from the white colonists who, intent on the fur trade, wanted the Indians left in their nomadic state and no obstacles placed in the way of the sale to them of liquor, the commodity for which the savages could be depended on to part with their best furs cheaply. Discouraged and disheartened by the situation and realizing that the task was beyond their resources, the Récollets decided to turn the work over to the richer and more powerful Society of Jesus. The first Jesuits, arriving at Quebec in June, 1625, included Charles Lalemant, Ennemond Massé, Jean de Brébeuf, and two lay brothers. Though warmly welcomed by the Récollets, they were very coolly received by the colonists.[8]

In their work in Canada, as elsewhere, the Jesuits mingled religion and politics. One of the first results of their arrival was the loss by the Huguenot uncle and nephew de Caens of their charter, the rights of which were taken over by the Company of New France.[9] The new charter

---

[8] Wrong, op. cit., Vol. I, p. 250.

[9] William and Emery de Caen, uncle and nephew, two Protestant merchants of Rouen, had secured a charter in 1620 with a monopoly to run till 1636. Richelieu, with slight regard to the granted rights, canceled this charter when he founded the Company of New France.

of this all-Catholic company expressly provided that expenses of public worship must be defrayed by the company and that three missionaries must be supported at every trading post. After 1632 the Jesuits were entrusted by the company with its religious obligations and came in great numbers to Canada, founding hospitals and missions, and permeating the whole colony with their influence. Only Montreal, formally founded on May 18, 1642, with the crusader-soldier, the Sieur de Maisonneuve, as its first governor, stood somewhat apart, becoming the center for the work of the active order of St. Sulpice.

The Jesuits especially addressed themselves to the task of Christianizing the Indians and soon showed that they were prepared to pour into this mission work both intelligent effort and great self-sacrifice. They first set their hearts on the conversion of the Hurons, establishing numerous missions in their settlements around Lake Simcoe and Georgian Bay. In this mission field Jean de Brébeuf, a Norman of aristocratic descent, iron constitution, great intellectual gifts, and extraordinary will power, labored for twenty years, building chapels and mission houses and sending annually a detailed "Relation" of his work to his superior. He was later joined by Father Lalemant and others. In all, twenty-five Jesuit missionaries labored among the Hurons, only in the end to have little to show for their efforts. On the whole the verdict of the Hurons on Christianity was, "It is good for the French but we are another people." Moreover, the Hurons had been marked down for extermination by the implacable Iroquois, and as the settlements were raided the missionaries suffered the fate of their flocks. At the time of the great attack on the Hurons by the Iroquois in 1649, Brébeuf and Lalemant were captured and put to death by torture, and by 1650 there was hardly a Jesuit mission left in all Huronia. Undeterred by this frightful experience and realizing that the Hurons and Algonquins were of low mentality as well as greatly inferior to their enemies in military powers and organizing ability, the Jesuits determined to carry Christianity to the Iroquois and "tame these human tigers." Father Isaac Jogues led the new undertaking and suffered tortures on more than one occasion. The Iroquois could not be tamed and in 1702 the "Mission of the Martyrs" was abandoned.

Work among the Algonquins, a wandering semiagricultural group, was somewhat more successful, especially after the introduction of royal government in 1663. Among both the Hurons and the Algonquins, the Jesuits tried to introduce the mission system and persuade the Indians to settle in native villages, become good farmers, and submit to the control of a missionary. Their object was to make "good Indians," a goal they sought to reach by isolating their charges as far as possible from the corrupting influence of the French traders and settlers. But with the economic interests of the French colonists against them, and the government itself opposed to such a policy of isolation and determined on continuing the liquor trade, and with other religious groups supporting a policy of gallicization of the Indians, the Jesuits' road was a hard one. Of them it can truly be said that they "bore themselves manfully and fought a good fight."

It is noteworthy that missionary efforts by the French Jesuits in Canada were carried out on an entirely voluntary, persuasive basis. There was no effort, as in Spanish America, to force the natives to become Christians. They were to be persuaded of Christian truths. Neither did the idea of the isolation of the native from the white man play the role that it did in South America. The permanent mission station, so characteristic a feature of the Spanish American system, was never so important in French Canada as in the dominions of Spain, though some modified mission posts for the more nomadic tribes were attempted. Further handicapping them in their struggle to convert the Canadian Indians, the French missionaries received only a small portion of the state support that Spain gave so lavishly to her missionaries. In Canada the mission fathers were not regarded as the shock troops of civilization—the forefront of the advance of the white man into Indian territory—as they were in Spanish America, and their success was very much more limited.

Reorganization under Louis XIV

In 1663 a new era opened for the French colonies. Following closely upon the death of Cardinal Mazarin, when Louis XIV became "his own prime minister," a royal edict completely reorganized the system of French holdings in America. The last shareholders of the Company of the One Hundred Associates were required to surrender their rights to the king, and Canada became the Royal Province of New France. Henceforth it was to be ruled as any other French province: by a governor, bishop, and intendant.[10] A Sovereign (later Superior) Council, made up of these three dignitaries and five to twelve other persons chosen annually by them, together with the attorney-general and registrar, was to act as an administrative body with power to carry on the government, issue local ordinances, function as a judicial court of second instance, and direct the fur trade. Presided over by the governor, with the bishop at his right hand and the intendant at his left, the Council—with its members in special costume—met once a week and regulated to the minutest detail the affairs of the colony. The king retained, however, the right to take direct action whenever he chose without reference to the Council. This political framework containing no element of either elective or responsible government, though

---

[10] The 1663 Edict made no mention of an intendant but the addition was soon made.

local opinion had real weight, was to remain practically unchanged until the end of French rule in Canada. With the encouragement of trade particularly in mind, Canada was placed the following year (1664) within a new and all-encompassing commercial framework for all French colonies fronting on the Atlantic. This enormous trading territory was given to the French West India Company, whose rights were thus extended over the west coast of Africa, South America from the Amazon to the Orinoco, and North America from Florida to Canada, with all the French West Indian islands also included. At the time that this reorganization took place, Canada consisted of the three settlements of Quebec, Montreal, and Three Rivers and had a total French population of perhaps twenty-five hundred, practically all of whom were priests, officials, and traders.[11]

This fundamental reorganization of French holdings in the New World brought new life to Canada. It was largely the work of Jean Baptiste Colbert who, after the demise of Mazarin, for two decades was Louis XIV's most trusted servant. A man of bourgeois birth who had received both a legal and a business education, Colbert was one of a number of ably trained and highly gifted public officials bequeathed by Richelieu and Mazarin to their sovereign. He possessed immense organizing ability and driving power and, though parsimonious, was competent and industrious in public affairs. Believing in wealth as the source of power, he thought it could be wrung from a world empire and a world commerce, which he held to be inseparable.

While Louis, seeking to dominate Europe by war, seized the opportunity offered by the poverty and weakness of Spain to humble the Hapsburg power, Colbert planned to dominate the world by trade. The French colonies, he thought, should be made paying business enterprises and woven into the fabric of a French state that would be wealthy, not merely self-supporting. Thinking in the terms of the era, Colbert planned that prosperous, monopolistic trading companies should serve as links between the colonies and the homeland. International trade required, he believed, the revival of shipbuilding and the development of a merchant marine; in addition it demanded, he was sure, the strengthening of the French navy so that it could provide the national trading companies with the transport and protection necessary for success. Also fundamental in his extensive plans were the encouragement of emigration to the colonies and their internal financial reorganization to be carried out under the minute direction of a powerful and imaginative intendant. Generally, he sought to curb waste and inefficiency and to encourage industry and commerce within France itself. To give Colbert an opportunity to carry through his pro-

---

[11] At this time the fourteen French colonies in the West Indies had a population of 15,000 whites and as many Negroes and mulattoes. *Cf.* Priestley, *op. cit.,* p. 73.

gram, Louis XIV made him comptroller-general of finances, minister of the marine and of the colonies, and secretary for both the royal household and the navy.

On the whole, Colbert's colonial policy was not only enlightened but successful, despite the handicaps under which he had to work: namely, the king's absorption in plans for European conquest and glory, the indifference of the nobility, the whole weight of social prejudice against trade, and the average Frenchman's distaste for colonization. Colbert's grandiose *Compagnie des Indes Occidentales* lasted ten years. It has been said that it was granted every privilege except that of being left alone to carry on its business in its own way; [12] but despite the handicaps that despotism imposed, it recovered Guiana in South America, took possession of the islands of Martinique, Guadeloupe, and Saint Domingue, established a prosperous trade in sugar, and opened rich markets to French goods. By the time it was dissolved in 1674 the company had achieved many of the goals for which it had been created.

In measuring Colbert's success it must be borne in mind that throughout his ascendancy Louis XIV was the "sun king" of a glamorous and extravagant court at Versailles, and abroad was dictator of Europe, going from triumph to triumph in wars against the Dutch and the Spaniards. These and other showy enterprises drained away most of the money that Colbert's economic and administrative reforms produced, deprived them of their due effect in improving the welfare of the French masses at home, and in the colonies obstructed the influx of money and men that might have laid solid foundations for a lasting French empire in America.

Before his early death in 1683, Colbert was depressed by a sense of failure and a foreboding of disaster as he watched his rival, Louvois, the minister of war, supersede him in the king's favor. Two years later his enterprises received their heaviest blow in the revocation of the Edict of Nantes (1685) which struck at the very classes of the French community on whose business activity and cooperation the success and stability of his policies rested. This measure dispersed to Holland, Prussia, England, and the English colonies in America those elements of economic strength which, if they had been retained and employed at home or in the colonies, might have made enduring the glories of *le Grand Monarque,* but which henceforth served to strengthen France's political rivals.

Meanwhile, within Canada, during Colbert's regime, reorganization, careful new appointments, and the prospect of increased court interest in colonial matters had brought new hope and real revival. The first royal governor was the Sieur de Courcelles who arrived in 1665 accompanied not only by a new set of able officials, but by the Carignan-Salières regi-

[12] Concerning its privileges and obligations see Wrong, *op. cit.,* Vol. I, pp. 366-69.

ment, the first body of regular soldiers to be sent to Canada. Though only 1,100 in number, these troops promptly relieved the wretched colonials from the Iroquois terror which had seemed on the point of engulfing the colony. These Indians were now not only driven from the French settlements, but pursued to their own country where their towns were put to the torch with such effect that their chiefs were soon suing for peace. This was but the first of many benefits that this famous regiment brought to Canadian life.

Canada's new organization called for leadership by three officials: the governor, bishop, and intendant. The king and Colbert soon made it clear that it was the intendant to whom they really looked to rule the country. The governor was to have general supervision and be the military commander-in-chief, but the intendant, in theory subject to the governor, in practice was to provide the guidance in detail and act as the business manager of the new system. The arrangement had its origin in the domestic situation in France where the traditional abuse of power by the aristocratic provincial governors, relics of the semi-independent feudal nobility, had made the appointment of a representative of the crown, drawn from the bourgeois class of career men, a desirable innovation in the interests of efficiency and centralization. In America, with no such past, the situation might well have been deemed to call for a single ruler rather than the deliberate creation of rival powers, but the king and Colbert had decided to follow the French model exactly. The title of "Intendant General of Justice, Police, and Finance in New France" gave only a slight indication of the multitude of duties and the wide powers that this official was expected to wield. The supervision of the whole administration of justice, of colonial finance, of the provisioning of the military forces as well as the allocation of land to new settlers were among his duties.

The first intendant was Jean Talon, whose prodigious and indefatigable love of detail, combined with breadth of vision and imaginative enterprise, are reminiscent of Colbert's own qualities. He dominated the first decade of royal rule in Canada, arriving in the colony in 1665 and returning to France in 1672. His first concern was to increase the population,[13] and in this he was encouraged by Colbert who wrote in 1665: "I pray you to commend it to the consideration of the whole people, that their prosperity, their subsistence, and all that is dear to them depend on a general resolution, never to be departed from, to marry youths at eighteen or nineteen and girls at fourteen or fifteen, since abundance can never come to them except through abundance of men." [14] Talon did his best to encourage

---

[13] In the spring of 1666 Talon took a census which showed that there were 3,215 French in Canada, of whom 2,034 were males. Quebec, the largest settlement, had a population of 547. Cf. Wrong, op. cit., Vol. I, p. 384.

[14] Quoted in T. Chapais, The Great Intendant (Toronto: 1914), pp. 55-56.

early marriage and large families by giving generous bounties and by severely taxing bachelors—indeed treating them like public malefactors, forbidding them by law to hunt, or fish, or trade with the Indians, or even go into the woods. Through his Canadian years he constantly pleaded with the government at home to help him with this population problem. As voluntary immigrants could not be attracted, he begged the home authorities to dispatch more and more state-assisted and compelled colonists. A few hundred a year arrived: in all 1,828 subsidized immigrants were introduced, of whom several hundred were unmarried women. These latter were supposed to be drawn from orphanages or from peasant families, and usually arrived in the care of nuns. When the ships came in, an amazing marriage market scene was enacted in which the soldiers and laborers sought wives among the good, bad, and indifferent newcomers. By such strenuous efforts, Talon succeeded in doubling the population of New France. With his departure immigration into Canada practically ceased.

As supervisor of the seigneurial system, Talon carried through a number of interesting policies. For example, he persuaded many of the soldiers of the Carignan-Salières regiment to take their discharge in Canada and settle as a military colony on generous grants of fertile land along the Richelieu River, hoping in this way to close the southern road by which Iroquois and English raiding parties were accustomed to travel. In assigning other lands Talon tried to mingle experienced pioneers with newcomers and thus provide skilled artisans for village groups. He also did his best to encourage spinning and weaving in the rural communities. To point the way to improvement and diversification of agriculture and to improve stock raising, he established a model farm near Quebec. A number of special industries, based on the peculiar resources of Canada as well as the needs of France, received his attention. Fishing, shipbuilding, iron, coal, and copper mining, tanning, shoe manufacturing, weaving, hemp raising, and the potash industry all felt his hand.

The intendant by no means confined his energies to the old settlements on the St. Lawrence, but encouraged the exploration of the interior with generous state aid. He had partly in mind the development of mining and fur trading, partly pure expansion. He would have liked to see New France expand to Mexico on the southwest and to Hudson Bay on the north. To shut in the Spaniards and the English and prevent their further extension he supported the policy of taking formal possession of the entire drainage basin of the Great Lakes as well as of the canoe routes to the "South Sea," though as yet no one knew how to reach the latter from the St. Lawrence system. On June 4, 1671, in a great ceremony at Sault Ste. Marie on the eastern shore of Lake Superior, a cross was set up and a royal plenipotentiary announced that France claimed "all territory from Montreal to the South Sea covering the utmost possible range and extent." [15] Talon also urged upon the home government the bold step of the acquisition of New Netherlands, pointing out that the Hudson River would be invaluable in the fur trade.

It was in Talon's time that, with government support and license as a fur trader, Robert Cavelier, Sieur de La Salle, the greatest of all French explorers, a member of a wealthy bourgeois family of Rouen who had come to Canada a year after Talon, embarked on the course that, fifteen years later, found its triumph when he succeeded in following the Mississippi to its mouth. Selling his seigneury at Lachine, near Montreal, the explorer set out in 1669 to look for the great river of the southwest of which there were many rumors. With fourteen men and four canoes and accompanied by the Sulpician missionaries, Dollier de Casson and René de Bréhant de Galinée, he made his way to Lake Ontario, hearing on the way of Niagara Falls. Near modern Hamilton the party met Louis Joliet, an explorer who had been in the west looking for a copper mine near Lake Superior and had just completed a notable journey by a new route through Lake Huron, the Detroit River, and Lake Erie. Joliet told the missionaries of the great need for them in the Lake Michigan region and they then left La Salle's party.[16] The exact route of his further wanderings on this journey is not known, but it is probable that in the course of them he discovered the Ohio River and paddled many miles along its course towards the Mississippi. Years of extraordinary hardship, misfortune, and persistent effort were to elapse before he was to crown this early work with ultimate achievement.

Canada's first intendant not only struggled to lay the foundations of a large, carefully regulated and flourishing colony along the St. Lawrence, but would have liked to see established between Canada and the motherland a free and growing commerce. Towards the end of his career in the New World when the West India Company, of whose charter he never approved, had relinquished control of Canadian trade, he had a freer hand in commercial matters and tried, among other projects, to inaugurate a triangle trade between Quebec, the West Indies, and the homeland similar to that already flourishing in the New England colonies. Building a ship on the St. Lawrence, he loaded it with Canadian produce, chiefly fish and other salted products, and dispatched it to the French West Indian islands where it took on sugar and tropical products in exchange for the original cargo and, carrying these to France, exchanged them there for European manufactured goods needed in Canada.

---

[15] For a more detailed discussion of Talon's interest in the West and a fuller account of the country about Sault Ste. Marie, see D. G. Creighton, *Dominion of the North* (Boston, 1944), pp. 69-71; also *cf.* W. T. Morgan, "English Fear of Encirclement," in the *Canadian Historical Review*, March, 1929.

[16] *Cf.* Coyne, "The Pathfinders of the Great Lakes," *op. cit.*, pp. 87-94.

In his relations with the other officials of the government, Talon quarrelled at times with the governor, though friction between the two was not continuous. With the bishop his relations were rather cool. Being Gallic in religious outlook, he was thoroughly opposed to Jesuit domination. The outstanding Catholic figure of this time in Canada was Bishop Laval,[17] who arrived in 1659 and for the next half century was to reside there, except for an occasional visit to France. Jesuit influence had been behind Laval's appointment as the first bishop and many believed it was chiefly he who had persuaded the king to take over the colony.

An aristocrat of the great house of Montmorency, Laval as a statesman was far-seeing and courageous, though of irascible and intractable disposition, quite willing to fight governor, intendant, and traders whenever he thought it necessary. On the burning issue of Church and State Laval was an ultramontane, determined that the Catholic Church in Canada should owe allegiance directly to the Pope and not be considered merely a part of the jurisdiction of the Archbishop of Rouen. At first he bore the title—not Bishop of Quebec—but "Vicar Apostolic and Bishop of Petrea *in partibus infidelium*"; in 1674, however, Quebec became a separate diocese and Laval took the title of the see with the king's consent.[18] One of his earliest activities was the establishment at Quebec of a seminary (later Laval University) for the training of a distinctly Canadian clergy. As a member of the all-powerful Sovereign Council, and in his relations with the secular power generally, his attitude was wholly imperious. He insisted that the Church should be regarded as the full partner of the state in all of whose activities its voice should be heard, though the state was not to presume to interfere in Church matters.

After Laval's arrival the long-standing controversy over the sale of liquor to the natives became increasingly bitter. The traders wished to have the Indians left free to roam and gather furs and themselves left at liberty to entice them to French trading posts with brandy. Laval roundly denounced this traffic, even excommunicating those taking part in it. The government long played the part of an uneasy third in the controversy. Jean Talon at first agreed with the bishop's view, realizing that his contentions were true that the traffic would lead eventually to the destruction of the Indians and the extinction of the fur-bearing animals, but later he came to the conclusion that this policy was unpractical. If the French did not sell liquor to the Indians, for which alone they would part with their furs cheaply, the English and Dutch would supply their wants and secure the profits. The French, he concluded, might as well have the fur trade.

---

[17] For a short, vivid account of Bishop Laval see C. Colby, *Canadian Types of the Old Régime, 1608-1698* (New York: 1908), chap. viii, pp. 260-90.

[18] See F. Parkman, *The Old Regime in Canada*, p. 160.

Talon's return to France in 1672 marked the end of an epoch. On his arrival in Paris he found Colbert's influence already waning and that of Louvois rising. Louis XIV was embarking on his long contest with William of Orange; henceforth commercial Protestant England would replace decadent Catholic Spain as the great enemy. There would be less money for Canada and the colonists there would have to depend on their own resources.

The last three decades of the seventeenth century in Canada were dominated by the figure of Count Frontenac, who was to direct the fortunes of New France through two terms of office. He first arrived in Canada in 1672 as governor and lieutenant-general of all dominions of France in North America, just as Talon was preparing to leave. A man of fifty years, whose career had been divided between court life and military camp, Frontenac was a born leader. A man of fine presence and great dignity, a good orator and a courageous and far-seeing statesman, he was fond of pomp and display, intolerant of opposition, arrogant, and possessed of complete confidence in himself. He provided admirably the vigorous central authority that the paternalistic government of New France needed. He grew to know the Indians well and learned to manage them with consummate skill.[19]

In matters of internal colonial policy Frontenac was in agreement with much that had marked Talon's administration. Concerning the issue of relations with ecclesiastical authorities, he agreed that the state should be dominant, not the handmaiden of the Church and of the Jesuits who represented it. In other matters of major policy, the new governor, believing exploration to be of primary consequence, sought to develop and extend it in every way; the fur trade was similarly encouraged and supported.

Frontenac's first administration, 1672 to 1682, was marked by long debates with Talon's successor, Duchesneau, over the ill-defined and overlapping powers of governor and intendant. It was finally on this account, when the colony had become almost distracted by the never-ending disputes, that he was recalled in 1682, along with his rival, to receive sharp censure from his royal master. But in the ten years of his first administration Frontenac had accomplished much. Though deprived of any considerable military support from home, he had succeeded in driving back the Iroquois and making friendly treaties with other Indian tribes, an achievement which did much to restore the fur trade to prosperity. His construction of Fort Frontenac at the outlet of Lake Ontario provided visible evidence of French power to the western Indians and served as a

[19] *Ibid.*, chap. ix, pp. 291-319, and also C. W. Colby, *The Fighting Governor* (Toronto: 1915).

base for explorations around the lakes. The governor had supervised its construction in person and inaugurated it with as much circumstance and magnificence as he could contrive.

As a result of the governor's support of exploration, achievements in this field were both extensive and important. In 1673, the year that Fort Frontenac was built, the explorer Joliet and the missionary Marquette, setting out from Michilimackinac and entering the Mississippi from the Wisconsin, had followed the great river south to within four hundred miles of its mouth, reaching natives who were in touch with the Spaniards and learning beyond a doubt that the Mississippi led to the Atlantic by way of the Gulf of Mexico and was not a water highway to the Pacific. Upon learning this news, Frontenac urged that a line of forts be constructed from Lake Ontario to the Gulf of Mexico. However, it was not until the year of the governor's recall that La Salle, having set out from Fort Frontenac and entered the great river from Lake Michigan by way of the Illinois, reached the mouth of the Mississippi on April 9, 1682. Here the explorer proclaimed Louisiana and the entire Mississippi basin to be possessions of the French king.

Difficulties with the neighboring English colonies made Frontenac, as had Talon before him, advise the court to obtain, by negotiation or force, Lake Champlain and the Hudson River. Louis XIV's preoccupations in Europe, however, prevented this advice from being taken.

Seven years elapsed before Frontenac was sent back to Canada for a second term as governor. During the intervening years French expansion westward went steadily forward, despite protests and warnings from Versailles, which was reluctant to assume further heavy responsibilities. The activity of fur traders and missionaries, however, drew the French ever westward and forced the creation of additional posts and forts for their protection. To help the friendly western tribes hold their own, the French continued to build more and more fortified posts. By the end of the 1680's France held an enormous extent of Canadian territory and maintained two chains of forts, one running from Montreal to the mouth of the Mississippi and another stretching westward from the St. Lawrence to the Saskatchewan. Their upkeep was a severe drain on the strength of the colony on the St. Lawrence and resources were stretched ever thinner. Meanwhile, the Iroquois grew increasingly troublesome as they fought to dominate the whole region west to the Mississippi in order to serve as middlemen between the western tribes and the English. On the St. Lawrence the leadership of Frontenac's successors was weak and inadequate while a thieving intendant and his friends plundered the public treasury. As the Iroquois gathered in ever greater numbers above and below Montreal to harass and massacre, and the War of the League of Augsburg broke out in Europe, the king, in 1689, decided to send Frontenac back to Quebec to save the colony from ruin.

Before Frontenac left France to serve his second term as governor, he had clearly decided upon his lines of general policy. The principal feature was to be a series of raids on the English settlements extending from Albany to New York, carefully timed to coincide with the activities of a French naval unit to be dispatched from France to New York. The king would promise no reinforcements of regular land troops, and consequently Frontenac must depend for defense on French Canadian militia and Indian allies. It was in these desperate circumstances that he determined to adopt savage methods of warfare—the surprise night attack, massacre, and the offer of rewards for scalps. Early in 1690 he organized three bands that set out from Montreal, Three Rivers, and Quebec, and plunged into war in its most atrocious form against France's enemies in the New World. One party fell on Schenectady, another on Casco Bay, and another on Salmon Falls near Portsmouth, on Dover, and on other Maine and New Hampshire settlements. These English communities were wiped out with all the accompaniments of fire, carnage, torture, and other savage atrocities. In the following summer Frontenac successfully held off an avenging naval expedition against Quebec, sent from Boston under the command of William Phips, and also repulsed a land raid from New York, under the leadership of John Schuyler, aimed at Montreal. Meanwhile, Frontenac waged unrelenting war against the Iroquois, allies of the English, constantly raiding and burning their villages. He also re-enforced the French garrison at Michilimackinac and renewed his alliance with the Indians of the west. By 1696 he had put the Iroquois definitely on the defensive, broken their power as a dominating confederacy, and forced them to realize that to drive the French from the St. Lawrence was beyond their power.

From the standpoint of the immediate needs of the French colonies Frontenac's war policy, essentially defensive in nature, was an undoubted success, but its long-range wisdom, especially the advisability of the savage character he deliberately gave to the fighting, is open to serious question. The ultimate result of all the bitter warfare of his second administration was to evoke in France's enemies an implacable hatred, and to harden the determination of the English colonists to drive the French from North America.

Frontenac himself realized the essential disparity in numbers and resources between the French and English colonies, and understood that when the English were ready for the final struggle nothing could save the French but adequate help from France. For this he begged constantly, asking for troops, supplies, and money for fortifications. But only in miserably insufficient proportions were they conceded. Fortunately for his reputation, the English in his time were too disunited and absorbed in their own problems to undertake successfully the conquest of Canada. In 1697, after seven hard years, the peace of Ryswick brought a breathing space to the contestants in the New World as in the Old. In this interval of peace Frontenac died (November 28, 1698), having succeeded in defending Canada from both savage and civilized foes.

II. FRENCH LOUISIANA

Although colonial French Louisiana was to have a history of little more than half a century, its establishment involved issues big with destiny for the three major colonial powers of North America. Lying directly athwart the path of western expansion for the English colonies, separating Spanish Florida from the rest of Spanish North America, and impinging on the northern coast of the Gulf of Mexico and so challenging Spain's exclusive claims there, Louisiana embodied French determination to encircle the English coastal colonies and seal off Spain from future northward thrusts from Mexico. At the same time it crystallized France's own ambitious scheme of creating a vast North American empire resting on the control of the two greatest water highways of the continent, the St. Lawrence-Great Lakes waterway and the Mississippi River system. Curiously enough, though a pawn in a great international game throughout its short history, Louisiana was to see comparatively little of the large-scale fighting that its emergence as a colony helped to provoke.

Neither the English nor the Spanish were blind to the issues involved. Nor were they inactive as France sent forth its great explorers in all directions from the forward base of the Great Lakes. Both realized clearly the goal of the French imperialists, from Champlain and Richelieu in the early seventeenth century to Talon, Colbert, and Frontenac under Louis XIV. Well expressed by Champlain in writing to Richelieu, this policy sought by "possessing the interior of the country . . . to expel our enemies and compel them to retire to the coast," in order (added Talon) "that the Europeans may lose all desire they may feel to share with his Majesty so beautiful and so vast a country."

The Spaniards were increasingly active throughout the century in pushing explorations and missions northward, from both Mexico and Florida, and showed no sign of abating their claims to the Mississippi, which de Soto and his Spanish followers had been the first to discover.

As for the English colonists whose colonial charters gave them title to a nebulous area the limit of which was vaguely described as "to the South Sea," they had hardly landed at Jamestown before they started to

15. New France and Her Neighbors in the Eighteenth Century

search for this mythical destination which, Indian reports assured them, lay not far to the west. Though their progress through the wilderness on foot was slower and more difficult than that of the French who were able to push their canoes along great waterways, by the middle of the century small parties of Virginians, encouraged by Governor Berkeley and the Virginia Assembly, frequently penetrated far into the western hinterland. They seemed to sense the urgency of not being forestalled and thus closed in from the rear. After 1663, when a charter was granted by Charles II to some English gentlemen to establish Carolina from the 31st to the 36th parallel "extending west and southwest in a direct line as far as the South Seas," the Virginians had some able assistance in western exploration from this more southerly colony. By 1671 the piedmont in both colonies was well known, the summit of the Blue Ridge had been reached, and a number of parties had gone well into the valleys belows. Marquette and Joliet in 1673 reported that the tribes of the Mississippi, from the mouth of the Ohio southward, were trading both with the English to the east and the Spaniards to the west. Thus at the time of La Salle's famous journey down the great river (1682), the English possessed well-established contacts with the Indians of the lower Mississippi basin.[20]

La Salle's expedition, and his later disastrous attempt to establish a colony on the Gulf which would control the river's mouth, aroused both the Spaniards and the English. The Spaniards sent out no less than nine expeditions, by sea and by land, to try to locate and destroy this menacing French settlement; to prevent such attempts in the future, they founded Pensacola. As for the English, the decade of the 1680's saw Dongan, the enterprising governor of New York, seeking to checkmate the French by establishing forts to secure the line of the Ohio; a strategy which was met by countermoves on the part of the French governor of Quebec.

In the last year of the century, rumors of an English plan to establish a colony of Huguenots along the lower reaches of the Mississippi induced the Quebec governor to commission Pierre le Moyne, Sieur d'Iberville, one of eleven sons of a Canadian *noblesse,* to frustrate the undertaking. Arriving on the scene, Iberville encountered an English ship with the prospective colonists on board, and forestalled their landing. The would-be settlers were thereupon forced to take refuge in the English coastal settlements. Iberville placed a French colony of some two hundred people at Biloxi on the Gulf, nearer the mouth of the Mississippi than Spanish Pensacola. Two years later this colony was transferred to nearby Mobile, a healthier location. Its supervision was placed in the hands of Jean Baptiste le Moyne, Sieur de Bienville, a brother of Iberville, who was to be associated with the development of Louisiana for over forty years.

---

[20] Wrong, *op. cit.,* Vol. I, xx.

Friendly relations and trade with the Indians of the basin were quickly established, but the colonies so languished for lack of French immigrants that Louis XIV decided to see what private enterprise could accomplish and in 1712 granted a Louisiana monopoly for fifteen years to Antoine Crozat, a wealthy business man. The charter gave Crozat exclusive rights to all trade, except in beaver skins, with permission to import Negro slaves from Guinea, and imposed on him the obligation of bringing in at least a score of colonists each year.[21] The king on his part undertook to furnish government salaries for nine years. With eyes on the pearl fisheries, profits from rumored mines, possible trade with Spanish Mexico, the proceeds of a slave trade, and the chance to sell supplies to settlers, Crozat hoped for riches; but by 1717 he was glad to surrender his charter and withdraw from his bargain. He had given little attention to colonizing or agriculture, and the population at his withdrawal was a mere seven hundred.

Soon after Crozat's departure, Louisiana became the kingpin in the magical financial scheme of John Law, a Scotsman, who in 1719 succeeded in persuading the French government that he could free France from the heavy public debt with which Louis XIV's wars had saddled her, and at the same time create a wonderful colonial empire in the heart of America. His plans called for the taking over of Crozat's monopolies, and the creation of a great Company of the West, or Mississippi Company, which should enjoy a monopoly of the fur trade for twenty-five years, the prospect of a lucrative general trade with both the Spaniards and the Indians, and the exploitation of the mines which were assumed to exist in the interior. Huge land grants and titles of *noblesse* were also to be part of the picture. All France became wildly enthusiastic, and the shares of the new company soared to forty times their face value.

Although the "Mississippi Bubble" burst within two years, and the Company of the West along with the rest of Law's gamble collapsed, while the mania of speculation lasted Louisiana secured a real start in the arrival of several thousand immigrants and the expenditure of a considerable capital on its development. By 1725, although no longer in the limelight, Louisiana was enjoying modest prosperity. The Company of the West had been refurbished along more reasonable lines; the country had a population of 5,000 whites and 250 Negro slaves; and, on a number of the new land grants along the river, crops of rice, indigo, and tobacco were being tried out. At key points north of New Orleans a number of small forts provided protection for the whites and local centers for Indian trade. One of the most important of these was Fort Chartres, from which was administered the area north of the Ohio. The capital of the whole area was New Orleans, which had been founded by Bienville in 1718 to

21 *Cf.* N. M. M. Surrey, *The Commerce of Louisiana* (New York: 1905), pp. 157-59.

supersede Mobile. It was located on relatively high ground in the marsh-lands a hundred miles from the mouth of the Mississippi. Though described by a French traveller in 1722 as "a hundred or so huts without order or beauty," the city was soon regularly laid out in lots. Its houses of cypress wood were constructed high above the ground and had steep roofs designed to withstand the torrential rains and hurricanes of the area. As the fur trade and Indian barter of the whole area came to center at New Orleans, the city took on a growing importance.

Company rule lasted in Louisiana until 1731 when it became a French crown colony. In form, the government was very similar to that of Canada, consisting of governor, intendant, and council, all with overlapping and ill-defined functions that caused bitter internal strife and unseemly disputes. Bienville again became governor in 1733 but, after three unsuccessful wars against the Chickasaw Indians, was withdrawn in 1743. Through the remaining two decades of French rule there were no great changes.

The relations of Louisiana with both her Indian and her two European neighbors were always strained. The long narrow country was bordered on the southwest by the dominions of the Spaniards who were disposed to contest every foot of French advance westward, especially infiltration south of the Red River line. A second obstacle to French expansion westward was the fierce opposition of a number of Indian tribes. Established across the westward tributaries of the Mississippi, and blocking advance to the "South Sea" as well as to possible silver mines, were the Apaches on the Red River, and the Comanches located on the Arkansas and the Missouri. In the northwest the Fox-Iroquois wars delayed French progress. For obvious reasons the Indians regarded the westward advance of the semi-agricultural colony of Louisiana with greater hostility—and opposed it more fiercely—than had the Canadian natives the advance of the fur-traders from Quebec. East of the Mississippi the French faced an equally determined resentment and resistance from Indian and European. English traders in the hinterlands of the Atlantic coast colonies unceasingly pressed the Indians of that region—the Chickasaws, Cherokees, Creeks, and Choctaws—against the French lines and outposts to force them back upon the Mississippi.

Despite the utmost these various enemies could do, however, the French explorers and *voyageurs* pressed steadily outwards, especially towards the west. They were seeking mines and suitable locations for trading posts and continually operated far beyond the sphere of political authority or military protection. Among the most notable were the establishment of Fort Orleans in Missouri in 1723, and the penetration of eastern Texas. Farther north the La Verendryes, father and sons, after 1733 were engaged in establishing a series of forts in the upper Missouri country, and by 1743 were within sight of the Rockies.[22] To their work, and that of others like them, was due the predominance of French influence in the whole western region north of the Red River line.

Life in French colonial Louisiana differed in many ways from that in New France. The Mississippi colony fell more definitely into distinct sections than did its parent colony of French Canada. With the inauguration of Law's great Company of the West, the lands north of the Ohio—the "Illinois country"—came under the government of Louisiana, but remained a community distinct in many ways from the regions of the lower Mississippi around New Orleans. The northern area, reaching from the Ohio to the Great Lakes and stretching from the Alleghenies westward well beyond the Mississippi, was administered from Fort Chartres. It included such settlements and trading centers as Kaskaskia, Cahokia, Vincennes, and Sainte-Genevieve. Developed from Canada and primarily a land of Indians and voyageurs where fishing and hunting were the order of the day, it nevertheless contained a fair proportion of successful small farmers who were interested in the growing of wheat on lands held in freehold. Sharing with the Quebec habitants the love of litigation and great respect for "the robed priest and the uniformed officer" at the top of society,[23] the whole population of this Illinois country differed profoundly from the more varied cosmopolitan society of the lower river.

Here along the southern Mississippi, Negro and Indian slaves and white *engagés* (indentured servants) mingled with free Rhinelanders, German Swiss, West Indians, Acadians, and various types of European French to form a conglomerate colonial society—a forerunner of the American melting pot of nations. The land, held on a seigneurial tenure, was divided into narrow strips running back, often two miles or more, from the river to the cypress swamps in the rear. Different nationalities showed an early tendency to settle in racial groups, a practice which soon gave a stratified aspect to the river bank. Immediately north of New Orleans for some fifteen miles was "the Chapitoula coast," where large plantations, worked by Negro slaves for aristocratic and often absentee landowners, formed the usual type of holding. Beyond came "the German coast," where many Rhinelanders and German Swiss were settled, and where the smaller holdings were so intensely cultivated as to give the appearance of a continuous garden to this section of the river. Farther north lay "the Acadian coast" where many of the exiles from Nova Scotia eventually found a home.[24] In the warm, humid climate of the lower river rice, tobacco, indigo, and, later, sugar became the principal crops. Some attention

---

[22] Coyne, "Pathfinders of the Great Lakes," *op. cit.,* pp. 117-37.
[23] Priestley, *op. cit.,* 227.
[24] *Ibid.,* p. 225.

was also given to silk culture; while corn and beans were raised for local sustenance or for export to the West Indies.

River life in this lower area provided considerable interest and excitement. Fur-laden bateaux from the Illinois country, rowed or sailed down the river and on the return journey often hauled with main force by two tow ropes, presented a picturesque sight. This traffic served also to build up the port of New Orleans as a marketplace for the exchange of the natural products of the colony for French manufactured goods; here the Illinois traders could obtain a better rate of exchange than at Montreal or Quebec. The frequent menace of floods provided recurrent excitement along this lower stretch of the river, and was early responsible for the building of fifty miles or more of levees, twenty to thirty feet wide, which required constant watchfulness and repair. The presence in the community of a large proportion of Negro slaves, needed for work on the plantations and in the cypress saw mills, meant constant fear of a servile rebellion, and called for vigilance against miscegenation. To guard against these dangers, Governor Bienville imposed regulations in his "Code Noir" which, among other things, prohibited Negro assemblies and forbade the colored men the use of arms; but frequent Indian wars and sporadic raids which necessitated the arming of slaves for the protection of the colony made impossible the strict carrying out of the code.

Cosmopolitan as this Louisiana society was, its tolerance, so evident in regard to divergence in race, did not extend to matters of religion. Jews and heretics were forbidden entrance from the beginning. Religious life, much as in the case of French Canada, was under the direction of religious orders. In the northern part of the colony the Jesuits and Sulpicians dominated, whereas farther south religious work was carried on largely by Carmelites and Capuchins.

Louisiana as a French colony had only a short life and never achieved any considerable importance in its own right; but in the wider strategy of the colonizing powers of the age, as a factor in the interplay of international forces, probably no American colony played a more significant role.

III. THE FRENCH WEST INDIES

While throughout the seventeenth century the French colonies on the North American mainland languished for lack of colonists, French activities in the West Indies were popularly supported and attracted a striking number of immigrants. In the preceding century the French had been among the earliest and most persistent of the corsairs infringing on the Spanish monopoly, discovering, like the English and the Dutch, that the Spanish American theater of operations offered advantages not to be found elsewhere. Although Spain, in that century of her greatest power, had been able to counter with some success these encroachments of her envious rivals by such devices as a convoy system, a local naval patrol, and the meting out of stiff sentences to captured pirates, nevertheless her enemies had been far from routed. In 1588, their position was immensely strengthened by the heavy blow dealt Spanish sea power by the defeat of the Spanish Armada; by 1600 Spain's enemies in the Caribbean were more eager and hopeful of success than at any time since the discovery of America. On the death of Philip II in 1598, the Spanish crown, now carrying with it the Portuguese as well as the Spanish inheritance, passed to the weaker Philip III. Throughout his long reign the new king, like his father, was to be enmeshed in a fatally ambitious foreign policy and at the same time was to show himself equally blind to the economic needs of both Spain itself and the Spanish Indies. Though near the turn of the century both France and England signed treaties of peace with Spain, it was soon evident that neither power considered that these instruments limited their activities "beyond the line." [25] The French, though Roman Catholics like the Spaniards and not moved by the bitter religious animosity that inspired the English and the Dutch, were nevertheless as fully determined as the Protestants to secure commercial advantages at Spain's expense for their own enrichment.

As the seventeenth century opened, the traders and buccaneers of the three northern powers, with more or less support from their respective home governments, set out on a policy of establishing permanent bases within the Caribbean area by taking possession of islands and coastal regions hitherto neglected by Spain but long familiar to themselves as convenient piratical hideouts. The strategically located crescent of the Lesser Antilles,[26] or Caribbee Islands, guarding the eastern entrance to the Caribbean Sea, the semiderelict area of the Guiana coast lying on the South American shore between the mouths of the Amazon and the Orinoco rivers, the small islands off the coasts of Venezuela and Nicaragua, and the western half of Española, or Haiti, all appeared ripe for seizure by enterprising rivals. These intruders later justified themselves, not merely by the plea of "no peace beyond the line," but on the further pretension of a natural right to found colonies in any American lands that were not "effectively occupied" by another Christian nation. They desired these lands not only as

---

[25] For a discussion of this policy and the treaties involved, cf. A. P. Newton, *The European Nations in the West Indies, 1493-1688* (London: 1933), pp. 122-27.

[26] In modern usage the northern portion of the chain, Martinique northward to Puerto Rico, constitutes the Leeward Islands; those from St. Lucia southward to the mainland are the Windward group. An older classification, however, gave the name Windward to the whole chain from the Virgin Islands southward to Tobago and Trinidad, reserving the name Leeward to Margarita, Curaçao, Oruba, and lesser islands along the shore line of the South American mainland. *Cf.* Priestley, *op. cit.,* footnotes, pp. 76-77.

bases from which to continue their raiding and contraband trading operations in the Spanish area, but also wanted them as permanent plantation colonies where the new colonial commodities, now so highly valued in Europe, might be grown. Thus the opening of the seventeenth century saw the inauguration of a new era in which were mingled with the old piratical ambitions a modern colonial policy directed towards the establishment of permanent settlements for the production of colonial goods. Spain, on the other hand, did not change her objectives, but in this century continued to cling to her original colonial design of emphasizing the production and possession of the precious metals.

The first area to receive the colonizing attention of the interlopers was that of the Windward and Leeward Islands of the Lesser Antilles. Spain had never occupied these islands, partly because they contained no silver or gold, and partly because they were inhabited by fierce Carib Indians who preferred to die fighting rather than to be forced into practical slavery. The first island taken over in the new program was St. Christopher or St. Kitts Island. Here, in 1624, under the leadership of Thomas Warner, some fifteen English settlers landed and were presently joined by a group of French buccaneers whose captain was the celebrated privateer, Pierre d'Énambuc. The combined forces were sufficient to drive away the protesting Caribs, and the two intruding nationalities were able to divide the island between them on the peculiar plan of the English taking the center and the French the two ends—an arrangement that was to persist, though with considerable friction, until the eighteenth century. Within a short time many new settlers poured into both French and English St. Kitts; Negroes were introduced in considerable numbers and the planting of tobacco began. Though driven away by a Spanish fleet in 1629 the settlers soon returned. The French were particularly active in exploring operations and rapidly spread to the neighboring islands of St. Martin, Barbuda, Guadeloupe, Marie-Galante, and Martinique.

During the 1620's a group of some six hundred French and English buccaneers settled on Tortuga island off the northwest corner of Española. In 1635 they were driven off by the Spaniards who hanged all on whom they could lay hands.[27] For a time the colony languished but presently started up again, this time as a French colony which soon acquired importance as the nucleus from which settlers, in the second half of the century, spread over the fertile western half of the larger neighboring island of Española. As French Saint Domingue this latter colony became the most prosperous of the French West Indies, with the basis of its wealth the cultivation of sugar cane.

---

[27] Newton, *op. cit.*, p. 175, estimates that six hundred persons were executed.

These early seventeenth century French colonizing activities in the Antilles received the countenance and a certain amount of direction from Cardinal Richelieu who, in 1635, encouraged the organization by some Dieppe merchants of the Company of the Isles of America. The chief contribution of this commercial company, before its demise in 1648, was the dispatch of some five hundred colonists to the island of Guadeloupe. Under two leaders who were unwisely given equal authority, the history of this rich island for a time was one of internal dissension, the miseries of a "starving time," and fierce Carib warfare. Within a few years, however, this, like other French islands, attracted a rapidly increasing number of colonists who eventually achieved prosperity by raising plantation products. Some planters engaged on the side in buccaneering but very few attempted regular trading. The latter occupation was left almost exclusively to the Dutch who, down to 1665, specialized in the transportation to Europe of the new colonial products such as tobacco, sugar, cotton, indigo, cochineal, hides, etc., gathered from the French and English islands, as well as through contraband channels from Spanish America.[28] The Dutch islands of Curaçao, Buen Aire, and Aruba off the Venezuelan coast, and St. Eustatius and Saba in the Lesser Antilles, became great local entrepôts. But the prosperity and power of the Hollanders, always precariously based on a tiny home population of three millions, vanished in the second half of the seventeenth century under the combined blows of English Navigation Laws and three commercial wars waged against them by their French and English rivals.

When Colbert came to power in 1662, he found France possessed of some fourteen plantation colonies in the West Indies, with a population of fifteen thousand.[29] He determined to make them units in a great trading enterprise and meanwhile to fit them into a closely-knit administrative framework. His first step was the creation of a new commercial company, the West India Company, which he launched with a great deal of circumstance. The new company was given a monopoly embracing all the French colonial holdings bordering on the Atlantic, inclusive of Canada and the West Indies. The head of the company, a noble and distinguished soldier, the Marquis de Tracy, was made lieutenant-general of all French dominions in the West and, escorted by a naval flotilla, was sent on an eighteen months' inspection tour of the colonies. In the course of a year spent in the West India area, Tracy visited the Guiana coast and compelled the surrender of Cayenne which France had been claiming for the greater part of a century but which the Dutch had been occupying. His

---

[28] Newton, *op. cit.*, p. 154, states that Dutch illegal trade outstripped the Spanish fleet trade five or six to one.

[29] *Cf.*, Priestley, *op. cit.*, p. 73.

later visit to Quebec inspired Talon with enthusiasm for the idea of a rich Canadian-West Indies-European triangle trade.[30]

Tracy's departure from the Caribbean marked the beginning of a most distressing period for Spanish colonies in the area. Then the buccaneers became most daring and most effective in their depredations, an activity which continued unabated through the 1660's, 1670's and 1680's. The Caribbean area was ravaged from end to end by piratical flotillas made up of men of all nationalities, often under French leadership. The unfortunate inhabitants of the Spanish coastal towns were either slaughtered indiscriminately or cruelly tortured to force them to reveal the whereabouts of their wealth, while the cities themselves were reducd to smoking ruins.

The practices of the "Brethren of the Coast," responsible for these activities, were developed into a recognized technique and their customs into a professional code. The leader of a single-ship expedition was usually called the "captain," while the head of combined operations of several vessels was known as the "admiral." The individual buccaneer maintained a certain independence, except when actually engaged in battle, taking service under prearranged conditions and sharing in the spoils in a recognized proportion. For a number of years as many as fifteen hundred to two thousand of these rovers were constantly at sea. They might easily have been suppressed by the French and English navies if the respective governments had cared to take serious measures instead of winking at the villainous activities of the buccaneers as a means of curbing the maritime power of Spain and of forcing open the American seas—goals which piracy materially helped to achieve.

Spasmodically the Spaniards put up stout resistance and, at times when the odds were not too overwhelmingly against them, even succeeded in repulsing attacks and defeating the pirates. But while they could manage this and also cause all foreign settlements in the Caribbean to live in imminent danger of dislodgment, as a matter of fact the Spanish colonial authorities seldom possessed naval strength enough either to recoup their chief losses or to follow up any local success. As her competitors grew stronger, their activities more extended, and her own strength at home declined, Spain's position in the West Indies became progressively more hopeless.

Eventually His Catholic Majesty was compelled to sue for peace and sign with his chief colonial rivals a series of treaties which recognized their claim to the sovereignty of colonies within the American sphere. In return for this coveted legal status which was tacitly conceded by Spain in the Truce of Ratisbon of 1684, France undertook to curtail the activities of the

---

[30] Tracy was in the West Indies from June, 1664, to June 1665. He returned to France in August, 1667.

buccaneers. With the re-affirmation of the same principles in the general pacification at Ryswick in 1697, open piracy, at least during intervals of international peace, could no longer count upon the support of any of the western powers. For another century, however, at every outbreak of war the old-time buccaneers were likely to reappear under the more respectable guise of privateers armed with letters of marque which allowed them to fight under their nations' flags. It is to be noted that the suppression of open piracy at the close of the seventeenth century by no means implied the disappearance of its old companion, contraband trade. On the contrary, illicit trafficking at Spain's expense took on enlarged proportions in the eighteenth century.

Political organization in the West Indies showed many of the same features that marked the administration of French Canada. In both, unsuccessful company government was eventually superseded by direct control on the part of the crown. Richelieu, imperialistically inclined, sponsored monopolistic companies for each set of colonies. The first West India Company, established in 1626, and reorganized in 1635 as the Company of the Isles of America, was parallel in many ways to the Company of New France, bestowing many of the same privileges on the stockholders and involving many of the same obligations, though the Canadian company was more pretentious and longer lived. The Company of the Isles of America petered out in bankruptcy in 1638, and its holdings were sold to private proprietors. After an interlude, both Canada and the West Indies were reorganized in 1664 by the mercantilist Colbert and included in his huge West India Company. The reluctant proprietors in the French island were compelled to sell out to the new company.[31] The French West India Company lasted until 1674, by which time it had, like its predecessor, become utterly bankrupt and lost its monopolistic privileges, the crown taking over direct control as Colbert had always intended that it should.[32]

It is to be noted that the pattern of the French monopolistic company rule, dominant in West India history up to this time, presents a marked contrast to that of the contemporary English trading companies. To a very considerable extent, the French companies were creations of France's chief ministers who laid down their policies and carefully scrutinized their activities. Furthermore, the French crown expected to share directly in the profits of the various undertakings. In the case of the English companies, the initiative and direction normally came from a group of individuals or a private person who, having applied for a royal charter, might

[31] Priestley, *op. cit.*, pp. 88-89.
[32] S. L. Mims, *Colbert's West India Policy* (New Haven: 1912), pp. 179-81, points out that the company had served its purpose of providing a transition from the period of Dutch supremacy to that of a substantial growth of French commerce in the area.

be granted privileges of exploration and settlement with wide powers in both political and economic matters, as well as the right to reap the profits. The crown was not expected to exercise much direct control and to be satisfied with the general prosperity that might accrue to the mother country through increased trade and such direct revenues as might come in the way of taxes and excise.

Now that Colbert was able to set up direct governmental control by the crown, Martinique became the center of government, both for the West India Islands and the settlements on the Guiana coast, with a resident governor-general, intendant, and a sovereign council, much on the pattern prevailing in Quebec. Subject to this authority, each of the constituent units had its own lieutenant-governor. Both before and after the reorganization there was a succession of able governors. While the administration had centered in the French portion of St. Christopher, a picturesque and vigorous naval captain, Philippe Longvilliers de Poincy, had wielded firm authority as governor-general from 1636 to 1660; and from the appointment of Tracy with an over-all authority in 1664, down to 1690, capable men filled the governor's position in Martinique.

Economically, the West India Islands were fundamentally plantation colonies, raising tropical crops for an export trade. Tobacco was at first the great staple, but by the middle of the century was being overtaken in importance by sugar, for which the demand and the price were steadier. Other tropical goods such as indigo, cacao, cochineal, cotton, and logwood were also exported. Very little interest was displayed in producing the more prosaic food crops which could be secured more easily, along with European manufactured goods, from the Dutch traders who also supplied the Negro slaves needed for work on the plantations. The change from a regime of small proprietors growing a variety of crops with the help of indentured white labor to the system of large plantations worked by gangs of Negro slaves was not made so rapidly or so completely in the French islands as in those under the British flag. The smaller amount of French capital available for colonial speculative investment forced a slower transition from the old to the new system. The resident owners of the small farms therefore hung on longer, and social and economic displacements were not so severe. The island communities suffered less from the evils of absenteeism and continued to possess a larger proportion of white residents genuinely attached to their colonial homes. With trade less burdened by the frightful waste and heavy overhead charges of the almost universal absenteeism of the English system, French sugar prices could be kept consistently lower than those of their British competitors.[33] With

---

[33] L. J. Ragatz, *The Fall of the Planter Class in the British West Indies, 1700-1763* (New York: 1928), p. 4.

the removal of the incubus of the monopolistic company, the development of the sugar plantations, and the opening of a certain number of free ports for foreign trade, the French West India islands had entered by the close of the seventeenth century upon an era of great prosperity.[34]

The social scene reflected the economic interests of the islands. At the top were the officials, planters, and clergy; at the bottom, the white engagés and Negro slaves.[35] The engagés, theoretically at least, were voluntary immigrants who came under three-year contracts to work out their passage cost. Actually many had been shanghaied in European ports by ship captains who delivered them to the West India planters for 1,000 pounds of tobacco. At the end of their term of service they were supposed to be given 500 to 1,000 acres of land and a sum of money, or its equivalent in tobacco; but were frequently cheated out of these rewards for their labor. Their lot, little better than that of the Negroes, was one of extreme hardship, and many ran away. By the end of the century their cost had become prohibitive, and they were gradually replaced by Negroes; those in service were turned adrift to find a living for themselves as best they might. The fate of the Negro slaves, despite the existence of a *code noir* which prescribed a minimum of food and clothing, was little better at any time than one of extreme misery; it grew even worse in the second half of the century as the plantations became larger, sugar replaced tobacco, and absentee landlordism became prevalent. Cruel punishments, revolts, and brutal reprisals were the order of the day. Many fugitives, known as Maroons, roamed the interior in groups, and the whites were in constant fear of their attacks.

Education and missionary work among both the Negroes and the Carib Indians were much neglected. Though some members of the religious orders worked on the islands, missionary enterprise played no such important part as in Canada, with the result that gross ignorance and superstitious practices were widespread and deep-rooted. The French treatment of the Indians in this area was certainly better than that meted out by the Spaniards and the English, but their relations with the natives were not nearly so intimate as in Canada and Louisiana. There was less inducement for cordial relations in the West Indies than in those North American areas where the Indians so frequently opened the way to exploration and were the principal agents in securing the immense wealth of the fur trade. Towards the African Negroes the French planter's attitude, while not nearly so arrogant as that of the Spaniard or the Englishman, was never-

---

[34] In 1674 no less than 131 French private trading vessels were engaged in the West India trade. Mims, *op. cit.*, p. 180.

[35] The population of the French West Indies, shortly after Colbert's death, was 47,321 of which 18,888 were white. The most populous of the islands was Martinique with 16,254, followed by Guadeloupe with 8,698 and Saint-Domingue with 7,993. Among 28,534 blacks and mulattoes, 27,000 were slaves. *Cf.* Priestley, *op. cit.*, p. 91.

theless distinctly harsh, though he managed to bestow upon them a thin veneer of the French language and ways of life.

Among the various white groups in the islands there was a good deal of social activity which gave a certain air of liveliness to the scene. French officials continued to infuse into the colonial surroundings many of the amenities and a good deal of the social atmosphere of the French homeland. Much visiting back and forth among the islands and frequent entertainments on a pretentious scale, marked by considerable formality and ceremony, provided a pale reflection of the pomp and circumstance of Versailles.

Chapter 9

THE ESTABLISHMENT OF THE ENGLISH COLONIES

I. THE FOUNDING OF THE THIRTEEN COLONIES

Political Foundations

Elizabeth's policy eventually carried England into an open war with Spain which outlasted her reign. That conflict opened the seas to English ships but, so long as it continued, it absorbed all English energies so that none of the wealth in the rich American treasure-house could be garnered. The colonies that were planned in the sixteenth century by Gilbert and Ralegh were associated with the war effort of that age and were designed as bases against the Spaniards rather than as profitable commercial enterprises. With the accession of James I, peace with Spain, though not popular, became practical politics and was established by the treaty of 1605; once more Englishmen gradually gave their full attention to trade. Like the Spaniards, the English longed to draw riches from the New World; but by the beginning of the seventeenth century they realized that, unlike the Spanish lands, North America had no stores of gold and silver, and that the inhabitants were too poor and too primitive to trade with profitably. If worth-while resources were to be tapped in that part of America, permanent English colonies must be established. This commercial motive was one of the principal factors back of the new colonial drive, which speedily assumed the form of establishing permanent plantations on American soil north of that region which Spain had already appropriated. In the period from 1606 to 1620, this commercial motive was assuming a place of first importance.

Another motive which, as the Stuart age wore on, came to occupy as important a rôle as trade was religious dissatisfaction. In the period from 1620 to 1640, this became the predominant factor, and continued to be of first importance through the forties and fifties while England was either locked in civil war or living under the rule of Oliver Cromwell. In this period political discontent also added a considerable quota to emigration. With the Restoration and the more hopeful outlook in England that accompanied it, the new emphasis on expansion stressed the commercial factor.

The earlier religious element in American migration arose from the dissatisfaction of many Englishmen with the Elizabethan settlement of the Church question. Under the stress of the Protestant Reformation, the pendulum of religious opinion had swung violently back and forth a number of times, and the compromise, in the form of the Established Church which Elizabeth enforced, inevitably left many dissenters. The Roman Catholics, who refused to abandon the papal connection, constituted one minority group. The so-called "Separatists," who insisted that each religious congregation should be allowed to control itself, were far to the left on the Protestant side; while not numerous, they constituted a very vocal nonconformist body. To the right were the Puritans, most numerous of the dissenters; while they professed to be dissatisfied with the Established Church, they wished to remain a part of it and be allowed to reform it from within, swinging it closer to continental Protestantism.

As the first two Stuart kings threw in their lot with the more conservative elements of the Established Church, convinced, as James I put it, "No Bishop, No King," the dominance of Parliament came to be regarded as the chief protection of all the dissenting groups. In the decade of personal rule of Charles I, which followed the events of 1629,[1] the wave of emigrating dissenters rose to a flood. The civil war in the forties added to the exodus; many persons whom religion alone would not have moved became so troubled at the state of politics at home that they were prepared to face the hardships of the American wilderness in order to create there the kind of community that they desired for themselves and their children.

The first permanent colonies to be successfully established in America were planted under a charter granted by James I in 1606. Two different groups of merchants, one centering in London and the other in Bristol, Plymouth, and other towns, applied for such a document,[2] and the king granted one to both groups under the general name of the Virginia Company; organized as subsidiary companies, the two groups were called, after their respective places of origin, the London Company and the Plymouth Company. The charter, like all such documents, roughly defined the boundaries of the respective jurisdictions, and in addition to wide commercial privileges, bestowed certain rights of government. The London Company was given rights on the Atlantic coast of America between the 34th and the 41st parallels of latitude; the Plymouth Company's lands were farther to the north and were described as between the 38th and the 45th

---

[1] In 1629 the relations between the Court and Parliament became progressively worse; disputes over the religious issue, the tax known as tunnage and poundage, and the imprisonment of Parliamentary leaders were among the issues involved. Finally this Stuart king embarked on eleven years of rule without the assistance of Parliament.

[2] Among those petitioning were: Sir George Somers, Richard Hakluyt, Edward-Maria Winfield, Sir Thomas Gates, Raleigh Gilbert.

degrees.[3] In the middle portion, where their jurisdictions overlapped, the companies were given equal rights with the provision that neither should establish any settlement within 100 miles of one begun by the other. To both companies were granted such rights as those of assigning land, opening mines, providing for defenses, coining money, and importing certain articles for seven years free of duty.

The ultimate authority over any colonies planted was vested in a royal council called the Superior Council of Virginia, consisting of thirteen persons appointed by the king and resident in England. In addition to

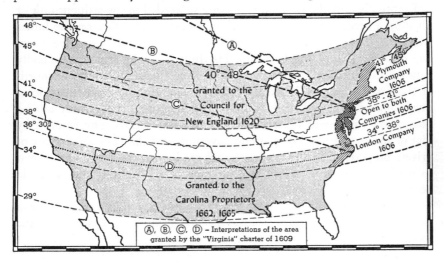

16. THE ROYAL GRANTS

this Superior Council, which was to represent the king's authority, there was provided for each of the two founding companies a council of thirteen members, appointed by the company, to be resident in America. Each local council was assigned certain rights and privileges: to make ordinances for the colony which must not be repugnant to the laws of England or the king's instructions; to sit as a court of justice; to appoint minor officials; and generally to exercise the functions of local administration. To the settlers the king promised "all Liberties, Franchises, and Immunities— as if they had been abiding and born, within this our Realm of England, or any other of our said Dominions." [4] As the charter creating the colonies

---

[3] Combined, the two grants covered the region between Cape Fear River and Bangor, Maine. In this charter of 1606 King James was apparently recognizing the right of Spain to lands in occupation, but not the papal bull of 1493; under this definition the Windward and Leeward Islands and Guiana lay open to English colonization. See Andrews, *The Colonial Period in American History*, I, pp. 82-83.

[4] First charter of Virginia, April 10, 1606. Quoted in H. S. Commager's *Documents of American History* (New York: 1934), pp. 8-10.

was from the king and not from Parliament (under the principle of English law that all ungranted land belonged to the king), it followed that it would be the crown, acting through the royal council, or an especially appointed body, and not Parliament, that would supervise them. The money for the enterprise was to be provided, however, not by the crown, but by private individuals. It is to be noticed that in the grants of 1606 there is evident a conception of a colonial system of government considerably in advance of that set forth in the charters of the sixteenth century.[5]

Eventually only the London Company succeeded in the arduous task of planting a permanent colony, founding Jamestown, in 1607, on the James River with 105 settlers. The history of this settlement in its first few years was one of suffering and hardship. The Indians of the region were badly handled and unfriendly. There was so much sickness that barely one fourth of the first two expeditions survived. The adoption of a system of joint ownership of land and stock functioned disastrously. It was only after a "starvation time" and the replacement of local council government by that of the strong hand of a single governor, and the re-establishment of private property, that a more prosperous era began; the settlers got down to work, a successful money crop in tobacco was found, and Virginia became a thriving colony.

As the settlements spread from the Tidewater region into the interior, a large measure of self-government was speedily granted. In 1609 and 1612 the sponsoring company was reorganized under new charters as a joint-stock company with enlarged rights and territories, and thereafter is known as the Virginia Company. The royal council resident in England was eliminated and all powers of government were entrusted to the Company. After trying the experiment of single-governor rule for a number of years, the Virginia Company under the leadership of the liberal-minded Sir Edwin Sandys in 1619 issued a charter of liberties to its colonists decreeing that the local government in Virginia should henceforth be composed of a governor and six councilors appointed by the Company to exercise executive functions and act as an Upper House, and a House of Burgesses with legislative functions, to be made up of representatives elected by the people of the various settlements.[6] In its main feature this form of government with its representative element, thus early granted to Virginia, became the model for all royal colonies until the Revolution. But within five years of the enlightened grant of these liberties, the Virginia Company met disaster. Dissentions among the leaders, financial difficulties, disputes

---

[5] *Cf.* J. S. Bassett, *A Short History of the United States* (New York: 1931), p. 45.

[6] For the considerations that led to the setting up of this first American legislative assembly, see Andrews I, ix.

over the tobacco monopoly, and suspicions by the king that the Company was overstepping its authority finally led to a commission of inquiry and an appeal by the crown to the courts, where in 1624 the charter was declared null and void.[7] Virginia thereupon became a royal colony, with its governor and council henceforth appointed directly by the king. Strangely enough, the House of Burgesses was retained, partly because James I died within a year and his successor, Charles I, had many other things to think about, and partly because the representative element in the government was seen to be a popular feature that helped to attract settlers and provided an easier way of securing the local revenue. The assembly, however, did not meet for legislative purposes until 1628 and did not receive the full approval of the crown until 1639.

North of Jamestown a number of other colonies, founded for the most part from religious motives, made their appearance along the Atlantic coast. In 1620 a group known as the Pilgrims settled at Plymouth. About a third of them were Separatists who some years earlier, in disgust at religious conditions in England, had migrated to Holland. There, however, they had so missed their native language and institutions that they had decided to cross the Atlantic and create in the American wilderness and under their own flag the type of community they sought. Accompanying these Separatist "Saints" were a larger number of "Strangers" who for the most part were lowly people from London and southeastern England, many of them members of the Established Church.[8] All had known poverty and were hoping to improve their lot in the New World. They discovered on arriving in Cape Cod Bay on the *Mayflower* in November, 1620, that their charter from the Virginia Company was invalid, as they had been blown north to a region beyond its jurisdiction. To meet this emergency, forty-one male settlers of the 102 persons on board drew up the Mayflower Compact (November 11, 1620), forming themselves into "A civil Body Politick . . . unto which we promise all due Submission and Obedience." [9] In this action, the Pilgrim Fathers probably had in mind the church covenants long in use among Separatists. In designing the Compact they were primarily intent on preserving the status quo and had no thought of writing a new charter of democracy; nevertheless their

---

[7] For greater detail on the reasons for the downfall of the Virginia Company, see Andrews, *op. cit.*, I, pp. 174-79.

[8] The three Pilgrims of later literary fame—Myles Standish, John Alden, and Priscilla Mullins—were almost certainly "Strangers," not Separatist "Saints." For greater detail see G. F. Willison's *Saints and Strangers* (New York: 1945), pp. 130-33. Only three of the Separatists on the Mayflower were originally from Scrooby—William and Mary Brewster and William Bradford.

[9] In the absence of a charter, the Mayflower Compact remained the basis of government in Plymouth until the union of the colony with Massachusetts in 1691. On the significance of the Compact see: Willison, *op. cit.*, 142-44.

document involved the acceptance of revolutionary principles of government that were to be more fully realized in a later time.

Ably ruled by governors of their own choosing, John Carver and later William Bradford, the Pilgrim settlers at Plymouth, though never numerous and at first suffering great hardships, soon became self-supporting. In 1621 the Pilgrims secured a new grant of land from the Council for New England [10] (a successor to the old Plymouth Company) [11] and as early as 1627 bought out the London merchants who had provided the funds for their expedition. Their colony grew and prospered steadily, if slowly, proving that an independent group without continued financial backing from home could settle in America and survive. Near the end of the century Plymouth was absorbed into the Colony of Massachusetts.

This colony of Massachusetts was settled by a group of Puritan Separatists who in 1629 applied to the king for a charter, which was granted under the name of the Governor and Company of Massachusetts Bay in New England. The original intention had been commercial, but the discovery of certain peculiarities in the wording of the charter gave the idea to some Puritan gentlemen that the governing body did not have to stay in England, like the old London and Plymouth companies: that the charter and governing body might be transported to America and made to serve as a framework of government for a colony of completely self-governing people who could set up any type of society that pleased them. The language of the charter referred to "freemen," instead of "shareholders" or "adventurers," and omitted to mention that the sessions of the governing council of eighteen "freemen" must be held in England. It seemed feasible to take the council to America and establish a Puritan commonwealth in a new world. John Winthrop, a wealthy and influential Puritan, was induced to act as leader for the 840 immigrants who landed near Boston in 1630.

After the usual initial struggles with the new environment and the settlement of dissensions springing from an effort by the first-comers to keep the government in the hands of a narrow oligarchy, by 1634 Massachusetts had achieved a stable and unique government. This consisted of a governor, deputy governor, and assistants, together with a General Court, which met four times a year. This Court in one session was made up of all the "freemen" and elected the executive officers; in the other three sessions

---

[10] The Council for New England was set up in 1621, with a grant of land from parallel 40 to 48 and "from sea to sea."

[11] The Plymouth Company, less wealthy and powerful than the London Company, had a shorter and less fortunate history. In May, 1607, it dispatched two ships with 120 men under George Popham and Raleigh Gilbert and established a settlement on the coast of Maine at the mouth of the Kennebec River, then known as the Sagadahoc River. This venture did not prosper and was abandoned after a year's trial. The Company then turned its attention to the fisheries along the Maine coast, which proved profitable.

it consisted of representatives of the towns and functioned as a legislative assembly. Massachusetts was thus a self-governing commonwealth, but the franchise was limited to church members; the founders of the state intended Massachusetts to be a Puritan stronghold and proposed to keep political power in the hands of those whom they regarded as virtuous and godly men. Non-Puritans, if they remained, were expected to be quiet and were not given the franchise; if they sought to spread their views, they were sent out of the colony as quickly as possible. Needless to say, difficulties soon arose from the presence of dissenting Puritan elements within the colony. Presently groups of these either migrated voluntarily or were banished as heretics. Among the most notable were Roger Williams who founded Providence in 1636, Anne Hutchinson who fled to Providence and later founded Portsmouth (1638), Rev. John Wheelwright who led a group to Exeter in New Hampshire, and Thomas Hooker who went to Hartford. In other words, religious dissent, springing from the intolerant policy of the strict Puritans in Massachusetts, led to new settlements that became the centers of other New England states. Of these, the Connecticut settlements secured a separate charter in 1662, Rhode Island in 1663, and New Hampshire in 1679. Massachusetts continued to claim jurisdiction over Maine until 1820, when separation was finally effected.

Besides charter (or corporate) colonies and the royal colonies, there soon appeared a third type called the proprietary colony. The first successful one of these was founded when Charles I granted a charter, carrying with it extensive lands and governing privileges, to Cecil Calvert, Lord Baltimore, a representative of that group of nonconformists of the Roman Catholic faith in England with whom the Stuarts had so much sympathy. The first of these colonists arrived in Maryland in 1634. The colony, having at once been granted religious toleration and representative government to all comers, throve from the beginning.

There had thus been developed, in the first twenty-five years of English settlement, three types of colonies: 1. The royal colony, in which governor and council were appointed by the crown and the assembly was elected by the people (this kind of colony was more directly under royal control than other types, and it became the king's policy to try to mold all colonies into this pattern); 2. the corporate colony, exemplified by Massachusetts Bay Colony, in which the freemen acting as the shareholders constituted a self-governing corporation which, under charter from the king, elected not only its own legislative assembly, but the upper house and governor as well; 3. the proprietary colony, in which the charter was granted to an individual, like William Penn or Lord Baltimore, who took the place of the king in appointing governor and council and by whose permission the legislature was elected.

17. THE THIRTEEN COLONIES

With the Restoration there came a new surge of imperialism and a new wave of colony planting that was aimed at filling the gaps left in the chain of English colonies along the Atlantic coast and at pushing the Spanish frontier as far back as possible. In 1663, the Carolinas were granted to a group of eight proprietors who had been prominent in effecting the Stuart restoration; in 1664, advantage was taken of the Dutch war to secure New York, which was presently made into the two proprietary colonies of New York and New Jersey; in 1681, Pennsylvania and Delaware were granted to William Penn as a refuge for the Quakers. The list of the Atlantic colonies was made complete by the granting of Georgia in 1733 to a philanthropist, James Oglethorpe, who hoped to make it a refuge for English debtors and persecuted German Protestants. All the southern colonies were founded with the clear knowledge that their acquisition invited trouble, since the region had long been claimed by Spain. From this aspect, the southern colonies of the seventeenth and eighteenth centuries continued the challenge thrown down to Spain by the sea dogs of the sixteenth century.

Toward the close of the Stuart period, the English crown embarked on a potentially important experiment, involving greater colonial consolidation. The change was the outgrowth of a variety of factors: numerous complaints poured into London from the non-Puritan colonists of Massachusetts concerning the intolerance and arbitrary behavior of their elected governors, in whose election they had had no voice; insistent demands came from the English merchants for better enforcement of the trade laws in New England; there was an ominous lack of unified defense measures against the growing menace of French and Indian raids. All these considerations finally induced the king, in 1684, to revoke the Massachusetts charter and take steps to form a union of the more northern Atlantic coastal colonies. Consequently, Massachusetts, Plymouth, Maine, New Hampshire, and part of Rhode Island were all united in the so-called "Dominion of New England" with provision for the later inclusion of Connecticut and Rhode Island. Moreover, in 1686, Sir Edmund Andros arrived in America commissioned as governor to put into effect an even larger union, embracing not only all New England, but New York and New Jersey as well. These schemes of colonial unification, which marked the last four years of the Stuart regime, were intensely unpopular among the bulk of the English colonists and, with the success in England of the "bloodless revolution" of 1688, fell into abeyance.[12]

---

[12] The standard work on this most important experiment in colonial consolidation ever embarked upon by England is *The Dominion of New England,* by Viola F. Barnes (New Haven: 1923).

The succession of William III and Mary brought Massachusetts, in 1691, the grant of a new charter, this time of a modified royal-colony pattern.

In local organization and administration, the English colonists were influenced both by English traditions and by the character of the lands on which they settled. In New England, where the ground was hard and agriculture unprofitable, the population tended to settle in villages and set up a town form of organization. In the typical New England town, once the site had been decided upon, a meeting house would be built, a portion of land reserved for a common, and the lands around it parceled out. Ungranted lands were held by the town trustees for common use until they should pass into private ownership. To the town meeting all must come or pay a fine, and from the community representatives would be sent to the colony's legislature. Within the town, religion and politics tended to fuse, and the local proprietors considered that they had the right to accept or refuse permission to later comers to settle within the town limits or share equally in the original privileges.

In the southern colonies, where agriculture was the normal occupation and settlement tended to be by single families, town organization was not found suitable, and the shire or county form of organization was used instead. The county court meeting, held at the crossroads several times a year, was a center at which social and business matters, as well as legal affairs, were attended to. The counties in turn were subdivided into parishes, each governed by a vestry which attended not only to church affairs but also to minor judicial cases, looked after the poor, and collected local rates. The counties were created by the colonial assembly and were by no means equal in size, nor did they wield the same amount of influence in the legislature. The older counties of the coastal area tended to be smaller than those in the interior and to have an unduly large number of representatives in the assembly, where they used their weight to delay as long as they could the creation of "back counties," and to make these, when created, as large as possible with the least number of representatives. This practice led to prolonged conflicts and built up a class bitterness as the back counties filled with poor people, mainly of German and Scotch-Irish descent, who resented the continued political dominance of the aristocracy of the favored coastal area. In the north this conflict between the old and the new settlements had its counterpart in the differences over many issues between the conservative and wealthy business interests of the east and the small farmers of the interior. The newer community stood for the new democratic practices and equalitarian views that long seemed to the aristocrats of the east dangerous, demagogic, and subversive of the best values that tradition and experience had taught; to the western farmers, the conservatism of the east seemed selfish and obstructive of progress. Throughout the history of the United States, these two forces were to act as rival influences on the course of events. *farmer, aristocrat*

The middle colonies, drawing inspiration from both north and south, combined in their form of local government ideas that were drawn from both the town and county organizations and fused them into a system in which both were important. By the close of colonial times the county system of administration had been extended to all the colonies, though in New England it was of secondary importance in comparison with the older town unit of local government.

Within one or another of these forms of political framework, each colony worked out its political history in the century or more between its planting and the Revolution, and its leaders gained that invaluable experience in practical affairs of government which made them ready to carry on without a pause when, at the close of the eighteenth century, the revolutionary movement brought independence. On the whole, in developing their political machinery, the English colonies clung tenaciously to the body of rights and liberties that they had brought with them. Besides their charter rights, these included the English common law and a vague body of ideas which the colonists spoke of as "the rights of Englishmen." All these were based on Magna Charta, the Petition of Rights, the Bill of Rights, Habeas Corpus, and the principle of no taxation without representation. From the beginning there was a considerable degree of self-government. The earliest charters were themselves liberal, and became the basis of the provincial governments that everywhere granted to the freemen the right to elect representatives to sit in legislative assemblies. As time went on, these freemen demanded more and more rights and came to think of each of their colonial assemblies as a little House of Commons in which they struggled to exert influence over executive action, through their control of the budget, as their forefathers had done in England. By the close of the seventeenth century, deadlock between the elected legislature and the appointed executive had become the normal state of affairs in most English colonial capitals.

By the eighteenth century, it had become the settled policy of the king to bring all proprietary and charter colonies directly under the crown by transforming them all into royal colonies, supervised by the Board of Trade. On the whole, the colonists preferred to be under the crown to being under a private proprietor. The English Parliament, at swords' points with the kings through much of the eighteenth century, showed itself suspicious of these royal moves; but when, after 1760, Parliament took into its own hands the government of the colonies, it only increased the difficulties of the colonists; Parliament's record of mismanagement was to prove far worse than that of the king had ever been.

Economic and Commercial Structure

The commercial structure of England and her colonies in the seventeenth century falls within the general pattern of the economic practices of the mercantile system. National self-sufficiency and a favorable balance of trade were the goals at which all nations aimed, and the primary purpose of colonies was thought to be the making of a considerable contribution to the welfare of the motherland and of the empire of which they formed a part. England was proclaiming no novel doctrine, therefore, when she insisted that all trade within her empire should benefit nationals and not foreigners; that it should be so organized as to make the merchants of the mother country the chief beneficiaries; and that a revenue should accrue to the English exchequer as some compensation for the expense involved in the establishment and continued defense of the colonies.

It is to be noted that this system assumed that trade regulations were the proper concern of the national government. Gone was the medieval view that trade was the business of the municipality, and not yet conceived was the nineteenth century theory of laissez faire, under which it was to be held that economic affairs flourish best when they are left to the unregulated activities of individuals pursuing their own best interests. The seventeenth century frankly believed in commercial regulation on a national scale, took the subject very seriously, and, in the field of the relations of colonies to motherland, worked out a more logical system than the one they contrived in the parallel field of political relations. It was the dream of that mercantile age to make England the center of a great self-sufficient empire, the component parts of which would not compete with each other. That the mother country who initiated the whole process, who supplied the capital and population, who planted, sustained, and defended the colonies, should be the chief beneficiary was taken for granted.

The colonies on the North American mainland were only a part of the empire. Other colonies with completely different needs, and designed to serve very different purposes, were scattered around the globe. In a general way, the American colonies were thought of as supply points from which many kinds of raw materials, needed for the navy and for British manufactures, would naturally come; in return, they would take goods manufactured in England and be given a protected position in the English market. As this system worked out in English practice, it produced economically a good deal of satisfaction to both sides. A group of colonies grew up that enjoyed a prosperity unexampled in the contemporary colonial world. The basic economic facts were sound: namely, that the colonies were interested primarily in agriculture, lumbering, and the extractive industries; therefore, as exporters, they needed to dispose of the surplus raw materials, and, as consumers, they required manufactured goods. Where private interests clashed, these tended to adjust themselves in the general well-being. The worst rub came from the fact that the regulations for this commerce were made in England and in decisions relating to them the colonists could exercise very little control. As most of the restrictions, however, were only superficially enforced, the pressure was not very heavy; also tending to silence protest was the fact that the colonies were in desperate need of defense—from the French on the north and west, the Spaniards on the south, and the Indians on every frontier—and this protection the mother country alone could provide.

In England there were two centers of colonial control—the crown and Parliament; a consequent difficulty was that the relationship of these authorities to each other, in the matter of colonial jurisdiction, was never completely clear. In general, as the seventeenth century wore on, Parliament tended to gain at the expense of the crown. In granting the original charters for the creation of colonies in America, the king had reserved for himself ultimate jurisdiction over all colonial possessions; colonization was to be an undertaking primarily dependent, at least politically, on the king rather than on Parliament; consequently, it was the crown acting through the Privy Council, and not Parliament, that provided the instructions and attempted to exercise general supervision over the affairs of the new settlements. Both James I and Charles I tried hard to make this reserved authority effective, and, on a number of critical occasions, appointed special commissions to investigate colonial conditions and to make reports upon which remedial measures could be based. Both monarchs, however, were too involved in the constitutional struggle at home to be wholly effective in so distant a field as colonial administration.

During the Civil War and Commonwealth periods, Parliament, in this field as in others, took over the prerogatives of the crown; thereafter it exercised not only political authority over the colonies, but also proceeded to lay down commercial regulations governing the economic relations of the colonial settlements with the motherland. From earliest days Parliament had claimed the right to determine the extent to which the king could interfere in financial matters, and in the Cromwellian period, when the Whig merchants and the county squires constituted the dominant element in the government, it was only to be expected that Parliament would stiffen economic control over an empire which they regarded as primarily a commercial undertaking, and provide rules that would safeguard their own interests. While more liberal than that of any other empire of the seventeenth century, the English legislation that produced the first of the navigation laws was based on no other conception than the view that colonies should be in a subordinate position to the motherland.

With the Restoration, the crown came back to some extent into its own. The responsibility for seeing that the terms of the colonial charters were carried out, and that the royal duties involved in the crown's right of ultimate supervision were really performed, was placed in the hands of an advisory committee of the Privy Council, called a Council for Foreign Plantations. In 1675 this body was replaced by a standing committee of the Privy Council called the Lords of Trade, which functioned until the Revolution of 1688. While these bodies had no executive authority, and were obliged constantly to refer to the Privy Council or the Secretary of State to secure definite action, and were therefore slow and uncertain, and at times corrupt, nevertheless they were staffed with important public men who, on the whole, were well-informed and genuinely interested in the welfare of the colonies.

In 1696, under William III and Mary, the Lords of Trade were superseded by a body independent of the Privy Council, called the Commissioners of Trade and Plantations, or the Board of Trade, under the nominal supervision of the Secretary of State of the Southern Department who was answerable to Parliament. Like the committees of the Privy Council before it, the Board of Trade had no independent executive power, and its decisions had frequently to wait on the pleasure and energy of the Secretary of State. The impotence of this body through long periods has been held by some students to have been a fruitful source of weakness of the old empire. As the cabinet system developed in the eighteenth century, the duties of the Board of Trade tended to slip away from it; and eventually, in 1768, a Colonial Secretary of State became the head of colonial affairs, a step which marked the final triumph of Parliament in its contest with the crown for direct supervision over the colonies. On the American side of the Atlantic, the chief agencies through which the Board of Trade or one of its variants functioned were the royal governors, judges, customs collectors, and vice-admiralty courts. The chief defect of these bodies, as that of the Board itself, was lack of expert training and consequent lack of system, with inefficiency and annoyance being the inevitable result.

It was in the period of the Protectorate that the Navigation Ordinance of 1651, the most fundamental of all English economic measures affecting the colonies, became law. This was passed by Parliament partly to strike at the Dutch, in whose hands hitherto had been most of the carrying trade of the world, and partly to please the English merchants who had played a prominent role in the revolutionary movement that had brought Charles I to the block, and whose interests were represented by the dominant element in Parliament. The obvious purpose of the law was to restrict

English and colonial trade to English and colonial shipping and so increase the naval and commercial strength of the empire. Earlier laws of the same general import had been in existence for years, but had been less complete. The most important clauses of the new legislation provided: (1) That goods produced in Africa, Asia, or America, including the colonies, could be brought to English ports only in English or colonially owned and manned ships, under penalty of forfeiture of goods and ships; (2) that European products could be taken to England or British possessions only in English or colonial ships, or in ships of the country in which the goods originated; (3) British coasting trade was limited to British ships; (4) salted fish, oil, or whale products might be brought into British possessions only in English ships, and also exported only in such ships. To a great extent this Navigation Ordinance of 1651 fulfilled its purpose; shipbuilding in both old and new England was encouraged, the number of ships and sailors was increased greatly, and presently pre-eminence in the carrying trade of the world was to pass into English hands.

After the Restoration, the influence of the merchants was still strong enough to secure not merely the continuance but a strengthening of the policy of Cromwell that had been so favorable to them. The Ordinance of 1651 was not only re-enacted in stronger form in the act of 1660, but with the important addition that certain enumerated colonial products—at first tobacco, sugar, indigo, cotton, wool, ginger, and dye woods—destined for a foreign port, must first be landed in England or Ireland, or in some colony other than that from which these goods had originated. This amendment aimed at depriving of a return cargo any foreign vessel that might carry their own goods to colonial ports; the object was either to eliminate entirely or greatly reduce that trade. The law also forced colonial vessels to carry these enumerated goods, if destined for European markets, to British ports first, and so gave English middlemen the business of handling the colonial goods and the English revenue the benefit of customs duties.

A supplementary act of 1663 provided that European goods destined for America, with but a few exceptions, could be dispatched to the colonies only from England in English or colonial ships; in other words, this law placed the handling of the colonial import trade completely in the hands of English merchants. As evasions were numerous, a third act of 1673 required that every ship loading enumerated commodities must either give bond for landing them in England or pay the stipulated duties on the spot. Taken together, these laws meant that colonial enumerated commodities could be sold only in England; and that European goods, with few exceptions, could reach the colonies only through England and in English and colonial ships; and that, consequently, most of the colonial importations would be English goods. In other words, the laws were designed to benefit English industry as well as the king's revenue, with little consideration for the interests of the colonies.

So far as the northern colonists on the American mainland were concerned, this policy of enumeration affected their export trade at first only slightly. Tobacco was the only enumerated article of the earliest list that was produced in mainland colonies. Their other exports, such as fur, fish, lumber, wheat, pork, beef, and other food products were not affected for a good many years, except through increased freight rates. On the other hand, the trade in the opposite direction, the import trade, was materially involved as the result of the acts was practically to confine American purchases to English goods, regardless of price, and make it generally true that colonials must sell their raw goods cheaply while paying high prices for English manufactured goods.[13]

The one section of the colonies that was struck hardest from the beginning by the new law was the South. It seemed strange to the people of Virginia and Maryland that these new laws and new customs duties on tobacco, enacted so soon after the Restoration, should strike particularly hard at the basic product of those colonies whose loyalty to the Stuart house had been particularly strong. The decades following the Restoration were economically black years in the southern colonies, partly because of the new regulations and partly because of overproduction. Bacon's Rebellion (1676) was an expression of widespread dissatisfaction in Virginia with post-Restoration economic conditions, as well as a protest on the part of the back counties against the neglect of frontier interests by a colonial legislature unfairly dominated by the richer eastern counties.[14] When rice was added to the enumerated list in 1706 another southern colony, South Carolina, was badly hit; the price was so raised that for a time she lost the important portion of this trade that had gone to Spain and Portugal, one tenth of the total export. The northern colonies were adversely affected when additional articles, placed on the enumerated list in the early eighteenth century, included molasses, naval stores, copper, and beaver skins. A Molasses Act of 1733 that struck hard at a profitable West Indian trade from the northern and middle colonies by laying prohibitory duties on molasses, sugar, and rum imported from foreign colonies would have done still more damage, but it became a dead letter soon after its passage because of general evasion and nonenforcement. Other trade and tariff acts, intended to protect English agricultural and industrial interests and

---

[13] On the Navigation Laws and their effects, cf. J. S. Bassett, op. cit., pp. 78, 81, 142-45; also H. U. Faulkner, *American Political and Social History* (New York: 1948), pp. 79-81.

[14] For an interesting study of this movement, see T. J. Wertenbaker's *Torchbearer of the Revolution; the Story of Bacon's Rebellion and its Leader* (Princeton: 1940).

A cattle fair, Bowling Green, founded by William Kieft, 1641. Central panel in a tapestry portraying life in early New Amsterdam. (Courtesy of the American Museum of Natural History)

Scenes representing outstanding events in early Pennsylvania history. (*Above*) A late nineteenth-century reconstruction of the landing of William Penn painted by J. G. Ferris. (*Below*) William Penn's treaty with the Indians. (Both courtesy of the American Museum of Natural History)

to restrict colonial industrial development by prohibiting the export from the colonies of woolen goods, beaver hats, and manufactured iron were limiting and annoying rather than serious. Another field where regulation was much resented was the financial, in which the British, with a view to safeguarding British merchants from loss due to depreciated or otherwise unstable currency, forbade the issuance of paper money. This regulation kept the colonies perpetually short of a medium of exchange.

But while to the colonists these limitations in the old mercantile system were a source of increased prices in consumer goods, and caused much annoyance and friction, it should not be overlooked that the system brought them certain definite advantages. Some of these were: a real share for colonial ships in the monopoly of the English carrying trade; a practical monopoly of the English market for tobacco; a preferential tariff in their favor for certain of their important products such as iron, silk, and molasses; a sure market, with bounties, for naval stores; employment for their shipyards; and certain refunding tariffs on goods sent to the colonies from England. While these benefits were real and collectible, the restrictions in the navigation laws against the colonies remained for the most part unenforced and unenforceable, and consequently affected their prosperity only slightly until the very close of the colonial era. The colonists justified the widespread and continued evasion by claiming that the laws were unjust, and that they had not their due share of influence in their making. British officials themselves, through inefficiency, lack of interest, vague policy, or graft, winked at these violations. Certainly, despite all limitations, colonial trade flourished greatly and colonial ports grew in population and wealth. From the ports of New England, Boston, Providence, Newport, Portsmouth, New Haven, New London, and many smaller places, a brisk export trade was carried on in naval stores, lumbering, shipbuilding, codfish, cod and whale oil, horses, and cattle. From the middle colonies through New York, Philadelphia, Baltimore, and other ports, went chiefly flour, wheat, and salted pork; and the South, through Charleston, made money in tobacco, rice, indigo, lumber, naval stores, and shipbuilding.

The most profitable trade developed in colonial times was the "triangle trade," in which the West Indies played a key rôle, and in which the northern and middle colonies were particularly active. The southern colonies were not so involved—carrying on their principal trade directly with England. There were three principal trade "triangles." Ships from New England and the middle colonies, loaded with their characteristic raw products—fish, flour, lumber, and foodstuffs—carried these to the West Indies; here the colonial products were exchanged for tropical goods which were then taken to England and bartered for the manufactured articles for which there was a ready sale in the colonies; in this three-cornered arrangement there were handsome profits. A second "triangle" was one formed by carrying the colonial products to southern Europe, either directly or by the West Indies, and here an exchange was made for wines, fruits, and currency, which then were invested in manufactured goods in England to be taken home to America. The third "triangle" that brought large profits was one in which rum from New England was bartered on the West African coast for slaves, gold dust, and palm oil; the slaves thus secured were carried to the West Indies and there exchanged for sugar and molasses, which in turn were in great demand in the colonies for the making of rum.[15] So great was the demand for slaves in the West Indies that in 1760 a slave costing £12 on the African coast brought £35 in Jamaica.[16] This third "triangle" involved a large illegal molasses and sugar trade in the West Indies; there the British islands (the only legal source) not only charged a higher price, but did not produce enough molasses and sugar for the New England rum-makers, who consequently sought and secured much of their needed supply through contraband trade with the French and Dutch islands. It was complaints from the British West Indian sugar planters that brought about the passing of the Molasses Act of 1733, so notoriously evaded through many years.

In assessing the advantages and disadvantages to the colonists of the mercantile system, the theories of which dominated the old British Empire, it must be borne in mind that the American colonies were in an early stage of development and were interested primarily in agricultural and extractive industries; that, consequently, a system laying emphasis on the exchange of colonial raw products for the manufactured goods of the mother country was one that met the fundamental needs of the situation; and secondly, that many of the evils inherent in the restrictive provisions were largely absent in practice because they were not enforced. All, therefore, went fairly well until Great Britain, at the close of a series of expensive wars—designed at least in part to free her colonies from their external enemies—reduced by half the duties provided by the Molasses Act and other trade measures and really undertook to enforce them.

II. THE ENGLISH AT HUDSON BAY

The eager and persistent search for a northwest passage to the Orient by English navigators who followed Cabot's trail to the New World in the sixteenth and early seventeenth centuries dotted the waste lands and frigid waters of the far north with English names and served to establish

---

[15] On the "triangle trade" cf. Faulkner, op. cit., p. 54.
[16] Bassett, op. cit., p. 145.

England's claims in that barren region. Hudson Bay itself was a seventeenth century discovery. Though Martin Frobisher's fleet had entered the strait that leads to it in 1578, it was not until 1610 that Henry Hudson, backed at the time by English capital, sailed the entire length of the strait [17] and entered the bay itself. After a winter of starvation spent on the southeast shore of James Bay, a mutiny which brought death to both Henry Hudson and his son prevented further exploration of the shores of the great inland sea. Convinced, however, that the prize of the northwest passage was practically in hand, interested parties in England continued the quest, dispatching a succession of expeditions in the following years: that of Thomas Button, 1612-1613; those of Robert Bylot and William Baffin, 1615 and 1616; and those of Luke Foxe and Thomas James as late as 1631.[18] But finally the disappointing conclusion had to be accepted that no one could find any westward route out of the bay leading towards the Pacific with its silks and spices.

For the next four decades, interest in Hudson Bay languished. In these years English overseas adventurers turned their attention southward to the founding of the Thirteen Colonies in the more temperate zone on the American mainland north of Florida, and to the conquest and development of a number of tropical plantation colonies among the West Indian islands of "the American Mediterranean."

Both in the West Indies and on the mainland these same decades saw the French enter into stubborn competition, disputing every English move. In the region between New England and Hudson Bay, which the French claimed as peculiarly their own, the rivals competed jealously for the fisheries off Newfoundland and in the Gulf of St. Lawrence. In Acadia, along the St. Lawrence valley, and by the shores of the Great Lakes the French established a string of colonies; still farther into the interior went the voyageurs along the various tributaries feeding these waters. In 1663, after an early period of company rule, all New France was brought under the direct control of the crown as a royal province, giving evidence of a new determination on the part of Louis XIV to support more strenuously the exploring and colonizing efforts of his subjects in the New World. Two years later Jean Talon arrived in Canada as Louis XIV's chief businessman. He was to prove an ardent imperialist and an effective instrument in establishing the new dispensation.

It was in the late 1660's that in both England and France popular interest in Hudson Bay suddenly revived, stimulated once more by the prospect of great riches. This time they were to be drawn, not from the spices

---

[17] The strait is 450 miles long.
[18] For details of these voyages, see J. A. Williamson, *Short History of British Expansion* (New York: 1931), Vol. I, pp. 236-39.

and gems of the distant East through the long-sought northwest passage, but from northern furs, a natural product of the Bay region itself and the foundation of a trade more in keeping with the prosaic spirit of the later age.

Strangely enough, it was the initiative of two discontented French adventurers, Pierre Esprit Radisson and Médard Chouart, Sieur des Groseilliers, that drew English attention once more to the Bay. Disgusted with what they regarded as a grossly unfair fine imposed upon them by the French authorities at Quebec for having embarked on a profitable fur-trading expedition without government license, the two voyageurs left the French colony, and in 1666 after various misadventures appeared at the English court. Here they successfully urged English material support for extensive fur-trading operations in Hudson Bay,[19] offering their own detailed plans and experienced leadership. It is almost certain that in their American wanderings they had personally reached the Bay by way of one of its several western tributaries.[20] They could therefore speak with circumstantial knowledge of the advantages to be derived from the establishment of fur-trading posts on the western shores of an inland sea reaching halfway across the North American continent. From vantage points so placed, they pointed out, it would be perfectly feasible to tap the very source of the wealth of the fast-growing French fur empire of the interior, undisturbed by hostile Iroquois, and at the same time enjoy the advantages of a direct, cheap, sea route to European markets.

They had arrived at a fortunate time, just as the Restoration had given a new impulse to English colonial ambitions and when many members of the English nobility, driven by poverty brought on by the events of the two previous decades, were turning to the promotion of trade and overseas expansion. If these could take the direction of curbing the dangerously growing ambitions of Louis XIV, or of deflating the Dutch, or both, so much the better. The recent capture of New Amsterdam had served to start rumors of the immense wealth that the Dutch had been gathering from the fur trade along the Hudson River. To Englishmen the very name of Hudson conjured up thoughts of wealth. Charles II and his courtiers were thus in a frame of mind to listen with interest to the two Frenchmen. Not only were they affably received and given a retaining fee to hold them in London, but presently (1668) two English vessels, one with Chouart and the other with Radisson aboard, were dispatched on a preliminary expedition to Hudson Bay. When one of these returned with an immensely

---

[19] Cf. D. MacKay, The Honourable Company (London: revised edition, 1938), p. 36.
[20] Cf. Agnes C. Laut, The Adventurers of England on Hudson Bay (Toronto: 1921), pp. 29-31; also see MacKay, op. cit., p. 21. For a more skeptical view see T. G. Marquis, "The Adventurers of Hudson Bay" in Canada and Its Provinces (Toronto: 1913), Vol. I, p. 160.

rich cargo after a winter spent in James Bay, there was little further hesitation. On May 2, 1670, King Charles bestowed a charter upon his popular cousin,[21] Prince Rupert, and a score of associates, mostly from the nobility and landed gentry. The corporation thus founded was given the name of "The Governor and Company of Adventurers of England Trading into Hudson's Bay." The charter, whose terms were drafted on a magnificent scale, made the members absolute proprietors of all the territories drained by waters flowing into Hudson Bay, and gave them a monopoly of all trade, as well as control of all minerals, furs, and fish of the entire region. Neither the king nor the Company could have conceived either the vast sweep of territory included in Rupert's Land or its immense wealth. The Hudson's Bay Company's charter also bestowed wide governmental powers, giving the associates the right to rule all the inhabitants, to make laws, erect forts, maintain garrisons, use the necessary force to expel enemies, and to arrest and send home to England all interlopers.[22] As a consideration, the Company bound itself to pay to the king "two Elkcs and two Black beavers whensoever and as often as Wee our heires and successors shall happen to enter into the said Countryes." [23] The Company's first governor was Prince Rupert, an old cavalier of the English Civil War and a distinguished soldier of the Protestant cause on the continent, who had settled in England at the Restoration and was widely respected as a man of versatile ability. The second governor was the Duke of York, until his accession as James II in 1685, when he was succeeded by the famous John Churchill, later Duke of Marlborough.

As a trading organization, the Hudson's Bay Company flourished from the start, although after the outbreak of official war between England and France in 1689 [24] there were long intervals when no dividends were declared.[25] The Company, however, enjoyed from the beginning two great and solid advantages over the French traders: cheaper, more durable English manufactured goods in steady supply, and immensely lower transport rates by sea into the very heart of the best beaver country. From the beginning the Company wisely adopted a policy of honesty and fair dealing with the natives, paying them fixed and reasonably good prices and encouraging them to take substantial and lasting articles in exchange for their

---

[21] Prince Rupert's mother was Elizabeth, Queen of Bohemia, and a sister of Charles I.

[22] Cf. D. M. Wrong, The Rise and Fall of New France (New York: 1928), Vol. II, p. 595; also MacKay, op. cit., p. 39.

[23] MacKay, op. cit., p. 40. The last occasion on which this was paid was at Winnipeg in the summer of 1938, during the visit of King George VI and Queen Elizabeth to Canada.

[24] Known in Europe as the War of the League of Augsburg and in America as King William's War.

[25] No dividends were paid from 1691 to 1717. Cf. MacKay, op. cit., App. D, p. 339.

furs, rather than worthless trinkets.[26] Until the pressure of French competition became too great, the policy was to keep the consumption of intoxicating spirits to a minimum. Although the Hudson's Bay Company, unlike the French fur traders, did not encourage its servants to make friends with the Indians and learn their language, and although it frowned upon any form of intimacy at its forts, where it permitted only three or four natives at a time to enter the barricades, the Company to a remarkable degree continued to hold the Indians' respect and cooperation. This was in part due to the fact that, for nearly a century, it did not stir up Indian resentment or alarm by penetrating the hunting grounds of the interior in search of furs or by establishing settlements far inland from the coast; instead it merely maintained posts at the river mouths around the Bay where its factors waited for the natives to bring in their furs. Until the fall of New France, colonization and inland settlement were definitely discouraged as inimical to the Company's main business, and even purely exploratory journeys were undertaken only occasionally.

It was as traders, rather than colonizers, that the Hudson's Bay Company won its fame and secured its profits. Annually several ships, loaded with tools, firearms, and other trading goods coveted by the Indians, departed for the Bay, later to return home heavily laden with a cargo of magnificent northern furs. The profits were often enormous. On the famous scouting expedition of 1668, when only one of the two ships completed the voyage, the trading goods are said to have cost £650, while the furs taken in exchange sold for £19,000.[27] While these phenomenal profits were not maintained every year, the Company through its first two decades financially did well. At the time of incorporation the total investment amounted to only £4,720, but by 1675 the total subscribed capital of £10,500 had been paid up,[28] a series of high dividends had made the Company's reputation, and it was able to begin the building and equipment of a string of needed forts. Over each was placed a local governor with instructions to manage the trade of the locality, maintain strict discipline, and keep an exact journal.[29] At home the Hudson's Bay Company carried on its business with great dignity and ceremony. Directors' meetings were often held in the royal palace, and sumptuous feasts marked the occasion of its great fur sales which were attended by the aristocracy and the wealthiest of the land.[30]

---

[26] MacKay, *op. cit.*, pp. 85-86, gives a list of the standard prices. Laut, *op. cit.*, p. 46, also gives a table of prices in relation to beaver skins. Examples: 1 gun = 12 beavers; 1 pistol = 4 beavers; 1 lb. of shot or 8 cannon balls = 1 beaver; 1 kettle = 1 beaver; 5 lbs. sugar = 1 beaver; 2 awls = 1 beaver; 20 fishhooks = 1 beaver.

[27] MacKay, *op. cit.*, p. 36.

[28] By 1720 the original capital had been increased tenfold.

[29] MacKay, *op. cit.*, pp. 36-40, discusses the charter.

[30] *Cf.* Wrong, *op. cit.*, Vol. II, p. 600.

The earliest of the forts established by the Company on Hudson Bay was Fort Charles at the mouth of the Rupert River in James Bay. It was early attacked by the French, who reached it from the Saguenay River and Lake Mistassini.[31] Shortly recaptured by the English, Fort Charles was to become famous as Rupert's House. Farther west on James Bay was Moose Factory, the natural goal of those coming overland from Montreal via the Ottawa and Moose Rivers. The third fort, Albany House on the Albany River, was naturally reached from Lake Superior. These forts on James Bay were all within reach of the jealous French who frequently raided them from their settlements on the St. Lawrence; but posts along the western rim of Hudson Bay itself were beyond the reach of the French, except from the sea. Here the most important of the early establishments was Fort Nelson, later York Factory, which occupied a strategic spot between the mouths of the Nelson and Hayes rivers, streams draining Lake Winnipeg and eventually the whole Saskatchewan River system. Farther up the western side of the Bay, but not established until fifty years later, was Fort Prince of Wales (now Fort Churchill) at the mouth of the Churchill River. Built of massive masonry and heavily fortified by Marlborough's engineers, and enjoying the one really good harbor on the west coast, this port tapped an immense area of the richest northern furs. Plundered and burned by the French during the American Revolutionary War, it was later replaced nearby with a less elaborate structure.

The most serious of the Company's early troubles came from the violent jealousy of the St. Lawrence French, vexations aggravated by the vacillating behavior of the two renegade promoters, Radisson and Chouart. Apparently disappointed at the monetary rewards that fell to them from the not-too-generous English company, in 1674 Radisson and his brother-in-law passed over to France and were received and forgiven their former sins by Colbert; presently the two adventurers found their way back to Quebec. Here Radisson formed the French *Compagnie du Nord* and in 1682 led a couple of armed trading ships into Hudson Bay. His appearance at the mouth of the Hayes River in the rôle of an enemy to his old Company opened a period of intermittent hostility between the French and the English in the Bay region which marked the remainder of the 1680's. On the expedition of 1682, Radisson captured the English governor, together with a Company ship and a group of prisoners from Old and New England and took them back to Quebec. Here, however, as there was no official war, the French authorities, to Radisson's disgust, released the ship, sent the prisoners home, and rewarded the conqueror with a heavy fine. In 1684, Radisson again deserted to the English, took an oath of fidelity to

---

[31] This expedition was sponsored by Jean Talon. See map 15, p. 243.

the Company, was given a larger salary, and presently was back on Hudson Bay, where to the bewilderment of the fort population, he succeeded in restoring to the English the post which he had formerly captured for the French. For the next ten years he made many voyages to the Bay where he frequently became involved in quarrels with the younger fur traders.[32] His last years were spent in England grumbling over his pension of £100 a year. He died in 1710.[33]

One of the most considerable episodes in the prewar period was the surprise attack and capture, in 1686, by a war party of French Canadians of all the English forts on James Bay, leaving the Hudson Company represented by a single post—Fort Nelson. One of the bold leaders of this raid was the famous Canadian, Pierre le Moyne, Sieur d'Iberville, who henceforth became the most relentless and daring of all England's enemies in the far north. During King William's War (1689-1697), when the two contestants were fairly evenly matched in Hudson Bay through years of raid and counter-raid, when the key post of Fort Nelson changed hands nearly every season,[34] d'Iberville was the scourge of the English. The local battles, on the whole, went in favor of the French; but always the Company managed to cling to at least one of its trading posts. By the terms of the Treaty of Ryswick (1697) the French were left in possession of most of the Hudson Bay region, the English company continuing to hold only Fort Albany. During the War of the Spanish Succession (1701-1713), which followed a peaceful respite of only four years, there was little or no fighting around Hudson Bay where the Company was decidedly on the defensive. Elsewhere, however, Queen Anne's War went in favor of the English, and the Treaty of Utrecht (1713) more than reversed the conditions left by the Treaty of Ryswick. Not only were all its former possessions restored to the Hudson's Bay Company, but France withdrew all claims to Hudson Bay as well as to Nova Scotia and Newfoundland.

Having weathered a half-century of intermittent conflict, the next fifty years (1713-1763) were the most fruitful of the Company's history. In the years following the death of Louis XIV both England and France, in Hudson Bay as elsewhere, turned to the development of the possessions which the spasmodic fighting of the preceding half-century had left in their hands. The Hudson's Bay Company recovered slowly, continuing to follow very conservative lines, emphasizing trade and discouraging settlement. Financially it did well.[35] In the middle of the century it was importing into England furs to the value of £23,000 to £30,000 annually,

[32] For the details see Wrong, *op. cit.,* Vol. II, p. 606.
[33] Groseilliers had died in Canada in 1691.
[34] For the details of these years see *Canada and Its Provinces,* Vol. 1, pp. 181-87.
[35] From 1721-1783 the Company never missed a dividend. MacKay, *op. cit.,* p. 126.

with costs averaging £19,400. At this time its stock was valued at £103,950 and was held by only ninety-eight shareholders.[36] It employed a small staff of 120 officers and servants and owned outright only three or four vessels. The Company had but one inland establishment and this—Henley House on the Albany River—was not more than 150 miles from the shore of the Bay.

Particularly profitable in the eighteenth century was the Company's trade which poured through York Factory and Fort Churchill, representing as it did the fur wealth of the Lake Winnipeg and Saskatchewan areas. Rumors of this immensely rich fur country aroused the envy of the French traders of Montreal and Quebec and stimulated the imagination and energy of a number of French explorers of whom the greatest was Pierre Gualtier de Varennes, Sieur de La Vérendrye.[37] This intrepid traveler, accompanied by his three sons and a nephew, undertook the bold exploit of blazing a trail to the "western ocean." Failing in his efforts to obtain money from the French government, La Vérendrye found it necessary to meet the expenses of his exploration by establishing fur-trading posts as he advanced. He and his sons moved westward towards Lake Winnipeg via the difficult route of Rainy Lake and Lake of the Woods; by 1734 he had established a fort on the Red River, not far from Lake Winnipeg. From here they continued westward to the Saskatchewan River system and were in a position, with a line of forts behind them, to tap the Hudson Bay kingdom from the rear, break its monopolistic hold on the interior, and claim a share of the wealth of the region for the key industry of New France.

The work of the Vérendryes was preliminary to the complete change in the Hudson's Bay Company's position that resulted from the absorption of Canada into the British Empire following the Treaty of Paris (1763). The former French voyageurs now became fellow British subjects with the proprietors of the Hudson's Bay Company, and many entered the Company's service. The coming of peace released a fund of energy not only for trading but for exploration. Henceforth the activities of the Company were no longer confined to the Bay region, but reached, through the efforts of Samuel Hearne and Peter Pond and others, as far as Great Slave Lake (1771) and Lake Athabaska (1778).

The next great conflict, the American Revolutionary War, brought further changes. Not only did France take advantage of this war to attack the Company's central position in the Bay, destroying Fort Prince of

---

[36] *Ibid.*, p. 75.

[37] The birthplace of La Vérendrye, as of so many French-Canadian explorers, was Three Rivers (1685). He died in 1749. Volume 19 in The Chronicles of Canada series entitled *Pathfinders of the Great Plains* by J. L. Burpee bears on the work of La Vérendrye and his sons. See map 15, p. 243.

Wales and York Factory, involving a monetary loss of £500,000, but when the war was over jealous trade competitors, many of them Scotsmen, and others, refugees from the Thirteen Colonies, organized themselves into private companies which eventually amalgamated, in 1784, into the North-west Company. Operating from Montreal as a center and using old French Canadian routes and guides, this company embarked upon a dramatic race across the continent from the Great Lakes to the Pacific, having as its principal goal the diversion at its very source of the fur trade to the St. Lawrence River route instead of to Hudson Bay. Before the war, Montreal had drawn its chief supply of furs from south of the boundary line assigned in the Treaty of Versailles to the United States. If the Montreal fur trade was to survive it must develop its initial tenuous hold over regions of the northwest and the far west gained for it by the Vérendryes. The richest of all was the country around Lake Athabaska known as the "Northwest."

The Hudson's Bay Company now found that it must finally abandon its old practice of waiting at the Bay for the furs and engage in a fiercely competitive transcontinental struggle. A wild, lawless trade war followed, filled with murderous episodes and sullied by a general debauching of the natives as the two rival companies, using fair means and foul to secure the Indian trade, raced into the northwest and across the mountain divide into the far west.[38] Many famous names of the period are those of the men associated with the Northwest Company. In its service Alexander Macken-zie, starting in 1789 from Lake Athabaska, explored the Mackenzie River by canoe as far as its mouth in the Arctic; then, in 1793, by ascending the Peace River canyon, he crossed the Rockies and reached the Pacific at the mouth of the Bella Coola River, the first white man to cross the continent north of Mexico.[39] Simon Fraser, the explorer of the Fraser River, and Donald Thomson, the surveyor of the Columbia River, were also men of the bold and vigorous Northwest Company.

This phase of the Hudson's Bay Company's history was not over until 1821 when the two rival fur companies merged, the Hudson's Bay Com-pany buying out the Northwest Company and taking many of the North-west men into its employ, some of whom reached positions of policy-mak-ing influence. The great figure in the new era was George Simpson, a vigorous far-sighted and tactful Scotsman who became known as the "little Emperor." Following a complete reorganization, Montreal lost its pre-eminence as a fur-trading center and Hudson Bay once again became the chief exit for Canadian furs.[40]

---

[38] MacKay states that between 1754 and 1774 the Hudson's Bay Company ordered as many as sixty inland voyages. *Op. cit.,* p. 91.

[39] For further details see MacKay, *op. cit.,* pp. 111-16.

[40] *Ibid.,* chs. xii and xiii.

III. THE ENGLISH IN THE WEST INDIES IN THE
SEVENTEENTH CENTURY

As the seventeenth century dawned, Englishmen like Frenchmen in their West Indian ventures began to conceive of tapping new sources of wealth to supplement the booty of their raiding activities against Spanish shipping and coastal towns. Hitherto piracy and illegal trading had been combined with the search for the romantic El Dorado; now the prosaic business of establishing settlements and raising plantation crops—especially the much coveted tobacco, ginger, cotton, and sugar—seized their imagination by the promise of enticing rewards. Throughout the sixteenth century, Europeans had grown to regard the new colonial commodities as indispensable and were prepared to pay a high price for them. As a further magnet, there was the additional advantage that permanent Caribbean colonies, such as the steady production of tropical products called for, would also serve as bases conveniently near the Spanish settlements for an enlarged and steady contraband trade in gold, silver, pearls, fine woods, dyes, gums, spices, and other coveted luxuries. A consideration that appealed to the government and populace at home and helped to secure their cooperation was the prospect that permanent Caribbean settlements would serve as places of refuge to provide new opportunties for the distressed and embarrassing surplus of indigent folk thrown out of employment by the enclosure movement.

This program of course blandly ignored the contention by Spain that prior discovery and papal sanction had given His Catholic Majesty the sole valid title to all America and its surrounding waters, and completely disregarded Spanish refusal even to discuss the theory that effective occupation was necessary. The King of Spain, however, no longer held the strong position that had once been his. Events of the later sixteenth century had at least made him anxious for some relaxation of hostilities. Within two decades of the defeat of the Spanish Armada, Spain signed a series of peace treaties with France, England, and Holland in which the issue of monopoly in the Caribbean was passed over without mention, implying a tacit acceptance of the continuation of the rule of "no peace beyond the line." Spain's rivals realized, of course, that King Philip was consoling himself with the reflection that under these arrangements any traders whom he could catch west of the first meridian and south of the Tropic of Cancer could be held to have gone there at their own risk and might be dealt with as pirates without jeopardizing international peace in Europe.

It was natural that the first of the new settlements should be made in the Windward and Leeward Islands of the Lesser Antilles. This eastern Caribbean rim of small volcanic islands, running in a crescent from Puerto Rico to the northeastern corner of Venezuela, had long attracted the attention of English sailors as they had come and gone on adventurous voyages, under Ralegh, Harcourt, Leigh, and others to "the wild coast" of Guiana. While "the Caribbees" were known to possess neither gold nor silver, and to be full of fierce cannibalistic Carib Indians, the islands also bore the reputation of being exceedingly fertile and beautiful. Furthermore, they possessed the advantage of never having been effectively occupied by Spain, and yet to be near enough to the Spanish coast to make excellent bases for carrying on a steady illicit trade with the Spanish American mainland.

The leader of the earliest settlement, Captain Thomas Warner, had been associated in 1620 with one of the vain English efforts to establish a tobacco colony on the Guiana shore. Exploring the Caribbees, island by island, and making actual experiments to test the suitability of the soil for tobacco-raising, this practical man finally decided that the small island of St. Christopher, situated well to the northern end of the chain, would be the best for his purpose. Securing from a group of English merchants the promise of financial backing and assistance in marketing the future crops, Warner landed his first English colonists in 1624, and started St. Kitts on its career as a commercial colony. So sensibly planned was the venture that a year later Warner had a crop of tobacco on the English market for which he received a good price.[41]

In this same year (1625) an Anglo-Dutch firm, the Courteen Brothers, interested in the smuggling trade with Brazil, sent out a ship under Captain John Powell which on its homeward journey touched at the island of Barbados, situated to the east of the Caribbees and off the usual route of Spanish ships. Struck by the many advantages which this flat, uninhabited, fertile island, covered with logwood or dyewood trees [42] and possessed of a magnificent harbor, seemed to offer as a location for a plantation colony, Powell proceeded to take possession of the island in the name of the English king. Two years later his brother, Henry Powell, led a group of eighty colonists to the new island. By 1630 Barbados was safely launched on its career as an agricultural colony.

Meanwhile, at St. Kitts the original English settlers had been joined by a French element which was to give that island a curious bi-national

---

[41] For further details on the settlement of St. Kitts, see A. P. Newton, *The European Nations in the West Indies, 1493-1688* (London: 1933), pp. 142-43.

[42] On the importance and use of logwood, or "Brasil" wood, consult Newton, *op. cit.,* pp. 144-45.

character. The captain and crew of a French privateer which happened to stop at the island accepted Warner's suggestion that they should vary their buccaneering activities with some tobacco planting, and meanwhile help to fend off expected attacks from the Caribs. Subsequently, when settlers of both national groups had increased in number, they came to an agreement to divide the twenty-three-mile-long island between them; the English took a broad strip in the more fertile center and the French, as later comers, occupied the two ends. Needless to say the divisional arrangement did not function smoothly, though it continued in existence until 1713 when the island became wholly English. Though wiped out in 1629 along with its daughter colony on the neighboring island of Nevis by a powerful Spanish fleet, St. Kitts was soon re-established and presently became fairly prosperous.

The subsequent destinies both of Barbados and of the English portion of St. Kitts followed a very similar course and were closely interwoven. Founded at approximately the same time, the two island settlements were to become fountainheads from which two streams of English settlement poured over the Caribbean islands. In 1627 and 1628 both colonies were granted to two noblemen of the court of Charles I under conflicting royal patents. One was a grant issued on July 2, 1627, to James Hay, Earl of Carlisle, making him Lord Proprietor of the Caribbee Islands, including St. Christopher, Nevis, and Barbados. This document ignored a patent, issued two years earlier, recognizing Warner as the King's lieutenant with rule over St. Christopher, Nevis, Montserrat, and Barbados. The dilemma was solved, however, when Warner was pacified with a knighthood and a life appointment as governor over the island of St. Christopher. On February 25, 1628, another palatine grant was issued to the Earl of Pembroke, acting for the Courteen interests. It bestowed upon Pembroke the islands of Barbados, Tobago, and Trinidad. As Barbados was included in both the Carlisle and Pembroke grants, there was again much heartburning, and, on the island itself, a good deal of open brawling between the two parties before the Carlisle interests were successfully established.[43]

In the first fifteen years several thousand English colonists moved into Barbados, although social conditions in the island long remained unsatisfactory. By 1645 it had a white population of 36,500, and as its total area was only 166 square miles, it was densely populated.[44] Many of the newcomers arrived as indentured servants, sent over by the investing merchants of the Carlisle interests who cared for nothing but the profits

---

[43] On the conflicting patents see P. A. Means, *The Spanish Main* (New York: 1935), pp. 154-59. At the time of the grant, Pembroke was Philip Herbert, Earl of Montgomery; the later title, by which he is usually known, came to him in 1630.

[44] Newton, *op. cit.*, p. 194.

that they hoped to wring from the tobacco, cotton, and other crops that the island could produce. Defense measures were wholly neglected and there was much idleness, drinking, and disorder. Fortunately for the future English sovereignty in Barbados, the Spaniards were so reduced in strength from the great financial loss incurred when in 1628 the Dutch had succeeded in capturing the entire annual treasure fleet [45] that they could not invade the island. As the two original islands filled up, others in the Caribbee group were occupied, Antigua and Montserrat being among the earliest.

Another early center of British activity in the Caribbean developed around two small, semiderelict islands, about 160 miles off the Nicaraguan coast at the western end of the Caribbean, known to the Spaniards as Santa Catalina and San Andrés. Seized by the English in 1629 and renamed Providence and Henrietta, they had an exciting and unique career. Their pioneer promoter was Robert Rich, Earl of Warwick, a Puritan nobleman who in 1615 had been heavily involved in the Somers Islands Company which had settled the Bermudas.[46] That venture, through local mismanagement and dissension, had not been especially successful, and Warwick was persuaded to try the new undertaking, partly as a relief measure for the dissatisfied elements of Bermuda, partly to create a place of refuge for Puritans who were unhappy in England on both political and religious grounds. "The Governor and Company of Adventurers of the City of Westminster for the Plantation of the Islands of Providence, Henrietta, and the adjacent islands lying on the coast of America" was set

---

[45] This capture off Matanzas Bay, Cuba, by a Dutch fleet of 31 ships commanded by Piet Heyn, realized an age-old dream of all sailors to the West Indies. The Spanish silver fleet on this occasion included 9 large merchant ships and 4 armed treasure galleons, bearing 200,000 lbs. of silver, 135 lbs. of gold, and large quantities of pearls, besides rich cargoes of spices, dyes, cacao, hides, and other characteristic Spanish American colonial goods. The exploit produced 15,000,000 guilders for the Dutch West India Company, enabling it to declare a 50 per cent dividend—the richest reward of the long naval war between Spain and Holland. For a discussion of the effects on later Dutch and Spanish policy, consult Newton, *op. cit.*, 152-55.

[46] The Bermuda or Somers Islands got their popular name from a Spanish sea captain, Juan de Bermudez, who is said to have been shipwrecked there with a cargo of wild hogs early in the sixteenth century, and later to have visited them again. They secured their second, and official, name from an Englishman, Sir George Somers, who in 1609, while in charge of a company of adventurers intended as a reinforcement for Jamestown, Virginia, was wrecked by a hurricane on the shore of the islands. After some months his people were able to continue in newly built ships to Jamestown where their supplies saved the starving colony. In 1612, by an amendment to the charter, Somers Islands were included within the jurisdiction of the Virginia Company. Two years later they were transferred to the crown and in 1615 a new charter was granted to the Governor and Company of the City of London for the Plantation of the Somers Islands. A prime mover in this reorganization was the Earl of Warwick. This Bermuda Company sent out a number of settlers. The second general colonial assembly established within the British Empire met at St. George's in Bermuda in 1620. The Company went through many vicissitudes until 1684 when the Company was abolished and the Islands became a royal colony. The history of Bermuda in the colonial age is curiously entwined both with that of Virginia and of the English Caribbean islands.

up in 1630. It was strongly Puritan in membership with John Pym as its leading light, six of whose relatives or protegées were members of the first Council for the colony. The first governor was Philip Bell who had been governor of Bermuda and had brought with him to Providence a contingent of ninety Bermudians. The first colonists landed in 1631, and five years later had increased to 540 in addition to 90 Negroes.[47] Strenuous efforts were made to avoid the mistakes of other Caribbean settlements by at once planting food crops and taking early steps to provide for adequate defense.

Life on Providence and Henrietta soon settled into the mold characteristic of other tropical islands, with plantation crops cultivated by Negro labor the principal reliance, though substantially supplemented by contraband trade with neighboring Spanish territories. The nearby Mosquito Coast of Nicaragua, extending from the mouth of the San Juan River to Cape Gracias a Dios in the north and inhabited by Indians who claimed never to have been conquered by Spain, provided an unusually rich field for illicit trading operations. In return for arms, munitions, and *aguardiente* (liquor), these Mosquito Indians served as agents for a considerable contraband trade with the Spaniards of the interior provinces in cacao, tortoise shell, salted tortoise, other products of the region, and Indian slaves. Socially there was much friction between the two incongruous elements of the Bermudians and the Puritans, and a good deal of brawling, gambling, and disorder. It soon became obvious that the tropical setting had induced a religious decline and moral deterioration.

In 1631 the Providence Company took under its wing an English colony set up on Tortuga Island with Anthony Hilton as leader. This former shipmaster had been driven away by the Spaniards from the island of Nevis to which he had led a colony from St. Kitts. Determined to combine planting and piracy, Hilton had fixed upon Tortuga as a likely site, assembled a number of English and French adventurers of like mind, and had then gone to England and persuaded the Earl of Warwick to back his venture. The fortunes of the two Warwick colonies, founded at the same time, were naturally entwined though the populations differed fundamentally in character. Tortuga had no such Puritan element as had originally marked Providence; its inhabitants were largely fugitives and desperadoes of many nations, mostly French and English, who were wanted elsewhere for their crimes. In many ways they were as savage as the wild cattle and swine they hunted, as tough as the hides which they exchanged with passing ships for guns, ammunition, utensils, and liquor. From their *boucans,* or crude gridirons on which they broiled their meat, came the

---

[47] *Cf.* Means, *op. cit.,* pp. 177-82.

term buccaneer which fitted most of them perfectly. Needless to say, little planting was carried on in the island, most of the inhabitants preferring the more exciting occupations of cattle hunting, logwood cutting, and piracy. Disorders and carousals of every kind were the normal state of affairs.

In 1635 the Spaniards fell on both the Warwick colonies. At Providence the attack was beaten off for a time, the strength of the defenses combined with the naturally strong position of the islands behind a maze of rocky reefs rendering the settlement almost impregnable. At Tortuga the Spaniards succeeded temporarily in overwhelming the colony and wreaked a terrible vengeance on the prisoners who fell into their hands. However, a few months later many of the old colonists, joined by other rovers, were back on Tortuga. Both colonies continued for another five years, mainly as bases for buccaneering and contraband trading; any plantation operations were carried on by Negro slaves. Their European supplies were secured mostly from Dutch traders who were paid in goods looted from the Spaniards. Now and again, merchant vessels came from New England looking for profitable tropical cargoes. In 1638 Captain Nathaniel Butler, an enterprising new governor, arrived in Providence. A former governor of Bermuda and an old enemy of the Spaniards, Butler was soon personally leading raids against Spanish coastal settlements in the Gulf of Honduras and building up a trade with the Mosquito Indians. At the mouth of the Sequia River, leading towards Lake Nicaragua and the rich interior of Central America, there was presently established a settlement named Bluefields, so called from a Dutch captain, Abraham Blauvelt, who was a boon companion of Captain Butler.

In the early 1640's the English lost both old Providence and Tortuga. In 1641 the Spaniards with a large force of twelve sail and 2,000 men seized Providence, taking a booty of 500,000 ducats.[48] Tortuga, on the other hand, was lost to the French. Governor Poincy of French St. Christopher in 1640 commissioned a certain Calvinist, M. Le Vasseur, to lead a considerable group of French Huguenots (recently arrived after the fall of La Rochelle) to Tortuga where he succeeded in throwing out the ill-organized English. A skilful engineer, the new leader systematically fortified the island, making it an impregnable piratical fortress. From it the French began presently to spread into the western part of Española, long deserted by the Spaniards who by the middle of the seventeenth century were concentrated around the town of Santo Domingo on the southern shore of the eastern part of the island. The French western section of the island became known as "Saint Domingue."

---

[48] Newton, *op. cit.*, p. 192.

"A Design to represent the beginning and completion of an American settlement or farm. Painted by Paul Sandby from a Design made by his Excellency Governor Pownall. Engraved by James Peake." London, 1761. (Courtesy of the New-York Historical Society, New York City)

Typical scenes illustrating trades in the early English colonies. (*Above*) The first hand paper mill, Milton, Massachusetts, 1717. (*Below*) Boston shoemakers petitioning for a consolidation of their craft so that "all boots might be alike well made." 1648. (Both courtesy of the American Museum of Natural History)

Shortly after these events, the Earl of Warwick acquired the patent rights of the Earl of Pembroke in the Caribbee islands and tried to colonize Tobago and Trinidad, off the northeastern coast of Venezuela, with former colonists from Bermuda, Providence, and the now crowded islands of St. Christopher and Barbados, as well as new arrivals from home. His efforts met with little success, mainly because the English Civil War was absorbing the wealth as well as the surplus population that had formerly been moving overseas.

All the English colonies in the Lesser Antilles, founded in the 1620's and 1630's, were by 1650 overpopulated and suffering a depression resulting from soil exhaustion and a decline of the price of tobacco in European markets where the island leaf had to compete with the better quality Virginia tobacco. Experiments with cotton and indigo were as yet not sufficiently successful to meet the situation. Presently, however, the islanders turned to sugar planting for a solution. They were encouraged in this by the Dutch who furnished the necessary capital on a long-term basis, expecting to profit not only as general traders but as monopolists of the trade in slaves which they realized would be required to supply the labor for the new product. At first the planters met with little success, but after methods developed by the Portuguese in Brazil had been studied and applied, profits began to come in.

The crop change brought in its wake a social revolution. Hitherto the islands had been cultivated in small holdings. These were now bought up by the relatively few planters who could furnish the capital, and transformed into great plantations. It was soon found that the labor of the white indentured servants, the engagés, was unsuitable and too expensive, and these unfortunates were turned off in droves, while African Negroes, secured through the Dutch, were imported so rapidly that within five or six years their numbers rose from a few hundred to more than twenty thousand. The smaller planters and the indentured servants, for whom there was no longer a livelihood, began to leave the islands in large numbers—twelve thousand going inside of a decade. Of these, two or three thousand joined the English colonists on the North American mainland, a few helped to start Jamaica, but the majority probably perished.[49]

During the tumultuous years of the English Civil War and the establishment of the Commonwealth, the Caribbean islands bulked large in English thought, both because of their highly prized trade and because they offered a place of refuge for English political and religious fugitives, first the Puritans and later the Royalists. When Cromwell came to power, he found the English Caribbees in the control of English Royalists and

---

[49] *Ibid.*, pp. 197-98.

sent a Commonwealth fleet in 1652 to secure their surrender. The Protector developed very ambitious views in regard to England's future in the West Indies and embarked on a determined and long-range policy affecting that part of the world. The primary objective was the ruination of the Dutch carrying trade, which he first attacked by means of the Navigation Ordinance of 1651. The effect of the new law was to make the trade of the English colonies as much an English monopoly as was Spain's in her holdings. As the result of the first Dutch War (1652-1653), which this act provoked, the Dutch were forced to acquiesce in their exclusion from the trade of the English colonies, and much of their traffic passed into the hands of English merchants. Cromwell's second step was to take measures to put into operation his long meditated "Western Design," which involved a direct military attack on Spanish power in the Caribbean. He hoped this would be so crippling that a large part of Spanish territory in America, especially in the Central American and Caribbean areas, would eventually fall into English hands, the Spanish treasure route would be blocked, and the New World would be "cleansed of popery." [50]

After making demands on the Spanish courts which he knew would not be accepted, Cromwell in December, 1654, dispatched to the Caribbean a considerable naval and land force under General Robert Venables and Admiral William Penn. While the naval side of the expedition, consisting of some 38 sail, was well turned out, the large army it carried was a hastily assembled and badly trained force and was made worse when to it were added, in overcrowded Barbados, several thousand volunteers who were little better than human derelicts.[51] The inevitable disaster followed. In an attack on the first Spanish objective, Santo Domingo, a few hundred determined Spaniards succeeded in driving the much larger English force in headlong flight back to its ships.

Passing westward to Jamaica and finding that island occupied only by a small garrison and some fifteen hundred Spanish colonists, the discomfited English commanders with their formidable force easily took possession of the island. This inglorious but important victory proved to be the only fruit of the ambitious expedition; so disgusted was Cromwell that both Penn and Venables on their return to England were sent to the Tower. The Protector, however, clung tenaciously to the possession of Jamaica as a base for future operations. Contemporary activities of the British fleet under Commodore Blake in European waters prevented ade-

---

[50] An inciting influence on Cromwell's West Indian plans was exercised by Thomas Gage, an Englishman who, as a member of the Dominican Order, had spent years in Central America and the West Indies and on his return to England abandoned Roman Catholicism for Puritanism. His famous book, *New Survey of the West Indies,* published in 1648, set forth the view that Spain's dominions in America could be easily conquered. See Newton, *op. cit.,* pp. 214-15.

[51] The total force amounted to 6,873. Means, *op. cit.,* p. 193.

quate assistance being dispatched from Spain to reinforce the insufficient resources in Cuba for the recapture of Jamaica. After the restoration, Charles II, who like Cromwell was much under the influence of the mercantile classes, continued to refuse to listen to any price for the return of Jamaica short of the legal admission of British trade to a share in the commerce of the Caribbean—a price which no Spanish government would grant.

The early years of Jamaica as an English colony were inauspicious and unsavory. Cromwell was determined that it should have a sizable population quickly, and persistently urged judicial authorities, as well as special emigration commissioners, to dispatch all sorts and conditions of men to the new colony. Its first settlers were therefore drawn from the flotsam and jetsam of the West Indies and the slums of London. Within three years a population of six thousand had been gathered. Health and sanitary conditions were of the worst, the island continuing to justify its old reputation of being one of the plague spots of the Caribbean for dysentery, yellow fever, and other scourges of the tropics. Some of the early governors made efforts to give the island some economic interests other than those centering in outright buccaneering, and to some extent succeeded. One of these was Sir Thomas Modyford, a planter of Barbados who became Governor of Jamaica in 1664, with instructions from home that were deliberately vague and obviously discretionary. Under his rule Jamaica became an emporium where slaves brought from Africa were reconditioned while awaiting sale in the Spanish colonies or in the English mainland settlements; it also became a port of deposit for English manufactured goods awaiting disposal, through contraband channels, in Spanish colonial markets. Ship repairing and boat building were likewise developed. At the same time encouragement was given to a small class of planters interested in large-scale raising of tropical crops cultivated by Negro labor.

Despite efforts to establish more conventional activities, buccaneering long continued to be the principal Jamaican occupation. Denied the use of regular naval forces, the governors found it necessary to use pirate fleets to ward off Spanish efforts to reconquer the island; and this alone tended to make Port Royal the headquarters of the "Brethren of the Coast." When, now and again, the governors tried withdrawing the letters of marque and cracking down on the buccaneers, the island's prosperity at once "decayed" and its commerce fell into mortal danger of being preyed upon by its erstwhile defenders. The decades of the 1660's and 1670's were the heyday of the Port Royal-based buccaneers. In single vessels, or fleets, bearing at times as many as a thousand or twelve hundred men, they ranged the Caribbean and mercilessly scourged the Spanish towns of Cumaná, La Guaíra, Río Hacha, Maracaibo, Santa Marta, Cartagena,

Porto Bello, Granada, Trujillo, and other settlements. These raids reached a peak in Henry Morgan's savage and ruinous sacking of the rich city of Panama in January, 1671,[52] when it was estimated by the English that a booty of £10,000 "besides other rich goods" was taken away; the Spaniards placed their losses at over six million crowns.[53] In all, it is said, between the conquest of Jamaica and Morgan's raid on Panama, eighteen Spanish cities, four towns, and thirty-five villages were sacked.

Not until the end of the second Dutch war (1665-1667), in which the buccaneers once more proved to be a poor and unreliable substitute for a regular naval force, did the British government finally come to the conclusion that tolerance of piracy in the Caribbean did not pay. Decisive action followed. In the Treaty of Madrid of 1670 Spain recognized Great Britain's right to "have, hold, keep and possess forever, with full right of sovereignty—all the lands, regions, islands, colonies, and dominions situated in the West Indies or in any part of America which the said King of Great Britain and his subjects at present hold and possess." In other words, Spain in this treaty gave up her old claim to monopoly in the New World, recognizing in effect her rival's contention that prior discovery of a territory was not enough, and that continuous and effective occupation alone secured possession.[54] Having thus gained Spain's recognition of her position among American colonial powers, England was ready to suppress the buccaneers who were becoming a general nuisance. Stringent orders went to Jamaica and the other English colonies to put down piracy.

For a time the only effect of England's action was to transfer buccaneering headquarters from English Port Royal to French Tortuga; but the French government, too, finally came to the conclusion that piracy was not worth while and, in 1684, also signed a treaty with Spain which marked the beginning of the end of French support of buccaneering activities, at least during periods of peace. Piracy was made a felony, and the hanging of pirates at Jamaica became a common sight. The most successful and richest of the former buccaneers, Henry Morgan, to the scandal of Spain, was made a knight and thrice appointed lieutenant governor of Jamaica, in the hope, presumably, that he would know how to suppress his former boon companions. Finally a number of fast-sailing frigates and a powerful squadron were dispatched to the Caribbean in the 1680's to aid in the work of clearing the American seas. By the time William III had gained the English throne and was ready to give a new direction to its policy, an end had come to the golden age of buccaneering. In 1692 a great earthquake and tidal wave engulfed two thirds of Port Royal—a divine retribu-

---

[52] For a description of this famous raid see Means, op. cit., pp. 211-13.
[53] Newton, op. cit., p. 275.
[54] For a fuller discussion of this treaty, see Newton, op. cit., pp. 269-71.

tion, many said, for its share in the many crimes that had been initiated there.

Though the War of the Spanish Succession brought a recrudescence of buccaneering disguised as privateering, English public opinion had definitely accepted the view that corsairing was contrary to the country's true commercial interests. Henceforth, buccaneering and contraband trading tended to separate more and more into two distinct activities. Piracy declined, while contraband trading took an upward turn and developed a specialized technique and etiquette in dealing with Spanish governors and customs officials. Many buccaneers turned to the logwood trade and later to mahogany cutting along isolated and deserted portions of the Spanish coast, especially in the Bay of Campeche, along the Caribbean coast of Yucatan, and in the Gulf of Honduras about the River Belize. Of this logwood trade Jamaica became a center, as of all other branches of illicit commerce which took on increased volume and importance during the eighteenth century as piracy declined. Certain Spanish American territories, located at a distance from the political and commercial administrative centers, became especially notorious as rich smuggling areas. Besides the Belize River and Mosquito Coast regions, which during this period became practically English colonies administered from Jamaica, the coastal stretch between the two, especially the sixty leagues of shore extending from Trujillo to Tres Puntos known as the Costa del Norte, was frequently visited by illicit traders from Jamaica. In this stretch of smugglers' territory, high mountains shut off the interior from a fertile coastal plain, across which flowed numerous rivers that served as highways for a rich illegal trade in gold, silver, hides, cacao, sarsaparilla, tobacco, and balsams. The Bay Islands, near Trujillo in the Gulf of Honduras, were spasmodically held by English intruders who at times cultivated plantations on them. Other Jamaican ships, looking for profitable contraband cargoes, traveled as far east as the Venezuelan coast where illicit trading opportunities were also plentiful.[55]

While practically all Jamaican activities for a century after the English conquest centered in relations with the neighboring Spanish American territories, the two other English governments of the West Indies (those of Barbados and the Leeward Islands) were most affected by the proximity of the Dutch and French. Outstanding through the thirty years following 1650 was the common interest shown by the English and French in ousting the Dutch from their leading position in West Indian commerce. But after

---

[55] For further details on eighteenth century contraband trading based on Jamaica, see my articles, "Contraband Trade: A Factor in the Decline of Spain's Empire in America," *Hispanic American Historical Review*, VIII, No. 2, May, 1928; "The South Sea Company and Contraband Trade," *American Historical Review*, XXXI, No. 4, July, 1926.

the third Dutch war (1672-1678) and the dissolution of the Dutch West Indian Company, a change of long-range significance ensued. Holland and England drew together, partly because William of Orange mounted the English throne in 1689, and partly because the Dutch decided that only as a complacent junior partner under England's wing could Holland secure protection for her remaining West Indian possessions and retain Britain's somewhat reluctant acceptance of Dutch predominance in the East Indian trade. This revival of Anglo-Dutch friendship was accompanied by a recrudescence of bitterness in French and English relations, which through the earlier years of the century had been remarkable for mutual forbearance. Not only had the French, much to England's disgust, shifted sides during the struggle against the Dutch and after the peace been slow to make restitution to England of captured territory, but commercial rivalry had naturally tended to sharpen as Dutch competition was eliminated. These friendships and enmities, manifesting themselves among the competing powers in the West Indies, had a considerable share in producing the pattern of international relations of the eighteenth century.

Thus in the course of the seventeenth century all three of Spain's European rivals had come to share a common outlook as to how to make American colonization pay: all reached the conclusion that settlements in the New World were likely to be profitable only if they were developed as agricultural colonies producing colonial products for Europe and serving as markets for home-manufactured goods, or if they were so placed as to be capable of use as emporiums through which European manufacturers could reach the huge and half-starved Spanish American market. Spain, on the other hand, continued to cling to her old idea that the only true form of wealth to be extracted from the colonies consisted of gold and silver. All four held to the mercantilist principle that colonies should trade exclusively with the motherland; all especially prized the trade of the West Indies, considering that it offered a combination of advantages not to be found together anywhere else in the world, providing at once the greatly needed new tropical products, a market for manufactured goods, and a supply of the precious metals. Spain, in the course of the century, was forced to relinquish her old claims to monopoly and acknowledge the right of other nations to colonize in the American sphere. Despite this, however, her actual territorial losses in the West Indian area were not great; only one of the Greater Antilles—Jamaica—slipped from her grasp, though she also had bitter reason to regret her earlier neglect of a string of smaller islands—the Lesser Antilles—which, coming under the occupation of her rivals, were not only unexpected sources of wealth to them, but proved to be a permanent threat to the security of other Spanish possessions.

In the realm of government, the British West Indian colonies of the seventeenth century showed many of the same features that marked the mainland colonies; identical political traditions and the same spirit of self-reliance led the inhabitants of both to secure their rights and liberties as Englishmen by means of strikingly similar institutions and practices. From the first, however, the bond uniting the West Indies with the motherland was closer and more intimate. It was natural and imperative that this should be so. The Caribbean settlements owed their development to English merchants, capitalists, and younger sons of the rural aristocracy who not only had no special grievance against established Church or State, but on the contrary were generally royalists in sympathy and hoped, after making their fortunes in the tropical colonies, to return home to end their days; meanwhile, they expected to prosper through a trade in goods complementary to, and not competitive with, those produced in the British isles.[56] Primarily, however, the close association was caused by the exposed position of the West Indian settlements. Located in the heart of the most bitterly contested of all colonial regions, the West Indian colonists were forced to recognize that most essential among all considerations was the need to keep intact at all times the lifeline with England, from whence alone they could secure the vitally necessary naval protection against national enemies and jealous trade competitors. Far from decreasing with the years, this dependence on the motherland for essential defense grew as the proportion of whites to the total population declined and less and less reliance could be placed on the local militia. Very few of the islands had permanent garrisons or shore defenses of any strength. As every major conflict during the century after 1650 was reflected in the West Indies, military dependence was an obvious and ever-present factor in every situation, a never-to-be-forgotten element in every dispute.[57] This constant precariousness of life and insecurity of riches naturally introduced a restlessness and get-rich-quick gambling spirit into West Indian society that was one of its outstanding characteristics.

These fundamental differences, combined with a unique geographical environment, operated in time to produce in the constitutional picture of the Caribbean settlements a number of variations from the mainland model. The rapid establishment of the royal type of government in the West Indies sprang partly from motives of military safety. The crown assumed proprietary rights of government in the Lesser Antilles within a year of the Restoration (1661), and two years later took over all the other

[56] *Cf.* F. Pitman, *The Development of the British West Indies, 1700-1763* (New Haven: 1917), chap. i, "British West Indian Society in the Eighteenth Century."

[57] *Cf.* E. A. Benians, "The Colonies and India," in *The Cambridge Modern History*, V, pp. 687-90; also, L. Penson, "The West Indies and Spanish American Trade, 1713-1748," in *The Cambridge History of the British Empire*, I, p. 330.

remaining privileges that had been bestowed by early royal patents upon private proprietors.[58] Jamaica never had a proprietary period, being set up immediately upon its conquest (1655) as a royal colony. In 1671 the eastern islands, all originally under a governor resident in Barbados, were divided into the two groups of the Leeward and the Windward islands.

In their domestic government, the Caribbean colonies gravitated towards a common framework, consisting of an appointed governor, a nominated advisory council, and a representative assembly elected on the basis of a property qualification. The council, varying in size from six to twenty members, served in the double capacity of an executive council to the governor and an upper house of the legislature. The councilors, occupying positions of great dignity in the colonial community, were generally subservient supporters of the governor. The assemblies, also differing considerably in size, were elected by the white freeholders of the various parishes into which each island was divided, each parish returning two members. Every island had its assembly which regarded itself as a local House of Commons and, like the assemblies in the Thirteen Colonies, used every indirect method conceivable to force the executive under popular control. Its chief weapon was always its control over the finances. In Jamaica, for example, the assembly fell into the practice of granting supplies for three months only; while the Jamaican policy was extreme, most of the island assemblies ensured annual meetings by the device of voting the budget for not more than one year. The governors, of whom a number in this century were very capable, were in frequent conflict with the local assemblies and found themselves able to carry on the administration only through a series of bargains and compromises.[59]

The theme of most constant complaint from the West Indian assemblies, as from those on the mainland, bore on commercial restrictions, especially the tendency of the Parliament at Westminster to devise trade regulations with the interests of the home merchants rather than those of the colonial planters and traders in mind. A stream of complaints from the extremely vocal West Indian interests concerning sugar duties and the oppressive practices of the slave trade monopolists was constantly flowing into London.[60] In the eighteenth century, the powerful lobby of the West Indian planters repeatedly succeeded in procuring protective legislation, like the Molasses Act of 1733 and the Sugar Act of 1764, that had repercussions far beyond the Caribbean.

---

[58] H. Wrong, *Government of the West Indies* (Oxford: 1932), p. 30.

[59] For details of the old representative system as evolved in the West Indies, see Wrong, *op. cit.*, pp. 36-47.

[60] E. A. Benians, *op. cit.*, p. 689.

Chapter 10

COLONIAL AMERICA: A BALANCE SHEET

I. SPANISH AND PORTUGUESE COLONIAL SYSTEMS COMPARED

The discovery of America came to Castile as a thrilling surprise, an unexpected gift dropped into her lap, challenging her to the same kind of adventurous and imaginative action as had the just-completed task of driving the Moors from Spanish soil. The experience gained in this struggle of seven hundred years was her principal qualification for the new rôle that the discoveries by Columbus thrust upon her. The conquest and control of the Canary Islands in the fourteenth century had added some slight experience in colonial management, but in a theater of small scope and relatively near home. In the government of vast, distant, transmarine possessions she had no experience, nor had that part of Spain directly involved, namely, the lands of the Castilian crown, much background in naval operations or trading activities. But with high courage she instantly seized the new opportunities. Before Columbus had reached the royal court to make his report he had orders to prepare a second expedition, and the Spanish ambassador at the Vatican was making sure of papal recognition of Spain's claims to the new lands, whatever they might turn out to be. Royal leadership in the American adventure was vigorously asserted from the start. Indirectly this sprang from the Moorish wars which had greatly exalted the prestige and authority of the crown. The character of Spain's advance on the American hemisphere was also a result of that struggle, taking the form of a great military conquest carried out by adventurous elements of Spanish society left foot-loose by the close of the Moorish wars and burning for new worlds to conquer. With the crown and the soldier, as in the medieval crusades, was immediately and closely associated the Spanish Church, which under Ferdinand and Isabella had become very much of a national church, though in close spiritual union with Rome.

To Portugal, the news that Christopher Columbus brought back was a stunning blow. Not only did it call into question the wisdom of King João II in having rejected the proposition of the sailor trained in his own service, but it seriously jeopardized the results of more than a century's persistent and intelligent exploration along the west African shore. These efforts had made Portugal a pioneer in maritime exploration and a much more experienced colonial and trading power than her Iberian neighbor, and one better fitted to profit from the prospects opened up by Columbus' discovery. Ferdinand and Isabella's wise acquiescence at Tordesillas in a compromise settlement of colonial claims and prospects on the one hand, and, on the other, Vasco da Gama's success in winning for Portugal the race to the real Indies stilled to a considerable extent the earlier heart-burning and provided scope for the energies and ambitions of both Iberian powers.

Indeed, so engrossed was Portugal in reaping the rewards falling to her adventurers as the first Europeans to reach the East Indies by sea that the national reaction to Cabral's discovery of Brazil in 1500 was so negligible as almost to amount to indifference. This was in striking contrast to the speed with which Spain reacted to the first news of Columbus' landfall, and to the dispatch with which Ferdinand and Isabella acted to consolidate their claims. Except for extracting a few loads of brazilwood and the dumping of some undesirables upon the conveniently distant shore, Portugal made practically no effort for three decades to do anything with Brazil. Her full energies were absorbed in the East, and so long as the future was bright there she had neither men nor resources to expend upon a second undertaking. Here her national weaknesses showed themselves. While more experienced than Spain in the planting and management of colonies and in trading operations on foreign shores, Portugal suffered from having to support her efforts abroad with a much smaller home popu-lation—she entered the sixteenth century with not more than 1,120,000 people as against Spain's 7,000,000. She was also handicapped by the poverty and smallness of the home base. In any test of strength, these fundamental discrepancies were bound to tell.

When, in 1530, the Portuguese crown took the first steps towards the development of Brazil, pressing considerations had moved the king to action. Not only had the prospects in the East become less glamorous, but the relation of America to the rest of the world had been clarified by Balboa's crossing of the Isthmus and Magellan's voyage around the world; meanwhile the reputation of America, as desirable on her own account and not merely as a halfway house to Asia, had been immensely enhanced by the discovery of Mexico by Cortés and the later rumors of the existence of a golden Peru. Finally, the constant reports of Spanish voyages along the Brazilian coast and in the La Plata estuary, and rumors of French exploring and trading activities in the vicinity of the neglected Portuguese possessions in America, aroused jealous fears in Lisbon, resulting in remedial action.

For both Portugal and Spain, conquest and settlement in America were royal undertakings, with the crown in each case initiating the enterprise and footing the bills; the sovereigns, however, quickly devised ways of sharing the burden, as well as some of the profits, with private individuals. Both nations started with the sanction of papal authority, in return for which they undertook certain religious obligations. Both enterprises had in them something of the spirit of the medieval crusades, though in this respect there was an enthusiasm and thoroughness in the Spanish effort that was not so marked in the Portuguese. With more maritime experience and a livelier commercial atmosphere at home, Portugal's adventure into the New World partook more of the nature of a national business undertaking supported by the agricultural, industrial, and commercial elements of the nation, whereas for Spain it was an enterprise chiefly of interest to soldiers, missionaries, and adventurers. Both nations, from their understanding of the nature of colonization and in harmony with the prevailing mercantile theories, were committed to the policy of exploiting the new-found possessions for the benefit of the homelands.

Once under way, the respective conquests and settlements followed patterns different from each other in many ways. In the first place, Portugal's methods of conquest were much less spectacular. The Spanish conquest was in many respects a great military pageant reaching its high points in a number of brilliant marches directed against the seats of old, established, native kingdoms whose capitals, as in the case of Mexico City and Cusco, were located hundreds of miles from the coast on which the invaders landed. These strongholds required for their capture a series of great battles in which a few hundred Spaniards, equipped with horses and modern weapons, were pitted against thousands of semicivilized natives wielding archaic weapons. The Portuguese in Brazil, on the other hand, were opposed only by seminomadic savages whose fierce opposition, while long, annoying, and costly, could leave no doubt of the ultimate issue. Secondly, the Portuguese conquest of Brazil was at first carried out much less thoroughly. The white settlements for years clung to the shoreline, while the rest of the land remained largely unexplored and unoccupied. The Spaniards, on the other hand, though always establishing port cities, tended to occupy also the inland centers of native power, as well as to follow old Indian trails into the interior in search of rumored riches.

Again, Brazilian colonization in the early years was more closely associated with a prosaic business motive than was the Spanish. The primary objective of the Castilians was gold, which they sought to acquire as spoils of war, secured at first from the Indian hoards and later from the captured mines which they forced the Indians to work for them. The primitive Brazilian Indians had no gold, nor were any mines discovered for nearly two hundred years. In the meanwhile, the Portuguese migrated to Brazil with the intention of making their fortunes in sugar. Immediately on arrival they laid out plantations along the tropical northeast shore and equipped them as soon as possible with sugar mills. This primary product was soon supplemented by cotton, tobacco, and other large-scale agricultural crops suitable for export. It was partly because of the need for port facilities that the Brazilian settlements clung so long to the coast. The prevalence of this plantation type of economy helps to explain why city life was a less predominant feature in Brazil than in Spanish America. In the Spanish area the agricultural unit also was a large estate, but it was less often devoted to a single crop, and it held a secondary, not the primary place, in colonial economy. Another result of the primacy of plantation economy in Brazilian life was that it attracted great numbers of the landed nobility and the well-to-do middle class of the homeland to the colony, thus providing it with a powerful landed aristocracy. In Spanish America wealth was more likely to be in the hands of the mine owners, who were not always resident in the colonies and so frequently failed to provide the local leadership which might have been expected from the class drawing the largest share of the riches.

Brazilian settlements quite early presented a permanent aspect, occupied as they were by immigrants a large proportion of whom had definitely cut their ties with home and thrown in their lot with the new country. Spanish settlements, on the other hand, suffered for years from the nostalgia of the many residents who were counting the days until they could return home with colony-made fortunes. Moreover, the long years that passed before minerals were found in Brazil, necessitating a continuing agricultural economy, tended to bring about a greater degree of colonial self-sufficiency. This in turn developed an independence of outlook absent from Spanish America, where the easily available gold and silver were immediately transferred to the motherland and inevitably postponed the coming of age of those colonies.

A further contrast is seen in the organization of labor in the respective colonies. Both mines and plantations required an immense labor force. Neither the Spaniards nor the Portuguese had any intention themselves of performing the work from which they drew their riches. Both equally disdained manual labor, drawing this view from their common medieval background in which hard work was associated with the despised infidel. The more numerous, more docile, semicivilized Indians of the Spanish area were a better source of human energy than was available to the Portuguese in Brazil. The latter did their best to enslave the wilder aborigines of their area; but, as these literally preferred death to enslavement and offered an almost unconquerable opposition either by fighting or in passive resistance, resort to African Negroes came relatively earlier and on a greater scale than in Spanish America. The result was that in Brazil, at the close of the colonial period, the blacks were not only more numerous but also more widely dispersed through the whole colony.

In both colonial realms the Church tried to stand between the native Indians and their enslavement by planter and miner. The effort met with greater success in the Spanish area, partly because there was no parallel development in Brazil of the semifeudal encomienda which, with all its weaknesses, at least preserved the Spanish American Indian from outright legal slavery. The Portuguese crown also seemed less interested in giving strong support to the clergy and missionaries in their efforts to Christianize and preserve the liberties of the aborigines. This was perhaps because the missionary task in Brazil seemed psychologically more hopeless and economically less practical, while the missionaries themselves were not the indispensable agents of frontier expansion that they became in Spanish territories. Furthermore, the ethical problem of whether the whites had the moral right to enslave the natives appears to have worried the Portuguese less. Their longer experience with slavery in Africa had inured them to the institution and made them less sensitive to such questions. Indian slavery, legally abolished in Spanish America by 1542, continued in Brazil throughout the colonial period. The organized razzias into the interior in search of slave labor for sale to the planters and miners of the coastal areas, which became a regular feature of Brazilian life strongly supported by public opinion, had no parallel in the Spanish region; nor was the relation of native and mestizo as bitter on Spanish soil as in the homeland of the mamelucos where the frontier was carried forward, not by missionaries, but by the bandeirantes.

In devising systems of government for the new lands, both nations naturally followed traditional trends of political thought and practice. The Spanish sovereigns started from the familiar concept of groups of territories severally attached to the crown. Spain itself for centuries had been such a group, made up of several kingdoms and countries on whose affairs the crown was advised by a number of royal councils, each concerned with a separate part. The Indies naturally took their place as another group of such kingdoms, related to the other Spanish realms merely through a common allegiance. Distance, of course, necessitated certain modifications: it was early decided that the king must be locally represented in America by a viceroy who would be his *alter ego;* the first regularly constituted viceroyalty was that of Mexico, set up in 1529. It was also in line with national development that Ferdinand and Isabella should take early steps leading eventually to the appointment of the important royal advisory councils to be resident in Spain—the Casa de Contratación and the Council of the Indies—which were intrusted with ultimate authority under the crown in different classes of colonial problems. It was in Ferdinand's later years that the first audiencia opened its doors in Santo Domingo in 1511. This was a collegiate body to be resident in America especially charged with high judicial authority on the model of the Castilian chancellería, though again because of distance, allowed more extensive authority.

By the time that the American discoveries had come to embrace Mexico and Peru, the Emperor Charles V, grandson of Ferdinand and Isabella, reigned over all Spanish territories as one of his several inherited realms. It was under this ruler, who was personally more familiar than any previous Spanish sovereign with the general idea of many kingdoms under one crown and perhaps less interested in encouraging unification than the Catholic Kings might have been, that the Spanish American realms were made into two viceroyalties having little contact with each other save through the crown and its royal councils. The process thus begun continued until, by the close of the eighteenth century, the Spanish American viceroyalties had increased to four and in addition had developed four captaincies-general, political units that were practically as independent of each other as were the viceroyalties. To the Hapsburg mind, this was a completely natural development, but the later Bourbon rulers were rendered uneasy by this fissiparous tendency and sponsored measures to create greater unity within America, as well as to strengthen the ties of all sections with Spain.

Portugal, in the late fifteenth century, drew quite different political concepts from her past. Since her origin as a national state, through separation from Spain in the twelfth century, she had been a single political entity; it was natural that in her colonial organization she should eventually adopt this same principle. After a short-lived and disastrous experiment of intrusting political power to some twelve semifeudal landlords (the donatarios), she settled down to the plan of having one supreme governor-general over all Brazil and clung to this arrangement, except for two short periods, throughout colonial times. In the homeland, unlike Spain, Portugal set up no special royal councils for colonial affairs but administered her American possessions through the existing general royal councils and other national bodies. Not until the Spanish king, Philip II, inherited the Portuguese crown in 1580, when Portuguese institutions became subject to Spanish influence, was a Portuguese Council of the Indies created; this body was later renamed the Transmarine Council. Thus in the case of Spanish America the nexus was between the king and a number of separate kingdoms; whereas, in Portugal's arrangement, Brazil was more truly a colony of the Portuguese nation. The subsequent history of Hispanic America is foreshadowed by the colonial divisions; Spanish America was eventually to emerge as a number of independent states, with boundaries largely determined by the colonial administrative pattern of many units; whereas modern Brazil was to retain the unity that marked the old colony.

Both Spanish and Portuguese governments in America were absolutist in character, with the fundamental laws and vital decisions all made in the Iberian Peninsula. In neither system was there anything approaching a cortes, or representative assembly, on either a colony-wide or provincial scale. Only in the sphere of municipal government had the colonists a voice, and here they were carefully watched by the crown to see that neither camara nor cabildo strayed beyond the narrow limits set for their functions, a temptation ever present in the case of both institutions. In Brazil, royal officials presided at the election of camaras and could almost always determine the membership; in Spanish America, the governor or some other royal official of the province presided at cabildo meetings, and officiales reales had ex officio seats. In both Spanish and Portuguese colonial systems the elective process tended to degenerate with time; in both, the municipal bodies were oligarchic rather than truly democratic in character but were the only elements in the government containing any representative feature. In both systems the royal authority was omnipresent and paramount at every level, though perhaps marked with a more personal note in the case of the less schematized Portuguese organization. In the matter of official personnel, the Portuguese monarch was more fortunate than the Spanish in attracting men of real ability into top-ranking positions in the colonial service. The lower ranks in both services were in general poorly paid and venal. In the realm of justice Portugal kept her system more centralized, reserving to courts of the home country for decision all cases of consequence or involving sums of any importance; Spain, on the other hand, leaning on the efficiency of the audiencia courts, strictly limited judicial appeals to the Council of the Indies.

In neither Spain nor Portugal was commercial machinery ever as wisely conceived or efficiently carried out as were their political institutions, a discrepancy that was reflected in colonial administration. The Portuguese economic and commercial system was neither as carefully planned nor as rigidly supervised as the Spanish, more initiative being left to the individual. The elaborate Spanish fleet system, for example, found no parallel in Portuguese practice; nor in economic life generally were the arrangements insuring royal control and crown participation in wealth so close and elaborate. Perhaps it was for this very reason that the Portuguese were the more successful traders in the long run. As the result of an attempted monopoly as rigid as could be devised, Spain emerged with a commerce mercilessly preyed upon by contraband traders and shot through with corruption. Although Portugal, too, had corruption to deal with and suffered from illicit trading by the English, French, and Dutch, her losses were, at least to some extent, made up by her own free and easy trading activities. At sea, Spanish losses tended to be much greater because the notorious preciousness of the cargoes of the silver fleets offered more tempting bait to the freebooters, especially in the seventeenth century after Spain had lost control of the sea lanes and could maintain only inadequate naval patrol. On land, in the same century, Portugal lost an immense proportion of her potential wealth through the encroachments of the English, French, and Dutch rivals who settled on her territory along the northern and northeast coasts of Brazil and at the mouths of the Amazon. But the postponement in Brazil of the discovery of valuable minerals until the eighteenth century, when the great age of piracy had passed, not only meant that the wealth of Brazilian mines was not subject to the heavy toll which had been levied upon Spain's treasure trove, but also gave time for the building up of a colonial self-sufficiency through agriculture and its allied industries. Portugal's more liberal and tolerant immigration policy, which welcomed even Jewish and unorthodox elements and their fruitful abilities into the colonial population, contributed measurably to this natural prosperity and provided a solid basis for a colonial life strong enough to withstand the gold rush of the eighteenth century.

It is curious to observe that of the two sets of colonies, both acquired about the same time, both located in tropical and subtropical regions of America, both despotically ruled from home through very similar institutions for three hundred years, and both finally caught in the whirlpool of the Napoleonic upheaval, the more strictly controlled Spanish colonial system left the motherland impoverished and feeble and her colonies deprived of their natural maturity in self-sufficiency and self-government; Portugal's more easy-going imperial system, on the other hand, produced a sufficiently loyal, prosperous, and secure Brazil to provide in a great national emergency an adequate refuge for the temporarily exiled royal court.

II. FRENCH AND ENGLISH COLONIAL SYSTEMS COMPARED

Through the sixteenth century, while America remained firmly in the hands of the Iberian peoples who had discovered it, French and English efforts to break into the monopoly were confined to spasmodic and irregular ventures; their seamen alternated between the hope of finding a northwest passage through or around America to the "spice islands" of the East and the more immediate prospects and satisfactions of gain to be had from preying upon the commerce of their older colonial rivals. In the case of France there was the additional motive of alleviating her vexing Huguenot problem. England's first attempt at permanent settlement was a phase of Elizabeth's undeclared war against Philip II, an effort to secure an American base for more effective predatory operations against Spanish commerce and Spanish American colonial coastal towns.

The sixteenth century efforts of the two northern powers differed from each other in that England's colonial activities were carried on under the parsimonious Tudors and had to be financed entirely by private capital; whereas French adventurers enjoyed a more liberal amount of official support, either from the king himself or from his ministers of state. On the other hand, the two movements were alike in the high caliber of many of the men who provided the leadership of the overseas ventures. Many of these came from the class of landed gentry or the educated upper middle class. The English Sir Humphrey Gilbert and Sir Walter Ralegh along with the French Jacques Cartier, Jean Ribaut, and Villegagnon, are outstanding examples of able, humane, and high-minded men who strove to establish the earliest outposts for their respective nations in the American scene. But despite their efforts, in the sixteenth century neither France nor England succeeded in founding a single permanent colony. Wars in Europe or religious and political controversies at home were too distracting, financial resources were too limited, and the dominance of the Spanish navy was too complete to make success possible. The adventurers of the age, however, laid far-flung bases for future French and English territorial claims, while at the same time training a large and active group of expert mariners, pirates, and contraband traders who, in this and succeeding centuries, contrived to divert an increasing stream of American gold and silver into other coffers than those of Spain and Portugal.

Both England and France planted their first permanent colonies shortly after 1600, and in the course of the seventeenth century developed their distinctive colonial systems; they were working, sometimes deliberately, sometimes unconsciously, towards a dramatic climax to be reached in the eighteenth century when their two rival systems would become locked in a gigantic struggle of a hundred years' duration, which had as its goal imperial supremacy, both in North America and the Orient.

By 1600 the driving forces behind European colonization had changed considerably. Religious strife had been the dominant note of the sixteenth century. At its close the lines were drawn; the Christian world of western Europe had become divided into two camps, one Protestant, the other continuing to acknowledge the supremacy of the Pope. By the time of Elizabeth's death it was evident that England was not to be drawn back into the Roman system but was to remain a leader among antipapal forces. In France the liberal-minded Henry IV, through a profession of Catholicism to please the majority of his subjects and the issuance of the Edict of Nantes to quiet a vociferous Huguenot minority, had achieved a religious equilibrium which, though uneasy, was to last for several decades.

In the sphere of international politics, the balance of power had shifted. The domination of Spain had been fatally shaken: at sea by the defeat of the Spanish Armada, on land by the successful revolt of the Dutch. In both England and France a new royal house held the throne; in each case the ruler was disposed to modify the established trend of national development. Such efforts, however, were to meet with only temporary success. Henry IV in France was to arrest but briefly his country's progress towards extreme centralization of power, monarchical absolutism, and religious unity. In England, the Stuarts, preaching the divine right of kings and obviously leaning toward Roman Catholicism, were to precipitate civil war; but the end of the century was to see the country once more marching toward parliamentary government and predominant Protestantism. The social upheavals associated with these profound religious and political changes were to produce in both countries large groups of people both prepared and anxious to face the hardships of life in a wilderness if only they could establish homes in surroundings free of these distractions.

By 1600 England and France had also acquired, though in different degrees, the further indispensable conditions for overseas empire: effective sea power and an influential, predominantly town-dwelling middle class. In regard to the first, the defeat of the Spanish Armada freed the seas for both powers, but as it was essentially an English triumph it was English naval strength that was most profoundly benefited. With respect to the rise of town economy and its effect on colonization, here again the future prospects seemed about equally bright for the two North Atlantic powers, though it was England that eventually proved to have the advantage. Both countries had recently emerged from a purely medieval economy which, with its wealth frozen in land values, could not have provided the fluid capital needed for colonizing distant North America; such an enterprise called for a large-scale business investment for which feudal landlords would have had neither the inclination nor the ready money. It took the seventeenth century's more restless, imaginative, and adventurous bourgeoisie, a product of the commercial revolution, to carry through successful colonization across the Atlantic. In both France and England, this middle class had become strong and numerous. Furthermore, a new economic device, the joint-stock company, made it possible to enlist the wealth of this group in the community in support of the new colonial ventures. These were never fully effective until the idea was hit upon of combining the new form of organization with monopolistic trading privileges which the crown might be induced to grant. Here again fortune favored the English. While English town economy was probably not more advanced than the French, English national economy as a whole was less enmeshed than the French in the shackles of feudalism; perhaps for this reason English use of government-chartered monopolistic trading companies came earlier, and was more successful than in French hands.

As powerful undercurrents of seventeenth century European life moved behind the tide of colonization from France and England, the motives actuating adventure in America changed considerably from those of the generation earlier. Although such sixteenth-century activities as fishing, piracy, slave-trading, and the search for the northwest passage continued in the seventeenth century, the new emphasis was on the pursuit of the fur trade, the raising of plantation crops, the acquisition of land, and the finding of religious freedom in a new home.

In the first half of the seventeenth century, French and English colonization was not, as in the case of Spain and Portugal, primarily a royal enterprise, but had its beginning in private initiative. The drive in both countries came from private companies holding charters from their respective governments. The latter were too preoccupied to undertake the ventures themselves but demanded, in return for state recognition, the assumption of such heavy obligations that many companies were unable to fulfil them. Both countries possessed large discontented groups that could provide excellent material for populating overseas colonies. As events fell out, however, one country was prepared to use this surplus, the other, for religious reasons, was more reluctant to do so.

England encouraged the emigration of every type of dissatisfied or downtrodden individual, religious dissenters, both Protestant and Roman Catholic, as well as social and political malcontents; France, on the other hand, after the first twenty-five years during which colonial enterprise was in the hands of companies either wholly or partly Huguenot in personnel and resources, prohibited all non-Catholics from going to New France. The effect was to divert French undertakings on the American mainland from becoming a true colonizing movement into an exploring and fur-trading venture; for, apart from the unhappy Huguenots who were not allowed to go, France had no considerable group desirous of settling down in the Canadian wilderness. Her peasants were still deeply encased in the feudal system, were too ignorant to organize, and were too frugal (or too poor) to help finance a venture in emigration; her middle class, still broken into exclusive guilds, had too little fluidity and enterprise. Also the frequent wars kept the population down so that there was no surplus available for emigration above the number who normally could find subsistence, even though meager, in France. Because of this lack of colonists, French trading companies, one after another, came to grief; they were unable to meet their charter obligations requiring the transportation and maintenance of a given number of colonists, even though the streets and jails were scoured to make up the necessary lists. Practically no family groups would migrate; only single men—transient fur traders, fishermen, soldiers, officials, and missionaries—could be induced to take ship for New France. The government canceled charter after charter for nonfulfilment of the settlement quotas, but all to no effect. New France, after a quarter of a century of strenuous effort, had fewer than one hundred French settlers in all.

Meanwhile, from a homeland with a population only half that of France but in the throes of a religious and social revolution that was breaking down old ties and securities, there poured into the English colonies—in family groups that proposed to stay—a goodly stream from all classes, including a small element from the nobility. Puritans, Quakers, Pilgrims, Huguenots, and Catholic refugees as well as debt criminals arrived in great numbers; poor folk generally, and a sprinkling of orthodox and moderately well-off people, landed on American shores prepared to work hard to create homes for themselves. Virginia alone, by 1627, had a population of more than four thousand, and enjoyed a flourishing trade with the mother country in tobacco, while on the New England coast a number of other enduring colonies had been founded. Though the original motive behind the colonizing efforts of both English and French chartered companies was the same, namely, the establishment of profitable trade, diverse national temperaments and a different political setting at home promptly gave wholly unlike aspects to the two contemporary developments. The French movement, as long as it was in company hands (until 1663), remained a predominantly trading enterprise; the English venture broadened out immediately, though company rule and private proprietorship long continued, into a general colonizing movement.

The French in Canada from the first carried on, in addition to their fur trading, magnificent exploring operations. The earliest companies examined Acadia, the St. Lawrence basin, and the Great Lakes, founding Port Royal, Quebec, and Montreal, and established themselves in the fur trade of these regions. They likewise explored, and had every opportunity to settle, the Atlantic seaboard from Cape Breton to Cape Cod before the English got there. Their trading interests, however, made them prefer the north. Later, under royal auspices, these operations were pushed southward to embrace much of the Mississippi River system, and westward to the Saskatchewan waterways. The combination of fur trading and inveterate roving was one that appealed especially to the Bretons and Normans who provided the majority of the French interested in Canada. In time there arose among French officials in America the grandiose idea of a great New France based on a control of the two magnificent water systems of the St. Lawrence and the Mississippi, a development that would limit the English colonies to a narrow Atlantic strip; but this idea at no time received effective support from home. Meanwhile, exploration in the seventeenth century received less attention in the English colonies. Established along the Atlantic coast, in touch with the sea and to some extent with each other, shut off from the interior plains by the Indian-haunted Appalachians, the English colonists had not such a consuming curiosity as to what lay beyond. The movement westward took the form of an advancing agricultural frontier, pushed slowly forward by family groups rather than by brilliant single exploits of exploration.

Company rule in Canada, tried out for fifty years, was not a success either in the early form of mixed Huguenot and Catholic organizations or the later all-Catholic companies and was replaced in 1663, under Colbert's influence, by royal government, administered by a governor and council appointed by the crown. On the other hand, charter government in the English colonies, associated everywhere with some form of popular assembly, had a longer and more successful history; though the tendency, from early days, was in the direction of transforming both corporation and proprietary colonies into royal ones.

By the close of the seventeenth century the two rival colonial dominions on the North American mainland presented very different aspects. The English Atlantic settlements, in a dozen different political units—some royal, some corporation, and some proprietary colonies—were each ruled by a governor, a council, and an elected representative assembly, with the latter empowered to make laws that were not inconsistent with the laws of England. The outstanding issues everywhere were the relationship of the colonial legislature to the colonial executive, and of both to the home authorities. The French settlements along the St. Lawrence formed a single unit under a royally appointed governor and council who executed laws made in France. In the council, the three important persons—the governor, intendant, and bishop—all had ill-defined and overlapping powers so that much of their time was consumed in disputes over their respective jurisdictions. The only reason for having the double secular executive of both intendant and governor apparently was that the provinces of Old France were thus administered, and Louis XIV claimed that New France held a parallel relationship and should be governed accordingly. In other words, in governing policy France made no effort to create a new political system or to devise a system that would solve the special problems involved in governing a distant dependency. For the same reason the seigneurial system was introduced, although already antiquated in France. The agricultural aspect of this semifeudal regime was supported by strenuous efforts of the crown whose full weight of authority was turned, after 1663, to dispatching agricultural settlers across the Atlantic, bribed with enormous grants of land to leave their beloved homeland and settle in Canada.

The outstanding features of French royal colonial government were paternalism, close colonial supervision, and minute economic direction. Not the slightest trace of elective institutions was tolerated. Louis XIV believed heart and soul in absolutist government; Laval was an ultramontane; Colbert was a mercantilist who considered that colonies should not only pay their own way but contribute to the wealth of the mother country and should be directed from Paris to that end. After a hundred years of effort, Canada was a country with a small population of about seven thousand persons—habitants, priests, and fur traders—living, for the most part, around the three settlements of Quebec, Three Rivers, and Montreal. There were no Protestants, no elected assembly, no town meetings, and trade was wholly controlled in the interests of the homeland.

Religion played a totally different part in the two sets of colonies. In the English colonies it provided the determining motive for the migration of most of the colonists to America, and later for the splitting off of groups from the parent colonies to form new settlements. It was an immense force in everyday living for the whites, but it hardly touched the relations of the colonists with the natives. Missionary enterprise played but a very modest rôle, though the English were in touch with the same Indian groups as the French. A large proportion of the colonists were Protestant dissenters and they had not the same driving belief in the sacramental value of baptism to urge them forward as had their Roman Catholic neighbors; nor had they such an organized missionary force at hand as the religious orders made available to the French. The extension of their faith to the red man had little part in the programs or interest of the English colonists. In fact, many of them were hardly convinced that the Indians had souls at all, and they were certainly not prepared to consider educating them for incorporation into their social structure, though a few Indian schools were founded. In the French colonies, missionary efforts constituted perhaps the most admirable aspect of the whole colonial movement. There is nothing more heroic in colonial annals than the stories of the Huronic and Iroquois missions, though their net results were very small. In their efforts to win the Indians to Christianity the French missionaries, unlike the Spanish and Portuguese, used persuasive methods only; neither was it considered so necessary to isolate the native, though in late colonial times a measure of segregation was favored for the wilder and more nomadic savages. The great struggle revolved about the liquor question. Should the government prohibit the sale of liquor to the Indians by the traders who used it as a bribe to induce the red men to bring in their furs to the forts? The missionaries threw their influence in the scale of prohibition. In the

English colonies the sale of liquor to the Indians hardly became a question, though there the traffic was of much smaller dimensions and so of less relative importance.

In their whole attitude toward the American native, the French differed from other colonists; and of all the white men, the Indians preferred the Frenchmen. Not only was the French colonial economy with its emphasis on fur trading a benefit rather than a menace to the Indian hunter, in contrast to the English and Spanish colonial systems in which the farmer, with his hunger for land and emphasis on forest clearance, relentlessly pushed the red man back and circumscribed his ancestral hunting grounds, but socially the Frenchman was more congenial. In intercourse with them, the French neither treated them, as did the Spaniards, as minors or "wards" whose every action and opinion must be supervised, nor did they despise them as the English obviously did, even while recognizing their title to the soil and their right to bargain and make treaties. The attitude of the French was more like that of an older brother who might coax, scold, punish, deceive, or seek to impress his primitive kin, but who never attempted to enslave him or behave contemptuously towards him. Though the French took careful measures to protect themselves against outbreaks of savage violence—building numerous fortified trading posts, and not so recklessly exposing themselves on isolated farms and in undefended villages as did the English—they seemed to possess a genius for securing and retaining the cooperation and good will of the natives. In peace they utilized the skill of the Indians as fur gatherers, and in war leaned on their prowess as warriors in the unending struggle with the English.

The Indians repaid the friendly French by constantly leading them to the discovery of new avenues of exploration and new sources of wealth; and, it is to be observed, it was in this field of endeavor that the French made their greatest contribution to the opening up of the North American continent. They were the outstanding pioneers in discovering mountains, lakes, woods, and rivers, and in the establishment of trading routes all over the northern continent. Their skill in clearing forests, their powers of endurance, and their ability to live tranquilly and cheerfully under hard conditions were unrivalled by the people of any other European nation.

In addition to their primary settlements in Canada and along the Atlantic coast, by the close of the seventeenth century France and England had each established a stake in a second mainland area: England at Hudson Bay; France in Louisiana. Both enterprises were to see their principal development in the eighteenth century. They differed widely in character. The English venture at Hudson Bay was primarily a trading enterprise whose promoters made no effort to link its fortunes with those of the

Thirteen Colonies. Its survival despite repeated and determined attacks from the French, who felt that its existence threatened to hem them in between two British developments as well as drastically to cut into the profits of the northern fur trade, is an impressive tribute to the inherent strength of the English commercial company. With a solid foundation in the farsighted planning, the organizing ability, and the financial stability of hard-headed London businessmen, the "Great Company" proved that it possessed the staying power and resiliency to tide over long periods of adversity. French Louisiana, on the other hand, was a mixed colonizing and trading venture, closely associated from the beginning with French enterprise in Canada and, though separately administered, woven with the northern colony into a single pattern in the imperial dreams of La Salle, Frontenac, d'Iberville, and other French imperialists.

The activties of the two powers in the West Indies were very similar in character; these were primarily trading ventures based on the development of plantation colonies and were supplemented by contraband trading with the nearby Spanish possessions. If anything, the English colonies were more purely commercial than the French, reversing the situation on the mainland where French enterprise had in it a greater trade element than the English. The French West Indies were, however, more closely tied in with an over-all design for all French holdings in America, as well as more directly associated with European events, than were the English Caribbean settlements. While a profitable triangle trade developed between the Thirteen Colonies and the West Indies area, the relationship was rather a venture in smuggling than in empire planning; officially the connection was so loose that the two developments might have been under different flags. The French in America, at least through long periods, had a grand design; the English had not.

III. GENERAL REFLECTIONS

Spain and Portugal discovered and settled their American colonial empires in the sixteenth century, Spain, of the two, getting off to a quicker and more dramatic start; the planting of the French and English colonies were contemporary developments of the seventeenth century, with England rapidly outpacing France. The Iberian colonial ventures, having their immediate background in fifteenth-century life and events, were a hundred years nearer medieval times and, in the emphasis on the crusading aspect of their colonial undertakings, were reminiscent of the "age of faith." The French and English settlements, on the other hand, receiving their dominant impulse from sixteenth-century religious dissensions and the commercial revolution, were definitely more secular in spirit and closer in character to the modern world.[1]

Of the four enduring colonial systems, three were founded on absolutist principles, both in religion and politics; while the fourth, the English, had its basis in the Reformation struggle for religious liberty and in the political upheavals of the Stuart age when England was struggling to revert to the main stream of her long constitutional evolution towards parliamentary government and to regain and solidify her challenged liberties. The migrating colonists naturally carried overseas these casts of contemporary thought, along with their languages and other elements of culture, with the result that in these early foundational years were laid broad distinctions which may be traced in the complexion of today's American continental pattern. The political status of all four imperial systems has of course completely changed. Only one European power holding dominion in colonial America is represented in any strength today, and in this case the holdings are principally those of eighteenth century conquest and not of original settlement. But while the nexus with Europe has completely altered, it is to be observed in the Spanish, Portuguese, and French communities that in domestic government, wherever democratic principles in politics, religion, the press, and speech have succeeded in establishing themselves, it has been at the cost of unending struggle against the constantly threatening resurgence of dictatorship and authoritarianism; whereas in the peoples of North America sprung from the Thirteen Colonies, political evolution along democratic lines has proceeded fairly smoothly, "broadening down from precedent to precedent."

Colonial economic theory was not to be so tenacious of life as were political and religious concepts. All four colonial systems were established within the circle of the then prevailing mercantilist ideas, in which colonies were expected to minister to the needs and support the power of the mother country, the homeland providing protection but demanding in return that its own interests should be considered paramount. In the colonial centuries, Spain tried hardest to carry through this system to the limit, and suffered most heavily from challenges to her claims. This was due not only to the perpetual economic warfare that mercantilism naturally brought in its train, but to the fact that her ships and ports were the ones most worth plundering, as through them flowed a stream of precious metals from the only rich colonial mines of the sixteenth and seventeenth centuries. The same mercantile system under which such great stores of American treasure were transferred to Spain—though to her small ultimate advantage—operated in less spectacular fashion in the case of Eng-

---

[1] *Cf.* S. A. Zavala, *The Spanish Colonization of America* (London: 1943), p. 3.

land and her colonies, but nevertheless was an insidious cause of mounting irritation which was to lead finally to a fatal break in established relations. It had a less direct effect in bringing about the separation of the French and Portuguese empires from their respective mother states. It was, however, during the revolutionary epoch that mercantilism was replaced by other economic concepts.

These changes in economic theory have their explanation in part, of course, in the inevitable changes that had been taking place meanwhile in Europe as a natural result of the whole colonizing movement. The repercussions of the planting of European life in America brought about revolutionary changes in every department of life in the homelands. Besides the startling effects on prices and commercial transactions in general produced by the sudden accession to the world's store of an immense amount of specie from the American gold and silver mines, the opening up of great sources of supply of all other kinds of raw materials naturally had a revolutionary effect upon the static economy of the Old World. The prospect of new and expanding overseas markets gave a great impetus to industry and commerce, and accelerated the growth in importance of towns and ports at the expense of the old rural economy. In the intellectual world, wider geographical horizons turned men's thought away from preoccupation with the glories of the past and encouraged them to look forward to a brightening future. Another kind of "other worldliness" from that of medieval times attracted men's thought and desires to the New World across the Atlantic.

PART III

COLONIAL LIFE AND CULTURE

Chapter 11

SOCIETY IN COLONIAL SPANISH AMERICA

I. THE SOCIAL PATTERN IN THE SIXTEENTH AND SEVENTEENTH CENTURIES

At the close of the first century of colonial times, Spanish America presented the aspect of a vast territory dotted here and there with a number of towns in which the white population was largely concentrated; surrounding each one was a considerable territory which was under its control. From the first, Spanish colonization in America had turned upon the founding of towns. This was natural considering the nature and origin of the colonial movement which, while primarily a conquest for the exploitation of mineral wealth, was also a fervent religious crusade for the conversion to Christianity of the pagan aborigines. For the furtherance of both these objects, there was needed the support of firmly established local bases such as the closely knit municipality alone could provide. Moreover, for the Spaniard the municipal unit was historically the natural unit of organization. The Romans long ago had taught the Iberians to be town dwellers and had deeply implanted the root of municipal government. By the time of the Discovery, it had become by far the most successful political unit in the peninsula, the only one indeed truly national in character. Compared to his *ciudad, villa,* or *pueblo,* provincial and national organization meant little to the average Spaniard. Once across the Atlantic, the Spanish conquistador naturally reverted to that type of organization in which he felt most completely at home. Furthermore, the Spaniards came to America, not in family groups seeking lands suitable for domestic habitations and agricultural operations, but for the most part, and especially in the earlier years, they arrived as individual adventurers loosely organized in conquering bands about the person of a leader; a municipality obviously suited the needs of this type of settlement.

Ordinarily, among the first acts of a conquistador on arriving within the area that he proposed to conquer was the establishment of a town at some strategic site—at a harbor, or a point commanding a river, or one possessing some other natural advantage. Proceeding to lay out his municipality, he would begin with a *plaza mayor* or principal square in the center, on which later would front the church, town hall, market, and other public buildings and monuments. From this square and following

317

a geometrical plan prescribed by royal ordinance he would trace a number of streets running from north to south and from east to west. The town area was thus divided into rectangles, each usually forming four lots which the leader assigned severally to his followers who became vecinos, or burghers, of the new settlement and were expected to erect dwellings on their assignments. Around the settlement, if local circumstances seemed to require it, would be thrown a wall for defense purposes, the vecinos acting as a garrison, each with the obligation to keep arms and a horse. At times, however, a plot of land within the town would be reserved for a fort and barracks, with special soldiers or horsemen assigned to garrison duty.[1] Beyond the area allotted for building purposes, land was usually set aside to serve the community as common and pasture land. Outside the town limits, grants of farm lands would be made to the vecinos that extended for a considerable, often an indeterminate distance from the settlement. In early days, with such grants usually went encomiendas of local Indians to provide needed labor. The vecinos were expected to cultivate and police their holdings and, as encomenderos, to civilize and Christianize the natives entrusted to them. From the Indians, the encomenderos might legally exact tribute in specie or in kind, or—down to 1549—require its equivalent in personal labor; after the prohibiting decree of that year, this demand for service became unlawful, although it was often made and enforced. As householders, the vecinos, at least in the first half of the sixteenth century, usually had the right to elect the alcaldes and regidores of the cabildo, whose jurisdiction within and without the city was limited only by that of the governor or viceroy. The boundaries of these city areas were never adequately defined, with the result that, as new communities were founded nearby, bitter jurisdictional disputes became inevitable.

Many colonial towns went through a long period of very slow development or suffered stagnation for many years. Colonial growth took place in the increase in number rather than in the size of towns. As the tide of conquest advanced, many inhabitants left established communities to form settlements on the new frontier. There was also a steady drain through the frequent violent deaths of the conquistadores or their return to the homeland. The Indian population was also kept small by hardships, cruelties, and decimation from the white man's diseases. Moreover, the natural growth of the colonial towns, which might have been expected from the acquisition and accumulation of wealth, was stunted by the draining off of their resources to fill the coffers of Spain. A further factor preventing the rapid increase of city populations was the stringent control of emigration exercised by Spain—the most rigid carried out by any power. Once the

---

[1] B. Moses, "Colonial Society in America," American Historical Association, *Annual Report 1911* (Washington: 1913), vol. I, p, 143.

Casa de Contratación was in full operation, one of its principal duties was to handpick the emigrants for America and see to it that neither political malcontents, heretics, foreigners, nor criminals took ship for the New World; inevitably, however, a fair number of these undesirables managed to slip through the net. As a result of this screening process the colonial population, through the first century at least, largely consisted of adventurous individuals who expected sometime to return to Spain, there being no obstacle to prevent their doing so. With this outlook on the part of the whites, the Spanish settlements were naturally slow to assume the aspect of permanent and developing towns. Not until there arose, towards the end of the sixteenth century, a considerable class of creoles—or colonial-born Spaniards—with naturally stronger ties to America than to Spain, did the Spanish American cities take on both a permanent and a distinctly American character. Colonial cities, even colonial capitals, were quite unequal in importance and varied similarly in the amenities of existence. Throughout the three colonial centuries, the two earliest viceregal capitals, Mexico City and Lima, far outdistanced all others in importance, not only as foci of political life, but as centers for educational, artistic, literary, and religious activities.

An outgrowth of the closeness of the tie with Spain and of the comparative absence of the spirit of criticism and protest inherent in the selected colonial population was the determination to preserve as completely as possible Spanish traditions and ways of doing things. Not only was the fundamental plan of the city and its government modeled on the Spanish pattern, and the white element in its population maintained at a high level of religious orthodoxy, but Spanish artistic, literary, educational, and architectural forms, as well as types of amusement, were clung to tenaciously even long after they had been abandoned in the mother country. The Spanish colonies of course were not unique among colonial societies in preserving an antiquated conservatism in things of the mind and spirit, while beating out new paths in the world of action; but the Spanish American cities seemed to be especially strongly marked by this characteristic.

By the close of the sixteenth century Spanish colonial society had become highly stratified. The first steps in this direction had been taken when the crown created an aristocracy among the earliest comers. Among other rewards, the king had bestowed titles of various degrees of honor upon successful conquistadores, the majority of whom had come from the middle class, though there was among them a sprinkling both of the nobility and of the dregs of society. Another major factor in producing gradation in colonial life was the early intermingling of Spanish and Indian blood. During the early decades, nearly all Spaniards arrived without their women, and unions with Indian women soon produced the new social group of Indian-whites, or mestizos. A third factor insuring Spanish America color problems and inequalities to the end of time was the arrival soon after the Discovery of large numbers of African Negroes; subsequent crossings of blacks with whites, as well as with Indians and mestizos, were inevitable. The fact that the Negroes were not spread evenly over the whole of Spanish America but were massed chiefly in the Caribbean area, and even there were mainly along the coasts, further diversified the picture.[2] It was not, however, only in color of skin that inequality early showed itself everywhere in Spanish colonial society; in education, wealth, political and professional opportunities, and even in legal standing, privilege and discrimination were universal. For large groups even economic independence was impossible, to say nothing of economic equality. To a certain extent religion held men together in a common profession of faith; but as an organization, the Church itself was a highly privileged body with great inequalities within its own ranks.

In the colonial caste system, seven important groups may be distinguished. At the highest level of society were the peninsulares, the peninsula-born Spaniards to whom the colonists gave the uncomplimentary names of *gachupines* (spurred ones) or *chapetones* (tenderfeet). To this group, a considerable number of whom belonged to the large class of Spanish gentry, was intrusted most of the high governmental and ecclesiastical posts of the Indies in the gift of the king. The majority came out to the colonies for only a short time; and then, usually after making a fortune, they returned home often leaving behind them the impression that they despised the American-born colonists, even though the latter might be of the noblest and purest blood. There is no evidence to suggest that the peninsulares had any monopoly of talent; they obviously owed their privileged position to the king's belief that from their group he was most likely to receive dependable, loyal allegiance.

The second position in the social hierarchy was occupied by the creoles, the American-born Spaniards. Though legally equal with the peninsulares, in practice they were admitted only to minor, usually local, offices in the government and Church. Apparently the king did not quite dare to trust his precious Indies to those born there; he feared, perhaps, that local patriotism might triumph over loyalty to a distant sovereign. Bernard Moses points out that, among the 166 viceroys and 588 captains-general, governors, and presidents, only eighteen were creoles.[3] The record in the

---

[2] E. J. Bourne, *Spain in America,* pp. 278-81, estimates that at the close of the eighteenth century Venezuela had five hundred thousand Negroes to New Spain's twenty thousand and Peru's eighty-two thousand.

[3] B. Moses, *Spanish Dependencies in South America,* 2 Vols. (New York: 1914), Vol. II, p. 398.

Detail of a Holy Week procession, Lima. A water color attributed to Pancho Fierro (1803-1879). (Courtesy of the Hispanic Society of America)

Lima street scene. From *Voyage autour du monde exécuté pendant des années 1836 et 1837 sur la corvette La Bonite* by Auguste N. Vaillant, Paris, no date.

Seventeenth-century Mexican pottery fountain. (Courtesy of the Hispanic Society of America)

Seventeenth-century incense burner of silver and parcel-gilt.

Eighteenth-century silver maté cup. (Courtesy of the Hispanic Society of America)

Church was similar. The most important political outlet for the ambitions and abilities of the creoles was the cabildo, which they controlled nearly everywhere.

In general the creoles, many of whom were educated in Spain, filled the professions and the ranks of the large landowners, rich miners, and wealthy merchants of the community. Within their own class there were sharply-drawn social lines; the descendants of the conquistadores, for example, formed a colonial aristocracy, while at the bottom of the creole ladder were some of the more prosperous artisans and traders. In the group generally there was much heart burning and dissatisfaction, with jealousy and hatred of the peninsulares on the one hand, and on the other, scorn, or at least complete lack of sympathy, for the mestizo and other colored groups. Many creoles apparently inherited the pride, militaristic outlook, and detestation of manual labor that had marked the social group in Spain from which so many of the conquistadores had come. Though as individuals often hospitable, kindly, and generous, the creoles as a class seemed to lack the self-control and perseverance that responsibility in high office might have produced. In the hopeless limitations of their lot under the colonial regime, they were notorious for indolence, instability, extravagance, love of empty honors, fondness for display, and openness to corruption and venality. The two white groups, peninsulares and creoles, who controlled most of the wealth of the Indies so far as this remained in America at all—were predominantly city dwellers.

Below the creoles were the mestizos, the descendants of mixed white and Indian unions, often suffering from the stigma of illegitimacy. From the beginning the Spanish crown had deliberately encouraged the blending of races in the colonies, prohibiting the imposition of any obstacles to it and strictly forbidding the emigration of unmarried Spanish girls to America unless they were daughters, or servants, of migrating families. The fact that the mestizos were usually the offspring of Spanish men and Indian women and generally despised their mothers as belonging to a conquered, colored, and primitive people, had an unfortunate effect on the estimation in which women generally were held in Spanish America. As a class the mestizos, who were excluded from higher education and therefore the professions, provided most of the artisans, small farmers, free laborers, overseers, small tradesmen, and the considerable body of professional beggars. Though a good type physically, they were grossly ignorant and frequently a prey to superstition; and there was much lawlessness, drunkenness, and gambling among them. Within their large and rapidly increasing group, there were many gradations according to the degree of color. With few privileges and shockingly low wages, they generally hated their social superiors and despised and abused the pure-blooded aborigines and the African slaves.

The mulattoes, part white and part Negro, and also usually illegitimate, were in a less favorable social position than the mestizos and suffered under greater restrictions and an even lower standard of living. Many were indolent and destitute, and considerable numbers crossed the line into crime or beggary. Like the mestizo, the mulatto was a cruel and bitter enemy to Indians and Negroes. To escape from their down-trodden groups, both mestizos and mulattoes were given to pretending to be creoles; some purchased royal patents declaring them to be white men, a practice bitterly opposed by the American-born Spaniards who hated this intrusion into their ranks. Between them, these two partly white groups did much of the hard work in the colonies, especially in the cities, and becoming increasingly standardized in type through intermarriage in their own ranks, were obviously preparing to take a place of growing importance in the structure of Latin American society.

The zambos were of mixed Indian and Negro blood, a combination which the government tried to prevent by the imposition of the cruelest penalties. These unfortunates not only suffered all the disadvantages attached to both the racially pure Indians and Negroes and the half-breed groups, but were regarded by society in general as naturally addicted to vice and likely to be guilty in any question of crime.

Among the racially pure colored groups, the Indians, though overworked and economically exploited, were much better off than the Negroes. After the New Laws of 1542, no Indians could be legally enslaved. Furthermore, as wards of the crown they enjoyed special protection before the law and were not subject to the Inquisition. At the close of the sixteenth century, the majority in the areas of Spanish settlement lived in their own villages, or in special sections in the white towns, under the rule of their own caciques, with a royal officer, the corregidor, especially charged with their protection, and with a resident cura to instruct them in the fundamentals of Christian living.

The number of African Negroes in Spanish America by the close of the sixteenth century was considerable, but they were very unevenly distributed. Only in the West Indian islands, the tropical coastal lowlands of northern and northwestern South America, and along the Atlantic shores of Central America and Mexico was the Negro element a dominant one. It was possible for the slaves to purchase their freedom, and a considerable number contrived to do so, thus constituting another social group of freedmen. Though Spanish American history was marked by a number of servile rebellions, on the whole the Negro seems to have been an industrious and cheerful element in society; and his lot under the Spaniards certainly was not worse than under other white masters.

The relative strength of the different groups at the close of the colonial era is indicated by Baron von Humboldt's estimate that, of the seventeen million people in Spanish America, three and a half million were whites, five and a third million were mestizos, seven and a half million were Indians, and three quarters of a million were Negroid.[4]

The contrasts and clashes between the various social elements of Spanish colonial society were reflected in the external aspect of the colonial cities and in the interplay of the daily routine of its inhabitants. By the end of the sixteenth century, the general pattern of the colonial city and its tempo of life had taken form. It was one that offered sharp contrasts of ostentatious splendor and dismal squalor. The plaza mayor, with the imposing public buildings and great cathedral of magnificent ornateness calculated to impress the simple minds of the colonial populace with the glory and power of Spain and of its Church and the ruling classes, was usually surrounded by a network of filthy, unpaved streets. The latter were completely innocent of any sewerage system or other plan to carry off the refuse daily thrown into them, except for the efforts of swarms of buzzards, dogs, and swine that infested them. In matters of sanitation, the cities of contemporary Europe were of course very little better.

The one decently paved and tree-lined street, the *alameda,* provided a setting for the popular late afternoon promenade which, in its display of the fine clothes of the carriage folk and the costly trappings of riders, accentuated the drabness of garb of the workers and the rags of the beggars. The houses of the wealthy, facing on the alameda, were usually one-story structures, flush with the street, enclosing in Spanish style one or more open courts or *patios.* These were the centers of such activity as custom permitted to the aristocratic Spanish and creole ladies who, following Spanish tradition, seldom appeared in public except on the way to and from Church. With no learning, even if there had been any books of interest to them, and with practically no other occupation than fine embroidery and the exchange of gossip, the colonial women led secluded lives which contrasted drastically with the habits of the men. The latter spent much of their time, when not engaged in such business as must be attended to, in the social amenities associated with drinking, gambling, and attending such sports as bullfighting, cockfighting, and horseracing and occasional excited attendance at a public flogging or an *auto-da-fé.* Meanwhile, the Negro slaves, the lowly Indians, and the half-breed laborers toiled to produce the comforts of the wealthy and their own hard-earned daily bread.

---

[4] A. Humboldt, *Political Essay on the Kingdom of New Spain,* translated by J. Black (London: 1911).

The essential monotony of colonial city life, almost entirely shut off as it was from contact with the outside world, probably found its greatest alleviation in the frequent festivals and religious holidays when there would be gorgeous spectacles of religious drama and ceremonial, and the city gave itself up to a gay round of festivity. Now and then, the holiday took on a more national aspect when, to mark such events as the accession of a sovereign or the birth of a royal heir or the coming of a new viceroy, the town was decorated with banners and floral arches, and bands provided music for military and civic processions.

The predominant influence in moral and intellectual life in a Spanish colonial city, as in that of the colony generally, was the Church. From the first, the strongest force, next to gold-getting, behind the whole Spanish colonial movement had been religious. Everywhere in western Europe, in one form or another, religion was the most vital concern of the age. Nowhere was it more intimately bound up with national life than in Spain where, for seven centuries, the struggle to free Spanish soil from the invading Moor had been inextricably associated with the crusade of the Cross against the Crescent. In that long struggle the Church and the crown had worked very closely together; and it was natural that they should be intimately associated in the new venture across the sea which opened in the very year that saw, in the fall of Granada, the collapse of the last Moorish stronghold in Spain. The energies of the one movement poured naturally and easily into the other and to a considerable extent tended to flow along accustomed channels. The sails of colonial ships bore the sign of the Cross, and the Discoverer landed on American soil under the two banners—the Cross and the royal standard of Castile. In his second voyage Columbus brought with him, under royal command, a number of missionaries to open the work of conversion in the New World.

The task the churchmen set themselves was to carry to the new dominions of their sovereign the orthodox religious traditions of Spain. Religious liberty was not within the scope of their thought; there was none in Spain. Ferdinand and Isabella held the view that religious unity must underlie political unity; to enforce this combination in state policy, they had introduced the Spanish Inquisition. Partly through its efforts the great world currents of the Renaissance and religious reforming zeal destined to carry on their crest the barque of political liberty were stemmed and, to a great extent, passed Spain by. The few nonconforming Spanish heretics were rather easily silenced. Colonial governing agencies were strictly ordered not to allow heretics to enter Spanish America, and the missionary task there was neither weakened nor embarrassed by doctrinal disputes.

In the colonies, Church and state maintained a unity of policy in ideals and practical aims even more complete than in the motherland. In neither theater was there any doubt as to which of the two possessed the dominating voice. Alexander VI, in recognizing the Spanish claim to the Indies, had done so on condition that the Spanish crown should assume the responsibility for converting the American aborigines. In a series of bulls issued between 1493 and 1508, the Pope specifically bestowed upon the Catholic Kings the *patronato real* which gave them not only the right of appointment to all ecclesiastical offices in the American dominions, but other privileges which elsewhere the Pope retained for himself.[5] Turning over to the king the right to receive the tithe,[6] the Pope asked in return that the crown should assume the financial responsibility for the support of the clergy and the work of the Church.

With these papal concessions in hand, it is difficult to see how any sovereign could have possessed more absolute control over an organization than the Spanish king held over the Church in the Indies. He was the highest ecclesiastical as well as the supreme secular authority. No cleric might go to America, or move about while there, or return home without license from the king; no papal bull might be published without his consent, no synod held, nor any church or monastery or other ecclesiastical building erected, or enterprise undertaken, without royal approval. Only in being allowed its own courts, to try the clergy under canon law, and deal with cases involving spiritual matters was the Church to any extent free of secular control. The result was an extraordinary degree of harmony in the relationship of Church and state so far as authority was concerned. There was, however, a certain amount of overlapping of secular and ecclesiastical jurisdictions, and consequently a good deal of rivalry and jealousy among local potentates. Fundamentally, however, the sovereign could hardly resent or fear the immense wealth and power of a Church so fully under his control, for its glory and success ministered directly to his own. Its tradition sanctified his own absolutism, and its clergy taught that loyalty to Church and crown were but two aspects of one allegiance.

From the first, the religious work in the Indies fell naturally into two fairly distinct major categories: that in the towns which for the most part was entrusted to the secular clergy, and that of the missions among the more remote Indian settlements, which was largely given over to the religious orders. In the towns, the work fell into the two divisions: parish work among the whites, and labor as curas or *doctrineros* among the In-

---

[5] For a detailed discussion of the issues involved in the *real patronato de las Indias*, see J. L. Mecham, *Church and State in Latin America* (Chapel Hill: 1934), ch. I.

[6] The tithe was a tax of 10 per cent on the income from agricultural and pastoral industries. The total amount collected in New Spain in the decade 1769-1779 was nearly 13,500,000 pesos, in the following decade nearly 18,500,000. *Cf.* C. H. Haring, *Spanish Empire in America*, p. 190.

dians living in the nearby suburbs or in native villages under the rule of their own caciques and supervised by Spanish officials.

Over many of the white towns the clergy were able to cast an aura of ecclesiasticism. The most important colonial cities were seats of the immensely wealthy and influential archbishops, of whom there were five by the close of the sixteenth century. Provincial capitals of lesser note were the seats of the twenty-seven bishops [7] and the sites of most of the numerous monasteries and convents.[8] The streets of the cities usually bore the names of saints or commemorated an event or doctrine in the Christian story. In some towns every household was encouraged to have a patron saint whose image was placed over the door. Most of the citizens were organized into *hermandades,* or religious brotherhoods, each devoted to the cult of some sacred image in whose honor members of the brotherhood, equipped with its own costumes, floats, and banners, took part on special occasions in great processions and colorful ceremonies. Caracas, one of the smaller capitals, was described in the middle of the eighteenth century as possessing fifteen churches and forty hermandades.

The chief architectural features of every town were the imposing and numerous ecclesiastical buildings—churches, episcopal and other ecclesiastical residences, monasteries, schools, and convents. Spain's Golden Age in art corresponded with the first hundred and fifty years of colonial history and many of the colonial buildings of the late sixteenth century, when the necessity was past of having buildings serve as fortresses, were handsome and dignified examples of the Renaissance type of architecture. Some, following the plateresque style so popular in Spain, showed fine sculptured façades and were decorated with wrought-iron grills protecting doors and windows. Occasionally, the colonial designs showed Indian motifs, an indication of the hands that, under Spanish supervision, really did the work. Roofs were usually in red tiles, though at times they, as well as the domes and tops of the twin towers that were frequently a feature of the colonial churches, were covered with brightly glazed tiles. These roofs, when combined with the rich natural coloring of many of the colonial building materials, gave variety and beauty. In the elaborately decorated interiors much gold and silver were used, not only in intricately carved reredoses, altars, pulpits, railings, screens, and pillars, but at times gold leaf was spread over great expanses of wall space. As the colonial age wore

---

[7] A list of the sees of seven archbishops and thirty-five bishops at the close of the eighteenth century will be found in J. L. Mecham, "The Church in Colonial Spanish America," in *Colonial Hispanic America,* A. C. Wilgus, ed. (Washington: 1936), p. 216. *Cf.* C. H. Haring, *The Spanish Empire in America* (New York: 1947), p. 184.

[8] Mecham, *op. cit.,* p. 225, gives the number and distribution of monastic establishments in 1800 as follows: Mexico, 250; Peru, 115; Chile, 45; Buenos Aires, 64; New Granada, 66; Caracas, 12.

on, architecture was to become more and more elaborate, passing from the plateresque into the baroque style of the seventeenth century, and later into the churrigueresque [9] of the eighteenth century. But even in the comparatively simple buildings of the sixteenth century no wealth was spared to make them witnesses of the Church's power and grandeur. All this exuberant display had its serious economic aspect. Within a few years of the Conquest it was found that a large part of the choicest municipal property had passed into the hands of the ecclesiastical corporations. As early as 1578, the cabildo of Mexico City complained that the Dominicans and Augustinians possessed the largest and best part of the property in the city, and urged the king to prohibit further acquisition of real estate by church organizations.[10] In 1748, it was reported of Lima by special royal investigators that, of a total of 2,806 buildings in the city, 1,135 belonged to religious communities.[11]

What the king did not clearly foresee and forestall with sufficient determination was that the excessive numbers of the clergy, both secular and religious, would eventually impose an almost unbearable incubus upon the economic life of the colonies. As more and more property, under the principles of mortmain, came into the inalienable and untaxable possession of the Church,[12] and as this fact became more glaringly apparent, a popular resentment would be generated that could undermine the acquiescence with which the absolute authority of the crown had been traditionally accepted. The growing wealth of the Church and the glaring inequality with which that wealth was distributed through the ranks of the hierarchy—salaries running from 130,000 pesos for the Archbishop of Mexico to 125 pesos as the wage of one of the humbler priests [13]—not only were the cause of bitter criticism but provided an inducement for many unworthy characters to seek the comparative ease, luxury, and power which clerical rank could bestow. In turn, these unworthy entrants lowered the whole moral tone of clerical life and gave ample justification for public censure on the score of venality, worldliness, concubinage and general unchastity. In justice it should perhaps be said that glaring faults are always remembered, while the many virtues that result in unselfish and heroic service are often unnoticed or taken for granted. It should also be remembered that neither faults nor virtues were confined to the clergy of the cities, nor indeed to the clergy as distinct from society at large.

---

[9] A style of architecture, named after its Spanish creator and especially popular in Mexico, marked by an elaboration of curves and counter curves, twisted columns, a variety of motifs and great exuberance.

[10] Mecham, *op. cit.*, p. 227.

[11] Jorge Juan and Antonio de Ulloa, *Noticias Secretas de América* (London: 1826), pp. 523-25.

[12] *Cf.* Haring, *op. cit.*, p. 191.

[13] Mecham, *op. cit.*, p. 228.

In general, the program of the Church for the natives, both in the towns and in the frontier missions, called for mass conversions, early incorporation into the Church through the formality of baptism—to be accepted voluntarily if at all possible—and then long training under the Church's guidance in religious practices and ceremonial, along with instruction in Spanish speech and in the rudiments of civilized living. From the first, the Church set its face against enslavement for the American natives and, in spite of a good deal of local opposition but with the backing of the crown, finally won the battle for Indian freedom.

In their gigantic task of conversion, the churchmen were somewhat assisted by a certain similarity to Christian forms in the rites, beliefs, legends, and practices held sacred among the Indians. They found, for example, that the underlying concepts of heaven, baptism, the cross, confession, and absolution were familiar, and that the stories of the Garden of Eden, the flood, and the Tower of Babel were known to large groups, as well as the legend of the visit to earth once upon a time of a reforming culture hero whose promised return was eagerly expected. But all the discouragements inseparable from pioneer work among primitive peoples were also experienced by the intrepid missionaries. The Pope, in 1527, rendered the official decision that the Indians were men, presumably possessed of souls; but the missionaries often felt hopeless of assisting an appreciable number of them to any real comprehension of Christian doctrines. Still more unattainable seemed the goal of imposing even a superficial appearance of Christian civilization on Spanish America as a whole. Great areas, especially in interior South America, were occupied by headhunters and cannibals who seemed little above the animal level. But despite all the disappointments, the terrible hardships, the loneliness of frontier life, and the crown's practice of refusing permission to return to Europe under ten years of absence, the adventure of missionary work in America appealed to a surprisingly large number of both secular and regular clergy. Some showed themselves capable of great fortitude and devotion, carried through at times to the point of martyrdom, on the farthest outposts of the empire; others, often men of high culture, worked hard in the older Spanish settlements to establish schools, workshops, and churches.

Of the religious orders, the Dominicans, Augustinians, Franciscans, and Jesuits were early on the scene, and in time became associated with the evangelization of special areas. The Dominicans were the first to arrive and, while Spanish colonization still centered at Santo Domingo, formed the vanguard of those forces opposing the enslavement of the natives. They were also active in the early missionary work along the northern coast of South America and in Central America. The pioneer Jesuits first labored in the Florida area, where Father Martínez was martyred in 1556; but later, the order became especially associated with the missionary efforts in the territories northwest of Mexico City. New Spain was made a Jesuit province in 1572, with Pedro Sanchez as provincial. He and a band of fifteen followers spent twenty years in setting up churches and educational institutions in the Mexican capital and other centers before beginning their missionary labors among the wild tribes of the Northwest. Starting with the pacification and conversion of the Chichimecos, just west of the capital, the Jesuits worked their way into the mining area of Zacatecas and then moved on into Nueva Vizcaya. In the course of the next two centuries the modern states of Durango, Chihuahua, Sinaloa, Sonora, Lower California, and southern Arizona became "Jesuit land," explored, christianized, and effectively ruled from numerous mission stations scattered throughout the whole area. In the wake of the missionaries followed the white miners and ranchers. Northeast of Mexico City the religious work fell primarily on the Franciscans whose missions served large areas in Florida, New Mexico, Texas, Nuevo León, and Coahuila. It was the Franciscans who, after the expulsions of the Jesuits in 1767, took over the work in the West and extended it to Alta California. In South America, in the region of the Guianas, the hinterlands of Cumaná, Caracas, and Bogotá, on the eastern slopes of the Andes, and along the great rivers that empty into the Orinoco or Amazon, all the great orders, at one time or another, established a footing. But Paraguay, like Lower California, became an exclusively Jesuit field.

The Indian frontier missions, that in the seventeenth century became an integral part of Spain's scheme of conquest and conversion, were of varying sizes. Ideally, at least two missionary fathers supervised each mission; living at a central pueblo, they pushed forward, as occasion offered, other missionary outposts, or *visitas,* which in time might form the nucleus of new missions. In some areas, however, one missionary might be found supervising three or more mission pueblos, as well as caring for a large visiting area. The inhabitants of the mission were natives of the area who had been persuaded to accept baptism and take up life voluntarily in a mission village where they would be taught the rudiments of agriculture, instructed in simple crafts, and drilled in Christian doctrine and practice. Once having given their agreement, the Indians usually found that there was no legal escape until the government should declare the mission at an end. As a nucleus of the new settlement, it was usual to bring a few families of Christian Indians from an older mission to serve as models and teachers.

In theory the mission belonged to the Indians and was ruled by native officials, but in reality every detail of life was controlled by the resident missionaries. These benevolent despots labored not only to train their charges in ways of civilized living but to make the mission economically self-supporting as quickly as possible. Each well-organized mission tried to make itself a complete frontier agricultural unit, and sought to acquire ample farm lands and buildings, cattle ranges, herds, pack trains, orchards, and gardens as well as blacksmith and carpenter shops and, possibly, spinning and printing establishments. The heart of the pueblo was always the church, built by the natives under the supervision of the missionaries; nearby was the residence of the priest. In hostile areas there was usually a strong wall around the whole mission, with military towers that made the unit virtually a fortress. These precautions served the double purpose of protection against attack from without and prevention of escape from within. While the natives were nearly always friendly at first, they often became resentful and restive as the boredom of daily labor and other restraints on their liberty pressed home, and as they realized the uprooting of their ancestral customs. If they tried to run away they were pursued, brought back, and punished. Partly to appeal to the pride of the natives, specialization and organization in the work of the mission was often carried to great lengths. Under an elaborate roster of native officials, the mission Indians worked as cowboys, muleteers, ox drivers, gardeners, bakers, carpenters, painters, and at other similar occupations. The daily routine for all included drill in the catechism, prayers, and church music. As much drama and pageantry as possible were employed, and a great deal was made of church festivals. In the visitas, the mission fathers were in charge of religious work, but the inhabitants were otherwise free.

The missionaries had the close cooperation of the crown, which provided salaries, building funds, and above all military support. As quickly as possible after the organization of a mission, a *presidio,* or military post, would be established in the district. Many missions had a small permanent guard of five or six soldiers. On the Spanish frontier the missionary and the soldier were close companions. The missions were not intended to be permanent but in time were expected to be transformed into doctrinas and given over to the care of the secular clergy. Nearly always a struggle ensued between religious and secular authorities as to when the proper time had come for secularization. As soon as a large region was sufficiently under control to warrant the measure, and the white settlements among the Indian pueblos had reached a safe number, the district was organized as a province with a governor appointed by the king, or ad interim, by the viceroy, as its official head. This officer usually resided at the principal presidio and exercised both civil and military authority. Under him were lieutenant governors commanding troops in less important presidios.

The most famous pioneer in the mission field of New Spain in the seventeenth century was the Jesuit father, Eusebio Francisco Kino. An explorer, astronomer, map maker, cattle king, all-round competent frontiersman, builder of many missions, and devoted priest, this "padre on horseback" was the most picturesque and effective of the many able men who spent their lives on Spain's farflung American frontier. Born in the Austrian Tyrol, educated in Germany, a traveler in Spain, Kino arrived in Mexico in 1681 and six years later, after a short time in Lower California, entered the field of his later work, Pimería Alta. Here in present-day Sonora and southwestern Arizona, in an area bounded on the east by the San Pedro River beyond which dwelt the fierce Apaches, on the west by the Gulf of California, on the south by the Altar River, and on the north by the Gila River, Kino spent twenty-four fruitful years. His first mission at Dolores became the mother of many other missions and visitas, over all of which Kino kept a fatherly eye and helped with his keen business acumen to become economically prosperous undertakings that would be capable of assisting in the work of further mission expansion. Rich gifts of thousands of cattle, swine, and sheep were dispatched to aid his friend and successor, Father Salvatierra, in his labors in the cactus desert of Lower California.

More than fifty journeys, all on horseback, taken in every direction from Dolores, made Kino one of the greatest explorers of the southwest. His greatest achievement in this field was the discovery that Lower California was not an island, as hitherto thought, but a peninsula. This came about in an interesting way: while on the Gila River, an Indian made the much-loved missionary a present of some blue shells, such as the father knew belonged to the Pacific shore of Lower California and felt sure could be found nowhere else; as the Indian had not crossed the Gulf, Kino realized that there must be an all-land road. A number of hazardous and exciting journeys proved the correctness of his assumption.[14] By the date of Kino's death (1711), the northwestward-moving missions had reached the general line of the Gila, well to the south of the Colorado River. Further to the northwest, Alta California, the present state of California, remained a little-known region. Though now and again it was explored for a few miles inland from the beaches by the curious from the Manila galleons homeward bound to Acapulco, its incorporation in the rest of New Spain awaited the opening of a permanent land road from Mexico which was only accomplished in the late eighteenth century.

To the northeast of Mexico City there was no such quick advance of the frontier as in the west. The effort in this area, in the seventeenth century, was largely aimed at holding what had earlier been won. In the wake of Juan de Oñate, who conquered present-day New Mexico in 1598 and remained in that country until 1610 exploring northeastward to the Arkansas and as far west as the Colorado River and the Gulf of California, went Franciscan missionaries who established numerous missions. Follow-

---

[14] H. E. Bolton, *Rim of Christendom* (New York: 1936), chaps. xxiv-xxv, pp. 424-91.

ing them, Spanish settlers slowly moved in. By 1680, at Santa Fe, El Paso, and other settlements in the area of New Mexico and western Texas, some three thousand whites had become established. In that year, one of the most serious native revolts ever encountered by Spain broke over the region. Bitterly resenting a demand for tribute, the Indians under the leadership of one Popé, a medicine man of Santa Fe, suddenly rose en masse, slew four hundred Spaniards, and drove the rest southward to the El Paso district. The northern area was reoccupied in the 1690's, and New Mexico was restored to Spanish control.[15]

In Texas, rumors of journeys by Marquette and Joliet in 1673, and the one by La Salle which brought him to the mouth of the Mississippi in 1682, and reports of French projects of permanent settlement in the river and gulf area caused the Spaniards to send a number of expeditions between 1686 and 1689 to search for the French and to establish some temporary missions in eastern Texas. All of these, however, were abandoned by the end of the century, after the Spaniards had learned that La Salle's expedition by sea had been a failure; and gradually the French scare passed. The permanent occupation of Texas did not come until the next century.

On the frontiers of savagery in South America there was only one region where the soldier, and not the missionary, was the foremost figure. This was in southern Chile where the unsubdued Araucanian Indians, "the Iroquois of the South," carried on relentless warfare against the white man. Elsewhere in the southern continent, as in the northern, the missionary was Spain's advance agent of religion and civilization. In the tropical hinterlands of New Granada, Venezuela, Ecuador, and Peru, a great army of "crusaders of the jungle"—as the missionaries of these regions have been picturesquely called—battled against almost overwhelming odds to bring the most primitive of the Spanish-American tribes to some conformity to white man's ways.

In the backwoods of the Río de la Plata, the seventeenth century saw a long-drawn-out contest between the Jesuits and the Brazilian and Argentinian frontiersmen for the control of the Guarani Indians. In 1608, Philip III, who was king of Portugal as well as sovereign of Spain, assigned to the order, already established in Paraguay, the task of converting and civilizing the Guarani Indians in the Portuguese area of Guaíra, lying to the east of Asunción on the Paraná River above the Iguassú Falls. Within five years, 119 missionaries were working in the region; and in two decades their converts were said to number forty thousand. By learning the native dialect and dramatizing the Christian doctrine, the Jesuits succeeded to a remarkable extent in making their faith appeal to the native mind. To

---

[15] Cf. Bolton, *The Spanish Borderlands* (New Haven: 1921), chap. vi, "New Mexico," pp. 178-81.

make the conversion and the newly-acquired civilization permanent, the Jesuits believed that instruction should cover a number of years and that during this period the natives should be isolated from all contact with other white men of the region who would be anything but examples of the Christian virtues.

The most violent opposition to this plan came from the Paulistas, frontiersmen of the Portuguese province of São Paulo, most of whom were Portuguese-Indian halfbreeds. These men had long made their living by raiding the interior areas for slaves whom they sold to the miners and planters of the coastal areas. The fury of the Paulistas against the Jesuits, whom they hated both as protectors of the Indians and as Spaniards, knew no bounds. Finally in 1629, a series of fierce raids against the unarmed Jesuit missions—raids that brought death or enslavement to thousands of Indians and destruction to the mission buildings—forced the missionaries to withdraw from the Guaíra territory and retreat down the river with twelve thousand of their charges. Eventually, in the territory between the Paraná and the Uruguay rivers, in an area which came to be called the *Missiones,* the Jesuits found sanctuary and started their work once more. Here, where they secured permission of the crown to arm their charges, they built a theocratic state of missions, or "reductions," with a center at Candelaría. In each village lived two Jesuit fathers whose orders were carried out by native officials. The surplus products of the missions were traded by the fathers in the Spanish settlements for needed manufactured goods. Economically, the undertaking was a success. The Indians became peaceful and apparently happy; but through a century and a half the opposition of Portuguese and Spanish planters and miners, as well as of the Paulistas, never relaxed. Eventually they had their way; the Jesuits were expelled from all South America in 1767 by orders from the courts of Spain and Portugal, and the Indians were left to the mercies of the whites.

The most serious criticism of the mission system has been that it left the Indian unable to face white competition successfully—although it may be doubted whether any system could have succeeded in achieving this end.[16] The missions, with their double role of extending Christianity for religious reasons and advancing the frontier of white settlements for reasons of national security, were a characteristic and symbolic feature of Spanish colonial policy.

Fortunately for the intellectual life of the Spanish colonies, the ecclesiastics were interested in learning as well as in the conversion of the Indians and the establishment of a strong colonial church. Though some of the conquistadores were college graduates, and many of the viceroys and high officials were men of culture and learning, it was the clergy who

---

[16] For a discussion of the effects of the mission system see Haring, *op. cit.,* 200-02.

constituted the bulk of the educated class and were the primary agents in the transference to America not only of the spiritual but of the intellectual culture of the homeland. As it was chiefly the churchmen who founded and largely staffed the schools and universities and wrote most of the books, education and learning in the Indies came naturally to have a strong ecclesiastical and medieval tincture. The colonial clergy were of necessity chosen from the ranks of the unquestionably orthodox. Once in America, they were almost completely out of touch with current intellectual interests in Europe; thus it was that the weight of their influence confirmed and supported the natural colonial trend towards conservatism and the preservation of antiquated modes of thought and expression. Both in method and content of teaching, they tended to lean backwards towards scholasticism, rather than forward towards the more liberal humanism.

In educational policy, Spanish America followed the lead of the motherland where, in the sixteenth century, there occurred a pronounced revival in academic matters, manifesting itself in the erection of a multiplicity of schools and a large number of universities. Among the latter, Alcalá and Salamanca were of worldwide fame—Salamanca at one time possessing sixty professional chairs and an enrollment of more than six thousand students. The urban character of the Spanish colonizing movement in America favored the early establishment of educational institutions; practically every large town came to possess one or more *colegios,* or academies, either as separate foundations or attached to monasteries. At times, viceroys or other royal officials, cabildos, or occasionally private persons, set up academies; but for the most part, this work was in the hands of the religious orders. Educational facilities were very unevenly sprinkled over Latin America; regions like Mexico and Peru were relatively rich, while more remote provinces like Chile and La Plata were comparatively badly off. The aim was not to provide education for the masses, or to use the school for the purpose of raising the general cultural level of the community—such an idea was hardly extant in the then contemporary world—but to provide educational training for candidates for the ministry, to give facilities to the specially gifted and to those of high political and social position. Educational opportunities usually were offered only to sons of upper-class whites, a few prominent mestizos, and the sons of Indian caciques. The colored castes, the lower classes generally, and girls remained illiterate. Colonial education was thus distinctly aristocratic in character, catering to the favored few, and the emphasis was on secondary rather than on primary instruction.[17]

[17] *Cf.* C. K. Jones, "The Transmission and Diffusion of Culture in the Spanish American Colonies," in Wilgus, *Colonial Hispanic America* (Washington: 1936), pp. 285-91. For details on colonial education consult J. T. Lanning, *Academic Culture in the Spanish Colonies* (New York: 1940).

The first school in America was for the sons of conquistadores and was established in the monastery of San Francisco in Santo Domingo. An early foundation in Mexico City was a school for Indian boys set up by the zealous, competent, and beloved Belgian missionary-teacher, Pedro de Gante, in which such practical trades as carpentry, blacksmithing, and shoemaking were taught concurrently with religion, music, fine arts, and "the three R's." Another famous Indian school, the Colegio de Santa Cruz, representing the combined efforts of Mexico's first viceroy and her first archbishop, gave instruction in some of the principal Indian tongues, reading, grammar, rhetoric, philosophy, and native medicine, as well as in religion and good manners. The school of San Juan de Letrán, designed especially for mestizo foundlings, was also established through the efforts of Viceroy Mendoza, who financed it rather appropriately by assigning for its support the proceeds of the sale of stray cattle. In Lima, another early viceroy set up a school for the sons of caciques. This institution, like many of the best and most enduring of the colonial schools, was long managed by the Jesuits who were famous for their pedagogical skill and their sedulous interest in Indian languages and customs.

The royal decree establishing the two earliest universities was issued in 1551, and provided for the setting up of the Royal and Pontifical University of St. Paul in Mexico City and the Greater University of St. Mark in Lima; both were designed primarily for the training of the clergy and modeled upon and possessing the same privileges as the famous European University of Salamanca. By the close of the colonial age, Spanish America had some six or eight universities. Most of them had libraries, and all taught at least theology and arts; in arts, the degrees of bachelor, licentiate, and master were conferred, and in theology, bachelor, licentiate, and doctor. In the larger institutions, faculties of medicine and law were also provided. Theology, however, was everywhere the paramount subject, with emphasis still on scholastic philosophy. Practically all professors in all faculties were members of the clergy, and the instruction was in Latin. In nearly all these institutions endowments were small, degree fees were high, and professors' salaries so low that university teaching was an avocation rather than a profession. Besides the regular universities and colleges, there later came into existence schools of special study such as, in Mexico City, the School of Mines, the Botanic Garden and, devoted to painting, sculpture, and architecture, the Academy of San Carlos.

Some fifteen years before the University of Mexico was founded, the first printing press in America was established in Mexico City in 1536 by the first viceroy, Antonio de Mendoza, who brought the equipment with him. The first printer was an Italian, Giovanni Paoli, and the first book was *La Escala Espiritual* by Juan Clímaco, followed shortly by a series of primers, catechisms, and other books of religious instruction, most important of which was a volume entitled *Doctrina Cristiana* written by Bishop Zumárraga. In all, this pioneer press issued some 116 books in the sixteenth century. Fifty years later than in Mexico, in 1583, the press was introduced into South America by a certain Antonio Ricardo, who was given to boasting that he was "the first printer in these Kingdoms of Peru." [18] Early in the seventeenth century some missionary Jesuits near Lake Titicaca were using a printing press to produce dictionaries and other works in the Aymara tongue, as well as to supply their need for religious manuals; later in the same century, the order was operating presses in some of its missions in Paraguay to assist in the study of the Guarani tongue. These mission printing shops were naturally primitive; type setting was by hand, the type was cast locally, and the printers were natives; but despite all handicaps they turned out some very creditable works, which are today treasured by book collectors and museums. Buenos Aires had to wait for its first printing press, known as the Foundling Press, until late in the eighteenth century. By the close of the colonial period, there were eight printing presses in operation here and there about Spanish America; though in some provinces facilities for printing were entirely lacking.[19]

On the whole, throughout the colonial period the production of books in Spanish America was slow, inadequate, expensive, and heavily shackled by restrictions from both Church and state. Paper was scarce and the bookseller's market was poor because of the narrow circle of educated people. But the heaviest handicap on both author and publisher was the double censorship imposed by Church and state in both Spain and the colonies in order to maintain the purity of the faith and an unquestioning allegiance to the crown. In this endeavor, a watchful and suspicious Inquisition acted as a thoroughly efficient agent; whole fields of writing were either prohibited entirely or severely restricted. For example, a law of 1543 forbade the printing, sale, or possession of romances of chivalry, currently so popular in Europe; another ordinance (1556) ordered that before being printed any book dealing with the Indies must be examined and approved by the Council of the Indies. Book shops operated under extreme difficulties; they were required to keep a catalogue of prohibited books (in which were listed some of the works of the greatest thinkers of the age); they had to furnish the Inquisition with a list of all volumes offered for sale, as evidence that they were importing no books without the license of that body; houses and shops alike might be searched at any time for

---

[18] Raimundo Lazo, "Early Printing in Spanish America," in *Pan American Bulletin,* November, 1937.
[19] *Ibid.*

Sor Juana Inés de la Cruz. In Museo Nacional, Mexico City. (Courtesy of the Museo Nacional de Historia)

"Los Rancheros," with a view of Zacatecas. A lithograph by Pierre F. Lehnert in *Album pintoresco de la Republica Mexicana*, published by Julio Michaud y Thomas, 1853. (Courtesy of the Hispanic Society of America)

unauthorized volumes. Actually, however, many forbidden volumes were smuggled into the colonies and eagerly passed from hand to hand; nevertheless, the prohibitions and inhibitions of the strict censorship inevitably exercised a stultifying and crippling effect on colonial intellectual activity.

As for journalism, newssheets had to wait for the eighteenth century, and even then were short-lived. As late as the close of the colonial age, only Lima had regular newspapers; these, however, carried little more than statements of fact and were far from being expressions of public opinion. More important were the scientific and literary journals, of which the most distinguished among the pioneers was the *Mercurio Peruana* of Lima; this was devoted to literary and historical matters and was inaugurated under the patronage of the viceroy.

The scarcity of published books is no indication of a paucity of scholarship. Many books were written that remained long in manuscript. Though few were remarkable for originality of thought, and many were old-fashioned in form when compared with contemporary European productions, they give evidence of a considerable intellectual activity which flourished largely in the viceregal capitals, Mexico City and Lima, though Bogotá and Quito made notable contributions. The earliest literary forms were the letters, diaries, chronicles, and reports by explorers, such as the *Journal* and *Letters* of Columbus and the *Letters* of *Cortés*. The conquistadores and their companions were often men of culture who not infrequently reached distinction in literary style in the reports of their activities and the descriptions of the new things that came under their notice. Treatises on plant and animal life by the early friars, and later by scientists who were attracted to America by the wealth of new forms in fauna and flora, constitute a notable contribution to the learned literature of the colonial age.

Another form of Spanish American writing that attained early distinction was historical narrative. The two foremost works in this field, belonging to the first century after the Conquest, were the *Historia Verdadera de la Conquista de la Nueva España* by Bernal Diáz del Castillo and *Los Comentarios Reales* by Garcilaso de la Vega. The former was the work of a genial old soldier, who in his younger years had been a follower of Cortés; his *Historia,* partly written in later years, is a fascinating account of the thrilling events in which he had taken part. Garcilaso de la Vega was of Inca ancestry through his mother, and the son of a Spanish conquistador. Brought up in Cusco where he learned Indian lore from his mother's people and Spanish culture from a friar, Garcilaso was in later life a captain in Spain in Philip II's army, and was thus uniquely equipped to interpret the culture of Inca Peru to the Spanish reading public of his day. The literary merits of the *Comentarios Reales,* published in 1609, as well as the peculiar interest attaching to the authorship and the contents as a contemporary chronicle of aboriginal culture, sufficiently accounts for the book's position as the first Spanish American volume to win a permanent place in Spanish literature.

Of more imaginative literature, epic poetry or rhymed historical chronicles long enjoyed a popular vogue. Given a local setting and relating some phase of the thrilling history of the Age of Discovery, or telling of the heroic deeds of missionaries and saints of the church, these poems—frankly imitative in style of the *Orlando Furioso* of Ariosto—were numerous and widely read. Among the better known were *La Araucana* by Alonso de Ercilla y Zúñiga (published 1569-1590), based on the author's personal adventures as a soldier in the Araucanian wars in Chile; *Peregrino Indiano* by Antonio de Saavedra Guzmán (1599), relating the deeds of Cortés; and *La Cristiada* by Friar Diego de Ojeda (1611), one of the many religious epics.

Lyrical poetry was also very popular, though much of that submitted in the frequent public poetry contests held in Mexico and Lima was artificial and of poor quality. There were, however, a few colonial writers of genuine merit. The earliest to produce work that won high praise abroad was the Mexican creole, Juan Ruiz de Alarcón y Mendoza, born in the late sixteenth century. His comedies, of which there are twenty-five or more, were enthusiastically received in Spain when they appeared on the stage there in the early seventeenth century and were compared favorably with the work of Lope de Vega and of Calderón. This lyrical tradition was to be carried to a high degree of perfection in the second half of the seventeenth century by the greatest of the Mexican poets, Juana Inés de la Cruz (1651-1695), who, before she insisted on retiring to a convent at the age of sixteen, was hailed by the admiring viceregal society of her day as "the tenth muse." When she died in an epidemic at the age of forty-four, her Latin works filled three volumes and in poetry she had experimented with love sonnets, epigrams, comedies, occasional and religious verse. Her style was strongly influenced by the prevailing Gongorism [20] of Spain but her work was inspired with real feeling. An older friend of the Mexican poetess was Carlos de Sigüenza y Góngora who also represented the flowering of an early tradition, though in his case it was the scientific interest in archeological and astronomical studies in their New World setting. The most noted Spanish American scholar of his day, a man of cyclopedic knowledge, Sigüenza was professor of mathematics at the University of Mexico City, and for many years bore the title of "royal cosmographer." On one occasion his special interest in the study of comets and his scientific view,

---

[20] Gongorism was a literary style named from the Spanish poet Luis de Gongora y Argote, 1561-1627, and marked by a complexity of verbal devices.

expressed in a tract, that these heavenly bodies were not a manifestation of divine wrath, brought him into a famous public controversy—the first waged in America—with the great missionary-scholar, Father Eusebio Kino, whose data the Mexican challenged in a work entitled *Philosophical and Astronomical Book*. Another contemporary scholar of great learning in both scientific and literary fields was the Peruvian Pedro Peralta de Barnuevo, born in Lima in 1663.

Thus, although Spanish America, like all other colonial societies, was the home of "men of action" rather than of "men of thought," there is evidence that the transplanted culture of the homeland took root in the new environment and flourished there with considerable vigor and variety of form. In the realm of poetry there was a noticeable retention of somewhat antiquated forms brought from the homeland, but these were often interestingly combined with a content drawn from the American surroundings. In prose writing, especially in the field of history, there was a greater degree of originality in form. Types of composition—letters, diaries, and the like, hitherto regarded as mere documentary material, entered the domain of literature.

Considered as a whole, the history of Spain in America in the seventeenth century does not show so definite a decline from the sixteenth-century standard as does the parallel story in Europe. Nevertheless, in their overseas possessions the reigns of Philip III, Philip IV, and Charles II witnessed an unmistakable exhaustion of the national vitality that had accomplished such amazing results in the first century of colonial times. Spain's great effort to lead the Catholic forces in Europe to victory in the religious conflicts of the sixteenth century was felt, not only in Spain itself, but in the American lands from which the wealth for the undertaking had come. Within the colonial structure, the whole tempo of life became slower as resources in men and money were drained away. In the older settlements consolidation replaced pioneering change, and paternalism pressed home its blighting weight on all political, intellectual, and economic life; on the frontiers the missionary replaced the *adelantado,* advance became slower as the stiffer resistance of wilder tribes was encountered, and the Spanish banner was carried forward only at the expense of heavy fighting. Furthermore, the spirit behind expansion changed; it was no longer inspired primarily by the urge for discovery or the desire for new riches; aside from the religious motive, it was pressed forward as a defensive advance in the interests of security designed to anticipate the explorations and claims of other European nations, and to protect gains already won.

It was on the fringes of her vast colonial realm that the changes became most noticeable, and that Spain became most painfully conscious that she no longer possessed a monopoly of the Western Hemisphere. In the Caribbean and along all her continental coast, increasingly serious encroachments from European rivals made evident the fact that the defeat of the Spanish Armada had left the seaways to America open to rising maritime powers of the North. As the century progressed, territorial losses occurred as Guiana, Jamaica, western Española, and the Lesser Antilles slipped from her grasp into the hands of the Dutch, French, and English. The area of the fiercest conflict was the West Indies, through which Spain's Atlantic trade had to move. From newly acquired island footholds, especially Jamaica, the buccaneers in this heyday of their marauding successes preyed upon the Spanish fleets and raided Spanish colonial harbors, forcing the Spaniards to withdraw their cities, ranches, and plantations as far inland as practicable, with the hope of escaping the almost constant coastal devastations. Furthermore, encouraged by their fabulous gains in the West Indies, the buccaneers extended their operations to the south and west until they succeeded in almost encircling Spain's New World empire, penetrating far up the Pacific coast. Along the western shore line there had been a growth of prosperity, springing in part from an extensive development of the pearl fisheries in the Gulf of California, and in part from an increase in Asiatic trade resulting from the government's permission for a measure of intercolonial exchange between Acapulco and Lima. This new wealth acted as a magnet, drawing into the comparatively undefended and hitherto largely unmolested area a number of devastating piratical expeditions, most of which had for their ultimate goal the capture of the Manila galleon.

The desire to protect New Spain from Pacific pirates, the hope of finding a good northern harbor for use as a naval station and as a place of refuge for the homing Manila galleons, and the fear that the French or English might arrive overland through the chance discovery of the fabled "Strait of Anian" and so take Mexico from the rear, all served to stimulate Spanish exploration by land and sea towards California. Among the most notable of the resulting expeditions was that of Sebastian Vizcaíno, who headed a painstaking survey (1602-1603) of the west coast from the northern point of the peninsula of Lower California northward to Cape Mendocino. He and his party missed the magnificent harbor of San Francisco, and merely reported favorably on the advantages of the port of Monterey. In the Atlantic, Spain's costly activities in Florida had the same defensive aims as her efforts in the Pacific. In the seventeenth century Spain was no longer undisputed mistress in the American world and was chiefly concerned to forestall further depredations by constructing bulwarks around those areas which the conquistadores had seized in the sixteenth century.

II. THE EIGHTEENTH CENTURY: REFORM AND STRUGGLE
AGAINST THE FOREIGNER

Many of the features that marked the last century of colonial times in Spanish America sprang from Spain's involvement in the second Hundred Years' War between England and France, a conflict which constituted the central drama of the age. On the whole, except for the informal warfare constantly carried on against pirates and buccaneers and strife with the natives on the frontiers, the seventeenth century had been a period of peace for Spain's vast colonial dominions. The wars of Philip III and Philip IV against the Dutch, Portuguese, and French, though resulting in serious territorial losses in Europe, had only minor repercussions and losses in the Indies. For the most part, except in the Cromwellian period, England and Spain—much taken up with other matters—lived at peace with each other while British merchants took advantage of the opportunity to win for themselves the first place in the commerce of the Spanish peninsula.[21] A new order of things, however, came at the turn of the century with a change in the dynasty on the Spanish throne. The death of Charles II in 1700 brought to an end the Hapsburg line that had ruled in Spain since the death of Ferdinand the Catholic in 1516. When the half-witted Charles II, under pressure from his French wife's relatives, left his throne by will to Philip of Anjou (a member of the house of Bourbon, the grandson of Louis XIV, and the probable heir to the French crown), the fundamental balance of power was disturbed and Europe was plunged into a general war. In this conflict—the War of the Spanish Succession (1702-1713)—England headed an alliance that supported the rival claims of the Archduke of Austria, a scion of the Hapsburg house. Henceforth, throughout the eighteenth century, in a frequently renewed struggle every phase of which had its reflection in America, England was the foremost enemy of Spain. Not until Spain broke with France in Napoleon's time were the two nations again at peace for any length of time. This century-long Anglo-Spanish war was so dwarfed, however, by the heroic proportions of the contemporary struggle between England and France, which began earlier and lasted longer, that the importance of the lesser conflict has received comparatively little attention.

Reasons for the long-drawn-out hostility were not all on one side. England was principally moved by the view that a Frenchman on the Spanish throne threatened an overwhelming coalescence of power in both

---

21 For details see my article [Vera Lee Brown], *Studies in the History of Spain in the Second Half of the Eighteenth Century,* chap. ii, "Anglo-French Rivalry for the Trade of the Spanish Peninsula, 1763-1783," in *Smith College Studies in History* (Northampton, Mass., October 1929-January 1930), Vol. XV, Nos. 1-2.

Europe and America; Spain was perpetually haunted by the fear of having to face, unsupported by a powerful ally, the startling increase of English colonial power. Spanish fears mounted considerably after the War of the Spanish Succession cost her the Spanish Netherlands, her Italian possessions, Gibraltar and Minorca, as well as the forced concession to England of the Asiento agreement. Also the British in America had for some time been steadily encroaching on Spanish boundaries and interests: off Newfoundland, English fishermen had long disputed Spanish fishing claims; in Honduras Bay, English logwood cutters had been camping for years in Spanish territory; in Florida, Spanish settlements and missions had long been seriously threatened by English aggression from the Carolinas; St. Augustine itself had suffered a siege in 1702. Furthermore, English contraband trade, so far from having been eliminated by Spain's grant of the Asiento, was soon seen to have been stimulated by that measure. All these considerations, coupled with the desire to retrieve the prestige so grievously damaged at Utrecht, induced the court at Madrid to adopt the policy of the Family Compact [22] under which, first in 1733 and later in 1761-1762, Spain signed treaties that were to carry her as an ally of France into every major conflict of the period.

Until the time of Charles III (1759-1788), colonial issues on the whole continued to be of secondary importance. Philip V, in the first half of the century, spent his not inconsiderable energy in intrigues that had for their chief result the establishment of two Spanish princes in Italian principalities, and so he regained some of the ground lost in that direction. In the multiplicity of European interests, Philip tended to underestimate the significance of colonial issues. England, on the other hand, bore them steadily in mind and repeatedly, in the first half of the eighteenth century, went to war to enforce her rights under the Asiento contract which it was Philip's policy to minimize and obstruct to the greatest possible extent. By the terms of the Asiento, England had the right to supply the Spanish colonial dominions with Negro slaves and to send each year one ship of 500 tons with merchandise to Porto Bello and Vera Cruz. In the hands of the South Sea Company, the concession was regarded as doubly valuable because, in addition to the legal gains it assured, it also afforded opportunities for a heavy increase in contraband trading which speedily came to permeate every phase of the company's activities.[23] In the "permission

---

[22] The Family Compact was a policy under which the Bourbon sovereigns of France, Spain, the Two Sicilies, Parma, and Piacenza entered an agreement to follow a common foreign policy aimed at guarding each others' possessions.

[23] This trade is treated in my articles, "The South Sea Company and Contraband Trade," in *American Historical Review*, Vol. XXXI, No. 4, July, 1926, and "Contraband Trade: A Factor in the Decline of Spain's Empire in America," in *The Hispanic American Historical Review*, Vol. VIII, No. 2, May 1928.

ships" and in the Negro packet boats, every conceivable device of false measurement, excessive crowding, and supplementary vessels was employed to increase the cargo space, while all the sailors and other employees carried on private trade as far as their resources would permit. The result was that a great stream of illicit traffic was carried on surreptitiously under cover of the South Sea Company's legitimate trade. This was in addition to another strong current of illegal commerce that flowed from the activities of private traders operating from Jamaica, Barbados, and other English West Indian islands.

The irritations and complaints associated with the Asiento and its illegitimate offspring were finally responsible for the so-called "War of Jenkins' Ear" that, breaking out in 1739, became merged in the following year with the general conflict, named in Europe the "War of the Austrian Succession" and in America "King George's War." Spanish Florida was drawn into this war by raids under General Oglethorpe from the recently planted English settlement in Georgia; in 1740-1743, St. Augustine was twice attacked. Central America also was deeply involved; for the English extended their trading and raiding activities along the entire coast line from the Bay of Campeche to Costa Rica. In the southern section of this area, the Mosquito Indians, whose claim of independence had long made them a thorn in the side of Spain, were now openly taken under the aegis of the English governor of Jamaica, an English superintendent was appointed and a body of soldiers sent to their shore; in the Bay of Honduras the Bay Islands off the Spanish port of Trujillo were seized; farther north, an area around Belize—long a center of a contraband trade in logwood—became another focus for hostilities. Other parts of the Caribbean saw a number of attacks by British ships on Spanish harbors. The most notable of these raids was led by Admiral Vernon in 1741 against Cartagena. Here, after an initial success in capturing the famous harbor and dispatching the news of his triumph to England, Vernon was finally driven off, his forces decimated by disease—that deadly eighteenth-century ally of local inhabitants. Another famous episode of this war was Admiral Anson's incursion into the Pacific Ocean where he captured the Manila galleon— a profitable enterprise leading to many later acts of aggression in the "Spanish Lake." The War of the Austrian Succession and its American counterpart were still in progress when in 1746 Ferdinand VI succeeded Philip V as king of Spain; two years later the international conflict reached a temporary lull with the signing of the Treaty of Aix-la-Chapelle. Henceforth, as long as Ferdinand lived, official peace endured and his country enjoyed a breathing time that enabled the second Spanish Bourbon sovereign to leave to his successor that rarest of all Spanish legacies, a surplus in the treasury.

Under Charles III, who succeeded his half-brother Ferdinand in 1759, emphasis was shifted from European interests to imperial concerns. Charles had been brought up in Italy and, as King of Naples, had been associated with Spain chiefly in her aspect as a world power. He had both the outlook and the means to adopt a wider policy than his two predecessors. Intelligent and enlightened, he was an excellent example of the benevolent despots of his age and like them was devoted to his *metier de roi*. He not only gave old Spain an administration that considerably revived her failing prestige but, as ruler of her American possessions, he came near to making a success of colonial government in an age when other colonial systems were shaking with radical changes.

As Charles assumed the Spanish crown, the great obstacle in Spain's path was the rising strength of England as an imperial power, just then reaching an apogee of might in the Seven Years' War. Hearing "with emotion" of the fall of Quebec and realizing its implications, Charles tried to steady the international balance by casting in his lot with France, signing, in 1761 and 1762, two treaties that revived "the Family Compact" or "Bourbon System." When England declined his mediation in the Seven Years' War, he joined the conflict on the side of France, a step which not only failed to avert the complete defeat of his ally but which also brought heavy loss of prestige and territory to Spain herself. Habana and Manila, Spain's overseas naval headquarters in the Atlantic and Pacific oceans, were captured by the English. To regain them, in the Treaty of Paris (1763), Charles was obliged to cede Florida to England, thus giving his rival a footing on his jealously guarded Gulf of Mexico. Other forced concessions were the relinquishment of fishing rights in Newfoundland and the grant to English logwood cutters of the privilege of operating in Honduras Bay. The compensatory cession of Louisiana by France to Spain, though it laid to rest a border problem that had long disturbed the relations between the two Latin nations, proved to be an embarrassing gift. Its acquisition posed for Madrid a number of serious problems: it involved the serious administrative task of providing an acceptable government for a protesting foreign population; it tied her more tightly than ever to the French alliance; it meant for the future a Spanish frontier abutting on English territory which contained a restless westward-yearning population.

The most threatening consequence for Spain of the disastrous Seven Years' War, however, was the elimination of France as an American power, for it left the Iberian nation alone—with her military weakness known and her coffers empty—to face the English menace. It was obvious that she lay athwart England's future pathway in many directions; her closely pressed monopolistic theory of colonial commerce closed two thirds of the New World to an ambitious nation of traders whose ships now dominated the seas; on the Mississippi, she stood fairly across the course of English advance overland from the Thirteen Colonies to the Pacific; in the South Atlantic, her wide claims under old papal bulls closed the sea routes to the Pacific, the new area of geographical exploration. The future of Anglo-Spanish relations wore in 1763 a decidedly unpromising aspect.

It speaks well for the courage of Charles III that he appeared neither dismayed or confused, but immediately set in motion a program of fundamental reforms for his American possessions that aimed at strengthening the defences of the colonies, increasing the royal revenue, and in general improving Spain's chances of survival as an imperial power. That his calculations were not seriously in error the final record of his reign was to prove, for when, after sixteen years of uncertain peace, he again went to war with England, the outcome was decidedly favorable to Spain.[24]

To carry his colonial reform program into effect, Charles dispatched to America a group of his ablest administrators to carry out thorough surveys of the needs of the colonies, and, on the basis of such information, to make the needed changes. The most noted of these envoys was José de Gálvez. He arrived as visitador general in Mexico in 1765 and remained for six years, instilling reform and vigor into every branch of the government. Through the first half of his term Gálvez devoted himself primarily to reforming the financial administration of the central provinces, improving the collection of taxes, considerably reducing official peculation and rapacity, and establishing the valuable tobacco monopoly for the benefit of the crown. In the later years, by a rearrangement of frontier presidios, he succeeded in forcing a measure of peace on the hostile border Indians—the Apaches and Comanches—under whose attack the whole northern frontier had been shrinking since the beginning of the eighteenth century. He also took vigorous steps to push the line of Spanish advance farther northward along the west coast, where the eventual occupation of Alta California was to a considerable extent due to his energy.

The interest shown by Gálvez in the work of discovering and appropriating new lands formed one phase of a general movement in which all the maritime nations of Europe took part and which centered around the Pacific Ocean. After the close of the Seven Years' War, France and England dispatched expeditions to the Pacific, and at the same time Russian fur traders worked their way southward from Bering Strait. This active foreign interest in California, rumors of which were always reaching Gálvez, was the primary consideration that urged the visitador into a policy of expansion. In the event that the Spanish monopoly of the Pacific could

[24] I am here following closely an early piece of research, "Anglo-Spanish Relations in America in the Closing Years of the Colonial Era," in *The Hispanic American Historical Review*, Vol. V, No. 3, August 1922.

not be maintained, he wished at least to stake out Spanish claims to as much of the Pacific coastal region as possible. His most ambitious undertaking was a joint sea and land expedition entrusted to the supervision of Governor Gaspar de Portolá who had with him for missionary work the Franciscan friar, Junípero Serra. It got under way in 1769 and resulted in the establishment of colonies and missions at San Diego and Monterey, as well as the discovery of San Francisco Bay. After Gálvez' departure from Mexico in 1771, the policy of westward expansion was carried forward by the exceptionally capable viceroy, Don Antonio María Bucareli (1771-1779). During his viceroyalty, Captain Juan Bautista Anza, through two remarkable expeditions, succeeded in opening an overland route from Sonora to San Francisco; but perils of the desert and hazards from Indian attacks long enforced the continued use of the sea route as the principal means of communication between Mexico and California. Along the coast, Spain moved steadily northward from one strategic point to the next. Her most northerly point was reached in 1789 when, in a violent dispute with England over Nootka Sound on the west coast of Vancouver Island, she was forced to withdraw her pretensions. From that time on her line began to recede southward.

When Gálvez reached Spain in 1771, the king made him Minister of the Indies so that his reforming ideas, acquired by experience in Mexico, could be generally applied to all Spanish possessions in America. The three greatest administrative reforms which he sponsored were: (1) the introduction of a system of intendants; (2) the final abandonment of the old Cádiz fleet system; (3) a further subdivision of the viceroyalties. All three changes had as their goal the strengthening of the defenses of the empire and increasing royal revenues. The new administrative divisions were intended to provide more effective local oversight of danger spots in the colonial defense system. The old policy of trade monopoly maintained so long in the interests of the homeland and enforced by fleets, fairs, and a restricted port system, was now with Gálvez' support replaced by a more liberal system. Although with some restrictions, trade was henceforth open to all Spaniards, whether living at home or in the colonies. The old fleet system, with its heavy import and export taxes, was definitely discontinued; individual ships were allowed to sail from any Spanish harbor for America without naval escort. This new "free trade" plan was put into effect first in the less important colonies and then gradually extended to the more important. The effect of the Reglamento of 1778—the decree stating the new policy—was to break the monopoly of the Cádiz merchants and bring smaller traders into the commercial field. This change in the character of the trade between colony and motherland was accompanied by a lifting of restrictions on intercolonial commerce. The net result of these liberalizing reforms in the trade laws was a great increase of general prosperity.

Since the early eighteenth century, the need for better defense arrangements in South America had been clearly recognized. It had been with the desire to guard the Caribbean more effectively that the viceroyalty of New Granada had been created, first as an experiment in 1717, and later when it was permanently established in 1739. [See Chapter 6.] To add further strength, Venezuela was made a captaincy-general.

Applying the same reasoning to the situation farther south, Gálvez created in 1776 the viceroyalty of La Plata. [See Chapter 6.] He took this step partly with the view to centralizing efforts against the Portuguese of Brazil, who for a hundred years had carried on extensive smuggling operations from Colonia del Sacramento on the northern banks of the La Plata. Gálvez' policy of reorganization was justified within a year, when the court at Lisbon proved willing to sign a treaty (1777) by which Spain acquired possession of Colonia and secured a generally favorable settlement of the whole Brazilian boundary question. The new viceroyalty of La Plata was also designed to stimulate the colonization of southern Argentina and to help in guarding the seaways to the Pacific. The danger in this latter direction had been made especially evident by the establishment in 1764 and 1765 of French and English colonies on the Falkland Islands, which had precipitated a crisis in Anglo-Spanish relations that brought the two nations to the verge of war in 1770 and 1771. To strengthen the Pacific outposts still further, Chile was made a captaincy-general in 1778 and her governor was given special instructions to take an active interest in Pacific exploration.

In 1776, the same year as the establishment of the viceroyalty of La Plata, a similar measure was taken in North America. Here the northern and western provinces of Mexico were erected into an independent commandancy-general under the military and political control of a Commandant-General of the Interior Provinces, who was made independent of the Mexican viceroy, although he might call upon him for assistance in emergencies. [See Chapter 6.] By this change it was hoped to secure the benefits of a new viceroyalty, but without the name and at less cost. Again, the primary motive was defense—to guard against aggressions from the English, French, and Russians, and to keep the border tribes in better order.

The chain of strengthened defenses provided by the newly consolidated provinces, an increased number of presidios and missions, and an enlarged colonial army, was fairly complete when the opportunity came to take advantage of England's trouble with her colonies and regain lost possessions and prestige. From 1776 onwards, Spain took an active part in the American Revolutionary War by furnishing arms, munitions, and money to the colonists. Finally, in June 1779, though not without misgivings as to the ultimate effect on his own dominions of thus encouraging revolution, Charles III followed France into open war with England.

As a belligerent Spain concentrated her efforts in the Gulf area. For twenty years, the English and Spaniards had jealously faced each other across the Mississippi on whose waters they possessed, under the Treaty of Paris, equal rights of navigation. Upon early information of the declaration of war, young Bernardo de Gálvez, nephew of the Minister of the Indies and at the time governor of Louisiana, struck with lightning speed and succeeded in capturing the English posts on the east bank of the lower Mississippi. Two years later he also took Mobile and Pensacola. By the terms of the peace the English were expelled from the Gulf territory, a time limit was placed on log-cutting in Honduras, and the Floridas were returned to Spain.

These changes meant that henceforth the Spaniards would have the Americans rather than the English across their frontiers in North America. The new American-Spanish line of demarcation stretched from the mouth of the St. Marys River on the Atlantic westward to the Mississippi, and followed the course of the river to its headwaters. To prevent the Americans from crossing this border, Spain imported Canary Islanders and British "loyalists" as colonists, and even tried counter colonies of Americans themselves. These experiments, however, failed to achieve their purpose. The difficulty was temporarily removed when Napoleon, in 1800, induced Spain to re-cede Louisiana to France for military purposes; but after holding it only three years, he sold the territory to the United States. With her old Texas and New Mexican frontiers restored, and keeping a precarious hold on Florida far to the east, Spain found her problems springing from a common frontier with the Americans to be worse than ever. But long before the disastrous sale had occurred, Charles III and his able minister, José de Gálvez, were both dead; weak Charles IV (1788-1808) and Godoy ruled in their stead. The new rulers faced in Europe a storm of war and in Spanish America a rising tide of disillusion and resentment, as new opportunities of enlightenment enabled the Spanish colonists to compare their lot with that of their already emancipated and prosperous fellow Americans in the new United States.

Chapter 12

LIFE IN NEW FRANCE

The French, other than fishermen and missionaries, at first came to Canada almost exclusively for two purposes: exploration and the fur trade. These interests determined the location of New France in the far north and for a long time provided its most striking characteristics. In the sixteenth century, Frenchmen had learned to their cost that the Iberians were in solid possession of the southern two thirds of America, and that only in northern latitudes were they likely to be left in peace to roam and explore at will. Moreover, it was only in the north that the fur-bearing animals flourished in perfection; and only in the fur trade could the work of the North American savage be profitably turned into gold.

The first permanent white settlements were established by the French explorers and fur merchants to give their operations in Canada essential local bases; these also provided the government with visible evidence of French possession which it needed to forestall any possible interference by foreign rivals in this valuable trade. Neither party was at first very enthusiastic. The merchants, especially, became progressively more skeptical as the difficulty of securing immigrants became increasingly evident; short of hiring colonists, they could find no way of fulfilling their charter obligation of carrying to New France each year a specified number of settlers. The government, however, first under Richelieu, an ardent mercantilist, and later under Colbert, who held similar economic views, were determined to make colonization in Canada a feature of state policy. But it was long before any of the white settlements really flourished. The four of greatest consequence were Port Royal in Acadia, and, on the St. Lawrence River, Quebec, Three Rivers, and Montreal. The first three were founded by Champlain in 1605, 1608, and 1634 respectively. Montreal was established in 1642 as a frontier post and religious center by the Sieur de Maisonneuve, acting as an agent of a small religious society. All four long continued to be little struggling communities, consisting of a few government officials, trading agents, soldiers, and clergy.

Agricultural settlement was definitely discouraged by the two dominant interests of exploration and fur trading. Both called for the services of vigorous single men, rather than the immigration of settling families whose prosperity would depend on developing, and not merely exploiting, the

349

resources of the country. Furthermore, the success of the explorer and fur trader was contingent on friendly intercourse with the Indians, and the latter could hardly be expected to accept the taking over and clearing of their ancestral hunting grounds to provide the white man with arable land for agricultural settlement.

Primarily, however, the lack of growth of the towns and rural communities in French Canada resulted from a lack of willing immigrants. This sprang from deep roots. The vast majority of French people in the seventeenth century, as now, were home-loving farmers who preferred a fertile homeland to immigration to a distant colony, especially one in the cold wilderness of northern America. The typical French peasant and small bourgeois, however meager his means or unpromising his future, ignorant and shut off as he was from much knowledge of the outside world, preferred above all else the sociable life of the villages of old France where the houses were clustered together "within sound of the church bell." Actual starvation from natural increase in population did not threaten them, for the frequent wars of ambitious monarchs and ministers could be relied upon to carry off any serious surplus of population. Nor did long-drawn-out revolution over parliamentary and religious rights (such as shook contemporary Stuart England, uprooted thousands of Britons, and sent them streaming across the Atlantic) disturb seventeenth-century France; on the contrary, French absolutism and social stability deepened as the century wore on. The one discontented element—the Huguenots—had its privileges, so hard-won under the Edict of Nantes (1598), progressively reduced. Their oppression, however, which might have produced a true colonizing group, was fruitless because, just as the first quarter of the seventeenth century closed, Cardinal Richelieu came to power and forbade heretics to migrate to New France. His decision, like that of the Spanish kings, was based on the idea that colonial life must be built on religious unity. Henceforth, therefore, there were practically no French available to form the nucleus of permanent colonies in North America. Not until imperious Louis XIV for a few years threw his full authority behind a drive for agricultural colonists for Canada could a few thousand be collected; after Talon's time, even this trickle dried up and New France became solely dependent on its own natural population increase.

Meanwhile exploration and the fur trade continued, year after year, to attract a number of adventurous individuals, especially the Bretons and the Normans, the least French of all French. These groups inherited from their Celtic and Norse forbears strong roving instincts which were reinforced by their geographical position on the northwest coast with its strong sea-going traditions and its remoteness from the rest of Europe and the

wars that absorbed the ambitions of the rulers in Paris. Even the majority
of the peasants who later were dispatched to Canada under pressure from
Louis XIV were predominantly Norman. So overwhelming was this element that by 1680 it was estimated that four fifths of the French in Canada
had Norman blood in their veins, despite the fact that the "King's girls,"
who were sent for the Quebec marriage market, came from all over France.

Once transplanted, the hardy, adaptable Normans were willing to endure untold hardships in a life of adventure and excitement. They made
magnificent explorers, traders, and frontiersmen. The least amenable to
colonial discipline were the voyageurs and *coureurs de bois*. These were
primarily independent Indian traders who, often without benefit of license,
traversed the woods far beyond the lines of settlement and forts, making
friends with the Indians whose language they learned, whose pelts they
bargained for, and to whose social level they were often content to sink,
clinging only to their cherished freedom. They were responsible for the
growing half-breed population and, though making no direct contribution
in the way of organized exploration, they gave useful service as guides and
interpreters as the frontier advanced westward.

The authorities did their best to limit the number who sought this
exciting life, even going to the length of drawing up a code of fearsome
penalties for those whom they could catch; whipping, branding, and labor
in the galleys were among the punishments inflicted for major crimes, with
heavy fines imposed for the avoidance of marriage responsibilities as well
as for unlicensed trading. Not many, however, were caught. They avoided
the white posts and settlements, except for occasional visits for hilarious
carousals and to secure the liquor and European goods needed for barter
on the next journey into the forest. Although the voyageurs, as distinct
from the coureurs de bois, were licensed small-scale Indian traders, the
terms were often used interchangeably, that of voyageur being more common along the Mississippi frontier, and coureur de bois on the St. Lawrence.[1]

The explorers, like the Indian traders, were likely to be lone figures, only
spasmodically securing state support. After Champlain's death (1635) and
Richelieu's absorption in the French phase of the Thirty Years' War, there
was little over-all organization of either exploration or planned settlement
of new areas throughout the three decades preceding Talon's arrival. In
this period occurred the decimation by the Iroquois of the Huron settlements and missions, and the flight of the remnants of these nations to the
west, a movement which carried the whole course of exploration westward
to center henceforth about Lakes Michigan and Superior. From there ex-

---

[1] R. M. Saunders, "Coureur de Bois: A Definition," *Canadian Historical Review*, Vol. XXI,
No. 2, June, 1940.

ploration radiated southward across Wisconsin and Minnesota to the head-waters of the Mississippi; northward along the rivers, especially the Albany, that empty into Hudson Bay, and westward in the first tentative steps towards Lake Winnipeg.

Among the outstanding men of this time whose activities were characteristic of the period were the two enterprising, fortune-hunting fur traders of Three Rivers: Pierre Esprit Radisson, daring, adaptable, plausible; and his brother-in-law, Médard Chouart, Sieur des Groseilliers, shrewd, practical, and experienced in Indian traffic. In 1658 these two set out from Three Rivers on their second trip into the wilderness. A skirmish with the Iroquois dispersed the originally large party and Radisson and Groseilliers went on alone. Going via the Ottawa River, Georgian Bay, and along the northern shore of Lake Huron, they finally reached Sault Ste. Marie and Green Bay. After visiting for a time the remnants of the Hurons in this vicinity, they continued southward, examining river after river. They may have reached the Missouri, or possibly may even have been the first white men, after de Soto, on the Mississippi. Learning a great deal of the Crees and the Sioux, but finding that the best beaver was not on the Mississippi but to the north, they retraced their steps, making great efforts along the way to unite the Indians of the northwest against the Iroquois. They traded as they traveled and eventually took a fleet of sixty canoes with a freight of 200,000 livres' worth of furs to Montreal in the summer of 1660. They were welcomed hilariously as having saved the season's business and opened a prospect for revived traffic through the Ottawa-Nipissing canoe route to the great western fur grounds of the upper lakes country. Another trip in 1661 and 1662 carried them back to the Sioux country in Minnesota, and in its later stages, probably to Hudson Bay from Lake Superior via the Albany and Moose Rivers. On their return to Montreal with a fleet of 360 canoes filled with beaver skins, they were infuriated to be fined one third of their profits for having slipped away without licenses. It was this treatment that drove Radisson into the arms of the English when he helped them to establish a foothold on Hudson Bay.

Along with the explorers and fur traders went the missionaries, who were not only as intrepid in facing the loneliness and hardships of the wilderness and the dangers from the savages, but also planned their activities even more intelligently and showed greater purpose and continuity in carrying them through. In their zeal for the conversion of the Indians they present a parallel in America to the self-sacrifice and enthusiasm of the agents of the Counter Reformation in Europe.

Among the missionary orders that followed the pioneer Récollets, most prominent were the Jesuits, whose center was at Quebec, and the Sulpicians who, after 1642, were established at Montreal. Both were represented in the

The St. Lawrence River and the Eastern Seaboard, 1689. A contemporary map by Pere Coronelli, engraved by I. B. Nolin, Paris. (Courtesy of the Royal Ontario Museum of Archaeology)

View of Quebec. Aquatint by J. C. Stadler, from a drawing in George Heriot's *Travels Through the Canadas*, London, 1807. In the Sigmund Samuel Collection. (Courtesy of the Royal Ontario Museum of Archaeology)

"Minuets of the Canadians." Aquatint by J. C. Stadler from a drawing in George Heriot's *Travels Through the Canadas*, London, 1807. In the Sigmund Samuel Collection. (Courtesy of the Royal Ontario Museum of Archaeology)

"Circular Dance of the Canadians." Aquatint by J. C. Stadler from a drawing in George Heriot's *Travels Through the Canadas*, London, 1807. In the Sigmund Samuel Collection. (Courtesy of the Royal Ontario Museum of Archaeology)

Seminary at Quebec, 1829-1830. A water color by James P. Cockburn in the Sigmund Samuel Collection. (Courtesy of the Royal Ontario Museum of Archaeology) *

Manor house in St. Roche's suburb, Quebec, 1829. A water color by James P. Cockburn in the Sigmund Samuel Collection. (Courtesy of the Royal Ontario Museum of Archaeology) *

mission field by men distinguished both for their piety and their vigor as explorers and pioneers. Preventing close cooperation between these two orders, however, was the difference of their views on Indian policy. The Jesuits sought to make the natives Christians and "good Indians"; to this end they advocated the isolation of the red men from the whites, even to the length of not teaching them the French language and discouraging visits to the French trading posts. The Sulpicians, on the other hand, believed that the more practical course was the gallicization of the Indians and their incorporation as quickly as possible into a new half-caste society. Champlain, Colbert, Talon, Frontenac, and other government leaders strongly supported the gallicization theory, and finally took sharp issue with the Jesuits on the subject.

With Talon's arrival in 1665, exploration once again became a feature of state policy as directed from Quebec, and remained so for the rest of the century under the two administrations of Frontenac. Both men, dreaming of a great and expanding French American empire that would seal off both the English and the Spanish holdings from further extension, gave as much support to the explorers and traders as they dared in the face of lack of interest and discouragement from a home government which was absorbed in other projects and reluctant to assume further responsibilities in America. Stimulated by Talon and Frontenac, exploration leaped ahead under the leadership of such men as Marquette, Joliet, Dollier de Casson, René de Brehant de Galinée, LaSalle, Jacques de Noyon, and Daniel Greysolon Dulhut. Throughout the remainder of the seventeenth century their energetic and heroic work laid a broad foundation for an impressive French dominion in North America based on the two great interior water systems of the St. Lawrence and the Mississippi. Over this vast area there were scattered a number of small posts and missions able to control local areas. But between these lay great stretches of unpeopled and uncontrolled territory; and ominous for the future were the facts that already many promising early Canadian adventures had not been followed up for lack of Frenchmen, and at home a preoccupied government was not greatly interested.

While the explorers, traders, and missionaries played their colorful and active roles on the fringes of the French colony, the home government was encouraging the building up of a solid core of more prosaic colonial life

---

←* "Lieutenant-Colonel James Patterson Cockburn (1779-1847) came to Canada with the Royal Artillery in 1826. . . . During his stay in Canada he made a great number of drawings and paintings, covering the country from Quebec to Niagara; . . . . His work displays most careful and accurate representations of the landscape and the buildings of the period. In some instances his drawings are the only pictorial records we have of certain local features since disappeared. All add immensely to our knowledge of the period." From the catalog of the Sigmund Samuel Collection, *Canadiana and Americana,* by Charles W. Jefferys, The Ryerson Press, Toronto, 1948, p. 56.

in the white settlements. A period of marked growth came with the establishing of royal government in 1663. Of the towns, Quebec was the largest with a population, on Talon's arrival, of some 547 persons.² The settlement had two centers: a lower town near the wharves where stood the warehouses and other buildings of the old Company of One Hundred Associates, and a number of the meaner kind of houses; from here a steep road led to the famous high cliff that gave Quebec the strength of an American Gibraltar. In this upper town were the fortifications that guarded the city, and near by, grouped about a principal square, were the governor's castle, the Chateau St. Louis, and the residences and institutions that housed the most important members of the colony. The Roman Catholic Church, that openly claimed dominance in all spheres of colonial life, was visibly represented by a number of prominent buildings. Near the Chateau St. Louis was the Jesuit College, founded in 1636 for the instruction of French and Indian youth. In the midst of a spacious garden was the convent of the Ursuline nuns where, under the leadership of Mère Marie de l'Incarnation, a school for girls flourished. In a *Hôtel-Dieu* the work of a nursing order of nuns, the *Hospitalières,* was carried on. Added to these buildings, following the return of Bishop Laval, was the famous group of institutions which he endowed: one called the *Séminaire des Missions Etrangères* for the education and training of priests was intended to serve as a nucleus for the ecclesiastical life of the colony; another, *La Petite Séminaire,* was designed as a boys' school. These two foundations were later to be crowned by a university called by the Bishop's name. Two miles away on the bank of the St. Charles River stood, within its palisade, the Jesuit house of *Nôtre Dame des Anges,* the base for Jesuit operations in New France.

While seventeenth-century Quebec had something of the air of a provincial city of Old France, it was more self-conscious and pretentious in its preoccupation with matters of ceremony and precedence. Society as well as political life was shot through with the rivalries and jealousies of governor and bishop and their respective entourages. The dualism of Church and state, familiar to contemporary European courts, was in colonial Quebec a matter of daily vexation and unseemly endless disputes over trifling details of etiquette and privilege. Colonial Quebec society, though containing very few members of the old French aristocracy, had a considerable number, especially among the ecclesiastics, of men of culture and good birth. The governor's chateau was the center of a social life, reflecting in its elaborate and punctilious formality something of the color and tone of the court of Versailles. The dignity of elaborate receptions and

---

² G. M. Wrong, *Rise and Fall of New France,* 2 Vols. (New York: 1928), Vol. I, p. 384. The total number of French in Canada in the spring of 1666 is given as 3,215.

banquets, however, was lightened at times by the gaiety of dances and dramatic and musical entertainments. On great occasions, such as the arrival of a new governor, the birth of a royal heir, or major religious festivals, the town gave itself up to holiday. The royal standard was raised to salutes of artillery, church bells were rung, ceremonial visits were paid, and elaborate civil and religious processions, in which the colorful military uniforms of the governor's guard vied with gorgeous ecclesiastical banners, canopies, and vestments, provided a spectacle of never-failing interest to a mixed colonial crowd. Here were jostled together the stolid Indian, the blue-cassocked seminary student, the voyageur back from his long trail, the coureur de bois paying a surreptitious visit to town, and colonial dames in their quaint cumbersome garments, surrounded by their bevies of children.

The two other important French settlements lay farther to the west. On the north bank of the St. Lawrence, nearly a hundred miles above Quebec, was Three Rivers, guarding the approaches to the capital. Located at the mouth of the St. Maurice River, which served as a highway for Indians coming from the north, the town had been settled in 1634 by a number of fur traders and by 1666 had a population of 455.[3] A fort and small garrison gave its inhabitants a precarious security from the not distant Iroquois to the south, whose jealousy of the settlement's northern trade always menaced it with extinction.

If life was precarious in Three Rivers, it was doubly so in Montreal which was situated on the very fringe of Iroquois country. But somehow the town's frail defenses under the command of its indomitable governor, the ardent crusader-soldier Maisonneuve, sufficed to beat off the frequent attacks made during his twenty-two years' regime which lasted until the inauguration of royal government. Within the walls of this advanced post, a famous *Hôtel-Dieu* under the heroic Jean Mance provided nursing care for the settlers, while the first school for girls was opened by a nun, Marguerite Bourgeois, who later also founded the convent of the Congregation of Nôtre Dame and secured funds for Bon-Secours church.[4] In 1663 the *Société de Montréal*[5] transferred its interests and its feudal fief of the island of Montreal to the Sulpician order, which presently came to oppose the Jesuits on the crucial matter of Indian policy, as noted above.

The future prospects of these white settlements on the St. Lawrence were immensely improved by the welcome arrival, in the summer of 1665, of the Carignan-Salières regiment of 1,200 men and officers. The colony had

---

[3] Isabel Foulché-Delbosc, "Women of New France," *Canadian Historical Review,* Vol. XXI, No. 2, June, 1940.

[4] On the work of these early French Canadian women see Wrong, *op. cit.,* Vol. I, pp. 292-93.

[5] On this organization consult E. R. Adair, "France and the Beginnings of New France," *Canadian Historical Review,* Vol. XXV, No. 3, September, 1944.

always suffered for lack of adequate royal troops, and this feature of the new regime was at once a gratifying recognition of the growing importance of the settlements and an indication of the royal determination to put an end to the Iroquois menace. The construction of three new forts on the Richelieu River and the dispatch of several expeditions into the Iroquois country were sufficient to impress the Iroquois with the superiority of French power and to induce them in 1667 to make a peace sufficiently enduring to relieve the harassed French settlements from Indian raids and permit their inhabitants to give their attention to matters other than defense.

The dominant institution of French Canada, and one that especially affected rural life, was feudalism, an institution already dying out in France when it was introduced into the American colonies. A feature of Canadian life from the very start, feudalism was at its height in New France from 1663 to 1750. In Champlain's day a few seigneuries were granted, but the early companies were absorbed in trading operations and gave little attention to their obligations and privileges as land proprietors. The Company of New France gave out some sixty seigneuries; but most of them went to directors of the company who had no intention of living in New France, wishing merely to hold land there for an increase in value. Not half a dozen of all grants made were in occupation in 1663 when the royal government took over the company's powers.

Under the new intendant, who became the supervisor of the whole land system with a wide commission to "order all things as he may think just and proper," all seigneuries not developed were gradually confiscated. Talon's first care was to have a proper survey made and a considered plan for development drawn up. Only then would he begin to confirm old seigneuries or give out new ones to officials, army officers, the Church and its affiliated institutions, and other applicants. Anyone above the rank of peasant who had a little money and was willing to assume feudal obligations could apply and was usually awarded a grant. The size of the seigneury depended on the applicant's social rank, wealth, and ability. Some allotments stretched a dozen miles along a river, others were a tenth of that size, and others still smaller. Though much more restricted than those of earlier days, Talon's grants proved to be larger than their seigneurs could cultivate. Nearly all had frontage on a river, the only practical highway, and ran back into the woods of the foothills, with boundaries vaguely drawn. Since by the "Use of Paris"—the code of laws adopted for New France—all children were entitled to inherit equally, and as all wished to build on the waterfront, there came in time to be a subdivision of the grants into numerous narrow strips running back from the rivers. The most popular of these water highways, the St. Lawrence River, in time assumed the appearance of a continuous village street.

There was much to be said for the introduction of feudalism into Canada. It was the form of land tenure with which the French were most familiar; it provided a needed social organization and local leadership; and it offered a measure of protection in a land where attacks from Indian enemies were a daily menace. As feudalism worked out in New France, some of its worst features in Old France were eliminated or greatly reduced. Absentee landlordism, with all its attendant evils, ceased to be a serious problem after the institution of royal government, when it was ordered that the seigneur must live on his seigneury. Moreover the seigneur in Canada was kept more conscious of his relationship to the central government and held more closely to his military obligations. Furthermore, no impassable caste barrier separated the seigneur from the habitant; for although Louis XIV, to help Talon with his population problem, inaugurated a Canadian noblesse, most of the seigneurs were not nobles in the European sense. As a class, they were fundamentally landowners, charged with special communal responsibilities. While the ordinary seigneur might live in a somewhat more pretentious dwelling, he was often little richer, and no less hard-working, than one of his tenants whose daughter he might well have married. The Canadian habitant was not in the position of the European serf; he had entered the seigneurial contract voluntarily and was not bound to the soil. His relationship with the seigneur had something in it of a patriarchal character, much as the government of the colony was paternalistic.

Finally, feudal dues were very light. On taking possession of a new grant, the habitant ordinarily paid nothing, all dues being remitted for the first few years. But once established, there were three principal sets of feudal payments.[6] First came the *cens et rentes*. The cens was a money payment of a few sous a year in recognition that the whole farm was held from seigneur; the rentes, another annual payment, was the real rent and might be paid in money, in kind, or in both. For the average farm of sixty acres, the rentes would amount to ten or twelve sous, and half a dozen chickens or a bushel of wheat paid after the harvest was in on St. Martin's Day, November eleventh. Secondly came the tax known as the *lods et ventes*. This was a mutation fee to be paid when the farm changed hands; it was supposedly one twelfth of the value of the land, but by custom usually one third of this was rebated. Unless a village or town happened to grow up on his land, this feudal right netted but a small amount to the seigneur.

---

6 Wrong, *op. cit.*, Vol. I, pp. 404-06.

A third set of dues consisted of the *banalités et corvée*. The banalités were feudal dues, paid in kind in return for certain special services which the seigneur had the exclusive right to render. The only two of importance in New France were those for the use of the grist mill and the baking oven; one fourteenth of the grain was the traditional fee. As the mills were expensive to equip with the necessary machinery, which had to be brought from France, the seigneur's obligation to maintain one was often felt to be a burden rather than a welcome source of funds and was frequently put off until public complaint had become too loud to be disregarded, or until the king had agreed to aid in its construction. This state help was the more readily given as the mill building, often of stone, served the purpose of a fort in time of danger. As private ovens early came into general use in a land where wood was plentiful, the tax from this source soon vanished. The habitant was also expected to surrender one fish in each eleven caught; but both hunting and fishing in Canada came early to be looked upon as natural rights, and the collection of any dues in connection with them was resented and seldom inforced. Contrary to the attitude toward the banalités, the corvée was a highly valued feudal right.[7] At certain seasons of the year the seigneur might require labor from the habitants on his land; nominally, this corvée might amount to a levy of six days' work a year, but actually rarely more than three were exacted.

Besides these various dues, every seigneur had a judicial prerogative with its accompanying right and duty to establish a court, appoint judges, and put the fines in his own pocket. In Old France, these judicial fines were an important part of the seigneur's revenues; but in New France, although the seigneur held the three grades of "high, middle, and low" justice, and at times held court in his manor house, he usually remitted all except minor cases to the king's court in Quebec. His revenue from fines, therefore, amounted to little. There were practically no complaints from the habitants to indicate that the seigneurial system weighed heavily on them; on the contrary, as long as defense was needed, it was generally regarded as indispensable.

The seigneur's duties to the state from which he held his land were likewise light: they consisted primarily of a ceremony of fealty and homage performed before the governor in Quebec. On coming into possession of his land, the seigneur swore on bended knee to be faithful and give due obedience in all lawful matters, and to defend the king if called upon to do so. He did not pay for his land as in a freehold system. His chief obligation, if the seigneury were new, was immediately to survey his land into farms and try to procure settlers. If he were inheriting an old seigneury,

---

[7] *Ibid.*, p. 406.

he was expected to make a report, accompanied by a map, stating the size of the holding, the number and state of the buildings, the number of livestock, the amount of land under cultivation, and a census of the inhabitants. In actual practice, the Canadian seigneur left the obligation to procure settlers largely to the state; although he would attend in person as the boats came in and try, by presenting the good points of his seigneurial holdings, to persuade settlers to go thither. Taken as a whole, Canadian feudalism as a land system was a generous one from every point of view. Indeed the crown erred in being too generous; of the land in some three hundred fiefs, granted between 1663 and the close of the century, not one tenth was developed. By 1712 only 50,000 acres were in cultivation, most of them on the north bank of the St. Lawrence River between Quebec and Montreal.

Life in the villages fell naturally into a simple pattern. Everyone lived along one long street paralleling the river. The dwellings were thatched or shingled one-story cottages of wood, usually having a stable partitioned off from the living quarters of the family. A huge fireplace equipped with iron spit and hooks provided the only means of heating and cooking, and oiled paper or thin parchment covered the windows, as only the wealthy in the early days could afford glass. Built-in bunks served as beds and backless benches for chairs until the later advent of the large square beds and rush seats. Chests of all sizes were among the most useful articles of furniture. As there was little earthenware, pewter provided the table equipment of plates, cups, porringers, spoons, and forks. Much of the food came from the gardens, the cows, the pigs, and the chickens which were all tended by the women. Until late in the seventeenth century there were no hand looms or spinning wheels, and no available wool, flax, or hemp. Textiles had to be brought from France, and from these, selected for their wearing qualities rather than for their appearance, the women made their own simple heavy dresses. Many of the men's hats and outer garments, other than those of fur or leather, were also long imported from France, and were so scarce and costly that they were likely to be regarded as heirlooms.[8]

On the farm, all methods were primitive: almost no fertilizers were used and even rotation of crops was little practised, seeds were poor and implements hand-made, and in consequence production was very low; there was little attempt to raise more than the quantity needed for the sustenance of a single family. As these conditions prevailed throughout the colony, there was never enough to feed the whole nonfarming population, and food had constantly to be imported from France. Manufactures were

---

[8] For details on life in the French Canadian village, see Foulché-Delbosc, *op. cit.*

practically nonexistent until Talon's strenuous efforts effected the introduction of a number of simple industries. As there was little hard money, furs serving generally as a standard of values, trading largely took the form of barter.

In each village the curé, usually drawn from a habitant family but somewhat better educated than the majority of his flock, provided, along with the seigneur and the captain of militia, a natural leadership. The militia captain was an interesting village personage whose duties embraced the oversight of many local activities. Instituted by Frontenac during his first administration, this officer was charged with the special responsibility of instructing in musketry all men and boys in his settlement or parish, and training them to act as skirmishers, or scouts, in Indian warfare. Gradually the *capitaine de milice,* or the *capitaine de la côte,* took on other significant local functions, and came to hold the first place among the habitants. Acting as superintendent of roads, local recorder, intermediary between habitants and seigneur or curé, official host to important visitors, as well as watching over local interest generally, he was at once an agent of the central government and a mouthpiece of the local folk. Appointed by the governor, he served without pay, finding his reward in the deference and honor paid to the office he held.[9] Local leadership was especially needed as few habitants had any formal education. Here and there in the larger centers there were a few schools attached to convents, but hardly one in five hundred of the habitants could read. Of the women, a few became nuns; for the rest, marriage, usually occurring at the age of thirteen, completely determined their lives, which were often hard and laborious. The housewives were frequently left alone to look after the farm and their large families, through prolonged periods while their men folk were off fighting Indians, or had gone into the woods, as often happened, to trap or trade for furs.[10] The family claimed the first loyalty from its members who tended to be a sensitive, easily offended, and excessively property-conscious people; litigation was frequent to the point of absurdity; and cases involving boundary disputes, trespass, and damages filled the calendar of the courts.

While life in seventeenth-century New France impressed travelers as that of a static and backward agricultural society unduly dependent on the homeland, and though it was notorious that Frenchmen had to be practically bribed to emigrate to Canada, French Canadian village life had its gay and pleasant side. Close settlement had many advantages: there was little of the loneliness that beset so many of the English colonists on their

---

[9] B. Sulte, "The Captains of Militia," *Canadian Historical Review,* Vol. I, No. 3, September, 1920.

[10] Foulche-Delbosc, *op. cit.*

isolated farms; quick measures for defense against Indian raids could easily be taken; an active social life centered in the family and church, in which assemblies of the community for christenings, marriages, and religious festivals alternated with others associated with the seigneurial relationship. St. Martin's Day, on which the payment of cens et rentes was due, early became a festive occasion, the tenants gathering at the manor house where they were received by the seigneur in the best room, and refreshments and other good cheer were provided; a May pole ceremony, originally a duty, was also made a gala social affair marked by songs and dances, and New Year's day likewise found a group of villagers at the manor house. Thus, in the settled communities of New France social life presented a pale reflection of the mores and social activities of the simpler elements of the society of Old France from which it originally stemmed. On the frontiers, on the other hand, the coureur de bois, the explorer, the soldier, and the missionary showed a greater adaptation to the stresses of the new environment.

Chapter 13

SOCIETY IN THE THIRTEEN COLONIES

I. THE GENERAL PICTURE

As first planted in the seventeenth century, there was a high degree of homogeneity in the twelve English colonies stretching along the Atlantic coast of North America, which by 1700 possessed a population of a quarter of a million people. The large majority of the original settlers were English, most of them townsfolk in origin and outlook. Here and there were scattered islands of foreigners, like the Dutch in New York, the Swedes and Finns on the Delaware, French Huguenots in South Carolina; and, behind the coastal settlements, especially though not exclusively in Pennsylvania, growing groups of Germans and the distinctive, though not foreign, element of Scotch Irish. These infused groups, though adding to the variety of contemporary life and promising an enriched heritage for the future, were not numerous enough to change the fundamental tone and pattern of colonial society. Even the increasing flood of non-English population in the eighteenth century was to prove incapable of overwhelming the dominance of English ways of life. Not only did the original settlers maintain their population superiority through a comparatively high birth rate—so that, to the end of colonial times when the total population numbered two and a half to three millions, the foreign elements failed to constitute a majority in a single colony—but the cultural foundations of the English language, law, and political practice were nowhere seriously threatened.

At the same time, it was characteristic of the English colonies that they did not consciously form an American England, nor think of themselves as members of a unified transatlantic commonwealth, as did New France and, to some extent, the Spanish colonies. While all acknowledged a union of sentiment and loyalty with England, the British colonies tended to regard themselves as separate enterprises, connected with each other only through their common tie with the motherland. When not openly jealous, they were surprisingly indifferent to each other's well-being; not merely did they frequently hesitate to come to the help of a neighbor in trouble, but only with the greatest difficulty could they be induced to cooperate in the face of such common dangers as invasion from French or Spanish territory, or the horrors of a general Indian uprising. Efforts on the part of English statesmen or colonial leaders, designed to effect even limited administrative unity, met with suspicion and opposition.

Despite such divisive factors, however, the English colonies unconsciously exhibited strong family likenesses: all cherished the rights and privileges of English common law; all, in distinction from other transatlantic colonies, clung to the traditions of representative government, even though in most cases there was such a high property qualification as to deny the franchise to the majority of the population; [1] all jealously guarded the right of self-government through duly elected representatives; every colony insisted on looking upon its own particular house of assembly as a replica of the English House of Commons, the mother of parliaments. Another family feature was the craving to own land, which was regarded as the most permanent and secure form of wealth, and desirable as conveying a certain title to respectability and social standing.[2] Even men engaged in seafaring, or townsmen occupied in industry or commerce, wanted land and regarded agriculture as the foundation of the country's wealth. Unlike his counterpart in the French or Spanish systems, the average farmer in the English settlements was not the lowest unit in a semi-feudal order of society but an independent and largely self-sufficient landowner, living on his own isolated, moderate-sized, freehold farm on the frontier or in a small village community.

Another national trait persisting in all colonies was to be found in the marked social cleavages, only less pronounced than in the mother country itself. The leading families everywhere were those of successful merchants or planters: all, except for a few Germans in Pennsylvania and some Dutch families in New York, were English, and immensely proud of their national inheritance; most of them were self-made men whose social ideal was that of the English gentleman; descendants of early comers and possessing the greatest economic stake in the country, they regarded as natural and right their own claim to leadership in all phases of colonial life; they were generally in control of the local legislature and close to the counsels of the colonial governor. Sharing political power, though not social position, with the wealthy merchants and large planters was a growing colonial middle class composed of well-to-do farmers, small merchants,

---

[1] J. F. Jameson in *The American Revolution Considered as a Social Movement* (Princeton: 1940), p. 39, estimates that property qualifications usually amounted to between $150.00 and $250.00. There was, however, much diversity among the various colonies in this respect; Massachusetts, New Hampshire, and North Carolina, for instance, were fairly liberal, South Carolina highly restricted. Property qualifications for officeholding were much higher than for the simple franchise. *Cf.* Morison and Commager, *The Growth of the American Republic* (New York: 1936), p. 39.

[2] For a short and scholarly discussion of the part that landownership played in American colonial society and the revolutionary movement, see Jameson, *op. cit.,* chap. ii, "The Revolution and the Land."

tradesmen, and lesser professional folk. Below this middle group there was the great mass of the poor and unprivileged, including many indentured servants, transported criminals, and, in the southern colonies as the eighteenth century advanced, an increasing number of slaves. Fortunately for social well-being, the nearness of the open frontier with its opportunities for the individual to develop and express his own capabilities tended to mitigate social bitterness, give emphasis to the dignity of the individual, and offer unlimited rewards for imaginative enterprise and hard work.

Education also followed the English pattern in its restrictive as well as in its constructive effects: educational opportunity was considered a privilege for the wealthy rather than a universal right; the curriculum, which was based on the classical-mathematical-philosophical pattern of Oxford and Cambridge, aimed at a general culture rather than anything resembling specialized or vocational training. The planters and rich merchants generally spared no pains to educate their sons, employing tutors for the early years, and later either sending the youth to Oxford or Cambridge or maintaining them at one of the colonial universities. These institutions, however, affected only a small proportion of the colonial population, unsupported as they were by an adequate school system. They were designed especially to meet the growing need for an educated clergy.

The colonial religious picture was extraordinarily diverse, and this diversity was one of the chief factors, as time went on, separating section from section and colony from colony. It was wholly consonant with English tradition that these religious differences should show themselves in the colonies. Ever since the Reformation, the tendency in England had been for every man to claim the right to worship God as he pleased and, as one satirist has added, "to require everyone else to do the same." The principal reason for the coming of many of the colonists was the hope of escaping the disabilities and persecutions to which they were liable at home. There control in matters of religion was exercised by the central and supreme authority of the realm, whereas in those colonies where restriction was in practice, at least it was exercised by the local authority, and the victim had recourse by a relatively short and easy migration to a more favorable environment. In the broad spaces of America there might well be ample room for freedom of conscience and worship, either in the safety of solitude or in the congenial society of fellow religionists. It was only in communities completely dominated by one particular sect that religious intolerance continued for any length of time; in others, men rapidly learned the new lesson of the possibility of people of different faiths living together, if not with charity at least with tolerance. This broad principle of freedom of religion came shortly to be as distinct a feature as was representative government in marking off the English colonies from the French to the north and the Spaniards to the south.

As the colonial period wore on, distinctions between sections, and between colonies within the sections, tended to become stereotyped—differences in soil, forcing different means of livelihood; lack of roads, isolating one community from another; the arrival of new racial elements, especially after 1680—all these, and other factors already dwelt upon, combined to effect the classification of the colonies in three major groups—the Southern, New England, and Middle colonies—each with its own peculiar characteristics.

II. THE SOUTHERN COLONIES

The section in which landowning counted most was the South. It was clear from the earliest days of settlement in Virginia that agriculture was to be all-important. A fertile soil and a long growing season pointed the way. Jamestown was hardly five years old when the planters discovered a stable and profitable crop in tobacco. Later on, rice, indigo, and cotton, and still later, sugar, played the same rôle in the Carolinas and Georgia as tobacco in Virginia and Maryland. These were the crops that it was profitable to export; and they presently came to be raised on large plantations, whose owners set the tone of social life and culture of the southern tier of colonies.

By no means, however, were all farms in the South great plantations. On the contrary, the average holding, at least in the seventeenth century, was small.[3] On these moderately sized freeholds, in contrast to the big plantations, diversified farming was carried on. Life was relatively easy and pleasant; land was cheap, gardens flourished with little labor, cattle could be kept in pasture throughout the year, while small home industries, such as flour milling, glassmaking, and home spinning gave a large measure of self-sufficiency. This middle group had its own social life, much of which centered in the gay country fairs with their wrestling and shooting matches, cock fights, games, and sports. On this social level there was little intellectual life or education, though there existed a few free or endowed schools. As the eighteenth century approached its end, the increasing competition of the large planters forced many small farmers to join the trek westward. Of those who remained at home, many became poverty-stricken and sank to the class of poor whites; the indolent ease with which a bare living could be secured tended to undermine morale; and the stigma attached to labor, as it became associated with slavery, worked the ruin of many small farmers.

---

[3] This point of view is elaborated in T. J. Wertenbaker, *The Planters of Colonial Virginia* (Princeton: 1922), pp. 45-57, also, P. A. Bruce, *Social Life of Virginia in the 17th Century* (Richmond: 1907), p. 135.

Between the small farmer and the planter yawned a great economic and social chasm, though the planters, at the top of society, were by no means all aristocrats; few members of the great English aristocratic families, or even the gentry, migrated to America. The majority of the planters were originally men of small means who rose gradually through their own efforts to a position of affluence. As a class they maintained close contact with the homeland, with which travel and traffic were easier and more frequent than with the other colonies. They looked to England for their market, furniture, clothing, and other supplies. Many of them sent their children to England for education and travel, and at home duplicated as closely as possible the life of English squires. Most of them belonged to the Anglican Church which had been established in Virginia from the beginning.

The diaries of the age depict the enjoyable social life that centered around the Big House: hunting, horse racing, grand balls, and assemblies, long theatrical seasons, and hospitality on a lavish scale, all had their part.[4] Charleston, the one great city of the South, was the center of this life, and was long noted for its pleasurable winter "seasons."[5] The scale of living was extravagant. The mercantile system of the day forced the planters "to sell cheap and buy dear"; the period between the dispatch of the crop and the payment for it was necessarily long, consequently the planters were practically always in debt to their London agents. This condition of perpetual debt to creditors in England was probably as responsible as anything else for the fact that the southern planters, though long attached to the English crown and English tradition, were to be found on the side of the rebels in the Revolutionary War.

The estates of the planters tended always to increase in size. This was primarily because the crops of tobacco, rice, and indigo soon exhausted the soil. But there were also other factors. Without scientific fertilizing or the rotation of crops, a large part of the acreage had to be permitted to lie fallow; furthermore, many planters, besides trying to secure as much land as possible for present and future crop needs, were ardent land speculators; they used their influence in the legislature to secure great tracts of land which were destined not for cultivation but for sale or rent to later comers. For many reasons, both utilitarian and aesthetic, every planter tried to secure water frontage on rivers or tidal inlets deep enough for ocean-going ships—often belonging to the planter himself—that would carry the tobacco from the planter's own wharf to the market in England. These numerous waterways of the South were essential for both trade and travel.

---

[4] For a description, see Bruce, *op. cit.*, chaps. x-xiv.
[5] Charleston's colonial life is admirably described by T. J. Wertenbaker in *The Golden Age of Colonial Culture* (New York: 1942), chapter on "Charleston."

What roads existed for the most part paralleled the coast and connected the towns of the coastal area. Development of east-west roads was very slow; in the beginning these were traversed only on horseback or on foot and became practically impassable in bad weather. Not until water frontage was no longer available and poorer men had to take up the interior lands did road building develop on any extensive scale.

The greatest problem of the southern planter was how to secure sufficient labor. The crops he raised demanded not the skilled work of a few, but the hands of the many. In the seventeenth century this problem was solved largely through the use of indentured labor, a form of contract probably suggested by the apprentice system of England. The services of an immigrant too poor to pay his own way across the Atlantic—an expense which ran from £6 to £10 and represented more than an ordinary English workingman could save in a lifetime—would be sold to a planter for a period of four to five years.[6] During this time the indentured man, in return for his labor, was entitled to food, clothing, care, and perhaps a little pocket money. At the end of his term of service he became a free person and was usually given fifty acres of land and a small outfit;[7] he then could become an independent farmer or join the stream of those moving westward. The term "indentured" came from the form of contract entered into between the servant and the man to whom he was selling his services. This document was drawn up in duplicate on a single sheet of paper with a broad space between the two identical versions. It was then irregularly cut into two, each party taking half of the paper, which could later be legally identified by the fitting together of the saw-toothed edges.

The indentured labor system introduced a number of curious elements into American society. While there were many voluntarily indentured servants drawn from the huge class of the unemployed folk of seventeenth-century England who had been tempted by the representations of an entrepreneur, others were kidnaped by agents or "spirits" employed by planters or shipowners who rewarded them well for their efforts. Probably five hundred kidnaped persons a year reached the colonies; most of these went to the West Indies, especially Barbados, but Virginia and Maryland received a good many. Such abuses became so serious that the English Parliament attempted to intervene, but its efforts were largely ineffective because English society was glad to be rid of the vagabond elements and the colonies had real need of their services. Among the indentured servants

---

[6] A. M. Schlesinger estimates that "perhaps one-half of all the white immigrants during the larger part of the colonial period were unable to pay their expenses." See *New Viewpoints in American History* (New York: 1928), p. 4. For further details on conditions of service, see Wertenbaker, *The Planters of Colonial Virginia*, pp. 31-34.

[7] On the indentured person's doubtful legal right to this, see Wertenbaker, *op. cit.*, p. 61.

there was a considerable criminal element. The barbarous laws of the age provided the death penalty for more than three hundred offenses and many judges were glad to substitute for such sentences a period of indentured servitude in the colonies. For this class of involuntary servant, the period of servitude was usually eight years. With the revolutionary upheavals of the second half of the seventeenth century, a considerable number of political offenders were dispatched to the colonies as indentured servants. From all sources probably some fifteen hundred to two thousand indentured persons arrived annually.[8] Many of them eventually obtained wealth and political influence and became the founders of estimable colonial families. This upward process was easier in the seventeenth century than in the eighteenth when class lines became more rigidly drawn—the wealthy growing wealthier and the poor becoming poorer. By this time the stream of indentured servants had dried up to a mere trickle as slavery supplanted it as a source of labor for the great plantations. These had increased from an average of 446 acres in the middle of the seventeenth century to 650 acres at the opening of the eighteenth.

As early as the seventeenth century there were, to be sure, some slaves in all the colonies: in the northern and middle colonies their use was largely restricted to domestic service, but in the South they were beginning to be used for agricultural labor as well. Throughout this century, however, slaves were very expensive, costing from £18 to £40, even after prices fell when the Dutch monopoly was taken over in 1648 by the English Royal African Company. It cost the planter approximately four times as much to buy a slave as to import an indentured servant; he therefore generally preferred the latter—though he had to face the prospect of losing valuable services after a few years, just as his man had become adequately trained and useful.

The flood of slaves to America started around the beginning of the eighteenth century, and increased greatly with the signing of the Treaty of Utrecht in 1713. A section of the treaty, known as the *Asiento,* transferred to English hands the monopoly for supplying slaves to the Spanish colonies.[9] This helped to bring about an expansion of the slave traffic in the English colonies as the South Sea Company, operating the English contract, liked to have the southern plantation absorb the surplus from the West Indian trade and secured government backing to that end. At first there was some opposition from the planters, as the Negroes were wild,

---

[8] *Ibid.,* p. 35; also *cf.* Schlesinger, *op. cit.,* chap. i.
[9] The introduction by British subjects into Spanish America of 144,000 slaves in the course of thirty years (at the rate of 4,800 per year) was provided for by the terms of the Asiento treaty signed on March 16, 1713.

"A South Prospect of y. Flourishing City of New York," by Thomas Bakewell, March, 1746. (Courtesy of the New York Public Library)

Church and Market Streets, Albany, 1805, by James Rights. (Courtesy of the New York Public Library)

County Fair, 1824, by John G. Woodside. (Courtesy of Harry T. Peters, photograph by the Metropolitan Museum of Art)

Arch Street Ferry, Philadelphia. "Drawn, engraved & published by W. Birch & Son," 1800. (Courtesy of the New York Public Library)

mutinous, and difficult to handle. But as the sources of indentured servants tended to dry up while the expanding plantations demanded more and more hands, and as Africa offered a continuous supply, early objections faded and black slaves took the place of the white indentured servants of the previous century. The trade itself came largely into the hands of Yankee traders whose vessels visited the Senegal and Gambia sections of the African coast. Here, in exchange for rum and American munitions, they bought Negroes whom the Arab traders had purchased or captured in the interior and were holding at the ports for sale to the masters of the slave ships. The mortality rate in the terrible journey across the Atlantic, known as the "middle passage," was so frightful that it was estimated only one in four survived. Most of the slaves were taken first to Jamaica for rehabilitation, and then many re-exported to the English colonies; some however were brought directly from Africa. By 1760, two fifths of the population of the South were Negroes, and their influx was producing a number of important social and economic results. Among these, class lines became greatly sharpened as prosperity came to depend increasingly upon slave labor which the poor man could not afford to buy but of which the rich man had a superabundance; consequently many of the smaller farmers, growing discouraged or discontented, pulled up stakes and moved westward into the Piedmont area.[10]

This Piedmont section came to be distinguished from the Tidewater area in a number of respects. The racial elements that composed it came from a number of different sources and gave it a less homogeneous character than the Tidewater region. Immediately to the rear of a generally English population, some of whom were former indentured servants, was a considerable settlement of Germans who had originally lived along the Rhine. These Rhineland folk, mostly sturdy Protestant peasants, had left the Palatinate under religious and political pressure when Louis XIV of France had embarked upon an expansive war in that country and endeavored to turn them all into Catholics. Some migrated directly to America, others went first to England, and still others to northern Ireland. In England and Ireland the refugees found a certain amount of religious liberty, but neither political freedom nor economic prosperity; and so for the second time determined to migrate, this time to America, where they presently joined the stream of German immigrants flowing directly from the Palatinate and other parts of Germany. Many entered through the port of Philadelphia; others came by way of New York. The majority settled permanently in Pennsylvania; others moved southward into the Piedmont

---

[10] There is an interesting chapter on this subject in Wertenbaker, *op. cit.*, chap. viii.

regions of the southern states, especialy of North Carolina. Many in the German group brought with them a deep sense of injustice against the British agents from whom they had suffered much on the long voyage to their eventual home. Honest, industrious, and pious, they soon prospered in their new setting; about three quarters of them remained indefinitely on the lands they originally settled, and the others moved nearer the frontier.

To the west of the Germans were considerable numbers of Scotch-Irish, some of whom had been inspired by the German movement to migrate to America from northern Ireland. As Scottish and English Presbyterians, they had been settled in Ireland by the government of James I in order to keep that country under English control. Like the Germans, they had found that the Test and Corporation Acts, and other English religious laws, weighed heavily on all who were not members of the established Anglican Church, and further that English trade laws closed the English and Scottish markets to inhabitants of Ireland. Once in America, the Scotch-Irish moved southward in the footsteps of the Germans, settling in the mountains and foothills generally to the west of the German settlements.

Many fundamental issues between the inhabitants of the Piedmont and those of the Tidewater counties resulted in early conflicts. Racial differences made for trouble. Quarrels over land were numerous, mostly arising from the efforts of the Tidewater aristocracy to grab up the land west of their actual plantations which they then sold or rented at high prices to the newcomers. Religious differences added their quota of disturbance, for the Tidewater people belonged mostly to the established Anglican Church, whereas the frontiersmen were dissenters and nonconformists. Different views as to the proper treatment of the Indians also were a source of trouble; the Tidewater folk constantly cheated the Indians; whereas the frontiersmen, living in close contact with the natives, were most anxious that Indian contracts should not be violated as they were the ones to suffer the consequences when the aroused Indians retaliated. Finally, constant trouble was caused by the determination of the Tidewater counties to maintain political control of the assembly by postponing the creation of new counties or by giving them unduly small representation. It was too much to expect that an arrogant Tidewater aristocracy, one based on money rather than birth, keenly interested in land and bent on exploiting the rest of the population, should live in harmony with an ultra-democratic and poverty-stricken back country made up of many pushing, restless elements that were determined to assert themselves.

III. PURITAN NEW ENGLAND

The New England colonies were originally planted by persons having very different motives from those that moved the gentlemen adventurers and the middle-class farmer immigrants who settled the southern tier of colonies. The goals of most of the latter were land and immediate riches; whereas the guiding idea of the Puritans as a group was to found a Bible commonwealth in which they might both carry out an experiment in Christian living and control political conditions so that these would at least not be antagonistic to that ideal.

The Puritans originated as a radical party within the Church of England. They were dissatisfied with the Elizabethan settlement, considering that it had merely substituted minor reforms and illogical and faint-hearted compromise in doctrine for the worse evils of the Roman Church. Strongly influenced by the Protestant movements on the Continent, the Puritans wished to see a whole-hearted return to the practices and doctrines of the primitive apostolic church—a purification of the whole process of living— and not merely minor changes in doctrine and ceremonial in a form of worship. The increasing secularization of thought and the growing worldliness around them alarmed them profoundly. At first they did not desire to leave the established Anglican Church but wished only to reform it from within; it was obstacles that they met with in seeking to carry out this program that drove them into the position of nonconformists and separatists, and finally induced many of them to emigrate. They left England, however, not merely to escape religious persecution, but with the constructive program of reaching a new land and there building up a new Canaan in which all conditions, including a new state, a new church, and new schools, would be conducive to the type of daily living they believed to be alone worth while.

Nor was religion their only motive; they were moved by political and economic considerations as well. Many were alarmed at the absolutist trend of English government and the narrowing economic opportunities at home. Under able leaders, the great migration began about 1630 and continued strongly for a decade, falling off rapidly after 1640. At its height, some fifteen thousand persons were migrating annually. They first established themselves in the colony of Massachusetts Bay, but eventually were responsible for the founding of Rhode Island, Connecticut, and New Hampshire, claimed jurisdiction in Maine, and early incorporated within their own state of Massachusetts the colony of Plymouth which had been founded by the Pilgrim Fathers. Throughout colonial times, Massachusetts continued to hold a place of pre-eminence among the New England colonies and was inclined to conduct her relations with the others in a haughty and overbearing manner which was frequently resented.

Towards the mother country, the persistent policy of the Massachusetts authorities was to have as little as possible to do with the King, the Privy Council, and the Lords of Trade, carrying on Massachusetts affairs as though the colony were an independent and sovereign state. Under the terms of the charter there was no royal governor and no question of interference from a London board. The General Court, acting in the double capacity of a board of directors and a legislature, not only issued laws, imposed taxes, and provided for local defense, but also assumed such sovereign prerogatives as coining money and imposing the death sentence without reference to England.

Within Massachusetts the Puritans made an earnest effort to put their religious ideas into practice. Fundamentally, the state was a kind of theocracy where, for sixty years, only those who were church members could exercise the franchise that controlled the state-regulated belief. Thus Church and state in the Bible commonwealth were practically synonymous, with the government exercising strict discipline over the lives of all individuals. A religious oligarchy of godly men exercised all power, indeed to such an extent that nothing less than a royal command could secure for a member of the Church of England the privileges of a freeman, and then only if he could secure a certificate of character from a Puritan minister. Thus, in the beginning the whole conception was aristocratic and antidemocratic; any leveling influences within the new environment were sternly suppressed.

The state thus organized imposed a scriptural standard of conduct and belief upon everyone and undertook to regulate dress, diet, drink, and behavior. Order and conformity were the major virtues; frivolity and lack of seriousness were the major vices. Harsh rules punished severely such faults as lying and swearing, strictly regulated the Sabbath, and put a ban on Christmas day and May day festivities, as well as on theaters and amusements. As a famous historian said of their fellow religionists in England, they objected to bear-baiting, not because it was cruel to the bear but because the spectators enjoyed it. In the enforcement of these standards, the clergy were more zealous than the officers of the law. They functioned as moral guides and as licensed teachers of religion, ethics, and politics rather than as priests of sacramental mysteries. Such a system inevitably encouraged among private members of the church a great deal of espionage which led to many accusations and controversial feuds. In business, as in private life, strict state regulations prevailed: a "just" price was a fundamental idea, and wages were rigidly controlled; frugality and thrift were praised, pauperism regarded as a stigma, and laziness condemned and punished.

In their relations with their neighbors—the Indians and the French—the Puritan leaders accepted the necessity of war. In fact, not only was war condoned so long as it was a "just" war, but military training for all above eighteen was imposed, and a number of savage wars waged in which the prisoners taken were often brutally treated. As for the Indians, the Puritans made little effort to convert or civilize them; indeed they were regarded by many as peculiarly possessed of the devil. To this general view John Eliot was an early and notable exception. As a missionary he went among the Algonquins, translated the Bible into the Algonquian tongue, and established a number of towns of converted Indians that became known as the "praying towns." [11] His work was later followed up by Eleazar Wheelock and others. In the late eighteenth century, the famous Puritan divine of Northampton, Jonathan Edwards, also showed deep interest in trying to convert the Indians to Christianity and personally labored to do so for some time from a center in Stockbridge, then a frontier settlement.

The religious faith that supported this stern regime—all the stronger and sterner because it had come through the fires of persecution—was one in which the theological views were based on a Calvinistic conception of God, a belief in the depravity of human nature, and a code of morals largely drawn from a literal interpretation of the Bible. From men the Deity demanded absolute and implicit obedience; because of the fall, "men were sinners in the hands of an angry God" and deserved damnation but through the mercy of the Redeemer a few elect persons, chosen by God, would be saved. On the great subject of election, man could but search his conscience and the Scriptures for assurance. This led to increased study of the Scriptures, absorption in theology, introspection, and tortuous self-examination.

Preoccupation with theological problems led to a great emphasis on education and intellectual activity. Massachusetts not only laid the foundation of the public school system of America by requiring in a law of 1647 that every town of fifty householders appoint and pay a teacher, and communities of one hundred families maintain a grammar school, but in 1636 also founded the first university in English America, Harvard College in Cambridge. Two years later the first printing press was established in Boston (1638), and presently that Puritan city became the second greatest

---

11 For an illuminating essay on John Eliot, see S. E. Morison, *Builders of the Bay Colony* (Boston: 1930), chap. x.

publishing center in the British Empire.[12] It is probably true that the best of the original thinkers of the seventeenth century in America were Massachusetts Puritans. Foremost among them were the four eminent divines, John Cotton and the Mather dynasty, Richard, Increase, and Cotton Mather, who wrote profusely, preached eloquently, and exercised enormous influence in a wide circle. Jonathan Edwards, another Puritan of intellectual genius, was a great evangelist and theologian who by his preaching and writing started the "Great Awakening" of the colonies in the eighteenth century.[13]

It is to be observed that the early Massachusetts Puritans made no pretense of toleration in any field; on the contrary, they prided themselves on being inflexible, believing that tolerance came from lack of fervor and uncertainty in belief. They conceived themselves to be possessed of the truth in its fulness and its purity, and thought of themselves as the chosen people of God. Those who were not content to receive guidance and give strict obedience had "the liberty to stay away from us." Dissenters like Roger Williams and Anne Hutchinson, who would not conform and did not voluntarily migrate, were driven out; while those who persisted in returning, as did the Quakers, faced the danger of execution. Each must conform for the good health of all; the issues at stake were too serious to be compromised. But even in Massachusetts the early rigidity of the Puritan regime gave way with the passage of time to a more liberal outlook and political practice such as had grown up meanwhile in the rest of New England.

Quite early, the whole New England group of colonists developed a complex economy. Besides cultivating such arable land as was available or could be brought into cultivation, mostly in comparatively small freehold farms, the colonies, for additional resources, turned their attention to the sea. Fishing, both off their own coast and as far away as the Newfoundland Banks, provided for local needs and for a growing export trade to the West Indies and southern Europe. These activities called for the development of shipbuilding, for which materials were readily at hand and which at once received encouragement from the home government, whose naval requirements provided a limitless market for masts, spars, rough-hewn timber, and other construction materials. For a time, every little settlement along the New England coast was busy turning out ships that in size ran from fishing smacks to ocean-going vessels; later, however, towards the end of the seventeenth century, ship construction and repairs, as well as

[12] On education in New England consult Merle Curti, *The Growth of American Thought* (New York: 1943), chaps. iv and v, and Carl Bridenbaugh, *Cities in the Wilderness* (New York: 1938), especially pp. 121, 123, 280-83, 289-92, 442-46.

[13] For illuminating studies of these theologians, their writings and influence see V. L. Parrington, *The Colonial Mind, 1620-1800* (New York: 1927), pp. 27-37, 98-117.

commerce in naval stores, fish, and furs, tended to be concentrated in a few large centers, of which Boston became the most important.[14] Meanwhile, Yankee ships filled with New England produce became a familiar sight in the ports of the other colonies and of the West Indies, as well as in English, European, and African harbors, while New England whalers and sealers plied the seas far to the north and south on highly profitable ventures.

Many New Englanders had brought with them from the old country highly developed skills in a diversity of trades and crafts, and manufacturing for home use began immediately. Saw mills, grist mills, tanneries, iron foundries, glass and pottery works, and brickyards were set up; while home spinning was universally practiced, soon providing clothing for two thirds of the population. As soon as larger manufacturing ventures requiring mills in the coastal towns began to develop, the jealousy of English manufacturers was aroused. This resentment, supported by accusations of numerous infringements of the Trade and Navigation Laws, especially in connection with the "triangle" trade in which New England was deeply implicated, provided a basis of constant remonstrance from the home government and eventually became a major factor in bringing about the withdrawal (1684) of the Massachusetts charter.

In population, New England was the most homogeneous of the three tiers of colonies; all her early settlers, except a few French Huguenots, Jews, and Negro slaves, came from the British Isles, and mainly from the lower middle class. Immigration was carefully controlled, as was the making of land grants, in the interest of an established Puritanism, with the result that the stream of settlers was diverted to more hospitable and tolerant regions father south, and New England was left to depend on its own natural increase for population and to crystallize in its own social and intellectual pattern. Social and political leadership, provided originally by the Puritan ministers, soon came to be shared by laymen of the prosperous merchant group. Throughout New England this class was free from the competing interest of the landed gentry whose influence counted so heavily in the middle and southern colonies, while, at least in Massachusetts, it was also exempt from the patronage of royal officials; thus it soon found itself everywhere in an unassailable position of dominance. Contrary to the practice elsewhere the normal unit of settlement in New England was the compact town community which not only provided the pattern of original organization, but also dictated the procedure under which new territory was opened up and occupied. Application to the legislature for land grants was normally made, not by the individual settler,

14 Wertenbaker, *The Golden Age of Colonial Culture*, chapter on "Boston."

but on behalf of a group proposing to set up a new town; the newly constituted community decided on individual allotments and established church, school, town hall, and other public institutions. At the time of the Revolution one hundred such towns had been set up in New Hampshire, fifty-four in Vermont, and more than twenty in Maine.[15] Thus, by the close of the colonial period, this northeastern group of English colonies presented the aspect of a community exceptionally homogeneous in population and politically mature. Its democratic organization was well adapted to its needs and intelligently put into practice. Possessed of an economy varied, complex, and to a large extent self-supporting,[16] it was also in educational matters well nourished and intellectually alert. All in all, New England appeared well fitted to take her place in the vanguard of the forthcoming march to freedom.

IV. THE MIDDLE COLONIES

The Middle Colonies, lying between New England and the Southern Colonies, shared certain features of each of the other groups and yet possessed a distinctive character of their own. All were originally proprietary colonies and all, except Maryland, were post-Restoration grants. Their proprietors had the disposal of all ungranted lands, charged what in other parts would have been considered a high price for them, and demanded in addition an annual quitrent—a vestige of feudal claims much disliked by the colonists.[17] It was a method of land tenure marking off all the proprietary holdings from the corporate colonies of New England where land could be acquired without these obligations.

In variety of population, the Middle Colonies were the most American of all—if the melting pot is accepted as the symbol of the future nation—for here was the heaviest concentration of non-English population elements which were eventually to become absorbed into the national amalgam. The Dutch, incorporated by conquest in 1664, continued until the end of the seventeenth century a dominant, though relatively declining, group in Manhattan, on Long Island, along the Hudson to Albany, and in northern New Jersey. The Swedes on the Delaware numbered about a thousand at the close of the seventeenth century and by that time, like the Dutch, were gradually abandoning their language and customs as they adopted those of the descendants of the original English settlers.

---

[15] Morison and Commager, *op. cit.*, p. 61.

[16] Morison and Commager, *op. cit.*, p. 59, point out that "the economic solidarity of the New England seaboard explains why four New England colonies came into the revolutionary movement as a unit" despite the presence of many diversifying factors.

[17] Jameson, *op. cit.*, p. 33, states that in the various colonies these dues "ranged from a penny an acre to a shilling a hundred acres per annum." They were often evaded and were abolished at the Revolution.

A still larger foreign group was German. Pious, industrious, largely a peasant people from the Rhineland, driven overseas by the poverty ensuing from the Thirty Years' War or the military ambitions of Louis XIV, the Germans early settled in considerable numbers on fertile farming soil in Pennsylvania, making their homes to the west of the English Quakers who had already occupied the three eastern counties of Philadelphia, Bucks, and Chester. In time their farms spread along the valleys of the Delaware, Schuylkill, and Lehigh rivers. They clung tenaciously to their language, folkways, and styles of architecture and furnishings. Though some moved southward, the majority held on to their first settlements and many of their descendants, known as the "Pennsylvania Dutch," are to be found there today. By the time of the Revolution, the Germans in Pennsylvania numbered about 90,000, and constituted a third of the population of the colony.[18] As the pioneering Scotch Irish moved into the frontier regions to the west, the Germans found themselves wedged in between two very different British groups. Becoming, through industry and thrift, economically as well as geographically a middle group in possession of considerable political power, they chose to align themselves with the English Quakers who dominated the Assembly, and in this way managed to secure various coveted goals.

Another foreign element represented in the Middle Colonies, though the largest group settled in the Carolinas, was that of the French Huguenots. Like the Rhinelanders, they had been driven from their homes by the activities of Louis XIV whose revocation of the Edict of Nantes sent many Frenchmen fleeing across the Atlantic in search of religious freedom and a peaceful opportunity to practice their skills in the silk and wine industries. The Scotch Irish, though not a foreign group, provided another distinctive element in the population of the Middle Colonies, especially of Pennsylvania. Racially, these people were descendants of English and Scottish settlers of northern Ireland. On becoming discouraged with their prospects in Ireland, they poured into America in thousands, chiefly through the ports of New York and Philadelphia; beginning their migration in the late seventeenth century, they came in increasing numbers through the eighteenth. Finding the eastern seaboard already occupied, they settled, largely by squatter right, on the less desirable lands back of the earlier comers. Sentimentally unattached to Europe, enterprising and vigorous, they made superb frontiersmen and bore the brunt of Indian raids as well as the first impact of French and Spanish attacks. By the time of the Revolution the Scotch Irish, like the Germans, constituted a third of the population of Pennsylvania.[19]

---

[18] Morison and Commager, *op. cit.*, p. 52.
[19] *Ibid.*, p. 52.

In matters of religion, the Middle Colonies showed an even greater complexity of elements. The majority of the settlers were refugees of the Reformation and post-Reformation movements, coming from lands where the fighting was hottest and religious feelings ran highest. English and Welsh Quakers, Roman Catholics, Scotch Irish Presbyterians, Calvinists of various types and nationalities, Dutch and Swedish Reformers, German Lutherans, and French Huguenots, all sought, and nearly always found, an American home where separation of Church and state was a reality and religious toleration prevalent. For both Maryland and Pennsylvania, the one founded by a Roman Catholic proprietor and the other established by a Quaker—each leader representative of a religious minority proscribed in England—freedom of religion was a matter of enlightened self-interest. Toleration was desirable not only from the point of view of internal peace but also as providing a strong inducement to those European groups most likely to make good settlers. These two colonies, together with New York where the terms of Dutch capitulation secured a measure of toleration, set a pattern not only for all the Middle Colonies but one eventually to be followed by all the states of the Union.

Economically, the Middle Colonies early reached a high level of material comfort, made possible by a diversified economy. The lavish products of field, forest, and mine of this region secured comfortable living standards for its inhabitants and provided a large margin of wealth in exportable goods. Rich cargoes of flour, wheat, packed meat, timber, furs, and naval stores were available for dispatch to profitable markets in the other colonies, in the West Indies, and in England. Especially through the operation of the "triangle" trade, the Middle Colonies were able to maintain for many years a brisk and profitable interchange of colonial products for European manufactured goods. When, in the eighteenth century, the English Parliament undertook to enforce the Navigation Acts, the Middle Colonies, like New England, suffered severely in a curtailment of trade and prosperity. Maryland, with much of her wealth invested in tobacco, suffered less, as did the Southern Colonies, with their simple one-crop economy.[20]

The constantly growing flow of trade through the Middle Colony ports induced in this area a rapid development of urban life, which brought in its train a flourishing industry. In this as in other respects, the most rapidly developing of the colonies was Pennsylvania, which possessed in Philadelphia (population 30,000 in 1770) the largest of the colonial cities.[21] New York's growth was long delayed. This arrested development was partly due to the continued occupation of central New York by the

---

[20] Wertenbaker, *The Founding of American Civilization: The Middle Colonies* (New York: 1938).

[21] Wertenbaker, *Golden Age of Colonial Culture,* chapter on "Philadelphia."

Iroquois tribes which long confined European settlements to the comparatively narrow limits of the Hudson and Mohawk valleys; furthermore, the perpetuation of antiquated Dutch traditions, as well as the huge land grants made to the favorites of the Duke of York, tied up the most desirable lands in great manorial estates and caused the stream of immigrants to shun the colony and turn southward. New York City at the time of the Revolution had a population of twenty thousand, about equal to that of Boston. Considered as an economic unit in the American scene, the Middle Colonies, though marked by strong racial and political sectionalism, were conspicuous for a balanced development of urban and rural prosperity.

Politically and socially, the dominant class in the Middle Colonies was composed of rich merchants and planters, descendants of early English settlers except for a few Dutch families in New York and a few Germans who had risen to wealth in Pennsylvania. Their stately mansions, filled with fine furniture and served by slaves, lined the Hudson River and Chesapeake and Delaware bays. In Pennsylvania, the English Quakers of the eastern counties, long after they had become a minority group, continued to exercise political dominance largely through their ability to persuade the enfranchised Germans that it was to their interests to support them in the General Assembly. Eighteenth-century currents, however, tended to undermine the leadership of the Quakers, dominant in a more peaceful age. Their doctrine of pacificism and nonresistance unfitted them to provide the dynamic leadership needed when population began to move inland and the critical issue of the age became the clash of interests in the Ohio and Mississippi valleys where international rivalry, particularly Anglo-French, called desperately for settlement—if need be by armed force. Furthermore, as education and enlightenment spread, the back counties increasingly resented the combination of an unduly heavy share of the military burden of defending the frontier with outrageously low representation in the General Assembly. But the colonial age was long past before democracy in its fullest flower came to prevail in the Middle Colonies.

Chapter 14

COLONIAL AMERICA: THE GROWTH OF NEW SOCIETIES

Western Europeans, migrating under various flags into the New World, were speedily surrounded by a multiplicity of novel circumstances and influences, human and environmental, that were to create within a few generations new and widely varying human societies. Differences in the immigrating white group—racial, regional, social, political, and occupational—were very great. The degree of closeness in association with the American native, the cultural differences in the native groups that came in contact with the whites, and the extent to which the African Negro was admitted into colonial society varied greatly, not only from one set of colonies to another but even from one community to another under the same flag. The blending of these numerous and varying racial factors with differing geographical, climatic, and economic influences in the several colonial areas had ensured a highly diversified social picture long before the close of the colonial age.

Broadly speaking, in the vast areas south of the Rio Grande—mostly Spanish and Portuguese—there had been from the earliest days racial fusion on an almost universal scale. It was naturally greatest in the heavily populated areas where the natives had attained the highest cultural level, and lowest in the frontier regions where the fiercer tribes were encountered. Where Negroes were numerous, as in the tropical lands of the Caribbean and along the coastal plantation regions of Brazil, the fusion of whites, Africans, and Indians proceeded apace, with a resultant elaboration of castes and colors. By the close of the colonial era, the hybrid classes—mestizos, mulattoes, mamelucos, zambos, and others in an intricate nomenclature—far outnumbered the rest of the population: at one end of the scale the whites—the relatively diminishing groups of peninsulares and creoles—and at the other, the pure-blooded Indians and Negroes. The fact that the incoming Spaniards were for the most part, especially in the early years, single individuals embarked on an adventurous search for gold, did much to produce the racial intermixture; moreover, the Spanish government definitely approved and encouraged the absorption of the American natives into colonial society through white and Indian unions. On the other hand the Spanish authorities prohibited, under severe penalties, the crossing of Indians with Negroes, believing that the descendants would inherit the poorer qualities of both.

In Brazil, a number of factors affected the racial picture and varied it from that in Spanish territories: the government hand-picked its white colonists less carefully, and allowed the inclusion of a greater variety of nonnational European elements; there was also a larger proportion of white women, and so a greater possibility, in early colonial days, of pure-blooded descendants; the economic goal for the first two centuries was the securing of riches from plantation crops, and, in consequence, colonists were more likely to arrive in family groups than was the case in Spanish territories where a mining economy was uppermost; the greatest differentiating factor, however, was the immensely greater number of Negroes incorporated into Brazilian society. The introduction of Africans into the Brazilian labor market was due to the unsuitability for hard manual toil of the Indians in the Portuguese territory, who were more primitive and less adaptable than those of the Spanish area, and simply died at their tasks when put to hard labor on the plantations. Neither Indians nor white men could bear plantation labor under tropical conditions and, if the work was to be accomplished, the hardier black man from Africa had to be imported.

In the highly graded Hispanic colonial society, both Spanish and Portuguese, occupation and opportunity depended to a great extent on the racial group to which one belonged; the higher the percentage of white blood the easier the upward path. Speaking generally, all the higher government and church offices were limited to whites of European birth whose close connection with the homeland seemed to the sovereign a surer pledge of loyalty. Their privileges were a cause of jealous heartburnings to the American-born whites, especially in Spanish America, where the implication of inferiority in loyalty and capacity were bitterly resented. Land and mine ownership, the professions, and petty government offices were the usual avenues open to the better class of American whites. Absenteeism and the crowding of the upper-class whites into cities, so outstanding a feature in Spanish America, did not constitute serious problems in the Portuguese colonies where the economic emphasis for two hundred years was on plantation living rather than on mining operations. The poorer sort of European immigrants made up a large proportion of the commercial class; those of mixed blood filled the army, the lesser trades, and the smaller industrial jobs; all the hardest labor in mine and field fell to the Indians and Negroes, the latter, of course, much more numerous in Brazil than in Spanish lands.

North of the Rio Grande, racial amalgamation played no such spectacular rôle in the process of building a new society as it did in the lands of the Spaniards and Portuguese. In the French colonies, this Latin people mingled their blood to some extent with that of the Indians in the frontier areas of Canada, in Louisiana, and in the West Indies; while in the two more southern areas under French sovereignty a certain amount of Negro blood also produced a mulatto class in these communities. On the whole, however, miscegenation was a comparatively minor factor in the French mainland colonies compared with the important part it played in Hispanic and Portuguese societies. The compactness and self-sufficiency of the white agricultural settlements in Canada discouraged racial amalgamation; the chief agents of such crossings as occurred were the coureurs de bois and the voyageurs.

Among the English in the Thirteen Colonies, miscegenation involving the Indians was negligible (the relations of these races were normally too hostile to permit such racial fusion), and the late arrival of the bulk of Negro slaves in the eighteenth century delayed the appearance of any considerable group of mulattoes until colonial times were well advanced. The gulf between the whites and the more savage Indians of North America led to much misunderstanding and prejudice: the English, especially, had very little understanding of Indian ideas in any field; indeed to them the redman's concept of property rights, land ownership, nature worship, religious symbolism, and ritual, and his passive acceptance of fate, were all beyond comprehension.

There was definitely a greater conscious effort in the Hispanic lands to harmonize divergent racial elements into a new social structure than in either the English or French areas. Especially was the Spanish government early aware of the serious social implications of the presence of the Indians, and it made zealous efforts to cope with the problems involved. It began by regarding the Indians as a conquered, subject people from whom tribute was due, apparently never dreaming of treating them, as the French and English later did, like independent nations with whom military alliances could be made and treaties concluded. Numbers in the Spanish area alone probably made the latter attitude impracticable; the sedentary nature of many of the Indians, their comparative mildness, their developed skills, the presence of gold, and the need for their services, all suggested a different procedure. In general, as far as economic pressure allowed, the plan adopted was to leave the Indians in their native communities, ruled by their own caciques under the supervision of royal officials. In meeting the problem of labor the government early attempted to solve the complex situation through the compromise institution of the encomienda, definitely rejecting outright slavery for the American natives. Despite violent opposition from the conquistadores and encomenderos, who felt that as they had largely financed their own expeditions they were entitled to the rewards, the crown gradually won the contest. As early as the middle of the sixteenth century the encomienda as a labor system had legally, though by no means in practice, ceased to exist, and gradually other phases of the institution were modified. In the law courts, the natives stood in the position of wards or minors, and the Inquisition was permitted no jurisdiction over them. In the field of religion, the Spanish sovereigns took more seriously than either the French or the English their obligation to Christianize and civilize the natives under their rule; they were influenced in this policy not only by religious considerations but also by their determination to make the Indians a permanent and acceptable element in Spanish colonial society. In the various phases of this grand scheme, the Church was the crown's chief agent, providing curas for the native towns and missionaries for the missions and visitas with duties that definitely included the training of the neophytes in the elements of Spanish civilization, as well as in Christian doctrine.

The Portuguese also found themselves faced by a native problem of great complexity. If anything, the Brazilian colonists showed themselves more determined than the Spaniards to put the natives to work, despite the fact that the more primitive level of the Brazilian natives made labor on the plantations, and later in the mines, more irksome and deadly than it proved in Spanish territories. The Portuguese kings showed no such sense of social and religious obligation in relation to the Indians as did the Spanish sovereigns; not until the numbers of the native population failed did the Negro definitely replace the Brazilian Indian as the source of slave labor.

In North America, the native was important to both the French and English as the chief supplier of fur; but on the whole he represented a frontier problem and did not, as in Hispanic lands, live in close daily contact with the whites. Both French and English supplied him with arms and liquor to induce him to work hard for them. French missionaries made serious efforts at evangelization, but they had little success when compared to their Spanish brethren. For one thing, the crown gave less consistent support to the missionary effort; for another, while the French coureur de bois and trader were congenial figures, the natives came to fear that the missionaries were but the forerunners of the French farmers, whose coming they recognized as a threat to their way of life.

Among the English, some of the more conscientious felt impelled to try to Christianize the Indians and save them from the devil in whose possession they were held to be. These pious folk supported a few missionaries in the frontier settlements; but the Protestant emphasis on ability to read the Bible and the lack of any organized missionary force such as the religious orders provided among Latin peoples made failure almost inevitable. Furthermore, the hunting economy of the Indians and the agriculture of the advancing English farmer rendered all attempts to bridge the gap between the two peoples practically hopeless from the start. Most of the English colonists considered the Indians simply brutal savages, incapable of receiving civilization or Christianity. In the case of the Negroes, the more intimate association of master and slave not only brought more racial fusion but also induced a stronger sense of responsibility to Christanize and instruct, at least to the point of teaching the English language. In their turn, the Negroes had a more considerable influence on the whites than had the Indians; they not only strongly affected the speech of wide areas, but their slave status gave emphasis to the idea of social caste and lowered the general concept of the dignity of manual labor.

Organized religion was in a different position in the four colonial societies. In the English colonies, the predominant spirit was definitely Protestant from the start; tolerance varied in degree and kind from colony to colony. Among the three Latin peoples, the Roman Catholic Church, even apart from Indian and Negro mission work, played a pre-eminent role. Its relationship to the state reflected the situation in the respective motherlands; in New France, the Church pretended to, and on the whole realized, equality and independence; in both Spanish and Portuguese possessions on the other hand, the Church, especially in relation to patronage and salaries, was definitely under control of the state. There were, however, great differences in the Church's standing in Portuguese and in Spanish America. In Brazil, partly because clerical salaries were early fixed at a low figure, the Church did not attract as many men of outstanding ability and never became as immensely wealthy and powerful as in Spanish America; nor was its work as intimately associated with secular government and policy. The original obligation to furnish religious instruction was taken more seriously by the Spanish sovereigns, and this in itself necessarily implied a closer working partnership; furthermore, in Spanish America greater emphasis was placed on orthodoxy, with the result that independent tribunals of the Inquisition were introduced into Spanish America; they were never permitted in Brazil, though agents from the Holy Office in Portugal were occasionally allowed to officiate in the colony.

By the close of the colonial age the population pattern of the Americas had been set and the cultural trends established. The French, Spanish, and Portuguese colonies, for upwards of a century, had received little more than a thin trickle of European immigration. The French settlements along the

The Americas in 1749. A contemporary map by "les Srs. Sanson, Geog. ordin. du Roi," engraved by Delaye. From the Sigmund Samuel Collection. (Courtesy of the Royal Ontario Museum of Archaeology)

St. Lawrence had remained practically static since the close of the seventeenth century, except for the natural increase from the original colonists. Only Louisiana received appreciable accretions from Europe. The Iberian colonies had evolved in the direction of new racial amalgams, formed from a comparatively small white element crossed with a wide variety of Indian stocks, varied here and there, especially in Brazil, by an increasing tincture of Negro blood. In the English colonies, there was a striking difference; so far from immigration's having ceased with the close of the first colonial century, the stream of new settlers had swollen to the proportions of a flood; not only had the original English stock received large additions from the British Isles, but considerable contingents from other northern European peoples had poured in, diluting the original English population; as yet, however, such foreigners remained in more or less isolated pockets, and left political and social dominance with the descendants of the original Anglo-Saxons.

The gulf separating all Americans from their respective European homelands had steadily widened, though in different respects in the four sets of colonies. In the French possessions the separation consisted of a time lag; the colonists, having changed little from the days of Louis XIV and Frontenac, had failed to keep pace with political and intellectual progress in old France. In the Spanish and Portuguese colonies, the change had come predominantly in racial composition. In the Thirteen Colonies, the gulf consisted in the psychological separation from homeland conceptions caused by a developing maturity of political and economic ideas, their elements inherited indeed from their English past but radically modified in practice through colonial outlook and experience.

The over-all picture of the Americas presented a composition of three major masses in interesting relations and contrasts. South of the Rio Grande the Hispanic peoples were evolving a new American physical type, combining southern European, African, and Indian elements; culturally, they exhibited an amalgam of intellectual, artistic, religious, and emotional qualities inherited from the Iberian Peninsula in combination with the highest achievements of Indian America; politically they suffered from a delayed development which would eventualy result in a long period of constitutional instability. North of the Rio Grande, and to the north and west of the English and Spanish groups, were the French colonies. Here the absolutism of the old regime and a modified feudalism dominated the internal economy while, externally, policies of aggrandizement at the expense of the neighboring English and Spanish empires were so persistent as to constitute the most disturbing feature of the whole North American scene. In the Thirteen Colonies, northern European groups were maintaining almost complete racial purity and were constantly receiving reinforcements from their European sources. The dominant element, the Anglo-Saxon, was self-reliant, enterprising, and politically experienced —and preparing itself to offer a democratic leadership to the whole continent.

PART IV

SECESSION OF AMERICA FROM THE OLD WORLD

Chapter 15

THE FALL OF NEW FRANCE

The separation of the French colonial empire in America from the motherland was not the result of a revolutionary movement within the colonies, but came in the wake of military defeat in a series of four wars between France and England in the eighteenth century. This conflict opened in 1688, when "the bloodless revolution" in England replaced Catholic James II by Protestant William III, who, as Stadtholder of Holland, had been the most persistent opponent of Louis XIV's policy of European expansion and supremacy. As all three powers had vital and conflicting overseas interests, wars involving them naturally became world wars. The core of this hostility was Anglo-French rivalry, and through the century-long contest it remained true that, whatever might be the European origin or complications of the dispute, before the fighting had continued long the struggle would resolve itself fundamentally into a duel between England and France for control of North America.[1] The Dutch, having suffered ruinously since the middle of the seventeenth century from the deliberately hostile policy of the French in Europe, the West Indies, and on the seas, were prepared to throw their weight on the English side in the culminating struggle.[2] Each phase of the giant conflict was a double war, bearing one name as a European conflict, and another in its American character.

The scales seemed fairly evenly balanced. Colbert, at his death in 1682, had left France in a commanding position in America: holding possession of a varied colonial empire that comprised a vast and rich fur kingdom in Canada, a fertile agricultural colony in Louisiana—both with unlimited horizons to the west—and, in the Caribbean, a number of choice plantation islands strategically placed for contraband trade with the Spanish American dominions. Based on the two greatest water systems of the continent, the St. Lawrence and the Mississippi, the two mainland holdings obviously possessed great strategic strength, which a unified command operating from Quebec could fully exploit to the disadvantage of an English rival whose territory was divided into a dozen political units hav-

---

[1] The fundamental thesis that Anglo-French colonial rivalry provides the one satisfactory basis of unity in eighteenth-century history was first advanced by J. R. Seeley in his work *The Expansion of England: Two Courses of Lectures* (New York: 1891), Lecture II.

[2] A. P. Newton, *The European Nations in the West Indies, 1493-1688* (London: 1933), especially pages 293-94, 300-307, 337-38, 347.

ing conflicting ambitions and programs. A powerful French navy, counting at least one hundred and twenty warships and manned by some seventy thousand trained sailors, promised quick and adequate sea support.[3] A third advantage was France, itself, which possessed a population three times that of England and correspondingly larger revenues.

From other angles, however, the prospect of success for France, in a prolonged struggle, was not so certain; indeed, the dice seemed loaded against the French. Colonial population figures were unpropitious: the English colonies possessed over two hundred thousand inhabitants compared with the little more than ten thousand in the French territories.[4] Furthermore, the character of the English settlements gave promise of greater staying power. A population of farmers and middle-class mechanics, voluntary immigrants fleeing unsatisfactory political and religious conditions at home, gave both a stability and a dynamic quality to the Thirteen Colonies which, combined with a large measure of self-government, had produced an extraordinary measure of self-reliance and individual initiative. The French colonies on the other hand, while possessing some frontier elements of driving force, suffered in the older settlements from debilitating paternalism and graft in government, from feudalism in social life, and monopoly and strict control in commerce and industry and, above all, from a crying need for permanent colonists.

The greatest handicap of the French empire in the colonial race, however, was the king's absorption in European issues; if he could win decisively in Europe he was confident he could at the peace conference arrange the colonial map to suit himself. To England and Holland, however, the issues seemed sufficiently in doubt to justify them in uniting with other powers to check the ambitions of Louis XIV. Since 1688 the English and Dutch had been firmly allied under a single leadership, and so were able to swing the heavy club of the combined sea power of their two strong navies. The first phase of the conflict was the War of the League of Augsburg, or as known in America, King William's War (1689-1697).

Rivalry between England and France had long been gathering momentum and, with war declared, it broke out at all points.[5] These elements of conflict were not only territorial but also commercial, diplomatic, and religious in nature. In North America, boundary and area disputes were inevitable. The Mississippi boundary became the greatest issue. Colonial English charters read "from sea to sea," while the French were determined

---

[3] J. Stern, *The French Colonies* (New York: 1944), p. 49.

[4] These figures are given for the year 1683 by L. B. Packard in *The Commercial Revolution, 1400-1776* (New York: 1927), p. 66. For the year 1714, H. I. Priestley estimates the English colonists as numbering 250,000 to Canada's 20,000, in *France Overseas Through the Old Regime* (New York: 1939), p. 155.

[5] *Cf.* A. H. Buffinton, *The Second Hundred Years' War, 1689-1815* (New York: 1929), pp. 7-11.

to connect, by means of a line of forts along the Ohio, their holdings bordering the St. Lawrence and Great Lakes with their possessions along the Mississippi, thus confining the English to a region between the Alleghenies and the sea. With the acquisition from the Dutch in 1664 of New Netherlands [6] stretching northward along the Hudson River to Albany, the English had begun to move westward, and to compete with the French for the Indian fur trade in that region. By 1680, the French, English, and Spaniards had reached the territory around the mouth of the Mississippi while, farther north, the English had worked their way in considerable numbers into the Ohio valley. The future would obviously rest with those who should most quickly and permanently settle this great river region.[7] Another zone of conflict followed the Quebec-New England border, where frequent Indian raids inflamed national hatreds and aroused in the English the desire to conquer Canada, and in the French the wish to drive the English into the sea. A third contact region, causing perennial difficulty, was that of New England and Acadia; here the New Englanders felt "overlooked" by the French settlements in Nova Scotia which jeopardized their sea routes to England and menaced their fishing interests, while their Protestant principles were outraged by such near papist footholds. The seventeenth century had seen a number of English attacks on Acadia and periods of English occupation, all of which whetted the New Englander's appetite to a hope of permanent possession. The Hudson Bay region was a fourth area in dispute and the scene of numerous conflicts after the establishment of the Hudson's Bay Company in 1670. A fifth storm center was the West Indies in which, after the ruin of the Dutch in the 1670's, there developed increasing antagonism.

In the commercial field, both France and England were mercantilist nations tending to regard trade at all times as a kind of war in which one nation's gain was necessarily another's loss. By the close of the seventeenth century, like Spain, both were restricting colonial trade as closely as possible to the markets of the homeland; both were using the monopolistic

---

[6] For an account of the New Netherlands—the region from the Connecticut River to the Delaware and northward to and including Albany—and reasons for the easy English conquest, see C. M. Andrews, *The Colonial Period in American History* (New Haven, 1937), Vol. III, chaps. ii and iii.

[7] For an illuminating discussion of the steady penetration of the British into this area, see A. T. Volwiler, *George Croghan and the Westward Movement, 1741-1782* (Cleveland, 1926), pp. 20-21. The author points out that "during the generation preceding 1754 the most dynamic and significant phase of Anglo-French rivalry in the Indian trade was in the central and upper Ohio valley and in the region south of Lake Erie." The French, he says, moved eastward into this region from their earlier main line of communication from the Great Lakes to the Mississippi that until then had been along the Fox-Wisconsin route. By 1731 they had a number of forts on the Wabash and the Maumee rivers. By 1750 English traders were numerous in this region and the French realized that if they were not to be cut off from Canada they must somehow secure sole control of the Ohio country.

commercial company; both were rivals for the native Indian trade, though this traffic meant infinitely more to the French, as it was their chief means of financing New France. The English, however, had the advantage of cheaper manufactured goods for general trade and, as the principal bribe in the Indian fur traffic, a plentiful supply of rum, much cheaper than the French brandy; on the other hand, the French were willing to travel into Indian territory to make their sales and were personally more congenial to the red man. From the military and diplomatic point of view, the support of the Indians was of crucial importance to both nations, for neither France nor England kept large standing armies in America. The Iroquois were at this time busy constructing an empire around the Great Lakes, depending like the French on the profits of the fur trade.[8] As this consolidating movement cut across the French line of expansion westward from Montreal, these Indians became the natural allies of the English. The French meanwhile held the allegiance of most of the other Indian tribes, who felt less threatened economically by French fur-trading activities than by the advancing agricultural frontier of the English colonists.

King William's War continued from 1689 to 1697. In Europe it consolidated William's position in England, crushing the last Stuart hope of regaining the English throne. In America it was marked by features that became characteristic of all eighteenth-century wars. From the St. Lawrence, guerrilla bands of French and Indians drove deep into English territory and struck terrible blows at Schenectady in New York, Dover in New Hampshire, Fort Loyal in Maine, and other outlying English settlements, burning buildings and slaughtering inhabitants, and earning the undying hatred of all the colonists who, in retaliation, encouraged the Iroquois to fall on the French. More ambitious reprisals were an expedition of New Englanders under a Massachusetts merchant, Sir William Phips, which captured and plundered Port Royal (Annapolis) in Acadia, May 11, 1690, and a later expedition of twelve hundred men which Phips led up the St. Lawrence to Quebec. This force arrived late in the year and found the great citadel too heavily fortified and garrisoned to be captured; after a week's bombardment, Phips had to withdraw in failure.

The Peace of Ryswick in 1697 interrupted hostilities. Its conclusion was a success for Louis XIV, who was anxious to give France a breathing time, break up the alliance of his enemies, and give his full attention to French interests in Spain, where it was evident that Charles II, the last of the Hapsburg dynasty, was nearing his end. The terms of this colorless treaty practically ignored the situation in America and settled nothing: no

---

[8] A. L. Burt, *A Short History of Canada for Americans* (Minneapolis: 1942), p. 37.

frontiers were defined nor were rivalries eased.[9] The *status quo ante bellum* was re-established; to the disgust of the New Englanders, Acadia was given back to the French, who were also allowed to remain in Newfoundland and share its fisheries; while in Hudson Bay, where the leadership of Pierre le Moyne, Sieur d'Iberville, had won a number of local victories, the Hudson's Bay Company found small comfort in retaining a mere token possession in the field of their vast monopoly; Fort Albany alone was restored to them by the peace. On the whole, the French position in America was strengthened at the close of this period of conflict. No territory or other advantage had been lost to the English; and, in relation to the Indians, Frontenac for the second time had sharply chastised the Iroquois, so severely this time that they never wholly recovered. Shortly after the peace d'Iberville effectively occupied Louisiana.

The second phase of conflict—in Europe, the War of the Spanish Succession, in America, Queen Anne's war (1702-1713)—opened like its predecessor on the European continent. This time, Louis XIV was faced by a Grand Alliance of England, Holland, the Emperor, and other princes. This combination had formed when the *Grand Monarque* had followed a spectacular acknowledgment of his grandson, Philip of Anjou, as King of Spain (by which he signified his embarkation on a program of uniting the French and Spanish realms), by the further steps of acknowledging, as he had promised at Ryswick not to do, the son of James II as lawful sovereign of England, and by an overt act of war against the Dutch.

General war quickly followed. While the commanding English general, the Duke of Marlborough, and the emperor's generalissimo, Prince Eugene of Savoy, were winning brilliant victories against French armies in Europe, Queen Anne's War was being fought out in America. Again, barbaric raids of French and Indians swept English frontier settlements. This time New England rather than New York suffered: Deerfield, Wells, Saco, and Haverhill were almost wiped out. Near the war's end, the Iroquois definitely became English allies, but their power was not what it had been and they played no prominent part in this second war. Again, after two unsuccessful attempts, a New England expedition captured Port Royal (1710) and renamed it Annapolis.[10] Once more an attempt was made on Quebec, this time by an English squadron of some seventy ships sailing from Boston with twelve thousand men. It did not, however, even reach the fortress, meeting disaster in the fog on the rocks near Anticosti

---

[9] This was of course not true outside America. In Europe France lost all the advantages gained by Louis XIV in the preceding two decades. For a discussion of the exhausting effect of The War of the League of Augsburg on French resources and vital energies, see A. T. Mahan, *The Influence of Sea Power upon History, 1660-1783* (12th ed., Boston: 1896), pp. 197-200.

[10] A. G. Doughty gives a description of this event in *The Acadian Exiles: a Chronicle of the 'Land of Evangeline'* (Toronto: 1916), pp. 20-23.

Island, with the loss of a thousand men.[11] Desultory fighting also occurred in Hudson Bay and at Newfoundland. But the decisive blows, those that forced Louis XIV to sue for peace, were struck in Europe.

The Treaty of Utrecht (1713) profoundly changed the political geography of America. France was forced to give up her claims on Newfoundland, Hudson Bay, and Acadia (rechristened Nova Scotia), except for the islands of St. Jean (Prince Edward Island) and Cape Breton. The treaty marked the beginning of the withdrawal of France from North America and greatly strengthened England's commercial position,[12] giving her a favored-nation status in France and Spain and transferring to her the trade concession in the Spanish American territories known as "the *Asiento*." [13] When this treaty was signed in 1713, neither side thought the struggle over; but general peace endured for a generation, though in this interval feverish military and diplomatic preparations went on in the certainty of an eventual renewal of open fighting.

In America, the French used the interval for fort building. On Cape Breton Island, Fort Louisburg, designed by the finest French engineers, was erected [14] as a better Port Royal to be "a watch dog" over the Gulf of St. Lawrence and "an official observer" of activities in New England.[15] Farther west a series of new forts were built, or old ones strengthened; at Chambly on the Richelieu, a new fort blocked the route from Lake Champlain to Montreal; farther south, the French erected a second fort at Crown Point; Fort Niagara arose, though it was soon matched by the English Fort Oswego; and Fort Detroit guarded the strait between the upper and lower lakes. By 1750, no less than sixty French forts had been erected between Montreal and New Orleans, marking the rapid development of schemes of expansion and settlement consolidating French sovereignty in this Mississippi-Louisiana area and fomenting envy and alarm in the British Thirteen Colonies.[16] To the northwest the French took steps to cut off the fur trade from the Hudson Bay area by going into the region west of Lake Superior around Lake Winnipeg and the Saskatche-

---

[11] G. M. Wrong, *Rise and Fall of New France,* 2 Vols. (New York: 1928), Vol. II., pp. 574-79.

[12] The fostering care with which England associated an expanding commerce with a strong navy—an outstanding feature of the Treaty of Utrecht—is considered by Admiral Mahan (*op. cit.,* pp. 225-31) as a primary factor in England's rise to the position of the first sea power after the War of the Spanish Succession.

[13] An authoritative treatment of this aspect of the Treaty of Utrecht is A. S. Aiton, "The Asiento Treaty as Reflected in the Papers of Lord Shelburne" in *Hispanic American Historical Review,* Vol. VIII, No. 2, May, 1928, pp. 167-177.

[14] Fort Louisburg, commenced in 1720 and completed in 1744, enclosed an area of one hundred acres and possessed walls two and a half miles in circumference.

[15] Despite their disapproval of this French fortress, the New England traders carried on with its builders, and later with its garrison, a considerable smuggling trade. See W. Wood, *The Great Fortress: A Chronicle of Louisburg, 1720-1760* (Toronto: 1915), pp. 7-8.

[16] On the forts in this region see Priestley, *op. cit.,* pp. 243-44.

wan River, thus tapping the peltry traffic at its source. This program was
to a remarkable extent successful in confining the English within a great
French crescent extending from Hudson Bay to the Gulf of Mexico.

England went to war with France for the third time in 1744 in the War
of the Austrian Succession. In the European phase of this conflict, England
fought for Maria Theresa of Austria against France and Prussia and other
states. In America, this conflict was reflected in King George's War (1744-
1748). Its only remarkable incident was the capture by New England
militia of the fortress of Louisburg in June, 1745. Inspired by a kind of
Puritan crusading zeal against a place which they regarded as a papal
stronghold, "a Catholic center of the devil in the New World," a motley
force of some four thousand poorly equipped men, mostly from Massachusetts, in forty-eight days reduced, with the help of a blockading British
squadron [17] and great good luck, the famous new "American Gibraltar." [18]
An English observer of the "eccentric siege," watching the colonials and
their unorthodox but effective tactics, remarked that "given pick and
shovel they would dig their way to hell and capture that fortress." Having
entered the stronghold, to their credit they allowed the French garrison
to retire with military honors; the zealous Puritans with their axes then
chopped away altars and images.[19] When this "darling conquest of the
people" was given back to the French at the peace of Aix-la-Chapelle in
exchange for Madras, New England suffered a stunning disappointment
which it never wholly forgave or forgot.

Again, a general war had been indecisive, and the treaty concluding
it proved only a truce. The ensuing short-lived peace was broken first in
America, not, as formerly, in Europe; and this time the fighting would
settle permanently the outstanding issues. In the interval between the wars
a fever of fortress building again possessed the French. The westward
drive of the English through the Alleghenies must, they felt, be blocked
at all costs; the line between Canada and Louisiana must be made strong
enough to hold, or Louisiana would be surrounded. They rushed up a
line of new forts in western Pennsylvania, the most important being Fort
Duquesne (now Pittsburgh) at the forks of the Ohio. Here there had been
an English fortification, erected by the Ohio Land Company to protect a
projected English settlement in the Ohio valley. When young George
Washington, dispatched by the governor of Virginia with a small force
of militia, arrived to warn off the French and to reinforce the English, he
found that he was too late; the French were in effective control and the

---

[17] A fleet of ten vessels carrying four hundred guns under Commodore Warren. The siege
began on April 30, 1745, and the capitulation came on June 16, 1745.

[18] For a description see G. M. Wrong, *Conquest of New France* (New Haven: 1918), pp.
80-94. Also, Wood, *op. cit.,* chap. ii.

[19] G. M. Wrong, *op. cit.,* p. 86.

recently constructed English Fort Necessity had to be surrendered in July, 1754.[20] These events decisively launched the contest for possession of the Ohio valley and became the immediate cause of the French and Indian War (1754-1763), which in its world setting was the American phase of the Seven Years' War (1756-1763), a struggle that was not to close until France had been eliminated as an American power.

The year 1755 was marked by three important events. The first was the defeat in the early summer of an army under General Braddock. The British government had been alarmed at the rise of Fort Duquesne and sent a respectable force of regulars and colonial militia to demolish the fort. Unfamilar with frontier fighting and disdaining the precautions urged by colonial leaders, the British general was trapped in an ambush by the French and Indians as he approached the fort, fell mortally wounded himself, and his army, suffering heavy losses, scattered in panic. Farther north, on Lake George, a band of British colonists seized the French fort at Crown Point and built Fort William Henry, forcing the French to retire to Ticonderoga where they proceeded to construct a new fort. In the east occurred the deportation of the Acadians. This tragic event was closely associated with the return in 1748 of Fort Louisburg to the French, who had promptly rebuilt the stronghold and made it again the center of French influence for the maritime area. Its strength had recently been reinforced by the erection of Fort Beauséjour on the Isthmus of Chignecto, near where Sackville now stands. Both forts represented French hope of regaining Acadia, whose inhabitants were encouraged by French priests and other agents to refuse an oath of allegiance to the British government to whom Acadia had been assigned by treaty in 1713.[21] To offset the menace of Louisburg, Halifax had been founded as a British naval base in 1749. Now, in 1755, with a decisive war pending, it was felt by Governor Lawrence and his council, half of whom were New Englanders, that the Acadians represented too grave a menace to tolerate. Advantage was taken of the presence of a large force of New England militia, which had come north to capture Beauséjour, to deal drastically with the Acadian problem. The British government was not consulted. The Acadians, both at Beauséjour and at Grand Pré on Minas Basin, were given a last chance to swear allegiance; those who refused, some six thousand, were placed in ships, and scattered among the English colonies along the Atlantic coast from

---

[20] For an account of Washington's skirmish with a French detachment at Great Meadow and the later surrender of Fort Necessity see Wrong, *Rise and Fall of New France*, Vol. II, pp. 752-55.

[21] On the matter of the oath of allegiance, see Doughty, *op. cit.*, chaps. iii, vi, viii, ix; also J. B. Brebner, *New England's Outpost: Acadia Before the Conquest of Canada* (New York: 1927), chap. viii.

Maine to Georgia.[22] About one third went to South Carolina; some found their way to Louisiana and there joined their compatriots; some in later years managed to return to their old homes in Nova Scotia. They represent an unfortunate group caught in an international crisis between two contending giants.

Until 1758, two years after Britain entered the Seven Years' War, the French held the upper hand, despite the fact that the English population in America numbered more than double that of the French. The early English military failures were due in part to the fact that the French government early dispatched large regular French armies to the American scene, partly to the unified French command in contrast to the dispersed and often incompetent English direction, and partly to the brilliant leadership of General Montcalm.[23] This distinguished French officer, the descendant of a long line of able French commanders, arrived in Quebec early in 1756 with the commission to defend and hold New France. Two of his early successes were the capture of Fort Oswego in August, 1756, and Fort William Henry in the following year. Early in 1758 a British attack on Fort Ticonderoga failed; but later in the year, with a change in British leadership, the tide turned.

William Pitt the Elder (later Lord Chatham) was now a member of the British cabinet where he quickly brought about a profound change of policy in the conduct of the war. Henceforth, the great organizer decided, England would concentrate on the colonial and maritime aspects of the struggle and leave her ally, Frederick of Prussia, to conduct the European part of the struggle, with English assistance limited to money subsidies. As part of this major plan, Pitt dispatched strong forces of regular troops to the American colonies under the command of young and capable military leaders. Sir Jeffrey (later Lord) Amherst, a man of forty, was made commander-in-chief Sept. 1758; James Wolfe, the second in command, was only thirty. The latter was a tall, slight man with wretched health but possessed of a dauntless spirit and real military genius.[24] Victories soon began to fall to the English. In the west, Fort Duquesne was captured in 1758 and renamed Fort Pitt; Fort Frontenac, strategically placed on Lake Ontario, fell in the same year. In August 1759 Forts Niagara and Ticonderoga were taken within a day of each other. All were among the vital links in the chain binding to Quebec distant Louisiana and the French western posts. In the east, a regular siege by overwhelming military and

---

[22] Doughty, *op. cit.*, p. 137. Priestley, *op. cit.*, p. 246, gives the total number of those expelled as 10,000. On the wider aspects of the expulsion of the Acadians, see Wrong, *Conquest of New France*, chap. vii.

[23] Louis Joseph, Marquis de Montcalm, was of the ancient nobility of Languedoc.

[24] On Wolfe's earlier career and his family relationships see W. Wood, *The Winning of Canada: A Chronicle of Wolfe* (Toronto: 1915), chaps. i and ii; also F. E. Whitton, *Wolfe and North America* (Boston, 1929), chaps. ii, iv.

naval forces armed with powerful artillery brought the surrender after 52 days of Louisburg on July 26, 1758.[25] Two years later this mighty fortress—which had been "a pistol pointed at Britain's head"—was ordered razed and became the picturesque ruin that it remains today, leaving Halifax to reign without a rival as the fortress city of the Maritimes.

In the summer of 1759 came the turn of Quebec, strongest fortress in the New World. Under the command of Admiral Charles Saunders, a fleet of twenty-two ships of the line with accompanying five frigates, eighteen sloops, and a fleet of transports and store ships carrying an army of 8,535 regular troops under General Wolfe sailed from Louisburg June 6.[26] To the amazement of the French, this armada succeeded in making its way without disaster up the difficult river channel of the St. Lawrence; it came to anchor (June 26) before Quebec, the most impressively strong fortress in America, situated on a high rocky cliff overlooking a narrow stretch of the river.[27] For a time Wolfe bombarded Quebec from Levis, on the opposite shore, but it was clear that only a land operation could effect the capture of the stronghold. How to reach the heights was the problem. At first it was planned to attack from the east, but operations from Montmorency were unsuccessful and for weeks Montcalm could not be enticed from his fortress.[28] Meanwhile, disease and sickness were weakening the English forces and autumn with its threat of river ice was approaching. After an attack on Beaufort, on the river below the fortress, had been repulsed, Wolfe learned that this attempted landing had so alarmed Governor Vaudreuil, who was always at odds with General Montcalm, that he had transferred troops from the west to guard the Beaufort marshes.

The British general took immediate advantage of this action to attempt a daring plan. There was an ill-guarded winding path, formerly used by the French as a supply route, that led up to the Plains of Abraham from a little cove, Anse de Foulon, some distance upstream from the fortress. Here in the darkness of the early hours of September 12-13, with fine

---

[25] A British fleet of 150 vessels under Admiral Boscawen cut off the fort from the sea for two months. Sir Jeffrey Amherst was in charge of the attack on the fortress. One of his three brigadiers was James Wolfe; 12,000 troops were engaged including 500 colonials. The French strength was 3,800 men in the fort, supported by five ships of the line and seven frigates manned by 3,000 men.

[26] These figures are from Whitton, *Wolfe and North America* (Boston, 1929), p. 246; Wrong, *op. cit.*, Vol. II, p. 821 places the total number of ships at 250 and says that there were twice as many sailors and marines in the fleet as in Wolfe's regular troops.

[27] Whitton, *op. cit.*, pp. 253-4 estimates that Montcalm at the time of Wolfe's arrival had 10,000 troops, exclusive of the 1,500 effectives comprising the garrison of Quebec, but points out that there is "an astounding discrepancy" concerning numbers among the authorities consulted—"some giving the number as twelve, fourteen or even sixteen thousand, of all ranks."

[28] General Wolfe wrote to his mother August 31, 1755: "The Marquis of Montcalm is at the head of a great number of bad soldiers, and I am at the head of a small number of good ones, that wish for nothing so much as to fight him, but the wary old fellow avoids action, doubtful of the behaviour of his army," quoted in F. E. Whitton, *op. cit.*, p. 268.

cooperation between navy and army, Wolfe landed his men from small boats, overpowered the few guards, and by dawn had 5,000 men in orderly array on the heights above, a mile west of the city. In the Battle of the Plains of Abraham that followed, the opposing forces were of approximately equal numbers; but the better discipline of the British regulars, the element of surprise, and the lack of cooperation Montcalm received from the various French civil officials quickly decided the issue. Unfortunately this decisive battle for the control of the New World cost the lives of the two commanding generals. Wolfe, thrice wounded, fell on the field of battle, but learned before he expired that victory was his; Montcalm was carried mortally wounded into Quebec, to die with the bitter knowledge of defeat.[29]

The fortress surrendered three days later. All hope of reinforcement from home was lost when a great French armada, preparing to sail for Canada, was destroyed in Quiberon Bay in October, 1759, by the British Admiral Hawke. In 1760 three British armies—one from Quebec, one from Lake Ontario, and one from Lake Champlain and the Richelieu River—closed in on Montreal. Facing hopeless odds, the French governor signed articles of capitulation (September 8, 1760), surrendering all New France without offering resistance. The American phase of the Seven Years' War was over; but, as fighting continued elsewhere, it was not until 1763 that a general peace was signed.

In other parts of the world, French disasters paralleled those suffered in New France. India saw the triumphant campaigns of the English Robert Clive against the French Governor Dupleix; and in Europe, the military genius of King Frederick the Great of Prussia won a series of brilliant victories against France and her ally Austria. These and other reverses induced Louis XV to call for assistance from his cousin, Charles III of Spain. The latter, who had declared that the news of the fall of Quebec "made his blood run cold" and who feared that in the future Spain would be left to face alone the rising might of the English world, signed in 1761 a close defensive alliance (the Family Compact) with the other Bourbon states—France and the two Sicilies—and the following year entered the struggle. But this counsel of despair proved worse than useless; the English speedily captured Habana (August, 1762), the center of Spanish naval strength in the Caribbean, and two months later, Manila in the Pacific. In the peace negotiations, these losses made it possible for the British to exact, as the price for the return of Cuba and the Philippines, the cession of Spanish Florida, as well as other concessions.

By the terms of the Treaty of Paris, France formally ceded to England

---

[29] A description of the Battle of the Plains of Abraham is given in W. Wood, *The Passing of New France* (Toronto: 1915), pp. 97-142.

her territorial rights in Canada and the Maritime Provinces, those in the
valley of the Ohio, and all her claims from the Mississippi eastward except
the city of New Orleans and, off the coast of Newfoundland, the two small

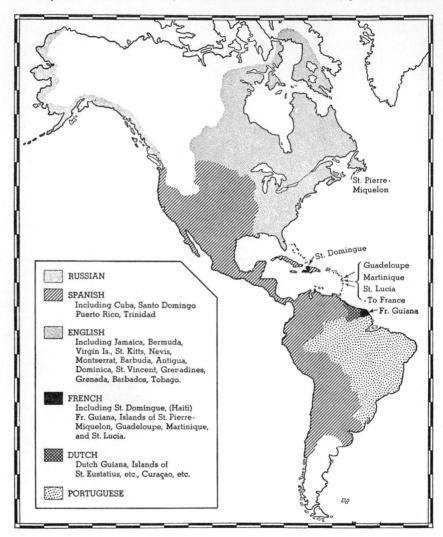

RUSSIAN

SPANISH
Including Cuba, Santo Domingo
Puerto Rico, Trinidad

ENGLISH
Including Jamaica, Bermuda,
Virgin Is., St. Kitts, Nevis,
Montserrat, Barbuda, Antigua,
Dominica, St. Vincent, Grenadines,
Grenada, Barbados, Tobago.

FRENCH
Including St. Domingue, (Haiti)
Fr. Guiana, Islands of St. Pierre-
Miquelon, Guadeloupe, Martinique,
and St. Lucia.

DUTCH
Dutch Guiana, Islands of
St. Eustatius, etc., Curaçao, etc.

PORTUGUESE

St. Pierre-
Miquelon

St. Domingue

Guadeloupe
Martinique
St. Lucia
-To France
Fr. Guiana

18. THE NEW WORLD IN 1763

fishing stations of St. Pierre and Miquelon. To her Spanish ally, in compensation for insisting on bringing the war to a close while Spain was still
convinced that the military situation could be bettered, France ceded New
Orleans and all her holdings west of the Mississippi. Thus, in the long
contest with England, the French empire in America with all its vast

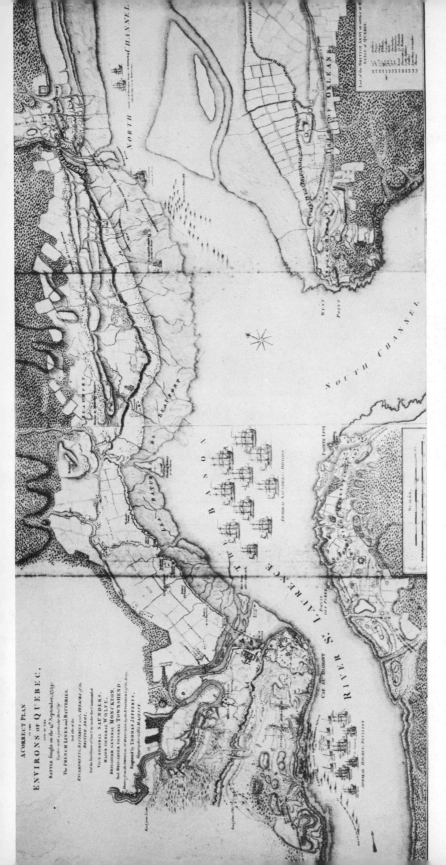

"A Correct Plan of the Environs of Quebec, and of the Battle fought on the 13th September, 1759." Engraved and printed by Thomas Jefferys, Geographer to his Majesty, London. From the Sigmund Samuel Collection. (Courtesy of the Royal Ontario Museum of Archaeology)

General James Wolfe. Mezzotint engraving by R. Houston after a sketch made at Quebec by Captain Hervey Smyth. From the Sigmund Samuel Collection. (Courtesy of the Royal Ontario Museum of Archaeology)

Death of General Wolfe at Quebec. Mezzotint engraving from the painting by Edward Penny, 1763. R. Sayer and J. Bennett, London, 1779. From the Sigmund Samuel Collection. (Courtesy of the Royal Ontario Museum of Archaeology) potentialities had been reduced almost to the vanishing point. France retained two tiny islands off Newfoundland, useful only to fishermen; she had in the West Indies, a few small islands, principally Guadeloupe and Martinique—the latter returned to her at the peace; and, on the South American mainland, she still held an unprofitable tract of tropical Guiana. Offered a choice of the cession of Guadeloupe or Canada, England hesitated for a while, but eventually chose the North American mainland possession.

From this pinnacle of colonial power, England could look back over two centuries of strenuous rivalry with other western European powers intent on expansion in the New World. On one after another, in the long drawn-out contest, she had inflicted a series of severe defeats: Spain in the sixteenth century, the Netherlands in the seventeenth, and France in the eighteenth. Of them all, France suffered most heavily. Spain and the Netherlands still held valuable colonial possessions, though they could no longer aim at the monopoly either of colonial dominion or of world trade; France had been forced out of practically all her overseas possessions—in the Orient as well as in the New World—and her world trade had been much reduced. England now practically shared the New World only with Spain and Portugal. On the sea no other nation could safely challenge her might.

England, however, turned from the victorious peace table to face serious colonial problems and responsibilities. In the field of administration, there was the problem of devising for French Canadians, now British subjects who had neither tradition nor experience in self-government, a workable form of government which would not be entirely out of line with forms and practices in the rest of British America. In the domain of religion arose the difficulty of how to induce two sets of colonists, long bitter enemies, but now under one allegiance, to live side by side in peace when one was rabidly Protestant and the other intolerantly Roman Catholic. Another major issue was presented by the acquisition of the western lands: should they be opened at once to the English colonists who considered that they had made their contribution to the late war largely in order to win access to them? They might well be enraged if these territories were closed; on the other hand, it was obvious that to open the land at once promised fierce and bitter Indian fighting through all western America. Another factor, always lurking in the background of English political thinking, was the knowledge that neither France nor Spain regarded the issues of the late war as closed, but were grimly determined to take the first opportunity to reopen the struggle. The scope of England's triumph had been great, the anxieties and burdens it imposed promised to be proportionately heavy.

Chapter 16

THE AMERICAN REVOLUTION

I. THE BACKGROUND

The loss by France of her American possessions, as a result of the Seven Years' War, marked the opening of an era of war and revolution lasting somewhat more than half a century in the course of which the remaining "old colonial empires"— those of the English, the Spaniards, and the Portuguese—disappeared from America. All these empires had been founded as a result of the discoveries of the sixteenth century, and represented a hundred and fifty to three hundred years of the most strenuous and dramatic efforts on the part of the most advanced nations of Europe. There was to be some difference in the completeness and finality of the changes. France's loss, despite a convulsive movement towards recovery in Napoleon's time, was eventually to prove final and, except for a foothold in the Guianas and some island fragments, was complete. The separation of Brazil from Portugal, though almost bloodless when it came, was also final; Spain's loss was complete on the mainland, but not in the Caribbean until after the Spanish American War a century later. In the case of England, the situation was somewhat different. When the revolutionary storm was over the Thirteen Colonies were gone; but England still held the Hudson Bay territories and her eighteenth-century conquests in Canada, as well as her West Indian possessions. These holdings in the Western Hemisphere, when combined with other eighteenth- and nineteenth-century conquests and discoveries in other parts of the world, were to form the basis of a second British empire even more extensive than the first. But at the close of the eighteenth century, England, like all the imperial powers staggering from recent losses, was thrown into depression, disillusioned with the idea of empire, and inclined to believe the French saying that "colonies were like fruits which when ripe drop from the parent stem"; it was to take more than three quarters of a century for more optimistic views toward overseas expansion to gain wide support and a new age of imperialism to open. Taken as a whole, the secession movements beginning in the eighteenth century were the first significant nationalistic reaction against modern imperialism; they were closely connected with each other, and it is to be observed that the first blow was struck at that mother country whose colonial policy, in actual practice, had been the most liberal and tolerant; her colonies were the first to be ripe for self-government.[1]

The crisis in the relations of England and her colonies followed close upon the termination of the Seven Years' War. In removing the French menace from the northern and western borders of the Thirteen Colonies and so putting a stop to the encouragement that had long been given from Quebec to Indian attacks, this war conferred immense benefits on the inhabitants of the Thirteen Colonies. At its close, in addition to relief from the daily terror of Indian raids, they suddenly found themselves in possession of a liberty of action in relation to the mother country that they had never known before; no longer was the protection of the British fleet and troops so absolutely necessary as it had always hitherto been.[2] Military and naval protection had been one of England's most vital contributions to the empire, in return for which she had exacted trading opportunities; with this protection no longer so urgently needed, the colonists immediately showed a disposition to restrict their contribution to the imperial bargain. Until this time, they had been generally satisfied with the imperial system as it had worked out in actual practice. Regulations from England, prior to 1763, had related usually to the colonies' external relations; though based on the mercantilist theories, they had conferred benefits as well as burdens; where they had pressed most heavily, they had been allowed to remain largely unenforced. In internal affairs, the colonists had enjoyed from the beginning a large measure of self-government—probably to a greater degree than was allowed to the people of the British Isles—certainly incomparably more than any other colonists of the world, and by the middle of the eighteenth century they had attained unexampled prosperity. However, by this time distance and the slowness of communication with England and the new overseas environment had had profound effects in modifying the outlook, ideals, and attainments of the colonists: the constant battle with frontier conditions had developed independence, self-reliance, and a patriotic loyalty to the new American home; long accustomed to running their own affairs politically and economically, they had come to regard self-government as a right, and wished nothing better than to be allowed to preserve the status quo.

It was England that felt the need of change. During the course of the life-and-death struggle with France in the Seven Years' War, as well as in the serious Indian uprising known as the Conspiracy of Pontiac that had followed the war and wiped out the settlements west of the Alleghenies, the

---

[1] C. H. Van Tyne, *The Causes of the War of Independence* (New York: 1922), chap. xviii, "The Freest of Peoples Were the First to Rebel."

[2] G. L. Beer, *British Colonial Policy, 1754-1765* (New York: 1907), p. 313, "In the annals of the British Empire during this decade, the most vital fact was the conquest and subsequent retention of Canada. It made the American Revolution inevitable."

precarious nature of the ties which bound the colonies to the motherland had been forcibly brought to the attention of English statesmen. It was clear to them that the English government possessed no effective control, political or economic, over the American continental colonies. It had been found impossible during the war to raise any considerable number of colonial troops to fulfil, even partly, the old tacit obligation that the colonies would make every effort to protect themselves on land while the mother country furnished the necessary naval strength. There had been much indifference to appeals for such help, as well as great unwillingness to cooperate with each other in common military action. It seemed evident that the colonies could not be trusted with their own self-defense in the future, let alone be relied upon for any effective assistance in keeping down the conquered French, or even the restive Indians so recently allies of the French.[3] Neither had the colonists been willing to give money; and, as far as trade was concerned, throughout the war they had carried on a traffic with the French enemy, and had sent their surplus food supplies to the French sugar-growing islands in the West Indies.[4] War profiteering in food prices had indeed gone to such lengths that it had been actually cheaper for the English army to send to England for food than to buy it from the American colonists.[5]

Clearly, it seemed to English statesmen in 1763, steps should be taken to tie the American colonies more securely into the imperial system. Furthermore, though the government had just brought to a close one of the most successful wars in England's long history—really the climax of nearly a century's rivalry with France—victory had left the responsible officials in London in a very serious frame of mind, with many problems of great magnitude on their hands. A national debt of unprecedented size, most of it incurred in the late war, made new taxes inevitable; [6] there was the necessity of maintaining a large army and navy with which to offset the bitter hostility of recently defeated enemies and the machinations of other powers, jealous and fearful of the great accumulation of strength in English hands; the newly won territories of Canada, the Mississippi Valley, and the Floridas on the American mainland, as well as the island acquisitions in the Caribbean, had to be reorganized; effective and equitable arrangements would have to be devised to control and satisfy the numerous and greatly alarmed Indian tribes menacing the western borders of all the settlements in order to furnish some security for the Thirteen Colonies; moreover, means had to be invented to finance the whole program. It would have been little short

---

[3] Beer, *op. cit.*, chap. i, "Theory and Practice of Imperial Defense," treats this general topic.

[4] For details consult Beer, *op. cit.*, chap. iv, "The Requisition System during the War," and chap. vi, "Colonial Trade with the Enemy."

[5] Beer, *op. cit.*, p. 103.

[6] *Ibid.*, pp. 271-73.

of miraculous if in the solution of these problems, of which so many touched American interests closely, the mother country had not aroused and alarmed her older group of American colonies.

The political reorganization that established the four new royal provinces of Quebec, West Florida, East Florida, and Grenada in the West Indies, and somewhat modified the boundaries of Newfoundland, Nova Scotia, and Georgia, aroused no particular colonial excitement. The effort to deal with the Indian problem struck closer home. A royal proclamation of 1763 forbade settlement west of a line drawn along the headwaters of the rivers that flow into the Atlantic, and set aside as an Indian reservation all the land west of this line and north of Florida. This territory was to be under the care of two royal superintendents by whom Indian relations were to be controlled and trade licensed, one functioning for the tribes north of the Ohio River and the other for those living south of that stream. This Proclamation settlement of the Indian problem was not intended as a permanent check to western settlement from the colonies, but merely as a temporary measure to keep the situation in hand until orderly arrangements could be made.[7] In time it was hoped that the Indians could be induced to cede their claims in these western territories, but meanwhile clashes with the natives could be avoided and the stream of American settlers directed into the poorly settled areas of Nova Scotia, Florida, and the still empty parts of the original colonies. Impatient colonial land speculators, however, felt cramped by the imposition of the new line, and a number of land companies and other colonial associations sprang up and besieged the British government with petitions to bend the line westward. Step by step the government gave way. In the years 1768 to 1770 the Americans secured the cession of land between the Ohio and Tennessee rivers, and numerous settlers poured into the region between the Kentucky and Monongahela rivers, where a fourteenth colony to be known as Vandalia was projected. While there was considerable trespassing by squatters south of the Tennessee as well as north and west of the Ohio, the Indian reservation on the whole remained intact in these areas until the Revolution. Meanwhile, the French villages along the Mississippi in the Indian country were ruled by mild military officials.

While this attempt to settle the issues of Indian trade and land stirred up a storm of protest, it was in the effort to solve the defense and financial problems of the colonies that the real trouble arose, for these involved a revision and a revitalizing of the whole system of colonial administration. In the interests of greater economic efficiency, as well as improved military protection, the English government undertook to make mercantilism really

[7] Cf, however, Morison and Commager, *The Growth of the American Republic* (New York: 1936), p. 20.

work as the basis of an effective colonial system.[8] The weakness of this plan was that it imposed certain restraints on the evasion of existing regulations that the colonists, long accustomed to an amiable indulgence, were to find exceedingly irritating. The regulations may well have been unjust, weighted heavily in the interests of the English traders and manufacturers as against the American colonists; but, assuming the desirability of maintaining the empire and accepting the prevailing political and economic views of the period, the program of colonial administrative reform worked out by the English ministers in the decade after the Peace of Paris, while blundering in many details, can hardly be accused of being either unintelligent or immoderate.

The head of the English ministry at this critical juncture was George Grenville who took office shortly after the treaty had been signed. A logical, prosaic, business-minded man, it seemed to him the most obvious conclusion that colonies, sharing in the benefits of empire, should help to meet the expenses of empire; and that it would be in the interests of defense and efficiency to bring greater centralization into the administration, and restrain the excesses of colonial irresponsibility that had been so obvious during the late war. To this end, he and his ministry devised a whole series of acts in the two years following the peace.

Convinced that adequate defense necessitated the stationing of British regular troops in America, Grenville dispatched ten thousand thither. One quarter of this force was to be kept in the Caribbean, and the remainder sent to various posts in the Thirteen Colonies. It was planned that the cost, estimated at £320,000 annually,[9] would be met for the first year entirely by Great Britain; after that the colonies would pay one third. To secure this extra revenue from the colonies, it was proposed to revise the navigation and other trade laws, and to make sure that the new regulations should not remain a dead letter as in former easy-going days. The prime minister had been shocked to learn that smuggling had gone to such enormous lengths that American customs revenue did not exceed £2,000 a year, and that it cost £8,000 to collect this amount! [10] Accordingly, measures were taken to reorganize the custom services; absentee custom officials were either dismissed or ordered to their posts, a general vice-admiralty court with jurisdiction over tariff infringements was set up for America, and a fleet unit was ordered across the Atlantic with strict instructions to break up smuggling.

---

[8] For the greater emphasis on colonies as markets for British produce after 1763, see Beer, *op. cit.,* pp. 139 and 155.

[9] *Ibid.,* page 267.

[10] Morison and Commager, *op. cit.,* p. 23.

In legislation, the most important measure was the Sugar Act of 1764, designed to replace the Molasses Act of 1733 that had long been notoriously ignored. The new act lowered from six pence to three pence a gallon the duty on foreign (i.e., French and Spanish West Indian) molasses on which the rum trade of New England and the Middle Colonies largely depended, and placed additional duties on foreign indigo, coffee, wines, and certain other luxuries, of which a comparatively small quantity was imported. These customs dues, which it was now proposed should really be collected, were designed not only to raise revenues but to restrict a trade that had been so embarrassing to the English in prosecuting the Seven Years' War. The duties of the Sugar Act, with the stricter revenue regulations accompanying it, it was believed, would furnish about half the revenue needed to pay the colonies' one-third share of the expense of "defending, protecting and securing the same." The remaining half of the needed revenue the prime minister proposed to raise through the Stamp Act, which became law in 1765.[11] Its terms required revenue stamps to be placed on all newspapers and on all legal, diplomatic, and commercial documents. England had long been accustomed to stamp taxes, and they were considered one of the least oppressive varieties of taxation; but in America revenue stamps were new. Another act prohibited the printing of paper currency in the colonies with the special purpose of preventing the payment of customs dues in worthless currency.

These various measures, and others aimed at the same goals, produced a storm of protest in America, where a post-war depression was promptly blamed on the new policy of interference from England. The new taxes struck especially hard at New England and the Middle Colonies and affected groups particularly able to express themselves. Massachusetts became the center of resistance. A large part of her wealth came from the triangle trade, on which the new Sugar Act would surely impose a heavy burden; it had always been possible to ignore taxes under the Molasses Act, and smuggling in the Bay State had become practically a matter of routine. As, however, the Stamp Act affected all colonies equally, Massachusetts was careful to keep this grievance in the foreground when she sponsored a Stamp Act Congress to meet in New York in October, 1765. This body drew up statements of rights and grievances which were widely circulated and dispatched to England as addresses to king and Parliament. Protests also took other forms: newspapers and lawyers vented their wrath in print; merchants formed nonimportation agreements or economic boycott associations, agreeing to apply a policy which today would be called "economic sanctions" against England; discontented artisans and laborers, who

---

[11] Beer, *op. cit.*, p. 286 states that the Acts of 1764 and 1765 were calculated to produce a total revenue of from about £105,000 to £145,000.

blamed the Stamp Act for their economic difficulties, formed Sons of Liberty associations and mobbed the customs offices, admiralty courts, and stamp offices, forcing the new officials to resign. Mob violence in Boston reached a climax in the sacking and burning of the residence and library of Lieutenant-Governor Hutchinson.

The English government was amazed at the storm it had aroused, not realizing the fears and hardships that the unfortunate sequence of the new measures imposed: the uneasiness caused by the arrival of garrison troops and a crowd of customs officials, the blow to the most flourishing branch of colonial commerce, the effect of the Stamp Act in draining away the all too-small supply of currency that the colonies possessed as a medium of exchange, and the hardships pressed home on the debtor class by the prohibition of printing paper money.

Under pressure from the violent addresses and advices from overseas and the loud protests from English merchants whose businesses were hard hit by the nonimportation agreements, as well as a recommendation from the king, Parliament gave way, reducing the sugar duties from three pence to one penny a gallon on all molasses (British or foreign), and repealing the Stamp Act. The repeal caused great rejoicing in the colonies. The Declaratory Act, passed at the same time, asserting the right of Parliament to make laws for the colonies "in all cases whatsoever," was hardly noticed. After all, it had been the collection of the duties, rather than the constitutional issue involved in their imposition, to which the Americans had objected. The colonies emerged from this encounter with the English Parliament proud of their victory and convinced that the lifting of the economic depression, which occurred at the same time, was directly connected with their triumph.

The new harmony was short-lived. This was largely because the colonial question had become a political issue in England, and a change of party brought into power a ministry that favored a more thoroughgoing colonial policy. An active member of this party was Charles Townshend who had taken the recent defeat much to heart as an unworthy concession to popular clamor. In 1766 he became chancellor of the exchequer, in a ministry which was nominally headed by the Duke of Grafton. Rashly, Townsend announced that he would bring in legislation to raise from the colonies the money needed for the support of the army that must be kept there. In May, 1767, he secured the passage of three bills. The principal act laid duties on certain British imports into the colonies: tea, glass, paper, and red and white lead. In the recent fracas over the Stamp Act, a distinction had been drawn between internal and external taxes; the latter the colonies generally admitted to be legal, and this was the type of taxation which the Townsend Act now imposed. A second measure created a board of commissioners to

A cartoon of 1766 celebrating the repeal of the stamp tax.

"The Hero of this Print is the gentle Mr. *Stamper* who is carrying . . . his favorite Child, in a coffin, Miss ᴀᴍᴇ-sᴛᴀᴍᴘ. *Anti-Sejanus*, who reads the Burial Service, is the first in the procession.—After him follow Two Pillars of the Law supporting Two Black Flags: on which are the usual stamps. . . . The Chief Mourner, *Sejanus*, follows Mr. *Stamper*. [Sejanus, a Roman who plotted to overthrow his emperor.] . . Upon the foreground are two large Bales of Black Cloth and Stamps returned from *America*. The unhappy Gang are separated from the joyous Scene . . . on the other side of the River *Thames:* where are *Open Warehouses* for the Goods of different Manufacturing Towns now shipping for *America*." (Courtesy of the New-York Historical Society, New York City)

The Battle of Lexington, April 19ᵗʰ 1775

A. Doolittle Sculp.

1 Major Pitcairn, at the head of the Regular Granadiers
2. The Party who first fired on the Provincials at Lexington
3 Part of the Provincial Company of [...]
4 Regular Companies on the road to Concord
5. The Meeting house at Lexington.

Washington, Lafayette, and Tilghman at Yorktown. Painted by Charles Willson Peale, 1786. (Courtesy of the State of Maryland, photograph by the Metropolitan Museum of Art)

Medals presented to Indian chiefs friendly to the British Cause. (*Above*) The "Lion and Wolf" medal struck in silver about 1766 and presented by General Amherst to friendly tribes at an assembly at Niagara after the Pontiac conspiracy. A wolf (Pontiac) is pictured snarling at the reclining British lion. The obverse, not shown, is a bust of George III. (*Below*) Obverse and reverse of a silver medal struck during the American Revolution to enlist the assistance of the Indian tribes to the British cause. (Courtesy of the Royal Ontario Museum of Archaeology)

stiffen the enforcement of the Navigation Acts. A third bill continued in somewhat modified form, the billeting of soldiers to which, especially in New York, there had been objection.

Again a storm of protest ensued. It was not as vociferous but more serious than in the previous instance. Again Massachusetts led the way. Nonimportation agreements were once more put into operation; the Sons of Liberty again went into action, this time concentrating on an effort to see that goods were landed without the payment of duties. The government tried to offset mob violence by sending troops to Boston to guard the customhouses. The relations between the townspeople and the soldiers were unpleasant, but for many months no serious clash occurred. Then, on March 5th, 1770, the so-called "Boston Massacre" took place. In an affray which began as an altercation between a town group and some soldiers guarding a customhouse, some five persons were killed and six others wounded. The incident left behind it bitter memories associated with "British tyranny."

This time England was in an economic depression and did not respond to colonial agitation so quickly; and, when the Townshend duties were eventually repealed in 1770, the step was taken not so much in response to colonial agitation as because of a change in economic theory. The government came to the conclusion that it was financially unwise to put taxes on goods from England and so cut down their consumption in the colonies; the Americans, on the other hand, did not realize the difference in motive, and believed that their nonimportation measures had again been successful. Peace again ensued and lasted for three years. During this time trade revived and radical activities were frowned upon, not only by colonial merchants who were again making money, but also by other conservatives who feared that America was in danger of being stampeded by irresponsible radicals; these groups argued that England had learned her lesson and the colonies need go no further to win their points.

The end of the truce came through the passing of the Tea Act of 1773. This was a measure primarily designed by the English government to assist its favorite corporation, the East India Company, which through poor management had a large surplus of tea on hand and was threatened with bankruptcy. By lowering the duty on the importation of tea into the colonies from seven to three pence a pound, and making it available at a price far below anything that the colonies had hitherto enjoyed, the government hoped that the satisfaction would be such as would recoup the company's finances. To their surprise a new colonial storm ensued. The measure provided the opportunity that the radical leaders had been hoping for. Through the establishment of Committees of Correspondence, men like Samuel Adams and Patrick Henry had managed to keep revolutionary groups in the various colonies in touch with each other and the spirit of revolution awake. They now denounced the Tea Act as a creation of a monopoly that might be indefinitely extended, and on this ground secured the support of the seaport merchants. It was clear to the traders that the Tea Act made smuggling with the Dutch Colonies unprofitable, and they listened to the argument that the creation of one monopoly might well lead to others.

When the ships with the cheap tea arrived, their reception at various American ports presented a bold challenge to the home government. The most violent action was taken in Boston, where, under Samuel Adams' leadership, a town meeting took steps to see that the tea should not be landed. On the night of December 18, 1773, a body of persons disguised as Indians boarded the vessels, and dumped the cargo of 342 chests of tea into the harbor. This "Boston Tea Party," with its lawless destruction of property, horrified many conservative elements in the city who felt that the extremists had gone too far.

Unwisely, the British government, under the leadership of Lord North, acted swiftly to punish the offenders. They rushed through Parliament four coercive measures which, when they became known in America, were promptly dubbed the "Intolerable Acts": the first closed the port of Boston until the tea should be paid for; the second modified the Massachusetts charter, bringing the colonial government more directly under crown control; the third changed the judicial system by providing that persons charged with capital offenses should be sent to England for trial; and the fourth was a new military billeting act. For good measure, the commander of the British troops in North America was appointed governor of Massachusetts.

A few months later (June 22, 1774), another measure, the Quebec Act, added fuel to the fire of American indignation; though in reality it had no relation to Boston events, but was the outcome of long study of primarily Canadian problems.[12] The arrangements made in this act, providing for the government of the territory conquered from France in the Seven Years' War and now reorganized as the Province of Quebec, offended many groups in the Thirteen Colonies. By this measure the new province was reattached to the region between the Ohio and the Great Lakes and so seemed to abrogate claims which a number of the colonies, notably Massachusetts, Connecticut, New York, and Virginia, possessed in this western region; the government established for the new province provided for no elective assembly, and recognized French civil law which allowed trial without jury, and so appeared to indicate a tendency in the direction

---

[12] For an able discussion of the Quebec Bill in relation to the American Revolution see R. Coupland, *The Quebec Act* (Oxford: 1925), pp. 116-22.

of autocratic rule; furthermore, the recognition extended by the act to the Roman Catholic Church also antagonized Calvinistic New England.

These various measures of 1774, with able assistance from the Committees of Correspondence, had the effect of solidifying American opinion and placing control in the hands of the radicals. From Virginia came a summons, supported from many quarters, for a Continental Congress "to consider the united interests of America." When this First Continental Congress met in Carpenters Hall in Philadelphia on September 5, 1774, all colonies save one were represented by many of the ablest leaders in America. With no thought of demanding independence, but simply of presenting a united front to the English government and making it back down again, the delegates united in refusing obedience to the coercive acts; they adopted a Nonintercourse Agreement, drew up a Declaration of Rights and Grievances, framed a Petition to the King, and composed Addresses to the people of Great Britain, Quebec, and the Thirteen Colonies; should their grievances not be redressed, the delegates agreed to meet again in the following May. Before that date, the dispute had passed from the political to the military sphere of action.

Thus, in the decade following the close of the Seven Years' War, the clash of interests between the colonists and the British government, which had long been brewing but had not been strong enough to manifest itself in an acute form as long as French power remained a menace, flared into open antagonism in a series of disputes that steadily increased in violence. As we look back upon it today, this early phase of the revolutionary movement is of great constitutional interest. While it is undoubtedly true that the majority of the people in both England and America directly involved in these disputes were concerned with practical goals rather than constitutional issues, we see now that constitutional principles of primary importance were at stake and that many of the more intelligent leaders on both sides realized this to be the case. But neither the king nor the Tory party then in power in England, it seems clear, had any particular designs against the liberties of colonial Englishmen; they were primarily concerned about the solution of practical administrative problems. Both Whigs and Tories, whatever their view of the wisdom of coercive measures, entertained no doubts concerning their legality or the responsibility of the British Parliament to legislate for the colonies, as it had been doing for a century and a half. In the minds of these eighteenth-century Englishmen, neither non-enforcement of previous enactments nor tacit allowance of actual colonial practice had impaired Parliament's rights of legislation for the whole empire.

In America, on the other hand, the colonists had long enjoyed practical self-government, and had built up a system of self-conscious political activity which they considered, by prescription at least, to have become their inalienable right; and they objected to effective interference in their affairs by the British Parliament. Furthermore, it must be borne in mind that much of the constitutional outlook of eighteenth-century America, stemming as it did from a period when colonial administration was based on royal charters and grants from the crown, really harked back to a period preceding the English revolution of 1689. At the accession of William and Mary in that year, a real revolutionary principle had been accepted in England; this declared the authority of the English parliament to be superior to the king's prerogative, not only for "the realm" but for "the dominions thereunto belonging." Samuel Adams, Patrick Henry, James Wilson, and other American leaders in the 1760's, maintained that this revolutionary principle of parliamentary supremacy had never been accepted by the people in the colonies and was therefore not legal in America, for, according to Locke's theory, a revolution only became legal when accepted by the people affected. On this assumption, the American people had a constitutional right, the leaders maintained, to resist British parliamentary legislation, at least that which affected their internal affairs; they contended that American representative assemblies should be regarded as "little parliaments" acting under the crown for American affairs and possessing an authority parallel to that exercised in Great Britain by the British Parliament.[13] It is interesting that this contention anticipates by more than one hundred and fifty years the principle laid down in the Statute of Westminster defining in somewhat similar terms the relationship of the autonomous units of the British Commonwealth of the twentieth century. A second British empire would put into operation a concept of equal partnership in an imperial structure that might have proved a saving device could it have been adopted in the eighteenth century for the first empire.

II. THE MILITARY CLASH

The first military clash in the gathering storm occurred on April 19, 1775, near Boston, where General Gage, the royal governor of Massachusetts and commander of the British forces in North America, anxiously watched the situation. Fearing an outbreak and believing that a show of force in the country might have a quieting effect, he decided, though an amiable, cautious, and somewhat timid man, to send a force of eight hundred to one thousand men to seize some military stores which the radicals had been collecting at Concord, eighteen miles away. His watchful oppo-

---

[13] For a full statement of this point of view and the arguments on which it rests see C. H. McIlwain, *The American Revolution: A Constitutional Interpretation* (New York: 1923), chap. i, pp. 1-17.

nents at once dispatched riders to arouse the militia. Among these riders was Paul Revere, who received his cue from a lantern in the tower of the North Church as to the exact time of the departure of the British troops from Boston. Other patrols took up the warning, with the result that when troops reached Lexington in the early morning of April 19 they found a body of some sixty militiamen drawn up on the village green. In the noise and confusion someone fired a shot, then a volley followed; after eight of their number had been killed and ten others wounded, the Americans

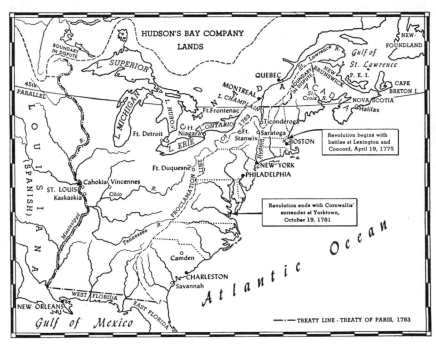

19. The American Revolution: War Areas

dispersed and the British pushed on to Concord. Here, a few "embattled farmers" opposed the British force at a bridgehead and further fighting took place. As the troops marched back to Boston with their object accomplished, at the expense of 247 of their number killed, they moved through a countryside thoroughly aroused; rumors were flying that a brutal attack had been made on peaceful villagers; minutemen fired from behind every vantage point; and ever-increasing numbers gathered to close in around Boston. Thus began a siege that was to last for eleven months and close only with the withdrawal of the British forces.

Beyond New England, Patrick Henry expressed the views of the more radical of the colonists when he declared: "It is vain, sir, to extenuate the matter. Gentlemen may cry 'peace, peace' but there is no peace. The war is actually begun! The next gale that sweeps from the north will bring to our ears the clash of resounding arms! Our brethren are already in the field! Why stand we here idle?"

It was in this atmosphere of rising excitement that, less than three weeks after the battles of Lexington and Concord, the Second Continental Congress assembled in Philadelphia on May 10, 1775. Here were gathered as distinguished a company of delegates as the Thirteen Colonies could produce. To preside over the assembly they elected John Hancock, a wealthy merchant of Boston. This congress was destined not to disperse until a long-drawn-out war had been fought and independence won, and was to act as the de facto federal government throughout the struggle. Independence was not, however, the object at which the majority aimed when the session opened. A "Declaration of the Causes and Necessity of Taking up Arms," composed jointly by John Dickinson and Thomas Jefferson, undoubtedly expressed the views of most of the delegates in stating, "We have not raised armies with ambitious designs of separating from Great Britain, and establishing independent states" but were determined to employ them "for the preservation of our liberties, being with one mind resolved to die free men rather than live slaves." [14] Years later Jefferson declared, "It is well known that in July, 1775, a separation from Great Britain and the establishment of a Republican Government had not yet entered any person's mind." While this aristocratic father of democracy may have had his own definition of "person," his statement was probably true for the majority in the country. On the other hand, the delegates were determined to cling to that union among themselves which in the First Continental Congress they had discovered brought such strength and produced so large a measure of redress. "We mean," they said, "not to dissolve that union which has so long and so happily subsisted between us." [15] To force the English government once more to back down and allow the colonists to govern themselves through their own little parliaments was their primary purpose.

But the logic of events speedily outran theory. In June, while the "Declaration of the Causes and Necessity of Taking up Arms" was still under debate, Congress found itself obliged to take into its service the militia besieging Boston and decided to appoint George Washington as the commander-in-chief of the American forces. The capture of Ticonderoga on May 10, 1775, by Ethan Allen's Green Mountain Boys, and the Battle of Bunker Hill on June 17, 1775, had already occurred. News of the latter

---

[14] "The Declaration of the Causes and Necessity of Taking up Arms," July 6, 1775, in H. S. Commager, *Documents of American History* (New York: 1934), p. 95.
[15] *Ibid.*

actually reached General Washington June 23 as he was leaving Philadelphia for Boston. These events were undoubtedly in the mind of the king when he refused to accept the petition addressed to him by Congress and, on August 22, issued a proclamation declaring the colonies in a state of rebellion.

In September, 20,000 Hessian mercenaries were dispatched to reinforce the regular British army in America and to assist in putting down the revolt. A blockade of the coast was also established. From the outset, the attitude of the British government was stiff rather than conciliatory; but of all measures taken, the employment of hired troops, though a typical European idea of the time, was the most resented in America. From the British government's point of view, it was necessary because of the lack of public enthusiasm for a war against the American colonists and the consequent difficulty of recruiting in such an unpopular cause. Many Liberals openly sympathized with the American rebels and blamed the government for mismanagement; they rejoiced to see the Tories discomforted, and a too-autocratic monarch suffer rebuff. Even the Tories had little enthusiasm for the war. Many military experts thought that reconquest was hopeless from the start; [16] with the theater of the struggle distant from the homeland a possible twelve weeks for the slow-moving troop transports of the age, and with the Americans in control of all vantage points to start with, land operations, they considered, were well-nigh hopeless; only a naval blockade stood a chance of success and this was handicapped through lack of adequate and convenient bases. However, to Lord George Germain, the arrogant and rather unintelligent colonial secretary, the problem appeared simple and the matter routine, calling for the reinforcement of a British army that had a task to perform. His view that the American war should be fought on traditional lines eventually prevailed.

Meanwhile, the colonists felt anything but sure of success. Many prominent men held a strong prejudice against a regular army and would have liked to fight through the struggle with militia only, serving under local leaders, in the traditional American manner; others realized the necessity for a trained force. But, in the country at large, there was little enthusiasm for such service or for the sacrifices that a regular army's training and maintenance required. Indifference and "the dearth of public spirit" were the source of constant complaint from Washington and other leaders. Patriotism—on more than a local scale—was indeed distressingly absent. New Englanders, for instance, felt little enthusiasm for serving in the Southern or the Middle Colonies, and men of other regions acted in the same spirit. At its peak, in the summer of 1776, Washington's army

---

[16] *Cf.* Morison and Commager, *op. cit.*, pp. 81-82.

numbered sixteen thousand men; but normally he had little more than five thousand under his command.[17] As the year 1775 wore on, it became evident that this time the English government was not going to back down and that the only alternative to complete surrender was to fight on to liberty; enlistment then picked up and bolder counsels prevailed.

The first major offensive operation decided upon by the colonists was no less than the invasion of Canada; a decision that was to prove of lasting continental significance. Decisive considerations were the strategic necessity of eliminating, if possible, the threat from the north of British invasion by way of the St. Lawrence, Lake Champlain, and the Hudson; and secondly, the hope of strengthening the revolutionary movement by inducing Quebec to join forces as the fourteenth of the revolting colonies. Towards the latter goal, organized propaganda had already prepared the way. Not only had the First Continental Congress, in the autumn of 1774, addressed a formal appeal to the inhabitants of the Province of Quebec for cooperation in obtaining redress of their "afflicting grievances," [18] but colonial agents in Canada for some time had been representing in the darkest colors the Quebec Act, which had just gone into effect, both to the habitants whom it professed to benefit and to the British traders in Montreal who were the real sufferers under its terms. Washington was well aware that in this contemplated enterprise the cooperation of the French Canadians was essential: "If they are averse, it must fail of success," he warned.

In the fall of 1775 two expeditions were dispatched to the St. Lawrence valley.[19] The western column,[20] led by Brigadier General Richard Montgomery, moved up the old route of Lake Champlain and the Richelieu River towards Montreal. The eastern column of some eleven hundred men under Benedict Arnold was to go north via the Kennebec River, then by Lake Megantic and down the Chaudière River to Quebec. It was known that Governor Carleton's equipment of British garrison troops had been recently depleted by two regiments sent to reinforce General Gage in Boston, and that his powers of opposition would depend on his ability to rally to the British cause the recently conquered French Canadian peasants.

At first all went well. Lake Champlain had already been opened by the victories in the preceding May at Ticonderoga and Crown Point; where Ethan Allen's Green Mountain Boys had failed in their attacks north of the Canadian border, Montgomery's men now succeeded. Fort Chambly

---

[17] *Ibid.*, p. 84.

[18] For a discussion of this address, see Coupland, *op. cit.*, pp. 144-51.

[19] Coupland, *op. cit.*, pp. 172-86, gives a concise account of the American invasion of Canada; see also A. L. Burt, *A Short History of Canada for Americans* (Minneapolis: 1942), pp. 74-81.

[20] The exact number in this western army is a matter of some doubt, and varied from time to time, *cf.* Coupland, *op. cit.*, p. 174, and also Morison and Commager, *op. cit.*, p. 89; the latter makes the force only "a little over a thousand men," the former four thousand.

fell on October 15, and Fort St. Johns on November 2. With these protecting posts in American hands, Governor Carleton decided not to try to hold Montreal but to fall back on Quebec. It was now clear to him that, despite all that the seigneurs and clergy could do, the habitants were not prepared to fight against the Americans; he was also well aware that the British traders in Montreal, whom he and his predecessor had sacrificed to his policy of conciliating the French Canadians, were disaffected. On his way down the river, Carleton lost his military escort in a surprise attack by a body of Americans, and it was only with the aid of a peasant disguise and a quiet rowboat that he was able to slip into Quebec, leaving Montgomery's men to occupy Montreal without opposition, on November 13. Three Rivers declared for the Americans as Carleton was passing downstream. In Quebec he had a mere eighteen hundred men of all ranks to help him maintain this last British stronghold until reinforcements should arrive from England.

By this time, Arnold had already arrived at Wolf's Cove after a frightful trip through the Maine woods, during which he lost 400 of his men. Despite these losses and the ragged state of his forces, he was bold enough to demand the surrender of the city on November 14 (1775). When this demand was treated with contempt by Carleton, who regarded Arnold and his men as "deluded rebels," the Americans, strengthened by the arrival on December 4 of Montgomery from Montreal, laid siege to Quebec. But winter was coming on, their forces were daily dwindling away as terms of service ran out, and the two commanders decided to risk everything on a direct assault. On New Year's Eve, 1775, in a blinding snowstorm, they attacked from two directions, but failed completely. Montgomery was killed, Arnold was wounded, and 431 men surrendered. Even after this disaster, however, the remaining American forces maintained the siege through the winter, while smallpox and the bitter cold took a heavy toll. The horrified Congress voted large reinforcements, but only a portion of these had arrived when, on May 6, three British ships, the first of a large convoy, hove in sight. The Americans hastily broke camp and withdrew up the river in some disorder, ahead of the British reinforcements.

Montreal, Chambly, and St. Johns were in turn all evacuated, and by the end of June the remnants of the American forces were back on the Hudson and the invasion of Canada was over. Recent studies have indicated that the retreat might well have ended in even greater disaster had Carleton moved with speed and used his new strength of ten thousand regular troops. It has been suggested that he deliberately let the Americans go, pitying them as "deluded subjects" who had been led astray by demagogues and who, if generously treated, might still "return to their duty." [21]

[21] Burt, *op. cit.,* pp. 80-81.

The military opportunity of gaining early control of the Lake Champlain-Hudson route that he thus threw away in the first year of the war was not to recur; when it was attempted a year later, the Declaration of Independence had been adopted, the revolutionary cause had gathered strength, and the decisive British defeat of the war ensued.

Meanwhile, the failure of the Canadian campaign of 1775-1776 meant for the American leaders the collapse of their chance to bring Canada into the American union, to extend their boundary indefinitely northward, and to set the stage for "one vast republic of North America." That failure had been due in large part to the conduct of the recently conquered French inhabitants of Canada, who had shown themselves unwilling to join the American colonists in a struggle to throw off the British yoke and strike out for independence along with the Thirteen Colonies. The habitants refused equally and decisively to fight either for the Americans or for the British. Had even a few thousand joined in the attack on Quebec that stronghold must have fallen, and with it all Canada would have been lost, at least temporarily, to the British crown. But the most that the Americans were able to obtain from the French Canadian peasants was acquiescence, and this was already beginning to change to open hostility before the last American recrossed the frontier. "As for the better sort of people," wrote one American officer, "seven eighths of them are Tories who would wish to see our throats cut."

The American lack of success in Canada was due then not merely, or even chiefly, to military reverses, but to the indifference and hostility of the French Canadian population. This hostility by no means meant friendship with Great Britain, but seems rather to have been a survival of a deeply rooted memory of old colonial enmities. The indifference may perhaps be explained by an inveterate racialism, and by the natural aversion to war on the part of a feudal peasantry which had nothing in common with the political aspirations of the Thirteen English Colonies.[22] However, this Canadian expedition was from the American point of view not altogether fruitless, for the appearance of an American force in Canada alarmed the British government sufficiently to cause it to divide its body of reinforcements between Canada and New York. Events in the following year were to prove that the American forces were strong enough to prevent a junction of these two British armies.

By March, 1776, when the remnants of the Montgomery-Arnold expeditions had returned to the Hudson, Washington had succeeded in forcing the withdrawal of the British from Boston, where Howe had recently replaced Gage. From Boston Washington took his army to New York,

---

[22] For an illuminating discussion of the French Canadian attitude see Coupland, *op. cit.,* pp. 151-72.

where its presence for a time prevented that colony from becoming a strategically placed British stronghold. Meanwhile things were going well for the insurgents in the south, where, in June, the British were successfully prevented from occupying Charleston.

With a background of these military successes, the radicals in Congress were strong enough by July 4, 1776, to secure after a terrific debate the adoption of an elaborate Declaration of Independence.[23] This courageous document, though largely the work of Thomas Jefferson, was officially prepared by a committee of Congress.[24] As justification for their course of revolutionary action, the authors pleaded before the world "the natural rights of man," as set forth in the political philosophy of the eighteenth century.[25] In a famous paragraph that was to be the inspiration of liberal minds for the next hundred years, they set forth:

We hold these truths to be self-evident, that all men are created equal, that they are endowed by their Creator with certain unalienable Rights, that among these are Life, Liberty, and the pursuit of Happiness. That to secure these rights, Governments are instituted among Men, deriving their just powers from the consent of the governed. That whenever any Form of Government becomes destructive to these ends, it is the Right of the People to alter or to abolish it, and to institute new Government, laying its foundation on such principles and organizing its powers in such form, as to them shall seem most likely to effect their Safety and Happiness.

The document listed twenty-seven grievances against the British king as proof that he had "in direct object the establishment of an absolute Tyranny over these States." To resist such tyranny and secure their natural rights the Americans declared their independence, and pledged to each other "our Lives, our Fortunes and our sacred Honor." [26]

Though delegates from all the states signed the Declaration of Independence, probably at the time fully a third of the population remained loyalist.[27] The persuasive pamphlet by Thomas Paine on the natural rights'

---

[23] A Resolution of Independence, submitted by R. H. Lee, had been voted on July 2 and C. Becker in his *Declaration of Independence* (New York: 1922), p. 3, points out that it was this resolution and not the later, more elaborate statement which was the official act in favor of separation from Great Britain.

[24] The committee consisted of Jefferson, Adams, Franklin, Sherman, and R. Livingston. Jefferson was chosen to draft the constitution because of his reputation of possessing a "masterly pen." Becker, *op. cit.,* p. 194.

[25] Becker points out that there is no mention in the Declaration of Independence of either "Parliament" or "the rights of British subjects," though those were the very subjects most debated in the preceding decade. For a brilliant discussion of the philosophy back of these significant omissions, see *op. cit.,* chaps. i. ii, and iii.

[26] McIlwain, *op. cit.,* pp. 1-2, points out that "to the summer of 1776" the Americans insisted that "their resistance was a constitutional resistance to unconstitutional acts." It become revolutionary, he says, only when the power of the Crown, and not merely parliamentary authority, was attacked.

[27] A. M. Schlesinger, *New Viewpoints in American History* (New York: 1928), chap. vii, p. 161.

philosophy, entitled "Common Sense," had been published six months earlier and had turned many wavering minds; but in spite of this, and of the influence of other radical writers, the bulk of the population had remained conservative or indifferent. From careful studies of contemporary materials, modern students have concluded that only in Massachusetts and Virginia was the bulk of the population in favor of revolution.

The regions of New York, New Jersey, and Pennsylvania, at least until the arrival of the Hessians, were "practically hostile territory to Washington's army." Resistance to revolutionary activities was naturally strongest in the upper strata of society, among the landowners and the professional and official classes, which had most to lose by any disturbance of the status quo.[28] Interest and temperament alike inclined this group to strive to hold the old empire together and frown on rebellions activities. Faulkner in his *American Political and Social History* states, "The Revolution was at first chiefly the work of an earnest minority composed principally of mechanics, sailors, small shop keepers, and small farmers, led by able young lawyers and discontented importers, the group as a whole representing the various elements that were not prospering under the existing political and economic regime," and adds, "generalizing broadly, it would be safe to say that the most cultivated, influential and wealthy inhabitants of the coast towns were likely to be loyalists." [29] It should not, however, be forgotten that as time went on many families and social groups were sharply divided, and leaders on both sides were drawn from some of the finest stock in the land with all social groups represented in each camp.

That the influence of the large loyalist group was not more effective in stemming the tide of revolution, so contrary to their interests, must be put down to two causes: in the first place, the ineptitude and inefficiency of the British government that marked the whole conduct of the war was nowhere more evident than in its tactless dealing with the loyalist groups whose assistance they failed to organize or adequately to appreciate; in the second place, the aggressive measures of the revolutionaries against the loyalists, involving systematic persecution, confiscation of property, disenfranchisement, and in many cases imprisonment, early robbed this pro-British group of any large measure of effective power.[30] With each military disaster for the English cause, great numbers of loyalists left the colonies. In all, some sixty thousand migrated northward; half of these settled in the Maritime Provinces and most of the remainder in what was to become

---

[28] J. F. Jameson, *The American Revolution Considered as a Social Movement* (Princeton: 1940), chap. i, "The Revolution and the Status of Persons," especially p. 16.

[29] H. U. Faulkner, *op. cit.*, p. 103.

[30] In justification of the harsh measures, it should be remembered that some twenty thousand Tories joined the British armies and fought against their fellow colonists. See Coupland, *op. cit.*, p. 259.

the province of Ontario; in these regions they established the foundations of a new British commonwealth. Thousands of others sailed for England or the British West Indies, especially the Bahamas.

Having succeeded in committing Congress in the Declaration of Independence to a complete separation from the British crown, the Whig minority, even though it lacked the support of large groups in the population, had now to set itself to win the war of independence. For a year and a half, this struggle remained a contest solely between England and the colonists. Through the first six months of this time, military events went badly for the Americans. Two days before the signing of the Declaration of Independence, large British reinforcements arrived in New York under the command of the two Howe brothers, Sir William Howe commander-in-chief of the army, and Admiral Lord Howe in command of the fleet. Whigs in politics, liberal-minded, and well-disposed towards Americans, the Howes, though sent to direct the war, came with a strong hope of putting an end to the fighting. Unfortunately for the cause of British and American unity, they had been empowered to offer practically nothing in the way of guarantees of future independence within the empire; all they might promise was leniency to rebels. As the Americans, largely through Franklin's influence, refused to negotiate save on the basis of independence, the struggle went on. The weight of numbers was now on the British side, royal troops numbering over thirty thousand men—not to speak of a navy—opposed an American force of eighteen thousand; strategic advantages, however, were still held by the Americans.

Howe succeeded in landing his army at New York in July (1776). Despite Washington's occupation of Brooklyn Heights, the British general in the Battle of Long Island (August 27) inflicted a defeat that necessitated the withdrawal of the Americans from the city and forced their retreat into New Jersey where an indecisive campaign filled the autumn months. By the end of 1776 the outlook was not bright: Washington's army numbered a mere five thousand, the rest having dwindled away, and General Charles Lee, a commander greatly favored by Congress, had been captured by Howe in the Jerseys. Had Howe been more energetic, he might well have wiped out the American army; but he moved in a leisurely fashion and depended on the strength of Tory sentiment and the dwindling popularity of military life among the Americans to win the final victory for him. As the year closed, however, Washington was in a strong position in the highlands of New Jersey about Morristown, while the British were back in New York.

In 1777 the British plan was to take advantage of reinforcements recently landed in Canada, to march eight thousand men under General Burgoyne down the line of Lake Champlain and the Hudson River to Albany, where he was to unite with an army from New York; [31] meanwhile, a simultaneous attack was to be made on Philadelphia. The capture of the American capital was effected as planned, on September 27, but the operations on the Hudson were frustrated. The great distances involved, difficulties of communication, poor coordination, a European-minded commander, and a completely hostile American countryside produced a series of British disasters culminating on October 17, 1777, at Saratoga, with the surrender to General Gates of Burgoyne's entire army of over five thousand men.

This decisive victory for the independence forces changed the whole character of the war. Hitherto the struggle had been between the colonials and the mother country, neither side fighting with great enthusiasm. After Saratoga, England's European enemies, only too eager for a chance to avenge the humiliations of the Seven Years' War and other struggles of the earlier part of the century, now entered the war. The news of Saratoga convinced them that the Americans were sufficiently aroused to make hopeful a campaign against England in America, while at the same time they realized that, unless they intervened, England would without doubt eventually win this war as she had its predecessors. Slowly a great coalition of powers was welded. From 1778 onwards, England was fighting old traditional enemies in the theater of her own colonies, but this time with the colonists included among her enemies.

From the beginning, the American revolutionary leaders had realized that without help there was small hope of ultimate military victory against the greatest imperial power of the world, and had set themselves to secure the needed foreign assistance. Early in 1776, agents of Congress, joined later in that year by the able diplomat Benjamin Franklin, were in France working to secure aid for their cause. Spain also was canvassed. Until the battle of Saratoga, French financial assistance and munitions of war were given only secretly through a dummy company, Hortales et Cie; while Spanish provisions were surreptitiously slipped through New Orleans and Habana. Four months after the victory of Saratoga, France signed an open treaty of alliance with the Americans (February 6, 1778); sixteen months later, in June, 1779, the Spaniards entered the war. The Spaniards came in as allies of the French rather than of the Americans, and gave their first attention in the Old World to besieging Gibraltar and in the New to regaining Florida and securing those sections of the old French holdings east of the Mississippi that had gone to England in the Treaty of Paris. However, an openly friendly New Orleans proved very useful to the

---

[31] *Cf.* Burt, *op. cit.*, p. 82, where it is stated that when Burgoyne left Montreal he already had the information that no help would be forthcoming from Howe and that consequently Burgoyne knowingly undertook the campaign single-handed.

Americans as a base for privateers, while Spanish military operations in Florida kept a considerable British force occupied there.

Formal entrance by France into the war not only brought a French fleet to American waters to challenge the British blockade, but further weakened England's strength by compelling her to disperse her forces, as the scope of the war widened, in order to provide protection to other parts of her far-flung empire. The British position steadily deteriorated as one after another of the nations that had formerly suffered at her hands either openly or secretly seized the opportunity to take their revenge. In 1780 Russia organized a League of Armed Neutrality, ostensibly to maintain the freedom of the seas; and later in the same year, the Dutch openly entered the war. England found herself fighting about half the world. It was not, however, until 1781 that cooperation between these various enemies was sufficiently effective to become decisive.

In the meantime, however, military operations were being carried on not only in America but as far away as India; naval engagements were occurring in the North Sea, the Mediterranean, the Indian Ocean, and the Caribbean. As far as the American forces were concerned, naval action was confined to predatory raids by privateers operating against British trading vessels and troop transports, or to gallant duels between single fighting ships or small squadrons. In this emergency the British navy showed itself to be at one of the lowest points of its history, corruptly managed by Lord Sandwich, the first Lord of the Admiralty, and inefficiently handled by his appointees at sea; the one brilliant exception was Admiral Rodney, and he was constantly harassed by interference from home.

In the colonies, after the British disaster of Saratoga had been followed by the withdrawal of Howe from Philadelphia, the land struggle shifted to the west and south. In the west, George Rogers Clark with a small force from Virginia succeeded in the winter of 1778-1779 in descending the Ohio and capturing the British forts of Kaskaskia and Cahokia on the Mississippi, as well as Vincennes on the Wabash, from which points the British were believed to have been instigating Indian attacks on American frontier settlements. Clark's exploits placed the Illinois country in American hands. Losing several of their footholds in the west and unable to make any headway in the north where the situation had reached stalemate,[32] the British hoped for a favorable decision in the south where loyalist feeling was strong and British sympathizers numerous.

From a headquarters in Savannah, occupied in December, 1778, and Charleston, taken in May, 1780, British armies marched hither and yon

---

[32] A discussion of why the entrance of France into the struggle did not bring about the conquest of Canada is given by Burt, *op. cit.,* pp. 83-84.

through Virginia, the Carolinas, and Georgia, despite the efforts of small patriot bands operating on guerrilla lines. A Congressional army under General Gates at first met with no better success than the guerrillas in checking the British army; but after Gates's defeat at Camden, South Carolina, in August, 1780, by a British force made up largely of loyalists, his men were placed under the command of General Greene, one of the most skilful of American commanders, who henceforth directed American operations in the south more successfully. Step by step the British army was forced to the seacoast. The main British army of the south under the command of General Cornwallis was finally manoeuvered into the York-town peninsula. Here the British commander with seventy-five hundred men was trapped by an effective cooperative movement, which combined siege by a land army of fifteen thousand French and American soldiers under the command of Washington and Rochambeau, with a blockade by the French fleet. This fleet, under Admiral Compte de Grasse, had recently succeeded in defeating a British naval force off New York and so temporarily held command of the sea. General Cornwallis found himself caught in a trap and was forced to surrender his entire army. This event, occurring on October 17, 1781, practically closed military operations on the North American mainland, although the final peace treaty was not signed until February 2, 1783. In the interval the struggle shifted to the West Indies where the French captured St. Kitts and Nevis and the Spaniards seized the Bahamas. Jamaica was saved for the British by a desperate naval battle won by Admiral Rodney.

The terms of the Treaty of Paris, negotiated for the Americans by Benjamin Franklin, John Jay, and John Adams, not only recognized the independence of the former Thirteen Colonies but conceded nearly everything for which they had the courage and foresight to ask. The definition of boundary lines constituted the weakest feature of the treaty; they were indeed so vaguely described as to require several subsequent treaties in the next hundred years to interpret them. They provided, however, a much more generous home for the new nation than the most optimistic patriot could have expected.[33] The western boundary was placed at the Mississippi though there was no reason why it should have extended west of the Appalachians, except the urgent desire in London for a quick peace and a vague British uneasiness of possible reawakening of French and Spanish ambitions in this area. The northern boundary, from a point west of Montreal, followed the course of the St. Lawrence River and then con-

---

[33] Morison and Commager point out that the British army at the time of the Peace of Paris still held Savannah, Charleston, New York, and seven posts in the Northwest, and commanded the sea where its position in relation to the French and Spanish was improving daily, while the American army was then in no condition to continue the war. For further details see Morison and Commager, *op. cit.,* pp. 105-6.

tinued through the Great Lakes westward to the Lake of the Woods, beyond which it was not defined. The northeastern boundary, between Maine and the Maritime Provinces and Quebec, followed a line drawn due north from the St. Croix River to the highlands and then westward along them to the 45th parallel; but which stream was meant by the "St. Croix" was not to be settled for sixty years. In the east the Americans were also granted a share in the Newfoundland fisheries. In the south the American boundary met territory in the East and West Floridas which, in other treaties, were simultaneously retroceded by Great Britain to Spain. Meanwhile, British demands for the payment of debts due to British subjects at the beginning of the war, and for the restoration of, or payment for, confiscated loyalist property were met by phrases to the effect that Congress would "earnestly recommend" to the several states restoration of property and would not hinder action in the courts for the collection of debts. The issue made unequivocably clear in the treaty was independence.[34] The war, at least from the Declaration of Independence onward, had been one for secession from the British Empire, and this was left in no doubt by the terms of the treaty. The former mother country and colonies reached these terms through direct negotiations and the signing of a separate draft treaty (November 30, 1782), whose terms however were not to become official until France too concluded peace, an event which did not occur till February 2, 1783.

A survey of the spoils of war falling to America's allies is of interest. France, whose assistance was the major, if not the decisive, factor in the military and naval operations in their final phases, emerged with little more than the satisfaction of having obtained revenge against an ancient enemy. A few West Indian islands added to those she already possessed, the prospect of a new ally, and the hope of new markets and revived trade were the only gains that could be accounted as assets. On the other side of the French ledger had to be placed a depletion of the treasury to the verge of bankruptcy by the colossal expenses of the war; within six years, France herself was to be in the throes of a revolution of which financial collapse was the initial stage.

France's ally, Spain, on the other hand, found herself immensely enriched at the close of the war. By the acquisition of East and West Florida, which had been in British hands for two decades, Spain had not merely wiped out the territorial losses in North America of the Seven Years' War, but once more had become mistress of the Gulf of Mexico. As she retained Louisiana, which France had ceded in 1763 in compensation for the Floridas, she was now in possession of the lion's share of habitable North

---

[34] For the exact treaty terms, see Commager, *op. cit.,* pp. 117-19.

America, in addition to her vast holdings in the southern continent. In North America, besides the Floridas, the Spanish flag flew over everything west of the Mississippi that lay south of an as yet undefined Canadian border. Having seen with relief, at the close of the Seven Years' War, the departure of France as a neighbor and rival in North America, she now watched with satisfaction the dismissal from the Mississippi valley and from her Florida borders of powerful England, and the latter's replacement by a young and comparatively weak new nation whose potentialities for expansion were as yet undreamed of.

This revolutionary movement in the English colonies proved to be the first of a series of New World colonial reactions against the imperialism of the Old World. This first revolution, as we have seen, had a very close relation to the removal of French imperial power from the St. Lawrence and the Mississippi, and its successful end was hastened by the French and Spanish desire for revenge which the Seven Years' War had left behind. It was to be followed within forty years by successful separation movements in both the Spanish and Portuguese colonies.

467
479

primary enjoyment of political and social equality with the peninsulares had hindered, disliked the extortions of commerce and

Chapter 17

THE STRUGGLE FOR HISPANIC AMERICAN INDEPENDENCE

I. SPANISH SOUTH AMERICA

The separation of the Spanish colonies from their motherland came a generation later than the parallel movement in the English colonies, and ran a longer and more hazardous course, occupying the years 1808 to 1825. In the background of this southern movement of emancipation, as behind the War of Independence in the north, lay profound dissatisfaction with the restrictions and oppressions of an outgrown colonial system, combined with an exalted enthusiasm on the part of many of its leaders for the ideals of "natural rights," "popular sovereignty," "equality before the law," and other slogans of the new theories of political relationships pervading the air in the closing years of the eighteenth century.[1]

The Spanish colonial structure—the most rigidly organized of American empires—had preserved almost unchanged from the first its characteristic features: royal absolutism and extreme centralization of authority centered in faraway Spain; no element of popular representation in any governmental unit larger than a municipality; legislation entirely from the homeland; overlapping powers and functions among appointed officials in the colonies; monopoly of commerce and economic life manipulated in the interests of the merchants of Spain, combined with a wasteful and scandalously corrupt fiscal system, keeping low the standard of living in America; and, last of all, a social and political hierarchy dominated by peninsulares and containing a discouraged creole group with a vast substratum of depressed classes.[2] In its basic principles the system ran counter to all the ideals of political and social freedom associated with the English revolution of 1688, John Locke, the French physiocrats, the encyclopedists, and the American and French revolutions.

The Bourbon reforms of the eighteenth century, designed to strengthen the bonds between Spain and the colonies as well as to improve the administration, had left most of the fundamentals unchanged. The creoles, whose

---

[1] On this aspect of the revolutionary movement see: John Rydjord, "The French Revolution and Mexico," in *Hispanic American Historical Review*, Vol. IX, 1929, pp. 60-65.

[2] *Cf.* W. E. Browning, "The Liberation and the Liberators," in *Hispanic American Historical Review*, Vol. IV, 1921, pp. 691-96.

primary grievance—lack of political and social equality with the peninsulares—had been left untouched, disliked the tightening of control and were further alienated.[3] The opening of interprovincial trade, the setting up of monopolistic commercial companies with exclusive rights in certain areas, the institution of intendancies, and the creation of two new viceroyalties, all, in spite of their original intention, served instead to strengthen the spirit of local pride and self-sufficiency. Meanwhile, side by side with these stresses and strains in the old system went the most lively interest in the new revolutionary doctrines emanating from France and the United States. Despite the utmost that a strict censorship by both Church and state could do, copies of the new revolutionary books circulated freely. Rebellious notions traveled along the well-worn routes of contraband trade and seeped across the boundary lines where eighteenth-century expansion into Florida and California had brought continuous contact with foreigners. An ever-widening circle of restive colonials discussed the implications of the new dynamic ideas and the changes in the other American systems. Inevitably the loss of colonies by Holland, France, and England served to suggest the possibility of the severance of Spanish America from Spain.[4]

Underlying the loss by Spain of her colonies was her too long adherence to an inadaptable and selfish colonial policy that by the close of the eighteenth century had made colonial status, if not unbearable, at least extremely irksome. But while discontent and new ideas were rife, and the chafing of old fetters would in time undoubtedly have been galling enough to provoke a general rebellion, the immediate cause of revolt did not lie in American conditions, but in events that took place in Europe. The usurpation of the Spanish throne by the French emperor was the immediate factor in precipitating the break. When in May, 1808, after treacherously forcing the abdication of the Spanish king and the renunciation of his rights by the crown prince, Napoleon marched powerful French armies into the Iberian Peninsula and placed his brother Joseph on the throne in Madrid, all Spain rose in a spontaneous movement of outraged patriotism that was to burn in the Peninsular War for five long years. These events left the Spanish colonies—in theory, holdings of the crown rather than possessions of the Spanish state—to shift for themselves. For a number of years all effective control from Spain was cut off, and by the time that Ferdinand VII was restored to his throne, through the defeat of Napoleon by the allied powers, it was too late to revert to the former relationship. In the interval a fortuitous separation had become a continent-wide independence movement;

[3] For a discussion of the fundamental causes of the Revolution consult C. Jane, *Liberty and Despotism* (Oxford: 1929), chap. v.

[4] C. H. Bernstein, "Some Inter-American Aspects of the Enlightenment," and also J. T. Lanning, "The Reception of the Enlightenment in Latin America," in *Latin America and the Enlightenment* by A. T. Whitaker and others (New York: 1942).

the sweets of freedom had been tasted and thereafter were not lightly to be surrendered.

The independence era in the Spanish colonies may be divided into two periods: (1) 1808-1816, and (2) 1816-1825. In the first period, revolutionary activities were generally under the direction of municipal bodies; in the second, events were dominated by two military geniuses, José San Martín and Simón Bolívar.

The opening of the first period, marked by the collapse of royal control, was preceded by a preliminary epoch filled largely with the activities of the greatest of the forerunners of revolution in Spanish America, Francisco Miranda.[5] This revolutionary was a Venezuelan, born in Caracas in 1754 of a well-to-do family originally from the Canary Islands. Following the usual practice of a wealthy creole, Miranda, after attending the University of Caracas for a time, went to Spain to complete his education. Here he began to gather his famous library, and came under the influence of French revolutionary ideas. Trained to arms, he secured a captain's commission and saw service under the Spanish flag during the North American Revolution. It was at this time that he is believed to have formed a determination to work for the independence of his own Spanish America. In the course of a checkered career he followed this lode star with devotion and persistence. Between 1790 and 1806 he made his headquarters in London and, while living on private loans or grants from governments unfriendly to Spain, traveled extensively in Europe and North America. In the course of visits to Paris, Berlin, Rome, Athens, St. Petersburg, Stockholm, Copenhagen, and Philadelphia, spreading anti-Spanish propaganda, dwelling on the future possibilities of the Indies, and organizing secret revolutionary societies, he solicited large-scale government aid with a view to revolution; to a remarkable extent he succeeded in focusing European interest on the discontent in Spain's colonial possessions. While persevering with this program through all manner of difficulties and discouragements, he was constantly occupied in drawing up scheme after scheme of revolutionary action and devising model constitutions for the new states he hoped to bring into existence.

In his search for foreign aid, Miranda came nearest to success in England where Pitt's government, then at war with France and Spain, seemed on two occasions to be on the very verge of embarking on his project, either in cooperation with the United States or alone, only at the last moment to relinquish the plan. Rendered desperate by the delay, Miranda in February 1806, after interviews with Jefferson, Madison, and other American leaders —though without winning their approval—recruited two hundred men,

---

[5] The standard biography of this controversial figure is W. S. Robertson's *Life of Miranda*, 2 Vols. (Chapel Hill: 1923).

20. HISPANIC AMERICAN INDEPENDENCE

secured munitions, and sailed on a filibustering expedition to the Venezuelan coast in the ship *Leander*. Forewarned of the approach of the incom-
petently managed enterprise the Spanish authorities at Puerto Cabello
had little difficulty in seizing the two small accompanying vessels and
compelling Miranda to flee in the *Leander* which only got away by throwing its artillery overboard. The popular rising that Miranda had expected
his presence to produce completely failed to materialize. A second effort
in August, 1806, under the aegis of a local British naval unit led to a
landing at Coro where Miranda proclaimed the revolution—thus firing the
first shot in the long struggle—but again a lack of local enthusiasm compelled the abandonment of the undertaking. When, four years later, the
true revolutionary movement opened, Miranda—"the Morning Star of the
Revolution"—was absent in Europe.

In this same year, 1806, which saw the failure of Miranda's two filibustering expeditions, an unofficial British escapade occurred and met with like
results. An English admiral, Sir Home Riggs Popham, whom Miranda
had fired with his own zeal for Spanish American independence, sailed
from Cape Town, apparently without orders, for the La Plata estuary. The
six ships of Popham's fleet carried sixteen hundred troops under the command of General Beresford. The plan was to free Montevideo and Buenos
Aires from the Spanish yoke and open their commerce to English trade.
The British force succeeded in marching practically unopposed into
Buenos Aires where Beresford proclaimed himself governor and exacted
an oath of allegiance to the British crown from all local officials. Six weeks
later, however, he was compelled to surrender by a force of colonials acting
under the leadership of Santiago de Liniers, a French officer who had been
for some time in the Spanish naval service and now cooperated with the
cabildo of Buenos Aires. In the following year another British expedition
succeeded in capturing Montevideo. After holding that city for seven
months, it failed in an attempt to retake Buenos Aires and finally evacuated
the whole region.

In spite of such evidence that the Spanish American colonists were not
in a truly revolutionary frame of mind, a British army of ten thousand
men was assembled at Cork in Ireland during 1807 for another expedition
to free Spanish America from Spain. This time the attack was to be made
via the Gulf of Mexico and to be under the leadership of Sir Arthur
Wellesley, but a treaty of peace and alliance with Spain in 1808, when the
crown and liberties of that country were openly menaced by Napoleon,
caused the diversion of these troops to fight the French in the Iberian
Peninsula. Further plans on the part of the British government to intervene in Spanish America were abandoned. These events contributed in
many ways to the later revolutionary development, giving the creoles

confidence in themselves, opening the prospect of foreign aid, offering a glimpse of the low prices and prosperous trade likely to ensue on the lifting of old-time commercial restrictions, and affording a seductive prospect of increased political power and prestige to the creoles.

The years immediately following the abdication of Charles IV (under French pressure) were filled with rumors and uncertainties throughout the Spanish colonies. It gradually became clear to the creoles that fate had presented them with the opportunity of leading a movement for independence without incurring the stigma of disloyalty. At first, Ferdinand VII was proclaimed king in many of the larger Spanish American centers. When French agents arrived with the news that Ferdinand also had abdicated and that Joseph Bonaparte reigned in his stead, they met with such uncompromising hostility that they hurriedly returned to Europe, convinced that the inhabitants of the Spanish Indies would not peaceably submit to the new regime.[6] Other disturbing communications also arrived. Among them, in 1808 and 1809, were letters and agents from the Central *Junta* of Seville claiming to represent the national government and asking for aid. Pressing offers likewise came from the sister of Ferdinand VII, Carlota, the ambitious wife of João, the Prince Regent of Portugal and Brazil, now living in exile in Rio, proposing to arrange for a provisional government for the colonies during her brother's detention by Napoleon. The sinister aspect of this proposal was emphasized by the dispatch in June, 1811, of a Brazilian army to Uruguay in support of a recently appointed Spanish viceroy whose pretentions were disputed by the Junta of Buenos Aires. The shadow of Carlota continued to hang over Argentina as late as 1817.[7] Meanwhile, in February, 1810, a proclamation from the Spanish Regency (successor to the Central Junta of Seville) invited the colonies to send delegates to a national cortes to assemble at Cádiz. The basis of representation however was such that the Spanish delegates would have an overwhelming majority.

Some of the peninsulares were in favor of giving strong support and practical aid in these efforts from Spain to hold the empire together while resistance was being offered to Napoleon,[8] but on the whole the creoles could not be induced to take much interest in constitutional proceedings in Spain. In the famous cortes of Cádiz which met in September, 1810, and constituted the de facto national government of Spain for the next three years, eventually producing the famous liberal constitution of 1812, Spanish America was represented by a few colonials who happened to be living in

---

[6] A. F. Zimmerman, "Spain and Its Colonies, 1808-1821," in *Hispanic American Historial Review,* Vol. XI, 1931, p. 440.

[7] *Ibid.,* pp. 441-44, a discussion of Carlotta's role in some detail.

[8] Money aid to the extent of approximately $26,000,000 had been sent from America by 1809. Zimmerman, *op. cit.,* p. 445.

Cádiz, and colonial affairs received a good deal of attention. But in America, political autonomy was becoming a reality, and this meant that there was an increasing unlikelihood that the Spanish cortes could offer any colonial privileges which would be acceptable as substitutes for self-government. The creole leaders insistently claimed that the American territories had been in the same relation to the crown as the other Spanish kingdoms and that the logical procedure was the formation of American juntas parallel and equal to those in Spain.[9]

As the year 1810 wore on and Napoleon's armies took possession of nearly all Spain, many of the larger municipalities throughout Spanish America formed governing juntas in the name of the king. For the most part of the juntas gubernativas were elected in cabildos abiertos,[10] and were usually presided over at first by the royal governor. Whatever the ultimate ambitions of some of the creole leaders, there was, as yet, no assertion of independence; on the contrary, they loudly proclaimed their loyalty to the crown and their immediate goal to be the preservation of the authority of Ferdinand VII. It is to be observed, however, that in the crisis the colonies had recourse to the most completely American of their institutions, the cabildo and its popular offshoot, the cabildo abierto, the only even slightly representative machinery they possessed. It also seemed a natural development that leadership should be assumed by the creoles, the American-born men who had long formed the dominant group in the cabildos. The influence of the more aristocratic audiencia, long the stronghold of the peninsulares, tended to recede further and further into the background as revolutionary sentiment grew stronger.

With the new access of power, the American governing juntas tended rapidly to become more openly revolutionary in character and the royal governors to be displaced as presidents. The next step in the transference of power to America was likely to be the issuance of an invitation by the junta of the capital city of each major political division—viceroyalty, captaincy-general, or presidency—to the other cities of the region to follow its example and set up local juntas and proceed to send representatives to a general assembly. The older the relationship among the subdivisions within such an area, the more likely were they to possess a spirit of unity and be willing to adopt common action.[11]

In the newest of the viceroyalties, La Plata, created as recently as 1776, the call for common action from the governing junta of Buenos Aires, on

---

[9] For a discussion of the relations of the cortes of Cádiz and the Spanish Americans, see Zimmerman, *op. cit.*, pp. 446-53, also Belaunde, *Bolívar and the Political Thought of the Spanish American Revolution* (Baltimore: 1938), chaps. vi, viii.

[10] See Chapter 6, p. 168.

[11] A study of the development of national consciousness during the colonial period will be found in Belaunde, *op. cit.*, pp. 11-15.

the initiative of a cabildo abierto set up in May, 1810, was only in part successful. Asunción in Paraguay, soon to set up its own independent junta with Dr. José Gaspar Rodríguez Francia in control, refused to cooperate with Buenos Aires except on a basis of equality. Córdoba in the distant west also resisted for a time as did, more successfully, nearby Montevideo in the *Banda Oriental* (Uruguay) where independence, through a number of confused local movements, was achieved under the leadership of José Artigas. Upper Peru (Bolivia) had little choice, being seized at once by royalists from Lima. Some of the interior provinces, especially Tucumán and Cuyo, acceded to the proposal and agreed to recognize the leadership of Buenos Aires. To compel acceptance of its program on the part of the recalcitrant sections and to quell the royalists who wished to maintain allegiance to the Regency in Spain, the junta in Buenos Aires mobilized its forces, and fighting was soon proceeding in many regions. It was to rage till 1815—with special bitterness in Upper Peru—with alternate victories and defeats for the patriot forces directed from Buenos Aires. The most famous of the creole generals in this civil war were Manuel Belgrano, Martín Güemes—an able guerrilla chieftain—and, after 1812, José San Martín.

By the time that the first constituent assembly gathered in Buenos Aires in 1813 the basic national issue had already become "unitarism" versus "federalism." Buenos Aires, of course, advocated the former, signifying as it did a program for a strongly unified government centering at the old viceregal capital city and principal port; "federalism," on the other hand, favoring a comparatively weak national government with powerful provincial governing units, was advocated by the outlying provinces, where the American Articles of Confederation of 1777 offered a precedent and suggested a form of constitution. Though by this time the outward symbols of royal authority had been generally discarded throughout the viceroyalty and there was little prospect of a willing return to royal government, there was no formal Argentine secession from Spain until 1816, when a congress of thirty-two delegates, representing ten cities and some regions of Upper Peru, met at Tucumán and on July 9 issued a declaration of independence.

The form of the future government and the whole question of whether a social and economic revolution would transform the old colonial system into a modern state were still problems of the future. Lack of confidence in democracy and lack of experience in self-government especially showed themselves in frequent changes in the form of the executive. Already a junta grande had succeeded a junta gubernativa, to be in turn superseded by two triumvirates, and these by a supreme directorate. Factionalism, inter-city rivalry, class jealousies, and personal ambitions helped to make these early years of Argentina's national history a period of political confusion and uncertainty, and at times almost complete anarchy.[12] In spite of all this, Argentina in 1816 possessed a political organization based on the oldest, most American, and most effective governmental unit of the old regime, namely, the town, and the independence movement, which everywhere else had been submerged, survived there.

Meanwhile, the neighboring captaincy-general of Chile had been having its own set of revolutionary and counterrevolutionary movements typical of the era. Because it was a region of great landowners with vast estates worked by gangs of servile laborers, the revolution in Chile, perhaps to a greater extent than in other regions, passed over the heads of the masses and was largely confined to the middle- and upper-class creoles and Spaniards. As everywhere, the Indians were largely royalist in sympathy, vaguely realizing that the issue for them was mainly a change of white masters, and that with independence they stood to lose, without compensating gains, the crown's traditional protection. The few Negro slaves, mulattoes, and zambos were not much concerned, and the mestizos only slightly more so; their turn must wait for another hundred years. As elsewhere, the early Chilean movement was fairly orderly and was marked by the use of familiar institutions. In September, 1810, a cabildo abierto in Santiago persuaded the captain-general to resign and established a governing junta dominated by the creole element. By July, 1811, a national congress, based on cabildo representation and provincial in scope, was in session in Santiago. Its members took an oath of fidelity to Ferdinand VII and also swore to support the constitution to be set up by the congress. Party divisions among radicals, conservatives, and royalists, as well as jealousies between the rival cities of Santiago and Concepción, ruined the effectiveness of this quasi-revolutionary government. Political confusion enabled a wealthy and ambitious aristocrat of some military training, José Miguel Carrera, to seize control and set himself up as dictator, with a program in which he was assisted by two other members of the Carrera family. Thus weakened by dictatorial tendencies within its ranks, the creole party was finally overthrown by a military force sent by the Peruvian viceroy to southern Chile. A royalist victory in the battle of Rancagua (October, 1814) marked the collapse of the early insurgent movement in Chile and sent the remnants of the patriot forces fleeing eastward over the Andes to swell the ranks of the army that San Martín was training in Cuyo.[13]

---

[12] Cf. J. F. Rippy, "Argentina," in *Argentina, Brazil and Chile Since Independence*, ed. A. C. Wilgus (Washington: 1935), chaps. v and vi.

[13] For a brief account of the earliest phase of the independence struggle in Chile, see I. J. Cox, "Chile," in Wilgus, *op. cit.*, chap. xxiv.

During these early revolutionary years, Peru stood apart from the rest of South America. Despite some ineffective opposition from creole groups, organized in secret clubs, the oldest of the South American viceroyalties, whose ties with Spain were especially strong, remained down to 1820 a royalist stronghold and served as a base from which strenuous and more or less successful measures were taken to stamp out revolutionary movements in other colonial centers. As late as 1822 the royalists of Lima were able to prevent the linking of the southern movements in La Plata and Chile to those of northern South America in the former viceroyalty of New Granada.

Efforts directed towards independence in the Caribbean area of northern South America were practically simultaneous with those in Buenos Aires, though much more violent in character. Venezuela and New Granada (Colombia), divided by the eastern Andes, and with viceregal administrative associations less than a century old, at first acted separately. As time went on, the currents of their two revolutionary movements merged, and then moved southward together into Ecuador to free the third member of the viceroyalty. Here in Ecuador, in 1822, the northern movement was to meet the upward thrust of the Argentinian-Chilean movement and set the stage for the overthrow of royal authority in Peru.

The revolutionary movement in the tropics centered first in Caracas, the center of the captaincy-general of Venezuela, where in April, 1810, on reports that hopeless defeat had been inflicted by Napoleon's forces on the patriot forces in Spain, the creole leaders persuaded the captain-general to call a cabildo abierto. This body insisted on the resignation of the representative of a king who was a prisoner on French soil, and created a creole junta to carry on the government in the name of Ferdinand VII. Other Venezuelan cabildos followed the example of the capital, and responded to its call to elect a constituent congress. This body met in Caracas in April, 1811, and on July 5 issued the first proclamation of independence in Spanish America. A few months later a constitution was adopted, making Venezuela a federal republic with Francisco Miranda as its first president. The famous revolutionary had been persuaded to return to his native land by a mission (of which Simón Bolívar was a member) dispatched to London to seek much needed aid against Spanish opponents both within and without the country. Although the English had made an alliance in 1808 with Spain against Napoleon and could not officially encourage rebellion in an ally's overseas dominions, they nevertheless gave the Spanish American envoys a favorable reception, prophetic of the interest and assistance that were to make Great Britain Spanish America's best foreign friend. Though early disclaiming any intention to take advantage of the confusion to make good her own recent colonial losses by annexing any part of an empire that Spain was letting slip from her grasp, England nevertheless was profoundly aware of the advantages to be derived if freedom of commerce could be established in those areas. Napoleon's Continental System had been especially devised to ruin England's European trade; here was a wonderful chance to recoup her losses and build up her depleted wealth, an opportunity which her seapower put her in unrivaled position to exploit.

Meanwhile, in Venezuela, civil war and bitter disputes over the form of the constitution raged continuously, bringing disaster to the first Venezuelan republic within a year of its creation. Neither Miranda nor Bolívar had approved its heavily weighted "federal form." But the greatest factor in the collapse of the young state was a terrible earthquake, occurring during the Easter season, on March 26, 1812, which devastated Caracas and a number of other republican cities while sparing all royalist towns. The calamity was represented by the clergy, who were bitterly opposed to the whole independence movement, as a demonstration of divine judgment on rebellion against the anointed king. All this brought confusion to republican ranks. Many ignorant and superstitious patriot soliders deserted; while the royalists, strongly supported by the hostile colored elements, who hated the local creole aristocracy, took heart and attacked the republicans with renewed vigor under the leadership of a Spanish lieutenant, Domingo de Monteverde. When Puerto Cabello, the republicans' most heavily fortified stronghold where most of their munitions were stored, was betrayed to the royalists, and Bolívar, who tried to save it, was forced to retire, Miranda despaired of a successful outcome and signed a capitulation on July 25, 1812. Through the connivance of a number of disappointed republican officers, among them Bolívar, who were furious at what they considered an unnecessary and cowardly surrender, Miranda was seized and turned over to the Spaniards. Sent as a prisoner to Spain, Miranda died four years later in a dungeon in Cádiz. From the evidence available, it seems that in signing the capitulation of San Matéo, which proved so disastrous to him, Miranda had probably intended nothing more than to retire temporarily from what he considered a hopeless situation and to renew the struggle at a later and more favorable time.

While these events were occurring in the eastern part of the viceroyalty, in New Granada proper the independence movement was following a more complicated and tortuous course. This was to be expected in a mountainous country which had been originally settled from several directions and peopled by widely diversified racial groups; it was a natural home of sectionalism. During the independence era, there were many rival centers of revolutionary activities and great diversity of opinion. Among the cities favorable to independence, Bogotá and Cartagena were rivals for the leadership of the revolutionary cause. On the other hand, at Santa Marta in the north and Popayán in the south, royalist forces long held out. Despite much discord, however, a loose league, bearing the name of "the United Provinces of New Granada," was in time formed, and succeeded in maintaining independence down to 1815, when a Spanish army of reconquest, some ten thousand men under General Pablo Morillo, made its appearence in the Caribbean.

It was to Cartagena that Bolívar had retired after the failure of the first Venezuelan republic. He had secured his safe conduct out of the country as a reward for his part in Miranda's capture. He was soon again forging to the front of the independence movement and rapidly became the most prominent leader in the north. Like Miranda, Bolívar was the son of a wealthy Venezuelan creole family. Sent to Europe to travel and complete his education, he had there been strongly influenced by the revolutionary ideas of the age. While in Spain Bolívar had fallen deeply in love, and, in 1807, had returned with his young Spanish wife to Venezuela, arriving just in time to take part in the stirring events that Napoleon's usurpation in the Spanish peninsula had thrust upon Spanish America.

At the time of Miranda's overthrow (1812), Bolívar was twenty-nine years of age, already a widower and bereft of family ties, he was now prepared to throw himself recklessly into a struggle to realize in America some of the ideals that in Europe had so quickened his imagination. A man of dynamic personality, quick judgment, and great eloquence, he was acknowledged to be as striking a figure in the assembly as on the battle front. Passionately devoted to liberal ideals, of driving energy and great personal courage, he possessed an extraordinary versatility in both arms and statesmanship. Despite his qualities of ambition, egotism, great arrogance, jealousy of his rivals, sensuality, and a streak of cruelty, he yet had an indefinable power of attracting and holding the affection of his friends and the devotion and loyalty of his followers. Despite his weaknesses, he was richly endowed to become the *imperator* of the revolutionary movement and the liberator of five republics.

Within a year of Miranda's overthrow, Bolívar had won his most highly prized title of "El Liberator." Raising troops in New Granada, he returned to Venezuela where he succeeded in seizing the capital and setting a second republic upon its feet. It survived, however, not quite a year, being overthrown in June, 1814, by attacks from some four thousand half-savage llaneros (horsemen from the plains of the Orinoco) led by a cruel and lawless Spanish commander named Tomás Boves.[14] After ordering the

---

[14] For a more detailed account of this terrible man, his followers and activities during the years 1813 and 1814, see G. Masur, *Simon Bolivar* (Albuquerque: 1948), xii and xiii.

massacre of all his royalist prisoners—the war had already engendered ruth-lessness on both sides—Bolívar retired once more to New Granada to assist in the independence movement there, and await more propitious conditions at home. That these might be long postponed he must have realized when the following spring brought a powerful Spanish fleet, with General Morillo's veteran army on board, to quench any surviving embers of revo-lution in Venezuela and to deal with the still active movement in New Granada.[15] By the middle of 1816 Morillo was able to boast that he had not "left alive in the kingdom of New Granada a single individual of sufficient influence or talents to conduct the revolution."[16] In the meantime, Bolívar, in May, 1815, moved to the West Indies where he found refuge and en-couragement in both Jamaica and Haiti.

At this juncture—the close of 1815—the outlook for the independence movement in Spanish America was gloomy in the extreme. Patriot forces had nearly everywhere been crushed. Only in Buenos Aires was a revo-lutionary government in power, and as yet it had not dared to issue a proclamation of independence. Morillo's forces held the line of the Carib-bean and the Spanish commander planned, when reinforcements should arrive, to move southward and join hands with the royalist forces in Peru. Peruvian armies were in control in Chile and Upper Peru, while in Mexico, as we shall see, only a few guerilla bands represented the cause for which Hidalgo and Morelos had given their lives. In Europe, from whence Miranda—now loaded with chains and dying in a prison in Cádiz —had hoped for aid, forces of reaction were in full swing: Napoleon was at St. Helena and the Congress of Vienna had established peace on the basis of legitimacy; Ferdinand VII, restored to his throne by the allied powers, was more reactionary than ever and was determined to bring the colonies to heel as of old, believing that there was more than a fair prospect that the Holy Alliance might be induced to extend the principle of legiti-macy across the Atlantic. Even England, always Miranda's best hope, was officially prepared to offer nothing more than mediation between Spain and her former colonies and was understood to favor a resumption of Spanish sovereignty, though on the basis of a generous measure of au-tonomy. The United States, the only free and acknowledged republic in America, was pursuing a policy of watchful waiting and nonbelligerency, though free in expressing sympathy. If the Spanish Americans could not beat Spain they did not deserve to be free, was the outspoken verdict of Monroe, then Secretary of State at Washington. Clearly, it was up to the Spanish Americans to decide their own destiny.

---

[15] Consult the interesting article "Morillo's Attempt to Pacify Venezuela," by Laura F. Ullrick in *Hispanic American Historical Review*, 1920, especially p. 541.

[16] Quoted by F. L. Paxson, *The Independence of South American Republics* (Philadelphia: 1916 ed.), p. 83. See also Ullrick, *op. cit.*, pp. 543-44.

For two more years there was little evidence of effective recovery. The reflections of the patriots were far from consoling. After seven years of effort the war for independence seemed over and a restoration to colonial status appeared inevitable. The royalists had displayed no great brilliance in plan or leadership, and yet they had met with general success because of weakness and divisions in the revolutionary ranks. Under predominantly municipal leadership, republican efforts had, generally speaking, met with no success on any but a local scale. New leadership in a new dimension was obviously called for.

The need was filled, dramatically enough, by San Martín and Simón Bolívar who, from 1817 onwards, placed themselves at the head of two revived independence movements that were separately conducted though complementary, one embracing the southern lands of South America and the other the tropical northern half of the continent. The southern movement, under General José de San Martín,[17] eventually brought freedom to Argentina and Chile, took naval control in the Pacific and began, but did not complete, the revolution in Peru. The northern movement under Bolívar [18] embraced the three divisions of the old viceroyalty of New Granada (Venezuela, New Granada, and Ecuador), and then completed the overthrow of royalist power in Peru and Upper Peru. The two creole chieftains, fighting for the same cause for twelve years, carried through their whole campaigns independently of each other. Beginning at bases as far removed from each other as the vast continent of South America permitted, their strategies gradually converged on the royalist stronghold of Peru. They met but once, when their respective tasks were all but completed. At Guayaquil in Ecuador, practically on the equator, in 1822 the Liberator of Colombia and the Protector of Peru held a brief conference and then drew apart again.

Let us look more closely at the two movements. First that in the south: its leader, José de San Martín, was the fourth son of a Spanish officer and was born in 1778 in an Indian mission village called Yapeyu on the Uruguay River in Argentina. As the family soon returned to Spain, the boy was educated in the peninsula and entered the army at the age of

---

[17] For a sympathetic short study of San Martín, see W. E. Browning, *op. cit.*, pp. 699-705. Also C. K. Webster, *Britain and the Independence of Latin America, 1812-1830* (London: 1938), Introduction.

[18] The most varied estimates have been held of Bolívar. A recent, objective and scholarly study is Gerhard Masur, *Simon Bolivar* (Albuquerque, 1948). The older works by Angell, Petre, Sherwell, and Ludwig are illuminating on certain aspects of the Liberator's career. In periodical literature: W. E. Browning, "The Liberation and the Liberators" in *Hispanic American Historical Review*, 1921, Vol. IV, pp. 705-12, is an objective estimate; see also J. F. Rippy, "Bolívar as Viewed by Contemporary Diplomats of the United States," in *Hispanic American Historical Review*, 1935, Vol. XV, pp. 287-97; for an early unfavorable opinion by an American journalist in 1818-1819 see Baptis Irvine's "Reports on Simón Bolívar," in *Hispanic American Historical Review*, 1936, Vol. XVI, pp. 360-73.

eleven. For twenty-two years he fought for the king in campaign after campaign in Africa, Portugal, and Spain. For his services in the famous battle of the Spanish patriots against the French at Bailén in July, 1808, he was made a lieutenant colonel of cavalry. No other Spanish American soldier of his age had such a long and systematic training, or was his equal in strategy. Filled with zeal for the cause of political freedom, on hearing of the revolution in South America San Martín relinquished his colonelcy and set sail for Buenos Aires where, landing in March, 1812, he immediately offered his sword to the revolutionary government. Confirmed in his former rank, he was soon playing an important role in civil and military affairs. For a time he commanded in the war against the royalists in Upper Peru, but became convinced that the defensive strategy underlying the military efforts in this area was wrong and at his own request was transferred in August, 1814, to the relatively obscure position of governor of the province of Cuyo with its capital at Mendoza. Underlying this change was a new plan which he had conceived for the winning of the war.

In Cuyo for two years, 1814 to 1816, in an independent and concealed position, San Martín patiently trained an army of Argentinian recruits and Chilean patriots while he completed his plans to strike with a disciplined army at the royalist stronghold of Peru from a base in Chile. His friend Pueyrredón, the Supreme Director of the government in Buenos Aires, gave him effective support, as did also the exiled Chilean leader, General Bernardo O'Higgins. Having laid cunning plans to deceive the enemy as to his intentions, San Martín in January, 1817, now commander-in-chief of the army of the Andes of the United Provinces of La Plata, led a force of five thousand men with supplies and artillery over the Andes, using principally the Uspallata Pass but also five others nine to twelve thousand feet above sea level, into the Chilean plains beyond.[19] This passage of the Andes is in itself one of the notable feats in military history. The royalists in Chile would not believe that it could be done. The passes they knew were so narrow that only a single man or animal could advance at a time, and they ran through mountains that were utterly destitute of forage and were held by hostile Indians who were devoted to the royalist cause. Yet San Martín accomplished the feat at the worst time of the year with very few losses, and, what is more, immediately afterwards succeeded in reassembling his divisions and striking an effective blow at the astounded royalists.[20]

---

[19] While detachments of San Martín's army used all six passes, the main army went through the Uspallata Pass to the south of the Aconcagua peak. The leader himself crossed with the reserves through the pass of Los Patos to the north of Aconcagua. See Browning, *op. cit.,* 702.

[20] For a description of this feat and how it was achieved see Browning, *op. cit.,* 701-03.

It was on February 12, 1817, that San Martín with the help of O'Higgins fell on the royalists at Chacabuco, defeated them, and forced them to evacuate Santiago. From the Chileans, who were by this time disgusted with the royalists and their oppressive regime, the Argentine general received a warm welcome and was invited to assume charge of the government. When he declined, at his suggestion a cabildo abierto elected Bernardo O'Higgins as Supreme Dictator of the state, and independence was formally proclaimed on February 12, 1818. It was not, however, until San Martín had routed the royalists on April 5 in the decisive battle of Maipú that Chilean independence was assured, although small royalist bands still held out in the far south for some time longer.

Having achieved independence for Chile, San Martín's next objective was his expedition against Peru, for which he proposed to use Chile as a naval base. In his struggle to create a fleet with which to transport and convoy his army to the environs of Lima the creole general was assisted by good luck as well as by the strenuous efforts of O'Higgins' government. A nucleus was secured when a Spanish frigate, convoying ten transports filled with troops intended to serve as re-enforcements to the royalists of Chile, fell into patriot hands. The addition of other vessels, purchased from the United States and England and manned by British and North American officers, finally gave Chile a small squadron to cruise the Pacific. This new fleet at the end of 1818 was placed under the command of Thomas Cochrane, Lord Cochrane, an English naval officer of great ability and courage who, through hot temper, had fallen into disgrace at home and been discharged from the British service. After capturing Valdivia and otherwise establishing control of the Pacific seaboard, Cochrane was ready in August, 1820, to transport San Martín's liberating army of Argentinean and Chilean troops—somewhat more than four thousand in number—from Valparaiso to Pisco on the Peruvian coast south of Lima. In the preceding year, 1819, a crisis had arisen which for a time threatened the whole expedition. The Buenos Aires government, alarmed by gaucho rebellions at home and terrified by the news that a huge Spanish army was assembling at Cádiz for the reconquest of the viceroyalty, had ordered its most distinguished general to return home. But San Martín, taking courage from the report that the troops at Cádiz had mutinied, refused to obey orders, declaring that destiny called him to Lima.

When he landed at Pisco San Martín found that the viceroy had been instructed to reach an agreement with him on liberal terms. Pending negotiations an armistice was concluded at Miraflores to the great disgust of the strenuous and ambitious Lord Cochrane who henceforth became increasingly critical of San Martín's strategy and eventually resigned. Even when he broke off negotiations with the viceroy on the ground that nothing short of independence was acceptable, San Martín did not at once attack Lima. Declaring that his mission was liberation and not conquest, he proposed to wait near the city until he should be invited to enter. Only minor military operations marked the campaign. Propaganda was San Martín's chief weapon and eventually it proved effective. The position of the royalists became untenable and under the viceroy, La Serna, they evacuated the city in July, 1821, and marched inland. The cabildo invited San Martín to enter the evacuated city which he did with great deliberation and without ostentation. A month later, on July 28, 1821, in the central plaza of the Ciudad de Los Reyes, Peruvian independence was proclaimed, severing the old tie with Spain. San Martín unfurled the new flag. Shortly afterwards he assumed by proclamation dictatorial powers over the new state under the title of "Protector." As the royalist forces, greatly outnumbering his own, were still intact in the highlands and the majority of the people were still royalist in sympathy, his position was by no means secure. He settled down to await reinforcements for the patriot cause from Bolívar's army which was approaching from the north.

The revival of republican fortunes in the north dated from Bolívar's return to Venezuela in December, 1816. This time the Liberator proposed a flank attack from the Orinoco Valley against the royalist enemy entrenched all along the coast. For his new campaign he secured aid from a number of quarters. President Petión of Haiti repeatedly gave assistance to the limit of the resources of his own recently freed republic. In England, Bolívar's commissioners, besides collecting substantial sums of money and arms, were able to enlist a considerable body of English and Irish veterans of Waterloo and other Napoleonic campaigns who, in the hard times of the postwar years, were glad of an opportunity to volunteer for service abroad. These foreign legionnaires, numbering some four or five thousand by the close of 1818 when they included a sprinkling of many nationalities, were a considerable addition to Bolívar's strength.[21] Though they included some mutinous and difficult elements, from among them Bolívar was able to develop a core of experienced officers and men on whom he could rely for efficient service in his later campaigns. A large proportion were to perish in the tropical lands they helped to free.

The discouragements of the years 1817 and 1818 were heartbreaking; little apparent progress in the revolutionary cause in the northern theater

21 Alfred Hasbrouck in his study *Foreign Legionaries in the Liberation of Spanish America* (New York: 1928), pp. 388-89, says that the total number of foreigners in Bolívar's army has been placed as high as 6,000 but that it is probable that "the actual number present in any campaign did not exceed 1,200." He points out, however that when all numbers were small, even the addition of a few hundred could be a decisive factor in a campaign. Furthermore, the knowledge of European tactics and discipline brought by the foreigners improved the morale and training of the American recruits, though their presence also created many difficult problems.

could be seen. Bolívar's fanatical zeal, however, never slackened and the royalists found that they could not drive him from his foothold on the Orinoco. Gradually the creole leader's army increased and took on a modicum of discipline. His most important reinforcements came from the llaneros of the plains who had been his worst enemies in 1814 but had since become alienated from the crown through harsh treatment by the royalists. Now, under the leadership of José Páez, an intrepid soldier of great natural talent but little education, they joined the patriot cause, contributing especially to the strength of its cavalry by their fine horsemanship.

On February 15, 1819, the second congress of Venezuela summoned by Bolívar to Angostura, his provisional headquarters, confirmed the Liberator in his position as commander-in-chief of the army and re-elected him as president of the Republic of Venezuela. With his political position thus strengthened and his army in better shape, Bolívar embarked on a daring move against the Spanish forces that were preparing to close in upon him. Leaving Páez to hold Morillo's forces in Venezuela, Bolívar, with a force of some two thousand men that included one hundred and fifty British, unexpectedly crossed the submerged tropical plains of southern Venezuela and then passed over the Andes into New Granada; there he joined the patriot guerrilla forces under the Colombian leader, Santander, thus striking behind the lines of the Spaniards' main strength. The passage across these bleak, trackless, most difficult northern Andean mountains, that rise to a height of 13,000 feet, in itself constituted a feat that rivaled San Martín's exploit in the southern Andes of two years earlier.

Taken by surprise, the Spaniards were decisively beaten in the battles of Pántano de Vargas and of Boyacá, a little to the north of Bogotá, August 7, 1819, and all serious royalist resistance in New Granada crumbled. Bolívar was unable to follow up this military advantage immediately and strike at Morillo's royalist forces on the coast because news of political dissensions at Angostura compelled him to make the long trip back to his headquarters on the Orinoco.

Shortly after his arrival at Angostura in December, 1819, the Venezuelan congress gave substance to the first phase of Bolívar's dream of political reconstruction by promulgating a fundamental law proclaiming the union of Venezuela and New Granada under the name of the Republic of Colombia. The law established a provisional government for the new state, named Bolívar as president, and issued a summons for a congress of both provinces to meet at Rosario de Cúcuta on the eastern frontier of New Granada. This body met in May, 1821.

The intervening months were largely filled with peace negotiations. The success of the 1820 revolution in Spain, with the acceptance by Ferdinand VII of the liberal Constitution of 1812, combined with several patriot successes in the Western Hemisphere, brought overtures from Spain for a negotiated peace. General Morillo was instructed by the king to open correspondence on the basis of the acceptance of the Constitution of 1812, which provided for colonial representation in the cortes, and, of course, implied a recognition of Spanish sovereignty; the creole leaders, however, were to remain in actual control of the provinces. Bolívar finally agreed to a six months' truce and sent peace commissioners to Spain, but with instructions to hold out for complete independence for the colonies.[22] When the Spanish government refused to negotiate on this basis fighting was again resumed. In this final campaign, the war centered in Venezuela. Caracas changed hands several times. The decisive patriot victory came on June 24, 1821, at Carabobo, where the British Foreign Legion greatly distinguished itself,[23] and the Spanish army was practically destroyed as a fighting force. Bolívar entered Caracas in triumph and the congress at Cúcuta pushed forward with greater assurance its task of drawing up a federal constitution. Bolívar took the oath of office as president for the third time in October.

Shortly afterwards, with his mind on the military problems involved in the incorporation of the third and most southern division of the old viceroyalty—the presidency of Quito—within the new Republic of Colombia, Bolívar transferred the capital from Cúcuta to Bogotá and began active preparations to move his army southward. The conquest of Ecuador was largely the achievement of General Antonio José de Sucre, Bolívar's warm friend and most trusted general, who early in 1821 had been sent southward by sea with a small force to keep the situation in hand until the Liberator could march thither by land. After one serious reverse, a battle fought on May 24, 1822, at Pichincha on the slopes of the volcano overlooking the capital city was such a decisive victory for the patriots that the Spanish commander shortly afterwards formally surrendered the whole province. A month later, Bolívar made a triumphal entry into Quito and proclaimed the territory a part of the Republic of Colombia, which at that very time was receiving recognition from the United States as a member of the family of nations. Its territory was now practically complete, for a few months earlier (November 28, 1821) Panama had broken ties with Spain and declared its adherence to the Colombian federation.

Two months after the battle of Pichincha, on July 26 and 27, 1822, the two great chieftains whose labors had brought independence to South America—the Liberator of Colombia and the Protector of Peru—met in

---

[22] On the peace negotiations and for an estimate of Morillo's work consult Ullrick, *op. cit.*, pp. 561-65.

[23] In this decisive battle Hasbrouck states (*op. cit.*, p. 240) that the patriots lost only 200 men of the 6,000 engaged and of the 200 casualties 130 belonged to the British battalion. Forty per cent of the royal army of 5,000 was killed, wounded, or captured.

Guayaquil. It was a momentous occasion. It is not known exactly what occurred at the meeting as neither participant left a specific record of the conference and both were careful to conceal their differences under a show of admiration and cordiality.[24] The two leaders discussed the general future of the independence movement and the form that government should take, as well as the immediate need of a Colombian army to overpower the royalist forces still in control of eastern and Upper Peru. Their views on these fundamental matters differed radically and no common agreement could be reached. Neither would Bolívar accept San Martín's offer to acknowledge the Colombian's leadership and serve under him, either convinced that such an arrangement would lead to future trouble or unwilling to share the glory. It is known that their political views at the time were far apart. San Martín wished to see the liberated colonies made into a number of constitutional monarchies ruled over by European princes; Bolívar believed that only the republican form was practical in the circumstances. No open breach occurred, but San Martín left the conference disappointed and convinced that the Colombian general would not furnish, under any joint arrangement, the aid to Peru that was indispensable.

The southern leader returned to Lima where in his absence there had been a revolution and his representative overthrown. Feeling that his work was done and that his continued presence would only complicate matters, he decided for the good of the cause that he had served for ten crowded years to withdraw himself entirely from the scene and leave the stage to Bolívar. Summoning a Peruvian congress and disregarding its protests, San Martín resigned his position as Protector and relinquished command of the army. As he departed in September he invited Bolívar to enter Peru and take up the work and honor that he was laying down. For a time he attempted to live in retirement near Mendoza in Argentina, but finding it impossible not to be drawn into politics, left Argentina in 1824 for exile in Europe. Attempting to return five years later, he was made to feel so unwelcome that he immediately went back to Europe where he spent the remainder of his life. He died in obscurity in France in 1850.

The Liberator did not arrive in Lima for a year after San Martín's departure. In the interval his coadjutor, Sucre, tried to quiet the political dissensions that distracted the country and to organize an army capable of facing the royalists. Even after Bolívar's arrival in Lima the situation did not greatly improve until the Liberator won the famous cavalry engagement against the royalists at Junín, and General Sucre inflicted overwhelming defeat in the final great battle of the war at Ayacucho in the highlands of Peru. In this decisive victory the last of the Spanish viceroys,

---

[24] Masur points out (*op. cit.,* p. 477) that San Martín arrived at this meeting without a card in his hand.

Simón Bolívar. (Courtesy of the Bolivarian Society of the United States, Inc.)

General José María Morelos

Miguel Hidalgo

Mansion of Emperor Iturbide

La Serna, was wounded and taken prisoner and the Spanish generalissimo signed a capitulation on December 9, 1824 for the whole army. Early in the following year, royalist forces had to be rooted out of Upper Peru. This last province, however, was finally declared independent on August 6, 1825, and renamed the Republic of Bolivia with a capital at Chuquisaca (now Sucre). The emancipation of South America was finally complete though it was not to be recognized as such by the mother country for many years.

II. MEXICO IN THE INDEPENDENCE ERA

In Mexico, as in South America, the struggle for independence was marked by two distinct phases. The character of the movement, however, in both its earlier and later stages, was different from that of the struggle in the southern Spanish colonies. From the outset the contest in South America was definitely a creole movement directed against the peninsulares, from which the Indians and Negroes generally held aloof or conservatively supported the old regime, while the mestizos played an unimportant part. In Mexico, on the other hand, down to 1821, the revolutionary forces were composed chiefly of Indians and mestizos, and the movement was primarily an uprising of the oppressed masses against white domination. In the years before 1815 this social insurrection was led by two parish priests.

The father of the Mexican revolution was Miguel Hidalgo y Costilla. Born in 1753 in a village of the province of Guanajuato, of old creole stock, Hidalgo was educated for the priesthood. Teaching for a time in a theological college, in 1810 he became parish priest in the village of Dolores, where he was much beloved for the interest he took in the social and economic well-being of the natives of the surrounding region, teaching them how to tan leather, make pottery, and even to cultivate the forbidden olives and grapes and experiment with silkworms. Early in his career, however, he fell under the suspicion of the Inquisition, by whose agents he was accused of holding heretical religious views, reading prohibited books filled with the doctrines of the French Revolution, leading an immoral life, and indulging in gambling and other vices.[25] His house, it was said, was "a little France," a center for the study and discussion of advanced ideas by a group of radical associates, among whom were two creole officers—Ignacio Allende and Juan Aldama.

The suspicions of the Inquisition were not entirely without foundation. After 1808 Hidalgo was certainly the leading spirit in a literary and social

---

[25] A. H. Noll and A. P. McMahon, *Life and Times of Miguel Hidalgo y Costilla* (Chicago: 1910), pp. 33-37.

club in Querétaro, which by 1810 had become a center of independence conspiracy. Before any detailed plans had been perfected, the plot became known to the authorities and an outbreak was prematurely forced. Warned by a friend—a Mexican Paul Revere—at two o'clock in the morning of September 16, 1810, that the authorities were on the move, Hidalgo decided to cast aside all further pretense. Striding to the village jail, he freed the prisoners and then rang the church bell to summon his followers. The *grito de Dolores* which arose from the crowd of assembled Indians signalized the beginning of the Mexican revolt against Spain.[26] A painting of the Virgin of Guadalupe, the Indian patron saint, acquired from a church on the route of march, became the banner of a movement to which the oppressed Indians and mestizos flocked in thousands.

From the first, however, Hidalgo and the other leaders seemed to have little or no program other than to make a passionate protest against social ills. After capturing and sacking the provincial town of Guanajuato, the undisciplined insurrectionary mass, armed for the most part only with machetes, moved on to engulf the larger centers of Guadalajara and Valladolid, and then advanced on Mexico City. Here, had he attacked at once, Hidalgo might have met with success, but he hesitated and gave his opponents a chance to organize resistance. By this time the excesses that marked the uprising had forced a union of all whites, as it seemed clear that Hidalgo's success would mean Indian domination. Eventually in 1811 a trained white army of six thousand men defeated the undisciplined hordes of some eighty thousand Indians at the Puente de Calderón. Hidalgo and most of his officers, attempting to find safety in flight towards the north, were captured and finally condemned and shot. Lack of military leadership, undrilled troops, division among the leaders, and lack of carefully formulated plans—both of revolutionary action and of government to follow—all contributed to the final disaster. The outbreak simply underlined the accumulated abuses and grievances under which the great masses of Mexicans suffered during the old regime, and started the ball of revolution rolling.

The execution of Hidalgo, Allende, Aldama, and other leaders of this first insurrectionary outburst failed to suppress the revolutionary movement. Another priest, José María Morelos y Pavon, rose to take Hidalgo's place. A man of more lowly social standing, a mestizo, son of a carpenter and one-time muleteer on the Acapulco-Mexico City trade route, Morelos had succeeded in securing an education at Hidalgo's college at Valladolid, and at thirty years of age was admitted to the priesthood. Attached to Hidalgo's revolutionary enterprise in its early stages, he was assigned the

---

[26] For events leading to the famous *Grito* consult Noll and McMahon, *op. cit.,* chap. xiv.

special task of capturing Acapulco. After his chief's death, Morelos evaded capture and was soon recognized as the leader of the most important of the many revolutionary guerrilla bands that maintained themselves, at first independently, in the rural regions of central and southern Mexico. Possessed of greater military and political ability, calmer and more practical than Hidalgo though less enthusiastic and inspiring, Morelos dominated the Mexican revolutionary scene from 1812 to 1815.[27] Under his leadership the movement, which under Hidalgo had been primarily an Indian insurrection against white landlords and oppressive living conditions, widened into a true independence struggle.

From a motley following of some six thousand men, Morelos slowly drilled an army able for some years to outmanoeuver a royal force of several times its number. Eventually Morelos succeeded in driving the royal troops out of large parts of southern Mexico, captured and held the large towns of Orizaba, Oaxaca, Vera Cruz, Guanajuato, and Acapulco, and, like Hidalgo, threatened Mexico City itself. In September, 1813, as a counter blast to the viceroy's promulgation in Mexico of the liberal Spanish Constitution of 1812, the revolutionary leader convoked a congress at Chilpancingo in Oaxaca, which he called the Congress of Anahuac. This body on November 6, 1813, issued a declaration of independence from Spain, and adopted a number of reform measures which included the abolition of slavery and Indian tribute, the cancellation of debts owed to Europeans, and the limitation and equalization of taxes. In the following year at Apatzingán, a congress drafted a republican constitution which, though it came into operation only for a short time in a limited area, served for six years as a source of liberal inspiration, and provides for later times the clearest expression we have of the form of political revolutionary thought of the first decade of the Mexican independence movement.[28] Its most interesting feature is the complete acceptance of the "centralist" principle.

The restoration of Ferdinand VII and the re-establishment of the old absolutism drove a number of liberals into the insurrectionary movement, but slowly the forces of the viceregal government under the leadership of the relentless Agustín de Iturbide pushed the independentists into the south. By deliberate self-sacrifice, Morelos was able to halt the royalist pursuit long enough for the recently constituted congress, under another leader, to retreat to safety; Morelos himself, however, was taken prisoner. Placed on trial in Mexico City for insurrection, he made the defense that, as Mexico was really independent, he as a loyal son had been merely defending her

<hr>

[27] H. I. Priestley, *The Mexican Nation* (New York: 1923), p. 239.
[28] J. L. Mecham, "Origins of Federalism in Mexico," in *Hispanic American Historical Review,* 1938, Vol. XVIII, p. 165.

liberties. Such arguments, however, did not save him. He was publicly degraded from the priesthood, branded as a heretic by the Inquisition, and shot by a firing squad on December 22, 1815. So fearful was the government, in view of the admiration of the masses for this warrior priest and patriot, that the execution was carried through secretly outside Mexico City. Tradition tells that at his death his prayer for the emancipation of his country closed with the words, "Lord, if I have done well, Thou knowest it; if ill, to Thy infinite mercy I commend my soul." [29]

With the passing of Morelos, the heroic period of the early revolution closed. Henceforth resistance to Spanish authority was represented simply by a number of independent bands of guerrilla fighters, who were barely disinguishable from banditti and who, one after another, were crushed by a government that seemed to most citizens the only guarantee of law and order. There was no further need, wrote the viceroy to Spain in 1819, to send more troops to Mexico.

In 1820 a curious situation arose when news arrived from Spain that the absolutist Ferdinand VII had been compelled by an uprising of his troops to accept the liberal Constitution of 1812, and was dispatching orders to Mexico to proclaim the document there. This, it was realized, would probably mean the dissolution of convents, the abolition of the Inquisition, the suppression of tithes, freedom of the press, reduced pay and importance for the army, possible attention to the agrarian grievances of the masses, and other liberal reforms associated with the suppressed independence movement. While many creoles were pleased, seeing increased importance for their class, the clergy, army officers, office holders, and the peninsulares generally were appalled. In their dilemma, they decided to take over the independence movement, which they had hitherto denounced and persecuted as heretical and traitorous, and reorganize, lead, and control it for their own ends. In the independent Mexico of the future, they proposed to see to it that, whatever happened to the connection with Spain, the privileges of their own groups would be safe.

To draw up plans for this curiously inverted, reactionary revolution, many meetings were held in the Jesuit church of the Profesa in Mexico City. Here it was decided to employ Colonel Agustín de Iturbide as commander of the troops. He was a very natural choice. A native of Valladolid and a mestizo, though generally regarded as a creole, he had once considered becoming a follower of Hidalgo but had thought better of the matter and joined the viceroy's army instead, where, in the years preceding 1820, he had distinguished himself for the unrelenting cruelty with which he had pursued the liberal guerrillas. Recently under a cloud for insubor-

---

[29] Noll and McMahon, *op. cit.*, p. 150.

dination, Iturbide was at the moment out of funds and ready for new adventure. Handsome, dashing, unscrupulous, vain, plausible in manners, and experienced in arms, he appeared to possess many of the qualities needed in the new leader. Through a ruse he managed to get himself placed in command of a body of troops by representing to the viceroy that Vicente Guerrero, the most outstanding of the revolutionary chieftains still in the field, was about to march on Mexico City. Commissioned to oppose the rebel, his real purpose was to seek a compromise with this independence leader and win him over to a plan for the emancipation of all Mexico, in which movement the conservatives should play the dominant rôle.

In a series of interviews, held in February, 1821, the famous Plan of Iguala was evolved. It was a pronunciamiento which was at once a declaration of independence from Spain and at the same time a plan for a provisional government for Mexico. To an assembly of army chiefs in the small village of Iguala in southwestern Mexico, on February 24, 1821, the famous Plan of the Three Guarantees was unfolded. It provided for the guarantee of religion, independence, and union in a Mexico free from Spain but governed as a constitutional monarchy by Ferdinand VII, or by some other prince of the Bourbon House. A Mexican congress would be summoned to draw up a constitution which must recognize Roman Catholicism as the only tolerated religion, with all the rights, privileges, and property of the church intact and would provide for equal civil rights for all classes in the community—Europeans, creoles, mestizos, and Indians. Finally, the new government was to be supported by the Army of the Three Guarantees, under Iturbide's leadership.

Support for the new scheme came from all sides despite the vigorous protests of the viceroy, whose objections were overruled and who was himself deposed. His successor, General Juan O'Donojú, thirtieth and last of the viceroys of New Spain, on arrival at Vera Cruz found that the Plan had obtained general acceptance throughout Mexico. In these circumstances, he was forced to agree to the embodiment of its main provisions in the Treaty of Córdoba, which he signed on August 24, 1821. By the terms of this document it was laid down that, if a Spanish prince did not accept the Mexican throne, the cortes of Mexico might elect a monarch. The victorious Army of the Three Guarantees marched into Mexico City, where presently a regency, of which Iturbide was president and O'Donojú a member, was set up to act as an executive until Ferdinand VII should be heard from. In May, 1822, when news arrived that the Spanish cortes had rejected the Treaty of Córdoba, soldiers and populace in a street demonstration proclaimed Iturbide as Emperor of Mexico. The following day a reluctant and intimidated congress, with many of its members absent, acquiesced in the popular decision, and on July 21, with great pomp and ceremony, Iturbide was crowned as Agustín I.

The new empire was short-lived, surviving approximately nine months. The new ruler showed little capacity for government, quarreling with and finally dissolving the constituent congress, and antagonizing his supporters by his lavish expenditures, forced loans, and general bad management. A new political star, Antonio López de Santa Anna, declared Iturbide's election illegal, and raised the standard of revolt in Vera Cruz. When Santa Anna demanded the establishment of a republic, not only the old republicans but a large part of the now dominant army went over to the new movement. Iturbide was forced to abdicate on April 19, 1823, and was sent into exile. When, seventeen months later, he foolishly attempted to return to Mexico he was arrested and executed near Tampico July 1, 1824.

Apart from its unique character, the most interesting thing about the only empire ever set up during the revolutionary age in Spain's dissolving dominions was its comparatively large size. It stretched from northern California to the Isthmus of Panama, embraced the whole continental portion of viceroyalty of New Spain, and included the former captaincy-general of Guatemala. The five provinces of Central America had realized the impossibility of continuing the Spanish connection after the independence of Mexico and Panama, and had declared their independence on September 15, 1821. The captain-general himself became the head of the new government, which in 1822 asked for annexation to the Mexican empire of Iturbide. The Liberals, however, were never satisfied with this arrangement, and when Iturbide abdicated the connection with Mexico was broken. In 1823 the Central American states formed their own Central American Confederation.

Meanwhile, in Mexico the republicans were in the saddle. A provisional plural executive of three members governed until a new constitution could be framed. In attempting to draft the new basic law, the republicans divided into two distinct groups, "federalists" and "centralists." The centralists represented the old Spanish tradition and would have continued the provinces as merely administrative units; the federalists, regarding centralism and autocracy as dangerously close companions, were determined to break with the old order of things and to place the emphasis on the autonomy of local units. According to the finally triumphant federalists, Mexico as a new nation ought to be under a new dispensation; they looked to the United States for inspiration, and the government which they established in the constitution of 1824 was federal in form and assured state rights for smaller territorial units. But under the influence of the Church, the landowners, and the army, many of the old centralist and reactionary habits of thought survived, determining the trend of national political development, so that the first truly liberalizing reform measures were postponed for a generation.

III. BRAZIL IN THE INDEPENDENCE ERA

The shadow of Napoleon fell earlier and more completely over Portuguese than over Spanish America, and brought events in its train as portentous for the future of Brazil as those that followed in the Spanish colonies the enthronement in Madrid of Joseph Bonaparte. It was on November 25, 1807, that an imperious message from the European conqueror arrived in Lisbon announcing that the Braganza dynasty was considered to have forfeited its throne, that Portugal was presently to be occupied by a joint French and Spanish army, and that it was to be divided between these two powers. The Portuguese ruler, Dom João, ruling as Regent for his demented mother, realized the impossibility of offering effective resistance to these nefarious plans of his two nearest neighbors. With the encouragement of Great Britain, his country's oldest ally, he made the momentous decision to remove the entire Portuguese government and court across the Atlantic to Brazil. This amazing armada, crowded to the rails with the royal family, soldiers, and government officials, with their archives and equipment, and accompanied by the whole court and a horde of retainers, left Lisbon November 29, 1807. It was convoyed to Brazil by British warships. Enthusiastic excitement, tempered by not a little consternation, marked the safe arrival of the huge flotilla first at Baía, and later at Rio de Janeiro where the general disembarkation of some fifteen thousand persons took place.

Brazil was pleased and flattered by the turn of events. On the whole the colony warmly welcomed the Regent and paid little heed to the severe criticism leveled at him by his courtiers as a vacillating, indolent, weak, and extravagant ruler. He might indeed have his failings, but he was good-natured, democratic in manner, cordial, well-disposed towards Brazilians, lavish in the distribution of honors and titles, and they liked him. His first decree to be issued at Baía, opening the ports of Brazil to the world's commerce and putting an end to Portugal's century-old monopoly of the colony's trade, confirmed both the Brazilians and the British—the chief beneficiaries—in their good opinion of Dom João. The Brazilians also approved of his energetic foreign policy which, in the north, presently brought about temporary occupation of French Guiana and, in the south, effected the incorporation of the Banda Oriental as the Cisplatine province.

In home affairs the Brazilians were pleased to find Dom João astute enough to choose able advisers and willing to select them impartially from both Brazilians and Portuguese. The Regent also won popular approval by his efforts to transplant an air of European culture and refinement to his new capital by opening a number of professional schools, establishing an academy of fine arts, founding a public library and a botanical garden, setting up the Bank of Brazil, permitting the establishment of a public press, and offering warm hospitality to such literary and scientific celebrities as could be induced to visit Brazil to explore and describe its riches, beauty, and promise. While Dom João thus made himself personally welcome, the thousands of arrogant and extravagant Portuguese hangers-on who had accompanied him lost no time in bringing upon themselves widespread criticism by their selfish and ambitious behavior. Despite the handicap imposed by the rivalry and jealousy of native Brazilians and immigrating Portuguese, Dom João made considerable progress in the difficult task of transplanting an Old World dynasty to a New World environment amid circumstances in which the traditional relationship of colony to motherland was practically reversed. Inevitably the legal status of the colony tended to change, and it spoke well for Dom João's political sagacity that he did not delay the recognition of this transformation. While still acting as Regent he formally announced, on December 16, 1815, that Brazil had been elevated to the rank of a kingdom. On his mother's death in 1816, he assumed the crown with the title João VI, King of Portugal, Brazil, and Algarve, thus recognizing the former colony as a co-ordinate kingdom.

Dom João's most important contribution to Brazilian welfare, however, was the reinforcement he gave to continued imperial unity. In the late eighteenth century, in Brazil as in other American colonies, there had been signs of a growing national consciousness and open evidence of serious dissatisfaction with the restraints imposed by the motherland. These impulses towards independence and republicanism varied in strength in different sections of the country. At first they were strongest in Minas Gerais where, in 1789, an open rebellion had broken out under the leadership of a certain Tiradentes. How greatly the government had feared that this example might spread was clear from the severity with which this first effort to break loose had been crushed. Further north, where the struggle against the Dutch in the seventeenth century had centered, Pernambuco was also an early focus of strong local patriotism in which independence and republican ideas were favorite topics of discussion. Here, in 1817, under the influence of stirring news from the neighboring Spanish American lands, an abortive republican movement got under way, but lacked a definite program and, securing little support outside the northern area, was easily suppressed. Considering the uneven development of the vast colony and the lack of communication between its parts, there might well have taken place by mere centrifugal force a breakup of Portugal's American dominion and the formation, as in Spanish America, of a number of independent states. The arrival of the monarchy in the person of the popular Dom João, and the pursuance by him of a generally acceptable policy, provided a powerful check to the growing forces of disintegration and strongly reinforced the idea of national unity.[30] Although under his rule no change was made in the direction of decentralizing the administration to meet the wishes of the provinces for greater autonomy, his government exemplified a mixture of practical democracy and theoretical absolutism; the king's mere presence prevented the development of those dispersive forces which would have made impossible a future great Brazil.

In 1820 Dom João's stay in America came to an end. A revolutionary movement in Portugal threatened his Portuguese crown and made it imperative that he should return to Lisbon. After postponing the move as long as possible, he took an affecting farewell of the country to which he had become strongly attached. As a parting gesture of friendliness he showered honors, medals, and decorations on all around him. To his son Pedro, whom he left as Regent of Brazil, he is said to have given the parting advice, "Pedro, Brazil will, I fear, ere long separate itself from Portugal; and if that happens, place the crown on thine own head rather than allow it to fall into the hands of any adventurer." [31]

It was not strange that he was filled with gloomy foreboding as he looked out upon the future. The new Regent was a mere youth of twenty-two who had been given no adequate training for the heavy task that now fell to him. His mother, Carlota Joaquina, a sister of Ferdinand VII of Spain, had never taken pains to conceal her dislike for her eldest son while she lavished affection on his brother Miguel. The easygoing father had also paid no heed to the education of his heir and had allowed him to grow up uncultured and untutored with little companionship but that of servants. He was more at home in the stables than in the palace; he had learned to be a fine horseman and a good mechanic, but in the art of government, knowledge of court etiquette, and in self-discipline he had been given little instruction and less practice. He was vain, ambitious, erratic, pleasure-loving, and immoral, and possessed only a slender equipment for the solution of the tremendous problems which his situation involved. It was, however, greatly in his favor that he had been brought up among his future subjects who were disposed to be lenient in their judgment of a handsome, vivacious, ardent, romantic young prince reputed to have a generous streak of the brilliance that had marked many men of his royal

---

[30] P. A. Martin, "Federalism in Brazil," in *Hispanic American Historical Review*, 1938, Vol. XVIII, p. 145.

[31] Martin, "Brazil," in *Argentina, Brazil and Chile since Independence*, edited by A. C. Wilgus (Washington: 1935), p. 158.

house.[32] His wife, whom he had married in 1817, was a strong factor in his early popularity, although his later ill-treatment of her was to be the basis of devastating criticism. This lady was Leopoldina of Austria, a daughter of the Emperor Francis I and a sister of Marie Louise, wife of Napoleon Bonaparte. Well-educated, friendly, and intelligent, she was from the first immensely popular.

On both sides of the Atlantic, the political situation facing the new Regent quickly assumed a threatening aspect. In Brazil an empty treasury and the growing unpopularity of the local Portuguese were the most serious factors. From Portugal the danger was still more menacing. The cortes, as soon as it had Dom João back in Europe, embarked on the shortsighted policy of trying to put back the clock and to reduce Brazil once more to its former colonial status. It refused to consider a separate legislative assembly for Brazil, annulled many of the Dom João's liberal laws, abolished many of the institutions created by him, tried to break up the unity of the country by attaching the different provinces directly and severally to the home government and, finally, proceeded to the humiliating measure of ordering the youthful Dom Pedro to Europe for the completion of his education. The immediate reaction in Brazil was a wave of loyalty to the young Regent and a flood of petitions from all sections of the population urging him to remain in the country. Faced with the painful dilemma of having to choose between the land of his birth and the country of his adoption, and fearful of sacrificing his rights to the Portuguese crown, Pedro finally decided to defy the cortes. On January 9, 1822, he formally announced his decision to a deputation from Rio de Janeiro in the famous words: "Since it is for the good of all and for the general happiness of the nation, I am ready; tell the people that I shall remain"—(*Fico*—I stay).[33] It is to be noted that the majority of Brazilians were not at this point clamoring for complete independence but only equality of status with Portugal as a co-ordinate kingdom. The mother country, however, did not grasp the situation rapidly enough, and the current swept on swiftly to the complete severance of the old bond.

At this crisis in his career, Dom Pedro was fortunate enough to acquire the support of one of the ablest statesmen Brazil ever produced. José Bonifacio de Andrada e Silva has been called "the Cavour" of the Brazilian independence movement. Behind him, giving advice and powerful support, were his two almost equally talented brothers, Antonio Carlos Bonifacio de Andrada and Martim Francisco Bonifacio de Andrada. Only recently, in 1819, José Bonifacio had returned from Europe where he had

---

[32] *Cf.* A. Manchester, "The Paradoxical Pedro, First Emperor of Brazil," in *Hispanic American Historical Review*, 1932, Vol. XII, pp. 177-79.

[33] Quoted by Manchester, *op. cit.*, p. 182.

gone for his education to the University of Coimbra. After leaving this great seat of Portuguese learning he had traveled widely in England and the countries of western Europe through the decade 1790 to 1800, becoming acquainted with the greatest thinkers of that remarkable epoch and making a name for himself as a mineralogist and a contributing member of many of the most learned societies of Europe. Settling in Portugal for a time as professor in his old university at Coimbra, he lived through the age of the regency and gradually came to the conclusion that the separation of Portugal and Brazil was inevitable. He returned to Brazil just in time to assist Dom Pedro to carry through the liberation movement without bloodshed and with a minimum of bitterness.[34]

Shortly after the *"Fico"* address, José Bonifacio was placed at the head of a new ministry. His first care was to strengthen the tottering unity of the country. To this end he persuaded the Regent to issue a call for deputies from all the provinces to meet at Rio de Janeiro in order to form a Council of State. When the response was only half-hearted, the minister dispatched young Pedro to make a horseback tour of some of the most populous and influential areas, especially of Minas Gerais and São Paulo, in the hope of arousing loyalty and enthusiasm. The measure succeeded beyond all expectation. The great landowners, as well as the powerful Masonic groups, gathered about young Pedro in great numbers and pledged their support, hailing him as a liberating hero. The problem of the Portuguese military forces still in the country was effectively disposed of when the Portuguese fleet and the greater proportion of the soldiers were persuaded by evident weight of popular disapproval to leave for Europe. Step followed step towards independence. In June, Dom Pedro issued a decree convoking a constituent assembly. Only a public proclamation of the virtually accomplished liberation remained to effect the constitutional change. This came dramatically on September 7 while Pedro was on a horseback tour of São Paulo.

As he paused with his suite to rest on the banks of the little stream of Ypiranga not far from São Paulo, the prince was handed some dispatches from the capital in which he was informed by Bonifacio of new decrees just received from the Portuguese cortes abolishing his new Council of State and peremptorily ordering him to Europe. An accompanying note from the astute Leopoldina carried the significant message, "the apple is ripe; harvest it now, or it will rot." Pedro took the momentous decision. Tearing the Portuguese colors from his hat and unsheathing his sword he cried to his escort: "The time has arrived: Independence or Death! We are separated from Portugal!"[35] This *grito de Ypiranga,* Brazil's declaration of

---

[34] Martin, "Brazil," *op. cit.,* p. 163.
[35] For quotations see Manchester, *op. cit.,* p. 185.

independence, was followed, on October 12, by the proclamation of Pedro as "Constitutional Emperor of Brazil," and this in turn was succeeded by his solemn coronation on December 1, 1822. The term "empire" was chosen because it was thought to savor less of the divine right of kings than the term "kingdom" and carried the connotation of conquest by popular revolution.

Although the horrified Portuguese cortes refused to acquiesce tamely and dispatched a naval force to cooperate with a loyalist group in Baía, all resistance to Brazilian independence was soon broken. This was accomplished largely through the efforts of the famous Thomas Cochrane, now Earl of Dundonald, a retired British naval officer, whose services Pedro fortunately secured as first admiral of his infant navy. Recently released from service under the Chilean flag, Cochrane secured the enlistment in the Brazilian navy of a number of British captains and seamen. With their aid he succeeded by the end of the year in lifting the blockade of a number of Brazilian ports and driving out, or forcing into surrender, the remaining Portuguese and loyalist troops. On the high seas he relentlessly pursued the Portuguese vessels back to Europe. Under British pressure, Brazilian independence was recognized by Portugal on August 29, 1825. Already a year earlier the United States had welcomed Brazil among the independent American nations.

Thus Brazil emerged from the colonial chrysalis easily and practically without bloodshed. In consequence, the independence era left behind it none of the bitterness of the parallel Spanish and English movements or the economic exhaustion of a prolonged military struggle. Neither did the movement, as in the neighboring Spanish American states, break the territorial unity of colonial times. From a comparatively mild experience as a colony, Brazil passed, without suffering, through a transitional period under the beneficent rule of Dom João into the light of full independence, easily secured under his son. Part of the country's good fortune was to arouse little antagonism in Europe by its appearance among the nations. Recognition, like independence, came without much struggle. Even Metternich admitted that "If ever the revolt of a colony against its metropolis has been justified such was the case of the uprising of the Brazilians." [36]

---

[36] Martin, "Brazil," *op. cit.*, p. 166. But, *cf.* W. S. Robertson, "Metternich's Attitude toward Revolutions," in *Hispanic American Historical Review*, 1941, Vol. XXI, pp. 550-58, with its emphasis on the fact that Metternich was careful that Austria should not recognize Brazil until Portugal had done so. For the influence of Canning on Austria's policy, see Webster, *op. cit.*, pp. 58-59.

Chapter 18

THE SEVERANCE OF COLONIAL TIES

In 1775 the entire territory of the American hemisphere was divided, as colonial dependencies, among the three largest of the world's empires, those of Spain, Portugal, and England. Twelve years earlier, two of these empires, the British and the Spanish, had absorbed the bulk of the American holdings of France. Fifty years later the whole scene was completely changed. By 1825 the maps of both North and South America had been radically altered; all the Americas, except Canada, the Guianas, and certain Caribbean areas, were independent. The Thirteen Colonies had become one unified republic now expanded to more than double its original size; on the other hand, the Spanish American empire had fallen into eight republican entities through a sort of cell-division process that was obviously not yet complete; Brazil, while retaining her colonial unity, had become an independent empire ruled as a constitutional monarchy by a scion of the royal house of Portugal. Of the European colonizing powers, only Great Britain continued to possess any considerable holdings on the American continents; Spain like France had been forced to withdraw from the mainland but, in the islands of Cuba and Puerto Rico, still kept a foothold in the West Indies; Portugal had departed entirely from the American scene.

The disappearance from America, practically simultaneously, of the four old colonial empires, which had differed from each other in many ways, indicates the presence of a common disruptive force. It is to be noted that colonial disintegration immediately preceded, or followed closely upon, the French Revolution, a relationship suggesting that the same explosive forces that were operating in western Europe were making themselves felt in America. The French Revolution marked in Europe the breakdown of a traditional order of society characterized by great social inequalities and, for the masses, intolerable economic burdens. Similarly, the American independence movements, in their underlying implications, were manifestations of the same impulse to break away from irksome obligations and restrictions on "natural" human rights. The colonial status as established by the European monarchs in the Age of Discovery was, broadly speaking, parallel to the feudal relationship of the Middle Ages. In this, most funda-

459

mental were certain reciprocal obligations—on the one side, implied protection, and on the other, service and allegiance. The knight fought and the serf labored for his overlord; neither knight nor serf owned his land or had the freedom to do with it (or with himself) exactly what he liked; in theory, at least, they existed to serve God and their overlord. The theory that ruled colonial relationships was basically similar; the king owned the newly acquired lands and afforded protection; in return he expected unswerving loyalty from all the inhabitants and took for granted the subordination of all colonial interests to the prosperity and power of the mother country. The same forces, which at different times and in various parts of Europe—but most notably during the French Revolution—had led to the overthrow of the last remnant of the feudal system, gradually undermined the foundations and finally swept away the structure of the old colonial systems with their disregard of the claims and aspirations of new and maturing overseas societies. When in any of the colonies the time came that self-determination was valued more highly than protection, the beginning of the end of the colonial phase had arrived. Even in those colonies that remained after the revolutionary storm was over, the tie to the motherland was henceforth to become more and more of a sentimental bond, rather than a relationship of recognized obligation.

In only one instance among the American empires had the revolutionary impulse no direct part in the events leading to secession from Europe. The severance of the French holdings from France came wholly as a result of military failure in the course of a series of wars between England and France. The actual cession by France of her North American holdings came in the treaties of Utrecht and Paris, signed fifty years apart. Her American undertakings had always been more closely tied to her European policies, more subservient to their ends, and more subject to their vicissitudes than was the case in the colonial enterprises of her rivals. It was wholly in character, therefore, that they should be lost by military conquest in wars which in their primary aspects were European conflicts.

In the three other groups of colonies—English, Spanish, and Portuguese—the climactic motive in bringing about the final rupture was the determination of the colonists to be free, though in no case was this of primary importance in the early stages. In the case of the Spanish and Portuguese holdings the spark was supplied by European events associated with the rise of Napoleon and his usurpation in the Iberian Peninsula. The fire thus kindled, however, was fed from true revolutionary sources. After an opening phase of experiment in governmental forms, when the voice of authority from overseas was silent or, as in the case of Brazil, became intolerable, the liberation movement aimed at providing adequate self-government on a national or a quasi-national basis. In the Spanish colonies, the struggle reached its consummation in determined and victorious war against the armed might of the mother country, resulting eventually in forced acknowledgment of complete independence.

Either negatively or positively, France was a major factor in determining the time and the course of all the American revolutionary movements. Before the rise of Napoleonic ambitions in the Iberian Peninsula set the time and pattern for the Hispanic revolution, the fall of France as an imperial power in North America had determined the time for revolution in the English Thirteen Colonies. In fact, none of the three groups of colonies could have dreamed of relinquishing the protection of the mother country so long as either the French or the Dutch continued to be a potential menace. The elimination of these two powers from the American scene gave a sense of security to the colonists, fortifying the boldness with which they dared to challenge the rights and privileges of their respective mother countries. Premature action at any earlier stage would have brought dangers with which revolting colonies or new-born states would have been wholly incapable of dealing. Had the Dutch still been on the Hudson, or ensconced in Pernambuco, neither English nor Portuguese colonies could have disregarded the hazard; but the peak of the Dutch menace had passed a hundred years before the revolutionary age. Had France remained on the Mississippi and able either to assist the Spanish government as a powerful ally or to take advantage of a conflict to extend her own possessions, the Spanish colonists could not have moved towards independence. It is also significant that the English colonies made no overt act of secession until the French flag had been hauled down on the St. Lawrence, the Mississippi, and the Ohio; then, with scarcely any delay, old grievances became vocal, new causes of irritation were seized upon, and constitutional theories debated with growing heat.

There were many specific causes, remote and immediate, for the breaking of the ties of empire in the several systems. Back of them all lay the primary fact that three thousand miles of Atlantic Ocean separated motherland from colony. In a period of slow and hazardous communications, this inevitably led to the realization that homeland and colony were really living in different worlds, and had become philosophically and emotionally incompatible, as well as geographically remote. The utterly different physical background of America, with the magnitude of its proportions and the challenge of its resources and demands; the grim task of wresting a livelihood from the virgin soil, often amid extremes of climatic conditions, and never free from the fear of the Indians; the inexorable law of "struggle or perish"; all these had brought a maturity and self-reliance that made tutelage irksome and dictation intolerable.

The three independence movements shared certain aspects in common. All were influenced by the politico-philosophical ideas current in England and France in the eighteenth century; in addition, the Thirteen Colonies based their great appeal and protest on the very sources of English liberties and the precedents of English law; the Spanish American and Brazilian revolutionary leaders were torn between their respect, on the one hand, for the development in England of constitutional liberties under a limited monarchy and, on the other, their admiration for the successful operation in the United States of these ideas in federal republican dress. All three movements were civil wars as well as conflicts with the mother country; all aimed at shifting control within the former colonies to American institutions and American-born men. This latter aspect was most pronounced in the Spanish colonies where many of the creoles resented the indignity of their implied political and social inferiority to the peninsulares more deeply than any other hardship suffered at the hands of Spain.

In the English colonies there was no class exactly comparable to the Spanish-born peninsulares; the persons displaced or impoverished—the American Tories or Loyalists—were for the most part the better-off, conservative, colonial upper class, who had most to lose in any political and social upheaval, and consequently were opposed to the use of revolutionary methods in dealing with the British government. These Tories also were proportionately a larger class than the peninsulares, probably constituting a third of the total population. Many were more American than their radical opponents in the sense of being the descendants of families long in America and of having the greatest stake in the country. Refusing to accept the revolution, persecuted and deprived of their property, the Loyalists in thousands left the country. Their departure, or the financial ruin of those who remained behind, brought a definite social overturn, and a shift in political control and substantial wealth from one class to another. The exile of both Loyalists and Peninsulares led in their respective communities to a general leveling of social life and political opportunity.

In the economic field, independence brought a chance for opening American harbors to foreign commerce and experimentation with freer trade regulations in an effort, first, to lower prices on European goods to the consumer, and secondly, to insure higher prices for colonial products through better opportunities of sale. For all the new states, the severance of colonial ties meant a chance to use the vast natural resources of a new continent without supervision from a jealous motherland beyond the seas, and without the vexation of being exploited for her benefit.

In the domain of government, independence led in all the new communities to the exhilarating pursuit of new constitutional ideals and forms which became at once the paramount subject of passionate discussion and debate on many levels. In seeking satisfactory government, the Spanish Americans had the most difficult and longest road to travel. With only absolutist rule in their past experience in any sphere larger than the municipality, they felt the necessity of weighing carefully the alternatives of constitutional monarchy or republican forms. The choice of the latter was eventually decided upon, largely by the pressure of ambitious creole generals, supported by the mass of the half-castes who were republican in sympathy. For the English colonists who had revolted against a constitutional monarchy, there was nothing left but a republic. The Brazilians, without bitter memories of an especially oppressive colonial age, retained monarchy under the name of empire, and concentrated on drawing up a constitution along modern lines. In all the colonial systems the colonists had had little experience in intercolonial relationships and none in international affairs.

In considering differences in the revolutionary movements, it is to be noted that the Spanish American movement was more complex in character and as a venture more hazardous than either the English or the Portuguese. The bond with the mother country was older and the white population in the Spanish colonies more carefully hand-picked for loyalty and orthodoxy, and therefore less ripe for revolution, than in the other two. The Spanish Americans were also handicapped by the disadvantage of more difficult lines of communication and a less compact territory. As in the Portuguese colonies, the presence in Spanish America of the constant menace from Indian and slave elements, strongly royalist in sympathy, had always to be reckoned with by the creoles in their bid for freedom. Furthermore, the Spanish American military leaders were under the pressing necessity of creating essential political institutions while they carried on the fight; whereas the North American army leaders had not only the support of experienced colonial assemblies which continued to function, but also the over-all authority of a newly called and generally recognized Continental Congress. In the case of Brazil, there was at hand a scion of the royal house with the competent advice of an experienced ministry to give an air of legitimacy to the separation movement; she could also count upon the support of the English navy to stave off interference from Europe.

The constitutional results of the revolutionary movements, as might be expected, were to be very different. The chief outcome in the English colonies was to be the federation of the separate units into a single nation. In Spanish territories, the revolutionary movement would have the opposite effect, producing a breakdown of a traditional unity; even the determined efforts of the best of the Spanish American leaders to hold together at least the former viceroyalties were to meet with only partial or temporary success. Brazil, for her part, was to be greatly aided in retaining her colonial unity through the strengthening of the spirit of nationality during the period when the Portuguese royal court was resident in the country. This unity was to be strong enough to survive both the separation from Portugal and the later collapse of the empire itself. The roads along which each set of colonies traveled varied in length and in the difficulties of the way; the goal of all was the same, independence and recognized nationhood.

PART V

THE SEARCH FOR SATISFACTORY FORMS OF GOVERNMENT AND RECOGNITION

Chapter 19

NORTH AMERICA

I. THE UNITED STATES, 1776-1789

The War for Independence in the English colonies having ended in victory, the major task was to organize a permanent government. This called, first of all, for the creation of adequate constitutional instruments, both federal and local, that in relation to each other would be acceptable to a people who had gone to war because of their dissatisfaction with an imperial system in which the extent of central control had been the main constitutional point at issue. Clearly the principal difficulty would be to contrive a satisfactory central government, strong enough to command respect abroad while possessing sufficient strength at home to direct competently the political affairs of common moment. At the same time enough power must be left to the several states to satisfy those sensitive political entities so tenacious of their "sovereignty" and the "rights" of their local assemblies, and jealous of the "natural rights" and "inalienable liberties" of the individual citizen. In other words, the people of the United States had to address themselves to a search for the perfect imperial system that Great Britain had failed to devise, but which must be found if the people of the former Thirteen Colonies were to look forward with confidence to "an indefinite and expanding future." [1]

The first efforts in this direction long preceded the formal peace. It had been obvious to the framers of the Declaration of Independence that logically its pronouncement must be closely accompanied by a frame of government for the new state; a drafting committee therefore was appointed by the Second Continental Congress at the time the famous Declaration was adopted. A week later, on July 12, 1776, a complete plan for the new federal government, called the "Articles of Confederation and Perpetual Union," was presented to Congress by its principal author, the chairman of the congressional drafting committee, John Dickinson, a distinguished constitutional lawyer of Delaware. After meeting with severe criticism and undergoing a number of alterations, it was finally accepted by Congress and submitted to the states for ratification on

---

[1] The population of the United States in 1783 was approximately three million, of which six hundred thousand were slaves.

November 15, 1777. It was not, however, until 1781, a few months before the surrender of General Cornwallis at Yorktown, that Maryland, the last of the states, gave its formal adherence and the new federal constitution went into effect. Meanwhile, through the revolutionary years the Second Continental Congress shouldered the responsibility of acting as a central government, holding the states to some semblance of a common course of action, directing the military forces, and conducting diplomatic relations.

Internal affairs in these war years fell to the care of the individual colonies, each of which, as it severed its relations with England, set up a state government. Even before May 10, 1776, when the Second Continental Congress advised this step, several of the colonies had already adopted new constitutions, and within a few years all the rest followed suit. It speaks well for the work of the authors that most of the states were to remain fairly content with these instruments until well into the nineteenth century. Many methods of procedure were followed in drawing up these documents. Two were the work of especially elected conventions and were later submitted to popular vote; others represented the labor of the regular legislatures, some of which were especially authorized for the purpose. In some cases the legislative bodies submitted their work to popular approval, while others proceeded to promulgation without referendum.

In content, a number of the new state constitutions showed only slight verbal changes from the colonial charters; others wore an almost wholly new face; though all alike leaned heavily for their principles on original charters, colonial experience, and Anglo-Saxon constitutional development through the centuries. Unlike less fortunate members of other colonial systems, freemen in all the English colonies had been familiar from the very beginning with the essentials of self-government; they were accustomed to popular elections, service in representative assemblies or in second chambers directly or indirectly elected, and even, in some of the colonies, to the election and control of the executive. With certain formal changes eliminating the distant sovereign, who through most of their history had not affected their daily lives much anyway, they were easily ready to carry on under the new conditions. In general, the form of the new state constitutions was the work of a relatively small group of talented and experienced men, well versed in the most advanced political philosophy of their time, well acquainted with the essentials of democratic government, and familiar with the pitfalls of the political system as it had been applied in the English colonies. Under their leadership, in an age when there were no models to follow, the American states acquired, from familiar democratic materials out of their own history, written instruments of government that were at once practical and abreast of the most advanced political thought.

Each of the state constitutions contained a Bill of Rights that paid homage to the theory of "natural" or "inherent" rights and protected individual liberties by insistence on trial by jury, free exercise of religion, and a free press. All laid down the theory of popular sovereignty, stressing the view that all governmental authority was merely delegated power and governing officials were but the servants of the people. All strove to set up systems of government in which the three powers of the state—executive, legislative, and judiciary—should be separate from each other and held in an elaborate system of checks and balances in which no one could grow too strong at the expense of the others. Bitter memories of the troubles of the colonial age were reflected in provisions that strove to prevent the power of the executive and the judiciary from overriding the legislative branch of the government. All but three of the states established bicameral legislatures. Suffrage was generally placed in the hands of those who had "a stake in the country," in other words in the hands of the propertied classes; nevertheless it was in these state instruments that greatest emphasis was placed on the safeguarding of the rights of the individual, however humble, and that the gains of the Revolution as a social movement were registered.

While the war was fought primarily for political goals, and as a social movement undoubtedly was one of the least revolutionary revolutions in history, nevertheless, as a sort of by-product, it had brought into prominence certain grievances of the common man against the privileged classes of well-to-do merchants and planters. These secondary ideals found in the new state constitutions an opportunity for expression and adjustment. The most notorious of the crass injustices had arisen from the evils of an unequal burden of taxation, quitrents, absenteeism, land speculation, the privileges of established as against dissenting churches, and the unequal representation of tidewater and back counties in local legislatures. The conflict with the motherland and the wholesale exodus of large numbers of the upper class had strengthened the hands of the radicals and helped to bring about more democratic conditions and a more liberal outlook. The confiscation of the lands of the Tories, especially in the Middle States and New England, had altered for the better the economic circumstances of many of the former lower classes and so had given them greater political strength. Probably the most important social results of the war were the broadening of the franchise, the reapportionment of representation between the old and the new counties, the abolition of quitrents, the disestablishment of churches, and the abolition of the laws of entail and primogeniture. Though complete political democracy was far from being established in the new constitutions, they registered a distinct advance in liberal ideas and gave evidence that the crust of custom had to some extent been broken by the war.

The years immediately following the peace with Great Britain were by no means a time of exaltation and rejoicing over a great triumph; on the contrary, they were filled with discouragement and constituted half a decade of gloom and turbulence that has been called the "critical period in American history." Problems of the first magnitude beset the new nation. Its constitutional machinery for central government, devised in haste and under pressure in a time of war, showed serious weaknesses, making it clear that the old problem of the relationship of central and local government had not been solved. Finances and the currency, both national and state, were also in confusion with ever louder cries from the debtor class for greater and greater issues of paper money. Taxes were heavy and unequal. A general economic depression had settled over the land with derangement of trade and commerce. Once the unifying pressure of the war was removed, the doctrine of state rights tended to reassert itself, and each of the former Thirteen Colonies showed a disposition to sink back into an isolationism which, in the economic field, led them to erect trade barriers against neighboring states and make regulations restricting interstate commerce. Meanwhile foreign nations showed themselves reluctant to conclude trade treaties on equal terms. Great Britain, on the ground that the United States government had not honored its treaty promises in relation to British debts and Loyalists' claims, refused to relinquish the military posts which she still held in territory ceded under the treaty terms. At the same time Spain signified firmly to Congress that she did not recognize the right of the United States to the navigation of the Mississippi, spoken of in the Anglo-American treaty, and negotiations with Madrid on the subject made little progress.[2]

Internally there hung over the country a great land problem affecting the region between the Appalachians and the Mississippi. In the area south of the Ohio River pressing Spanish claims and intensified Indian raids presented major difficulties; north of the Ohio, no less than seven of the states had conflicting and irreconcilable claims each dating back to original charters. For a time there seemed no possibility of avoiding a major conflict over these overlapping boundaries. The Congress of the Confederation, however, in a masterly handling of this matter scored its one great triumph, eventually succeeding in drawing up a "wise and noble plan" for all territorial expansion westward and providing for its organization and management in such a manner as to prove satisfactory and permanent.

---

[2] There is an enlightening treatment of the diplomatic aspects of the situation in A. C. McLaughlin, *The Confederation and the Constitution, 1783-1789* (New York: 1905), chap. vi, "Diplomatic Relations, 1783-1788," pp. 89-107.

This "question of the northwest" was brought to the forefront of political debate and so to the possibility of its solution owing to the drastic action of Maryland. This state positively refused to agree to the Articles of Confederation so long as other states asserted claims to the region beyond the Appalachians.[3] One by one the various claimant states between 1780 and 1786 expressed their readiness to cede their rights in the disputed area to the "United States" and allow the lands in question to be disposed of by Congress for the common benefit of all. By 1786 Congress held the title to all lands north of the Ohio River and on July 13, 1787, was able to pass the Northwest Ordinance,[4] one of the most important and farsighted measures in the history of the United States.

In this comprehensive scheme for the eventual settlement and government of western lands, which at that time had practically no population, there were incorporated two essential ideas which had evolved from various suggestions as the subject had been threshed out in Congress. First, there must be provision for a stage of temporary government with a generous measure of autonomy as soon as any considerable number of settlers arrived, and secondly, ultimate admission of the territory into the union as new states upon terms of equality with the original Thirteen States. The Northwest Ordinance provided for the eventual setting up of not less than three, and not more than five, states in the whole region. At the outset a governor, secretary, and three judges were to be appointed by Congress for the area. As soon as there were 5,000 free male inhabitants of full age in a given section, a territorial legislature was to be established which would possess the power to make laws for the territory as well as the right to send a nonvoting delegate to Congress. The government at that stage would consist of a governor, legislative council, and an elected house of representatives. A series of declarations provided a Bill of Rights, and a special clause prohibited slavery. When the population of the territory reached 60,000 it was to be admitted into the union on equal terms with the older states. The Ordinance passed Congress with but one dissenting vote. It established the principle that new western communities were to be regarded as an extension of the republic and not as subordinate colonies. Having secured in advance grants of land from Congress, and

---

[3] The details of the controversy between the states over the western land claims may be read in C. W. Alvord, *The Illinois Country, 1673-1818* (Springfield, Ill.: 1920), chap. xiv, pp. 382-87.

[4] The Northwest Ordinance had been preceded by another important measure deeply affecting the settlement of the west, namely, the Land Ordinance of May 20, 1785. This provided for the orderly surveying of land available for settlement in advance of its sale. The New England township unit of 6 miles square was taken as the unit. This was subdivided into 36 sections of 640 acres each, with one section in each township reserved for educational purposes and four set aside for the United States government. The average price was to be not less than $1.00 an acre. This Ordinance, though frequently amended, remained the basis of the land system until the Homestead Act of 1862.

with their political future clear before them, settlers were soon streaming into the Northwest.

For the region south of the Ohio, the principles underlying the Northwest Ordinance were also eventually applied, though the Congress of the Confederation played no such determining role in this area as in that to the north of the river. The physical features of the area and Indian problems were the major factors determining the development of this section of the country. As far back as the Treaty of Fort Stanwix, 1768, in which the Iroquois gave up their claims to the land between the Tennessee and the Ohio rivers, streams of settlers had been flowing westward and southwestward into Tennessee and Kentucky following river valleys and mountain gaps. At the same time new communities were developing beyond the Appalachian range in the western areas of Pennsylvania, Virginia, and North Carolina. These movements continued throughout the revolutionary and "critical" periods.[5] The first state in this region to be admitted to the Union was Kentucky which entered in 1792.

The year that saw the passage of the Northwest Ordinance, with its basic formula for the settlement of the western land problem, saw also a determined assault upon the even more formidable task of creating a satisfactory central government and the beating out of a truly workable relationship between federal and local administrations. Even before the peace with Great Britain had been signed, the Articles of Confederation had proved themselves to be an inadequate basis for a satisfactory national government.[6] They represented an experiment in the creation of a confederate republic of contracting states operating through a unicameral congress in which each state had one vote. They made no provision for a separate executive. At the time of the ratification of the Articles, all thirteen states considered that they had been most generous in the extent to which they had delegated powers of first consequence to a central governing body. But in actual practice these powers proved to be so limited and so hedged about with restrictions as to give a mere semblance of power rather than actually to provide the reality of national unity and strength. Under the Articles, for example, Congress might declare war, but had not the right to levy the taxes that alone could furnish the sinews of war; the federal government was in the position of having to ask and wait for grants from the states. It might not tax the individual in peace or in war, and consequently could not raise funds to pay the interest on the national debt nor protect public credit. Neither had it the right to regulate trade or

---

[5] Consult Constance L. Skinner, *The Pioneers of the Old Southwest*, in Chronicles of America, Vol. XVIII (New Haven: 1919), chaps. vi, vii, viii.

[6] Conditions under the Articles of Confederation are ably set forth in McMaster's *History of the People of the United States* (New York: 1920), Vol. I, chap. i; and also in McLaughlin, *op. cit.*, chap. xi, pp. 168-83, "Proposals to Alter the Articles of Confederation."

Washington's farewell to the officers of his army at the Old Tavern, corner Broad and Pearl Streets, New York, December 4, 1783. Currier and Ives, 1876.

John Jay by Gilbert Stuart. (Courtesy of D. K. Jay, photograph by the Metropolitan Museum of Art)

impose a tariff for the protection of infant manufactures against foreign price-cutting. Nor could it force the acceptance of a single stable medium of exchange and so remedy the confused currency situation. Again, while the "United States in Congress assembled" was made by the Articles "the last resort on appeal in any disputes between . . . two or more states," that body had no way of compelling the acceptance of its decisions. Effective government was also seriously handicapped by the fact that many important measures required the support of as many as nine states, while amendment to the Articles required the unanimous consent of all the states. So impotent in the face of grave problems did the central government appear by the middle eighties that many of the ablest men in the country refused membership in Congress or simply failed to attend its sessions.

In fairness to the authors of the Articles it must be remembered not only that they did their work in the midst of a war with Great Britain fought over this very issue of the relationship of central authority to local rights, but also that they were handicapped by certain traditions from the past. One of these was a deep-rooted conviction that a strong central government was an instrument of tyranny and must be held in check at all costs. They failed to give sufficient weight to a vital factor in the situation. The center of imperial power in colonial days had been thousands of miles away, well beyond the reach of effective influence or control by an unrepresented American public. It was perhaps natural that in setting up a substitute for that authority the former colonies should fear above all else to give the federal body too much power. Time and bitter experience were needed to teach men who had fought for freedom that if governing institutions were truly popular and within reach of the living voice they need not be feared; and that the central organization, like the local government, was capable of being made an instrument to be used in the service of the people. But as John Jay once remarked, "it takes time to make citizens out of subjects."

Another element contributing to constitutional feebleness in the Confederation Congress was the relative weakness of the conservative classes at the time of its inception. The Revolution, it must be borne in mind, was not merely a contest between the colonists and England; it was also, in some measure, a civil war in which a large proportion of the big businessmen and propertied classes were opposed to the movement and in its course were either killed, exiled, or ruined. In the work of political reorganization, the loss of their counsels was plainly evident, and nowhere more clearly than in the provisions of the Articles of Confederation. They were the elements in the population naturally most in favor of organs of government strong enough to maintain order and command respect for property, business, and sound money.[7] It was not until the radicals, who constituted the majority of those in power during the war years, had been replaced in influence by men very much like the old Tories, that a truly effective form of government was devised.

It was this group of business and commercial men, along with the bulk of the professional classes, who in the middle eighties became sufficiently disturbed over the economic and political situation to insist on the revision of the constitution. The typical American of the day, the small farmer, was satisfied enough with the Articles; the state constitutions guarded everything in which he was really interested. But the commercial group, whose economic interests languished, felt most acutely the lack of a central power capable of imposing terms on the several states and of making profitable business possible once again on more than a pitifully local scale. This business group was particularly disturbed by the loud demands voiced at every political meeting by the debtor class for more paper money. After these disturbances had reached a crisis in Shays' Rebellion in Massachusetts in July 1786, the political leaders of the country, as well as the substantial classes everywhere, were sufficiently convinced that the foundations of society were rocking to make effective action possible.

The first step was taken at a trade convention held in Annapolis in 1786 where a resolution, drafted by Alexander Hamilton, was adopted. This called for another, more representative convention to meet in Philadelphia in the following year "to devise such further provisions as shall appear to them necessary to render the constitution of the Federal Government adequate to the exigencies of the Union." Congress sanctioned the proposed gathering and the legislatures of all the states, except Rhode Island, elected delegates. In all, some seventy-two representatives were named to the Constitutional Convention, though only fifty-five actually attended the sessions. Most of these carried credentials empowering them merely to revise the Articles of Confederation. When the Constitutional Convention finally opened in Philadelphia on May 25, 1787, only twenty-nine delegates, representing seven states, were present and this number continued to be about the average in attendance at the sessions. Behind closed doors they toiled five hours a day through one hundred days of a hot summer.

Some interesting studies have been made of these "fathers of the Constitution" of the United States, now one of the oldest written continuing constitutions of the world. Of the fifty-five men only five had signed the

---

[7] Fundamental to an understanding of the economic and financial conditions lying behind the change from the Articles of Confederation to the new constitution is the scholarly volume by C. A. Beard, *An Economic Interpretation of the Constitution of the United States* (New York: 1913).

Declaration of Independence, though all but twelve had seen service in the Continental Congress.[8] About a dozen were of national prominence. The level of education was high; about half of the group were college graduates, thirty-three were lawyers, seven had been state governors, eleven were shippers or manufacturers, nine were planters, fifteen were slave owners. Not one represented the small farmer or artisan group. Thus the convention was anything but a gathering of political theorists or fire-eating demagogues. On the contrary it was an assembly of substantial business and professional men, practical politicians, and solid citizens who were determined to erect a workable central government that should have the will and the power to protect "property"—the key word of the constitution. They understood the necessity of compromise, and the rank and file of them could not be swept off their feet by oratory but knew how to listen and then when the time came "to vote right."

Washington, the most prominent man in the country, at this time fifty-five years of age, was made the presiding officer. He had been greatly disturbed by the disorders of the critical years and his heart was set upon the convention's devising a workable constitution. Though without a sense of humor, as a chairman he was possessed of graciousness, tact, and dignity, and proved able to draw out the best in the delegates. He also displayed a great ability to sum up in a few words the contents of a long debate. As president of the convention, he construed his task to be similar to that of the speaker in the British House of Commons and consistently used his position to keep discussion open and to the point. Next to Washington, Benjamin Franklin was probably the most outstanding figure. But he was at this time an old man of eighty-one, suffering from rheumatism, and had difficulty in making himself heard. His career in diplomacy had taught him the value of compromise and he threw his weight in that direction.

Of the younger men, Madison and Hamilton were outstanding. James Madison, the "father of the Constitution," at this time was a man of thirty-six and had been for some time the leader of a conservative party in the Virginia legislature. He was the meticulous scholar of the convention, having carefully prepared for it by studying earlier experiments in democratic government, especially Greek and Swiss models; he used his knowledge to warn his colleagues of forms that past experience had shown would not work. He was not an especially proficient speaker, but his words commanded great respect and produced more votes than those of any other delegate. In his Journal he kept the best account of the proceedings. The convention's greatest conservative, Alexander Hamilton, was the

---

[8] See F. Rodell's very readable volume, *Fifty-Five Men* (New York: 1936).

youngest man present and oratorically the most gifted. He was one of a delegation of three representing New York State. Hamilton stood for the forms rather than the reality of democracy. If he had had his way, the chief executive of the United States would have been one chosen for life by an elaborate system of indirect election; senators would have sat for long terms; the power of the lower house would have been severely restricted; and state governors would have been appointed by the national government. A national bank and a protective tariff were other features of his program. Though the constitution as finally resolved upon probably met his views less than those of any man present, he loyally accepted the instrument decided upon by the majority and, when the convention was over, worked hard for its ratification.

Other members of special interest included: John Dickinson of Delaware, the gifted "penman of the Revolution" and the author of the Articles of Confederation, through whose influence much of the old wording of the Articles was to be retained in the constitution; Edmund Randolph, Governor of Virginia, who introduced the "Virginia plan" supported by the larger states; and William Paterson, an able lawyer of New Jersey who became the spokesman of the smaller states and introduced "the New Jersey plan." The two Morrises of the Pennsylvania delegation are worthy of special note. Robert Morris was a financial expert, though in later times he was to languish for years in a debtors' prison. To Gouverneur Morris, a brilliant speaker and debater who became the chairman of the Committee on Style, the United States Constitution owes its distinguished, succinct phrasing. One of the ablest lawyers and steadiest workers present was the Scotsman, James Wilson of Pennsylvania. The greatest obstructionist was Luther Martin of Maryland, a wearisome speaker and obstinate lawyer, who refused to sign the completed document and later worked for its defeat.

Prominent American radicals who were not present at the Constitutional Convention were: Thomas Jefferson and Thomas Paine, both in Europe at the time; Samuel Adams, who was not elected; and Patrick Henry, who disapproved of its fundamental ideas and refused to serve. Two other prominent Americans, who were to have a large influence on the Constitution at a later date and also were not present, were John Jay, who as much as any man brought about the ratification of the Constitution, and John Marshall, first Justice of the Supreme Court, whose decisions were to set the mode of interpretation of the Constitution for all time.

It was soon clear to the men assembled in Philadelphia that the Articles of Confederation needed such drastic revision that their task would be simplified if they embarked on a completely new instrument. This they based upon a radically different conception from that on which the Articles rested. The first experiment had been a league of states; the new union, it was decided, must be a national government with direct authority over individuals and possessing the power of taxation. Another fundamental decision taken was that the national government, like the state governments, must be one of three branches, each separated and protected from the others by a carefully worked out system of checks and balances.

Different delegates had brought with them and proposed various schemes for the reform of the government; notable among these were especially the New Jersey plan which was supported by the smaller states and involved a unicameral system and a plural executive, and the Virginia plan which actually became, more than any other single document, the basis of the later Constitution. A discussion of these in detail led to a temporary deadlock between the larger and smaller states over the question of "proportional representation," further complicated by the problems of slavery and sectional rivalry between North and South. Eventually the "great compromise" was reached when it was decided that membership in the House of Representatives should rest on popular election while the second chamber should be representative of the equal sovereignty of the states.[9] In determining the population, slaves were to count as three-fifths of a unit for both purposes of representation and taxation, and Congress was to agree not to interfere with the slave trade for twenty years nor lay an import tax on slaves heavier than ten dollars a head.

The final document was a mass of practical compromises, designed not to meet any one person's theory or follow any particular plan, but aimed solely at the goal of producing a workable frame of government in which all legitimate interests should receive due recognition. This effort of the drafters of the constitution to find the middle road brought into being an instrument of government in which sectional and group interests were balanced against each other: large states against small states, county against town, raw materials against manufactures, and so on. With the final result of their labors none of the framers was completely satisfied, and only thirty-nine signed the final document.[10] It was then forwarded to the Confederation Congress which passed it on without recommendation to the states for ratification or rejection in specially summoned constitutional conventions. When nine of the thirteen states had signed it was, according to one of its own provisions, to go into effect.

Had the document been submitted either to the regular state legislatures or to popular referendum, there seems no doubt that it would have been

---

[9] On the "great compromise," consult McLaughlin, *op. cit.,* chap. xiv, pp. 221-35, and the admirably clear exposition in Max Farrand, *The Framing of the Constitution of the United States* (New Haven: 1913), chaps. v, vi, vii.

[10] For interesting reflections on the general character of the constitution and the forces that produced it, see Max Farrand, *op. cit.,* chap. xii, pp. 196-210.

rejected.[11] While the new constitution was under debate in Philadelphia the country had looked on without enthusiasm or faith that anything worth-while would emerge. In the debates on ratification in the various state conventions, every possible objection to the adoption of the new frame of government was advanced. A criticism that was general was that the document had no Bill of Rights; that property, not human rights, had received all the attention of the framers of the new document. The obvious reply that a Bill of Rights was a document extorted from a tyrant and had no appropriate place in the provisions of a government of delegated powers emanating from a sovereign people was logical but not convincing to the popular mind, and the promise had finally to be made that a Bill of Rights would be added in a series of amendments. Other critics pointed out that the document restored to the central government the very type of authority that the Revolutionary War had been fought to abolish. Another bitter objection was that it took too much power away from the states: "By what right," demanded Patrick Henry in the Virginia Convention, where the fight for ratification was closest, "had they to say 'We, the People . . .' instead of 'We, the States'?" Others complained that in making gold and silver the only legal tender, as also in prohibiting the states from passing laws impairing the obligations of contract, the delegates had been hard on the debtor class. The farmers thought that the commercial and business interests had been favored at their expense, and in the conventions the representative of the back counties showed strong opposition to ratification.

Powerful voices, however, were raised in behalf of ratification of the new constitution as the best that could be obtained. Among the most influential advocates were Madison, Hamilton, and Jay. In a series of eighty-five essays, later to become famous under the title *The Federalist,* but originally contributed to various New York papers, these statesmen undertook to explain the purpose and nature of the various aspects of the Constitution and to win over to its support the intellectual classes in the country. Their brilliant analysis of the constitutional issues involved set the temper of political thought for the next hundred years.

But despite the utmost efforts of the framers—and no group of men could have worked harder to secure the acceptance of their handiwork—the vote in many conventions, especially those of the larger states, was very close. An unexpected crisis developed when it was found that the first nine ratifying states did not include the two most important, New York and Virginia, strategically placed between North and South. Eventually, however, Virginia came in as a tenth state with a vote of 89 to 79 and New York entered as the eleventh with a majority of 30 to 28. The thirteenth

---

[11] H. U. Faulkner, *Political and Social History of the United States* (New York: 1948), pp. 132-33.

state, Rhode Island, held out until 1790, maintaining that, without unanimous agreement of all the states, the Articles of Confederation could not legally be thus fundamentally altered. Finally, under threat of tariff barriers established against her, the recalcitrant little state, that had suffered much since Revolutionary days, ratified and came into the Union. The fight for ratification, as the fight for the revision of the constitution and, indeed, the Revolution itself, had been won by a determined minority.

The Constitution of 1789 has remained the fundamental law of the United States until the present day. There have been twenty-one amendments. The first ten of these, forming a Bill of Rights, were adopted in 1791 and so became part of the Constitution. The eleventh and twelfth were perfecting amendments. The thirteenth, fourteenth, and fifteenth were added in the period of the Civil War, and all the rest bear on social justice and register a twentieth century point of view towards the relationship of government and society.

II. CANADA BECOMES ENGLISH, 1761-1791

Canada, which we now think of as the oldest of the British self-governing dominions, became predominantly English in a series of stages, and the growth of its constitution followed a similar development. The three decades, 1761-1791, which saw the rise, success, and governmental stabilization of the American Revolution, also produced a number of momentous constitutional changes in the heart of what is now the Dominion of Canada. Many of these changes were closely associated with events in the English colonies to the south. They carried the former French colonies of the St. Lawrence from the status of French colonial possessions of a paternalistic and semifeudal type, populated with a homogeneous people, largely Norman in blood, to the position of two British provinces, provided with representative government similar to the colonial pattern developed in the Thirteen Colonies, and inhabited by a mixed population of French Canadians and English Loyalists whose political experiences and aspirations were poles apart.

Other areas, now important parts of the Dominion but in the eighteenth century on the fringes of American life and not parts of "Canada" at all, were already British in 1761. In the Hudson Bay area, Nova Scotia, and Newfoundland, English activities and claims ran back to John Cabot, Martin Frobisher, John Davis, and other intrepid English adventurers. Around the Hudson Bay area these claims had found a focus and organization in the Hudson's Bay Company whose charter, granted by Charles II in 1670, embraced the territory drained by the rivers flowing into Hudson Bay. Thereafter the expanding operations of this great company had held in check French exploration to the north and west of Quebec and Montreal.

At the opening of the eighteenth century, England's success in the War of the Spanish Succession or, as it was known in America, Queen Anne's War, had forced an acknowledgment from France in the terms of the Treaty of Utrecht (1713), not only of Britain's claim to Hudson Bay territory but also of her sovereignty over Acadia and Newfoundland. After Utrecht, in this whole eastern region France retained only Cape Breton and Prince Edward Island, but had proceeded to construct at Louisburg, on Cape Breton Island, the most powerful fort in America. It was designed to serve as a naval and military outpost to guard the mouth of the St. Lawrence leading to "Canada" and to keep a watchful eye over English activities from Hudson Bay to New England. Relying on help and protection from this center of French power, the Acadians of the ceded territories had refused for half a century to reconcile themselves to their new political situation.[12] In 1755 this attitude resulted in the forced emigration of six thousand persons from the province.[13] Not until 1763, when England acquired in the Treaty of Paris the title to Cape Breton and Prince Edward Island, as well as a defined western boundary at the St. Croix River for the whole province of Nova Scotia, was Anglo-French rivalry in this maritime region, as elsewhere in North America, finally laid to rest.[14] Already, in 1758, English Nova Scotia had been given a representative assembly, and English immigrants had begun to pour in from New and Old England. The province by 1763 was a fairly typical English colony, one, however, marked by the presence of a minority of agricultural Acadians who, as Roman Catholics, though allowed the free exercise of their religion, were excluded from the franchise by English law. Like New England, Nova Scotia in the next few years engaged extensively in the rum trade with the West Indies and the profits of this trade, along with a certain amount of shipbuilding and business promoted by a resident garrison, gave the colony an air of prosperity and contentment.

Among the varied and widely separated American holdings of which England found herself in possession on the morrow of the Treaty of Paris (1763), to the north of the Thirteen Colonies, were Nova Scotia, Newfoundland, the Hudson's Bay Company's territory, and French "Canada," and to the south of her original holdings were the two Floridas, as well as a number of new islands in the West Indies.[15] Among all these, that

---

[12] For the part played by the Roman Catholic clergy as political agents of the French government, see R. Coupland, *The Quebec Act* (Oxford: 1925), pp. 13-15.

[13] See previous discussion, Chapter 15, pp. 396-397.

[14] After 1713 France had claimed that only the peninsula part of Acadia—not its mainland section, now the Province of New Brunswick—had been ceded. England's right to this area was now, in 1763, recognized.

[15] In the West Indies France ceded to England Grenada, Dominica, St. Vincent, and Tobago; England restored to France Martinique, Guadeloupe, Marie-Galante, and St. Lucia. See map 18.

section presenting the most difficult administrative problems was Canada. This new conquest from France included not only the present province of Quebec with its population of some sixty or seventy thousand French peasants, now heavily leaning on the clergy for leadership, but also, attached to it, two lines of fortified posts running through lands predominantly Indian. One line of these forts consisted of a series of trading posts strung out westward through the Great Lakes country toward Lake Winnipeg, and the other was a chain of forts leading southward from the St. Lawrence to the Ohio. As originally planned by the French, these forts had two objects: one had been to connect the two great water systems of the Mississippi and the St. Lawrence, and so to secure for French traders the riches of the fur trade of the interior plains; the second had been to confine the English settlements to the Atlantic coastal region and so prevent their expansion westward. While this latter menace vanished with the conquest, the Indian problem at once assumed greater urgency. Its seriousness was made evident by an Indian uprising known as Pontiac's Conspiracy which followed closely upon the Treaty of Paris.

In despair at the prospects ahead, inspired and organized by French traders and ably led by an Ottawa chieftain named Pontiac, the former friends and allies of the French lashed out at the new conqueror. The primary purpose of this native revolt, involving practically all the Indian tribes from Lake Superior to the Mississippi, was to confine the British to the Quebec area and cut them off from the outlying fortified posts and the territories which these protected. From this western area, British garrisons had been largely withdrawn after the war while the French traders had been unwisely allowed to roam there at will. In the course of the summer of 1763 some eight fortified posts on the Great Lakes, in the Ohio valley, and in the Illinois country, fell into Indian hands and were burned and most of the garrisons were massacred; Detroit and Fort Pitt alone held out, the former withstanding a five-month siege by Pontiac himself. For a time English influence almost vanished in the Great Lakes area west of Niagara, and was seriously threatened on the Ohio. But in August, 1763, the victory of the veteran Indian fighter, Colonel Bouquet, at Bushy Run relieved Fort Pitt and assistance by water enabled Detroit to hold out until October 30 when Pontiac was forced to retire. Scattered fighting, however, continued for the next three years before the red men were beaten into submission. Pontiac at Oswego on July 25, 1766, unwillingly signed a treaty of amity with the English Indian Commissioner, Sir William Johnson, recognizing that the new lords of the western country were too strong for his people to conquer. Two years later, by the Treaty of Fort Stanwix (1768), the Indians were forced to withdraw from large areas in the Mohawk, Allegheny, and Ohio valleys.

Meanwhile, the Proclamation of October 7, 1763, outlined the framework of a new Indian policy. Indian affairs were taken under the control of the imperial government and were henceforth to be administered from London. Beyond the so-called Proclamation Line, running north and south along the crest of the Appalachian highlands, and west of the Thirteen Colonies, no colonial governor was to grant any lands to white settlers "for the present, and until our further pleasure be known." Westward of this Line, the land was reserved for the Indians. Roughly, this Indian territory lay between the Hudson Bay territories on the north, the Floridas on the south, the Alleghenies on the east, and the Mississippi on the west. This arrangement was admittedly a temporary measure, designed to rid the white settlements of the menace of Indian raids by offering some satisfaction and security to the native tribes. In the future, it was hoped, sections of this territory might be secured peaceably for white settlements by purchase or treaty cession, and, in the meantime, white migration might be directed into the newly won lands to the north and south which were awaiting organization and settlement. The obvious weaknesses of the plan were: first, that this Indian reservation included some of the most attractive lands beyond the Alleghenies; secondly, that much of the designated territory lay within the charter limits of the older colonies; and thirdly, that land hunger at this time was so great that no mere paper Proclamation Line could restrain the westward surge of the pioneers.

Besides laying down a new Indian policy, the Proclamation of 1763 provided for the temporary government of four new provinces in the American hemisphere: Quebec, East Florida, West Florida, and Grenada in the West Indies. The boundaries of the first three were carefully drawn so as not to encroach on the older Thirteen Colonies. In fixing the boundary of Canada, which was now named the Province of Quebec, the British government sacrificed the hinterland of the old French colony in the interests of its new Indian policy and the desire to keep the French population well to the north. The province was made still smaller by restricted frontiers to the north and east.

The form of government provided for all the new provinces was for the time being to be of the typical crown colony variety. Each province was to have a governor, appointed by the crown, and advised by a council; the members of the latter, all of whom must be Protestant, were to be approved in London. The Proclamation further provided that a representative assembly was to be summoned as soon as circumstances should justify the step, and meanwhile the inhabitants were to enjoy the benefits of courts administering justice according to law and equity "as near as may be agreeable to the laws of England." These provisions, while undoubtedly meant to be generous and designed to give the new communities as soon as possible all the benefits that had been developed in the older colonies, proved in reality largely impractical. The English lawmakers of 1763 apparently failed to grasp the complexity of the constitutional problems that faced them. For years the majority of folk in all four of the new provinces would necessarily consist of Frenchmen or Spaniards, totally unfamiliar with British ideas of self-government. Moreover, considering that by English law no Roman Catholic could either hold office or exercise the franchise, to hold out the hope of a representative assembly was illusory. The only persons competent to sit in such a body, or even vote

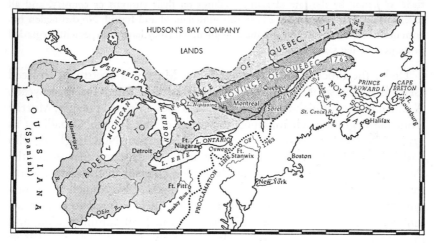

21. CANADA IN 1763 AND 1774

for it, would be a small Protestant minority of British traders, at least until such time as a large English immigration should completely change the picture.[16]

In Canada, the principal and immediate effect of the Proclamation was to substitute a civil regime for the military one in operation since the capitulation of Quebec and Montreal. Certain practices and policies of the military period, however, continued to have a considerable effect on the new administration. Under General Amherst, who had ruled as military governor of the whole territory in pre-Proclamation days, local administration had been entrusted to a considerable extent to French militia captains who acted as magistrates, with instructions to apply their old laws, on the principle that the laws of a conquered country remain in

---

[16] An ordinance of September, 1764 gave some relief, allowing French Canadians, despite their religion, to sit on juries and practice law in the Court of Common Pleas. For a detailed discussion of the legal aspects of the situation, see Coupland, *op. cit.,* pp. 37-40.

force until superseded by a new code. The promises made in the Articles of Capitulation to grant religious toleration and allow the practice of the Roman Catholic faith were also scrupulously carried out. There was much sympathy on the part of the English forces for the defeated French and the general attitude was genuinely conciliatory and protective.

"I feel the highest satisfaction," reported General Gage, who was in charge of the district of Montreal, in 1762, "that I am able to inform you that, during my command in this Government, I have made it my constant care and attention that the Canadians should be treated agreeably to His Majesty's kind and humane intentions. No invasion on their properties or insult on their persons has gone unpunished. All reproaches on their subjection by the fate of arms, revilings on their customs or country, and all reflexions on their religion have been discountenanced and forbid. No distinction has been made betwixt the Briton and the Canadian, but [they have been] equally regarded as subjects of the same Prince." [17]

Under the Proclamation, General James Murray, a Scotsman, replaced General Amherst as the first civil governor and ruled for three years. A warm-hearted, quick-tempered man who spoke French fluently, Murray from the beginning championed the cause of the French Canadians as against the few English-speaking traders, mostly from New England, who had followed in the wake of the army and now expected that under the Proclamation they would become the ruling element in the new government. Murray also carefully selected the members of his council from men sympathetic with the French Canadians, resolutely refused to call an assembly, continued to use the militia captains in local administration, and in matters of religion quietly overlooked many disqualifications such as were still imposed by law on Roman Catholics living in England.

Naturally, Governor Murray's policies were not popular with the English element. However content the French Canadians might be under a beneficent autocracy which represented the best that they had ever known, the British immigrants, mostly from the Thirteen Colonies, were very unlikely to be satisfied with a government which contrasted so strongly with what they had known before. Moreover, their uncompromising Puritan outlook upon the religion of the Catholic French was strengthened by a memory, burnt into their souls, of barbarous, French-inspired, Indian raids on their former settlements. Representative government was their demand, and the fact that it would work an injustice upon the overwhelming majority of a newly conquered population was of little concern to them. Their bitter criticism of Murray, who despised them for their shortsightedness, self-seeking, and intolerance, led to his recall in 1766, but they found themselves no better off under his successor. Thus from the very beginning of

---

[17] Quoted in Coupland, *op. cit.*, pp. 18-19.

English administration in Canada the racial issue constituted the major problem.

Murray's successor, Sir Guy Carleton, who had been with Wolfe at the capture of Quebec, was to play perhaps the most significant rôle of any of the English governors of Quebec. In general he approved of Murray's policies and, in particular, refused to call an assembly. A difficulty that he had to face at the outset was the imposition of English law as prescribed by the Proclamation. The carrying out of this provision had already been found by Murray in many respects to be impracticable. The French peasants knew nothing, and apparently could learn nothing, but their own legal system. For some years the courts struggled with the confusion wrought by the existence side by side of two languages and two codes of law. A further difficulty was the lack of local revenue due to the Council's inability to impose taxation in the absence of a representative assembly. These conditions made it evident that the settlement imposed by the Proclamation of 1763 must be reconsidered. A prolonged inquiry was set on foot and resulted in the famous Quebec Act of 1774. Carleton spent nearly four years in London working over this bill and it was largely his policy that the law embodied. Basically it rested on the conviction that Canada was to remain a French Canadian land. In expressing this view, he said:

> Barring a catastrophe shocking to think of, this country must to the end of time, be peopled by the Canadian race, who already have taken such firm root and got to so great a height that any new stock transplanted will be totally hid and imperceptible amongst them except in the towns of Quebec and Montreal.[18]

It was Carleton's view that France would probably at some time attempt to regain her former colony, or would support the Thirteen Colonies in "pushing matters to extremities," and therefore he felt it to be a matter of the first importance to secure the loyalty and support of the French Canadians.[19] This group, he realized, had no common interests with their neighbors to the south, and in the future, as in the days before the conquest, it might continue to be useful as a check on the revolutionary activities of the English colonists. At the head of his program of conciliating the French Canadians, Carleton placed religious toleration—a benefit not to be enjoyed by Roman Catholics in England for another fifty years. As a solution of the legal tangle he advocated the acceptance of French civil law along with the maintenance of the English law in criminal cases, a combination found by experience to work satisfactorily and to be acceptable to the French people. In view of the lack of interest of the French Canadians in the matter of a popular assembly and their complete lack of experience in

---

[18] *Ibid.*, p. 59.
[19] *Ibid.*, p. 60.

the operation of such a body, Carleton was definitely opposed to the establishment of representative government, in spite of the clamors of the six hundred-odd English settlers.[20]

In the form of government provided for Quebec, the bill secured all that Carleton desired. The measure declared that "whereas it is at present inexpedient to call an assembly," government was to be by a governor and a royally appointed legislative council of seventeen to twenty-three members; Roman Catholics were to be admitted to membership in the Council by the device of a substitute oath of allegiance which respected their religious scruples; the council might legislate by ordinance subject to royal approval on all matters except taxation, which was to be provided for in a subsequent Quebec Revenue Act. Carleton's ideas on a legal system were largely adopted, provision being made in the Act for a mixed English and French system of laws. When the absence of all mention of the rights of habeas corpus brought an outburst of especially bitter criticism from the English element, specific instructions were issued to Carleton, as he prepared to return to Canada as governor to administer the Act, designed to correct this glaring omission, as well as to meet other complaints of the English minority. The determined governor, however, thought proper neither to inform his Council of these orders nor to take the necessary steps to carry them out. The almost immediate outbreak of war must be taken as his excuse.[21]

The Quebec Act, passed in 1774, came into operation in May, 1775. It brought resounding repercussions immediately, not only from the English living in Canada who were especially resentful of its constitutional aspects, but from the inhabitants of the Thirteen Colonies, who felt themselves so adversely affected by the boundary changes it involved that they were soon listing the Quebec Act among the Intolerable Acts justifying armed rebellion. By the terms of the measure, the restricted frontiers of Canada, as laid down by the Proclamation of 1763, were abandoned in favor of the inclusion in the Province of Quebec, for administrative purposes, of a much wider area. Once more the old French colony's western hinterland—the area lying between the Great Lakes and the Ohio and the Mississippi rivers—was to be restored. This most criticized feature of the Quebec Act was held by its framers to be desirable in order to regulate the settlements and the trade in territory traditionally associated with Canada. Though the act definitely provided that "the boundary of the Province of Quebec shall in no wise affect the boundary of any other colony," neverthe-

---

[20] Various estimates of the French Canadian population at this time run from eighty to one hundred and fifty thousand. *Ibid.*, p. 74.

[21] *Ibid.*, pp. 128-35. See also A. L. Burt, *A Short History of Canada* (Minneapolis: 1942), p. 71.

less the Atlantic colonists felt convinced that in actual fact it would prove a powerful means of frustrating their steady westward movement.

At the time of the passage of the bill in the British Parliament, this colonial opposition had been foreseen and the Whigs had been bitterly critical. The elder Pitt from his place in the House of Lords denounced it vigorously; he feared, he declared, that "the bill might finally lose the hearts of His Majesty's American subjects." [22] In justice to Carleton and the other supporters of the bill, it has to be remembered that the measure was thought of by them primarily as a form of government for Quebec, whose population was wholly without experience in self-government. Furthermore, it was meant to be only a transitional measure: "As soon as Canadians shall be in a condition to receive an assembly it will be right they should have one," said Lord North.[23]

Despite the violent repercussions in the Atlantic colonies where it had the effect of stimulating the revolutionary movement, it seems undeniable that the contentious Quebec Act was originally conceived as an honest attempt to meet in an enlightened spirit the unprecedented and complicated problem of providing a suitable government for a people of alien race and traditions, and, at the same time, of settling the vexatious western question. Later on, in the light of experience, its supporters came to urge that at least the Act had begun the process of incorporating the French Canadians into the fabric of the British Empire. From the first, the former French colonists regarded the Quebec Act as their charter of liberties and were inspired by its safeguards to resist the most seductive blandishments from the south aimed at drawing them into the maelstrom of revolution. This in the long run was to give Great Britain a second chance at building a western empire on wiser and juster principles than those which at the time were about to cause her the loss of her first colonies in America.

The migration of the Loyalists to Canada at the close of the rebellion had the momentous effect of securing an eventual majority in the population of the new empire for English-speaking people, rather than French Canadians. In this respect, the future of Canada was just as truly determined by the outcome of the American Revolution as the destiny of the Thirteen Colonies. As a civil war, the American Revolution is unique in that the losers neither settled down in subordination to the victorious group nor were dispersed as politically impotent exiles; instead, they grasped the opportunity of settling as a coherent body in contiguous territory where they became almost at once the dominant group. Henceforth, they were able to begin the process of building a new state along the lines of that peculiarly British form of constitutional development from which

[22] Coupland, *op. cit.,* pp. 102-03.
[23] *Ibid.,* p. 108.

their former compatriots were making at that very moment a significant departure. The numbers involved in this migration were considerable, and the high educational and social character of the immigrants gave their movement an even greater importance than might be inferred from the actual figures.

John Adams estimated that "one third of the people of the Thirteen Colonies had been opposed to the measures of the Revolution in all its stages." While not all these Loyalists actually migrated, probably one hundred thousand in all left their homes to live under the British flag. Most of those financially able to do so returned to England; a considerable number went to the West Indies, especially to the Bahama Islands, which with their coming took on a new lease of life; but by far the largest group migrated to the Maritime Provinces or to Canada. The number of those entering what is now the Dominion, during and after the war, has been variously estimated as from sixty to seventy-five thousand. In later years the original Loyalists, especially those who settled around Lake Ontario and the Niagara peninsula, acted as magnets, drawing northward many of their old neighbors who, as land hungry frontiersmen, were attracted by the news of the free fertile land north of the border.[24]

That British North America was able to secure this large group of persons of substance and leadership was due in no small measure to the honorable and long-continued efforts of Great Britain to stand by those who had stood by her in the revolutionary struggle, and to her generous financial assistance in the difficult process of resettlement. In the peace treaty the British negotiators secured, despite the opposition of the American agents who looked upon all Tories as traitors, the insertion of three clauses meant for the protection of the Loyalists. One of these agreed "that creditors on either side shall meet with no lawful impediment to the recovery of the full value in sterling money of all bona fide debts heretofore contracted"; another agreed "that Congress shall earnestly recommend it to the Legislatures of the respective states, to provide for the restitution of all estates, rights, and properties which have been confiscated, belonging to real British subjects . . ."; a third agreed that "there shall be no future confiscations made, nor any prosecutions commenced against any Person or Persons for or by reason of the part which he or they may have taken in the present war . . . and that those who may be in confinement . . . shall be immediately set at liberty, and the prosecutions so commenced be discontinued."[25] Time was to demonstrate that the weak central govern-

---

[24] On the Canadian Loyalists in Upper Canada, consult C. Wittke, "Canadian Refugees in the American Revolution," in *Canadian Historical Review,* Vol. III, pp. 320-34: also, the same author's *History of Canada* (New York: 1931), pp. 57, 60-62, 65.

[25] Articles IV, V, and VI of the Treaty of 1783.

ment of the United States under the Articles of Confederation lacked sufficient power, even if it had the will, to enforce the cooperation of the state governments in carrying out these clauses of the peace treaty. The Loyalists were to save from the wreck of a lost cause only what the mother country could herself provide.

Meanwhile, the pressing need for a place on the American continent to offer as an alternative home to these persecuted people stiffened the attitude of the British government in refusing Franklin's suggestion that the northern border should be limited only by the North Pole. It is interesting to speculate what might have happened if the American revolutionaries had been more tolerant of those in their midst who had not seen eye to eye with them in the struggle, and if they had been more conciliatory toward them in the settlement. It is an open question as to whether, if there had not existed these thousands of Loyalists eager to migrate as fast as possible to a new American home under the British flag, North America might not have been one great republic. But with a large group embittered by their late experience firmly settled north of the line, it might easily have been foreseen that northward expansion would henceforth be most difficult. At the time of the peace treaty a disillusioned mother country might well have thrown in her hand and abandoned the American continent had the Loyalists not been a living argument against surrendering anything further. Rodney's victory late in 1782 over the French fleet in the Battle of the Saints in the West Indies, and the victorious defense of Gibraltar against a combined French and Spanish fleet, were other considerations stiffening British resistance and encouraging her to retain her Canadian holdings.

Meanwhile, orders had been sent to Sir Guy Carleton, who in 1782 had been made commander-in-chief of the British forces, to do his best for the protection of the Loyalists, whose lot after the peace was desperate. He proved their firm champion and determined protector, refusing to budge from New York harbor, despite the treaty's stipulation that it should be "evacuated with all practical despatch," until the last supporter of the lost British cause who wished to leave under the protection of the British fleet had been given a chance to do so in order and decency. To the pointed request from Congress for the date of his departure, he returned the reply that the more the Loyalists were persecuted the longer he would be obliged to stay. He finally sailed on November 25, 1783.

The British government not only recognized the obligation of providing free lands and free transportation for the Loyalists, but made generous grants for food, seed, stock, and implements to help establish the settlers in their new locations. At the same time, it set up a royal commission to deal with matters of compensation for losses of property and position. In all, it is estimated that the equivalent of $30,000,000 was expended in direct aid to the Loyalists over and above the land grants.[26] Despite, however, the utmost that could be done, great hardships were suffered by most of those involved in this great transplanting of people. Many had long enjoyed comfortable living standards and honorable employment in the larger cities and now had to face primitive pioneering conditions in log cabins and hard-won forest clearings.

The arrival in the British North American colonies of this multitude of English-speaking people whose general level of character, intelligence, education, and experienced political outlook gave them a position of natural leadership produced fundamental changes in every walk of life, but most particularly in the constitutional field. Two areas especially were affected, the Maritime Provinces and what is now known as the province of Ontario. To Nova Scotia, which then still included New Brunswick, went probably thirty thousand persons, increasing the population of this region threefold. The group that settled in this area comprised a large proportion of professional people: judges, lawyers, doctors, clergymen, and teachers from the cities and towns of New England and the Middle Colonies who preferred this region because it was already settled, though sparsely, and enjoyed representative government of the same kind with which they had long been familiar. Some ten thousand of the Maritime Loyalists settled along the St. John River north of the Bay of Fundy. These people soon complained that they were too far from the seat of government at Halifax to receive proper attention, whereupon the British government in 1784 set off this section as the Province of New Brunswick with its own governor, legislative council, and representative assembly, with a capital city soon established at Fredericton. Colonel Thomas Carleton, the younger brother of Sir Guy, was its first governor and continued in office for thirty years. To Cape Breton Island went some three thousand Loyalists, and they also were soon provided with a separate government of the crown colony variety. Some six hundred Loyalists joined the sparse population of Prince Edward Island, formerly the island of St. John, which had been already, in 1769, parted from Nova Scotia and made a separate colony. Thus what had once been the single province of Nova Scotia was by 1784 split into four separate colonies. In the Maritimes, therefore, the outstanding effects of the American Revolution were first, to treble the population, and secondly, to lead to the creation of two new provinces. In 1820 Cape Breton rejoined Nova Scotia, but the other divisions remained permanent.[27]

[26] Wittke, *op. cit.*, p. 60.

[27] On the Loyalists in the Maritimes, see Wittke, *op. cit.*, pp. 57, 62-64; also by the same author, "Canadian Refugees in the American Revolution," in *Canadian Historical Review*, Vol. III, pp. 320-34.

The effect of the migration into Canada was more far-reaching than that into the Maritimes. A more varied social group constituted the bulk of the new settlers in what is now the Province of Ontario. Most of these were frontiersmen from the back counties of the older colonies. Many came from the Mohawk Valley. Among these latter was a large group of Mohawk Indians who were led by their chief, Joseph Brant, into the region that is now Brantford, Ontario. On the whole, the Ontario settlers had less formal education, had left less behind them, and were more accustomed to manual labor. They, therefore, in many respects had a less bitter struggle to get to their feet in the new land, in spite of the fact that the country into which they came was itself more of an unbroken wilderness than Nova Scotia. Moreover, the immigration into this area, unlike that of the Maritimes, was continuous over a number of years. By 1791 some twenty-five thousand were said to have arrived. At first the plan of the British government had been to settle these people on the south side of the St. Lawrence in what are today the "Eastern townships," with the idea of setting up a kind of buffer state between the revolted colonies and the French Canadians. Carleton's successor, General Haldimand, however, convinced the British ministry that this policy might stir up new strife, and would work a hardship to the French Canadians for whom this land, he suggested, should be reserved as an area of future expansion. To some one thousand Loyalists he assigned lands near Sorel and on the Bays of Gaspé and Chaleur; others he settled in the cities of Montreal and Quebec; but with these exceptions he directed the movement into lands west of Montreal along the upper St. Lawrence, around the Bay of Quinte, and into the Niagara peninsula.

Associated with these Loyalist settlements of Upper Canada difficulties arose between the British government and the United States over the "old Northwest." The close of the war found the British in possession of the forts in this area. Historically and geographically the region belonged to Canada, though surrendered by the terms of the peace treaty. When the United States failed to carry out the terms of the treaty in respect to the Loyalists, the British government refused to relinquish the northwest forts, and in this attitude was encouraged by the Loyalists who faced this territory across the Lakes. Not until after the Jay Treaty was signed in 1794 were these posts relinquished by the British.

In 1786, while Loyalist settlements were still in progress, the British government undertook to tie into a closer union the several parts of British North America that still remained to the crown. The first effort was to effect this unity through a larger measure of executive cohesion. Sir Guy Carleton was made Governor-General of all the British provinces with authority extending from the far west to Cape Breton and Prince Edward

Island. In each of the several provinces a lieutenant-governor was substituted for the governor. But when Carleton, now Lord Dorchester, reached Canada he was faced with a great popular agitation for further constitutional changes of a fundamental kind, involving, among other things, the racial question. The English element throughout Quebec was crying aloud for representative government, which the French Canadians did not want. Moreover the Loyalists living in the new settlements west of Montreal were demanding not only an elective assembly but also a partition of the province and a separate government. This latter demand the English living in the eastern portion denounced as a completely selfish move which would leave them isolated in a hopeless minority. Eventually the westerners were to gain both their points, chiefly because the British Parliament was forced by the financial situation to take action. The Quebec Revenue Act of 1774 was producing an utterly insufficient sum, and yet the home government did not wish, after its experience in the Thirteen Colonies, to impose direct taxation. Consequently there seemed nothing for it but to set up a local taxing body. There was also the further consideration that transplanted Loyalists deserved to have a form of government at least as liberal as that to which they had previously been accustomed.

There were really three alternatives under discussion. The first was to keep Canada as one province but give it a representative assembly in which the English would indeed be in a minority, but a fairly numerous one. The second was to divide Canada into two wholly separate provinces, each with its own representative government, in one of which the English could control the future. The third was to federate all British North America, and so have fairly even representation of the two races in the central representative house. The most enthusiastic advocate of this third idea in Canada was William Smith, an outstanding Loyalist who later became chief justice; Carleton, on the other hand, wished to move more slowly and gave the idea of federation only very cautious approval. In England there was considerable support in high places for the federal proposal which so interestingly foreshadowed the British North America Act of three quarters of a century later.

Despite strong opposition from English merchants of Montreal and Quebec, it was the second plan, with certain modifications, that was finally decided upon. The British Parliament, under the leadership of the younger Pitt, put through the Canada Act or, as it is better known, the Constitutional Act of 1791. This measure separated Quebec into two distinct provinces, called Upper Canada and Lower Canada, divided from each other at the Ottawa River. Each province was given a government of the traditional eighteenth-century colonial type with its own lieutenant-governor functioning under an over-all governor-general, an appointive legislative council, and an elective assembly based on a limited suffrage. The idea was

proposed in England, in imitation of the British model, to create hereditary titles of nobility for the members of the upper house as a safeguard to
the interests of the crown and to serve as a check upon democratic tendencies that might develop too radically in the lower house; Carleton's objection, however, overruled the proposal. To make the bill more acceptable to
the English residents in Lower Canada, various saving clauses were in-
serted: thus, the towns of Montreal, Quebec, and Three Rivers were given
two members each so as to insure representation for the local English
merchants; various safeguards were provided to secure British interests
under the mixed legal system; matters of appointment and veto were left
in the hands of the governor; in land tenure it was provided that lands
outside of the seigneuries were to be held under the English system of
common socage; and one seventh of all crown lands was reserved for the
Church of England. In the field of commerce the crown reserved the right
of supervision, as it was realized that were this to be turned over to the
provinces, Lower Canada would, because of its possession of the great
forts and control of the seaway, have the power to impose financial ruin
on Upper Canada. The crown also retained control of naval and military
expenditures, for which, in any case, it would have to furnish the funds
for many years to come. Under the Constitutional Act of 1791, ultimate
power really rested in the hands of the resident governor, whose advisory
council was also in a strong position. The new measure went into effect
December 26, 1791. Only to the French Canadian representatives was the
central idea of representative government which it embodied entirely novel.

Basically, the Constitutional Act of 1791 really reproduced in Canada
the fundamental theories of the old colonial system of the Thirteen Colonies. No one apparently considered as feasible the introduction into colonial administration of the principle of "responsible" government. This
now seems strange, when we consider that the lack of responsibility of the
executive to the representative assemblies of the Thirteen Colonies had
been one of the rocks on which the old system had so recently foundered.
Moreover, that this enlightened procedure which might have avoided the
political pitfalls of the next fifty years was not incorporated in the government of the Canadas at the time now appears the more remarkable, as it
was the pride of British constitutional development in the homeland.
Consciousness of the problems presented by the political inexperience, as
well as the alien race and religion, of the large French element probably
furnishes the best explanation as to why the British lawmakers and their
advisers in 1791 did not take the step which, for the English constituents,
was the obvious next move in colonial constitutional evolution.[28]

---

[28] But *cf.*, the discussion of this question in Coupland, *The American Revolution and the
British Empire* (New York: 1930), pp. 276-87 for a different point of view.

Chapter 20

HISPANIC AMERICA

I. SPANISH AMERICA TO 1830: "PLOUGHING THE SEA"

In Spanish America, the search for a satisfactory form of government with which to replace the royal absolutism of the colonial age, as we have already seen, was older than the first declaration of independence. It began with the arrival of the news that the mother country had been overrun by French armies and the Spanish king and crown prince were prisoners in Napoleon's hands. The first general reaction was a vigorous refusal by peninsulares and creoles alike to accept French domination. French agents, soliciting colonial support for Joseph Bonaparte as "King of Spain and the Indies," were speedily convinced that the Spanish colonials were more royalist, if possible, than the European Spaniards, and that there was no possibility of securing countenance in Spanish America for the new regime. Meanwhile, following the theory that in the absence of the king sovereignty had reverted to the people, and leaning on the one bit of genuine constitutional experience that they possessed, many of the larger Spanish American municipalities, acting through their cabildos, set up provisional juntas gubernativas. To secure as wide support as possible for such a momentous step, the cabildos, or here and there the distracted viceroys or royal governors, made use of a device that had occasionally been resorted to in crises in the past, namely, the calling of a cabildo abierto, or open town meeting, in which a larger group of vecinos than those in the official cabildo could be heard on the vital issue under discussion. At first the juntas gubernativas very generally proclaimed loyalty to the imprisoned Ferdinand VII and professed to be merely holding the fort for him until he could return to his throne. As originally set up, they were usually presided over by the governor or other royal official.

But as the extent of the disaster in Spain became apparent, and as the creoles gained greater control in the juntas, these bodies tended to become revolutionary in character. Their leaders practically everywhere were well-to-do creoles, many of whom had been educated in Spain, had seen service in the Spanish armies or in the colonial militia, and were familiar with the machinery of the cabildo. By 1810, revolutionary movements were in progress in many parts of Spanish America, spreading from cabildo to

494

cabildo.[1] The juntas of the capital cities of most of the larger divisions tried to provide the needed leadership, not only urging the other cities of the area to organize themselves, but inviting the new juntas of the provincial towns to send representatives to a general congress to consider the issues of independence and organization on a national scale, along both military and constitutional lines. The first declarations of independence came from such congresses; that of Venezuela, meeting in Caracas, issued the first declaration of absolute independence on July 14, 1811.

Meanwhile, patriotic Spaniards in the homeland were by no means indifferent to what was passing in the overseas empire. Though beset by military problems of the first magnitude and staggering under great constitutional difficulties within the peninsula, successive provisional governments in Spain not only tried to grapple with the imperial issue involved, but sought such fundamental colonial reforms as would place the people of the Indies on a basis of economic and political equality with the inhabitants of the homeland. The Central Junta, meeting at Seville in 1809, asserted that the American kingdoms were "elements of the Spanish nation" and not merely parts of the monarchy and in the following year the Committee of Regency invited the Indies to send delegates to a cortes called to meet at Cádiz. This assembly likewise declared the Spanish dominions in Europe and overseas to form "one single and identical monarchy," and recognized the principle of equality of representation of Spain and the Indies whenever that should become a practical possibility.[2]

It is interesting to speculate what might have happened if, instead of adopting the theory of a unitary and centralized state, the Cádiz cortes had attempted a federation of Spanish kingdoms under a constitutional monarchy. At least in that case the activities of the congress might seriously have interested the leaders in the Indies. As it was, the concept adopted seemed so foreign to the political realities shaping colonial life that it apparently had little bearing on the actual situation. Regrettable or not, the inhabitants of the Indies had long thought of their tie with Spain as binding them to the king rather than to the nation. With a usurper on the throne, they felt that they must look for political direction to themselves alone. Few in the Indies paid much heed to what went on at Cádiz or elsewhere in Spain, being too much absorbed in the local scene.

The revolutionary impulse in the colonies varied considerably in

---

[1] For details consult V. A. Belaunde, *Bolívar and the Political Thought of the Spanish American Revolution* (Baltimore: 1938), chap. vii, "The Insurrection of the Cabildos" and chap. ix, "From Sovereignty to Absolute Independence."

[2] Eventually, thirty American representatives were present at this gathering, though the great majority had been chosen by Hispanic American residents in Europe. A number of far-reaching social and political reforms for the American territories were on the agenda, but the crucial issue was that concerning the nature of the Spanish states. *Cf.* Belaunde, *op. cit.,* chap. xvii.

strength in different areas. The capitals of the two older viceroyalties, Lima and Mexico City, were centers of conservative loyalty, rocks around which swirled the revolutionary currents engulfing the rest of Spanish America. For more than a decade Peru remained a stronghold of royalist sentiment and until 1822 succeeded in preventing the junction of the northern and southern wings of the independence armies in South America. Mexico City, the capital of the oldest of all the viceroyalties and the chief administrative center for the northern colonies, where the peninsulares were naturally in great strength, presented a somewhat similar obstacle in the path of the revolutionary movement to that offered by Lima; though the separatist movement in the Mexican viceroyalty as a whole ran a course distinct in many ways from that in South America.

The months immediately following the news of the Napoleonic invasion of Spain saw many political cross currents at work in the Mexican capital. When the viceroy, José de Iturrigaray, showed a certain sympathy towards the cabildo in its efforts to set up a provisional governing junta, thus tending to follow the same pattern as in the rest of Spanish America, he was forcibly seized by the peninsulares who were suspicious of his loyalty, compelled to resign, and finally deported from the country. By March, 1809, the peninsulares, now the dominant group, had recognized the supremacy of the Spanish Central Junta at Seville. For a time this European body tried to direct Mexican affairs through the local audiencia with the archbishop of Mexico acting as viceroy, but when the latter showed a propensity to lean too heavily on creole support, a new viceroy was sent from Spain, in September, 1810. With his arrival, the separatist spirit began to shift from the capital to creole groups in provincial centers where support from the mestizos and Indians could be relied upon. An insurrectionary movement in Valladolid was nipped in the bud in December, 1809. The really serious outbreak came in September, 1810, from the village center of Dolores under the leadership of the parish priest, Miguel Hidalgo y Costilla.[3]

In South America generally, the dominant creole groups in the various sections tried to ride out the storm, which in one aspect was a struggle for independence from Spain and in another a civil war against the peninsulares, by making use of their provisional municipal juntas and the new constituent assemblies. The task was enormous. Not only had the military campaign against the royalists to be planned and conducted, but the working principles on which the new states should emerge had to be beaten out and new practical constitutions framed. Both nature and history seemed to be against the patriots in their struggle for independence. The

---

[3] For a discussion of these early revolutionary events in Mexico, see H. I. Priestley, *The Mexican Nation: A History* (New York: 1923), chaps. xi and xii.

physical character of one of the most mountainous areas in the world, the almost total lack of serviceable roads, and the absence of accustomed lines of intercourse between the different parts of any one of the major divisions, to say nothing of communication between the larger colonial units, appeared to make common action hopeless. Lack of political experience on the part of the reformers was an even greater handicap. The centralized Spanish system had given the creoles nothing like a broad political experience on a provincial or national level. Furthermore, the graded class system of the colonial regime had produced a society with divided loyalties and interests, so that behind the creole leaders there was not a united people clamoring for independence and prepared for the sacrifices entailed; probably a very small percentage of the total population understood what the controversy was all about.[4] Some of the mestizos, increasing in number as time went on, were in favor of independence, but they possessed even less political experience than the creoles. The Indians, as wards of the crown, had enjoyed many special favors under colonial government and were generally royalists in favor of the status quo. The other colored groups were divided from each other and too ignorant and oppressed to grasp the issues. The struggle for independence was predominantly a creole movement; if it was to be won, the creoles, practically alone, had to win it.

In an attempt to gain strength and attract special groups to the cause of independence, or to weaken the royalist cause, the creole leaders, in their various centers, proclaimed a number of far-reaching social reforms. To placate the Indians, they were declared henceforth to be on a basis of equality with the whites, the obligation to pay tribute was repealed, and all forms of compulsory labor were forbidden. In a gesture to attract the Negroes, slavery was abolished. Other pronouncements promised freedom of the press, liberty of assembly, and the removal of restrictions on agriculture, commerce, and industry. Further to weaken the peninsulares, titles of nobility were done away with, while the royalist-minded Church was struck at through the abolition of the Inquisition, restrictions on religious orders, and rigorous pronouncements regarding the subordination of Church to state.

The two most powerful influences on the new constitutions, both national and provincial, taking shape in the period before 1814 were first, the liberal propaganda from abroad, holding up to admiration the ideas emanating from the eighteenth-century *philosophes* which had been recently embodied in the American and French revolutions and their republican constitutions; and secondly, long-standing familiarity with the Span-

---

[4] It has been estimated that in the Spanish American population of this age 45 per cent was Indian, 31 per cent Mestizo, 19 per cent white and the rest Negroes and Mulattoes. See J. F. Rippy, "Monarchy or Republic?" in *South American Dictators,* ed. A. C. Wilgus (Washington: 1937), p. 14.

ish centralized system. These opposing ideas eventually crystallized behind the terms "federalism" and "unitarism," respectively, and involved not merely constitutional opposites but a deep-seated social struggle. Federalism, in the Spanish American sense, stemmed from the cabildo tradition and, further back, from ineradicable Spanish regionalism, and expressed the loyalty of frontier folk and inhabitants of the smaller towns to local leaders. With its states' rights emphasis, federalism appealed to the provincial populace as the one form of political organization likely to give them any voice in the management of public affairs. On the other hand, the Spanish colonial tradition of a highly centralized government in the hands of a selected few was the real strength behind unitarism, for it seemed to the propertied classes, who for the most part resided in the larger cities, the only system likely to preserve order. Meanwhile, in every town junta and assembly there were pressure groups that strove to use the crisis to maintain old privileges or free themselves from old bondages, and were prepared to throw their weight in the scale for whichever set of theories would be most to their advantage. In many areas, differences among various revolutionary parties were accentuated by bitter feelings between rival cities, so jealous of their prestige that tumults between them frequently approached the fury of little civil wars fought within the framework of the general struggle going forward between royalists and patriots.

Another fertile source of bitter dispute in this period was the jealousy between the provisional town juntas of an area and the general congress. The range of activity assumed by the "national" congresses tended constantly to widen as they attempted to pose as the central authority for their respective regions—undertaking to direct the military struggle against Spain, conduct relations with foreign powers, draw up a national constitution, and make such all-important appointments as those of the chief executive and the generalissimo, at times combining both in the office of a "dictator." Naturally this process led to accusations of the usurpation of power and caused the breaking away in rebellion of one or more regional fragments which frequently proceeded to set up a separate congress. Expressive of this spirit of rampant localism, the doctrine of "communal sovereignty" became widespread and the multiplying of congresses was so great in some areas, notably in New Granada, as to be seriously crippling to all large-scale action in the main business of winning the war against Spain.

The fundamental question of size and boundaries of the emerging states was, to a great extent, determined by past alignments. In the colonial period there had been a considerable development of a feeling of unity within the various viceroyalties, captaincies-general, and presidencies. The best of the creole leaders felt that the new political units should follow the traditional lines, and they supported the recognition of the so-called principle of *uti possidetis juri* of 1810, by which the boundaries of the future should correspond to those of the several sections as they had existed at the time of the proclamation of independence. This by no means eliminated all boundary problems, but at least furnished a rough and convenient guide.[5]

It is noteworthy that the new constitutions give evidence of a widespread fear of a too strong executive, a reflection of the abuses of the highly centralized Spanish colonial system.[6] Venezuela, for instance, in her constitution of 1811, closely copied the Constitution of the United States of 1787, except that she established a collective executive of three persons instead of entrusting all executive power to one individual. New Granada, where regionalism ran riot, in her Constitutional Act of 1812 clearly followed the Articles of Confederation of the United States of 1777 with their weak central authority.[7] The numerous state constitutions of New Granada, as of Venezuela, showed the same determination to weaken the executive. In the La Plata area, where there was no declaration of independence or formal constitution until 1816, the junta gubernativa of Buenos Aires in the earlier period displayed a strong determination to dominate the political destiny of the rest of the viceroyalty through subordinate committees set up for the different provinces. As in northern South America, so here there was the same reluctance to entrust supreme authority to one individual and, in consequence, a succession of "triumvirates" functioned throughout the opening years. In 1814, however, under the direction of the first Argentine Assembly, this collective authority was replaced by a single Director.

Meanwhile, in the interior provinces federalism raised its head and became associated with "exaggerated personalism" as well as a tendency towards the fragmentation of the old viceregal domain. The district of Paraguay, leaning on the principle of the right of "free determination," refused to recognize the authority of Buenos Aires and set out on its own independent career; in the Banda Oriental (Uruguay) early local loyalties gathered about Artigas, but it was not till 1828, after years spent as a bone of contention between Brazil and Argentina, that the region eventually secured recognition as an independent state. In Buenos Aires itself, rival constitutional theories wrecked the effectiveness of the government. From the tendency towards the fragmentation of territorial jurisdictions under the spell of federalism, so marked in the constitutional development of

---

[5] Belaunde, *op. cit.,* chap. i, pp. 11-15, "The Spanish Background," and chap. xii, pp. 142-47, "Formation of the Nationalities."

[6] *Ibid.,* p. 148.

[7] *Ibid.,* p. 151.

southern Spanish America, Mexico stands apart. In her first revolutionary constitution, signed at Apatzingán in 1814 under the inspiration of Morelos, the unitary Spanish Constitution of 1812 was followed rather than the United States federal model. On the other hand in the provision made for a collective rather than a single executive,[8] the Mexicans exhibited the same fear of prerevolutionary conditions as marked contemporary South American constitutional documents.

Nowhere, except in La Plata, had any of these constitutions a chance of a fair trial, for before the end of 1815 the royalist cause had triumphed. King Ferdinand had been restored to his throne, "legitimacy" was in the saddle in Europe, and a strong naval force had been dispatched to the Caribbean to bring back the Spanish colonies to their allegiance. By the time the fleet arrived, the incipient republics were already bleeding to death from internal strife.

The years 1815 to 1825, forming the second period in the struggle for independence, were dominated in the constitutional as in the military field by the two great figures of Simón Bolívar and José de San Martín whose organizing genius and military abilities were to succeed eventually in turning disaster into victory. Both these men based their work on the principle of popular sovereignty as expressed in cabildos or popularly elected congresses, consistently showing the peoples' representatives an almost exaggerated deference. In their respective programs, political organization played a larger part in Bolívar's career than in that of San Martín. The Argentinian, through the greater part of his career as a Spanish American generalissimo, had behind him the support of the comparatively vigorous civil administrations of Pueyrredón in Buenos Aires and O'Higgins in Chile; Bolívar, on the other hand, had to create most of the assemblies and governments he served, and seems never to have had his mind free from political problems. Neither leader had any faith in the practicability of applying principles of absolute democracy to the Latin American scene. "The experience of the continent has proved," wrote Bolívar as early as 1812, "that pure representative institutions are not suitable to our character, customs, and present conditions."[9] Though both men were idealists, neither shared the delusion so common among doctrinaire radicals of their day that if only a perfect constitution could be devised, or an unexceptionable declaration of political principles arrived at, all would be well and society would flourish in peace and prosperity.

Bolívar especially excelled in devising ringing declaratory statements, and gave great attention to constitutional documents; but at no time did he

---

[8] Priestley, *op. cit.*, pp. 234-36.
[9] Quoted in C. Parra-Pérez, *Bolívar: A Contribution to the Study of His Political Ideas* (Paris: 1928), p. 20.

lose his grasp on the actual scene and its possibilities. He told the famous Congress of Angostura, in his opening address to that body on February 15, 1819, that that "system of government is the most perfect which produces the greatest possible measure of happiness, social security and political stability." [10] He never tired of denouncing "demagogic idealism" and "theoretical liberalism." No one realized better than the Liberator that a grossly ignorant people, wholly untrained in political thinking, could not use the vote with intelligence and would surely fall victim to designing factions and unscrupulous individuals. A workable constitution must, he knew, be designed to meet the needs of each particular people in its own environment and not merely be copied without modification from another state. "We are," he wrote, "a separate part of the human race; we possess a world apart, we are neither Indians nor Europeans but a species between the legal proprietors of the country and the Spaniards."

Both Bolívar and San Martín instinctively felt that the constitutional pattern that was working so amazingly well in the United States was not the right one for Spanish America. "It requires," declared Bolívar, "virtues and talents in politics very superior to ours." Both leaders grasped the fact that the constitutional problems facing the former Spanish colonies were, in many vital respects, the reverse of those that had confronted the North American constitution makers. The latter had had the problem of creating a strong national union out of already existing, practically independent, political state units. To imitate this system within their several kingdoms, Spanish Americans who had inherited a centralized system would have had to break down an existing unity in order to form states with which to start the federating process. Furthermore, the North Americans had set out with the tradition of a government in which the legislative branch had always been a very effective part of the governmental system; in England it had become the supreme authority to which the executive was responsible. In English colonial legislatures there had been a constant struggle towards this goal; the outcome of the American Revolution, and the constitutional debates that followed the close of the struggle, had been to make the legislative and executive branches separate and theoretically equal. In Spanish America, on the other hand, there was no tradition of a legislature at all, but merely of an overwhelmingly powerful executive. In setting up new governments, the former Spanish colonists not only had to create such legislatures from the ground up, but to devise a workable relationship between the two branches of government. They had to avoid, on

---

[10] The address of Bolívar to the Congress of Angostura, February 15, 1819, as translated by F. J. Yañes, is available in separate reprint, 39 pp. (Washington: 1919); large sections of the address are given in N. A. N. Cleven, *Readings in Hispanic American History* (New York: 1927), pp. 435-43. For a discussion of this address see Parra-Pérez, *op. cit.*, chap. iv, and Belaunde, *op. cit.*, chap. xv.

the one hand, the traditional pattern of giving overwhelming authority to the executive, and on the other, while seeking to escape this danger, avoid also the perilous error of withholding sufficient strength to enable the executive to function. Bearing in mind these and other political differences between North and South America, as well as the utter lack of resemblance in the two social scenes, neither Bolívar nor San Martín felt that the United States' pattern should be allowed to have as much weight as popular liberal propaganda sought to give it. San Martín definitely favored constitutional monarchy for the new states and, as dictator of Peru, dispatched a number of commissioners to Europe to look for candidates. His withdrawal from the scene before the military struggle had been completed made his contribution to the solution of political problems less extensive and significant than that of Bolívar.

The Venezuelan leader admired, above all others, the British constitutional system for effectiveness in actual operation, but instinctively felt that monarchy did not fit well into New World conditions. "I think that the Americans," he said at Angostura in 1819, "anxious for peace, the sciences, the arts, commerce, and agriculture, would prefer republics to kingdoms." He doubted that his soldiers would ever be willing to step aside and see European princelings exercising power in the states which their own arms had freed from European absolutism. "European princes in America," he said, "would be factors foreign to our race." Neither did he believe that a sufficient number of candidates could be found anxious to mount "royal scaffolds." For these and other reasons he favored a republic, but one with a strong central executive.[11]

Bolívar's political views were expressed especially clearly in four important documents: (1) The Manifesto to the People of New Granada,[12] issued from Cartagena in 1812; (2) a Letter to an English Gentleman from Jamaica. in 1815; (3) his Message to the Congress of Angostura, February 15, 1819; (4) the Bolivian Constitution, 1826.

The Bolivian Constitution which the Liberator was invited in 1826 to write for Upper Peru, the last of the five countries to be liberated by his armies, must be taken to express Bolívar's mature views of what was desirable and practicable in a constitution for a Spanish American state in his day.[13] For months he worked over the document, declaring in his introductory message to the Bolivian Congress, "I have employed all the

---

[11] See Rippy, "Monarchy or Republic?" *op. cit.,* also Belaunde, *op. cit.,* chap. xviii. For an interesting commentary on the difficulties in the way of monarchy in Spanish America, see Cecil Jane, *Liberty and Despotism in Spanish America* (Oxford: 1929), chap. vii, "The Establishment of Republics."

[12] There is a chapter on this famous Manifesto and its setting in Parra-Pérez, *op. cit.,* chap. i.

[13] On the Bolivarian constitution, consult Parra-Pérez, *op. cit.,* chap. ix, "The Constitutional System," and Belaunde, *op. cit.,* chap. xxi, "The Life-Term Constitution."

powers of my mind for the purpose of submitting to you my opinions . . . respecting the best method of governing Freemen."

The scheme proposed a republic of an ultraconservative but unique character in which Bolívar's earlier views were both modified and extended. The republic was stated to be of a representative centralistic type. The sovereignty of the people was to be exercised through four divisions of power—electoral, legislative, executive, and judicial. Provincial electoral colleges, resting on the suffrage of those citizens who could read and write and made up of one elector for every ten citizens, were charged with the duty of drawing up lists of names from which the legislature and various provincial and municipal functionaries would be chosen. The legislative power was to be exercised through three chambers: a House of Tribunes, serving for four years and given the right to originate laws respecting revenue, peace, and war; a Senate, elected for eight years and especially given charge of religion, law, and the regulation of patronage; and finally, a House of Censors, serving for life and given special control over education and public morals, including control of the press, encouragement of the arts and sciences, and bestowal of public honors. Bolívar likened the power of the Censors to that of the Areopagus of Athens and the Censors of Rome, and declared, "The most terrible as well as the most august function, belongs to the censors." The legislative houses, besides having each its own particular field of operations, had certain functions in common. As the agreement of two of the three houses would be sufficient to carry any ordinary measure, it was hoped that the difficulty of insoluble conflict between two contending chambers would not arise.

The executive power was to be wielded by a president who would serve for life. In the first instance, he was to be elected by the combined legislature, but was then given the power to name the vice-president who became his successor. "The President of the Republic is, in our constitution," declared the Liberator, "like the Sun, which, firm in its center, gives life to the universe." He was to be Chief of the Administration, Commander of the Army and Navy, and the "support of the whole system." This President, however, was to be accountable to no one. "On him rests all our order without being responsible for it," said Bolívar. Among the strong safeguards against abuse of presidential authority was the bestowal on the legislative body of most of the appointive power. Another check was a powerful vice-president who, as chief of the ministry, was made, along with the three secretaries who headed the administrative departments, responsible to the legislature and subject to impeachment before the Senate. The judicial power was also made wholly independent of the executive, the magistrates being elected by the legislature from names proposed by the electors. The power of the voters was also conceived as "a counterpoise put into the scale against the executive power."

In this constitution Bolívar returned to the colonial tradition of centering the chief authority, as well as the continuing element of government, in the executive. Six years earlier he had pressed at Angostura for a system in which a hereditary senate would provide the principal element of strength and permanence. Reflection and experience had served to change his mind as to the best method to resist the shock of "the two monstrous enemies . . . tyranny and anarchy" which are "constantly contending with each other" and "form an immense ocean of oppression rolling around a small island of liberty." For purposes of local government, Bolívar's constitution provided that the country should be divided into departments, provinces, and cantons; there was to be a prefect at the head of each department who would be selected from the electors' list by the central government. Thus the Liberator chose neither a federal system on the North American model nor one based on the old cabildos, but a quasi-federal system of provinces over which the central government would exercise control.

For this elaborate and intricate constitutional system Bolívar gathered ideas from the constitutional efforts and experiences of many ages and many lands. He leaned most heavily on Napoleon's consular constitution, although he also drew inspiration from Greece, Rome, Great Britain, the United States, Haiti, and the constitutional schemes of Miranda of Venezuela. He made a supreme effort to weave them into a coherent pattern which, while consonant with his idealism, could be approved by his long experience as practically applicable to the Latin American scene. While truly desiring a republic, he doubted the wisdom—for his people—of a federal one in the North American sense, and feared the danger of anarchy in a system based on contending municipal units. Experience had also convinced him that truly democratic and representative institutions were not workable in the Spanish America of his day. What was needed, he thought, was a centralized, paternalistic, and respected government beyond the reach of obstructing and paralyzing factions. It would contain institutions which, while satisfying popular aspirations with the symbols of power, would provide training centers in political action for large elements in the nation. He hoped that a veiled dictatorship, surrounded with safeguards and having within it the seeds of an enlightened future, would preserve the states, which he had labored so hard to free, from dissolving into utter anarchy.

Critics have pointed out that his system was cumbersome and expensive; that in ignoring the cabildo and providing for strict centralized control over local government through provincial organization, it nullified what little political experience Spanish America possessed; that it was at variance with his own earlier views; that in essential respects it was a contradictory blend of ultra-democratic and reactionary principles, and was in fact unworkable.[14] It is to be observed, however, that while open to criticism on many scores, this remarkable document incorporated the principal elements of Bolívar's political creed: republicanism, national unity, a congressional body, a strong executive, and an honored place within the government for the influence of cultural and religious forces. Bolívar himself long retained faith in his own handiwork, repeatedly declaring that the Bolivian constitution expressed his best judgment as to a suitable form of government for Spanish America.

This new fundamental law was immediately adopted in Bolivia and retained for two years under the presidency of Bolívar's friend, General José de Sucre, the hero of Ayacucho, who, however, refused to accept the presidency for life. Peru also accepted this constitution, and named Bolívar life president. However, on his departure for Colombia on news of revolution there, the adoption was declared by the Congress in Lima to have been illegal and a new instrument replaced it. Though answering to many of the realities of the political scene, Bolívar's supreme constitutional effort was in fact nowhere popular. In part this was because of the deficiencies in the document itself, but in large measure its rejection was due to the suspicion of many that it was designed to further imperialistic ambitions which the Liberator was believed to be cherishing.

The volume of criticism of the *constitución vitalicia* mounted higher as it became evident that the Liberator was thinking in terms not only of one country but of larger combinations of states. He had always done so. From his earliest efforts for independence, Bolívar had conceived of his own Venezuela in its larger viceregal setting. His military fortunes had no sooner taken a turn for the better in 1819, after the great victory won at Boyacá in New Granada, than he had hurried back to Venezuela and urged upon the Congress at Angostura—met to frame a new constitution for Venezuela—the adoption of a wider union to embrace all the lands of the old colonial viceroyalty.

Swayed by the magnificent oratory in which the great patriot urged the wider vision, the Congress decreed the union of the military captaincy-general of Caracas (Venezuela), the kingdom of Santa Fé (New Granada) and the presidency of Quito (Ecuador) into one republic to be entitled "Colombia," and issued a summons for a congress to meet at Rosario de Cúcuta in eastern New Granada to undertake the task of draw-

---

[14] Gerhard Masur calls the constitution an "amazing product of political imagination and extravagance," also "one of Bolivar's greatest blunders." See Gerhard Masur, *Simon Bolivar* (Albuquerque: 1948), pp. 560, 562.

ing up a constitution for the new united republic. As a result of the work at Cúcuta a fundamental law was promulgated in 1821, just a week after Bolívar's victory at Carabobo. It provided for a unitary state, with Bogotá as a capital, and a government featuring a four-year-term president, a bicameral legislature, and provinces ruled by deputies chosen by the executive. After taking oath as the first president and providing that the vice-president, Santander, should be in charge at Bogotá and General Páez his representative in Venezuela, the Liberator turned his thoughts to the military campaign in the south where the third member of the new republic, Quito, at that time still awaited liberation. The victory at Pichincha (1822) had had as one of its first fruits the completion of "Great Colombia."

Bolívar's arrival in Lima, September 1, 1823, was followed ten days later, by the bestowal on him by the Peruvian Congress of supreme military and political powers. For the next three years he remained Dictator of Peru, as well as President of Colombia, reaching the zenith of his power. After the victories of Junín (August 6, 1824) and Ayacucho (December 9, 1824) had been won, came the turn of Upper Peru to receive liberation at the hands of General Sucre, the special friend and favorite general of Bolívar. Following the principle of *uti possidetis juri*,[15] the Liberator would not permit the calling of a deliberative assembly in Upper Peru until the Argentine government had specifically authorized the independence of this former province of the viceroyalty of La Plata. The latter not only made no difficulty but sent representatives to help complete the reorganization. During 1825 Bolívar spent ten months away from Lima on a tour of inspection—in actual fact a kind of royal progress—in southern Peru and in the cities of Upper Peru. At Chuquisaca the deliberative assembly decreed a change of name from Upper Peru to the Republic of Bolívar in honor of the Liberator, bestowed on him supreme executive power and the honors of Protector and President, and invited him to draw up a constitution for the new state.

In this heyday of his power, as he worked in the early months of 1826 on his constitution for Bolivia, Bolívar's mind played with various projects for larger unions. Eventually much of his thought crystallized around a project for an Andean Confederation in which, under himself as life-term supreme president, all the lands his arms had freed—Great Colombia, Peru, and Bolivia—would form a close federation possessing one flag, one army, and a national capital at some central point, possibly Quito. A modified

---

[15] By this basic principle of Spanish American revolution, each nation was to preserve the territorial status quo of 1810, the year in which the movement for independence had been inaugurated. Upper Peru through the greater part of the colonial period had been a province of Peru, but in 1776 on the formation of the new viceroyalty of La Plata it became a part of that political entity. Bolívar believed therefore that Argentina must give her consent to the establishment of Bolivia as an independent state.

22. Latin America in 1826

constitución vitalicia would provide the fundamental law of this large state, as well as serve for the participating states, each of which would have its separate government with a life-term president at its head. Matters of war and foreign affairs were to be settled by the central government in which all sections would be represented. The plan called for dividing Peru into two departments, or states—Northern and Southern Peru; and partitioning Colombia into three, later four, departments—Cundinamarca, Venezuela, Quito, and Cartagena; Bolivia would enter as a single unit.[16]

During 1826 both Bolivia and Peru, historically long associated, accepted this project of union; but in Colombia, long politically severed from the more southern areas, the fusion plan encountered such obstacles and produced such discords that it eventually foundered completely. A number of public men, including Santander and Sucre, had warned Bolívar that a union of Colombia and Peru with Bolivia was impracticable; but he had no faith in a loose federation, the only apparent alternative. Though the gross ambition and boundless vanity ascribed to him by his enemies need not in this connection be taken too seriously,[17] there seems no doubt that the Liberator was influenced by a longing to contrive some political framework that would embrace all the lands whose freedom he had helped to win, and enable him to exercise over them a paternalistic control and help fend off those public enemies of tyranny and anarchy which he dreaded most.[18]

Before this project for "a perfect union" in the Andean Confederation had taken shape, a still larger project had been set on foot. On December 7, 1824, two days before the battle of Ayacucho, Bolívar had dispatched a circular letter to the independent governments of America and certain others proposing a Pan-American Congress at Panama. He had in mind the creation of a league or amphictyony, formed primarily in the interests of the Spanish American succession states, which abroad might be able to show a certain military and diplomatic front to the world, exert in the immediate future a combined force in making peace with Spain, and secure recognition from other states; and, at home, might perhaps aid in completing the revolution by freeing the Caribbean islands from the Spanish yoke, provide machinery to insure peace among the various states sharing a common background and carry through a program of reform in the interests of all. He also hoped that the proposed congress would draw up a code of laws regulating the relations between the member states. Of such a Pan-American league or federation he expected to be president.

Originally, the continent-wide character of the Congress seems not to have been of great concern to him. He thought at first of not including

[16] On the composition of the Federation of the Andes, see Belaunde, *op. cit.*, chap. xxiii, "The Andean Federation and Monarchic Plans." Reasons for its collapse are discussed in *ibid.*, chap. xxiv and also in Jane, *op. cit.*, chap. viii, "Freedom in Spanish America."

[17] On Bolívar's monarchial leanings, Masur, *op. cit.*, p. 570, says that he "is convinced that . . . he [Bolivar] was never tempted to follow in the steps of Napoleon" and wisely asserts that his reputation always meant more to him than "his power" and that this was "based on the title of Liberator."

[18] For a discussion of a suggestion by Bolívar that the Andean Federation might be placed under the protection of Great Britain, see Masur, *op. cit.*, pp. 585-86.

Brazil, Argentina, the United States, or Haiti. Of the latter two he remarked, "Both the North Americans and the Americans of Haiti, because of their foreign blood, have a heterogeneous character for us." [19] In his opinion the presence of Great Britain was the one great essential: "If we bind ourselves to England we shall exist; if we do not bind ourselves we shall be lost without fail." [20] He found, however, that Colombia, Mexico, and Central America were desirous of having the United States included, and that Sucre especially wanted the presence of Brazil; and eventually all were included with his approval. By February 1826, Bolívar was proclaiming with satisfaction: "The Congress of Panama will bring together representatives from all the governments of America and a diplomatic agent of his Britannic Majesty. This Congress seems destined to form the vastest league, the most extraordinary and the strongest which has ever appeared on earth. . . ." [21] He dreamed that "the New World would take shape in the form of independent nations, all joined by a common law which would control their foreign relations and would offer them a stabilizing force of a general and permanent congress. . . . The strength of all would come to the aid of any one which might suffer from the aggression of a foreign enemy or from anarchic factions within. . . ." He prophesied that "in the march of the centuries it may perhaps come about that only one nation will cover the universe—the federal."

The Congress was far from realizing Bolívar's high hopes; indeed, these had already faded before the delegates had assembled in Panama, and Bolívar did not personally attend to press the grand scheme. He had already turned his thoughts to the apparently more realizable project of the Andean Confederation.

The first Pan-American Conference, however, after long delay finally met in Panama, June 22 to July 15, 1826. Only Mexico, Central America, Colombia, and Peru sent delegates; though these four represent twelve present-day nations. Argentina and Chile were too suspicious of Bolívar's motives to risk participation, though their governments gave indications of adherence and approval of the project. The Emperor of Brazil accepted the invitation but also failed to send delegates. Paraguay, then in the grip of its extreme isolationist dictator, Dr. Francia, was not represented. Uruguay was too deeply engulfed in civil and foreign war to consider such amenities. Bolivia's representatives arrived too late.

Of the three non-Latin American powers invited to be present—England, Holland, and the United States—the first two sent observers. Two North American delegates [22] were dispatched after four months of sharp

---

[19] Belaunde, *op. cit.*, p. 260.
[20] *Ibid.*, p. 262.
[21] *Ibid.*, p. 265.
[22] Richard C. Anderson and John Sergeant.

debate in Washington; but one died on the way and the other arrived after the conference had closed. The British representative, Edward J. Dawkins, seems to have played an influential part behind the scenes. His instructions ordered him to encourage freedom of commercial intercourse, to impede the formation of a general league that might be dominated by the United States, and to oppose any military enterprise by Mexico and Colombia aimed at revolutionizing Cuba. Secretary Clay's instructions to the American delegates stressed the importance of securing equal trade opportunities for all foreigners, safeguarding maritime neutrality rights and religious liberty, and, like the British instructions, opposing any attempted conquest of Cuba and Puerto Rico.

In the three weeks of conference sessions that actually took place, a Treaty of Union, Alliance, and Perpetual Confederation was signed by all the delegates. This provided for a permanent confederation of Hispanic republics, with a central authority meeting every two years, to be supported by armed forces contributed by the member states. At this point, on the insistence of Mexico, ostensibly for health considerations, the meeting was adjourned. It was supposed to assemble again at Tacubaya in Mexico, but it was never reconvened—perhaps because Bolívar thought that the new location would imply overwhelming American influence. The greatest achievement of the conference, the Treaty of Confederation, was never ratified except by Bolívar's own state of Colombia. The first Pan-American Conference thus failed of its immediate objects; it finds its chief importance as a prototype of the future, and a symbol of the extraordinary prophetic vision of the great Spanish American statesman who invited to it the nations of the Americas.[23]

While Bolívar's largest project of union was thus proving itself too far in advance of its time to be practicable, his plan of an Andean Confederation was not only heading for disaster on the rocks of Colombian opposition, but was providing an excuse to the Liberator's critics to undermine the unity of Colombia itself. In these northern territories discontent had been mounting since the promulgation of the code of Cúcuta. New Granada, with its possession of the federal capital, exercised an ascendency which was bitterly resented in Venezuela. News reaching Bolívar that Venezuela and New Granada were on the verge of civil war obliged him, late in 1826, to leave Lima and undertake the long and wearisome journey to Bogotá. His days of triumph were numbered. The next four years of

---

[23] On the Congress of Panama, see Belaunde, *op. cit.*, chap. xxii, "The International Politics of Bolívar and the Congress of Panama" and the articles "Bolívar and the United States" by W. R. Shepherd in *Hispanic American Historical Review*, Vol. I, 1918, especially pp. 287-95, and that by Frances L. Reinhold, "New Research on the First Pan American Congress Held in Panama in 1826" in *Hispanic American Historical Review*, Vol. XVIII, 1938, pp. 342-63.

his life were to be spent in rushing from end to end of the member states
of Great Colombia in a vain effort to hold together this earliest and most
historically based of his political unions. No sooner, however, had he suppressed the separatist movement in Venezuela than he must retrace his
steps to put down rebellion in various parts of New Granada; and while
thus occupied he received news of an invasion of Ecuador and Bolivia
by troops from Peru, necessitating a war against the latter country.

Meanwhile, in New Granada divergent political parties were taking
shape around the leadership of Vice-president Santander and President
Bolívar, the first standing for "federalism" and the other for a strongly
centralized government. The Liberator's enemies now openly accused him
of aspiring to a crown, while he retorted that the "federalism" which was
sweeping the country and bringing anarchy in its train was a return to
medieval feudalism and would be "the sepulchre of Colombia." For a time
he hoped that the national convention, called to meet in March, 1828, at
Ocaña, for the purpose of reforming the constitution of Cúcuta, would
provide a remedy; but the rival political groups so successfully nullified
each other's efforts that the assembly finally dissolved for lack of a quorum
(June 11, 1828).[24] By this time disillusionment and pessimism had already
engulfed Bolívar: "I should like to know," he exclaimed, "what we can do
in a country where at each step the government dissolves or conspires
against itself. . . . We cannot form a stable government because we lack
many things, and, above all, men who can command and know how to
obey. Still less are we able to govern a vast and extensive empire with democratic laws." [25]

Following upon the dissolution of the Congress of Ocaña, Bolívar, on
August 27, 1828, in despair of a constitutional remedy and feeling obliged
to take some step in the constitutional impasse, proclaimed himself dictator
until another congress, summoned for January, 1830, should take the
situation in hand. That this step injured his reputation seemed to be
proved when, in September, 1828, an attempt was made to assassinate him.
"My enemies have succeeded in depopularizing me," mourned the Liberator.[26] In the following months as an incurable illness overcame him,
Bolívar grew more and more sensitive to critcism. "They call me tyrant and
reward me with vituperation. . . . All America resounds with denunciations against me." As he reviewed the scene throughout Spanish America he lost faith in the capacity of the former Spanish colonies to save themselves, and recommended to his council that it consider asking England,

---

[24] Ocaña is discussed in Parra-Pérez, *op. cit.,* chap. xiii, "The Great Convention." See also
Masur, *op. cit.,* pp. 630-40.
[25] Parra-Pérez, *op. cit.,* p. 172.
[26] *Ibid.,* p. 155.

the United States, or France to intervene and help establish internal order. "The government of Bolivia has declared itself for the League of Peru as was natural. . . . Buenos Aires has had, in five days, three presidents, having killed two of them. Chile is in very inept and vacillating hands. Mexico has had a major scandal and has committed the gravest crimes. Guatemala increases its difficulties. All this makes me believe that this world of anarchy needs foreign intervention which may serve as a mediator in our differences and our madnesses." [27]

As for a crown for himself, Bolívar declared in July, 1829, "There is no question about the project for a monarchy, for I do not wish and no foreign prince wishes to ascend a king's scaffold." [28] His outlook for the future was expressed in the famous words, "Our country, unable to support either liberty or slavery, will make necessary a thousand revolutions and these in turn a thousand usurpations." [29]

By the time that the new congress had been installed, January 20, 1830, Venezuela had already voted for separation from Colombia, and called Páez to supreme command; and it was evident that Ecuador was embarked on the same path. Bolívar presented to the Congress his definite and final resignation from power, saying, "Believe me a new magistrate is now indispensable for the Republic," and added sadly, "the American states look upon me with inquietude. . . . Even in Europe there are not wanting those who fear that I may discredit with my conduct the beautiful cause of liberty." [30] Joaquin Mosquera was elected president and the Liberator turned away to make preparations for his exile in Europe which, however, he did not live to reach. During the months before his death at Santa Marta on the Colombian coast, the anti-Bolívar reaction was in full swing. The efforts of Congress to reach agreement with Venezuela failed and on May 31, 1830, Quito definitely pronounced for release from the confederation. Great Colombia had thus dissolved into its several parts; the earliest and most logical of the political unions that the Liberator had sponsored lay in ruins. "In serving the cause of revolution I have ploughed the sea," he cried in despair; but nevertheless his dying proclamation to the Colombians was another forceful appeal to them "to labor for the inestimable boon of union." Through more than two decades, in spite of inconceivable difficulties, Bolívar had persevered on the battle field and in the council chamber to lay a foundation of national independence, representative government, and confederation in the five states in which his lot was cast, and beyond their borders had taken definite steps to encourage cooperation and fellowship among all the new-born republics of the whole American world.

[27] *Ibid.*, p. 183.
[28] *Ibid.*, p. 185.
[29] *Ibid.*, p. 191.
[30] *Ibid.*, p. 196.

II. BRAZIL UNDER PEDRO I

In Brazil an intensive search for a satisfactory constitution filled the first twelve years of the independent empire, proclaimed in 1822. Young Pedro I was politically astute enough to realize that if he wished to hold his country together and wear a crown for long, his empire must bend before the fashion of the hour and offer as great attractions in the matter of a written frame of government as did its Spanish American republican neighbors. Furthermore, the Liberal revolution of 1820 in Portugal was having repercussions in Brazil, awakening widespread clamors for political reforms especially in the direction of greater local control over provincial affairs. Wisely, therefore, one of Pedro's earliest acts as emperor was the summoning of a constituent assembly. It was formally opened on May 3, 1823. But the session did not proceed smoothly. At heart the Emperor was at most only a lukewarm democrat and found it extremely irksome to work with a popular body; moreover the delegates' outspoken hostility towards the Portuguese in the land annoyed him.[31] Finally in November, 1823, just as the draft of the new constitution was approaching completion, Pedro in great exasperation suddenly employed troops to enforce a dispersal of the assembly. Though he immediately ordered an appointed commission of ten to prepare another instrument of government "twice as liberal as that produced by the assembly," and in the following March proclaimed it as the basic law of the land, the Constitution of 1824 was off to a bad start. A modern, formal constitution, it was popularly felt, should not be the gift of the ruler, but the accepted product of an elected body.

The repercussions of dissatisfaction reached revolutionary proportions in the north. A movement displaying significant and prophetic characteristics engulfed the four provinces of Pernambuco, Paraíba, Rio Grande do Norte, and Ceará. These formed a so-called Confederation of the Equator, in which were significantly entwined the two ideas of federalism and republicanism. The inspiration for this union of the two principles came naturally from the nearby republic of Great Colombia which was just then taking form under the leadership of Simón Bolívar. Though the Confederation of the Equator was easily overturned by the arrival of royalist land and naval forces, the association of federalism with republicanism continued to hover about as a dynamic idea through the remainder of the imperial period.

Local liberties, inherent in the federal ideal, were those most lacking in the Constitution of 1824. Though the old provincial divisions, based for

---

[31] A. Manchester, "Paradoxical Pedro, First Emperor of Brazil," in *Hispanic American Historical Review*, 1932, p. 188.

the most part on the feudal captaincies of the colonial period, were retained for election purposes, they were allowed by the terms of the new constitution to have only small significance as units of local government, and in fact were merely administrative subdivisions of a highly centralized empire. Though each province was provided with an elective provincial council sitting in its capital city, the functions were restricted to the right of debate on a limited range of subjects and to recommendations bearing on these to the national parliament. Furthermore, high suffrage qualifications kept the electorate easily within the control of the central government which also determined all provincial taxation and expenditure. Elective municipal and district councils, though somewhat better off, were also lacking in vital legislative and financial powers. In fact, under the new regulations all real authority outside the national capital was wielded by provincial presidents who, as appointees of the emperor, took their orders from Rio de Janeiro. In the central government, legislative power was vested in a general assembly of two houses: a lower one, elected for four years, and an upper chamber of senators appointed for life by the emperor from a list voted upon by the electors. Executive power was vested in the emperor, who was expected to rule through cabinet ministers and a council of state, the latter composed of appointed life members. So glaring were the faults of the new constitution—with the threat of economic ruin and the mockery of political power for the provinces—that dissatisfaction rapidly mounted throughout the whole empire and helped to precipitate the abdication in 1831 of the ruler so eagerly supported nine years earlier when he had led Brazil into the circle of independent nations.

There were, however, other than constitutional causes for the disastrous termination of the reign of the first Brazilian emperor. The major element of weakness lay in Pedro's own character and poverty of statecraft. Thoroughly ill-educated, and without knowledge of the philosophy of government or of its practice outside of Brazil, he was unprepared to cope with the liberal political theories of his day. His own nature and the tradition of his house inclined him towards despotism, and the fear that decentralization of authority might result in the same kind of anarchy as had engulfed contemporary Spanish America impelled him in the direction of absolutism. Had he retained the services of the talented and liberal Andrada brothers, he might have been able to steer his ship safely through the dangerous currents of the time, but he exiled them at the very time that he dismissed the constituent assembly. Henceforth, surrounding himself with Portuguese courtiers, he ruled through a "kitchen cabinet" over the deliberations of which his mistress was popularly held to have great influence. His notoriously immoral life, his bad treatment of the popular

Empress Leopoldina, and his extravagant and corrupt court all brought him and his government into disrepute and thorough unpopularity.[32]

Furthermore, Pedro's regime was weakened by an unsuccessful foreign policy. A long-drawn-out war with Argentina over the Banda Oriental, incorporated into Brazil as the Cisplatine province in 1822, brought reverses on land and sea. This conflict eventually, to Brazilian disgust, resulted merely in the recognition of Uruguayan independence (1828) and the consequent creation of a buffer state between Brazil and Argentina.[33] The British, it was generally known, had pointed out to the Emperor the danger of the war's becoming a continental struggle between monarchial and republican ideas, from which his country might well emerge another Latin American republic. That British influence was held to have had much to do with Pedro's recognition of Uruguay as a separate nation only served to make his government the more unpopular, as the British at this period were widely disliked. This anti-British feeling was due partly to their long association with Portugal, but most of all sprang from their success in wringing from Pedro, in return for the recognition of his government, a treaty in 1826 promising to do away in three years' time with the profitable slave trade.[34] In 1831, as no move had been made to implement this undertaking, the British were applying pressure. In irritation and disgust at the numerous difficulties surrounding him, sensitive of the widespread criticisms of his life and policies, and uncertain of support even from the army, Pedro suddenly at 2 A.M. on April 7, 1831, without consulting anyone, wrote out his abdication.[35] Leaving the crown to his son, Dom Pedro, then only six years of age, he appointed as guardian of his children José Bonifacio de Andrada, who had returned to Brazil some three years earlier. The ex-emperor then left for Portugal where he spent the remainder of his life.

Abdication seemed a dismal end to the career of a prince who had achieved many great things for his country. In less than a decade Pedro I had carried to sucessful conclusion a bloodless independence movement; had secured the recognition of Brazil as a sovereign nation from the mother country, the United States, Great Britain and other great powers; had called the first constitutional assembly; had proclaimed the first constitution which, though later amended, was to be the basic law for Brazil through sixty-seven years and secured for the country greater liberty and

---

[32] *Ibid.*, p. 193.

[33] The difficulties surrounding Pedro, especially those springing from the Uruguayan war, are discussed in some detail by J. P. Calogeras, *A History of Brazil*, translated by P. A. Martin (Chapel Hill: 1939), chap. v, pp. 94-118, "Growing Discontent."

[34] For a discussion see Manchester, *British Preëminence in Brazil* (Chapel Hill: 1933), chap. viii, "The Price of Recognition, 1822-1827."

[35] Manchester, "Paradoxical Pedro, First Emperor of Brazil," *op. cit.*, p. 196.

a more generally satisfactory political life than any other nation in South America enjoyed; had negotiated advantageous commercial treaties with Great Britain and the United States; and had taken the first steps in ridding the country of slavery.

In the nine years of regency that intervened between the abdication of Pedro I in 1831 and the proclamation, in 1840, declaring the coming of age of Pedro II, Brazil had an opportunity of trying out what was practically a republic in disguise. In these years two political parties dominated the turbulent scenes, both of them former Liberals, whose pressure had brought the abdication. This party split into two bitterly opposed factions —the *Moderados* favoring the continuance of a constitutional but centralized monarchy, and the *Exaltados* who sponsored a federal republic. The regency, at first provisionally in the hands of three men chosen by the chamber of deputies, took the form of an elected permanent triumvirate. On the whole, it represented the views of the *Moderados* and failed to satisfy those demanding more fundamental reforms. Disorders became so serious that it seemed likely that Brazil would break into a number of parts as her neighbor, Great Colombia, had recently done. The danger, however, was averted in 1834 when the triumvirate was replaced by a single regent in the person of Father Diogo Antônio Feijó, who introduced fundamental reforms in the shape of an amendment to the constitution of 1824. This amendment, which is known as the *Acto Addicional*, accorded a measure of real autonomy to the provinces, and made possible the smooth functioning of the administrative machinery of the empire. By this famous measure, a unicameral legislative assembly, elected for two years, was set up in each province with functions embracing a fairly wide range of administrative and financial matters. One great change in the central government was the elimination of the council of state. Although the provincial presidents still remained the appointees of the central government, many laws in a wide field no longer required their signature.

Unfortunately, with a change of regents in 1837, provincial autonomy was greatly reduced by the central government's arrogating to itself all sources of revenue. The pauperized provincial bodies presently found to their dismay that they could be kept in subordination to Rio de Janeiro by the latter's insistence on political conditions in return for adequate financial subsidies. The prestige of provincial assemblies, as well as the calibre of the men who served in them, naturally declined, though they continued until the end of the empire to be an important training ground for statesmen and a school of self-government. The *Acto Addicional,* though thus somewhat emasculated, was of great importance in satisfying to some extent the craving for local autonomy, and probably to it was due the continuance of the empire. How seriously national union was threatened by the insistence on the states' rights element in federalism was made clear in the long rebellion—covering ten years, 1836 to 1846—in Rio Grande do Sul. When the last embers of that insurrection were extinguished, federalism ceased to be a political issue for twenty years. Brazil had found, for the time being, under the constitution of 1824 as amended by the *Acto Addicional,* if not a fully satisfactory, at least a stable form of government. In 1840 young Pedro de Alcántara, though only fifteen years old, was proclaimed of age and replaced the regent as head of the government. Brazil settled down to a period of comparative political calm.

Chapter 21

THE ESTABLISHMENT OF THE TWO SPHERES

I. THE WAR OF 1812

To bring the American scene into broad perspective we may now consider the train of circumstances that followed the period of constitution-making in North America. These events went far to establish for a century the general pattern of interrelations among the American nations themselves, and between them and the rest of the world. The two most crucial happenings were the War of 1812 and the promulgation of the Monroe Doctrine.

The War of 1812 was part of the backwash of the Napoleonic wars. The first impact of that world struggle on the American hemisphere had started the chain of reactions in Hispanic America that led to the independence of the Spanish colonies and the severance of Brazil from Portugal. Momentous repercussions were also felt in North America which eventually plunged Great Britain and the United States into war a second time, and threatened the British North American colonies with absorption by the United States. Thus the long-range results of the ambitions of the Corsican adventurer were felt in the Americas from the Arctic snows to the Falkland Islands.

In 1793, four years after the outbreak of the French Revolution, France, already at war with Austria, Prussia, and Spain, declared war on Great Britain. The immediate effects on the United States of the new involvement of Europe in a general war seemed at first advantageous. The huge demand by belligerents on both sides for American foodstuffs and raw materials brought a great economic boom, which not only set the new state on its feet financially but smoothed away much of the opposition to the new American Constitution, born in the same year as the French Revolution, if indeed it did not actually popularize that document. Exports, especially from the agricultural south and west, rushed ahead in leaps and bounds, rising from a value of $19,000,000 in 1792 to $108,000,000 by 1807, while in the same period imports increased from $29,000,000 to $247,000,000.[1]

---

[1] H. U. Faulkner, *American Political and Social History* (New York: 1948), p. 166.

In the realm of foreign relations, however, embarrassing complications soon developed. When the news reached America that England had joined the European coalition against France, the United States government, on the advice of Washington, issued a declaration of neutrality. This step was bitterly resented by France where it was regarded as a piece of rank ingratitude by a former ally whose independence French arms had done so much to win. The estrangement of the two former allies was accented when the American government found itself obliged to ask the recall of the French representative, Genêt, whose violations of American neutrality, in line with his instructions to involve the United States in war with England, became too flagrant to overlook.[2] The Jay Treaty of 1794 with England, settling a number of outstanding issues with that nation, so widened the breach with France that the United States actually found itself waging against its former ally an undeclared war, in which American frigates were frequently capturing French ships and apparently doing their best to destroy France's trade with her West Indian Islands. In retaliation, France seized American vessels in French ports, and pursued an insulting course toward American commissioners who had been sent to Paris to adjust differences. Not until 1800 was an acceptable treaty devised that settled temporarily the sharpest points at issue between the two nations.

Meanwhile relations with England also were far from satisfactory. A matter of violent dispute concerned American trade with the French West Indies. The French, knowing that they would be too weak at sea to defend their own trade with the islands, had declared their West Indian harbors open to the world, realizing that the islanders would sell their produce to the United States whose ships would carry much of it to France. England declared this traffic illegal, applying the so-called "Rule of 1756," which said that any trade not open in peace could not be opened in war. In enforcing this declaration, British warships seized numerous American vessels bound to or from the French islands and treated the crews roughly. Presently seizures were extended to all vessels carrying French goods of any kind.[3] So great was the indignation in the United States, whose contention was that "free ships make free goods," that there seemed a good chance that the two countries might actually drift into war over the issue. To prevent this, Chief Justice John Jay was sent by Washington to England in 1794 with powers to conclude a treaty.

The instrument that resulted, known as Jay's Treaty,[4] secured a promise of the surrender by 1796 of the northwestern frontier posts still in English

---

[2] On Genêt's activities, see S. F. Bemis, *Jay's Treaty* (New York: 1924), pp. 142-46.

[3] For a discussion on France's opening to neutrals of the French West Indies trade, see Bemis, *op. cit.*, pp. 152-60.

[4] For text see H. S. Commager, *Documents of American History* (New York: 1943), 3d ed., pp. 165-68.

hands, obtained the admission of small American ships to the trade of the British West Indies, and secured the abandonment of the British demand for a rectification of the Canadian boundary which would have changed that line from the 49th to the 45th parallel.[5] For these concessions England exacted in return large favors in the United States for British trade which was now placed upon a "most favored nation" basis, and provided for the continuation of fur trading over the Canadian border. Jay also acquiesced in Britain's definition of contraband, and agreed that the pressing matter of compensation for the seized vessels should be postponed and referred, with some other questions such as the Loyalists' debts and the Maine boundary, to mixed commissions for later settlement. Certain features of this treaty, especially the inauguration of the extensive use of arbitration for the settlement of questions involving a large technical element, were most forward-looking.

Although its terms actually embraced the principal items in the American negotiator's instructions, nevertheless in the United States the outcry against the treaty was loud and long. Many felt that its terms were humiliating; even the government hesitated, though it was well aware that seven eighths of American trade was still with England and that a break with her would be financially ruinous.[6] Eventually, however, the treaty was ratified. President Washington, in signing it, comforted himself with the reflection: "if this country is preserved in tranquility twenty years longer, it may bid defiance in a just cause to any power whatever; such in that time will be its population, wealth, and resources."

Washington also fully realized that the lot of a neutral in time of war is never easy, and that it was only to be expected that this would be particularly so in the case of a new nation not yet possessing the military power to enforce its demands. The President and his administration were also conscious that the mass of their fellow countrymen, where no immediate financial interest was involved, had instinctively given their sympathy to England in the European conflict then raging, believing, however reluctantly, that she and not Napoleon was the champion of right. To such people the British navy, whatever its shortcomings and oppressive behavior might be, represented a welcome rampart between American shores and French imperialistic activities. As the French revolutionary period merged into the Napoleonic era and the conflict spread, the involvement of important American interests had the salutary effect of softening to some extent

---

[5] On the project of the British government, in the years 1791-1795, to create a neutral Indian barrier state along the Canadian frontier taking in the territory north of the Ohio and shutting the United States away from the Great Lakes and the St. Lawrence, see Bemis, *op. cit.*, chap. vi.

[6] For a discussion of whether Jay might have secured a better treaty, see Bemis, *op. cit.*, pp. 267-71.

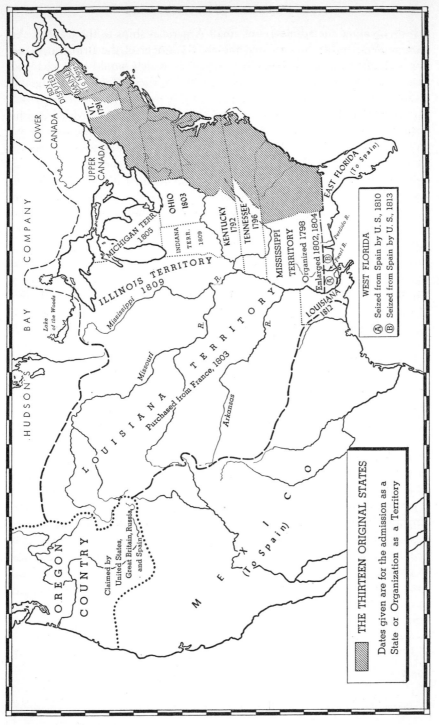

HUDSON'S BAY COMPANY

LOWER CANADA

UPPER CANADA

BDY. DISPUTED

VT. 1791

MICHIGAN TERR. 1805

OHIO 1803

INDIANA TERR. 1809

KENTUCKY 1792

TENNESSEE 1796

ILLINOIS TERRITORY 1809

Lake of the Woods

Mississippi R.

Missouri R.

Arkansas R.

LOUISIANA TERRITORY
Purchased from France, 1803

OREGON COUNTRY

Claimed by United States, Great Britain, Russia, and Spain

M E X I C O
(To Spain)

LOUISIANA 1812

MISSISSIPPI TERRITORY
Organized 1798
Enlarged 1802, 1804

Perdido R.

WEST FLORIDA

Ⓐ Seized from Spain by U. S. 1810
Ⓑ Seized from Spain by U. S. 1813

EAST FLORIDA
(To Spain)

THE THIRTEEN ORIGINAL STATES

Dates given are for the admission as a
State or Organization as a Territory

23. THE UNITED STATES, 1803-1813

the bitterness of the Revolutionary War, relegating its issues to past history. In domestic politics, however, party lines tended to divide according to sympathies in the world struggle: the Federalists on the whole sympathized with Great Britain and the Republicans with France, though the leaders of both parties were anxious to keep their young nation out of the struggle and maintain a policy of neutrality; in fact, they succeeded in doing so through twenty of the twenty-three years of its duration.

It was in this setting that Washington, as he approached the close of his second presidential term in September, 1796, summed up his political experience for the benefit of his fellow countrymen in a Farewell Address. In the field of foreign policy his advice was especially momentous, setting the pattern for many succeeding administrations. On the whole it followed the lines which his government was then pursuing. After the general admonition, "Observe good faith and justice towards all nations; cultivate peace and harmony with all. . . ." he passed to his famous doctrine of isolation: "Europe has a set of primary interests, which to us have none, or a very remote relation.—Hence she must be engaged in frequent controversies, the causes of which are essentially foreign to our concerns. Hence therefore it must be unwise in us to implicate ourselves by artificial ties in the ordinary vicissitudes of her politics or the ordinary combinations and collisions of her friendships or enmities. Our detached and distant situation invites us to pursue a different course. . . . It is our true policy to steer clear of permanent alliances, with any portion of the foreign world. . . . Taking care always to keep ourselves by suitable establishments, on a respectable defensive posture, we may safely trust to temporary alliances for extraordinary emergencies." [7]

Washington's immediate successors, both the Federalist, John Adams, and the Republicans, Jefferson and Madison, through the next fifteen years faced an international situation of increasing strain and growing difficulty. After 1805, with its balanced victories of Trafalgar and Austerlitz, the intensity of the titanic struggle heightened as the two major contestants became convinced that the economic weapon must be the decisive factor. Napoleon, unable to invade the British Isles and convinced that trade was the lifeblood of Britain, was determined on a great effort to cut England off from her markets. To forestall this the British government, during the three years beginning in 1804, issued a series of Orders in Council designed to apply an economic boycott to all parts of the continent under French control, finally declaring in 1807 that no neutral ship might trade with France or her allies without first stopping and paying duties at an English port. Napoleon replied with a series of decrees, notably the Berlin Decree of 1806 and the Milan Decree of 1807, establishing a blockade around England

---

[7] For text, see Commager, *op. cit.*, pp. 169-75.

and declaring any vessel sailing to or from a British port subject to French seizure. He further set on foot his "Continental System" which prohibited practically the whole of Europe from trading with his enemy. Faced with such a dilemma, the lot of the United States as the chief neutral became increasingly difficult; in fact, American commerce was almost driven from the seas. Both belligerents were offenders, but as England was mistress of the seas her actions were more notorious, immediate, and irritating, though recent investigations tend to show that French measures probably caused greater actual loss.

American grievances concerning the violations of international law multiplied around the three questions of blockade, contraband, and impressment. Under the law of nations, blockade to be legal must be effective, and with England after Trafalgar in undisputed control at sea it was obvious, the American government pointed out, that the French blockade of England was only a paper blockade and therefore illegal, as were also all the French seizures of American vessels based upon it. The Americans further contended that England's sweeping declaration that the whole coast of Europe was under blockade was likewise contrary to international law.

In respect to contraband, the situation was more complicated. International law recognized three classes of goods in wartime: absolute contraband, which included articles such as munitions, definitely designed for war use which the belligerent might seize if he could; noncontraband, comprising goods with no obvious relation to war, likewise raised no question; but the third classification, conditional contraband, comprising goods used in both war and peace and depending for their character on their use, was a most thorny issue. Americans hotly disputed the right of a belligerent to change the category of such an item in time of war; to alter the character of freight from the classification of "conditional" to "absolute" contraband, or from that of "noncontraband" to "conditional." In particular she objected to England's adding such articles as cotton and grain to the list of contraband goods. She felt bitterly sure that England's action was prompted not only by war's necessity but by the desire to cripple the growing mercantile strength of a lusty trade rival.

But of all the American grievances the greatest was that of impressment. The heart of this problem lay in the refusal of all European governments of the time to recognize the right of nationals to change their citizenship without the consent of their respective countries. It was aggravated by the great need of the time for seamen for service in the warships, where life was grim and conditions hard and cruel. Desertions from British warships were frequent in American harbors, where work was readily available in the expanding merchant marine, with wages higher and service conditions better. American naturalization laws encouraged foreigners to become American citizens in short order, and, if there was no time for formalities, forged papers were not difficult to obtain. The common language added to the ease of evasion. The British were adamant in their claim to stop and search foreign vessels on the high seas and impress any British subject they might find aboard. As the need for sailors to keep their ships at fighting strength became more urgent, British naval officers were not too careful to distinguish between English and American citizens, and waived aside certificates of citizenship, with the result that there were many scandals and much heartburning.[8]

The climax was reached in 1807 in the *Chesapeake-Leopard* affair, in which the British warship, the *Leopard,* overhauled the new American *Chesapeake* off the American coast. When the latter refused to be searched, the English warship fired three broadsides into the American vessel, killing and wounding a number on board, and proceeded to remove forcibly four seamen on the ground that they were British subjects. In the United States this fired patriotic indignation almost to the point of war.[9] Jefferson, however, now in his second presidential term, was a lover of peace. Believing that the need of both belligerents for American food was so great that he could use this means to force respect for America's rights as a neutral, Jefferson decided instead of going to war to embark on a policy of economic boycott. He inaugurated his program in 1806 with a Non-intercourse Act, prohibiting the importation of certain goods from England. In the following year he advocated and Congress passed a total Embargo Act (December 22, 1807), closing America's coasts and harbors to the whole world, and prohibiting American vessels from sailing to foreign ports for any reason whatsoever.[10] The immediate effects of this policy were more serious in the United States than in the offending foreign countries where the war issue distracted attention from all lesser ills. At home, commerce and business were soon on the verge of ruin. Ships by the score were laid up, unemployment became general, and distress widespread. New England, stronghold of the Federalists, was convinced that the Republicans were deliberately planning to ruin that section of the country and openly talked of secession and civil war.[11]

---

[8] The actual extent of the impressment in these prewar years is not known. Monroe in 1812 made a report to Congress in which he mentioned six thousand Americans as having been illegally seized for the British navy, but this number was discredited in Congress; fifty-one New England merchant shipowners of long experience declared that they could recall only twelve actual cases. See S. E. Morison, *The Maritime History of Massachusetts, 1783-1860* (Boston: 1941), p. 196.

[9] For a short, lively description of this affair with its background in the practice of impressment, see Allen Johnson, *Jefferson and His Colleagues* (New Haven: 1921), pp. 138-43.

[10] For the text of the Embargo Act, December 22, 1807, see Commager, *op. cit.,* p. 202.

[11] On the effect of the Embargo Act in New England and the sentiments it inspired there, see Morison, *op. cit.,* chap. xiii, pp. 187-94.

After fifteen months Congress relented and repealed the Embargo Act, and a little later the Nonintercourse Act also, without, however, having any alternative policy in sight. Jefferson signed the repeal of the Embargo Act (March 1, 1809), just before he left office. He was succeeded by his favorite follower, James Madison. For the next two years, in the midst of a complicated situation, Congress was without competent leadership and, in the face of a growing popular demand for strong action, finally allowed the passing of the Macon Bill No. 2 in May, 1810. This law restored relations with both Great Britain and France, but with the condition attached that if either agreed to withdraw its obnoxious measures against neutral commerce, then the United States would cut off all trade with the other.[12] Napoleon took immediate advantage of this stipulation and announced the repeal of his decrees. His actual course of conduct toward American vessels, however, remained practically what it had been. Despite this, Madison carried out his government's promise and revived nonintercourse, now directed solely against Great Britain.

Some students have maintained that if persisted in this policy might have been successful in averting war, pointing out that England, feeling the pinch, did finally revoke the offensive Orders in Council, though only four days before the American declaration of war.[13] It has been said that had there been a transatlantic cable at the time there would have been no War of 1812 between England and the United States. We are today not so sure of this. There were other causes than the violation of neutral rights at sea leading toward a conflict. It is to be noted that on the vexed subject of impressment England had given no indication of budging.

Another factor stirring up American antagonism, one for which there was no relief in sight, was the reappearance in the northwest area of the Indian menace which Americans suspected was due to the activities of British agents, who, in an effort to hold up the drive of the Americans westward, were encouraging the red man to attack the frontier settlements. Under two able leaders, Tecumseh and his brother, "the Prophet," the Indians of the Great Lakes region had formed a strong confederacy and were keeping the whole western border in terror. We now know that the British were as much afraid of the Indians as were the Americans, and that the primary factor in the Indian uprising was the despair of the Indians at the continuing loss of their lands, and the impossibility of making the white man keep his treaties. Though the Indians' situation was quite hopeless from every point of view, on November 7, 1811, they made a heroic stand at Tippecanoe, on a tributary of the Wabash, and made William Henry Harrison, governor of Indiana Territory and

---

[12] For the text of the Macon Bill, No. 2, see Commager, *op. cit.,* p. 204.
[13] Jefferson to his death believed this. See Johnson, *op. cit.,* p. 169.

leader of the American militia, pay dearly for a victory.[14] After a drawn battle the Indians retreated into Canada, and the way was open for the Americans to continue their advance westward.

As the white frontiersman's greed for land to the west pushed the Indian tribes into hopeless warfare, so his hunger for more land to the north and south was a large factor in producing the War of 1812. Canada and Florida, like the west, were tempting areas of expansion and were naturally linked in one dream. Not only would their absorption into the Union mean the elimination of irritating frontiers to the north and south, but the moment seemed ripe for the conquest of both of them. After 1808 England and Spain were allies in the war against Napoleon, and had their attention fully occupied in Europe. It had already, in 1810, proved possible to take advantage of Spain's preoccupation with the struggle against the French army in the Spanish peninsula and to annex West Florida as far east as the Pearl River,[15] and the chance to secure the rest of Florida seemed too good to lose. The same line of reasoning could be applied to Canada. With Napoleon at England's door, it was obvious that any war in America could be but a secondary consideration for Britain, too.

The demand for military action to secure Canada and Florida came largely from the frontier areas of the south, west, and north. For one thing, war promised an outlet and satisfaction for virile energies. But more specifically, these were the sections most interested in demanding unlimited room for agrarian expansion in the future, and were most affected by the restlessness that sprang from the great agricultural depression that had settled over America after 1806 when the European markets for wheat and cotton were closed.[16] One antiwar representative in Congress [17] cried out: "Agrarian cupidity, not maritime rights, urges the war. We have heard but one word—like the Whip-poor-will, but one eternal, monotonous tone —Canada! Canada! Canada!"

It was, therefore, from a background of intense national irritation and frustration, a strong element of frontier cupidity, and a great restlessness

---

[14] For the relationship of the British to the Indian menace and of the latter to the declaration of war, see J. W. Pratt, *Expansionists of 1812* (New York: 1925), pp. 41-59. See also an excellent article by C. B. Coleman, "The Ohio Valley in the Preliminaries of the War of 1812," in *The Mississippi Valley Historical Review*, Vol. VII, June, 1920, pp. 39-50.

[15] On October 27, 1810, President Madison issued a proclamation authorizing Governor Claiborne to take possession of West Florida as far as the Pearl River and govern it as part of the Orleans Territory, on the ground that West Florida belonged to the United States as part of the Louisiana Purchase. A declaration of independence had been issued from Baton Rouge by a local group of Americans on September 23, 1810, and incorporation into the United States requested. In 1813, West Florida from the Pearl River to the Perdido was added to the Territory of Mississippi.

[16] For a discussion of the war as a necessary measure for the economic relief of the West, see G. R. Taylor, "Agrarian Discontent in the Mississippi Valley Preceding the War of 1812," in *Journal of Political Economy*, Vol. XXXIX, No. 4, 1931, pp. 498-505.

[17] John Randolph.

growing out of economic depression, that President Madison, on June 1, 1812, sent a message to Congress calling for war. The war message was debated for eighteen days and then passed the House by a vote of 79 to 49 and the Senate by 19 to 13. The vote was almost entirely on sectional lines. The strongest affirmative vote came from the South but was backed up strongly by the "War Hawks" of the West. The East with its powerful commercial and shipping classes, though presumably most seriously affected by any invasion of maritime rights, was bitterly opposed to war. New England, especially, objected to the whole adventure. Her opposition was based partly on her desire to save what remained of her trade, partly on the belief that the Republicans were out to ruin New England as a center of Federalism, and partly on her disapproval of Napoleon and intense dislike of being on the same side of the fence with him. It was clear from the outset that the whole weight of this region, which had been the heart of the revolutionary struggle, was to be thrown against the prosecution of this second war with England. It evaded every draft law, traded with the enemy, hobnobbed with New Brunswickers, loaned money to the British, and finally, in the Hartford Convention in October, 1814, threatened to make a separate peace, or even to withdraw from the Union itself.[18]

Partly because the country was not united on the issue, the conduct of the war was a story of ineptitude and military disaster. Lack of military preparedness before the war started was followed by failure to set up the unified command needed to weld into an efficient force the newly authorized army of twenty-five thousand regular troops and fifty thousand state militia called out; this in turn was made worse by the corruptness of political contractors. The principal objective was possession of Canada. But the land expedition across the northern border was a total failure, despite the fact that the population of the British North American colonies was a mere half million, of which half were French Canadians, compared with the seven and a half millions in the United States. No advantage was taken of the fact that Great Britain, through the first two years of the struggle, was too preoccupied to spare many troops for the Canadian sideshow. American efforts should obviously have been directed immediately and forcibly at blocking the lower St. Lawrence, to cutting off any possibility of aid from England, and dividing Upper from Lower Canada. But plans for the conquest of Lower Canada collapsed, and the fighting in Upper Canada was largely confined to the Niagara peninsula at the extreme west end of the British settlements. The American invaders in this latter area expected to be assisted from within by a group of recent immigrants from south of the border who hoped to see the incorporation of their new

---

[18] The attitude and activities of Massachusetts during the war are interestingly set forth in Morison, *op. cit.,* chap. xiii, pp. 198-212.

holdings into the United States; moreover, a conflict here gave the westerners, who were so keen for the war in the first place, a chance to fight; but this choice of a fighting theater resulted in ignoring major strategic advantages elsewhere.

Eventually the American invasion in this Niagara section met its greatest obstacle in the determined resistance of a fiercely patriotic Canadian population, predominantly Loyalist, under the leadership of General Brock, who halted the American advance by a decisive victory at Queenston Heights. Previous to this engagement he had captured Detroit, and all the Northwest Territory between the Great Lakes and the Mississippi passed for a time under British sway. No American attempt whatever was made upon the Maritime Provinces, partly because of British seapower, and partly because antiwar New England shielded the land frontier. In fact, the attitude of New England did much to determine the character and the military operations of the entire war; not only did it shelter the Maritimes but, to a considerable extent, Lower Canada as well.

In the third year of the war, with Napoleon locked up in Elba, the English were able to dispatch reinforcements, and plans were made for the invasion of the United States at Niagara, Lake Champlain, and New Orleans. These plans failed. The Americans proved much more effective in defense than in their recent offensive operations. The British advance from Niagara was checked by an American victory at Chippewa on July 5, 1814; that by the Champlain route was stopped by an American naval victory on that lake; and the attack in the South was frustrated by a battle won at New Orleans by Andrew Jackson, who forced the British army of six thousand back to its transports. As this last engagement, the one considerable land victory of the whole war for the Americans, was won after the peace treaty had been signed, it had no effect on the settlement, though it did much to restore national morale, especially in the southwest.[19]

In the sphere of naval operations, matters went more favorably for the American cause, especially on the Great Lakes which were inaccessible to the main British fleet and where, on both sides, the engagements were between comparatively small, locally constructed ships. Here spirited battles provided an outlet for national feelings and did much to throw an aura of success upon the American cause.

At sea there were no general fleet engagements, though there were some spectacular single ship actions in which a number of units of the British navy were compelled to strike flag to American warships before the latter were finally bottled up in a complete British blockade of the Atlantic coast. The forays of a large fleet of American privateers did con-

---

[19] The military story of the war is well told in Morison and Commager, *The Growth of the American Republic* (New York: 1936), pp. 299-310.

Ceremony transferring Louisiana from France to the United States, New Orleans, 1803. (Courtesy of the American Museum of Natural History)

Lewis and Clark expedition in the western mountains. (Courtesy of the American Museum of Natural History)

MacDonough's victory on Lake Champlain, September 11, 1814. When the British lake fleet came up to aid their land forces in the attack upon Plattsburg, Commodore MacDonough joined battle with his fleet of three ships and several galleys and won a decisive victory. (Courtesy of the New York Public Library)

siderable damage to British trade. Faulkner mentions that 496 American privateers captured no less than thirteen hundred British ships with a value of thirty-nine million dollars.[20] But meanwhile the British blockading fleet held the Atlantic coastal cities at the mercy of their raiding operations.[21] The most notorious of these occurred in August, 1814, when Washington was captured and the White House, the department buildings, and the Capitol were set on fire.[22] As an excuse for this act of vandalism the British pointed to a similar action in the previous year by the Americans at the Upper Canadian capital of York, now Toronto.

The futile struggle, unwanted and unsupported by New England, and disliked by the British as a distracting, minor incident in the midst of a major world conflict, having reached a stalemate was finally closed by a treaty of peace of which the terms did little more than establish the *status quo ante bellum*. In the Treaty of Ghent there was no mention of the causes that had produced the conflict; neither maritime rights nor impressment were spoken of. Three commissions, however, were set up to deal later with certain technical matters. The abiding results, however, of the War of 1812 were to prove out of all proportion to the little fervor with which it was fought and the indecisiveness that attended its military and naval events.[23]

The treaty which said so little proved to be one of the strongest ever made and one followed by immense developments in many fields. The peace with Great Britain proved to be a permanent one, and carried with it a full recognition of an American independence, now complete and fully accepted as such by other world powers. The failure of the attempt to conquer Canada thoroughly discouraged any program for either annexation or seduction of British North America that had long haunted many American minds, and this dream gradually passed into the limbo of discarded ambitions. American expansion would henceforth take a western direction, which was facilitated by the fact that the close of the war was accompanied by the end of the Indian menace. Not only were the Indians finally pushed out of the Old Northwest, but farther south General Jackson's defeat of the Creeks at Horseshoe Bend opened up the southwest, while his invasion of Florida put an end to Indian raids from that direction.

In the domestic sphere, strangely enough, this war of predominantly western agrarian origin inaugurated an industrial era in which New England, so strongly opposed to the war from the beginning, benefited

---

[20] Faulkner, *op. cit.*, p. 180.
[21] Morison, *op. cit.*, p. 207.
[22] For a vivid description, see Johnson, *op. cit.*, pp. 228-31.
[23] *Ibid.*, chap. xii, pp. 239-64, "The Peacemakers." For the effects of the war from a Canadian point of view, see A. L. Burt, *A Short History of Canada for Americans* (Minneapolis: 1942), pp. 107-12.

most. An extraordinary revival of shipping and manufacturing brought a period of phenomenal prosperity to the eastern states. In the field of politics the war brought forward two prominent figures, later to become presidents, Jackson and Harrison. It also completed the ruin of the old Federalist party, which even before the war had been declining in power through its loss of touch with the common man. Henceforth all party alignments found it necessary to take account of the growing democratic West, and the postwar period is remembered as an "era of good feeling." With peace re-established, the United States felt at last free from Europe and independent of England's quarrels, and could turn to her own domestic problems. She now entered upon a period in which American eyes were to be turned westward, and American minds were to occupy themselves with problems of transportation, banking, and expansion. The War of 1812, inglorious as it was in many respects, proved to be a veritable second war of independence.

II. THE MONROE DOCTRINE

President Monroe's message to Congress of December 2, 1823, portions of which were to become immortalized as the Monroe Doctrine, played a major rôle, like the War of 1812, in focusing the eyes of Europe once again on the sole republic in America whose government, up to that time, the powers had recognized. The address served to make them uncomfortably aware that the newcomer was growing up. Despite its domestic American setting, Monroe's message was obviously a statement intended primarily for Europe. It clearly presumed to lay down in comprehensive terms certain limits within which must be confined all major European policies directed toward the other states in the Western Hemisphere just then emerging from their colonial chrysalis.[24]

Obviously part of the message was intended to counter a major tenet underlying the political program of the Holy Alliance. This concert of the European powers, an outgrowth of the struggle of Europe against Napoleon, after 1815 had assumed the direction of international affairs. It operated through a system of periodic congresses and, even after eight years beyond the close of that titanic struggle, still dominated Europe. In the guiding hands of Prince Metternich, Chancellor of Austria, and Tsar Alexander of Russia, the Alliance had dedicated itself to the principle of "legitimacy" as a criterion for the recogntion of any government. It constantly directed its efforts toward stamping out the whole body of liberal

---

[24] For the reaction at the courts of London, Paris, Madrid and Vienna, consult W. S. Robertson, "The Monroe Doctrine Abroad in 1823-1824," in *American Political Science Review*, Vol. VI, November, 1912.

ideas that had sprung from the French Revolution, whose resurgence in any form, it feared, might produce another world conflagration. To prevent this, the Alliance had promised to send armies into any country that seemed to be threatened by revolution, no matter how bad the legitimate government of that state might be. The one great power that had not given approval and support to this policy was Great Britain, the principal victor in the recent conflict. Although under a Tory government, England had shown herself increasingly opposed to the Alliance's policy of intervention in the domestic affairs of individual states. She had not, however, been able to prevent an Austrian army from being sent to Naples in 1820, or in the spring of 1823 to stop the allies from dispatching a French army into Spain to put down in that ill-governed country a liberal insurrection threatening the throne of the worthless Ferdinand VII. In disgust at the reactionary trend of events on the continent, the English government—first under the leadership of Lord Castlereagh, and later, after his death in 1822, under his versatile successor, George Canning—was tending to slip back into its traditional policy of isolationism toward European affairs.

What particularly disquieted English statesmen was the accumulating evidence that the Holy Alliance appeared likely to extend its policy of intervention beyond the Old World into the colonial field, making no distinction between the European and American spheres. Such a position was logical. Many European states—Russia, France, Spain, Holland, Denmark, and England—held possessions on the American continents or adjacent islands, and were in that sense American powers. Indeed, Russia was then actively engaged in extending southward her Alaskan holdings in America. The Allies professed to see no fundamental difference between intervening in the affairs of the American territories of these powers and taking similar action in relation to the home country in Europe. The question of intervention had been raised in active form by the course of events in the Spanish colonies.

Ferdinand VII had signalized his restoration to the throne on Napoleon's downfall, not only by instituting a reactionary regime of the blackest kind in Spain, but by embarking on a determined program to force the old yoke once more upon the shoulders of the former Spanish colonies in America. These colonies, under the spur of necessity in Napoleonic times, had established government by their own juntas and, at the time of Ferdinand's restoration in 1814, were enjoying de facto independence. Having tasted the strong wine of self-government, enjoyed for a time free intellectual intercourse with the rest of the world, and shared in the prosperity of a free commerce, they were in no mood for unconditional submission to Ferdinand. Taken, however, more or less by surprise, they were ill-prepared to meet the strong force that Ferdinand dispatched in 1815 across the Atlantic to re-establish Spanish rule; their new unstable regimes very generally and promptly collapsed. By 1817 all seemed lost for the cause of independence. In the following year, however, there came a turn in the tide: a remarkable revival of resistance in the next five years under the leadership of San Martín and Bolívar practically freed Spanish South America; in Mexico in 1821, the Spanish viceroy was unexpectedly compelled to acknowledge the independence of that colony; and in the following year the declaration of Brazilian independence further strengthened the cause of liberty in the whole Hispanic American area.

The rapid succession of these events presented to Europe the spectacle of an American continent, from the Canadian border to the Strait of Magellan, asserting its independence, and strong repercussions were felt in the chancellories of the Old World. As early as 1818 Tsar Alexander, alarmed by the first evidence of the revival of revolutionary strength in Spanish America and acting at the instance of the panic-stricken Ferdinand of Spain, suggested to the allies at the Congress of Aix-la-Chapelle that there should be armed intervention by European troops acting on behalf of Spain for the re-establishment in America of Ferdinand's legitimate authority. Lord Castlereagh, English representative at the Congress, strongly opposed this suggestion and it was rejected. Henceforth, however, the idea continued to receive consideration, and at the time of Monroe's message, seemed to most onlookers a distinct possibility for the future.

In regard to Spanish America, England had special interests and definite views. The development of a great commerce there during the Napoleonic War, as the old Spanish exclusive restrictions on colonial commerce lost their effectiveness, had gone far to compensate for the losses which Napoleon's Continental System had entailed and to make it possible to finance the war against him to a successful conclusion. During and after the war, the English merchants had continued to pour their goods and capital into Spanish America, had taken over many of the old Spanish investments, especially mining properties, and had received many new concessions. They were in no mind to lose the new markets and brought strong pressure to bear on the government to resist anything that might threaten such loss.[25] The government, however, was, as it had long been, in a delicate diplomatic situation in regard to Latin America and Spain.

Throughout the struggle for independence, the first object of the Spanish American revolutionary leaders had been to obtain British support. Although they never succeeded in getting this in any official form, strong British sympathy had unofficially been demonstrated through generous donations and through large public subscriptions to loans floated on the

---

[25] To such proportions had this trade developed that in 1822 British exports to South America surpassed in volume English exports to the United States.

London market, as well as in a good deal of volunteer military aid. The part played by Lord Cochrane, a sailor whom many considered scarcely inferior in ability to Nelson, has been referred to. Likewise reference has been made to the British soldiers who served as volunteers in Bolívar's forces and who constituted the "Old Guard" of his army. Officially, however, there was no open assistance, and could not be, as after 1808 the Spanish and English governments were allied against Napoleon, which prevented England from assisting Spain's colonies in their struggle for independence. In these circumstances, during the Napoleonic period, there had grown up a kind of passive contract between the Spanish and the English governments, which in practice meant that Spain would turn a blind eye on English infringements of old commercial restrictions in Spanish American harbors, while England would continue to deny political recognition to the revolting colonies.

. From time to time after the war, the British government had offered mediation and good offices for bringing about a settlement. The one that she preferred was the return of the colonies to Spanish allegiance through a peaceful agreement between motherland and colonies, with such liberal conditions as would place them upon a basis of practical autonomy. Should this eventually prove impossible, the English ministers favored the establishment of constitutional monarchies rather than republics. Naturally biased by faith in their own *via media,* they considered that the inclusion of a few crowns interspersed among the republics would be better than a continental system wholly republican and dominated by the influence of the United States. They were, however, unprepared to take decisive measures to implement their rather mild views, and British agents on the scene were instructed to allow the revolutionaries to make their own unhampered choice of governmental forms. The chief effect of all this was to delay British diplomatic recognition.

In regard to its own future in South America, the British government quite early reached two fundamental decisions from which it did not later swerve: first, that it was not desirable to attempt to acquire any of the American possessions of Spain in the event of that country's not being able to hold them herself; secondly, that in the event of independence, England would not demand exclusive preferential trade treatment. At the same time, however, she was determined not to see other states force the colonies back to Spanish allegiance; even less was she prepared to permit foreign powers to seize for themselves either the territories or their exclusive trade. She shrewdly suspected France of having the most ambitious designs, and of being strongly supported in them by Russia and Austria who were preeminently interested in forcing the principles of legitimacy upon the New

World as upon the Old. All these schemes George Canning, the British foreign minister, was determined to resist.

By 1822 Canning had reached the conclusion that independence of the Spanish colonies was inevitable, and that recognition by England was "a matter of time, rather than of principle." In September of that year, the Duke of Wellington, English representative at the Congress of Verona, was instructed to inform the powers that Great Britain had been obliged to extend commercial recognition by sending consuls to several Spanish American governments. This step practically detached England from the European alliance.

Six months before England took this step, the United States government, in a presidential message of March, 1822, had indicated its intention of extending full political recognition to a number of the strongest Spanish American states; shortly thereafter it recognized the five governments of Mexico, Colombia, Peru, Chile, and La Plata. This brought to an end the long-continued American policy of neutrality. Though not hampered, like the English, by any alliance with Spain, and naturally moved by a sympathetic fellow-feeling towards "the glorious spectacle of eighteen millions of people struggling to burst their chains and be free," the American government through the crucial years of that conflict had pursued a cautious and noncommittal policy. Liberty and independence were, it is true, still magic words in the United States, but the government was in the hands of realistic leaders who in this matter, as in others, did not lose sight of practical considerations. They fully realized that their own nation, however bright its future, was as yet only a small, undeveloped one of ten millions of people, and must feel its way.

In diplomacy, the American rule had been to follow Washington's warning and maintain a policy of isolation from European affairs. Most public men were fully convinced that along this path alone lay safety and prosperity. From time to time someone suggested that the corollary to Washington's doctrine of noninterference in European affairs was clearly nonintervention by Europe in the concerns of the American world, but circumstances for a public statement to that effect had not been propitious. For one thing, until February 1821, negotiations were in progress for the purchase of Florida from Spain and the transfer to the United States of Spanish claims in Oregon. Any favor shown to rebellious Spanish colonies would obviously not expedite these matters. A policy of neutrality clearly represented diplomatic wisdom, and this the government proclaimed and adhered to. Miranda and other diplomatic agents and filibusters from Spanish America could get audiences with individual American statesmen but no official action, though rebel privateers for years found it possible to make extensive use of United States harbors. Compared with that of Great

Britain, American neutrality probably covered fewer selfish commercial interests and was more sentimental in its nature; although it too, as far as possible, included insistence on an open-door trade policy.

By the autumn of 1822, it was clear that American and British policies in the Spanish American field were not far apart, although Canning was not yet prepared to extend full political recognition. Opposition in the conservative English cabinet, based on the dislike of openly flouting Spain and the Holy Alliance, as well as other considerations, was still too strong to make the step seem politically expedient. A year later, however, events had clarified the situation and helped to outline his plans. By this time the Congress of Verona had been held, French armies were on the eve of complete triumph in Spain, and France was proposing that the affairs of Spanish America should be settled in a conference of the allies. The dangers of an attack by the forces of legitimacy upon the New World seemed alarmingly closer. To ward off this danger, Canning determined to propose a joint Anglo-American declaration of policy on South American affairs. This he did in the course of a series of interviews held in August, 1823, with Richard Rush, then minister of the United States in London. Here Canning discussed the whole subject of Anglo-American cooperation. The points of his proposal he summed up in a note to Rush dated August 20, 1823: [26]

1. The English government conceived the recovery of the colonies by Spain to be hopeless.

2. It viewed their recognition as independent states to be one of time and circumstance.

3. It was not, however, disposed to impede an arrangement between them and the mother country, if such could still be had.

4. It did not aim at the possession of any portion of them for Great Britain.

5. It could not see any portion of them transferred to any other power with indifference.

"If these opinions and feelings are, as I firmly believe them to be, common to your government with ours, why," asked Canning, "should we hesitate? Would it not be mutually advantageous to confide them to each other and to declare them in the face of the world? Such a declaration," he urged, "would be at once the most effectual and least offensive mode of intimating our joint disapprobation to any projects which look to a forcible enterprise for reducing the colonies to subjugation on the behalf of, or in the name of, Spain, or meditates the acquisition of any part of them . . . by cession or by conquest."

Rush was favorably impressed with the proposal and offered without waiting for further instructions to sign such a joint declaration, but on the

---

[26] S. F. Bemis, *The Latin American Policy of the United States* (New York: 1945), p. 56.

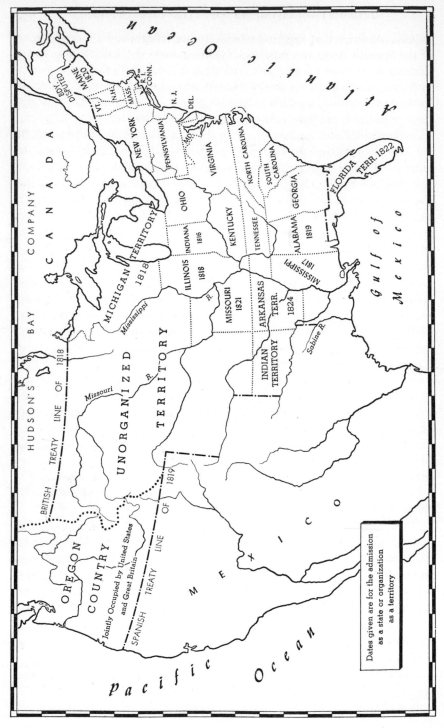

24. The United States in 1825

explicit condition that England would at once recognize the independence of the Spanish American republics. Canning, however, still could promise nothing more than a future acknowledgment, and Rush therefore merely undertook to forward the proposals to Washington. In his report he made the shrewd comment on current English policy: "It is France that must not be aggrandized, not South America that must be set free." [27]

Meanwhile Canning, fearful of the results of the imminent triumph of the French army then operating in Spain, decided to take steps himself to eliminate France from the Spanish American question. He was determined that that power should not be allowed to crown her military and political successes in Spain by a further adventure across the Atlantic. If only French designs could be thwarted, he felt sure that the plans of Russia—in no position at the moment to act alone—would be paralyzed. Early in October he summoned the French ambassador in London, the Count de Polignac, to a series of interviews in which, under some pressure, the Frenchman was induced to state in unambiguous terms his country's intentions concerning the Spanish colonies. Canning further insisted upon Polignac's signature to a memorandum setting forth the conclusions reached at the meetings, making up his own mind that the document should be circulated among the powers. As recorded in the memorandum, Polignac, under Canning's threat of immediate recognition by England of Spanish American independence, avowed that France "abjured, in any case, any design of acting against the colonies by force of arms . . . and disclaimed any intention or desire, on the part of France, to appropriate to herself any part of the Spanish possessions in America, or to obtain for herself any exclusive advantages." As for a European congress to discuss the destiny of Spanish America, the memorandum made it clear that Canning had stated that Great Britain would not be prepared to take part in such a conference without the presence of "a Power so eminently interested as the United States of America." [28]

This document was not published until the spring of 1824 but it was generally known in the European chancelleries in October.[29] Rush learned its terms from Canning on November 24, though not in time to allow their reaching Washington before the promulgation of the Monroe Message. They did not, therefore, affect the wording of that document. It was in Europe that the Polignac Memorandum, so adroitly obtained by Canning, had its great significance. Its positive and striking words made a convincing impression and successfully disposed of the French menace. By so doing,

---

[27] On Rush's suspicions of Canning's motives consult W. C. Ford, "John Quincy Adams and the Monroe Doctrine," in *American Historical Review*, Vol. VII, July, 1902, pp. 687-90.

[28] For the principles laid down in the Polignac Memorandum consult Harold Temperley, *The Foreign Policy of Canning, 1822-1827* (London: 1925), pp. 115-18.

[29] *Ibid.*, p. 119.

it undermined the whole project of European intervention in Spanish America and effectively paved the way for general acceptance of the Monroe Doctrine.

Canning, however, did not overlook the Spanish American scene. Immediately upon securing the Polignac Memorandum he dispatched copies of it to British agents in Mexico, Colombia, and Buenos Aires with instructions to bring it confidentially to the attention of the several governments, stressing the fact that in securing it England had thwarted all real danger of European intervention. It was not until the following summer, however, that the memorandum reached the Spanish American press. It was then widely and favorably commented upon and had the effect of claiming for England a share of the credit for warding off the dangers which Monroe's Message also had in view. Shortly after the Polignac interviews and the receipt of news of further French successes in Spain, Canning, on October 10, dispatched a number of consuls to important Spanish American cities and appointed two special Commissions of Inquiry to report on the readiness of Mexico and Colombia for British recognition.

It was on October 9, the very day the Polignac Memorandum was signed, that Canning's propositions to Rush reached Washington. The first American reaction was favorable. President Monroe forwarded them for advice to Jefferson and Madison with a covering note, in which he said that his own view was that they should be accepted. The two elder statesmen agreed with him, as did Calhoun.[30] The Secretary of State, John Quincy Adams, however, was of another opinion. As he pondered the whole matter he became more and more opposed to the suggested joint declaration. While he approved of "holding up a finger in warning to Europe," he disliked this to take a form which would make the United States appear subject to English leadership. He did not wish America to look like "a cock boat in the wake of a British man of war." Furthermore he disliked, especially as he thought of Cuba, to make long-range promises concerning the inviolability of Spanish American territories that later might be found to be embarrassing to the United States. He was also suspicious of British motives in proposing such a joint declaration,[31] especially as, judging from advices arriving through diplomatic channels from Europe, he had reason to believe that the danger of armed intervention was by no means imminent. In any case, it was clear from Rush's communication that the British navy could be relied on to deal effectively with that

[30] Ford, *op. cit.*, pp. 684-5; but *cf.* E. H. Tatum, Jr., *The United States and Europe, 1815-1823* (Berkeley: 1936), pp. 261-64, with its emphasis on Jefferson's desire "to tie the hands of England."

[31] J. F. Rippy, *Rivalry of the United States and Great Britain over Latin America, 1803-1830* (Baltimore: 1929), pp. 117-18, points out that in Adams' mind the Monroe Doctrine was "directed as much against England as any other Power."

contingency should it actually materialize. He grasped the fact that his own government was free from the political entanglements that were embarrassing Canning, and he came to the conclusion that if the United States had the courage to act independently, it might reap greater benefits than any partnership in a joint declaration could bestow, and, at the same time, could escape the embarrassment of an open affiliation with England. He therefore suggested to his colleagues that they issue independently, using the occasion of a presidential message, a purely American statement of principles bearing on the international situation. After some hesitation, his strongly urged advice was adopted and incorporated in the famous Message to Congress delivered by President Monroe on December 2, 1823.[32] Adams was responsible for its wording, though President Monroe gave to the final form his full approval.

The two major declarations of the document were:

1. The American continents were not to be considered as subjects for future colonization by any European power.
2. Any extension of the state system of any European power to any portion of the American hemisphere would be regarded by the United States as dangerous to her peace and safety.

These statements aimed at the two different elements of European policy toward America which Adams had recently been viewing with special dissatisfaction.

The declaration on "future colonization" had particular reference to negotiations that had for some time been in progress with Russia and concerned that power's pretensions along the Pacific coast. The statement immediately follows a reference in the Message to these negotiations. A Russian *ukase* of September 4/16, 1821, had extended Russia's Alaskan boundary southward to the 51st parallel, which brought it to Oregon. Added significance to the Tsar's claim was given by the appearance of Russian trading posts in the vicinity of San Francisco Bay. Off shore, Russia not only maintained that Bering Strait was a *mare clausum,* and demanded exclusive jurisdiction over the seas within 100 miles off such coasts as she claimed, but, beyond these specific areas, held the expansive theory that the waters of the northern Pacific Ocean and Bering Sea constituted a Russian sphere. In dealing with these claims, Adams had been taking a firm stand, finally telling the Russian minister on July 17, 1823—five months before the Message was penned—that in view of the fact that North America was fully occupied by Canada, United States, and Mexico, and that South America had now declared its independence, he considered the New World closed to future colonization. The Russian government,

---

[32] For text of the Monroe Doctrine see Commager, *op. cit.,* Vol. I, pp. 235-37.

in returning a reply in the following October, had not only refused to recognize this contention but had made some derogatory remarks concerning "expiring republicanism." In the colonization clause of the Monroe Message, Adams was thus returning to an old attack, and reiterating views already expressed.

The second declaration, that concerning the extension of the European political system to the American continent, bore directly on the rumored intentions of the Holy Alliance to intervene in the Spanish American situation in behalf of the claims of Ferdinand VII. Here the Message openly challenged a policy that had not only been under contemplation in the European chancellories, but for some time had been freely discussed in the lobbies of international congresses. If the American government should succeed in obtaining the acceptance of its views, it would insure at one stroke the corollary of Washington's famous doctrine. But this was much to expect. The original doctrine of American exclusion from Europe had been a self-denying ordinance; the corollary, that is the doctrine of European exclusion from American affairs, represented a limitation placed by the United States on the action of the greatest powers of Europe toward the whole American hemisphere, the most directly affected parts of which were neither under the sovereignty of the United States nor had been consulted on the issue involved; furthermore, the United States made no commitment as to any action she might herself regard as desirable. Very astutely the American government rested this daring policy on the simple basis of the nation's right of self-protection. On the face of it, the Monroe Doctrine merely professed to be a declaration by the United States of one aspect of its own defense policy.

The underlying concept, however, on which both the "colonization" and the "state system" clauses rested, was in fact revolutionary, for it involved an entire set of ideas that were to become known as the "Doctrine of the Two Spheres." [33] Briefly stated, this embodied the theory that there is a natural separation of the New World and the Old. It had inherent strength at the time because it corresponded to a large extent with reality. In a day of slow sailing vessels, it was a geographical fact that wide oceans to east and west were formidable factors of isolation between the Old and the New Worlds. It was at the time actually true that, economically, Europe was largely a world of manufacturing interests seeking control of markets for finished goods and, politically, was an area of old monarchical states whose governments rested on military force; whereas America was still in the colonial stage of having chiefly raw materials for sale and, politically,

---

[33] Rippy, *op. cit.,* p. 119, "The Doctrine of the two spheres, so much resented by Canning, was the doctrine of Adams perhaps more than any other man."

presented the picture of a region of experimentation in popular and republican forms of government.

A weakness of the "Doctrine of the Two Spheres" lay in the fact that the passage of time would inevitably modify these circumstances, or their significance. The element of distance, for instance, would lose its force with the development of better means of transportation and communication; while the commercial status would change with the introduction of large-scale machinery and the growing complexity of American economic life. Meanwhile, however, arguments based on the status quo seemed valid, and were difficult for European critics to gainsay. An obvious anomaly in the Two Spheres theory lay in the fact that several European governments actually at the time held colonial possessions in America. England, for example, ruled more territory in the Western Hemisphere than the United States itself. Against this weakness in the thesis, the American statesmen made careful provision in qualifying clauses in the famous Message which clearly stated, "with existing colonies in America of European powers we have not and shall not interfere." It was, however, obviously their intention that any extension of these European colonies, either at the expense of already organized American states or in unoccupied regions, would be considered an infringement of the basic prohibition. In other words, the Message established a kind of sacredness of boundaries in the Western Hemisphere, so far as European interests or designs were concerned. The Old World, the Message indicated, must consider that in relation to Europe the territorial status of the New World was fixed.

On the other hand, while the Message assumed that boundary changes within the Americas were henceforth no concern of Europe, the United States gave no guarantee that it would not itself expand at the expense of its Latin American neighbors; indeed, any such self-denying clause as Canning's proposed declaration would have prominently featured, was carefully excluded. There was, moreover, no undertaking on the part of the United States that it would, or would not, interfere to protect American states against each other or against disruption from internal causes. Retention of freedom of action in the future had been a strong inducement to Adams to take an independent line in relation to Canning's proposal. He was careful not to throw away such freedom in the words of the Message.

Besides the consideration of national defense moving the authors of the Monroe Message, there was also the question of national dignity, a subject on which young states are naturally sensitive. The United States in the previous year had publicly accorded to several of the Spanish American states political recognition of their independent sovereignty. To have this course of action ignored in Europe by discussion of possible armed intervention aimed at returning these states to their former colonial status was clearly a reflection upon the judgment and power of the United States. In Monroe's Message the view was clearly expressed that the United States, both because of geographical nearness and as the oldest of the republics of the New World, was in a position of special interest, obligation, and understanding towards Latin America. The whole document, indeed, was a manifestation of American regionalism under the aegis of the United States. It is important to note, especially from the point of view of later developments, that the policy enunciated was entirely unilateral. Both in its negative aspects as a prohibition of European interference while retaining freedom of action for itself, as well as in its positive assumption of its own paramount interest in the Americas, there was apparently no thought of any necessity to ascertain the views of the other American governments.

It was hardly to be expected that the full significance of the Monroe Message would be discerned by many contemporaries. Few, indeed, foresaw that it would become a guiding principle—if not, indeed, the most important statement—in American foreign policy for the next hundred years. Naturally the strongest reaction came from England. Canning realized at once that he had made a mistake in thinking that he could effect a policy of cooperation with the United States without first taking the step, already taken by Washington, of giving full political recognition to the Spanish Americas. The American statesmen, he perceived, had outwitted him, taken advantage of their more fluid situation, and made a clever regional adaptation of his own principle of nonintervention. He had meant the policy to be universal and accompanied by safeguards which would have applied to the United States as well as to the rest of the world. The substitution of an independent American statement, he realized, left the United States free in the future to proceed against the former colonies of Spain as it might see fit, and in the meanwhile enjoy the advantage of being able to press its warning to Europe without being prepared to fight, secure in the knowledge that the British fleet would enforce this policy. As for the colonization clause, which introduced an element that had not been included in his declaration, Canning disliked it most of all. He fully grasped, and viewed with alarm, the implications of this demarcation of "the Two Spheres." Without delay he took occasion to inform the American minister in London that England would not commit herself to unqualified acquiescense.[34]

As far as England's immediate continental policy was concerned, Canning perceived that the Message was all in his favor. England and the

---

[34] See W. F. Reddaway, *The Monroe Doctrine,* 2nd ed. (New York: 1905), pp. 92-93.

United States—mother and daughter nations—were supporting, albeit in separation, the same policy of insistence on nonintervention by Europe in Spanish America. In jubilation he wrote to another English diplomat, "Pozzo [Russian ambassador in Paris] may bustle and Ferdinand may swear. . . . the Spanish American question is essentially settled. There will be no Congress upon it and things will take their own course, which cannot be otherwise than favorable to us." [35]

In the European chancellories, so far as it was noticed at all, Monroe's Message can only be said to have aroused indignation as coming from an upstart young state that obviously had not the power in itself to enforce such a policy. Metternich called it "an impertinence." The course of events was not noticeably influenced. In actual fact the policy of intervention had already been laid aside, as no single power was really prepared to risk a military expedition. In Russia all serious ambitions by this time centered in the Balkans, and the government, for some months before the Message, had been ready to come to terms with the United States concerning expansion in the Pacific.

In Spanish America the reception of Monroe's Message was cordial.[36] At the time there were eight organized states that had declared their independence from Spain, though none of these could be said to possess a stable government or fixed institutions. Mexico was just getting rid of her temporary emperor; Central America had recently formed a confederation which was to prove ephemeral; the rest of the new republics were ruled by military men. All these states firmly believed in the actual danger of European intervention and all hailed Monroe's declaration as a pledge that the older northern republic would defend their liberties, if necessary by force of arms. The greatest of the Spanish American leaders, Simón Bolívar, the Liberator of Great Colombia, was at the time in Peru, his hands more than full with both political and military affairs. A royalist Spanish army was still in the field and was not to be defeated until the following year in the decisive battle of Ayacucho. Bolívar seems to have given little attention to the news from North America. It had been from Britain that he had received concrete assistance, and the Polignac Memorandum appeared to him of greater consequence than Monroe's Message. Other leaders, however, as well as the press generally expressed their satisfaction at the stand taken by the United States. None of them perceived any of the dangers that might be involved, or realized that the special interest that Washington manifested might in time lead on to intervention in the

---

[35] Letter from Canning to Granville quoted in Temperley, *op. cit.,* p. 129.

[36] This favorable reception in South America of Monroe's address is set forth interestingly in W. S. Robertson, "South America and the Monroe Doctrine," in *The Political Science Quarterly,* Vol. XXX, 1915, pp. 82-105.

domestic affairs of their own states; nor did any grasp the fact that the United States meant to be the judge of the occasions when the protection which the Monroe Doctrine apparently promised might be applied.

In the world at large, Monroe's Message marked the coming of age of his nation as an international power. Providing a coherent statement of national policy, both in relation to Europe and to the rest of the American hemisphere, and breathing an air of peculiarly American ideals, the famous Message, though not strictly a doctrine until after the Civil War, had really the importance of a second declaration of independence.

The Americas at the end of the revolutionary period. A contemporary map by the outstanding British cartographer, Samuel Arrowsmith, London, 1828. (Courtesy of the American Geographical Society)   (*over*)

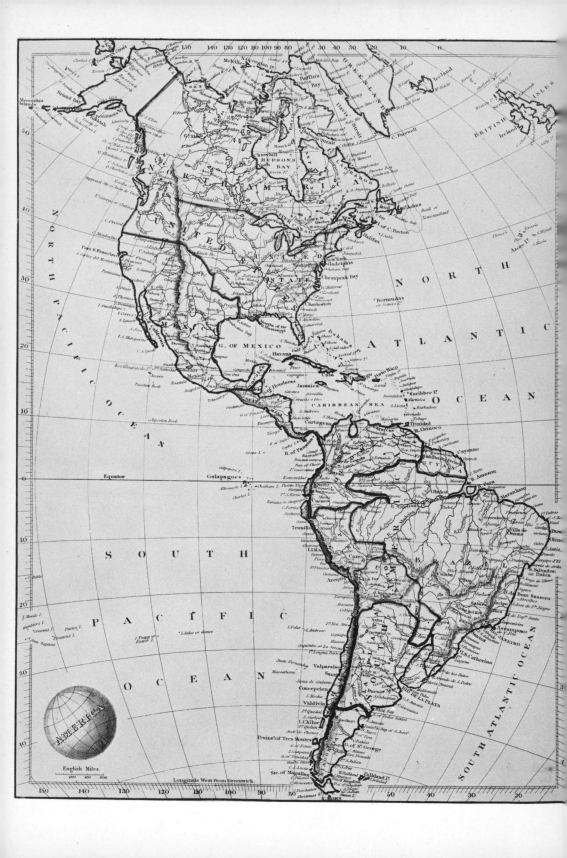

Chapter 22

EUROPE IN AMERICA: THE PATTERN SET

During the colonial centuries the western European peoples were transplanting their culture and a part of their population to the American hemisphere. Not all elements of their society were transferred, nor were those elements that crossed the Atlantic in the same proportionate relationship to each other as they had previously been in Europe; neither did all prove equally well adapted to New World conditions, nor similarly able, or willing, to blend with the differing native peoples and widely varying natural conditions found in America. Society in the New World was thus destined from the beginning to produce a social picture different from that of Europe.

The various migrating national groups showed a tendency to settle in areas in America most like their respective homelands. The Spaniards, with all America to choose from, showed an early preference for high tablelands resembling those of Castile, and, although they eagerly explored and overran all sorts of regions, the heart of their permanent holdings continued to be areas tropical and subtropical, and largely highland. Unlike the Spaniards who quickly investigated the interior, the maritime Portuguese, also settling in tropical and subtropical regions, long clung to the coast and the seaports. The trading, maritime, nonmigrating Dutch were interested in centrally placed and strategically located ports like Pernambuco, or in locations at the mouths of such navigable rivers as the Hudson and the Delaware, which were suitable for trade with the natives of the interior; or were attracted to islands that could serve as trade emporiums and were located, like Curaçao, Aruba, and Buen Aire, near a well-populated mainland; or, like St. Eustatius and Saba, were placed in the midst of heavily populated settlements of other nationalities in need of exporting and importing facilities. The French, from a northern European homeland intersected by navigable rivers with their fertile valleys, were at once attracted to the great rivers of temperate North America; they based their imperial strategy, as well as their exploring, fur trading, fishing, and farming economy on control of the St. Lawrence, the Great Lakes, the Mississippi, and the Ohio. The two bights of the Caribbean Sea and Hudson Bay also saw some French colonial activities. The seagoing English, with their northern traditions and varied economy of agriculture and handicrafts,

came from a homeland restricted in area and protected, though not isolated, from the rest of the world by the rampart of the sea. Across the
Atlantic they developed the roots of their American culture in the Thirteen Colonies, centrally located in the temperate zone, and shut off on the
west from their enemies, both native and European, by the Appalachian
Mountains but open on the east to sea communications. Here for more than
a hundred years they deepened their American roots and gathered their
strength before turning decisively on those rivals who would have liked
to confine them within the barrier of the Appalachians in order to prevent
their expansion westward. Traders, as were the French and Dutch, the
English also took a lively interest in the Caribbean Sea and Hudson Bay.

By far the greater proportion of all the migrating Europeans were
drawn from the middle class—the most adaptable and energetic of all
classes—and it was their standards that predominated in the new society.
Frankly interested in material prosperity, they quickly transported to
America such bases of Old World comforts and convenience as domestic
animals—in which the New World was singularly deficient—European
cereals, vegetables, fruits, flowers, and trees, and turned their inventive
industry to improving, by the application of European methods, the wealth
of new foods and plants that their American environment afforded. Crossing the Atlantic before the advent of the machine age, the first Europeans
endowed colonial America with a rich variety of practical skills and handicrafts. The urgent demands of a new environment not only maintained
these at high efficiency, but developed them in both theory and practice
as the necessity arose for applying these arts to more difficult tasks than any
hitherto dreamed of, and of teaching them to American natives.

As the professional classes were also heavily represented in the migrating groups, the new American world (at least its larger settlements) possessed the theoretical and professional talents needed for engineering and
building projects, the development of the decorative arts, the study of
strange plants, drugs, and other products of the new environment, and the
establishment of schools, universities, and printing presses for the propa-
gating of this knowledge. Under pioneering conditions there were wide
areas, of course, where none, or few, of the amenities of life existed. Here
the European settler had only his native ingenuity and enterprise to rely
upon, and geographical, climatic, and native influences were at their
strongest. It was in the English and Spanish colonies that the transfer of
European culture was most complete, the greatest number of professional
folk flourished, urban life counted for most, and in consequence education
and literary, artistic, and other cultural forms had their greatest development. Colonial Brazil was predominantly more rural, and among the
Dutch and the French the primary emphasis was on trade.

Of the professional classes, the most numerous were the clergy. In the Latin colonies the great attraction was the call from the limitless missionary field, to which response was made with courage, ingenuity, and perseverance. Other categories of clergy succeeded in casting over the white settlements, especially the urban districts, an atmosphere of ecclesiasticism. To these efforts of the Church, the state in the three groups of Roman Catholic colonies gave a strong, though varying, measure of support. This was most effective in the Spanish colonies where the crown's very title to American holdings was entwined with a papal mission to spread the faith. In all three, the blending of strong religious motives with military action and state policy is strongly reminiscent of the medieval outlook.

In the Thirteen Colonies, the motive of migration drawing the clergy in great numbers came from dissatisfaction with the religious settlement which followed the Reformation movement, not only in England and Ireland but in the persecuted areas of northern Europe. Numerous religious sects, predominantly Protestant, sought in the English colonies an opportunity to practise in peace their own interpretation of the recently opened Scriptures. As the colonial period wore on, the colonists under the British flag were to make the great discovery that religious toleration was a practical possibility. The prominence of the religious issue in colonial English America emphasized the fact that the primary motives of emigration to the Thirteen Colonies were either directly religious in character or were a response to an urge for economic betterment in an atmosphere free from religious and political disabilities; such waves of migration did not represent a mere overflowing of a surplus European population.

The colonial American social structure was, as in Europe, by no means free from class distinctions, but the gradations were on a different plane. Very few of the higher nobility emigrated to any of the colonies, except temporarily to assume administrative positions as representatives of royal authority. At home they constituted a privileged group and were naturally content to remain in Europe. The gradation of colonial social classes quickly accommodated itself to American circumstances, building up a typically American pattern of social strata. On the higher levels were likely to be found the original settlers, generally in the order of their wealth and education; below them were more recent comers, in the English colonies often of alien stock; in the middle ranks, especially in the Latin colonies, there grew up an entirely new element representative of racial crossings in various degrees, either with the indigenous population or, as time went on, with imported slaves. The colored groups were long to remain on the lower rungs of the social ladder. Social distinctions were most elaborate and clearly defined in the Spanish system, less so among the more easy-going Brazilians, and least of all in the English colonies where the Indian element was wholly outside the social structure. Because of greater mobility and more rapid changes in fortune there was, despite elaborate classifications, probably a greater fluidity in the social arrangement in America than under the more static European conditions. Everywhere the frontier was a strong equalizing factor (both socially and politically) that acted as a safety valve for restless elements, often making neighborliness a condition of survival, and working for rapid and robust Americanization.

In all the colonial ventures the presence of the Indians constituted a major problem. In some cases the policy was to ignore or exterminate them; in others to use them as military allies or fur gatherers; in still others to employ them in a servile capacity as miners, plantation workers, or in other humble occupations; but in all cases throughout the colonial period, the natives constituted the strongest influence tending to modify European ways of life and behavior. The Indians left their mark not only on arts and crafts, nomenclature and culture, but upon the racial fiber of the major portion of the Western Hemisphere through the admixture of their blood in immense, though varying, degrees.

Of all the colonizing powers, Spain showed herself most conscious of, and most concerned over, the Indian problem. As in contemporary Europe where Spain with fervent religious zeal supplied the leadership and most of the men and resources in the battle of Roman Catholicism against the forces of the Protestant Reformation, so in colonial America did she exhibit the strongest sense of mission, interpreted with imagination and sweeping inclusiveness. Not only did she make a determined effort to carry out the papal commission to Christianize the newly discovered pagans—though they turned out to be in such numbers as the Pope had never dreamed of— but also undertook to bestow upon them European civilization, ideas, and customs, and to incorporate them into a new society of blended Indian and Spanish elements. When it became evident that the economic temptations and need for labor were so great that the Spanish colonists would not give fair treatment to the Indians, the Spanish sovereigns took the drastic step of placing the American natives in a specially favored legal relationship to both state and Church, excluding them from the operations of the Inquisition and making their protection the first charge on all royal representatives in America. From first to last the Catholic Kings showed themselves the Indians' best friends, trying numerous experiments to determine their capacity and the types of institutions, officials, and organizations best suited to their needs. It was no idea of the sovereign that his new American Indian subjects should be placed in a servile position in relation to the conquering Europeans. The development of the semifeudal encomienda sprang from the determination of the Spanish conquerors and colonists in America to use the natives as a labor force, and was only countenanced by the crown to save the Indians from the worse fate of outright slavery. Negro slavery was likewise an outgrowth of American conditions and demands, and its introduction was not the idea of European rulers. As far as the Spanish sovereigns were concerned, it was disliked and discouraged and only grudgingly permitted in order to ease the lot of the Indians, while recognizing the economic needs of the colonists.

The other European nations took the fate of the Indians of their areas more casually, especially in the early years, and dealt with them as the needs of the moment seemed to dictate, while giving less thought to long-range policy and consequences. In the Thirteen Colonies the pressure of the red man on all the frontiers forced compactness and unity, along with an attention to military preparedness and a willingness to learn those new fighting techniques from the Indian which were especially effective in the New World. All this experience stood the colonists in good stead in their wars against European colonial rivals and, later, in their own struggle for independence. It is to be remembered that it was an increase in the seriousness of the Indian problem, brought about by the conquest of French Canada and the acquisition of the French lands east of the Mississippi, that produced one of the most serious of the issues leading to the struggle for independence.

Relics of feudalism imported by the colonists, which are apparent in such institutions as the Spanish encomienda, the Brazilian capitania, the French-Canadian seigneury, and the English proprietary colony, were all in their several ways modified or conditioned by American environment and ways of thought. The abundance of free land and the possibility of escape to the frontier were naturally inimical to the permanence of feudal institutions that had originated in the comparatively static conditions of medieval Europe. The encomienda ceased to be a labor system as early as 1549, at least in legal theory; the capitanea was brought under the control of the central government which absorbed its political and governmental functions; the proprietary grants in the English settlements one by one became royal colonies; and the French-Canadian seigneury took on, in American atmosphere, such a beneficent air as to make its disappearance at the English conquest rather a matter of regret than of congratulation to the habitants.

Economically, the Europeans headed for the New World were mercantilists, as were those they left behind in the Old. Many of the conceptions of this economic doctrine at first served the infant settlements well. Indeed, in everyone's view, colonies seemed to be the perfect answer to the essential problems posed by mercantilism. A protected market for both homeland and colony seemed to meet the difficulty of securing needed imports while at the same time finding an outlet for surplus goods without the necessity of parting with precious bullion to the foreigner. But early expectations soon proved over-optimistic. The system in practice was too heavily weighted in favor of the mother country. Many mercantilist regulations pressed so harshly upon American interests that violation and circumvention attained almost the sanction of moral right. As each of the imperial powers tried to balance its economy within its own monopolistic system— and as this could never be perfectly achieved—there was much smuggling, peculation, piracy, and discontent. Tropical and plantation colonies fitted into the mercantilist pattern best, but in the long run the very mercantilism that had provided one of the incentives to colonization proved a major factor in its disruption.

Associated with mercantilism in the English, French, and Dutch systems were the chartered commercial companies that were the actual agents making the first plantations. They were a new feature in the commercial life of Europe and provided a channel through which individual efforts of middle-class folk and the accumulated wealth of the investing public could be poured, with a prospect of quick returns, into the expensive task of establishing and maintaining overseas colonies. The governments acted through these agencies, entrusting them with wide commercial and political powers, and expected from them administrative services, the maintenance of the national prestige, and substantial gains for the royal coffers. Such companies had no significant development in the Spanish and Portuguese systems, although they did appear briefly in the eighteenth century. The Hispanic nations, discovering their colonial territories and setting up their systems nearly a hundred years before the commercial company system had become common and proved its efficiency, had necessarily to make other arrangements for carrying out the functions which later, in other nations, were performed for the crown by the private business organization. In the Iberian countries, the state itself (through royal councils) entered directly into the business of colonization, commercially as well as politically, and provided the organization, regulation, enforcement, and protection furnished in other lands by the commercial companies. It is to be noted that the French colonial system founded in the seventeenth century, although much like the Hispanic in many other respects, followed the northern model in the use of the commercial companies.

It was in the sphere of government that the strongest effort was made by all the colonial nations to transfer their ideas and the benefit of their experience across the Atlantic, but here as elsewhere the transfer was by no means complete, nor did the institutions fit the new conditions without great modifications. A tendency to let the colonies drift for long periods marked all the systems, and this allowed a natural growth in the influence of the local environment favorable to the Americanization of all institutions. But in the Spanish, Portuguese, and French empires there was sufficient bureaucratic control from the homeland to prevent the development of any local political institutions, or even aspirations, on any scale larger than the municipal. Of all the colonial systems, that of France, long a despotic monarchy, was held in tightest autocratic control and developed the least independence of thought and action. In overseas France, there was no significant democratic development even in the sphere of municipal government. In the Spanish colonies, deliberately denied their own cortes (the oldest national representative assembly in Europe) by a jealous crown only recently grown despotic and fearful of an effective center of colonial political action, there was at least a sturdy growth of municipal life. This was a development parallel in many respects to traditional Spanish political experience in the peninsula since Roman times. This municipal foundation of elementary popular government was ultimately to provide the very basis of articulate colonial self-expression leading to independence and the growth of new national states. Portugal, like Spain, took precautions that her colonists in Brazil should gain no independent political experience on any but a local scale. In all the Latin colonial systems, these autocratic political principles were accompanied by enforced orthodoxy in religion and a strict control of immigration, though both were less evident in the Portuguese than in the Spanish dominions. The Dutch settlements, except for a short period in the seventeenth century, hardly constituted a political colonial system, being more in the nature of trading factories oriented almost wholly towards business.

Only in the English system was there any considerable development of true self-government. Although brought out under the aegis of commercial companies, whose natural tendency was to emphasize the economic at the expense of the political, the earliest English colonists—those who set the pattern—gave immediate attention to the creation of political institutions in line with those long familiar at home. They strongly maintained that government should be regarded solely as an instrument for giving effect to the will of the people. The great flood of the earliest English colonists, mostly Puritans, left England when the theory of the divine right of kings, as asserted by Charles I, was being most hotly contested; needless to say, few had supported the king of whose religious policies many had been victims. Both the Anglicans who followed the Puritans (in the years when the English civil war and the establishment of the Commonwealth halted the Puritan flood) and the Independents, who came in a heavy migration after the Restoration, were unsympathetic towards the home government of the day. The majority of the early colonists left England before the conflict between the crown and parliament had been settled by the "bloodless revolution" of 1688 which secured the fruits of victory for the parliamentary forces. It was therefore consistent with their whole previous experience that the controversy between the executive and the legislature should be transferred to American soil, where it was reflected in the determination of colonial representative assemblies to control the royal governor and his policies by the old English constitutional device, the power of the purse. From the beginning, the colonists persisted in viewing each of their colonial assemblies as a little House of Commons. They were also strongly insistent, like their forefathers, on maintaining their fundamental rights as Englishmen which had been expressed in the whole range of English law from the Magna Charta to the Petition of Rights. These hard-won privileges, they realized, could only be safeguarded and preserved by due representation in parliament. The constitutional difficulties became more involved when, after the accession of William III, the English parliament, successful in its contest with the king, moved on to assert its assumption of the former functions and power of the crown in relation to the colonies.

Historical and constitutional events of the eighteenth century progressively carried the two groups of English people further and further apart and complicated the imperial relationship. Contemporary social changes, occurring within the American population, widened the breach. The new population waves arriving during the eighteenth century were either Scotch-Irish elements, greatly embittered against England by their experience in Ireland, or continental folk like the Germans and Huguenots who were naturally without English loyalties. Meanwhile increased imperial responsibilities, growing out of the wars of the eighteenth century, sharpened the English government's determination to insist that the colonies observe their colonial obligations and make their fair contribution to the defense of empire, though they offered no corresponding opportunity for colonial representation in the British parliament.

The severance of Old World ties, occurring in all the colonial systems within a period of sixty years, strangely enough did not arise directly from American grievances but was closely associated with general world wars. The first voluntarily to let go the apron strings of the mother country and become independent were the English colonies, politically the most mature of all and best able to fend for themselves. Their break represented, among other things, an indirect result of the Seven Years' War. That struggle had culminated in the absorption into the British empire of France's colonies. It was a victory that greatly complicated the British colonial system and made immensely more difficult the problem of maintaining its cohesion. The Spanish and Portuguese movements were aspects of the Napoleonic convulsion. The Portuguese, the last of the systems in which the break came, and the only one to take place without much violence, was one in which the tie with the monarchy had been strengthened by the temporary transference to America of the crown itself.

The military conflict was obviously but one phase of the struggle towards independence. It was everywhere necessarily accompanied by the problem of devising satisfactory constitutions to replace colonial systems, and the working out of relations at once dignified and secure with foreign powers. In the Hispanic area, the outstanding feature in the constitutional field was the emergence within the once-unified Spanish American empire of a number of independent states. All were republics from the start, save Mexico, which for a year experimented with an empire before finally accepting the republican form. Until his death in 1830, Bolívar strove to limit the amoeba-like process of division and hold in check political disintegration by successively creating Great Colombia, the Andean Confederation, and the first Pan American Conference. His efforts met with only temporary success. Portuguese America, unlike Spanish America, was successful in retaining its colonial unity. Here in Brazil the new state took the form of an empire. That it also faced immense difficulties was evidenced by the abdication of the first emperor before he had worn the crown for a single decade.

In America north of Mexico, the former Thirteen Colonies, after an unhappy experience with the Articles of Confederation, found themselver glad to bestow upon a central government many of the restrictive and regu-lative powers to which they had violently objected in the old imperial days when the political center had been London. With remarkable prescience, provision was made from early days for the incorporation of new territory, which might be added from time to time on the basis, not of colonies, but of new states with equal rights. Meanwhile, as the United States was working out its plan of a federal republic, still further north the "old colonial system" was being introduced into the conquered Canadian provinces where, hitherto, representative government had been wholly lacking. There the Constitutional Act of 1791 represented a great advance in democratic government for the French element in the population, but offered only a very meager justice to the Loyalists, accustomed as they had been to the practical democracy of the Thirteen Colonies. Obviously the migrants from south of the line had not improved their political status by the sacrifices which their British loyalty had involved.

In all these constitutional settlements of the post-independence era the acid test of the value of the political training that the colonial peoples had received would be found in the workability and permanence of the new forms of government which they set up.

The early establishment of stable government in both the United States and Canada, under the Federal Constitution of 1789 and the Constitutional

Act of 1791 respectively, left these countries free at an early stage to give their attention to pressing problems involving their relations with foreign powers. In treaties with France and Spain, the United States, within two decades of the opening of the nineteenth century, more than trebled its territory through the acquisition of Louisiana and Florida. Relations with England rather naturally did not proceed as smoothly as with the late allies. Though the Jay Treaty (1794) secured the relinquishment of the northwest posts and the re-establishment in accustomed channels of Anglo-American trade, it was not until the young nation had emerged from the War of 1812 with enhanced prestige that it attained its majority in the eyes of the former mother country and convinced a skeptical Europe that it was likely to survive and must be treated with respect. In America the same conflict pressed home the lesson that expansion must henceforth be turned westward and not northward, for Canada then demonstrated that she held firm political convictions that did not involve absorption by the United States, and had also begun her orderly march towards nationhood.

In relation to Hispanic America the United States took two bold steps within a decade following the War of 1812. The first was the extension of full political recognition to the emerging sister nations to the south; the second was the promulgation to an astonished world of the Monroe Doctrine as a corollary to Washington's nonintervention thesis. The earliest of the American republics thus assumed the primacy in safeguarding the integrity and destiny of all the Americas.

By the close of the first three decades of the nineteenth century the American nations had thus fairly well settled their state systems, their internal constitutional forms, and their international relationships. Having passed through a formative period as a congeries of dependencies of Europe, the American world had reached its majority and emerged among the world systems as an entity in its own right—a New World in a new sense.

BIBLIOGRAPHY

BIBLIOGRAPHY

For the great mass of historical materials that awaits the student of the history of the Americas, reference can be made only to the general bibliographies in the three principal fields. For the history of the United States consult H. P. Beers, *Bibliographies in American History: Guide to Materials for Research,* (New York: 1942); in the Latin American field refer to C. K. Jones, *Bibliography of Latin American Bibliographies,* (Washington: 2nd ed. 1942); for current publications since 1935 see the annual *Handbook of Latin American Studies,* (Harvard University); for Canada see R. G. Trotter, *Canadian History, A Syllabus and Guide to Reading* (Toronto: 1934).

For scholarly articles of historical character and book reviews reference should be made to the quarterly publications: *The American Historical Review, The Canadian Historical Review, The Hispanic American Historical Review,* and the bi-annual *Revista de Historia de America* of Mexico City.

Useful historical atlases are: J. T. Adams, *Atlas of American History* (New York: 1943); A. C. Wilgus, *Latin America in Maps,* (New York: 1943); L. J. Burpee, *An Historical Atlas of Canada,* (Toronto: 1927).

The following lists of suggested titles for further reading, arranged according to the topics of the individual chapters, are highly selective and simply represent the author's judgment of a group of useful books and articles probably available in a good college library. A few titles of books and articles written in Spanish that have a special bearing on the text have been added to appropriate chapters with the thought that they might prove enlightening to students able to read that language.

INTRODUCTION—UNITY IN AMERICAN HISTORY

The pioneer and premier exponent of the underlying unity in American history is Herbert E. Bolton, until recently Professor of History and Director of the Bancroft Library, University of California. His address on "The Epic of Greater America," made as President of the American Historical Association at the annual meeting of the Association in Toronto, December 27-29, 1932, is printed in *The American Historical Review,* April, 1933. It also constitutes the first of a series of essays by Professor Bolton on various aspects of Western Hemisphere history entitled *Wider Horizons of American History* (New York: 1939). Another collection of essays, originally lectures on the Harris Foundation, is published under the title *Inter-American Solidarity,* W. H. C. Laves, editor (Chicago: 1941). The first essay, "What Have the Americas in Common?" by H. Portell Vilá (University of Havana) and "Canada and Hemispheric Solidarity," by Frank Scott (McGill University), bear especially on the subject of this introductory chapter. An interesting symposium presenting varying points of view on the topic, "Have the Americas a Common History?" is printed in the *Canadian Historical Review,* June, 1942, XXIII, No. 2. It is composed of contributions from W. C. Binkley, G. Arciniegas, E. O'Gorman, and G. W. Brown. Reference should also be made to an article entitled "The Day of the New World," by Henry A. Wallace, printed in the Magazine Section of the *New York Times,* October 11, 1942. Three works of more general character are: *The Two Americas* by S. Duggan (New York: 1934); *A Short History of the Americas* by R. S. Cotterill (New York: rev., 1945); and *The Story of the Americas* by L. D. Baldwin (New York: 1943). Professor Bolton's *History of the Americas* (New York: rev., 1937) is a detailed syllabus with valuable bibliographical references. A recent study of current hemispheric problems and relationships, written with a realization of their deep historical roots, is the thoughtful volume *The Americas* (New York: 1949), by the late Laurence Duggan, formerly of the State Department in Washington.

CHAPTER I—THE AMERICAN SCENE

The physiographic background of Hispanic American history, with emphasis on its relation to settlement, is given in small compass in two excellent chapters by C. F. Jones in *Colonial Hispanic America,* edited by A. C. Wilgus (Washington: 1936), chaps. ii, iii. A brief but scholarly treatment of the northern Spanish American area is "An Outline of Basic Physical Factors Affecting Middle America," by O. G. Ricketson, Jr., in *The Maya and Their Neighbors* (New York: 1940). A. M. Schlesinger's *New Viewpoints in American History* (New York: 1937), chaps. i, ii, iii, is an interpretation of the effect of physical environment on the history of the Thirteen Colonies; a treatment on a broader canvas is the classic *American History and Its Geographic Conditions* by E. C. Semple (New York: rev., 1933), chaps. i, ii, iii. A very readable brief survey is *The Redmen's Continent* by Ellsworth Huntington (Chronicles of America I: New Haven: 1921). For fuller accounts of the geography of the two continents see J. Russell Smith, *North America: Men and Resources* (New York: 1925); C. F. Jones, *South America* (New York: 1930); P. E. James, *Latin America* (New York: 1942). J. Bryce, *South America: Observations and Impressions* (New York: rev., 1923) is still useful and illuminating. For a more elaborate treatment of the geology and geography of the Caribbean area, consult C. Schuchert, *Historical Geology of the Antillean-Caribbean Regions* (New York: 1935). The enlightening volume by C. L. White and E. J. Foscue, *Regional Geography of Anglo-America* (New York: 1943), gives an excellent idea of the disjointed geographical setting against which the Canadian and Mexican historical dramas have had to be played out, as well as the sectional character of the geographical background of the Thirteen Colonies. A useful and very readable geographical study emphasizing regional development in its bearing on historical events and noticing Spanish and French contributions is R. H. Brown's *Historical Geography of the United States* (New York: 1948).

CHAPTER 2—INDIAN AMERICA

E. R. Embree's *Indians of the Americas* (Boston: 1939) is a short but attractive account of the high spots in the history of the red man of the two continents. D. G. Brinton, *The American Race* (Philadelphia: 1901), C. Wissler, *The American Indian* (New York: 1938), and P. Radin, *The Story of the American Indian* (New York: 1927) are classics in the general field. C. Wissler, *Indians of the United States* (New York: 1946), as its title indicates, deals with a more limited area. A recent work of high scholarship covers the region north of Mexico to the time of the Conquest: P. S. Martin, G. I. Quimby, and D. Collier, *Indians before Columbus* (Chicago: 1947). P. Radin's *Indians of South America* (New York: 1942) places emphasis on the Amazonian tribes. P. A. Means' *Ancient Civilizations of the Andes* (New York: 1937) is the standard work in English on the Inca empire and its correlatives. A parallel work for the Aztecs is George Vaillant's *Aztecs of Mexico* (Garden City, N. Y.: 1941). For Mayan history see S. G. Morley's *The Ancient Maya* (New York: 1946) and a shorter older work, T. Gann and J. E. Thompson's *History of the Mayas* (New York: 1937). More specialized and lighter in tone is the description of excavation work at Chichén-Itzá in T. A. Willard's *The City of the Sacred Well* (New York: 1926). A readable volume on Pueblo culture is E. L. Hewett, *Ancient Life in the American Southwest* (New York: 1943). A book of great interest on a specialized aspect of Peruvian life is A. F. A. Bandelier's *The Islands of Titicaca and Koati* (New York: 1910). F. C. Hibben, *The Lost Americans* (New York: 1946) briefly and entertainingly reviews the story of the Folsom discoveries. The ethnographic monograph by R. Redfield, *Tepoztlan: a Mexican Village* (Chicago: 1930) gives a vivid sense of the timeless rhythm of folk life in an Indian village. Interesting short interpretive essays on the significance of the Indian background for Latin American history are: P. A. Means, "The Native Background in Latin American History," in *Colonial Hispanic America* (Washington: 1936) iv, and C. C. Griffin, "The Significance of Native Indian Culture in Hispanic America" in *Concerning Latin American Culture* (New York: 1940), C. C. Griffin, ed. In the vast and expanding field of anthropology and archaeology consult the *Handbook of South American Indians,* edited by J. H. Steward of the Smithsonian Institution (4 vols., 1946-48), and A. L. Kroeber's *Anthropology* (New York: rev. ed., 1948), an indispensable classic. See also the short vivid articles: "Maya Civilization—100% American" by S. G. Morley, *Forum,* LXXXVIII (August, 1927); and "What Is Civilization: Answer of Ancient America, Part I, Economic and Industrial; Part II, Intellectual and Artistic" by H. J. Spinden, *Forum,* LXXIV (August and September, 1925) and two collections of specialized studies by a number of technical scholars, *Early Man,* edited by G. G. MacCurdy (London: 1937) and *The Maya and Their Neighbors,* dedicated to Professor A. M. Tozzer (New York: 1940). A beautifully illustrated work on the art of Indian America is Pal Kelemen's *Mediaeval American Art,* 2 vols. (New York: 1944).

CHAPTER 3—THE SPIRIT OF DISCOVERY

For an understanding of the European movements and events of which the great Age of Discovery was a phase, E. P. Cheyney's *European Background of American History, 1300-1600* (New York: 1904) is still the most illuminating and readable. E. J. Payne's *History of the New World Called America,* 2 vols. (Oxford: 1892), Vol. I, Book I, covers the same field in a scholarly and stimulating interpretation. His chapter in "The Age of Discovery" in *The Cambridge Modern History* (Cambridge: 1902), Vol. I, pp. 7-36, is a masterpiece of condensation. For the background of Spanish history, especially the internal anarchy of the fifteenth century and the plans and purposes of reorganization by the Catholic Kings, see R. B. Merriman's *The Rise of the Spanish Empire in the Old World and the New,* 4 vols. (New York: 1918-34), Vol. II, chaps. xii-xv. A collection of learned essays on medieval overland travel is *Travel and Travellers of the Middle Ages,* edited by A. P. Newton (London: 1926); especially fine is chap. vii, "The Opening of the Land Routes to Cathay," by Eileen Power. Another collection of lectures that is now a classic is *Factors in Modern History* by A. F. Pollard (London: 3rd ed., 1932), especially chaps. i, ii, iii. A useful small volume on the economic background of the discoveries is L. B. Packard, *The Commercial Revolution, 1400-1776* (New York: 1927). On the motives and results of the discoveries a well-balanced, short treatment will be found in E. M. Hulmes's *The Renaissance, the Protestant Revolution and the Catholic Reformation in Continental Europe* (New York: rev. ed., 1915), chap. ix, pp. 175-85. On the events of the Portuguese and Spanish maritime voyages to America recent scholarship in fine literary style is represented by S. E. Morison's *Portuguese Voyages to America in the Fifteenth Century* (Cambridge: 1940) and his *Admiral of the Ocean Sea,* 2 vols. (Boston: 1942). Though all scholars will not agree with the point of view expressed, an interesting biography of the Great Discoverer written in English by a Spanish scholar is *Christopher Columbus* by Salvador de Madariaga (New York: 1940). An article of great significance is A. H. Lybyer's "The Influence of the Rise of the Ottoman Turks upon the Routes of Oriental Trade" in the *Annual Report of the American Historical Association, 1914,* Vol. I, pp. 127-33.

CHAPTER 4—DISCOVERERS AND EXPLORERS OF THE SIXTEENTH CENTURY: HISPANIC AMERICA

In addition to the well-written chapters in the textbooks on Latin American history by M. W. Williams, D. G. Munro, W. S. Robertson, C. E. Chapman, and T. B. Jones, fuller treatments on the Conquest are: E. G. Bourne's *Spain in America, 1450-1580* (New York: 1904); F. A. Kirkpatrick's *The Spanish Conquistadores* (London: 1934); P. A. Means's *The Fall of the Inca Empire and Spanish Rule in Peru* (New York: 1932); J. B. Brebner's *Explorers of North America* (New York: 1933) and H. I. Priestley's *The Coming of the White Man* (New York: 1930). Invaluable for their dramatic and literary qualities and as having awakened public interest in the field and, though much research has since been done, still of primary importance are the classics: *The Conquest of Mexico,* 3 Vols. (New York: 1843) and *The Conquest of Peru,* 3 Vols. (New York: 1847) by W. H. Prescott, and *The Discovery of America,* 2 Vols. (Boston: 1899) by John Fiske. In the biographical field may be mentioned S. de Madariaga's *Hernán Cortés* (New York: 1941) and the excellent, short, biographical chapters on Balboa, Cortés, and Pizarro in I. B. Richman's *The Spanish Conquerors,* Vol. II, in the Yale Chronicles of America series (New Haven: 1921).

Among the most valuable of the primary materials are: *De Orbe Novo: Eight Decades of Peter Martyr d'Anghera,* translated by F. A. MacNutt, 2 Vols. (New York: 1912), a lively contemporary account in the form of letters written between 1494 and 1526 by a noted Italian scholar, high in favor at the Spanish court, who met and talked personally with many of the early explorers; Antonio Pigafetta's *Magellan's Voyage around the World,* translated and edited by J. A. Robertson, 2 Vols. (Cleveland: 1906); Bernal Díaz del Castillo's *True History of the Conquest of New Spain,* Hakluyt Society Publications. Díaz was a companion of Cortés who took part in the conquest of Mexico.

For Brazil see the appropriate chapters in the general histories: J. P. Calogeras, *History of Brazil* (Chapel Hill, N. C.: 1939); H. G. James, *Brazil after a Century of Independence* (New York: 1925); and H. V. Livermore, *A History of Portugal* (Cambridge: 1947). More specialized works on the Portuguese voyages are: S. E. Morison, *Portuguese Voyages to America in the Fifteenth Century* (Cambridge: 1940), of primary importance; E. Prestage, *The Portuguese Pioneers* (London: 1933). Articles of special interest are: Mary W. Williams, "The Treaty of Tordesillas and the Argentine-Brazilian Boundary Settlement," in *Hispanic American Historical Review,* Vol. V, 1922; F. de Figueredo, "The Geographical Discoveries and Conquests of the Portuguese," in *Hispanic American Historical Review,* Vol. VI, 1926; and C. E. Nowell, "The Discovery of Brazil, Accidental or Intentional?" in *Hispanic American Historical Review,* Vol. XVI, 1936.

Chapter 5—discoverers and explorers of the sixteenth century: north america

On the Cabot and Cartier voyages, students should consult H. P. Biggar's two meticulously careful works: *The Precursors of Jacques Cartier, 1497-1534* (Ottawa: 1911) and *A Collection of Documents Relating to Jacques Cartier and the Sieur de Roberval* (Ottawa: 1930). The two best general treatments on France as an American colonizing power are G. M. Wrong's *Rise and Fall of New France,* 2 vols. (New York: 1928) and H. I. Priestley's *France Overseas through the Old Regime* (New York: 1939). A. G. Doughty's well-written chapter "The Beginnings of Canada" in the first volume of *Canada and Its Provinces* (Toronto: 1913) carries the Canadian story to 1543. A short, very readable biography of Jacques Cartier is Stephen Leacock's *The Mariner of St. Malo* in The Chronicles of Canada series (Toronto: 1922).

For the texts of the English voyages, R. Hakluyt's *Principal Navigations, Voyages and Discoveries of the English Nation,* to be had in many editions, is, of course, indispensable. The standard secondary work on English sea activities of the sixteenth century is J. S. Corbett's *Drake and the Tudor Navy*, 2 vols. (London: 1912). The same author's short biography of *Sir Francis Drake* (London: 1911) is also scholarly and entertaining. A. P. Newton's *The European Nations in the West Indies* (London: 1933) and P. A. Means's *The Spanish Main* (New York: 1935) bear on the history of both England and France in the West India area.

CHAPTER 6—THE SPANISH COLONIAL SYSTEM

A recent, scholarly, one-volume treatment of Spanish colonial history, arranged topically with emphasis on institutional history, is C. H. Haring's *The Spanish Empire in America* (New York: 1947). Two important works by Bernard Moses, a pioneer teacher in this subject, also cover the South American colonial field with a strong accent on institutions: *The Spanish Dependencies in South America* (London: 1914), 2 vols., and *Spain's Declining Power in South America, 1730-1806* (Berkeley: 1919). E. G. Bourne's *Spain in America, 1450-1580* (New York: 1904) throws the weight in early colonial events on those of special interest to North America. R. B. Merriman's *The Rise of the Spanish Empire in the Old World and in the New* (New York: 1918-1934), 4 vols., keeps to the forefront the close interweaving of European and American events with emphasis on the political aspect. Among more specialized studies of book length should be mentioned as indispensable: L. E. Fisher, *Viceregal Administration in the Spanish-American Colonies* in University of California Publications in History (Berkeley: 1926), Vol. XV; S. A. Zavala, *New Viewpoints on the Spanish Colonization of America* (Philadelphia: 1943), a series of scholarly studies with a new approach on "The Legal Claims of Spain in the Indies"; "Papal Bulls of Alexander VI"; "The Doctrine of Just War"; "Indian Slavery"; "The Encomienda"; "Social Experiments," etc.; L. B. Simpson, *The Encomienda in New Spain: Forced Native Labor in the Spanish Colonies, 1492-1550,* in University of California Publications in History (Berkeley: 1926), Vol. XIX; C. H. Haring, *Trade and Navigation between Spain and the Indies in the Time of the Hapsburgs* (Cambridge: 1918); A. P. Whitaker, *The Huancavelica Mercury Mine* (Cambridge: 1941); E. J. Hamilton, *American Treasure and the Price Revolution in Spain, 1501-1650* (Cambridge: 1934). Biographies of special interest are: F. A. MacNutt's *Bartholomew de Las Casas* (New York: 1909) and A. S. Aiton, *Antonio de Mendoza, First Viceroy of New Spain* (Durham: 1927). A contribution to the Las Casas literature, with emphasis on the ethical considerations that guided Spanish royal policy towards the Indians through the sixteenth century, is Lewis Hanke, *The Spanish Struggle for Justice in the Conquest of America* (Philadelphia: 1949). Among review articles of particular interest: C. H. Cunningham, "Institutional Background of Spanish American History" in *Hispanic American Historical Review,* Vol. I, pp. 24-39; C. H. Haring, "The Genesis of Royal Government in the Spanish Colonies," in *Hispanic American Historical Review,* Vol. VII, May, 1927; W. W. Pierson, Jr., "The Cabildo as an Institution," in *Hispanic American*

Historical Review, Vol. V, November, 1922; H. C. Lea, "The Indian Policy of Spain" in *Yale Review,* Vol. VIII, 1899; L. E. Fisher, "The Intendant System in America" in the *Hispanic American Historical Review,* Vol. VIII, 1928; A. S. Aiton, "Real Hacienda in New Spain under the First Viceroy" in *Hispanic American Historical Review,* Vol. VI, November, 1926; C. H. Haring, "Early Spanish Colonial Exchequer," in *American Historical Review,* Vol. XXIII, 1917-1918.

In Spanish see: Conde de Revillagigedo, *Instrucción reservada . . . a su sucesor en el mando, Marqués de Branciforte* (Mexico: 1831), an intimate account of the problems faced by a viceroy in New Spain in the eighteenth century; Juan de Solórzano Pereira (1575-1655), *Politica Indiana,* a judge in the Audiencia of Lima in the seventeenth century describes the condition of the Indians; Jorge Basarde, "El Régimen de la Mita," *Letras* (Lima: 1937), a modern Peruvian historian deals with an aspect of colonial policy; Silvio A. Zavala, *Origenes Coloniales del Peonaje en Mexico* (Sobretiro de El Trimestre Económico, vol. X, No. 4. Mexico: 1944); Roberto Levillier, *Don Francisco de Toledo,* 2 vols. (Madrid: 1935-40), a biography of the ablest of the sixteenth century viceroys of Peru; Ernesto Schäfer, *El Consejo real y supremo de las Indias* (Sevilla: 1935); Niceto Alcalá Zamora, *Impresión general acerca de las leyes de Indias* (Buenos Aires: 1942), a work by the noted exiled Spanish liberal.

Chapter 7—Brazil and the Portuguese Colonial System

In the textbook treatments of this subject, that by M. W. Williams is especially noteworthy. Somewhat fuller accounts will be found in J. P. Calogeras, *A History of Brazil,* translated by P. A. Martin (Chapel Hill: 1939) and H. G. James, *Brazil after a Century of Independence* (New York: 1925). Of the older, more comprehensive histories, the best is that by Robert Southey, *History of Brazil* (London: 1817-1822), 3 vols., which is continued in John Armitage's *History of Brazil, 1808-1831* (London: 1836), 2 vols. L. E. Da Costa's *Rio in the Time of the Viceroys,* translated by D. M. Momsen (Rio de Janeiro: 1936), gives a picture of social life in the colonial period. The same subject is dealt with in more general terms by G. Freyre, "Some Aspects of the Social Development of Portuguese America," in *Concerning Latin American Culture,* edited by C. C. Griffin (New York: 1940). A contemporary view of Brazilian Indian life in the sixteenth century is afforded by "The Captivity of Hans Stade of Hesse in A.D. 1547-1555 among the Wild Tribes of Eastern Brazil," Hakluyt Society Publications, 1st Series, Vol. LI. The following review articles are of unusual importance: A. Manchester, "The Rise of the Brazilian Aristocracy," in *Hispanic American Historical Review,* Vol. XI, 1931; and P. A. Martin, "Portugal in Brazil" in *Hispanic American Historical Review,* Vol. XIX, 1937. The history of Portugal in the colonial age—and Portuguese overseas expansion and policies—are the subject of a number of chapters in H. V. Livermore's *A History of Portugal* (Cambridge University Press, 1947).

CHAPTER 8—THE ESTABLISHMENT OF THE FRENCH COLONIES

Beside the histories of Canada by Wittke, Burt, Creighton, and Wrong, and the appropriate chapters in *Canada and Its Provinces,* edited by Shortt and Doughty, Vols. I and II (Toronto: 1913), the most scholarly of the general treatments of the French period are G. M. Wrong's *The Rise and Fall of New France* (New York: 1928), 3 Vols., and H. I. Priestley's *France Overseas through the Old Régime* (New York: 1939). H. P. Biggar's *Early Trading Companies of New France* (Toronto: 1901) is of more specialized interest. For the French in Louisiana, see A. Fortier, *A History of Louisiana* (New York: 1904), 4 Vols.; C. W. Alvord, *The Illinois Country, 1673-1818* (Springfield, Ill.: 1920); H. I. Priestley, *The Coming of the White Man* (New York: 1929), chap. x, "The Men of the Middle Border," and W. T. Morgan, "English Fear of Encirclement" in *Canadian Historical Review,* Vol. XII, March, 1929. For French activities in the West Indies, the best secondary accounts are those by A. P. Newton, *The European Nations in the West Indies, 1493-1688* (London: 1933); P. A. Means, *The Spanish Main, 1492-1700* (New York: 1935); S. L. Mims, *Colbert's West India Policy* (New Haven: 1912), and N. M. Crouse, *The French Struggle for the West Indies, 1665-1713* (New York: 1943). In the biographical material, attention should be called to the excellent short biographies in *The Chronicles of Canada* series, especially: C. W. Colby's *The Founder of New France* [Champlain] (Toronto: 1915); the same author's *The Fighting Governor* [Frontenac] (Toronto: 1915), and T. Chapais, *The Great Intendant* [Talon] (Toronto: 1914). Colby's *Canadian Types of the Old Régime* (New York: 1908) contains excellent chapter-length biographical sketches of many of the outstanding figures of the period. See also D. Ogg's *Louis XIV* (London: 1933), especially chap. iii, "Colbert," and Morris Bishop, *Champlain: The Life of Fortitude* (New York: 1948), a recent, judicious, and eminently readable biography with an appreciation of the explorer's relations to both America and Europe.

Francis Parkman's fascinating and indispensable volumes should be read, chronologically, in the following order: *Pioneers of France in the New World* (Boston: 1865); *The Jesuits in North America* (Boston: 1867); *La Salle and the Discovery of the Great West* (Boston: 1869); *The Old Régime in Canada* (Boston: 1874); *Count Frontenac and New France under Louis XIV* (Boston: 1877); *A Half Century of Conflict* (Boston: 1892); *Montcalm and Wolfe* (Boston: 1884), and *The Conspiracy of Pontiac* (Boston: 1851).

CHAPTER 9—THE ESTABLISHMENT OF THE ENGLISH COLONIES

Besides the appropriate chapters in the general text by H. U. Faulkner, *American Political and Social History,* rev. ed. (New York: 1948), there are a number of satisfactory one-volume treatments of the colonial period of United States history. Among the most useful of the more recent texts are: M. W. Jernegan, *The American Colonies, 1492-1750* (New York: 1929); O. P. Chitwood, *A History of Colonial America* (New York: 1948); and Curtis Nettels, *The Roots of American Civilization* (New York: 1938).

Classics in the field are the three works of George Louis Beer, *Origins of the British Colonial System, 1570-1660* (New York: 1908); *The Old Colonial System, 1660-1754,* 2 vols. (New York: 1933); *British Colonial Policy, 1754-1765* (New York: 1933); and the more recent four volumes by C. M. Andrews, *The Colonial Period in American History* (New Haven: 1934-1938).

Specialized volumes on colonial, political, and commercial development with a biographical emphasis are: G. F. Willison, *Saints and Strangers* (New York: 1945), an entertaining account of the Pilgrims and the Mayflower incorporating modern research in this field; William Bradford, *History of Plymouth Plantation,* Original Narratives of Early American History, Vol. VI (New York: 1906), an indispensable account of Massachusetts by an early governor; C. M. Andrews, *The Fathers of New England* (New Haven: 1921); J. T. Adams, *The Founding of New England* (Boston: 1921); S. E. Morison, *Builders of the Bay Colony* (Boston: 1930); S. H. Brockunier, *The Irrepressible Democrat, Roger Williams* (New York: 1940); W. I. Hull, *William Penn: A Topical Biography* (Swarthmore, Penn.: 1937); P. A. Bruce, *The Virginian Plutarch* (Chapel Hill: 1929), interesting sketches of colonial figures of the South. On constitutional aspects of colonial life see L. W. Labaree, *Royal Government in America* (New Haven: 1930); Viola F. Barnes, *The Dominion of New England* (New Haven: 1923); E. B. Greene, *The Provincial Governor* (New York: 1898). T. J. Wertenbaker, *Torchbearer of the Revolution: the Story of Bacon's Rebellion and Its Leader* (Princeton: 1940), a study of the economic distress, high taxes, Indian troubles, and inequitable representation leading to rebellion in Virginia (1676).

Enlightening short accounts of English activities in Hudson Bay will be found in D. G. Creighton, *Dominion of the North* (Boston: 1944) and G. M. Wrong, *Rise and Fall of New France,* 2 vols. (New York: 1928). The most readable single-volume treatment of the history of the Hudson's Bay Company with an elaborate bibliography is Douglas MacKay, *The Honourable Company* (London: 1938). The useful, well-written *Chronicles of Canada* series includes a volume, No. 18, by Agnes C. Laut, *The 'Adventurers of England' on Hudson Bay* (Toronto: 1914). Some five other volumes in the same series bear on fur trading and exploration in the far north, all more or less associated with the Hudson's Bay Company's history.

England's share in European rivalries in the Caribbean in the seventeenth century is discussed in considerable detail in A. P. Newton, *The European Nations in the West Indies, 1493-1688* (London: 1933) and P. A. Means, *The Spanish Main, 1492-1700* (New York: 1935). The same theme is carried through the eighteenth century in R. Pares, *War and Trade in the West Indies, 1739-1763* (Oxford: 1936). The working of the old system of representative government in the British West Indies and the first experiments in island federation are discussed in Hume Wrong, *Government of the West Indies* (Oxford: 1923). Two scholarly works emphasizing social and economic conditions of the eighteenth century are F. W. Pitman, *The Development of the British*

West Indies, 1700-1763 (New Haven: 1917) and L. J. Ragatz, *The Fall of the Planter Class in the British Caribbean, 1763-1833* (New York: 1928).

CHAPTER 10—COLONIAL AMERICA: A BALANCE SHEET

Among the most illuminating of the all-too-few studies that stress the comparative features, or dwell on the general characteristics, of the various American colonial systems are: Manoel de Oliveira Lima, *The Evolution of Brazil Compared with That of Spanish and Anglo-Saxon America* (Stanford University: 1914); S. Zavala, *New Viewpoints on the Spanish Colonization of America* (Philadelphia: 1943); B. Moses, *Spain Overseas* (New York: 1929), the comparative aspects of Spanish and English dependencies; F. de los Rios, "The Action of Spain in America" in *Concerning Latin American Culture*, C. C. Griffin, ed. (New York: 1940); H. I. Priestley, *The Coming of the White Man, 1492-1848* (New York: 1929); R. S. Cotterill, "British and Spanish Colonial America," chap. x, in his *A Short History of the Americas* (rev. ed., New York: 1945); T. Chapais, "New France: A General Survey," chap. i, in *Canada and Its Provinces*, Vol. I (A. Shortt and A. G. Doughty, eds., Toronto: 1913).

CHAPTER 11—SOCIETY IN COLONIAL SPANISH AMERICA

Beside a number of excellent chapters on social and intellectual development in the general texts: Mary W. Williams, *The People and Politics of Latin America* (rev. ed., New York: 1945) and B. Moses, *Spanish Dependencies in South America*, 2 vols. (New York: 1914); see also C. H. Haring, *The Spanish Empire in America* (New York: 1947), and C. E. Chapman, *Colonial Hispanic America* (New York: 1933) in which the emphasis is largely on constitutional development. In A. C. Wilgus, ed., *Colonial Hispanic America* (Washington: 1936) the following chapters are of special interest: J. L. Mecham, "The Church in Colonial Spanish America," chap. viii; I. A. Leonard, "Colonial Society," chap. ix; C. K. Jones, "The Transmission and Diffusion of Culture in the Spanish American Colonies," chap. x.

Among the most useful of the more specialized studies on the Church and missions are: J. L. Mecham, *Church and State in Latin America* (Chapel Hill: 1934), an impartial approach though limited in scope; J. F. Rippy and J. T. Nelson, *Crusaders of the Jungle* (Chapel Hill: 1936), a vivid account of mission work in the backlands of northern South America; H. C. Lea, *The Inquisition in the Spanish Dependencies* (New York: 1908); R. B. Cunninghame-Graham, *A Vanished Arcadia* (London: 1927), describes the Jesuit missions of Paraguay; H. E. Bolton, "The Mission as a Frontier Institution in the Spanish American Colonies" in *The American Historical Review*, XXIII, Oct., 1917, pp. 42-61; and by the same author, *The Spanish Borderlands: A Chronicle of Old Florida and the South West* (New Haven: 1921), chap. viii, "The Jesuits on the Pacific Coast"; *The Rim of Christendom: A Biography of Eusebio Francesco Kino, Pacific Coast Pioneer* (New York: 1936) and *Kino's Historical Memoir of Primeria Alta*, 2 vols. (Cleveland: 1919).

On intellectual life see especially P. Henríquez-Ureña, *Literary Currents in Hispanic America* (Cambridge: 1945) in which literary developments are closely related to political and social conditions and the impression made by America on sixteenth-century Europe is described; J. T. Lanning, *Academic Culture in the Spanish Colonies* (New York: 1940); B. Moses, *Spanish Colonial Literature in South America* (New York: 1922); I. A. Leonard, *Don Carlos de Sigüenza y Góngora, A Mexican Savant of the Seventeenth Century* (Berkeley: 1929), a fine biography illuminating many phases of colonial life; also, by the same author, "A Great Savant of Colonial Peru; Don Pedro de Peralta" in *Philological Review*, XII, No. 1.

For the changes in social life in the last century of colonial times, see: B. Moses, *Spain's Declining Power in South America, 1730-1806* (Berkeley: 1919); by the same author, *The Intellectual Background of the Revolution in South America, 1810-1824* (New York: 1926) and "The Social Revolution of the Eighteenth Century in South America" in *The Annual Report for 1915* of the American Historical Association (Washington: 1917); A. P. Whitaker, *The Spanish-American Frontier, 1783-1795* (Boston: 1927); H. I. Priestley, *José de Galvez, Visitor-General of New Spain, 1765-1771* (Berkeley: 1916) is an outstanding biography of the period of the reforms of Charles III in Mexico. Two famous contemporary accounts of later colonial times are: Jorge Juan and Antonio de Ulloa, *A Voyage to South America* [1735-1746], translated from the Spanish (London: 1806) and Alexander von Humboldt, *Political Essay on the Kingdom of New Spain*, English translation (London: 1811).

In Spanish see: Vicente G. Quesada, *Vida intelectual en la América española durante los siglos, siglos xvi, xvii, y xviii* (Buenos Aires: 1917), a classic; J. M. Ots Capdequí, *Instituciones sociales de la América española en el periodo colonial* (La Plata: 1934); by the same author, *El Estado español en las Indias* (Mexico: 1941); J. Torre Revello, *El Libro, la imprenta y el periodismo en América durante la dominación Española* (Buenos Aires: 1940); L. González Obregón, *México Viejo, 1521-1821* (Paris: 1900); J. M. Vargas, *Arte quiteño colonial* (Quito; 1945).

CHAPTER 12—LIFE IN NEW FRANCE

The most useful of the general histories of the French in Canada are G. M. Wrong, *The Rise and Fall of New France,* 2 vols. (New York: 1928), and H. I. Priestley, *France Overseas Through the Old Regime* (New York: 1939). More specialized studies of particular aspects are S. D. Clark, *The Social Development of Canada* (Toronto: 1922); on economic life, H. I. Innis, *The Fur Trade in Canada: An Introduction to Canadian Economic History* (New Haven: 1930), and by the same author, *The Cod Fisheries* (New Haven: 1940); M. C. Newbigin, *Canada, The Great River, The Lands and the Men* (New York: 1927); on feudalism, W. N. Munro, *The Seigneurs of Old Canada,* Chronicles of Canada No. 5 (Toronto: 1915). Of special biographical interest is Thomas Chapais, *The Great Intendant: A Chronicle of Jean Talon in Canada, 1665-1672,* Chronicles of Canada No. 6 (Toronto: 1914), and C. W. Colby, *Canadian*

Types of the Old Régime (New York: 1910). Outstanding articles in periodicals are: R. M. Saunders, "Coureur de Bois: A Definition," *Canadian Historical Review,* Vol. XXI, No. 2, June, 1940; Jean E. Murray, "The Early Fur Trade in New France and New Netherlands," *Canadian Historical Review,* Vol. XIX, No. 4, Dec. 1938; E. R. Adair, "France and the Beginnings of New France," *Canadian Historical Review,* XXV, No. 3, September, 1944; Isabel Foulché-Delbosc, "Women of New France," *Canadian Historical Review,* XXI, No. 2, June, 1940; B. Sulte, "The Captains of Militia," *Canadian Historical Review,* Vol. I, No. 3. September, 1920.

CHAPTER 13—SOCIETY IN THE THIRTEEN COLONIES

From the vast literature on life and culture in the Thirteen Colonies may be recommended as especially useful to the general student the following volumes: C. P. Nettels, *Roots of American Civilization* (New York: 1938), especially chaps. xii, xiii, xvii, xviii. In the History of American Life series, edited by A. M. Schlesinger and D. R. Fox, the following volumes: T. J. Wertenbaker, *The First Americans, 1607-1690* (New York: 1938); J. T. Adams, *Provincial Society, 1690-1763* (New York: 1938) and E. B. Greene, *The Revolutionary Generation, 1763-1790* (New York: 1943). T. J. Wertenbaker, *The Golden Age of Colonial Culture* (New York: 1942) has short and eminently readable chapters on social life and culture in Boston, New York, Philadelphia, Annapolis, Williamsburg, and Charleston.

On particular sections the following works may be consulted: For New England—S. E. Morison, *Builders of the Bay Colony* (Boston: 1930), *Maritime History of New England, 1783-1860* (Boston: 1941), especially chaps. ii and iii; S. E. Morison, *The Puritan Pronaos: Studies in the Intellectual Life of New England in the Seventeenth Century* (New York: 1936); Elizabeth D. Hanscom, ed., *The Heart of the Puritan: Selections from Letters and Journals* (New York: 1917); K. B. Murdock, *Increase Mather* (Cambridge: 1925); and A. C. McGiffert, *Jonathan Edwards* (New York: 1932). For the Middle Colonies— T. J. Wertenbaker, *The Founding of American Civilization: The Middle Colonies* (New York: 1938); J. Fiske, *The Dutch and Quaker Colonies,* 2 vols. (Boston: 1903); D. R. Fox, *Caleb Heathcote: Gentleman Colonist, the Story of a Career in the Province of New York, 1692-1721* (New York: 1926). For the South—T. J. Wertenbaker, *The Planters of Colonial Virginia* (Princeton: 1922); P. A. Bruce, *Social Life of Virginia in the 17th Century* (Richmond: 1907) and *Institutional History of Virginia in the Seventeenth Century* (New York: 1910); J. S. Bassett, *The Writings of Colonel William Byrd of Westover* (New York: 1901) in his introduction gives a well-written account of the lives of three generations of a large plantation family centering on the Byrd estate on the James River, Virginia, in the century before the Revolution; L. H. Gipson, *The British Empire before the American Revolution* (Caldwell, Idaho, and New York: 1936-1942), 5 vols., has separate volumes devoted to the different sections, emphasizing social and economic factors.

On particular aspects of colonial social life, the following volumes may be recommended: C. M. Andrews, *Colonial Folkways: A Chronicle of American Life in the Reign of the Georges* (New Haven: 1921), everyday life; Elizabeth A. Dexter, *Colonial Women of Affairs* (New York: 1924), a study of women in business and the professions in America before 1776; U. B. Phillips, *American Negro Slavery* (New York: 1918); Carl Wittke, *We Who Built America* (New York: 1939), bears on colonial migration as does M. L. Hanson, *The Atlantic Migration, 1607-1860* (Cambridge: 1940); Carl Bridenbaugh, *Cities in the Wilderness: the First Century of Urban Life in America, 1625-1742* (New York: 1938); F. J. Turner, *The Frontier in American History* (New York: 1920), a dynamic series of essays, written at different times, of aspects of sectionalism. The most famous essay, "The Significance of the Frontier in American History," was presented at a special meeting of the American Historical Association at the World's Fair, Chicago, July 12, 1893, and opened a new period in the interpretation of American history. Anne Grant [1755-1838], *Memoirs of an American Lady* (various editions), are sketches of manners and scenes in America as they existed previous to the Revolution. On intellectual life consult: V. L. Parrington, *The Colonial Mind, 1620-1800,* Vol. I in *Main Currents in American Thought* (New York: 1939), a brilliant synthesis of history and literature; Merle Curti, *The Growth of American Thought* (New York: 1943) and T. J. Wertenbaker, *The Golden Age of Colonial Culture* (New York: 1942). A useful selection of source material will be found in H. S. Commager, *Documents of American History, 1492-1934* (New York: 1948).

CHAPTER 15—THE FALL OF NEW FRANCE

Besides the works referred to in the bibliographical notes for chaps. viii and xii, see in the Chronicles of Canada series the following volumes: A. G. Doughty, *The Acadian Exiles: A Chronicle of the 'Land of Evangeline',* Vol. IX (Toronto: 1916) and William Wood, *The Great Fortress: A Chronicle of Louisbourg, 1720-1760,* Vol. VIII (Toronto: 1915); *The Passing of New France: A Chronicle of Montcalm,* Vol. X (Toronto: 1915); *The Winning of Canada: A Chronicle of Wolfe,* Vol. XI (Toronto: 1915). In the Chronicles of America series, see G. M. Wrong, *The Conquest of New France* (New Haven: 1921). By the same author, *The Fall of Canada* (Oxford: 1914) bears on the climax of the struggle. The Berkshire Studies contain three volumes useful for this period: L. B. Packard, *The Age of Louis XIV* (New York: 1929); *The Commercial Revolution* (New York: 1927) and A. H. Buffinton, *The Second Hundred Years' War, 1689-1815* (New York: 1929). Two other studies of special interest are J. B. Brebner, *New England's Outpost: Acadia before the Conquest of Canada* (New York: 1927), and A. T. Volwiler, *George Croghan and the Westward Movement, 1741-1782* (Cleveland: 1926), an illuminating monograph on the fur trade and international rivalries in the Ohio valley based on the career of an individual British trader. On the influence of seapower in procuring victory for England in the Second Hundred Years' War, the standard work is A. T. Mahan, *The Influence of Sea Power upon History, 1660-1783* (Boston, 12th ed.: 1896). It should of course be remembered that Francis Parkman, *A Half-Century of Conflict* (Boston: 1892) and *Montcalm and Wolfe* (Boston: 1884), 2 vols., are the indispensable classics for these Anglo-French wars of the eighteenth century.

CHAPTER 16—THE AMERICAN REVOLUTION

Among the many studies on the background of the American Revolution, for the general student reference may be made to the following works: G. L. Beer, *British Colonial Policy, 1754-1765* (New York: 1933), a classic, and still probably the best account of British problems and policy lying behind the Grenville acts; H. E. Egerton, *The Causes and Character of the American Revolution* (Oxford: 1923), a small, readable volume by an Englishman, professor of colonial history at Oxford; C. L. Becker, *The Eve of the Revolution* (New Haven: 1921), another small, eminently readable account, by an American scholar, in the Chronicles of America series; J. C. Miller, *Origins of the American Revolution* (Boston: 1948), a recent scholarly study in this field; C. M. Andrews, *The Colonial Background of the American Revolution* (New Haven: 1931), a series of four essays on British imperial problems by the dean of American colonial historical studies; by the same author, *The Colonial Period of American History*, Vol. IV, "England's Commercial and Colonial Policy" (New Haven: 1938) emphasizes the economic aspects; J. T. Adams, *Revolutionary New England, 1691-1776* (Boston: 1923) gives the New England background; A. M. Schlesinger, in *New Viewpoints in American History* (New York: 1937), chap. vii, gives the setting of the Revolution within a single essay.

On the constitutional aspects of the Revolution see: C. H. McIlwain, *The American Revolution: A Constitutional Interpretation* (New York: 1923), the emphasis is on the constitutional status of the colonies within the British imperial system and on British constitutional precedents; R. G. Adams, *Political Ideas of the American Revolution* (Durham: 1939), the stress is on contemporary American views of the British imperial problem of the eighteenth century. Other important specialized constitutional studies are R. Coupland, *The Quebec Act* (Oxford: 1925); and Carl Becker, *The Declaration of Independence* (New York: 1922), "in a class by itself"; Conyers Read (ed.), *The Constitution Reconsidered* (New York: 1938).

On the diplomacy of the period S. F. Bemis, *The Diplomacy of the American Revolution* (New York: 1935), is now the standard work. Carl Van Doren, *Secret History of the American Revolution* (New York: 1941) is an account of the conspiracies of Benedict Arnold and others.

The social and economic implications of the Revolution are treated briefly in J. F. Jameson, *The American Revolution Considered as a Social Movement* (Princeton: 1940). A lively and illuminating short essay is C. L. Becker's "The Spirit of '76" in *Everyman His Own Historian: Essays on History and Politics* (New York: 1935). This is a study of the supposed opinions and activities, during the years 1763 to 1776, of "Jeremiah Wynkoop," a New York merchant of Dutch-American stock, engaged in profitable business with the West Indies.

In the field of intellectual history V. L. Parrington, *The Colonial Mind: 1620-1800* (New York: 1927), especially Books I and II, presents a stimulating and masterly summary of prerevolutionary and revolutionary thought; see also Philip Davidson, *Propaganda and the American Revolution, 1763-1783* (Chapel Hill: 1941).

For the role of "the West," as won by the Seven Years' War, from 1763 to the Revolution, see C. W. Alvord, *The Mississippi Valley in British Politics: A Study of the Trade, Land Speculation, and Experiments in Imperialism Culminating in the American Revolution*, 2 vols. (Cleveland: 1917), also a later work in one volume that carries the story to the end of the Confederation period is T. P. Abernethy, *Western Lands and the American Revolution* (New York: 1937).

Recent well-written biographies cover the younger years of three great figures in the struggle for independence whose careers were to extend well into the post revolutionary period: (1) D. S. Freeman, *George Washington: The Young Washington*, 2 Vols. (New York: 1948), the story so far reaches only to 1758; (2) Dumas Malone, *Jefferson The Virginian* (Boston: 1948), the first of four projected volumes on Jefferson and covers the years to 1784; (3) Irving Brant, *James Madison: The Virginian Revolutionist* (Indianapolis: 1941) follows Madison's life to 1780. A short, useful biography of this period is G. M. Wrong, *Washington and His Comrades in Arms* in Chronicles of America Series (New Haven: 1921). Other important biographies include: J. C. Miller, *Sam Adams: Pioneer in Propaganda* (Boston: 1936); J. A. James, *The Life of George Rogers Clark* (Chicago: 1928); Carl Van Doren, *Benjamin Franklin* (New York: 1938); and H. S. Allan, *John Hancock: Patriot in Purple* (New York: 1948).

CHAPTER 17—THE STRUGGLE FOR HISPANIC AMERICAN INDEPENDENCE

An excellent summary and able interpretative treatment of the Spanish American independence movement as a whole, within the space of a single chapter, is F. A. Kirkpatrick, "The Establishment of Independence in Spanish America," in the *Cambridge Modern History*, Vol. X, chap. ix. F. L. Paxson, *The Independence of the South American Republics* (Philadelphia: 1903) is a useful, brief account of the movement in the southern continent. The underlying causes of the independence movement will be found ably discussed in two works by Bernard Moses, *South America on the Eve of Emancipation* (New York: 1908) and *The Intellectual Revolution in South America, 1810-1824* (New York: 1926). Confined to Mexico is Lillian E. Fisher, *The Background of the Revolution of Mexican Independence* (Boston: 1934). *Latin America and the Enlightenment* by A. P. Whitaker, R. D. Hussey, and others (New York: 1942) is a series of essays on the reception of eighteenth-century enlightenment in the Ibero-American world. A stimulating interpretive study of the independence movement will be found in Cecil Jane, *Liberty and Despotism* (Oxford: 1929).

Among the volumes, now growing fairly numerous, on European and United States' interest in Latin American independence, and the concomitant diplomatic relations may be mentioned: John Rydjord, *Foreign Interest in the Independence of New Spain: an Introduction to the Wars for Independence* (Durham: 1935), covers a wide field; C. K. Webster, *Britain and the Independence of Latin America, 1812-1830: Select Documents from the Foreign Office Archives,* 2 vols. (London: 1938), has an illuminating and well-written introduction on "The Causes and Character of the Struggle for Independence and the General Influence of Britain upon It," pp. 3-79; W. S. Robertson, *France and Latin American Independence* (Baltimore: 1939); A. P. Whitaker, *The United States and the Independence of Latin America, 1800-1830* (Baltimore: 1941); C. C. Griffin, *The United States and the Disruption of the Spanish Empire, 1810-1822* (New York: 1937); Alfred Hasbrouck, *Foreign Legionaries in the Liberation of Spanish South America* (New York: 1928); Bartolomé Mitre, *The Emancipation of South America;* a condensed translation by William Pilling of the History of San Martín (London: 1893), glorifies San Martín and is severely critical of Bolívar.

Among the best of the biographies are: W. S. Robertson, *Rise of the Hispanic American Republic as Told in the Lives of Their Liberators* (New York: 1928), a collection of short biographies of the revolutionary leaders, useful and reliable; the same author's two-volume *Life of Miranda* (Chapel Hill: 1929), is the standard work on this forerunner of the independence movement; on Bolívar the best full-length biography is now Gerhard Masur, *Simon Bolivar* (Albuquerque, 1948); a shorter, very readable volume is J. B. Trend, *Bolívar and the Independence of Latin America* (New York: 1948); the older works by H. Angell, G. Sherwell, and E. Ludwig will also be found useful; the Liberator's political philosophy is ably dealt with in V. A. Belaunde, *Bolívar and the Political Thought of the Spanish American Revolution* (Baltimore: 1938); R. B. Cunninghame-Graham, *José Antonio Páez* (London: 1929) is a readable biography of the Venezuelan leader; A. H. Noll and A. P. McMahon, *The Life and Times of Miguel Hidalgo y Castilla* (Chicago: 1910) is still the best available work on the Father of Mexican independence.

W. R. Manning, *Diplomatic Correspondence of the United States Concerning the Independence of the Latin American Nations,* 2 vols. (New York: 1923), contains contemporary material indispensable for the student of the period.

In Spanish see: Bartolomé Mitre, *Historia de San Martín y de la emancipación Sud-Americana,* 3 vols. (Buenos Aires, 1887). One of the best accounts of the wars of independence in South America. The author was president of Argentina, 1862-1868; Mariano Picón-Salas, *De la Conquista a la independencia* (Mexico, 1944). Contains some stimulating ideas.

CHAPTER 19—NORTH AMERICA: CONSTITUTIONAL ISSUES

Among the most useful of the general works on the constitutional aspects of the "critical period in American History" should be mentioned A. C. Mc-Laughlin, *The Confederation and the Constitution, 1783-1789* (New York: 1905), an illuminating and comprehensive survey; R. L. Schuyler, *The Constitution of the United States* (New York: 1923), a small readable volume presenting an objective view of the constitution in its historical setting and stressing the American contribution of federalism to constitutional thought and practice; John Fiske, *The Critical Period of American History, 1783-1789* (Boston: 1916), an attractively written popular narrative; J. M. Beck, *The Constitution of the United States* (New York: rev. ed. 1941), chap. iv, "Franklin Gives a Dinner," presents an enlightening symposium of characters and conversations; Max Farrand, *The Framing of the Constitution of the United States* (New Haven: 1936), "a brief presentation of the author's personal interpretation of what took place in the federal convention." For a more recent general study see Conyers Read, *The Constitution Reconsidered* (New York: 1938). A specialized study is Merrill Jensen, *The Articles of Confederation: an interpretation of the social-constitutional history of the American revolution, 1774-1781* (Madison, Wisc.: 1940). Indispensable for this period is *The Federalist,* a collection of essays by Alexander Hamilton, John Jay, and James Madison, interpreting the constitution as agreed upon by the Federal Convention, September 17, 1787 (numerous editions). For a useful source book for the whole period of the American Revolution—that includes, besides essential documents, state constitutions, and other formal papers, excerpts from debates, letters, pamphlets, et cetera—reference should be made to *Sources and Documents Illustrating the American Revolution 1764-1788 and the Formation of the Federal Constitution* (Oxford: 1923), edited by S. E. Morison.

A small, readable volume in the Chronicles of America series is Max Farrand's *Fathers of the Constitution* (New Haven: 1921); also stressing the biographical element is F. Rodell, *Fifity-Five Men* (New York: 1936); in the biographical field see also C. G. Bowers, *Jefferson and Hamilton* (Boston: 1925); Nathan Schackner, *Alexander Hamilton* (New York: 1946), and A. J. Beveridge, *The Life of John Marshall* (New York: 1929), 2 volumes.

For the economic aspect, the standard work of first-rate scholarship is C. A. Beard, *Economic Interpretation of the Constitution* (New York: 1936); A. M. Schlesinger in *New Viewpoints in American History* (New York: 1937) has a good chapter (viii) on the same theme.

On the western and land questions, consult T. P. Abernethy, *Western Lands and the American Revolution* (New York: 1937); C. W. Alvord, *The Illinois Country, 1673-1818* (Springfield, Ill.: 1920), chaps. xvii to the end emphasize government and settlement of the Old Northwest in the period following the Revolution; F. A. Ogg, *The Old Northwest: A Chronicle of the Ohio Valley and Beyond,* in Chronicles of America series (New Haven: 1921); Constance L. Skinner, *Pioneers of the Old Southwest,* in Chronicles of America series

(New Haven: 1919); A. P. Whitaker, *The Spanish American Frontier, 1783-1795: the Westward Movement and the Spanish Retreat in the Mississippi Valley* (Boston: 1927).

Among the notable special studies in the evolution of Canadian government in this same period may be mentioned two works by R. Coupland, *The Quebec Act* (Oxford: 1925) and *The American Revolution and the British Empire* (New York: 1930), the latter being a series of lectures of which numbers VII and VIII are especially relevant. On the significance of the Loyalist movement see W. S. Wallace, *The United Empire Loyalists,* in the Chronicles of Canada series (Toronto: 1914); C. H. Van Tyne, *The Loyalists in the American Revolution* (New York: 1929); A. C. Flick, *Loyalism in New York* (New York: 1901); and C. Wittke, "Canadian Refugees in the American Revolution" in the *Canadian Historical Review,* Vol. III, pp. 320-34. William Wood, *The Father of British Canada: A Chronicle of Carleton* (Toronto: 1916), a volume in the Chronicles of Canada series bears on the career of Lord Dorchester.

CHAPTER 20—HISPANIC AMERICA: CONSTITUTIONAL ISSUES

For the development of political thought and the evolution of governmental forms during the revolutionary years in Spanish America the outstanding work is V. A. Belaunde, *Bolívar and the Political Thought of the Spanish American Revolution* (Baltimore: 1938); an earlier, somewhat diffuse volume in the same field is C. Parra-Pérez, *Bolívar: A Contribution to the Study of His Political Ideas,* translated by N. A. N. Cleven (Paris: 1928), a series of studies of different episodes in the life of the Liberator profusely illustrated with long quotations. Gerhard Masur's biography *Simon Bolivar* (Albuquerque: 1948), gives considerable attention to constitutional matters. For shorter treatments, see in A. C. Wilgus, ed., *South American Dictators* (Washington: 1937), chap. ii, "Monarchy or Republic?" and chap. iii, "The Anguish of Bolívar," by J. F. Rippy, and chap. xvi, "Dictator José de San Martín," and chap. xvii, "Dictator Simón Bolívar," by N. A. N. Cleven; in the *Pacific Ocean in History,* edited by Stephens and Bolton (New York: 1917), pp. 311-16, see the article by E. Larrabure y Unanue, "The Monarchial Plans of General San Martín."

For early constitutional events in Argentina, see L. S. Rowe, *The Federal System of the Argentine Republic* (Washington: 1921), chap. iii, "The Basis of the Argentine Constitutional System," chap. iv, "Antecedents of the Argentine Constitution"; the parallel volume for Peru is G. H. Stuart, *The Governmental System of Peru* (Washington: 1925), chap. i, "Constitutional Development of Peru"; for Bolivia, N. A. N. Cleven, *The Political Organization of Bolivia* (Washington: 1940), chap. iii, "Establishment of the Republic"; on Mexican constitutional development the standard work is H. I. Priestley, *The Mexican Nation: A History* (New York: 1923); for this period see chaps. xi-xv.

A stimulating discussion of the fundamental concepts involved in the new constitutions will be found in Cecil Jane, *Liberty and Despotism in Spanish*

America (Oxford: 1929), especially chaps. vii and viii. For a discussion by a Spanish American writer see F. García Calderón, *Latin America: Its Rise and Progress* (New York: 1913), especially chap. iii "The Struggle for Independence."

On the constitutional history of Brazil under Pedro I general accounts will be found in J. P. Calogeras, *A History of Brazil,* translated by P. A. Martin (Chapel Hill: 1939), chap. v, and H. G. James, *Brazil after a Century of Independence* (New York: 1925), chap. iv. Two excellent special articles are available: A. K. Manchester, "Paradoxical Pedro, First Emperor of Brazil" in *Hispanic American Historical Review,* 1932, and P. A. Martin, "Portugal in America" in *Hispanic American Historical Review,* 1937; see also in *South American Dictators,* "Constitutional Dictatorship in Brazil" by A. K. Manchester, chap. xxiii, pp. 429-43.

For a comparative view of Brazil and Spanish America, see the distinguished work by M. de Oliveira Lima, *The Evolution of Brazil Compared with That of Spanish and Anglo-Saxon America* (Stanford University: 1914).

On the relations of Brazil with Great Britain and their repercussions on the constitutional situation, see A. K. Manchester, *British Preëminence in Brazil* (Chapel Hill: 1933), especially chap. viii, pp. 186-219, "The Price of Recognition." On the relations between Brazil and the United States, consult L. F. Hill, *Diplomatic Relations between Brazil and the United States* (Durham: 1932), and, in shorter form, for the period of Pedro I, see W. R. Manning, "Early Diplomatic Controversies between the United States and Brazil" in *Hispanic American Historical Review,* Vol. I, No. 2, 1918.

CHAPTER 21—THE ESTABLISHMENT OF THE TWO SPHERES

Satisfactory short general treatments of the War of 1812 and its background are H. U. Faulkner, *American Political and Social History* (New York: 1948), chap. xi, "Resurgent Nationalism," and A. L. Burt, *A Short History of Canada for Americans* (Minneapolis: 1942), chap. vii. More extended accounts are A. L. Burt, *The United States, Great Britain and British North America: From the Revolution to the Establishment of Peace after the War of 1812* (New Haven: 1940); C. P. Lucas, *The Canadian War of 1812* (London: 1906); W. Wood, *The War with the United States: A Chronicle of 1812,* in the Chronicles of Canada series (Toronto: 1915); and R. D. Paine, *The Fight for a Free Sea,* in the Chronicles of America series (New Haven: 1920). An indispensable special study is S. F. Bemis, *Jay's Treaty: A Study in Commerce and Diplomacy* (New York: 1924). Allen Johnson, *Jefferson and His Colleagues: A Chronicle of the Virginia Dynasty,* in the Chronicles of America series (New Haven: 1921) is a lively, biographical sketch of the period. More extended important biographical studies falling within this period are: Marquis James, *Andrew Jackson: The Border Captain* (Indianapolis: 1933), carries Jackson through the War of 1812 and the subsequent Florida adventure; Bernard Mayo, *Henry Clay: Spokesman of the New West* (Boston: 1937), follows Clay's career through the War of 1812; W. P. Cresson, *James Monroe* (Chapel Hill: 1946); S. F. Bemis, *John Quincy Adams and the Foundations of American Foreign Policy* (New York: 1949), concentrates on the career of Adams as a diplomatist and follows him into the presidency, therefore treating extensively the War of 1812 and the formulation of the Monroe Doctrine.

Sectional divergencies were a major feature of the war. New England's attitude in the prewar and war years is the subject of two excellent chapters in S. E. Morison, *The Maritime History of Massachusetts, 1783-1860* (Boston: 1941), chap. xii, "Federalism and Neutral Trade, 1789-1807," and chap. xiii, "Embargo and War, 1807-1815." The role of the West, with special emphasis on the part the Indian menace had in it, is set forth in J. W. Pratt, *Expansionists of 1812* (New York: 1925); agrarian, imperialistic ambitions as a motivating force is the theme in two important articles: G. R. Taylor, "Agrarian Discontent in the Mississippi Valley Preceding the War of 1812," in *Journal of Political Economy*, Vol. XXXIX, No. 4, 1931 and C. B. Coleman, "The Ohio Valley in the Preliminaries of the War of 1812," in *The Mississippi Valley Historical Review*, Vol. VII, June, 1920, pp. 39-50.

A short, scholarly treatment of the background, pronouncement, and effect of the Monroe Doctrine will be found in S. F. Bemis, *The Latin American Policy of the United States* (New York: 1945), chaps. iv and v. For a general review, consult Dexter Perkins, *Hands Off: A History of the Monroe Doctrine* (Boston: 1941). Special treatises of importance in their relation to the Monroe Doctrine are C. K. Webster, *The Foreign Policy of Castlereagh, 1815-1822: Britain and the European Alliance* (London: 1925); Harold Temperley, *The Foreign Policy of Canning, 1822-1827* (London: 1925); J. F. Rippy, *Rivalry of the United States and Great Britain over Latin America, 1803-1830* (Baltimore: 1929); E. H. Tatum, Jr., *The United States and Europe, 1815-1823: A Study in the Background of the Monroe Doctrine* (Berkeley: 1936). Indispensable is Richard Rush, *Memoranda of a Residence at the Court of London* (Philadelphia: 1845). Important articles include W. C. Ford, "John Quincy Adams and the Monroe Doctrine," in *American Historical Review*, Vol. VII, July, 1902, and Vol. VIII, October, 1902; W. S. Robertson, "The Monroe Doctrine Abroad in 1823-1824," in *The American Political Science Review*, Vol. VI, November, 1912; "South America and the Monroe Doctrine," in *The Political Science Quarterly*, Vol. XXX, 1915; "The Recognition of the Hispanic American Nations by the United States," in *The Hispanic American Historical Review*, Vol. I, August, 1918; W. F. Craven, Jr., "The Risk of the Monroe Doctrine," in *The Hispanic American Historical Review*, Vol. VII, 1927.

INDEX

Absentee landlordism, in Brazil, 381; in Canada, 357; in Spanish America, 381; in the Thirteen English Colonies, 469; in the West Indies, 254, 255

Academy of San Carlos, 335

Acadia and the Acadians, 224, 225, 247, 275, 308, 391; captured by English but restored to France, 229, 393; deportation of inhabitants of, 396, 480; French surrender, 394; menaced English settlements, 396; reclaimed by English by Treaty of Utrecht, 480; renamed Nova Scotia, 394

"Acadian coast," 247

Acapulco, Mexico, 181, 331, 340, 449

Acoma (pueblo), 56

Acto Addicional, provisions of, 516; and continuance of the empire, 516-17

Adams, John, helped negotiate Treaty of Paris, 424; quoted, 488; second President, a Federalist, 522

Adams, John Quincy, Secretary of State, opposed acceptance of Canning's proposals, 538, 539

Adams, Samuel, 409-10, 476; on Parliament and colonies, 412

Adelantado, of the South Sea, title awarded Balboa, 103; Pizarro, 120; Almagro, 123

Adobe, 54, 69

Africa, 83; exploration in, 81; simian types in, 33

African slaves; *see* Negroes in America, 196-97

"Age of Discovery," 75, 80, 81, 83, 85

"Age of faith," 313

Agincourt, battle of, 75

Agriculture, 21, 24; basis of Mayan culture, 36, 46-47; in Brazil, 204; in New France, 359, 545; in southern English Colonies, 266, 268, 365-70; of Aztecs, 52; of Chibchas, 61; of Incas, 65, 68; of Indians, 35-38; of Plains Indians, 57; rotation of crops, 37, 154; rotation disregarded in Southern colonies, 366; Spanish colonial economy based on, 184-90; *see* Cotton; Domestic animals; Fertilization of the Soil; Fruits and flowers; Grazing; Maize; Potatoes; Squash; Sugar; Tobacco; Tomatoes; Vegetables; Wheat and flour

Aguilar, Spanish Castaway, 107; interpreter for Cortés, 108

Ah Puch, the death god, 48-49

Ailly, Pierre d', French cardinal, author of *Imago Mundi,* 88

Aix-la-Chapelle, 343, 396; congress of, 532

Alabama, geography, 21, 23; visited by De Soto, 116

Alagoas (state), Brazil, Dutch hold, 218

Alarcón, Hernando de, 115

Alarcón y Mendoza, Juan Ruiz de, 338

Alaska, 18, 24; held by Russia, 531; route of Indians, 32, 33

Albany House, 279, 280, 391

Albemarle Sound, 23

Alberta, Canada, 22; cattle in, 22; wheat in, 22

Albuquerque, Jeronymo de, ended French ambitions in Brazil, 217

Alcabala, 188

Alcalá University, 334

Alcalde, 101, 164-67; Cortés made, 107; at Cusco, 123; elected by vecìnas, 318

Alcalde mayor, 174

Alcaldes ordinarios, 166

Alcaldia mayor, 174

Aldama Juan, 447, 448

Aldeas, or mission-villages, 214

Alexander I, Tsar of Russia, and Holy Alliance, 530; suggests European intervention in Spanish colonies, 532

Alexander VI, Pope, 131, 132, 188, 325

Algonquian Indians, allies of Champlain, 225; as fur traders, 227; attempts to christianize, 230; French missions among, 231; move west, 230; John Eliot, a missionary to, 373

Algonquian language groups, 40, 59-60, 226

Alhambra, 96

Allen, Ethan, 414, 416

Allende, Ignacio, 447, 448

Almadén mines in Spain, 185

Almagro, Diego de, 118-20; claims Cusco, 124; defeated in battle of Las Salinas, 125; governor of territory now Chile, 123, 126; governor of Tumbes, 120; returns to Peru, 124; shares in Atahualpa's ransom, 121

Almagro the Lad, son of Diego de Almagro, governor of Peru, 125

Alpacas, 27; wool from, 66, 68

Alta California; *see* California.

Altiplano, 24, 28

Aluminum, 17

Alvarado, Pedro de, conqueror of Guatemala, 107, 113; at Mexico City, 111-12

Alvares, Diogo, 136; known as Caramurú, 136

577